D1106080

WILLIAMS' GANG

William H. Williams operated a slave pen in Washington, D.C., known as the Yellow House, and actively trafficked in enslaved men, women, and children for more than twenty years. His slave-trading activities took an extraordinary turn in 1840 when he purchased twenty-seven enslaved convicts out of the Virginia State Penitentiary in Richmond with the understanding that he carry them outside the United States for sale. When Williams conveyed his captives illegally into New Orleans, allegedly while en route to the foreign country of Texas, he prompted a series of courtroom dramas that would last for almost three decades. Based on court records, newspapers, governors' files, slave manifests, slave narratives, travelers' accounts, and penitentiary data, *Williams' Gang* examines slave criminality, the coastwise domestic slave trade, and southern jurisprudence as it supplies a compelling portrait of the economy, society, and politics of the Old South.

Jeff Forret is Professor of History at Lamar University. He won the Frederick Douglass Book Prize for his book *Slave against Slave: Plantation Violence in the Old South* (2015) and has authored *Race Relations at the Margins: Slaves and Poor Whites in the Antebellum Southern Countryside* (2006), among other works.

JEFF FORRET

WILLIAMS' GANG

A NOTORIOUS SLAVE
TRADER AND HIS CARGO
OF BLACK CONVICTS

CAMBRIDGE
UNIVERSITY PRESS

CAMBRIDGE
UNIVERSITY PRESS

University Printing House, Cambridge CB2 8BS, United Kingdom

One Liberty Plaza, 20th Floor, New York, NY 10006, USA

477 Williamstown Road, Port Melbourne, VIC 3207, Australia

314–321, 3rd Floor, Plot 3, Splendor Forum, Jasola District Centre,
New Delhi – 110025, India

79 Anson Road, #06–04/06, Singapore 079906

Cambridge University Press is part of the University of Cambridge.

It furthers the University's mission by disseminating knowledge in the pursuit of
education, learning, and research at the highest international levels of excellence.

www.cambridge.org
Information on this title: www.cambridge.org/9781108493031
DOI: 10.1017/9781108651912

© Jeff Forret 2020

First published 2020

Printed in the United Kingdom by TJ International Ltd. Padstow Cornwall

A catalogue record for this publication is available from the British Library.

Library of Congress Cataloging-in-Publication Data
Names: Forret, Jeff, 1972– author.
Title: Williams' Gang : a notorious slave trader and his cargo of black convicts /
Jeff Forret, Lamar University.
Other titles: Notorious slave trader and his cargo of black convicts
Description: Cambridge : New York, NY : Cambridge University Press, [2019] |
Includes bibliographical references and index.
Identifiers: LCCN 2019015910 | ISBN 9781108493031 (alk. paper)
Subjects: LCSH: Williams, William H., approximately 1802–1858. | Slave
traders – Washington, D.C. – Biography. | Slave trade – United States – History – 19th
century. | Slavery – United States – History – 19th century. | Washington,
D.C. – History, Local.
Classification: LCC E442 .F67 2019 | DDC 381/.44092 [B]–dc23
LC record available at https://lccn.loc.gov/2019015910

ISBN 978-1-108-49303-1 Hardback

Contents

Figures

Abbreviations

AAS   US Slavery Collection, American Antiquarian Society, Worcester, Massachusetts

ADAH   Alabama Department of Archives and History, Montgomery

BLHBS   Baker Library, Harvard Business School, Cambridge, Massachusetts

BECHSA   Buffalo and Erie County Historical Society Archives, Buffalo, New York

LSA   Louisiana State Archives, Baton Rouge

LVA   Library of Virginia, Richmond

NA   National Archives, Washington, D.C.

NAMS   National Archives Microfilm Series

NARA   National Archives & Records Administration

NONA   New Orleans Notarial Archives

NOPL   New Orleans Public Library

RSPP, PAR   Race & Slavery Petitions Project, Petition Analysis Record

SHC   Southern Historical Collection, the Wilson Library, University of North Carolina at Chapel Hill

UNO   Supreme Court of Louisiana, Earl K. Long Library, University of New Orleans

Acknowledgments

When I finished my last book, I couldn't decide which project to do next. About that time, a former high school classmate, Guy Hill, whom I hadn't seen in twenty-three years, took a job a block away from my university, and so two former Calamus-Wheatland Warriors reunited and played catch-up over Japanese food, more than a thousand miles from where we first met. That conversation with Guy clarified matters for me and set this book in motion. Chronologically, then, Guy appears first in a long list of people I need to thank for their involvement in this undertaking.

I had first encountered slave trader William H. Williams and his shipment of enslaved convicts while researching an article on the Louisiana State Penitentiary many years ago. Few people knew about him, but I was aware of one who did: Marianne Fisher-Giorlando at Grambling State University. Since I did not wish to embark upon a book someone else was already writing, I immediately contacted Marianne to see if she had long-term plans for Williams. She said no and encouraged me to proceed. To get me off to a good start, she sent several sources about Williams that she had encountered in her own research. I have several times benefited from such generosity during this project. Michael S. Martin's invitation to present a paper on William H. Williams at a meeting of the Louisiana Historical Association gave the project its first public forum. That visibility invited unexpected but welcome contacts from several strangers enthused about the book and kind enough to supply information they had accumulated about the slave trader. Patsy Fletcher, Matthew Gilmore, and Melissa Howell all shared research on the Washington, D.C. side of Williams' story. Jimmy L. Bryan, Jr. and Tom Bartholow proved immensely helpful in teasing out genealogical matters.

Several librarians and archivists also deserve my gratitude: Minor Weisiger, Chris Kolbe, and the rest of the staff at the Library of Virginia in Richmond; Christina Bryant and Amanda Fallis at the New Orleans Public Library; Erin Albritton, Sally Reeves, Sybil Thomas, and Siva Blake at the New Orleans Notarial Archives; Bob Ellis at the National Archives; Connie Phelps at the University of New Orleans' Earl K. Long Library; John Fowler at the Louisiana State Archives in Baton Rouge; Tara Laver, Germain Bienvenu, and the whole staff at Hill Library on the Louisiana State University campus; Stephanie Braunstein at LSU's Middleton Library; Sean Benjamin of Tulane University; Frances Thomas at the Poynter Legislative Research Library; Nancy Dupree and the staff at the Alabama Department of Archives and History; Paula Webb at the University of South Alabama; Zennia Calhoun of the Mobile Municipal Archives; Trevor A. Brown at the Historic Natchez Foundation; Susan A. Riggs at the College of William & Mary's Earl Gregg Swem Library; Jessica Kincaid at the Southern Historical Collection on the University of North Carolina campus; and Jim Gerencser of Dickinson College. I also appreciate the helpful staffs at the Baker Library of the Harvard Business School, the Historic New Orleans Collection, the Library of Congress, the Mobile Public Library, the New York Public Library, the New York County Clerk's Office, the New York Historical Society, the Buffalo and Erie County Historical Society Archives, and the Kent County Courthouse in Chestertown, Maryland. Even when we came up empty, the archivists put forth a good effort. On my home turf, former Lamar University government documents librarian Theresa Hefner-Babb snooped around on my behalf even though she wears a different hat now, and Severa Norris in the LU interlibrary loan department kept me well stocked in necessary readings. Other professionals helped me answer crucial questions while writing this book. Attorney John McElroy puzzled through some legal terminology for me, and Ryan Shovar handled my accounting queries. Wendy Butusov of Washington, D.C.'s Glenwood Cemetery wielded her tape measure for my first paragraph, and Kristen Harbeson did some last-minute archival mining in Baltimore. Many thanks to all.

I offer my deepest thanks to Peter Kolchin, Josh Rothman, Richard Follett, and departmental colleagues Jimmy L. Bryan, Jr., Rebecca Boone,

Brendan Gillis, Mark Mengerink, Gwinyai Muzorewa, and Yasuko Sato for reading all or parts of the manuscript. I appreciate all of the feedback. Calvin Schermerhorn, Dan Dupre, Sheri Huerta, and Maria Montalvo offered wonderful advice, suggestions for sources to consult, and sometimes the sources themselves. Doug Egerton, Leigh Fought, and Josh Rothman all contributed to the process through which this manuscript found an agent in Cecilia Cancellaro and, thanks to her efforts, editor Debbie Gershenowitz of Cambridge University Press, who tightened the prose and eliminated various points of anticipated frustration for readers.

My gratitude extends to all of those audiences who have listened and asked questions at panel presentations and keynote speeches on Williams' gang, at the Organization of American Historians' meeting in New Orleans, the Gateway History Conference in Clinton, Iowa, and the British American Nineteenth Century Historians' meeting in Warwick, UK. Thanks to Erin Greenwald's invitation, I also gave several public talks in Louisiana for the *Purchased Lives: New Orleans and the Domestic Slave Trade, 1808–1865* traveling museum exhibit, curated by the Historic New Orleans Collection. The engaged audiences made all of those trips worthwhile. Closer to home, I was invited to share parts of my work on Williams' gang with the Texas Governor's School, the local Colonial Dames chapter, the Progressive Democrats of Southeast Texas, and the on-campus Cardinal Conversations series in the home of university president Kenneth Evans and his late wife, Nancy, who coordinated the event. All of these audiences contributed comments and questions that have shaped the final product.

I am grateful for the funding for my research through a National Endowment for the Humanities Summer Stipend and a William Nelson Cromwell Foundation Grant, in association with the American Society for Legal History. I thank Josh Rothman, Paul Finkelman, and Doug Egerton for writing recommendation letters on my behalf. The Leland Best Distinguished Faculty Research Fellowship, the University Scholar Award, and a Faculty Development Leave Grant, all from Lamar University, also kept me flush with travel money. I appreciate all of my colleagues across campus who made those awards possible.

Portions of this book have appeared in article form as "Before Angola: Enslaved Prisoners in the Louisiana State Penitentiary," *Louisiana History*

54 (Spring 2013): 133–171; "The Murder of James Carradus and the Case of *Commonwealth v. John* (1839)," *Southern Quarterly* 54 (Winter 2017): 130–141; and "'How Deeply They *Weed* into the Pockets': Slave Traders, Bank Speculators, and the Anatomy of a Chesapeake Wildcat, 1840–1843," *Journal of the Early Republic* 39 (Winter 2019). They are used here with permission.

I conclude with special notes of thanks for three people. Long-time administrative associate Patty Renfro in the Lamar University history department was nearing retirement as I finished this manuscript. Throughout my many long years at LU, I have always counted on her to help me complete travel forms, to keep me well stocked in office supplies, to perform the occasional book-related odd job, and to serve as late-day sounding board. Ever a competent and reliable champion of mine, I am sorry to see her leave.

Finally, my wife, Sharon, and son, Gabe. The career of a professor and its multiple, competing demands of teaching, research, and service are not particularly conducive to family life, and my family endures a lot, whether through my many absences, my presence, or my absences even when I'm present. I appreciate their patience, support, and love. I am excited, now that Sharon has embarked upon her new career as a professional educator, that our three schedules will now coincide in coming years as our adventure continues.

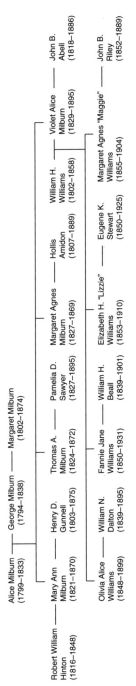

1 Williams–Milburn genealogy.

INTRODUCTION

The Slave Depot of Washington, D.C.

A T 2219 LINCOLN ROAD NORTHEAST IN WASHINGTON,
D.C., lies the entrance to Glenwood Cemetery. On lot 119,
adjacent to Central Avenue and near the chapel, stands an impressive
headstone, well in excess of eight feet tall, carved of Italian marble. The
marker is not so much massive as it is distinctive, bearing the shape of
a shield on the front and crowned by an ornate bell. This is the grave
of William H. Williams, slave trader and proprietor of a notorious
Washington, D.C. slave pen.[1]

From Williams' place of burial, it is approximately three miles to the
site of his slave jail, dubbed the Yellow House, which once stood on the
block now occupied by the Federal Aviation Administration's Orville
Wright Federal Building. In January 2017, the US government unveiled
a pair of historical signs at 800 Independence Avenue Southwest, across
the street from the Smithsonian's Hirschhorn Museum, to indicate the
location of Williams' slave pen. The charcoal- and yellow-orange-colored
panels supply curious passersby a cursory history lesson in Washington,
D.C.'s slaveholding past.[2]

At the Democratic National Convention in July 2016, when First
Lady Michelle Obama observed, "I wake up every morning in
a house that was built by slaves," she elicited gasps of indignation
from some listeners offended by her statement, however factually
correct it was. Slaves *were* involved in the construction of not only
the White House but also the Capitol and practically all public
buildings that went up in Washington, D.C. before the Civil War.
That was how it was: enslaved people were crucial to the literal and
figurative building of the United States. Though long overdue,

1

Americans are at last beginning to reckon with the centrality of slaves to the nation's history.[3]

The United States terminated its lawful participation in the transatlantic slave trade effective January 1, 1808, but Congress did nothing to restrict the buying and selling of slaves within the young nation. Once the introduction of bondpeople from abroad was banned and external sources of labor cut off, the domestic slave trade accelerated, to redistribute enslaved workers to locations where they were most needed. Masters in the Upper South states of Virginia and Maryland sold surplus slaves, rendered unnecessary for labor locally by generations of Chesapeake bondpeople's self-reproduction as well as by regional economic transformations, to traders who carried the excess bondpeople farther south and west, where the demand for labor outstripped supply. At first, the preponderance of the domestic traffic conveyed slaves from the Chesapeake to the South Atlantic states of South Carolina and Georgia. After about 1820, the trade turned more westward, to the recently added states of Alabama, Mississippi, and Louisiana. Fresh cotton lands and cane swamps beckoned.[4]

Slave traders drove bondpeople to the Deep South in overland coffles, chained together single-file or in pairs, but as the domestic slave trade professionalized in the 1820s to accommodate the insatiable labor demands of the burgeoning cotton and sugar economies, they increasingly transported slaves via water. The US government, explained US Minister to Great Britain and future president Martin Van Buren in 1832, "most sedulously and rigorously guards against the further introduction of slaves" from overseas, with Congress in 1820 declaring participation in the international slave trade a form of piracy punishable by death. Yet simultaneously, Van Buren added, the law "*permits* [slaves'] transfer coastwise from one of the States to another." The same March 1807 statute that outlawed the foreign slave trade authorized, protected, and regulated the saltwater domestic slave trade in vessels "over 40 tons burthen" sailing from one US port to another.[5]

Among the new generation of professional slave traders arising in the 1820s, Austin Woolfolk pioneered the coastwise domestic slave trade from his base at the port of Baltimore. His family-run operation, which shipped virtually all of its slaves by water, dominated the slave market until the emergence of Isaac Franklin and John Armfield in the late 1820s. Headquartered in Alexandria, then a part of the District of Columbia, Franklin & Armfield upped the ante by purchasing their own slaving ships. In addition to the self-named *Isaac Franklin*, they operated the brigs *Tribune* by 1831 and *Uncas* by 1833. The coastwise slave trade had matured into a regular system by the time William H. Williams began to participate extensively in the saltwater traffic. Starting in the mid-1830s, he established himself as one of the foremost slave traders in Washington, D.C.[6]

Congress carved the District of Columbia in 1790 from lands donated by Virginia and Maryland. Consisting of a square ten miles on each side and bisected irregularly by the Potomac into two unequal parts, the District originally encompassed precisely one hundred square miles, much of it swampland in need of reclamation. It would take another decade of planning and backbreaking labor before the city of Washington was readied as the site of the new US capital. Sandwiched between Virginia, the single largest exporter of slaves, and the slaveholding state of Maryland, the District of Columbia emerged logically in the 1820s as a major hub of a bustling domestic slave trade on the East Coast, one that rivaled Baltimore in its traffic. About 6,400 resident slaves lived in the District in 1820, almost one-fifth of its total population. They lived on small holdings and most commonly labored as domestic servants. But it was the bondpeople who merely passed through the District, from the surrounding countryside en route to destinations farther south, who supplied slave traders their livelihood. Washington City and Alexandria were not known for the quantity of sales transacted there; rather, both served as leading depots for the gathering, warehousing, and shipment of slaves. "[T]his District is the principal mart of the slave trade of the Union," proclaimed one congressman in 1835. It teemed with slave traders. One edition of the *National Intelligencer* in March 1836 included simultaneous advertisements from slave dealers Franklin & Armfield, James H. Birch, and J. W. Neal & Co., in addition to William H. Williams. Collectively, the traders desired more than 1,200 slaves for

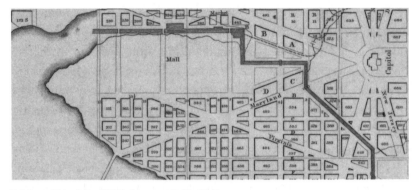

2 Map of "the Island," Washington, D.C., 1840
Source: F. C. De Krafft, Mrs. W. I. Stone, and William M. Morrison, *Map of the City of Washington* ([Washington, D.C.?]: Wm. M. Morrison, 1840), American Memory, Library of Congress, Geography and Map Division, Washington, D.C., www.loc.gov/item/886940 55/ (accessed November 26, 2018).

export. A September 1840 issue of the same newspaper listed not only Williams but also Jilson Dove on Pennsylvania Avenue, James H. Birch at the Steamboat Hotel, Robert W. Fenwick at Levi Pumphrey's Tavern at C Street and Sixth, plus George Kephart, across the Potomac in Alexandria, at Franklin & Armfield's former location on Duke Street. The slave trade, though certainly competitive, produced plenty of business to go around.[7]

William H. Williams established his slave pen and place of business on the Island, the name for that portion of Washington south of the City Canal, an artificial waterway connecting the Eastern Branch to Tiber Creek. (See Figure 2.) Opened in 1815, the Washington City Canal stretched northwards from the Eastern Branch, jogged northwest to skirt Capitol Hill, turned sharply west, north, and then west again as it joined a scooped-out and straightened Tiber Creek, which naturally flowed westward north of the Mall and emptied into the Potomac immediately to the south of the President's House. A Washington City ordinance mandated that, starting August 1, 1831, anyone wishing "to trade or traffic in slaves" obtain a license from the mayor for $400 annually, although enforcement of the provision proved lax to non-existent. According to one congressman in 1838, "for seven years, it has never been carried into effect." William H. Williams and his fellow

Washington slave traders may never have paid a dime for the privilege of peddling enslaved black bodies.[8]

This was how it worked. Sometimes, to the great convenience of the trader, sellers visited the slave pens with human merchandise to vend. Slave traders and their agents also roamed the surrounding Chesapeake countryside for slaves to buy. Paying for their purchases in cash, they escorted them to slave jails in the capital. "Private cells and prisons," such as William H. Williams' Yellow House, "have been erected by the slave traders in the District," observed a congressman in 1835. Bondpeople "are brought into this city, sometimes marching in double files, connected by chains passing through hand-cuffs or collars, and sometimes crowded into large wagons, like sheep for the slaughter" or, to use another analogy, "like droves of cattle." The slaves are then "driven through the streets of this city," past the US Capitol, and "deposited in the 'private jails' prepared for their reception."[9]

There the slaves awaited re-sale. Sometimes, but especially in the 1820s and early 1830s, dealers auctioned them off publicly within the District. "The District of Columbia is the great mart for the sale of men," complained one antislavery activist in 1834. It is home to "a vast and diabolical slave trade[. T]he red ensign of the auctioneer," customarily hung out to advertise the site of an impending sale, "is stuck up under the flag which waves from the towers of the Capitol." By the end of the 1830s, however, local sales in public spaces outside the pens had fallen into disrepute and diminished, replaced by private sales negotiated within the walls and behind closed doors. Still, the vastly greater number of enslaved captives occupying Washington's slave pens would not be sold to nearby masters at all but to strangers in distant lands, hundreds upon hundreds of miles away. In the Washington slave jails, explained one informant, "the negro is incarcerated until a cargo of slaves, of 'human chattels,' can be completed."[10]

Once traders accumulated a sufficient stock of bondpeople to constitute a shipment, they prepared them for departure. As one representative in Congress explained, they "gather together gangs of slaves, and then fasten them by a long chain, running between the pairs, and to this they are hand-cuffed, right and left, and so driven off, ten, twenty, and thirty in a drove." Thus bound, they exited the pen, navigated the streets of the capital, and crossed the Long Bridge over the Potomac, at the southwestern end of Maryland Avenue. "The number passing the bridge, in a year, was said to have amounted to hundreds," wrote one observer in 1825, and the scale of the slave trade only increased as the nation experienced the flush times of the 1830s. Whereas some slave coffles kept marching hundreds of miles, across state lines, to their final destination, William H. Williams guided his captives through Alexandria to the riverfront. "Scarcely a week passes without some of these wretched creatures being driven through our streets," grumbled one contemporary soured on the sight of slave coffles forcibly paraded down Alexandria's thoroughfares. "After having been confined, and sometimes manacled, in a loathsome prison, they are turned out in a public view, to take their departure for the South. The children, and some of the women, are generally crowded into a cart or wagon, while the others follow on foot, not infrequently handcuffed and chained together."[11]

Williams and other D.C. traders then loaded their human cargoes on to vessels participating in the coastwise trade. After pulling out of port in Alexandria, they sailed down the Potomac, into the Chesapeake, and out into the Atlantic. By the time Williams achieved preeminence as a trader, his coastwise slavers set out occasionally for the port of Mobile, Alabama, but more commonly for New Orleans. Traders such as Williams undertook these voyages seasonally. Slaving vessels usually plied the coastal waters from October to May, avoiding the hottest months of summer, the malarial season, and the frequent outbreaks of yellow fever that besieged the Crescent City almost annually. The coastwise slaving calendar reduced mortality and increased the odds of maintaining the health of human cargoes. Voyages to New Orleans aboard the "floating jails" took about four weeks. Once in port, the slaves would be placed in a pen, fattened, and prepped for sale at auction. Traders maintained ownership of the bondpeople conveyed to the South until the moment they finalized their sales.[12]

New Orleans ranked as the largest slave market in the Old South and in all of North America. From the 1790s to the 1860s, the domestic slave trade dislocated one million bondpeople from home and loved ones, more than two-thirds of that figure between 1820 and 1860 alone. About 100,000, or 10 percent of the total, passed through New Orleans. The

twin demands of cotton and sugar cultivation sucked slaves involuntarily into the city's pool of laborers for sale. The number of Louisiana
sugar plantations increased more than threefold from 1824 to 1830,
leading to a dramatic increase in the numbers of slaves toiling in the
legendary hell of the cane swamps. Through no coincidence, the value
of the cane crop more than tripled between 1820 and 1829. At the same
time, cotton became the leading US export in the 1820s, and the
expanding cotton frontier dispatched eager buyers to New Orleans on
a quest for an idealized labor force necessary to clear the land and make
a crop. Cotton prices "reached fifteen-year highs by 1835," spurring the
acquisition of ever more slaves. Professional slave traders accordingly
increased the scale of their operations to keep pace with demand. One
of every twelve slaves crossed state lines in the 1820s, and one of every
seven in the 1830s. Thirty percent of all bondpeople living in the
Virginia Tidewater that decade were yanked out of the commonwealth.
From 1833 to 1836 alone, 150,000 slaves were part of a sweeping, compulsory migration to the newer states of the Old Southwest. Large
numbers passed through the Crescent City, either with their masters
and onward to their new plantation homes upriver or as chattel for sale.
Between 1820 and 1860, the New Orleans slave markets disposed of
6,000–8,000 bondpeople each year to new owners, or about $11 million
worth of enslaved bodies annually. Many of these slaves produced the
cotton that transformed New Orleans into a commercial powerhouse
thoroughly enmeshed in an Atlantic capitalist economy. By 1850, the
bustling port was not only the largest city in the South but also the third-
largest in the United States. Measured by the value of its exports, it
outranked New York City as of 1834 and became the fourth-largest port
globally in the 1840s. Slave trading not only was big business: it made big
business.[13]

This book chronicles the misadventures of slave trader and slave pen
operator William H. Williams, who trafficked in commodified human
beings during a career that spanned from the late 1820s to 1850.
During that time, he sold untold thousands of slaves in Washington,
D.C., New Orleans, and other slave markets. His slave-trading activities
took an extraordinary turn in September 1840 when one of his agents

purchased a parcel of twenty-seven enslaved convicts – twenty-one men and six women – out of the Virginia State Penitentiary in Richmond. They had been convicted of a range of felonies and sentenced to death, but the commonwealth's governor exercised his legal right to reprieve them to sale and transportation outside the United States as an alternative to execution. He sold them to Williams' agent with the understanding that the enslaved criminals would, in accordance with Virginia law, be transported out of the country. Williams furnished the required $1,000 bond per slave as insurance that he would remove them beyond the limits of the United States, but six weeks later, he appeared in New Orleans with his human cargo in tow. His violation of an 1817 Louisiana statute against the importation of enslaved convicts set off a protracted legal battle in the state court system. Altogether, Williams was party to more than a dozen lawsuits, providing ample fodder for a book that weaves together strands of slave criminality, the coastwise domestic slave trade, and southern jurisprudence.[14]

Few scholars have ever mentioned William H. Williams or his fateful journey of 1840. Whereas some slave traders have had articles or entire volumes written about them, Williams has garnered only cursory examination, never earning more than a sentence or two and sometimes only a footnote.[15] And despite the explosion of research on the domestic slave trade over the past two decades, as well as the publication of landmark works in the new history of capitalism that situate the forced migration of slaves to the Old Southwest within the context of an expansive and rapidly evolving economic system, the legal history of the domestic slave trade remains little explored. With the notable exception of breach of warranty suits, in which slave purchasers sued traders after finding their newly acquired human property "unsound" in either mind or body, scholars have overlooked a host of legal issues resulting from the internal traffic in enslaved laborers. Williams spent the bulk of his adult life mired in litigation related to his profession. In 1840, his cargo of convicted slaves that arrived in New Orleans generated a sensation nationwide as it not only shed light on Williams' own sordid business dealings as human trafficker but also exposed multiple points of contention within the construction of Louisiana slave law. The tangle of legal issues raised by Williams' case would not be fully unraveled until after the Civil War and the abolition of slavery itself.[16]

Slave ships and their cargoes have inspired no shortage of studies. Unlike Williams' imbroglio in New Orleans, the vast majority of these contain an international dimension, examining the transatlantic slave traffic, outlawed beginning in 1808, and the Middle Passage from Africa to the Americas.[17] The fully lawful coastwise domestic slave trade produced its own share of memorable incidents, including shipwrecks and captives' shipboard uprisings. The Williams' gang slaves neither wrecked nor rebelled during their voyage, and their story does not share the same notoriety as other contemporaneous incidents, aboard such vessels as the *Creole* or the *Amistad.* It is nevertheless significant in that it offers the first detailed look at a shipment of enslaved criminals ordered sold and transported out of the United States. That the captives never made it outside the country reveals much about the functioning of the coastwise domestic slave trade in law and in practice. Williams' exploits with his enslaved transports attracted national attention by exposing the legal machinery that governed the realm of human trafficking.[18]

No simple biography, *Williams' Gang* is a roughly chronological story of not only a trader but also his enslaved cargo. Every act of sale told of one person's profit as it related a brief tale of another's heartbreak, tragedy, and misery. We learn about the convict slaves from Virginia transported by William H. Williams to New Orleans from a vast array of sources that collectively help identify the members of the Williams' gang captives by name, age, sex, and market value, and supply knowledge of the dates, locations, and natures of the crimes for which they were convicted. Surviving records permit the reconstruction of tumultuous and difficult moments for the accused bondpeople and offer a fleeting glimpse of their emotionally complex lives, filled with anxiety, suffering, deprivation, and loss. We also step inside the Louisiana State Penitentiary, where ten of the Williams' gang slaves spent years as property of the state, toiling at hard labor.

Before transfer to and imprisonment in Louisiana, Williams' gang was held in the notorious Yellow House slave pen, recreated in this book by drawing generously upon the accounts of visitors to the jail as well as

Solomon Northup's narrative *Twelve Years a Slave*. The Yellow House's most famous prisoner, Northup was held captive there only months after the Williams' gang slaves departed. We learn as well about Williams' early slave-trading career and the larger dynamics that sustained it. Slave manifests, mandated by the act of 1807 that outlawed the transatlantic slave trade as a bureaucratic means to deter illegal importations, listed such vital information as the names of the shippers or owners, the names and tonnage of the slaving vessels transporting the slaves coastwise, and the names, sex, age, height, and color of each enslaved captive on board, along with the ports of origin and arrival and the person or entity to which the shipment was consigned. Virginia governors' executive papers uncover the process of selling convict slaves, based on a system of competitive bidding. A Williams agent won the enslaved criminals, who were transported to Washington, D.C., briefly incarcerated in the Yellow House, and then shipped out of Alexandria.

After an aborted attempted landing in Mobile, Alabama, William H. Williams conveyed his cargo of enslaved transports to Louisiana. Newspapers and New Orleans notarial records supply the best evidence for what transpired. Notaries public documented the sales of slaves in New Orleans in heavy, massive volumes available for viewing by researchers today in the Orleans Parish Clerk of Civil District Court Office. But Williams did not sell his enslaved transports in New Orleans. New Orleans police records show that the convicts were confiscated from him, after which Williams gathered testimony from eyewitnesses and put their accounts on file with a notary public, thus preserving detailed information no longer found among the surviving court records of his case.[19]

Accessing court records is still essential to understanding slave dealers. Although some traders, such as Franklin & Armfield of Alexandria, Virginia, landed in court less frequently than others (most notably Theophilus Freeman, a defendant in some thirty lawsuits across three states), the nature of their business meant that they all ended up there eventually. Quite simply, slaves were valuable property, so their sales sometimes prompted litigation. Slave traders sued, for instance, to recover debts owed them by clients with unpaid balances on their slave purchases. Compared with that, William H. Williams' many brushes with the law proved far weightier and more complicated. Court records and related petitions from the District of Columbia chronicle Williams' long history of litigation, including a series of *habeas corpus* cases in which he was accused of the illegal incarceration of free people of color in the Yellow House.[20]

Other cases, plus newspapers and legislative reports, permit us to explore the relationships between slave trading, finance, and the emerging capitalist system of the antebellum decades. They unearth the involvement of William H. Williams and his cronies as both investors in and beneficiaries of suspect antebellum banking institutions in Maryland that sprouted up after the death of the Second Bank of the United States and the corresponding loss of its regulatory authority. Williams' use of unsound currency in the acquisition of slaves shortly before one institution's collapse landed him in court several times as sellers sued him, charging that he was aware of the bank's insolvency yet passed the near worthless paper knowingly to perpetrate fraud. Through Williams, the dynamic commercial webs that bound the older slaveholding states to the Old Southwest, the fishy institutional arrangements that undergirded the domestic slave trade, and the seedy internal dynamics and ethically questionable behavioral norms endemic to slavery's capitalism all come into sharper focus. The Chesapeake may rightfully stake its claim for placement alongside the cotton frontier at the vanguard of the new economy.

In the pivotal case of *State v. Williams*, the state of Louisiana prosecuted Williams for the unlawful importation of enslaved convicts. As the suit against him progressed from the First District Criminal Court of New Orleans to the Louisiana Supreme Court, Williams' difficulties, it became clear at trial, were the by-product of a clumsily written law that legislators had made in haste decades earlier. Simultaneously, the case surrounding the slave dealer's illicit cargo exposed multiple issues that transcended the relatively circumscribed realm of Louisiana's slave code to raise significant legal matters concerning the distinction between civil law and criminal law, the Louisiana Supreme Court's appellate powers, and the distinguishing characteristics of what constituted a "penal action."

Williams left behind no known diaries, account books, or business papers. He kept a ledger book detailing all of the enslaved prisoners held captive in his jail, but that, too, is not known to survive. Only some scant correspondence appears in Williams' hand. Newspapers, court cases, slave manifests, and notarized slave bills of sale fill the void, enabling us to track William H. Williams' slave-trading business from the last of the flush times of the 1830s to the "hard times" following the Panic of 1837 and beyond. While Williams' was bogged down in court in New Orleans, his younger brother Thomas Williams figured more prominently in running the family's operations starting in 1841. As a more robust economy returned by 1845, Thomas ran the family enterprise successfully while navigating his own courtroom encounters.

Williams' slave pen also figured recurrently in the context of American politics. The sight of slave coffles marched to and from the Yellow House, within the metaphorical shadow of the US Capitol, greatly offended abolitionists. "The inhuman practice" of the slave trade within the District of Columbia, wrote one antislavery publication, "is so shocking to the moral sense of the community, as to call loudly for the interposition of Congress . . . Humanity, justice, national character, consistency, all unite in demanding it." Petitions poured in to the House of Representatives calling for the termination of the slave trade in the District, but the gag rule stymied debates over them until 1844. That same year, a newspaper war erupted between the Whig and Democratic presses in Washington, D.C., as rival editors debated which party was responsible for hoisting a political flag over Williams' slave jail during the presidential election. Six years later, the Compromise of 1850, a collection of legislative measures designed to tamp down the rising tensions over slavery that were then plaguing the nation, ended the D.C. slave trade, forcing the closure of the Yellow House.[21]

After the state of Louisiana seized Williams' gang, the slave trader labored mightily for their return. Williams, still resentful of the verdict against him, circumvented the court system by petitioning the Louisiana legislature for relief. His efforts prompted yet another court case. Williams' unusual cargo of enslaved criminals in 1840 not only interfered with the terrible and routine business of human trafficking but also produced a series of courtroom clashes that permeated many different aspects of Louisiana law.

Williams died without a will, but a probate inventory cataloged his wealth. His widow, Violet, inherited both her deceased husband's riches and his legal troubles. As explained in the final chapter, as Violet Williams navigated wartime Washington and the 1862 emancipation of slaves in the District of Columbia, she was sued over the same enslaved convicts her husband had bought in Virginia more than two decades earlier. That case would be carried all the way to the US Supreme Court and conclude years after slavery's demise.

As much as the sources permit us to peer into William H. Williams' life and work, much remains a mystery. Some gaps in knowledge cannot yet be filled. Future discoveries of additional evidence may prove wrong some of the cautious speculation engaged in here. The commonality of the slave dealer's name complicates the process of tracking him down in the historical record. Was the trader the same William H. Williams who was a temperance advocate in Washington, D.C., in 1854? It seems out of character for him but not entirely out of the question. Was he the same William H. Williams of the Baltimore mercantile partnership of Shwartz & Williams, which dissolved in March 1855? Or the same William H. Williams living in Patuxent City, Maryland, who advertised for runaway slave John Briscoe the following May? Possibly. Was the sloop *William H. Williams*, which ran between the Chesapeake and New Orleans, named for the slave dealer, just as Isaac Franklin of Franklin & Armfield had bestowed his name upon one of his slaving vessels? Maybe so. That the slave-trading William H. Williams consistently used his middle initial permits us to eliminate him as a co-partner in the New Orleans confectionary business of William Williams & Co., but it is impossible to determine if he was related to either Edward Williams, Joseph C. Williams, George W. Williams, or John G. Williams, all of whom shared his occupation in the 1820s and 1830s. He was definitively related to his younger brother Thomas, whom he mentored in the business of slave trading and who became his most trusted ally in the slave trade.[22]

In some ways, the story presented here is unique, a tale of one highly unusual shipment of enslaved men and women and the captor who carried them into bondage of a different sort than the vast majority of slaves ever knew. Most captive laborers stolen from the Chesapeake were not convicted criminals, like those of Williams' gang. Most captive laborers conveyed to New Orleans arrived there legally, swept up in the lawful but involuntary exodus of slaves to the Old Southwest. Legally, Louisiana itself was singular among the states in that it followed a civil-law rather than a common-law tradition. Under the common law, explained Attorney General Christian Roselius of Louisiana, "all misdemeanors are punishable with fine and imprisonment at the discretion of the court; and all new offences are considered as misdemeanors unless they are declared to be felonies." Louisiana was different. Here, explained Judge François-Xavier Martin of the state Supreme Court, "we have no common law offences ... All crimes and offences against our law are created and punishable by statute." It was therefore incumbent upon the Louisiana legislature to identify and define each crime and attach a commensurate penalty. Any carelessness or neglect in these duties could generate future confusion over the law, as William H. Williams would learn. The trader's legal saga over the shipment of convict slaves, in short, could not have happened in any other state except Louisiana.[23]

Despite his case's exceptionality, William H. Williams serves as well as anyone as a window into the legal difficulties attendant in the slave-trading profession broadly construed. He not only imported convict slaves contrary to law but also illegally detained free black people in his Washington slave pen and completed shady transactions with worthless paper, among a host of other criminal or morally questionable activities. Williams endured a host of self-inflicted misfortunes, yet in the process made a fortune. He and other slave traders paid cash for slaves in the Chesapeake, where surplus laborers glutted the market and reduced their prices, and then sold them in southwestern markets, where enslaved workers were in high demand and expensive. Therein lay traders' profits, and for Williams and many dealers like him, it was a remunerative profession. Yet even though slave traders were in fact often among the wealthiest and most prominent men in the South, southern whites – slaveholders included – readily dismissed them in public discourse as categorically unscrupulous and disreputable. Slave traders' poor reputation in the public mind notwithstanding, they were crucial cogs in a great global machine. Occupying a world of relentless ambition, chicanery, fraud, and deceit, all of which were part and parcel of the emerging capitalist economy, they redistributed the labor force that kept the South's economic motor and Great Britain's cotton textile mills humming.

Williams' long but troubled career as a slave dealer active in the waterborne trade grants us access not only to the legal but also to the larger economic, political, and social landscapes of his time. The events leading up to and resulting from his imbroglio in New Orleans paint a colorful and dynamic portrait of the business of domestic slave trading, the booms and busts of the Old South's slave economy, and the national struggle over bondage. The result is a snapshot of the antebellum era, told through the lens of one slave dealer's life.

In all this, we must not lose sight of who Williams was and what he did for a livelihood. "[W]hat is the slave trade?" asked Vermont's William Slade in the US House chamber in 1838. "It is the making merchandize of men. It is . . . the buying and selling of men and women to get gain." William H. Williams never experienced a spiritual epiphany as did the mid-eighteenth-century transatlantic slave trader John Newton, who went on to become an abolitionist cleric and to compose the hymn, "Amazing Grace." Throughout his lifetime, Williams remained committed to the "abominable and disgraceful traffic" in enslaved bodies. Though commodified, the men and women ensnared in the slave trade were no ordinary commodities, akin to bales of cotton, hogsheads of sugar, bushels of corn, barrels of flour, or casks of molasses. They were fathers and sons, mothers and daughters, brothers and sisters, aunts and uncles. Many marched from the District of Columbia to the Deep South, chained in coffles, their two captive feet carrying them against their will. Williams, in contrast, transported bondpeople coastwise. Shipboard, each individual bondperson constituted a special type of cargo. Their names appeared clearly on the slave manifests of each voyage, a legal requirement that denied their anonymity and testified to their humanity. They had been stolen from family and friends. They survived a slave jail, described by one abolitionist congressman as "that infernal hell which once existed at the corner of Seventh street and Maryland avenue." They endured the journey to the Lower South and the horrors that awaited them. And so it is just to recover the stories of those victimized by the domestic slave trade and to resurrect them from the hard numbers and emotionless quantitative data of the human traffic, even as William H. Williams pursued a perverse, distorted brand of justice that would acknowledge them as his property.[24]

CHAPTER 1

An Ambush

J OHN ASHFORD'S ASSAILANTS LEAPT OUT FROM BEHIND
some bushes when they attacked him on a clear, starlit Saturday
night in 1840. Wielding clubs of locust wood and black oak, they administered repeated blows to the head and neck that rendered Ashford's
bruised and swollen face virtually unrecognizable. The assault must have
generated immense, if fleeting, gratification among the attackers, for all
of them were enslaved, and Ashford was a member of the patrol, one of
the Old South's many informal, community-based police forces tasked
with monitoring neighborhood bondmen's nocturnal activities and
sending back those who had strayed off the plantation.[1]

It was February 29 – leap day evening – at about 9 p.m. when
Captain Stephen B. Jones summoned brothers John and Francis P.
Ashford and their kinsman Francis Ashford "to make their round" on
patrol duty, as they had been doing the past fourteen months. During
that time, the company had conveyed three slaves to the local magistrate for punishment. Twice the patrol itself had taken the liberty of
punishing slaves, with consent of the master, without consulting the
magistrate. Nothing in their history of regulating local bondmen
could have prepared them for the magnitude of the events that
were about to unfold. The evening got off to an unexceptional start.
The four patrollers set off on foot, "entirely unarmed," in the performance of their duty. As they traversed the Fairfax County, Virginia,
countryside, they heard the ten o'clock "Bell, or Clock" reverberate
over the landscape from the nearby town of Alexandria, part of the
District of Columbia until 1846. Despite the late hour, the patrol
found the roads abuzz with activity, for tomorrow was Sunday, slaves'

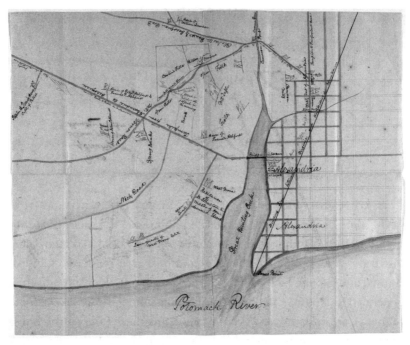

3 Map of the vicinity of the ambush.
Source: Map of the Contiguous Parts of Alexandria and Fairfax County, Virginia, Executive Papers, Thomas Walker Gilmer, Box 1, Folder 6, map 755.23 1840, Library of Virginia, Richmond.

customary day off from the work routines that structured their lives. Saturday night afforded bondpeople welcome opportunities for clandestine parties in the woods, dancing, drinking, gambling, and sex. While the patrol was taking a break at Hunting Creek Bridge, "Mr. Foote's negroes came up." (See Figure 3.) The white men requested to see their passes, the precious slips of paper indispensable for slaves desiring to travel unmolested off their home plantations. Upon inspecting their tickets, the patrol, satisfied, discharged the bondmen without incident. Throughout the encounter, the slaves "behaved very civilly," exhibiting the racial deference whites expected as their due.[2]

Not so the next group of slaves who approached. As John Ashford recalled, "some other negroes came up," including Alfred, Spencer, Henry, Taylor, Dennis, John Mudd, and two unidentified "boys" aged fifteen or sixteen, both of whom reeked of fish, having recently marketed their catch in town. The patrol demanded they all produce their passes. Striking a match, they lit a candle and, by its faint glow, examined the tickets the newcomers presented. As Jones and Francis P. Ashford scrutinized the passes, one of the bondmen – either Alfred or Spencer – boldly "walked up & whistled in Jones's face." Captain Jones barked a warning to "go off" or risk incurring a "slap ... in the mouth" or other punishment. The patrol took into custody the two enslaved "boys," each of whom lacked a pass, tied them up with a rope, and ordered the remainder of the company on their way. Alfred and Spencer, two bondmen who had gained reputations as "rude and impudent" during previous brushes with the patrol, appeared reluctant to depart, perhaps not wishing to abandon their erstwhile companions to the whims of their captors. Instead Alfred and Spencer loitered, resting against the rails at the south end of Hunting Creek Bridge as they grumbled in hushed tones about the white men oppressing them. Francis P. Ashford "spoke to them about it," and, after lingering momentarily, they begrudgingly ambled off into the night. The patrol, with two bound slaves now in tow, resumed its charge.[3]

By 11 p.m., the patrol arrived at Samuel Catts' tavern – a possible magnet for illicit frivolity on slaves' Saturday nights – to assure "that all was quiet." Following a brief respite, the patrollers moved on, fording Cameron Run, crossing paths with a hostile neighborhood dog, and arriving at a fork in the road. Rather than take the path to Occoquan, they tramped more than half a mile farther down the Mt. Vernon Road, in the Spring Bank neighborhood of Fairfax County. Around midnight or 1 a.m. on Sunday, Captain Jones halted his company so that his comrades might double-check the cords binding the two young slaves taken captive at Hunting Creek Bridge. As they did so, Jones detected a presence "in some thin bushes" alongside the road. Initially believing it foraging cattle, he did not realize in time that it was the second, troublesome band of slaves from the bridge, including the disgruntled Alfred and Spencer, crouched in ambush. Before Jones could utter a cry of warning, the slaves sprang upon the patrollers. The assailants first "attacked Jones," felling the captain with "several clubs." Francis P. Ashford was adjusting the enslaved prisoners' ropes when he heard the commotion and turned, only to find Jones sprawled out on the ground.

He rushed to intervene, but the insurgent slaves struck him too, knocking him senseless. Clutching a stick, John Ashford entered the scuffle and scattered the attackers, but the bondmen quickly regrouped and landed several severe blows on his skull. A final shot from Spencer sent the stunned and reeling Ashford to the ground, unconscious.[4]

John Ashford's desperate offensive allowed Jones a moment to recover, struggle to his feet, and battle the bondman John Mudd. The patrol leader seized "a stick from one of the slaves," but "Spencer knocked him down," commandeered the weapon, and used it to knock out Ashford. As Jones attempted to flee the chaotic scene, the rebellious slaves blocked the road in both directions, so he moved perpendicular to them, clambered over a fence adjacent to the path, and tumbled awkwardly into a field. According to the captain, "Spencer sprang up on the fence, struck him, and called out 'Damn you, I will kill you.'" But Jones frantically scrambled away, fearful for his life, "and made his escape," confident in his assumption that "two or three of the Patrol were killed" in the bedlam.[5]

Jones maintained enough of his senses to think to take sanctuary at the home of his brother-in-law, William Lawson, and to sound the alarm that a gang of slaves had waylaid the patrol. Lawson dispatched his son Charles to fetch Dr. Richard C. Mason to tend to Jones' wounds. Dr. Mason remained with Jones and sent Charles Lawson on horseback to investigate the scene of the fray. Mason would not go until he knew whether the Ashfords required his services. Perhaps, as Jones feared, they were already dead.[6]

Charles Lawson was not soon in returning, probably because he could not locate the Ashfords at the site of the attack. Dr. Mason returned to his home, where, at 3:15 a.m., Michael Ashford – father to John and Francis P. – and another neighborhood white man named John Collard roused the physician to alert him that the injured brothers had reached home. Quite possibly Francis Ashford, knocked down during the skirmish but apparently not as seriously hurt, got the "severely beaten" victims to safety. Dr. Mason tended to their wounds the next morning. He first called briefly upon Captain Jones, whom he had administered to the night before. Though "lamed by a blow" to the hip and bruised on his limbs, Jones was otherwise free of "any deadly or dangerous injury." Dr. Mason next journeyed to Michael Ashford's house, where the distressed father's two sons convalesced in the same room. The doctor found John Ashford "terribly beaten indeed." The slaves had inflicted "[o]ne very heavy blow," a three-inch gash "over the left eye brow" as deep as the bone, as well as another "on the left side of his neck." The swelling obscured John's vision and left him dreadfully disfigured in appearance. Lesser injuries included "sundry cuts and bruises" to the top of the head, mouth, and right side of his face. Francis P. Ashford suffered a contusion above his left ear and other head injuries. Both brothers had an "excited pulse," complained of intense, throbbing pain, and vomited profusely, indicating to the doctor a "high degree of disturbance of the brain." Mason bled both men "copiously" and administered to Francis P. "active purgative medicine."[7]

The physician then proceeded to the location of the assault. Mason observed the impressions in the sand where the melee occurred. He saw one indentation in the ground "covered with blood, not with a mere stain, but clotted in a cake." A slight distance away, he noticed "the spot where Francis P. Ashford" must have collapsed on to the sand: "there too was evidence of a free loss of blood." The doctor's examination left no doubt about the ferocity of the battle. Like the physician, the victims' father also visited the site of the attack on Sunday morning. A scuffle had obviously taken place there. Michael Ashford picked up from where they lay on the ground the clubs that the slaves had wielded as weapons so that they might serve as evidence in court.[8]

Antebellum Virginia did not permit slaves accused of felonies a jury trial. Instead, enslaved defendants in the commonwealth appeared before ad hoc courts of oyer and terminer, convened at the county level as the occasion warranted. At such courts, a panel of at least five justices of the peace heard evidence, determined the guilt or innocence of the accused party, and levied any punishment lawfully due the slave. Local authorities took into custody five bondmen identified by the victims of the attack on the patrol as perpetrators of the assault, and on March 11, 1840, less than two weeks after the ambush, they appeared for trial before a Fairfax County court of oyer and terminer, charged with beating and wounding with intent to kill Stephen B. Jones, John Ashford, and Francis P. Ashford. Four of the defendants – Alfred, Spencer, Henry, and Taylor – counted among the human property of Dennis Johnston, a prominent local planter and owner of almost fifty enslaved persons. Unlike the rest of his co-defendants, the "negro Dennis" belonged to the estate of the deceased Daniel Monroe. (A sixth alleged attacker, John Mudd, owned by minors but under the guardianship of Dennis Johnston, appeared at trial separately.) All of the accused pleaded not guilty to the charge levied against them.[9]

Prosecuting the case against a complement of five enslaved defendants proved a formidable challenge. The patrollers could not agree definitively on the identities of all their assailants. The attack unfolded at night, as "the Big Stars shone," bathing Fairfax County in gentle light – sufficient illumination for John Ashford to assert with certainty that he "recognized" the enslaved assailants "as the same negroes they had met at the Bridge" earlier in the evening. According to Ashford, Alfred, Spencer, Henry, and Taylor were all present. He believed Dennis was too, but that that bondman was preoccupied with the two "boys … who were tied," one of whom was his son whom he presumably hoped to liberate from the patrol's clutches. Whether as a result of the lighting conditions or the general pandemonium of the ambush, other patrollers did not share John Ashford's confidence. Captain Jones testified that he could not be sure that Henry, Taylor, or Dennis was involved in the fray at all, recalling only that Henry and Dennis had been at the bridge earlier in the evening. Francis P. Ashford remembered Alfred, Spencer, and Dennis from the bridge, but could not identify any of the assailants. Francis Ashford recognized only Alfred and Spencer from the night's mayhem. The accumulated testimony pointed most strongly toward those two bondmen. With the involvement of Henry, Taylor, and Dennis cast in some doubt, the magistrates holding court found those three not guilty and discharged them. But the terrible example set by the crime of assaulting the white men of the patrol could not go entirely unpunished. The court found both Alfred and Spencer guilty and, on March 12, 1840, condemned them to death. The pair of slaves – brothers, as it turned out – were to bide their time in jail until April 17, the third Friday of that month, at which time they would be escorted to Fairfax

County's "place of Public Execution" and be "hung by the neck until they be *dead*," sometime between the hours of noon and 2 p.m.[10]

The commonwealth of Virginia reimbursed masters the monetary value of any slave lawfully executed. Codifying its first compensation statute into law in 1705, Virginia set the precedent that masters of enslaved offenders should not suffer the full economic brunt of their bondpeople's criminal behavior. Southern, slaveholding colonies and states (except Georgia, after 1793) all adopted some variation of a compensation scheme. Some states established a maximum dollar value that the owner of a capitally convicted bondperson could receive. Others set compensation up to a specified fraction of the slave's market price. More generously, Virginia offered masters the "full value" of an enslaved convict, but the commonwealth's terminology was misleading. Many factors, including a bondperson's age, sex, occupation or skill set, general character, and overall health, contributed to a slave's sale price. Additionally, a Virginia statute newly implemented in March 1840 mandated that a convicted slave's valuation assume the buyer's "knowledge of his or her guilt," which automatically reduced, to some degree, the anticipated market price at public auction. The law specified that each of "the justices who shall condemn … [a] slave shall value him or her." The final payment to the enslaved convict's owner was determined by taking an average of the magistrates' appraisals. Alfred and Spencer would drain the state's coffers of $900 and $850, respectively.[11]

The court's pronouncement of sentence sparked an intense dialogue in Fairfax County over the propriety of the punishment. Such debates proved common in many instances in which antebellum Virginia's courts of oyer and terminer convicted slaves like Alfred and Spencer of capital crimes. As of 1801, Virginia law dictated that, in all cases in which slaves were condemned to death, a record of the court proceeding be forwarded to the governor and his council so that the executive might commute the sentence to sale and transportation outside the United States or, in very rare cases, grant a full pardon. The commonwealth's governors had occasionally reprieved slaves in the years before 1801, but after Virginia lawmakers codified the process for commutations of sentence into law, they virtually guaranteed that protracted, sometimes heated discussions would erupt in the affected communities over the ultimate dispensation of slave criminal cases. Like Virginia, other southern, slaveholding states, too, especially those of the Upper South, permitted the same alternative to hanging. In many cases, they realized, sale and transportation disposed of troublesome bondpeople as effectively as death but without the grisly spectacle of execution. What made Virginia different was the magnitude of the practice. The commonwealth sold and transported almost one thousand convicted slaves between 1801 and 1864. By law, masters were compensated for such bondpeople the same as if they had been executed at the gallows.[12]

Several prominent citizens of Fairfax County corresponded with one another and with two successive Virginia governors, David Campbell and Thomas Walker Gilmer, from mid-March to May 1840 to ensure that the state meted out the death penalty as set forth by the court of oyer and terminer. Dr. Richard C. Mason, the physician who saw firsthand the bloody aftermath of the slaves' attack upon the patrollers, strenuously championed Alfred's and Spencer's executions. He and George Mason – a planter in the vicinity of Alexandria, the committing magistrate in the bondmen's case, and likely Richard C.'s brother – juxtaposed the relative characters of the two slaves with those of their white victims. George Mason, responsible for organizing the patrol company in January 1839, took pride in its composition. He described its members as "all young men of good Families & Character, regular & orderly [in] Conduct, industrious, honest & worthy." He singled out for especial praise Captain Jones, "a man of much intelligence, integrity & courage," "a most valuable and faithful officer." Slave patrols occasionally drew criticism for the wanton abuse of slaves or for overenthusiastically correcting bondpeople's perceived misbehavior, but throughout their lengthy tenure on patrol, not a single Fairfax County slaveholder had lodged any complaint against Jones or the men under his command.[13]

In contrast to the unimpeachable character of the patrol, Alfred and Spencer had gained reputations as neighborhood troublemakers. According to various reports, "they have always been reputed as men of very bad Character," "not only Thieves, but turbulent & outrageous in their behavior." Spencer had committed an unrelated "Felony" as recently as June 1839. The enslaved brothers were locally notorious as a "roguish" pair. One of them was rumored to have violently attacked their former master, who was compelled to sell them as a consequence of their reportedly "turbulent and violent" natures. When presented with a petition encouraging Virginia's governor not to interfere with the slated execution of Alfred and Spencer, Dr. Mason, though sympathetic to the sentiment of the memorial, declined to add his signature, fearing "that the remaining brothers of these men would murder him in a spirit of revenge," for "the *ferocious temper* and *disposition to revenge*" was common "to the whole family." Mason was petrified of the ramifications should the brothers' kin "find out that he had signed that paper."[14]

Generally, whites in Fairfax County believed the scheduled executions of Alfred and Spencer the most appropriate fates for the enslaved brothers. As they saw it, the trial was undeniably fair. It had proceeded in accordance with the law and had been decided on the basis of the evidence. Plus, the court had reached a unanimous verdict, without "*a moment[']s doubt or hesitation.*"[15] In addition, the Masons argued, heinous crimes deserved death, and the assault upon the patrol proved so vicious, so "wilful and malicious," and so galling to public sensibilities, that nothing short of the bondmen's hanging could soothe a society unnerved and on edge. Richard C. Mason described the attack upon "the Police Patrol of our County" as a "flagrant case of insurrection, and rebellion against the lawful authorities of the Commonwealth." It must be met with "*exemplary* punishment" or risk "another Southampton Tragedy brought to our own doors." The deadly Nat Turner slave revolt referenced by Mason had erupted less than a decade earlier in Southside Virginia, resulting in the deaths of almost sixty whites. Memories of the rebellion lingered, still fresh enough to induce the frightening specter of another slaughter at the hands of marauding blacks. According to Mason, failure to punish Alfred and Spencer with due severity would set a dangerous precedent for the future, embolden the commonwealth's slaves, and spur them to additional crimes.[16]

Certainly many whites in the Chesapeake believed themselves under siege by the slave population. They often spoke nostalgically of days past when slaves were supposedly better behaved and more obedient than they were now. Slaves' "insolence and insubordination [are] greatly increased," grumbled one resident. To him, Fairfax County's close proximity to the nation's capital only exacerbated the challenges of enforcing slave discipline. "[T]he nearer you approach the district of Columbia the more unwilling the obedience ... of the slave," he complained. In the environs of the nation's capital, "our Slaves are hearing Abolition Doctrines ... preached every Day from the very Halls of Congress." Under such circumstances, only Alfred's and Spencer's executions and the undeniable message they would send could ensure the safety and security of the neighborhood.[17]

Proponents of execution dismissed the transportation of Virginia's enslaved convicts out of the United States as impractical and unviable. When the commonwealth's governors first accelerated the practice of commuting bondpeople's punishment to sale and transportation in the early nineteenth century, convict slaves often went to Spanish Florida. After the United States acquired Florida in 1819, slaving vessels increasingly carried reprieved bondpeople to the West Indies. After Great Britain initiated the emancipation of slaves in its Caribbean territories in 1834, traders necessarily funneled those slaves most commonly to Spanish colonial holdings in the region. By 1840, an overabundance of enslaved Africans in the Spanish West Indies meant that convict slaves sent there for sale brought "nothing more than half the price" they could have attracted on the US mainland. Contemporary observers implicitly understood and resigned themselves to the fact that, throughout the history of sale and transportation from Virginia, some slave traders carried enslaved convicts surreptitiously to the South to sell at auction within the United States, contrary to the commonwealth's laws, without divulging the circumstances of their removal from Virginia. The deception endemic to the slave trade meant that dealers could extract full price for convict bondpeople from buyers "ignorant of their crimes." William Branch Giles, governor of Virginia from 1827 to 1830, once indicated to the state legislature that "the negro Traders who purchased the negro criminals" were evading "the law of transportation." Likewise, William M. McCarty, during his brief tenure in 1827 as acting governor of the Florida Territory, complained to the legislative council that enslaved convicts "were brought into that Territory & there sold" contrary to statute. Lawmakers appeared at a loss to supply any legislative remedy for the illegal transport of convict slaves into Virginia's sister states, and the covert introduction of enslaved criminals into the Deep South continued apace.[18]

Alternatively, traders in 1840 might lawfully transport enslaved convicts to the foreign country of Texas, an independent republic since 1836, with a government friendly to slavery. For Virginians in favor of Alfred's and Spencer's executions, this solution, too, proved a source of "some uneasiness." Correspondents in the Old Dominion wrote glowingly of Texas. They heaped effusive praise upon its "milder climate" and "richer soil" than Virginia's, and readily contributed to the mythology that Texas was "a better country than any of our own." Fairfax County slaves "are all perfectly aware of the condition of Slavery in ... Texas," whites argued, the consequence of their "constant & extensive Commerce" "in the vicinity of Alexandria, the largest slave-mart in this part of the Union." With the lands of an idyllic Texas already the stuff of legend, some Virginia whites concluded that the transportation of convict slaves there "is scarcely a punishment, for a ... Location better suited to the black cannot be called a punishment." No doubt, they insisted, "in every possible respect their condition will be improved." Under such perceived circumstances, transportation to Texas seemed to some white observers "a reward for the outrage" the enslaved convicts perpetrated and would incite other Virginia bondpeople to commit crimes as well, knowing that transportation "is only to go to Texas." "[N]o slave, who has ever gone there," wrote one pair of correspondents to Governor Gilmer, "will voluntarily return to Virginia" (not that slaves enjoyed such freedom of movement). According to Virginia whites, bondpeople viewed the prospect of removal to Texas with such "pleasure" that it "is in truth a favourite idea with them," to the extent that slaves in the Old Dominion had purportedly run away from their masters, "placed themselves in the Jails of the Traders, & petitioned to be sold," even sacrificing family ties to do so. Although such proclamations strain credulity, certainly a sizeable number of Virginia whites adhered to the belief that sale and transportation as a punishment lacked sufficient "terror" and preferred both the security as well as the example to other slaves that the execution of enslaved criminals afforded.[19]

Just as forces rallied to guarantee Alfred's and Spencer's executions, others in Fairfax County launched a petition drive to gather signatures imploring Virginia's governor to commute the enslaved convicts' sentences to sale and transportation outside the United States. Spearheading the effort for a reprieve was Bernard Hooe, close confidant to the enslaved brothers' master, Dennis Johnston, and mayor of Alexandria throughout most of the 1830s and a portion of the year 1840. Within days of the court's sentence against the two slaves, Hooe drew up a memorial in favor of commutation that he presented on the evening of Tuesday, March 17, at the Fairfax Courthouse, with an invitation for area residents to sign. After that night, slaveholder Dennis Johnston, desirous of seeing his slaves' lives spared, carried it through the neighborhood in search of additional signatures. His quest was successful, attracting more than 350 likeminded citizens by April 10, one week before the scheduled execution. Some of those absent from home when Johnston stopped by later wrote the enslaved convicts' owner that they, too, supported transportation and authorized the addition of their names to the memorial.[20]

George Mason, among the avid supporters of execution, was appalled that hundreds of Fairfax County whites would consider a reprieve for the pair of enslaved criminals. Upon learning of the counterpetition advocating transportation, he immediately wrote David Campbell, who would step down as governor on March 31, urging him not to act on any petition on Alfred's and Spencer's behalf until "the voice" of the community could be fully discerned. On March 19, George and Dr. Richard C. Mason requested a copy of the counterpetition from Bernard Hooe and Dennis Johnston, under the assumption that it contained untrue statements or errors that they hoped to correct. Hooe replied two days later that he had not seen it since he "left it in other hands" at the courthouse on the seventeenth, despite conflicting evidence that it had been spotted in his office since then. By early April, the Masons complained to the new governor, Thomas Walker Gilmer, that they had been unsuccessful in their attempts to view the counterpetition for Alfred and Spencer. George Mason rifled a letter to Silas Burke, the presiding judge at Alfred and Spencer's trial, on March 27 seeking information about the court's impression of the enslaved brothers' character, the evidence arrayed against them, and any doubts the justices may have entertained as to their guilt. Judge Burke, Mason understood, had declined to sign Dennis Johnston's counterpetition for the reprieve of the two convicted bondmen, but Mason also wanted to know if any other justices were known to have committed their names to it. "These facts," Mason explained, "we wish to be possessed of under your Signature, as the highest authority, to refute, if necessary, the baseless assumptions, said to be set up" in the memorial bound for the governor's desk.[21]

Justice Burke replied on April 4. He had seen the petition for commutation in Bernard Hooe's office on March 19 but had declined to sign it. "[N]o member of the Court ... ought to sign it," Burke observed, "as the petition conveys the idea and holds out the impression that there was doubt on the minds of the Court as to the guilt or criminality of slaves" – doubt that the judge denied was present. "I think it improper or rather indecorous for the Court *who sat upon the trial* to interfere in any way," Burke continued. Nevertheless, he added, "many of the six justices that sat on the trial have signed the petition," indicating their belief that the circumstances of the case did not merit the death penalty for the two convicted brothers. One magistrate, John Millan, scribbled a brief message on the memorial next to his name: "I would most respectfully as a member of the Court who sentenced Spencer and Alfred to execution recommend them most *earnestly* to Executive clemency and desire the sentence to be commuted, although I believe from the testimony delivered, they were guilty of the offences charged." In refusing to sign the counterpetition, Burke and a fellow magistrate in the case, William H. Chichester, were the exceptions.[22]

All six of the Fairfax County justices present for the enslaved brothers' trial could agree, however, that the scheduled date for the hangings must be changed from Friday, April 17. The decision had nothing to do with the debate taking place in the community or the petitions then making the rounds; rather, after the court had adjourned, the magistrates realized that they had inadvertently slated the executions for Good Friday. The justices thought it religiously insensitive and morally offensive to hold the "tragic event" of a public execution on "a day held in high veneration in every Christian community." Although they did not mention it explicitly, the symbolism of putting two bondmen to death on Good Friday may also have too closely mirrored biblical accounts of Christ's crucifixion. The Gospels tell of a pair of criminals, traditionally identified as thieves but in some translations described as rebels or revolutionaries, executed on either side of Jesus. Escorting two convicted slave insurrectionaries to the gallows for a Good Friday afternoon execution, as few as sixty minutes before the hour Christ himself expired, surely smacked of irreverence and threatened to cast the law of Fairfax County into the discomforting position of antagonist in the unfolding, parallel drama. The six justices of the peace who convicted Alfred and Spencer begged Governor Gilmer for a five-week respite in "the execution of their sentences," until Friday, May 22.[23]

A further advantage of postponing the hangings of Alfred and Spencer concerned another of their alleged accomplices. John Mudd, purportedly the sixth enslaved assailant on the night of the attack, evaded the authorities far longer than had his companions. Arrested only in March, he was slated for trial in Fairfax County during the April term of court. By May 22, then, John Mudd's fate would be decided. The justices of the peace in Alfred and Spencer's trial believed it "most desirable that the case of *all* the offenders should be acted on at the same time." For the sake of convenience, they explained, "*if* the public execution of offenders be required," it would be preferable to hang them all "on the same day, rather than to have two such exhibitions on different days, within a few weeks of each other." Persuaded by the justices' arguments, Governor Gilmer on April 9 issued the requested respite to the latter half of May.[24]

The day after Gilmer delayed the executions of Alfred and Spencer, the executive received the counterpetition signed by hundreds of citizens of Fairfax County, including many slave owners, calling for the commutation of the brothers' punishment to sale and transportation. This memorial argued that Alfred and Spencer were "but little more culpable than their Associates who have been discharged." It denied "that the slaves meditated *Insurrection* or *Revolt*"; rather, they merely wanted "to rescue, from the custody of the patrol, two of their fellow servants belonging to the same Master." Although the bondmen's actions were unquestionably "highly improper," they were not worthy of the death penalty. They had previously been obedient, the petition continued, and the patrollers were not hurt as badly as originally thought. Bernard Hooe added in a separate letter to Governor Gilmer that "three fourths of the Magistrates" of Fairfax County – eighteen of them in total – appended their names to the petition for banishment as a preferable alternative to death, bringing the total number of signatures on Alfred and Spencer's behalf to almost four hundred. By contrast, the petition that George and Dr. Richard C. Mason spearheaded, calling for Alfred's and Spencer's executions, mustered only sixteen signatures.[25]

For a portion of the white population in Fairfax County, the executions of Alfred and Spencer became absolutely compulsory upon the acquittal of their enslaved compatriot, John Mudd, at his separate trial in April. The bondman's successful defense team included Alexandria mayor Bernard Hooe, the same man campaigning for Alfred's and Spencer's transportation. Mudd's innocence generated a "clamor" in the environs of Alexandria. A number of Virginians contended that the legal discipline of errant slaves had grown too lax. White bloodshed demanded exemplary punishment, they claimed. Absent execution, the criminal justice system became, to the slaves themselves, an object of mockery. George Mason indicated that, among the annoyingly smug "Slaves in this Neighbourhood," the "*impression, near entirely prevails*" – especially "*since the most extraordinary acquittal of ... John Mudd*" – that Alfred and Spencer "*will only be sent to the South*" and not executed. As a result, the enslaved brothers' "condemnation" produced "little effect" in striking fear into slaves and remedying their misbehavior. When another bondman in the spring of 1840 threw a rock at a Fairfax County patroller, he only magnified white impressions that northern Virginia's slaves were running amok, turbulent and unchecked in their behavior.[26]

The postponement of Alfred's and Spencer's executions until May 22 gave time for parties on both sides to make their final pleas to Governor Gilmer. When Bernard Hooe journeyed to Richmond to consult the executive personally, likely in late April, the governor assured him that he would not decide immediately on the enslaved brothers' fates so that further evidence would have ample opportunity to make its way to him. Those arrayed both for and against the execution of the pair of convicted bondmen believed themselves in the numerical majority of community opinion. "People here are generally in favour of transportation," wrote one citizen from Fairfax Courthouse to the governor. Dennis Johnston, owner of Alfred and Spencer, "has been quite successful in obtaining names to his memorial" for commutation, conceded Thomas H. Jones of Prospect Hill, Virginia, but that was "before the people in this remote part of the country were fully aware of the nature of the offence committed by his slaves." Jones labored under the impression "that it is the numerous wish of my neighbors that the execution of ... the sentence ... take its course" as determined by the court. Altogether, a new petition to the governor, dated May 8, "against the commutation of Punishment" for Alfred and Spencer garnered 355 signatures from among the citizens of Fairfax County. Gauged by the size of petitions alone, the number of residents supporting execution roughly equaled the number opposed.[27]

Like so many others in Fairfax County, Bernard Hooe waited anxiously for Governor Gilmer's decision on the enslaved brothers Alfred and Spencer. With so many arguments marshaled in favor of execution on one hand, or transportation on the other, with whom would Gilmer side? What factors would sway him? "A day does not pass without rumours of the determination of the Executive not to move in this matter at all," Hooe fretted. He resolved to send one final letter to persuade the governor to commute the bondmen's sentences to sale and transportation. In it, he shared with Gilmer the latest chatter from Fairfax County "that *Alfred* was not on the ground, at the time of the conflict with the Patrol, and that the violent beating which was inflicted on those officers was perpetrated by John Mudd and Henry who have been tried and acquitted, and by another negro, not belonging to Mr. Johnston." Hooe also added that his friend Dennis Johnston had already resolved, of his own accord, to send Henry and John Mudd "out of the limits of the United States," despite both bondmen being found innocent of the charges against them stemming from the attack on the patrol. Ever since his acquittal, John Mudd had remained in an Alexandria jail, "where Mr. Johnston intends to keep him, until he can obtain an order from the Court ... to authorize his sale." Because "orphan children and infants" were the lawful owners of John Mudd, and Johnston merely the acting master, he needed to surmount some legal hurdles before he could implement his plan. Hooe made his point explicit to the governor: "if it shall be your good pleasure to grant the prayer of the Memorialists for a commutation of the sentence against Alfred and Spencer, and to substitute *Banishment* from the country for their execution on the gallows," Johnston would happily oblige.[28]

In mid-May, the week before Alfred's and Spencer's executions and likely before Hooe's last missive arrived at the governor's desk, Thomas Walker

Gilmer reached a decision. Weighing so much evidence for and against the executions of the enslaved brothers, the governor ultimately split the difference: he commuted Alfred's sentence to sale and transportation out of the country but not that of Spencer. One attorney observed even before the brothers' trial that "the murderous intent in Alfred's case did not seem so clear as in Spenser's [*sic*]." The governor likewise recognized a distinction. Spencer M. Ball, the clerk of the Fairfax County court, may have proven instrumental in forging that impression. Ball remarked to Governor Gilmer in the latter half of April that "Alfred ... seems to have excited much sympathy. The general opinion being that he is much less culpable than others who were tried for the same offence – and were acquitted. His conduct previous to this affray had been good and orderly, and circumstances have transpired calculated to increase the interest in his behalf. I believe," Ball concluded, "there are few in this community who would refuse to join in an application as regards Alfred."[29]

Upon learning of Gilmer's commutation of Alfred's sentence, Dennis Johnston penned a letter on May 18 thanking the governor "for that merciful act" sparing his slave "a violent death." But Johnston then quickly pivoted to his other bondman, Spencer, still condemned to hang on May 22. He presented for the governor's consideration a petition alleging that "there is not such a difference between the ... negroes Alfred & Spencer in the degree of their guilt, as there is in the grade of their punishment." The fifty-four signers requested sale and transportation for Spencer as well. But Governor Gilmer's generosity had evaporated. After an additional, brief respite of less than two weeks, Spencer was taken from jail and executed on June 3, 1840. About two weeks before Spencer swayed lifeless from the noose, his brother Alfred had been carried some one hundred miles south, to Richmond. There, he bided his time in the Virginia State Penitentiary, awaiting purchase by a slave trader willing to convey him outside the boundaries of the United States.[30]

CHAPTER 2

The Yellow House

THE DOOR SWUNG OPEN TO SOLOMON NORTHUP'S DARK, underground cell, admitting a sudden flood of light. "[A] large, powerful man, forty years of age, perhaps, with dark, chestnut-colored hair, slightly interspersed with gray" entered. "His face was full, his complexion flush," Northup recollected, "his features grossly coarse, expressive of nothing but cruelty and cunning. He was about five feet ten inches high, of full habit, and . . . a man whose whole appearance was sinister and repugnant." Confused, Northup did not yet comprehend where he was or how he had gotten there. Born a free black man in New York, Solomon Northup had been lured away from his Saratoga Springs home in the spring of 1841 by two seemingly respectable gentlemen's promises of lucrative employment. Northup accompanied the well-mannered pair to Washington, D.C., where they lodged at Gadsby's Hotel on Pennsylvania Avenue. On the second day of their stay in the nation's capital, Northup's companions generously plied him with drink at local saloons. By evening, he began to feel unwell and that night suffered insatiable thirst before slipping into unconsciousness. But Northup had not over-imbibed; he had been drugged. When he awoke, he found himself handcuffed, fettered at the ankles, and chained to the floor of a dungeon, inhaling the "damp, mouldy odors" of his prison. The duplicitous gentlemen he had met in New York, it turned out, were confidence men who had executed an elaborate kidnapping. Northup heard the echo of approaching footsteps outside his cell and the key rattling in the lock before the heavy door opened to reveal the man now standing in front of him. He recoiled at the sight of his captor, a man he soon learned was Washington, D.C., slave dealer James H. Birch.[1]

Birch numbered among the plethora of slave traders operating in the US capital in 1841. By the time he stunned Northup with the news that he had purchased the northern-born free black man and intended to sell him in New Orleans as a slave, Birch had been an active human trafficker for years, gathering surplus slaves in the Chesapeake to transport via the domestic slave trade to the cotton frontier of the Old Southwest. Slave traders almost always paid ready cash to sellers, and throughout most of 1836, Birch offered "CASH FOR 400 NEGROES" of "both sexes, from twelve to twenty-five years of age." His advertisement encouraged "[p]ersons having servants to dispose of" to "give me a call," for he promised "higher prices, in cash, than any other purchaser ... now in this market." By 1838, Birch teamed up with slave dealer Theophilus Freeman. Stationed in New Orleans, Freeman sold the bondpeople that his partner sent him from Maryland, Virginia, and the District of Columbia. In the late 1850s, Birch would acquire his own slave pen in Alexandria for the warehousing of his unfortunate captives, but in 1841 he did not yet possess his own carceral facility. Therefore, after he purchased Solomon Northup from the free black man's abductors, he lodged his prisoner in the Washington, D.C., slave jail known as the Yellow House, owned and operated by fellow slave trader William H. Williams.[2]

Virtually nothing is known of Williams' early life or of any time prior to the year of his thirty-third birthday. He was born in April 1802 in Virginia. If his middle name, Hendrick, as it frequently appeared in notarized acts of slave sales in New Orleans, indicated his mother's maiden name, it would offer some clues about his possible birthplace. By 1810, a number of families with the Hendrick surname resided in Virginia's central and southern Piedmont, in such counties as Buckingham, Cumberland, Amelia, Prince Edward, and Charlotte. One of Williams' daughters, however, listed her father's birthplace as Charlottesville, in Virginia's Albemarle County, home of slaveholder and slavery critic Thomas Jefferson. When the master of Monticello won the presidency in 1800, census records showed no Williamses in Albemarle County, but by 1810 there were three such households. None can be conclusively shown to include the young William H. Williams.[3]

In his youth, Williams may have lived for a time in Alabama. He first surfaced as a minor player in the domestic slave trade in his mid-twenties.

At least four extant slave ship manifests from 1828 listed him as the owner or shipper of slaves departing from Mobile, Alabama, or Norfolk, Virginia, to New Orleans. The number of bondpeople he transported via the coastwise domestic slave trade at this early stage of his career was paltry – just twenty-four in total among the four voyages, an average of only six per vessel. One of the surviving manifests identified Williams as from Montgomery, Alabama, although that may have indicated merely the town where he had most recently traded in slaves. The strongest evidence of Williams' Alabama connection derives from his younger brother and slave-trading partner Thomas Williams, born about 1819. Never referred to as half- or step-brothers, the siblings apparently shared the same father and mother despite the seventeen-year gap that separated them in age. Thomas had a legal guardian in Montgomery as late as 1839 and frequently identified Macon County, Alabama, just to the east of Montgomery, as his home.[4]

How wealthy the Williams clan was is not known. For a future slave trader who, like all in his profession, virtually always paid for his purchases in cash, it would have helped William H. Williams to have come from a family of means, or at least one with a reputable enough name to command good credit. We do know that Williams owned property in Washington, D.C., by 1830 and began to establish himself as one of the city's preeminent slave traders in 1835. That summer, Williams announced in the newspaper that "I wish to purchase a number of servants of both sexes, for which I will pay the highest market price." His foray into the District of Columbia's active slave-trading market placed him in direct competition with such established dealers as James H. Birch of Birch & Jones or J. W. Neal & Co. Yet Williams' arrival also coincided – surely by no accident – with seismic changes underway in the Washington, D.C., slave-trading scene. In the mid-1830s, Franklin & Armfield, the single most prominent slave-trading firm in the South for several years, began gradually downsizing its massive operations. By November 1841, the company extracted itself from the slaving business altogether. Williams seized this moment of flux in the history of Franklin & Armfield to fill the void in the market left behind by the company.[5]

Williams' earliest advertisements as an independent slave trader in Washington offered no indication of even an office from which he conducted business. He instead urged "[p]ersons wishing to sell" their slaves "to give me a call, at my residence, near the National Hotel." In 1836, Williams issued a new summons for "300 NEGROES ... from the ages of 12 to 28," inviting sellers either to call at his residence on 6th Street West between F and G Streets, or to visit him at Alexander Lee's Lottery and Exchange Office on the north side of Pennsylvania Avenue, between 4½ and Sixth Street West. Promising "[t]he highest cash price ... for Negroes of both sexes," Williams' first slave-trading headquarters inside the lottery and exchange office was adjacent to William Nourse's apothecary shop and only "five doors east of Gadsby's Hotel," from which Solomon Northup would later be kidnapped.[6]

Although slave dealers such as James H. Birch often conducted business in hotels, inns, and "tavern barrooms," Williams' decision to base his operations initially at a lottery and exchange office made ample sense. Like slave traders, owners of lottery and exchange businesses understood money and grasped the inner workings of the economy amid the dramatic transformations of the market revolution. Even as lotteries were growing more disreputable in the 1830s and 1840s, proprietor Alexander Lee continued to sell chances and draw "Lucky Numbers" from a wheel. The geographic reach of Lee's business was sprawling. Customers from across the country visiting the nation's capital risked sums in search of wealth without work, and Lee accepted orders by mail as well. He also swapped for travelers the myriad currencies then circulating within the United States. For Lee, business was thriving, and at some point in the 1830s he partnered with William H. Williams in the lottery and exchange office.[7]

What bound Lee and Williams philosophically was the pervasive spirit of speculation that permeated American society at the time. Each man made a career out of a species of gambling. Whether by playing money markets or by human trafficking, they both pursued the maxim "buy low, sell high" as they profited through speculation. Neither partook in productive labor that resulted, at the end of the day, in tangible commodities to sell; rather, Lee and Williams each looked to turn quick and easy profits merely by moving and exchanging money in the form of either bank notes or enslaved bodies. Society held in contempt professional gamblers and slave traders alike, as unscrupulous, selfish, ruthless, and morally bankrupt individuals worthy only of scorn. But in another sense, they were simply capitalists who embraced and navigated an emerging market economy that many Americans in the 1830s were still struggling to understand. Lee and Williams willingly took the risks inherent in speculative ventures to reap the anticipated rewards. Sharing an affinity for the main chance, the two men naturally gravitated toward one another and co-occupied their location on Pennsylvania Avenue. In a metaphorical if not literal shadowy corner of Lee's lotto office, William H. Williams launched a sordid enterprise trafficking in human flesh, one that catapulted him to the forefront of a burgeoning culture of capitalism driven by cotton and slaves.[8]

The connection between slave trading and gambling was not unique to Williams. In the late 1820s, his acquaintance George Milburn, a Scottish immigrant and fisherman by trade, dealt in slaves out of his residence at Washington's Lafayette Tavern on F Street between Thirteenth and Fourteenth. Milburn also headed a thriving gambling enterprise, running an illegal faro bank in the nation's capital, for which he was eventually sentenced to "imprisonment at hard labour in the penitentiary of the district." As men cut from the same cloth, Milburn and Williams shared a penchant for speculation, surely knew each other, and may even have collaborated in business at some point. When Milburn died prematurely in 1838 at the age of forty-four, the consequence of lingering injuries sustained in a savage mugging two years before near Seventh and B streets, close to Williams' Yellow House, he left behind four living children from his first wife, the deceased Alice Milburn. The youngest of their surviving offspring was nine-year-old Violet, who would in time bloom into "a most popular belle of Washington." In 1848, Violet would marry William H. Williams, a man twenty-seven years her senior. Through his contacts with George Milburn, Williams had probably first met his future wife when she was only a young girl. He could certainly provide her a financially comfortable life; he may also have reminded her of her father.[9]

By 1836, William H. Williams was a man rapidly rising in the slave-trading business of Washington, D.C. In July, he promised "[t]he highest cash price" for four hundred "Negroes of both sexes, from the age of 12 to 28."

To transact business with him, Chesapeake masters wishing to dispose of surplus slaves could still visit Alexander Lee's Lottery and Exchange Office, but they could also call upon Williams at his newly purchased "place on 7th street, a yellow rough-cast house; the first on the right hand going from the market house to the steamboat wharf." By the fall, "William H. Williams & Co." of Washington City had purchased the *Tribune* and the *Uncas*, two of the three slaving vessels once owned by Armfield, Franklin & Co., then engaged in the process of scaling back its operations. On December 1, the *Tribune* docked in New Orleans, bearing a cargo of almost 160 bondpeople whom Williams had shipped from Georgetown. The following spring, Williams announced on April 5, 1837, that the co-partnership of William H. Williams & Co. had "dissolved by mutual consent." Future advertisements encouraged slave sellers to consult Williams solely, no longer at Lee's office but "at my residence," now "in the rear of Gadsby's Hotel" (the site of Solomon Northup's kidnapping), or at the Yellow House, "on 7th street, south of the Market bridge" on city block number 433.[10] (See Figure 4.)

By 1837, Williams had established himself as a fixture in the nation's capital. Owners of excess slaves recognized his name and knew to visit his establishment to do business. When a competing Washington, D.C., slave trader indicated his desire to purchase "any number of young and likely Negroes," he urged sellers to seek him out "at my residence, on the corner of 7th street and Maryland avenue ... opposite Mr. William H. Williams." Williams no doubt appreciated the free advertising from his competitor. Still, he issued his own continued calls for "200 NEGROES," promising to "give in cash the highest prices the Southern market will afford" for bondmen and -women alike. Williams must have forked over significant sums to the Washington newspapers that advertised his establishment daily for months on end. But this was a small price to pay, given the potential rewards. Williams spied his opportunity, and he was going to seize it. Franklin & Armfield had begun their gradual withdrawal from the domestic slave trade. Prior to 1835, that firm had been shipping 1,000–1,200 slaves annually to the Old Southwest. In one year alone, they had reaped an astronomical profit of $33,000, or nearly $850,000 in modern-day money, and their business had expanded still further after that. If Williams could occupy the vacuum left behind by the once-

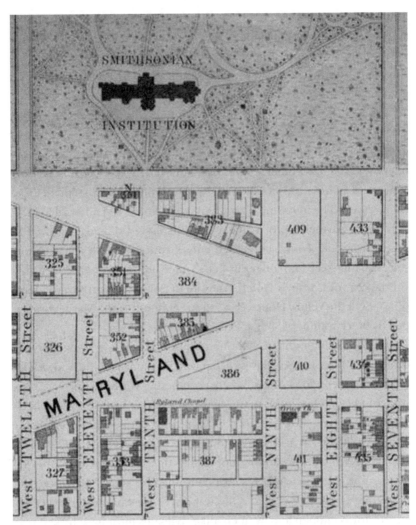

4 Site of the Yellow House, block number 433, Washington, D.C.
Source: A. Boschke and Julius Bien, *Map of Washington City, District of Columbia, Seat of the Federal Government: Respectfully Dedicated to the Senate and the House of Representatives of the United States of North America* (Washington: A. Boschke, 1857), American Memory, Library of Congress, Geography and Map Division, Washington, D.C., http://hdl.loc.gov/loc.gmd/g3850.ct006188 (accessed November 26, 2018).

powerful Franklin & Armfield slave-trading empire and capture even a significant fraction of its business, the future would bode well for him. Williams' economic prospects appeared bright.[11]

In the flush times of the 1830s, credit flowed freely for the purchase of both land in the Old Southwest and the enslaved men and women who would sow and harvest its cotton. President Andrew Jackson, self-proclaimed champion of the common man, had attacked the Second Bank of the United States (BUS) as a vestige of elite privilege that favored the interests of a select few to the detriment of the masses of working people. In vetoing the bank's re-charter in 1832, Jackson saw himself as opening economic opportunities for the very farmers and laborers who had swept him into office in the election of 1828. The BUS, however, had long served, under bank president Nicholas Biddle, as the one institution able to regulate the nation's money supply. It had made great strides in stabilizing the nation's currency. It issued millions of dollars in paper notes that American consumers knew were backed by specie – gold or silver – and redeemable for hard coin at any of the BUS's more than two dozen branches. The BUS further inspired confidence in the financial system through its policies on the paper money printed by various state-chartered banks. Over time, these notes filtered in to the BUS and its branches. The BUS promptly redeemed them with the issuing institutions, returning the state bank's paper in exchange for either BUS notes or specie. This process forced state banks to maintain in their vaults a supply of valid funds sufficient to cover their outstanding paper. The net effect was to restrain state banks' printing and lending of their own notes and to maintain a structurally sound economic system across the country.[12]

President Jackson saw fit to tamper with this system and the confidence it instilled. His bank veto message enumerated a litany of complaints against the BUS, but at heart was his contention that the restraints imposed by the institution limited the amount of credit available and thus inhibited the entrepreneurial spirit of the masses of people whom he claimed as his constituents. After Jackson vetoed the bank re-charter, assuring the death of the BUS in 1836, the president labored to hasten the institution's demise by withdrawing federal funds on deposit there and redistributing them to handpicked state banks dubbed "pet" banks. The move weakened the BUS's financial leverage over the nation's economy and, minus concerns over redemption of their own notes, spurred existing banks to print and lend money almost indiscriminately, with little regard for the concerns' specie reserves. The assault upon the BUS also prompted state legislatures to grant charters for new banking institutions, each of which would go on to print and push into circulation its own monetary issues. The number of state banks increased by almost four hundred between 1830 and 1836. By no coincidence, the total amount of paper money circulating in the nation's economy ballooned by 50 percent between 1834 and 1836 alone, giving enterprising Americans easy access to credit for the purchase of land and slaves.[13]

The new economic reality unleashed a speculative frenzy in the Old Southwest, as entrepreneurs poured into states such as Alabama and Mississippi, voraciously gobbling up lands recently vacated by the indigenous victims of President Jackson's genocidal Indian policies. The US government sold some 50,000 square miles of land to ravenous purchasers in the two years from January 1835 to December 1836. Thanks to rampant inflation and the exponential rise in land values, some investors turned around and sold their property within a matter of months or weeks for stunning profits; many others settled, committed to cotton cultivation. By 1835, the American South produced in excess of 500 million pounds of cotton valued at almost $65 million, easily the single most important US export. Enslaved laborers forcibly conveyed to the cotton frontier readied the soil for the valuable crop. With bondpeople driving the economic growth of the region, slave markets heated up accordingly. Sellers of surplus bondpeople in the Chesapeake could expect to receive handsome sums for chattel destined for the Old Southwest. Between 1835 and 1837, slave prices in Virginia increased 60 percent, after having already risen 60 percent between 1829 and 1835. But slave prices for buyers on the cotton frontier proved higher still. The wild, credit-fueled rush to the region enabled slave traders Franklin & Armfield to realize fantastic returns during the flush times. As the firm began its gradual withdrawal from the business, William H. Williams no doubt hoped to capitalize upon the same speculative wave.[14]

Unbeknownst to him, Williams entered the D.C. slave-trading scene at about the least auspicious moment possible. Dazzled like so many others by the economic sparkle of the flush times, the slave dealer failed to recognize how the fundamental shifts in the ways in which the nation's economy operated, orchestrated by President Jackson, portended disaster. The greatest casualty of Jackson's war against the Second Bank of the United States was the loss of nationwide economic stability. Absent the regulatory constraints of the BUS, the free flow of money available for loans deluded the masses into thinking that previous economic rules no longer applied. They purchased land and slaves with blissful abandon under the assumption that the structural foundations that undergirded the American economy had somehow changed. But they had not, and it was only a matter of time before the speculative bubble burst and those who trafficked in land and slaves were exposed as the de facto gamblers they really were. The Jackson administration's belated effort to rein in the speculative mania, the Specie Circular, issued in the summer of 1836, dictated that, henceforth, the public could pay for federal lands only with gold or silver rather than with paper, prompting a drain of specie from eastern banks to those in the South and West. With specie reserves reduced in the East, nervous bankers called in loans and tightened the availability of credit. Growing numbers of people discovered, much to their alarm, that they could not redeem their bank notes on demand for gold or silver coin.[15]

The sources of economic collapse were not entirely domestic, however, nor could they have been in an age of global capitalism fueled by slave-grown southern cotton. Several scholars have emphasized the international dimension of the imminent depression. In 1836, the Bank of England contributed to the looming catastrophe by raising interest rates and constricting credit to British merchants trading with the United States in the booming cotton market. The interdependent economic webs that bound together the European and American continents meant that disturbances on one side of the Atlantic inevitably reverberated to the other. Disruptions to the credit networks that linked England and the United States resulted in a 25 percent decline in the price of cotton between November 1836 and April 1837 alone, an ill omen for Liverpool and Louisiana alike. A constellation of factors, then, both foreign and domestic, conspired to bring the economy crashing down in the Panic of 1837.[16]

For slave traders such as William H. Williams, the financial crisis proved devastating to the gangbuster pace of business. The breaking of the credit chains that fueled the flush times seized up the markets for land and slaves both. Just as cotton prices plummeted dramatically, so, too, did the artificially inflated prices for the enslaved laborers forced to produce the crop. By the early 1840s, the value attached to black bodies on the auction block fell by more than 50 percent from their pre-panic highs. Banks pursued slave traders to recover hundreds of thousands of dollars they had lent the peddlers of bondpeople for the purpose of purchasing surplus slaves in the Chesapeake region. A slight rebound in the economy in 1838 momentarily augured well for slave traders' future fortunes, but 1839 brought a return of hard times. Slave dealers ultimately would not fully recover from the country's double-dip depression until the 1850s. Launching his D.C. slave-trading operation in 1835, Williams benefited from only the last seventeen or eighteen months of the flush times. Because a good chunk of his slaving career spanned the years after the Panic of 1837, during the continued depression of the first half of the 1840s, slave trading would never be as consistently lucrative for him as it once was for Franklin & Armfield.[17]

Despite the inopportune timing of his entrance into the slave-trading business of the nation's capital, Williams soldiered on through depressed economic times. In late summer of 1838, he expressed his wish "to purchase a number of Negroes for the Louisiana and Mississippi market," offering "the highest prices" in cash that "the market will justify." A similar advertisement during the renewed panic in 1839 invited sellers "of Negroes, of both sexes," to "call" at his place of business "on the west side of 7th street, between the Centre Market and Long Bridge." The Centre Market "occupied a vast plaza on the south side of Pennsylvania Avenue between Seventh and Ninth streets," where vendors hawked "a cornucopia of produce" from farmers' stalls. Walking southward from there down Seventh Street, across the National Mall, carried pedestrians past the Yellow House. A dogleg to the right next put them on to Maryland Avenue, toward the Long Bridge that crossed the Potomac to the Virginia side of the District. That was probably the route that Williams

44

took in November 1839 when he marched a shipment of fifty slaves, evenly divided between men and women, from the Yellow House to the brig *Uncas,* awaiting them in Alexandria for conveyance to New Orleans. The following year, Williams proclaimed his eagerness "to purchase immediately a number of house-servants and farm hands" for transport to the Old Southwest. The *Uncas* would again undertake the same journey to New Orleans in the autumn of 1840.[18]

Williams' personal economic fortunes were not tied exclusively to the financial success of his annual slaving voyages, for he also kept a private jail at the Yellow House. From their slave pen in Alexandria, it had been Franklin & Armfield who dominated the business of incarcerating black bodies in the District of Columbia up to 1836, but Williams' jail would soon overtake their facility to become the largest slave depot in the capital and give Williams "a virtual monopoly" over the internment of slaves there. Located immediately "south of the market bridge, on the west side" of Seventh Street, the Yellow House not only served as Williams' office but also functioned as a temporary incarceration facility. Inside, Williams detained those bondpeople he or his agents had purchased and planned to convey to the Old Southwest via the coastwise domestic slave trade. But he also invited others "wish[ing] to board their servants . . . on moderate terms" to make use of his establishment. Slave catchers or masters merely visiting Washington, D.C., and wanting to keep their slaves secure while they conducted business might avail themselves of the Yellow House's services. At the same time, one Washington visitor recorded, Williams also accommodated at the Yellow House slaves purchased by "five or six other regular slave-dealers in the city" who had "no jails of their own." Their bondpeople, too, dwelled within Williams' facility, for a fee, until their vessels or coffles were readied for departure. In the mid-1840s, slave dealer Richard R. Beasley of Lunenburg County, in Virginia's southern Piedmont, deposited at Williams' jail "3 negroes . . . for sale" on his behalf. To board "Negroes . . . from the country or town" at the Yellow House, Williams charged – "for all except children at the breast" – "the low price of 25 cents per day," 9 cents per diem cheaper than the 34 charged by the public jail. Furthermore, compared with the Washington city prison, Williams' private slave jail boasted "superior accommodations in respect to food and lodging." One traveler who visited both institutions observed that "the difference in comfort" for the captives fell "wholly on the side of the private establishment."[19]

Slave pens akin to those of Williams or Armfield in the District could be found at all major slave-trading centers across the South: Baltimore, Richmond, Petersburg, Norfolk, and more. Slave coffles heading southward over land from the Upper South sometimes departed slave pens in Lexington, Kentucky, or stopped at slave pens in Nashville, Tennessee. There, in the 1850s, according to Kentucky-born bondman Isaac Johnson, "The pens were divided into groups, women in one, men in another, girls and young boys by themselves." Farther south still, Jackson and Vicksburg, Mississippi, and the river port town of Grand Gulf, some thirty miles downstream from Vicksburg, all boasted slave jails of their own. The most notorious such facility in Mississippi, however, was the slave "pen 'tached to the slave market" at the Forks of the Road, located just east of Natchez at the intersection of the Liberty and Washington roads. But as significant as it was, the pens in New Orleans, the largest slave market in the antebellum United States, surpassed it in scope, in the sheer numbers of enslaved captives detained inside. In all of these places, proprietors of private slave pens like that of Williams rented space to clients ranging from individual masters to rival slave dealers without jails, to municipal governments requiring additional accommodations for prisoners. "Only the wealthiest or most powerful traders could afford to operate ... jails" of their own, observed one researcher, so having possession of such a facility "became an important status symbol."[20]

Slave pens might serve somewhat different purposes depending upon their geographic location. Across the South, they commonly functioned as sites of punishment for masters reluctant to lash slaves themselves. Owners could instead pawn off the grisly work of whipping, for a small fee, to jailers, who administered the specified number of stripes. Antislavery journalist and historian Richard Hildreth identified another purpose of some slave pens in his 1852 fictional work, *The White Slave; or, Memoirs of a Fugitive.* The Augusta, Georgia, slave pen described in the novel served as a site to prepare bondpeople for sale. "[T]he stock was kept to be fatted and put in order for market," Hildreth wrote. "Indulgence and plenty were the order of the day at the pen."

Hildreth's account contained more than a grain of truth. Former slaves' reminiscences about their experiences in slave pens made routine mention of the steps taken in advance of sale. The animal imagery contained in their accounts constantly compared the enslaved to livestock. The "nigger pen" of New Orleans was "a place like a stock yard where dey auction us off," recounted one ex-bondwoman. William Wells Brown saw one slave trader's "gang of human cattle" in the New Orleans pen "exhibited for sale." The process of dehumanization played out over and over again in the Old South wherever people were sold as slaves. Medical doctors compelled victims of the slave trade to strip – sometimes "men and women together naked in the presence of each other" – for examinations to determine those who were physically "sound" and suitable for the auction block. A former Mississippi bondperson documented the next step for slaves in the Natchez pen prior to display to potential buyers. "[Th]ey was fed an' washed an' rubbed down lak race hosses," he explained. "Den dey was dressed up an' put through de paces dat would show off dey muscles." Willing buyers flocked to the slave pens of Natchez, New Orleans, and elsewhere to select the most perfect bondperson to fulfill their fantasies of mastery.[21]

Unlike the bondpeople jailed while awaiting auction in New Orleans, Natchez, and other, smaller slave-trading centers of the Deep South, most of those held in D.C. slave pens awaited transport to another location prior to sale. A few were disposed of locally, but the overwhelming majority of slaves imprisoned temporarily in the District of Columbia, from a matter of days to a few months, were bound for the cotton frontier or the Louisiana cane fields. As one former bondwoman held briefly in the capital explained, they "stayed in Washington only a short time" before a trader either chained them together in a coffle for the grueling walk hundreds of miles south and west or deposited them aboard a vessel, likely docked at the port of Alexandria but possibly in Baltimore, for the slightly more costly but shorter and relatively less physically taxing journey coastwise, by ship, to the slave markets of the Deep South. In the 1830s, no network yet existed to transport bondpeople by rail from Washington slave pens to the Old Southwest.[22]

The District of Columbia played host to multiple slave jails in the mid-1830s, containing, according to one researcher, as many slave pens as did the entire state of Virginia. Franklin & Armfield operated their pen in Alexandria, but the greater concentration of such facilities lay across the Potomac in Washington City. Washington Robey ran one of these slave pens, adjacent to his tavern on the east side of "7th street, south of the Centre Market House," and B Street, near the intersection with Maryland Avenue. There, at Robey's Tavern, Joseph W. Neal & Co. based their slave-trading enterprise. English traveler E. S. Abdy visited Robey's slave pen in 1833. Unable to gain access to the interior, Abdy could only describe the external appearance of the "wretched hovel." The pen, he wrote, "is surrounded by a wooden paling fourteen or fifteen feet in height, with the posts outside to prevent [the] escape" of those incarcerated behind the walls. It was "separated from the building" – meaning the tavern, presumably – "by a space too narrow to admit of a free circulation of air." Abdy learned that the pen confined captives of "both sexes, and all ages," exposed alike to the scorching heat of summer and brutal cold of winter. Some had reportedly "actually frozen to death."[23]

Across Seventh Street from Robey's, William H. Williams opened his own slave pen in 1836. His Yellow House quickly became infamous. One contemporary observed that "you need never be at a loss to find that house, while there is a colored man in Washington to enquire of." Based on various descriptions of its location, the Yellow House compound probably consumed most if not all of the rectangular block between Seventh and Eighth streets and between B Street and Maryland Avenue, immediately south of the National Mall. The commencement of operations at Williams' establishment predated the opening of the Smithsonian Institution by a decade and the dedication of any presidential monument by a half-century. In an era before the memorials to Washington or Jefferson (much less the yet-unknown Lincoln) had been erected, D.C. travelers oriented themselves based on the Yellow House, which stood as a prominent landmark within the nation's capital. "If ever you have been to Washington," commented a correspondent from the *Lowell Journal* (Massachusetts), in 1843, "you have probably noticed a large yellow house which stands about a mile from the avenue, near the Potomac. – That is the slave prison ... owned by a celebrated slave trader, who has made a large fortune by following his hellish traffic" in enslaved people: William H. Williams.[24]

The Yellow House itself was three stories tall, built of brick, but covered in plaster and painted its distinctive color. According to Solomon Northup's description from 1841, an outdoor "yard extended rearward from the house about thirty feet." This central space, where slaves could be displayed to potential buyers, was "paved with brick" and "surrounded by a brick wall ten or twelve feet high." As Northup further explained, "The top of the wall supported" the lower "end of a roof, which ascended inwards," toward the courtyard, "forming a kind of open shed. Underneath the roof there was a crazy loft all round, where slaves, if so disposed, might sleep at night, or in inclement weather seek shelter from the storm." Northup likened the place to "a farmer's barnyard in most respects." Abutting the courtyard, reported a *Cleveland Herald* correspondent in 1849, an outbuilding constructed of brick served as the slave quarters. It was "two stories high, fronting ... one of the public streets of Washington," with "[w]indows grated and prison-like." Williams detained there "most of the slaves brought [to him] ... for sale or shipment elsewhere," although others "were kept in the dwelling house in a room adjoining the kitchen." The jailer could immobilize Williams' enslaved captives by shackling them to stout staples secured to the walls of both this room and the outbuilding where the majority of the enslaved prisoners stayed. Fearsome, ferocious dogs also patrolled the facility. The barking of the canine guards, added to the cacophony of clanking chains and cracking whips, filled the air with the sounds of brutal oppression. But the public face of Williams' slave pen was the Yellow House and the Yellow House alone. J. Miller McKim of Pennsylvania, writing to the New York City-based black abolitionist newspaper *The Colored American*, depicted Williams' dwelling as "large but lonely and desolated looking." In his advertisements, Williams observed that the Yellow House sat back from the road "on the west side of 7th Street," within a "large garden surrounded by trees." His portrayal made the pen's setting seem serene and tranquil, almost pastoral – an oasis within the hustle and bustle of District business. As Solomon Northup observed, "Its outside presented only the appearance of a quiet private residence. A stranger looking at it, would never have dreamed of its execrable uses," for the entire complex "was so constructed that the outside world could never see the human cattle that were herded there."[25]

The innocuous façade belied the dismay and horror felt by those confined in the interior. J. Miller McKim, a lecturer for the American Anti-Slavery Society, received a tour of the inside of Williams' slave pen in early 1838. When he "set out for W. H. Williams' Slave-factory," he explained, he doubted that he would gain admittance. He nevertheless made the attempt. Refusing on principle to masquerade as a slave buyer, McKim wrote, "I made up my mind to be perfectly candid and practice no kind of deception." He "rapped at the door" and was greeted "by a stout, thickset man, dressed in a pea jacket, coat and fur cap, with large whiskers and [a] stern countenance." Inquiring for Williams, McKim learned that the slave dealer was presently in Natchez. He then asked the unidentified proprietor "to see your establishment – if you have no objection," clarifying that "I don't wish to purchase any" slaves. Williams' agent invited McKim inside and spoke openly about the business. He "went to a window on one side of the room . . . opened the shutters – threw up the sash, and invited me to look out" upon the courtyard of the pen, McKim recalled. "I surveyed an area of about 40 feet square, enclosed partly by high jail walls built" to confine the slaves. There, he learned, bondpeople were permitted to exercise, and the enslaved children could play. But on the winter day of McKim's visit, "it was very cold," and the courtyard empty. The slaves "were all down in the cellar," Williams' agent noted. When McKim "asked to go down and see them," the proprietor obligingly "led the way through a winding passage out into a temporary enclosure which communicates with the 'pen.' He took out of his pocket a key [and] opened the lock of a huge iron cross-barred gate, which admitted us to the space within. He then opened a door which led us into the 'cellar.'" McKim viewed three "apartments," each "about 25 feet square." One held "about 30 slaves of all ages, sizes, and colors."[26]

In 1841, when the abducted free black man Solomon Northup regained consciousness following his drug-induced stupor, he occupied a room in the same basement prison McKim had toured three years earlier. Northup was wearing irons, "chained to the floor of Williams' pen ... and handcuffed." His cell "was about twelve feet square – the walls of solid masonry. The floor was of heavy plank. There was one small window, crossed with great iron bars, with an outside shutter, securely fastened. An iron-bound door led into an adjoining cell, or vault, wholly destitute of windows, or any means of admitting light." In "the room in which I was," Northup related, "The furniture ... consisted of the wood-en bench on which I sat, an old-fashioned, dirty box stove, and besides these, in either cell, there was neither bed, nor blanket, nor any other thing whatever." Northup would eventually learn that it was slave dealer James H. Birch who imprisoned him in Williams' basement.[27]

Northup recalled another white man who accompanied Birch deep into the bowels of Williams' slave pen. The free black hostage identified him in his narrative as Ebenezer Radburn and dismissed him as "a simple lackey ... who acted merely in the capacity of turnkey." In actuality, Ebenezer Rodbird functioned as "the keeper" of Williams' private jail. As the facility's jailer, Rodbird lived with Williams, from 1837 to 1841. He moreover served as his employer's occasional agent in the countryside, "purchasing negros" on Williams' behalf. Born in England about 1805, Rodbird in 1839 and 1840 counted among a cadre of "several" agents Williams dispatched "to purchase negroes for him in the states of Maryland and Virginia." Williams gave Rodbird and his other represen-tatives out in the field "various sums of money" – hundreds or thousands of dollars at a time – to buy slaves. The agents, in turn, wrote out receipts to Williams acknowledging their acceptance of those funds. Rodbird and the other agents then set out to acquire bondpeople in the Chesapeake region and to deliver them, along with the bills of sale that legalized the transactions, to Williams at his pen.[28]

Northup's most vivid recollection of Rodbird was of the jailer's complicity in a brutal lashing Northup received. After James H. Birch explained to Northup, still enchained in Williams' cellar, that he had purchased him to sell in New Orleans, Northup strenuously protested, insisting that he was a free man. Birch "flew into a towering passion" and heaped "blasphemous oaths" upon his prisoner, as Rodbird stood by in silence. "His business," as Northup understood of the jailer, "was, to oversee this human, or rather inhuman stable, receiving slaves, feeding, and whipping them, at the rate of two shillings a head per day." Birch, enraged by Northup's perceived insolence in continuing to assert his freedom, turned to Rodbird and "ordered the paddle and cat-o'-nine tails to be brought in." Rodbird fastened Northup's feet in chains. Then, "Drawing me over the bench, face downwards," Northup recalled, the jailer "placed his heavy foot upon the fetters, between my wrists, holding them painfully to the floor." With Rodbird assuring that Northup lay prone and vulnerable, Birch waled upon his victim with a paddle, stopping periodically to ask if he still claimed to be free. (See Figure 5.) Northup maintained his liberty throughout. Birch relented only when, "[a]t length[,] the paddle broke," forcing him to retrieve a rope to resume the thrashing. Rodbird eventually intervened, telling Birch "that it was useless to whip me any more – that I would be sore enough." Birch and Rodbird departed. The jailer returned to Northup's cell in an hour or two, observed that the prisoner "had received a pretty severe flogging," and, with feigned and patronizing concern, advised that Northup cease asserting his claims to freedom. As Northup recalled, Rodbird then "unlocked the fetters from my ankles, opened the shutters of the little window, and withdrew, leaving me again alone."[29]

Some time later, in the Yellow House yard, Northup met "a colored man," also destined for sale farther south, who informed him "that I was in William's [*sic*] Slave Pen, a place I had never heard of previously." D.C.-area slaveholders well knew of William H. Williams' private slave jail, however, and the services he offered. So did northern abolitionists. When the antislavery J. Miller McKim visited the Yellow House in early 1838, strictly out of curiosity he asked the agent – probably Ebenezer Rodbird – if he had "any negroes now on hand." The caretaker replied, "a few," but also noted, "We have very few slaves for sale of our own – most that are here belong to other people." Williams did offer some slaves for purchase in the District of Columbia, typically through private sales inside the Yellow House grounds rather than at public auction on the street. The slave trader was equally renowned for his prison that incarcerated bond-people for perhaps only a day or two but possibly for weeks or months on end, depending upon their circumstances. Slaves languished in Williams' jail only briefly when their masters wanted them punished

SCENE IN THE SLAVE PEN AT WASHINGTON.

5 Ebenezer Rodbird holds down Solomon Northup as James H. Birch administers a thrashing.
Source: *Twelve Years a Slave. Narrative of Solomon Northup, a Citizen of New-York, Kidnapped in Washington City in 1841, and Rescued in 1853, from a Cotton Plantation Near the Red River, in Louisiana* (Auburn: Derby and Miller, 1853), 45. AF Fotografie/Alamy

or as their owners conducted business in the nation's capital. The lengths of their detention likely increased if they were awaiting local sale or, especially, transportation to the Deep South. The respective slave pens of Williams and Robey in Washington and Franklin & Armfield in Alexandria collectively made the District of Columbia "the most active slave depot in the nation" in the 1830s.[30]

Still, for William H. Williams, like most Americans, the late 1830s marked dire economic times. Perhaps for that reason, in 1840 Williams embarked upon a fresh gamble. As a first step, he dispatched an agent named Rudolph Littlejohn to Richmond, Virginia, to launch the new speculative venture.

CHAPTER 3

Sale and Transportation

WILLIAM H. WILLIAMS COULD NOT HAVE ANTICI-
pated the outrage that awaited him as his brig *Uncas* sailed
into Mobile Bay. Although certainly not as bustling as New Orleans,
Mobile, Alabama, served as another notable port of entry in the coastwise domestic slave trade. Slaving vessels regularly docked there to
unload their human cargoes bound for the cotton frontier, so
Williams' arrival with a shipload of chattel warranted no surprise in
and of itself. His paperwork was all in order as well. In conformity with
an 1807 federal law, on October 9, 1840, the customs officer in
Alexandria completed a roll call to verify the accuracy of the slave
manifest and cleared the *Uncas* for departure. The manifest properly
recorded the sixty-eight captives on board. It identified their first and –
unlike most legal documents – last names and listed the sex, age,
height, and complexion of each, as required by law. The shipper
officially listed for the voyage of the *Uncas* was Alexander Lee, proprietor of the lottery and exchange office in Alexandria and Williams' one-
time partner and office-mate. Lee and master Nathaniel Boush, captain
of the *Uncas*, did each "solemnly, sincerely and truly swear" the mandatory oath that the slaves on board had not been illegally imported into
the United States since January 1, 1808 – the date the country terminated its constitutionally lawful participation in the transatlantic slave
trade – and were not entitled to their freedom. The captives were
consigned to trader William H. Williams, the destination Mobile.
Nothing about the slave manifest seemed untoward or suspicious in
the least. The official form gave no indication, however, that the first
twenty-six names enumerated therein were enslaved convicts purchased

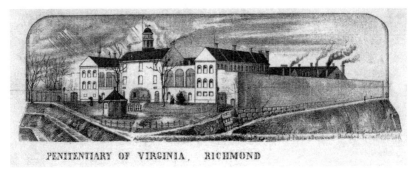

PENITENTIARY OF VIRGINIA, RICHMOND

6 Exterior view of the Virginia State Penitentiary, Richmond
Source: Auditor of Public Accounts, Condemned Blacks Executed or Transported,
Records – Condemned Slaves, Court Orders, and Valuations, 1846–1857, Misc. Reel 2554,
Frame 865, Library of Virginia, Richmond.

out of the Virginia State Penitentiary for transportation outside the
United States.[1] (See Figure 6.)

The Fairfax County bondman Alfred entered the Virginia State
Penitentiary in Richmond on May 21, 1840, to await sale and transportation, per Virginia law. He counted among the 455 enslaved men and
women, between 1815 and 1846 alone, who had been convicted of
various capital crimes in Virginia courts of oyer and terminer, only to
have the commonwealth's governors commute their death sentences to
expulsion beyond US boundaries. When Alfred arrived at the penitentiary, he joined some two dozen other slaves already there who would
share his impending fate. The longest serving had already languished in
the unpleasant confines of the penitentiary for twenty-one months.[2]

Alfred shared in the day-to-day routines of the other enslaved convicts:
listening for their names in the roll call every morning, wearing the same
prison garb, sweeping their cells daily, consuming carefully doled out
quantities of what passed as food, enduring reduced rations or whippings
as punishments, and facing a high risk of illness and death from such
diseases as cholera, a major outbreak of which, years before, claimed
three-fourths of the prison population admitted in 1832. Eight years
later, in 1840, when Alfred first set foot inside the penitentiary, at least
four black prisoners expired within its walls, from such conditions as
pulmonary consumption, apoplexy, and "congestive fever." All prisoners,
black and white, worked for their state captors, although at different

gender-specific tasks. But for those enslaved offenders whose sentences had been reprieved, incarceration in Richmond was from the start a temporary measure. Alfred and twenty-six other bondpeople detained in the Virginia State Penitentiary would gain their liberation from the institution on the very same day in September 1840. But, though out of prison, they were hardly free, for as they exited the pen, they fell into the possession of a slave trader's agent.[3]

The convict bondpeople fell into William H. Williams' hands after a protracted silent bidding war between professional slave traders. Only on rare occasions did private individuals purchase an enslaved convict out of the Virginia State Penitentiary for their personal use outside the country. Customarily, slave traders rather than private citizens competed for the convict slaves confined in Richmond. The process differed, however, from conventional slave auctions in which interested buyers vied with one another directly to outbid each other at the site of sale. As sometimes occurred in private auctions, the commonwealth of Virginia preferred to sell inmates reprieved to sale and transportation not as individuals but as groups referred to as "lots." Slave dealers were free to visit the penitentiary in Richmond, divine the values of the reprieved bondpeople imprisoned there, and then submit sealed bids to the lieutenant governor or governor and Executive Council for the executive's consideration. Over a period of several weeks, the commonwealth entertained offers for the lot of slaves available for sale and transportation outside the United States. The governor approved the highest bid, unless he believed he could elicit a more attractive sum by withholding sale until a later date. For the state, the purchase price for a lot of convicted bondpeople offset at least a portion of the expenses incurred in the reimbursement of masters whose enslaved property the law had confiscated for sale and transportation. The commonwealth of Virginia almost never came out ahead, occasionally broke even, and usually accepted less money for convict slaves – sometimes much less – than it shelled out in recompense.[4]

During the nine fiscal years from October 1, 1833, to September 30, 1842, the Virginia State Penitentiary detained 44 bondpeople awaiting execution but three times as many reprieved to sale and transportation. Of those 134, 4 died, including, on June 3, 1839, the bondman Peter of Augusta County. One escaped. Traders purchased the remaining 129, or about 14 per year, for sale abroad. No shame or stigma dissuaded slave dealers from acquiring convict slaves. Human trafficking was their business. They expended enormous sums, often in the thousands of dollars, to buy enslaved criminals for resale elsewhere. Whether they abided by the law and carried them to a foreign land or evaded the law and sold them domestically, they did not voluntarily divulge the personal histories of their cargo to potential buyers curious enough to ask. When the art of silence would not do, slave traders pressed to reveal the provenance of their shipment could always lie. Deceit was endemic to the profession. Dealers dyed or plucked gray hairs to disguise slaves' advancing age, dismissed as nothing telltale signs of slaves' serious illnesses, concocted false tales of barren bondwomen's fertility, and carefully coached bondmen and -women to deny past injuries, to proclaim their eagerness to do work they had never before done, or to otherwise mislead or deflect if asked direct questions by likely purchasers. Neglecting to mention bondpeople's criminal pasts conformed to the pattern of deception intrinsic to the business. Other than noting the presence or absence of lash marks and keloid scars on slaves' backs as a gauge of tractability, prospective buyers would almost never have thought to inquire specifically about any alleged slave crimes that warranted the attention of the southern legal system.[5]

From 1833 to 1842, more than a dozen different slave traders paid for convicted bondpeople out of the Virginia State Penitentiary. In the summer of 1838, Virginia had ten convict slaves available for sale and transportation, whom slave trader Nathaniel Matthews purchased for $5,800. By the spring of 1840, another sizeable lot of convict slaves had accumulated in the Virginia State Penitentiary. Slave trader James G. Lindsey opened the silent bidding with a quote "for the 22 negroes" then incarcerated in Richmond. He forwarded the governor and Executive Council a detailed invoice that listed "14 men sound," meaning healthy and ready for work. Another three he labeled "unsound," indicating physical or mental infirmity and, consequently, diminished value. The last of the eighteen total men was "old[,] say 50 or 55 years," and therefore also much depreciated. The remainder of the slaves were female: three women, plus "1 Girl about – 12 years." For this lot, Lindsey offered "Eight Thousand Dollars in cash," $3,750 immediately, with the balance payable in December. Thomas Walker Gilmer, the recently inaugurated governor, passed on the proposal. The commonwealth could do better.[6]

Hometown Richmond slave trader Robert Lumpkin, purchaser of a prior shipment of transports in the late 1830s, contacted Governor Gilmer on May 22 to do business again. By then, twenty-five enslaved convicts, including Alfred, were anxiously awaiting sale to parts unknown. "I will give for them the sum of thirteen thousand dollars," Lumpkin stated, "say six thousand and five hundred dollars in Cash" now and "six thousand and five hundred dollars in twelve months," by which time the shipment's sale would have put more ready money in Lumpkin's pocket. Surely to the delight of Governor Gilmer, Lumpkin was offering $5,000 more than had Lindsey, even though only three additional slaves were encompassed by the prospective arrangement. Subsequent bidding confirmed that the proposal was a good one. But if Gilmer took smug satisfaction in having previously turned down Lindsey, in hindsight he probably wished he had accepted Lumpkin's offer. It is not clear whether he passed on it because he got greedy and thought the total dollar amount too low or because he would have had to wait a year to complete the sale and replenish Virginia's treasury.[7]

Resolved to hold out for more, Gilmer patiently bided his time. Spring gave way to summer, and late August brought a spate of additional bids as slave traders sought to bolster their stockpiles of commodified men and women for the upcoming fall selling season. On August 29, John W. Coleman, another Richmond slave dealer, penned a letter to the governor and Executive Council proclaiming his willingness to pay $12,550 cash for the now "29 Negroes" confined in the penitentiary for transport. Three more bondmen and one bondwoman – Nan, found guilty of assaulting and attempting to kill Elizabeth Martin in Patrick County – had augmented the number of transports in the intervening months since Lumpkin's proposal in May. Having visited the penitentiary, though, Coleman observed that one of the twenty-nine was visibly ill. "[I]f he dies," he informed the governor, "you should deduct in propo[r]tion for him." Because Gilmer had already received a bid of $13,000 for a smaller quantity of slaves, he could not accept Coleman's offer.[8]

Gilmer rejected another, even lower bid, also made on August 29, from Washington, D.C., slave trader Thomas N. Davis. As late as 1838, Davis had a direct but difficult to pinpoint working relationship with William H. Williams. They bought and sold slaves at the same locations. "I can be found at the yellow house on Seventh Street," Davis explained in one advertisement for two hundred slaves, "or at Alexander Lee's Lottery and Exchange Office." After April 1837, Williams was advertising as an individual slave trader and not as William H. Williams & Co., so Davis may have been his employee or agent but not a partner. By early 1839, however, Davis had struck out on his own, establishing his headquarters "at John Brown's stage office, opposite Gadsby's Hotel" on Pennsylvania Avenue. In February, he issued a call for "FORTY OR FIFTY NEGROES," preferably "in families," for which he would "pay the highest cash prices." Eighteen months later, Davis tried to tempt Governor Gilmer with a parsimonious bid of $11,000 for the Virginia State Penitentiary's twenty-nine convict slaves. Although Gilmer was obliged to refuse the offer, Davis would maintain a hidden but ongoing role in the bond-people's unfolding story.[9]

Two days after Davis' and Coleman's proposals, yet another bid for the penitentiary slaves reached Governor Gilmer and the Executive Council, from Nathaniel Matthews, the winning bidder for the ten convict slaves in 1838. "I have Recently Examined the transports now confined in the State prison[,] twenty nine in number," Matthews wrote. "I have concluded to make you an offer of twelve thousand one hundred dollars for the twenty three men and six women." With stronger bids already in hand, Matthews' proposal seemed much less attractive this time around.[10]

Of the six known slave traders vying for the enslaved convicts, an obscure man with the distinctive moniker Rudolph Littlejohn emerged triumphant. Littlejohn remains an enigma. Born around 1808, he did not know his own birthplace. According to one correspondent out of Alexandria, Littlejohn "is not [formally] engaged in the slave trade but is said to be a gambler in Washington City." That he mistakenly submitted his bid for the convicts to the Richmond auction house of Messrs. Templeman & Dickinson, rather than directly to the governor or lieutenant governor and council as was customary, suggests he was misinformed or naïve, a newcomer to the process of procuring bond-people out of the penitentiary. Littlejohn's first bid, dated August 4, was $13,000 for the then "Twenty Eight negroes" confined there, a sum equal to the price Robert Lumpkin had been willing to pay two and one-half months earlier for four fewer slaves. Despite Littlejohn's inexperience, he had at least read up on Virginia statutes governing sale and transportation and accordingly pledged "to abide by the law by Giving Bond & security that they shall be carried out of the United States." More boldly, Littlejohn requested "an immediate answer[,] as it is out of my power to delay here [in Richmond] long." Apparently receiving no reply, he corresponded with Templeman & Dickinson again, two weeks later, from Baltimore, Maryland. This time, he reduced his bid to $12,600. Though $400 lower than his previous proposal, it was still $500 more than Nathaniel Matthews' and $50 more than John W. Coleman's. Governor Gilmer could no doubt see the proffered amounts tightening in the $12,000 range, and a mere fifty extra dollars gave Littlejohn the slightest of advantages.[11]

Still, the governor wanted assurances that he was obtaining the best possible price for the latest round of transports. He consulted auctioneer R. H. Dickinson of the firm Templeman & Dickinson and solicited his expertise in ascertaining the values of the enslaved prisoners in the penitentiary. Dickinson conducted his valuations for each inmate and presented them in a statement on August 16. By adding up the individual dollar figures he ascribed to them, he arrived at subtotals of $12,550 for the enslaved male prisoners and $2,250 for the enslaved female prisoners, for a grand total of $14,800 for all of the "29 Negroes ... now confined in the Penitentiary for transportation." None of the bids received were particularly close to this figure. But by the time Dickinson wrote Governor Gilmer on September 1 with the results of his inquiry, the auctioneer had reduced the estimated total value of the transports to $13,350. The majority of the updated dollar amount derived from the "14 men 18 to 30 years old[,] stout & likely," even though "some are badly scarred from whipping." Dickinson valued each of these persons at $550 apiece, for a subtotal of $7,700.[12]

The process of prognosticating convict slaves' individual dollar values at auction exposed the various medical maladies that plagued the imprisoned bondpeople. The twenty-five-year-old enslaved convict Jarrett of Loudoun County, Dickinson recorded, was "very sick." Slave trader Thomas N. Davis elaborated, noting that Jarrett suffered from a "bilious fever," an elevated body temperature accompanied by nausea, vomiting, and diarrhea. Davis observed, too, that the bondwoman Nan of Patrick County was "unsound in her feet." More graphically, Dickinson specified that she sported "one foot nearly burned off," perhaps the result of a tragic accident or a sadistic punishment. Two of the four enslaved inmates named John endured other unpleasant conditions. John Cooper was plagued by a "large wen or swelling on the neck," giving him a "Big Jaw," and another John was deemed "unsound" owing to a fistula.[13]

Illness and injury directly affected slaves' anticipated prices. R. H. Dickinson stated so explicitly in his communications with Governor Gilmer. Dickinson described the two Johns as "almost valueless" because they "would not be sold but at very low prices," probably no more than $250 apiece. He also noted that "one negro man" in his forties – Jacob from Mecklenburg County – was allegedly "at times somewhat deranged." During his sale, Dickinson feared, "disclosures might be made by him," revealing his condition and decreasing his value. Any "doubt of his being of sound mind" translated to a maximum purchase price of $400, the auctioneer predicted. Landon Carter, an enslaved blacksmith held in the penitentiary, possessed the specialized skills to make him a valuable and highly sought-after bondman, but Dickinson discovered that "he is whip[p]ed in a horrid manner[,] which is a great eye sore" and indicative of a troublesome character or temperament. His $800 valuation was hundreds less than it otherwise would have been with a pristine back. A final factor that reduced bondpeople's expected values was age. Advanced age meant lower productivity, a shorter remaining working life, and a commensurate decline in their worth. Whereas Dickinson priced young, healthy men in their prime at $550 each, the "four Negro men between 40 and 50 years old" he "value[d] at three hundred and seventy five dollars each." Enslaved women's value was predicated on their ability not only to produce, through work, but to reproduce, by bearing the next generation of labor. Dickinson's estimate for the "two old women, 38 to 40 years old," was a paltry "two hundred and fifty dollars (together)." One of these was Nan, whose damaged foot diminished her value still further.[14]

Despite the various debilities that depressed certain bondpeople's prices, Virginia still controlled a collective $13,350 worth of convict slaves – until forces diminished the commonwealth's human assets. Health concerns necessitated the adjustment and re-adjustment of the total number of enslaved inmates ready for transport out of the country. A notice dated September 5 stated that "Jacob from Mecklenburg," the purportedly mentally ill slave, "is not to be sold now." He was probably so obviously unwell that his disability would have thwarted sale. Nothing in the paperwork indicated whether Virginia State Penitentiary superintendent Charles S. Morgan, his medical staff, the governor, or auctioneer R. H. Dickinson made the final decision that shrank the available number of transports to twenty-eight. The same day Jacob was scratched off the list, the governor's council recommended that Rudolph Littlejohn's initial offer of $13,000 be accepted for the remaining twenty-eight convict slaves. But $13,000 was the trader's first, higher bid, which he later reduced to $12,600, for twenty-nine slaves, not twenty-eight. Just days later, the total number of transports dropped still further. On September 8, Superintendent Morgan informed Governor Gilmer that the ailing bondman Jarrett had died the preceding night of "Congestive Fever" after fourteen months' confinement in the penitentiary. Twenty-seven transports remained.[15]

Pending the sale to Rudolph Littlejohn, only a few convict slaves were left behind in the penitentiary. Those too ill for transport in 1840, such as Jacob, joined those otherwise ordered "not to be sold" to serve as seed for the next shipment, assuming they survived that long. By September 7, Charles S. Morgan was eager to see the bulk of the enslaved inmates depart and thereby liberate precious space in his overcrowded facility. He urged the governor's secretary to "[p]lease let me know if they are sold & if so when they will probably be taken away."[16]

Already the wheels were in motion. Rudolph Littlejohn had bid $12,600 in the middle of August for the transports. On Friday, September 4, R. H. Dickinson communicated to Governor Gilmer Littlejohn's interest in the enslaved convicts and his willingness to supply the legally obligatory "bond with good security" pledging "that the negroes will be carried out of the United States." Littlejohn was in a hurry. Not wishing to remain in Richmond until Monday, he requested a reply from the governor by 10 a.m. Saturday. "[I]n my opinion this offer ought to be accepted," Dickinson advised, "it is more than I had expected would have been offered." Yes, he acknowledged, there had been higher bids before when fewer slave inmates were held in the penitentiary, but "nearly all" of those enslaved prisoners were "likely," meaning healthy, of good quality, and ready for labor. Now, Dickinson explained, "Eight or nine" of the current twenty-eight convicts (Jarrett would not die for another three days) were weak, ill, or infirm. "[T]here is no doubt" that Littlejohn's "[is] a much better offer than has ever been made," he assured the governor, "and I am satisfied that the interest of the Commonwealth will not suffer should this offer be received." He requested news of Gilmer's acceptance or rejection of the proposal by 10 a.m. the next day.[17]

The governor consented to do business with Littlejohn, but bureaucracy moved at a slower pace than the rookie trader preferred. The commonwealth of Virginia and Littlejohn agreed to a sale price of $12,500 for the twenty-seven transports, so apparently some last-minute negotiating discounted the slave trader $100 from his most recent bid, a deduction likely linked to the loss of the bondman Jarrett on September 7. Still, the sale was not yet concluded. On September 14, Dickinson recommended that Gilmer not present Littlejohn the order authorizing the slave buyer to pick up "the negroes now confined in the Penitentiary" until the monetary exchange with the commonwealth had been fully completed. Wait "untill [after] I receive the money for the sale ... & pay the ... commonwealth" with it, he advised. Littlejohn had technically paid for the transports already, in full, and had gotten a receipt for the transaction, but he purchased the convict slaves, in part, with "two Bank drafts." The slave buyer claimed the notes were "undoubted," by which he meant drawn on a solvent bank with the financial resources to pay the amount of the drafts, but in the wake of the Panic of 1837, with so many financial institutions going under and wildcat banks popping up to print worthless bank notes without scruple, Dickinson could not be too cautious. Because he harbored some reservations about the validity of the funds Littlejohn proffered for the sale, prudence dictated that he verify the bank drafts were worth their face value before finalizing the sale. Dickinson's message to the governor was simple: Littlejohn's financial obligation to the commonwealth must be legitimately fulfilled and confirmed prior to taking delivery of the transports. Once the funds were guaranteed and in Dickinson's hands, the auctioneer would notify the state.[18]

Littlejohn's money was good. No small sum, the final purchase price of $12,500 equaled roughly $350,000 in 2016 dollars, yet it paled in comparison to the $20,485 the commonwealth had expended in compensation to the masters of the twenty-seven bondpeople seized for sale and transportation. In disposing of the lot to Littlejohn, the state treasury incurred a financial loss of $7,985.[19] (See Appendix A.)

Virginia prescribed that traders buying slaves out of the penitentiary post a bond in accordance with a state law passed on March 2, 1819. If Littlejohn failed to carry the enslaved convicts outside the United States per the statute's provisions, he would be legally obligated to surrender $1,000 per slave to the commonwealth's literary fund. With a shipment of twenty-seven slaves, the penalty would be exorbitant, the equivalent of $750,000 in 2016 dollars. Like virtually all Americans, Littlejohn lacked such copious financial resources. But he was working as an agent for someone who did, slave trader William H. Williams of Washington, D.C. How the two men had become acquainted is open to speculation. If Littlejohn was the gambler he was reputed to be, perhaps he had met Williams in Alexander Lee's Lottery and Exchange Office on Pennsylvania Avenue. Williams trusted Littlejohn enough to dispatch him to Richmond to buy the transports, but Williams followed to serve as security for the purchase. Appearing in person before justice of the peace James Evans on September 12, Williams "made Oath that he is worth Thirty thousand dollars after all his just debts are paid," more than enough to cover the $27,000 in potential fines should the traders prove derelict or unfaithful in fulfilling their duty to ship the transports out of the country. Isham Puckett testified that "I have been . . . acquainted with Mr. Wm. H. Williams for a number of years[.] I [k]no[w] him to be a gentleman of property, and that full confidence may be given to the [certificate]." Puckett and Thomas Howard both served as witnesses to the signing of the official bond that bound Littlejohn and Williams to the commonwealth. Governor Gilmer accepted the bond on September 15, ordered it formally recorded and filed, and transmitted it to Virginia's auditor of public accounts. That same day, the auditor's office received from Littlejohn the receipt for the $12,500 he paid into the Virginia treasury for the purchase of the twenty-seven enslaved inmates now his to dispose of abroad.[20]

On September 16, Littlejohn took delivery of twenty-one male and six female convict slaves. They had been held prisoner in the penitentiary as long as two years and one month and as briefly as two months. They came to the penitentiary from nineteen different Virginia counties, the largest number coming from Fredericksburg and arriving on the same day, convicted of a burglary in which all were complicit. Two Virginia masters formerly owned more than one slave among the sample of twenty-seven. The slaves themselves ranged in age from fourteen to forty-two, with an average age of twenty-five. They were valued at between $250 and $1,500 apiece, with an average valuation of $759.[21]

The transports made their way to Washington, D.C. Perhaps they trudged, chained together in a coffle as was the custom for slaves traveling over land, more than one hundred miles northward, or maybe they boarded a ship in Richmond and proceeded by water down the James River, out into the Chesapeake, and up the Potomac to the port of Alexandria. Regardless of the route, their destination was William H. Williams' Yellow House. At the jail, Williams or one of his associates entered each bondperson's name in one of the ledger books kept since he opened his pen in 1836. Jailer Ebenezer Rodbird, purported keeper of the books, recalled in 1843 that the ledgers also listed "the names of every person depositing negroes there[,] when they [the slaves] were brought [in,] & to whom they belonged." The same single volume contained the data for all prisoners held captive in the Yellow House from 1836 to 1842. None of the ledger books is known to have survived, however. Already in 1843, Rodbird explained, the first volume "is nearly detached from the corner, and the ha[l]f containing the entries from September 1840 to June 1841 appears to have been torn out" – "that is the only leaf which has been torn out of or is missing from the said book." Direct evidence of the twenty-seven transports' entry into the Yellow House therefore does not exist, although their subsequent history suggests that they must have been hostage there for almost a month.[22]

When a newspaper correspondent identified only by the pseudonym Pilgrim visited the Yellow House in early 1849, he found that the private jail "contained some 30 inmates, of both sexes, and various ages." Pilgrim did not arrive at the peak of the trading season, so the quantity of inmates then confined there was unimpressive. In contrast, the transports from Virginia must have arrived in the third week of September 1840, as Williams was amassing as many bondpeople as possible for his fall voyages to the slave markets of the Deep South. Those inmates would have experienced much more crowded conditions, for as abolitionist J. Miller McKim learned during his impromptu tour of the Yellow House complex in early 1838, described in Chapter 2, Williams could cram at least one hundred additional prisoners into his facility. Accommodations were grim. Although McKim never identified by name the jailer who escorted him through the compound, presumably it was Ebenezer Rodbird who showed him three basement apartments. One was designated "as a sleeping apartment to the females." Eleven years later, Pilgrim likewise learned that "[t]he 'girls' occupied separate apartments." (See Figure 7.) All the enslaved prisoners in the Yellow House – men, women, and children – slept in the cellar. "[T]hey lie upon the floor," the keeper explained, "– each one has got a couple of blankets." Solomon Northup's experience in the Yellow House in 1841 more or less squared with the jailer's description but infused a harsh dose of lived reality. "At night I laid down upon the damp, hard floor," he remembered, "without any pillow or covering whatever." Eventually, he did get blankets, at some point prior to the expiration of this two weeks in Williams' slave pen. J. Miller McKim marveled that the sleeping quarters could accommodate the forty-odd slaves he saw during his visit. "O Lord, yes, sir," replied the jailer, "three times as many! – last year we had as many as 139 in these three rooms." McKim was incredulous: "I could hardly see how this was possible without their lying on each other."[23]

Accommodations were rivaled in their dreadfulness only by the food. The jailer showed McKim in 1838 "a table at one side of [an] enclosure where [prisoners'] meals were served up. It was in the open air, with no

VIEW OF THE INTERIOR OF THE JAIL IN WASHINGTON.—FANNY JACKSON.

7 Interior view of a Washington, D.C., jail.
Source: "View of the Interior of the Jail in Washington," *Slave Market of America* (New York: American Anti-Slavery Society, 1836), Broadside Collection, portfolio 118, no. 26c, Library of Congress, Rare Book and Special Collections Division, Washington, D.C.

other protection than a covering from the storm." Slaves ate outdoors, taking "their meals in the open air summer and winter." As it was wintertime during McKim's visit, he inquired, "don't they suffer very much from the cold?" The jailer scoffed at such a notion. "O Lord, no, sir," he replied, "they squat down and eat in ten minutes." Slaves' limited their exposure to the elements, in other words, by gobbling down their food quickly. Inmates of the Yellow House ate twice per day, at 9 a.m. and 3 p.m. "We give them plenty of substantial food," boasted the keeper, "– herring [probably pulled fresh from the Potomac], coffee sweetened with molasses[,] and corn bread." Solomon Northup recalled mealtime at the Yellow House differently. He ate in the cell where he was confined and did not feast from the menu the jailer described to McKim three years before. Rodbird gave Northup, "on a tin plate, a piece of shriveled fried pork, a slice of bread and a cup of water ... Punctually, twice a day, [he] came in, with his pork, and bread, and water."[24]

The grim circumstances infiltrated and darkened the souls of most of the Yellow House's inmates. During his visit, J. Miller McKim observed that "[t]he very small children were gamboling about unconscious of their situation; but those of more advanced age were the most melancholy looking beings." He spoke to one prisoner bound for Alabama whose tone of voice expressed "the deepest sadness." The man's wife, tending their baby, never dared make eye contact with McKim during the encounter. Many other captives cast "wistful, inquiring, anxious looks" at him during his tour, assuming the abolitionist was a potential buyer. "[T]hese poor things," empathized McKim. Their gazes "were hard to endure . . . I soon turned away."[25]

Compared with McKim, Pilgrim, the pseudonymous correspondent touring the Yellow House in 1849, took a more sanguine view of life in the pen. After the enslaved men ate dinner, he explained, someone – the jailer or a guard, perhaps – barked a command, and the inmates arranged themselves "in a line in the yard for inspection." Afterwards, "they engaged in marbles and other sports, and were apparently as contented and happy as so many schoolboys." The "girls," too, "were frolicking and laughing together without a visible shade of care." These comments on enslaved prisoners' leisure time were not the remarks of an abolitionist like McKim. Their visits separated by eleven years, the two guests at Williams' jail emphasized vastly different features of the Yellow House experience.[26]

The convict bondpeople in the Yellow House labored under unspeakable anxiety and fear over what the future held for them. Inmates shared a common apprehension as they imagined what type of person their new owners would be. But some felt their concerns even more acutely than others because they did not know *where* they were going. "Many of the slaves held by Williams in his Seventh Street prison were already sold," J. Miller McKim informed his readers, and were "awaiting delivery to new owners in the deep south." Williams and other slave dealers in Washington, D.C., or Baltimore "often acted as agents for buyers in Mississippi, Alabama and Louisiana," McKim continued. Slave traders scoured the Chesapeake to fill slave owners' requests for a specific type of bondperson – an expert blacksmith, a skilled carpenter, a good cook, a first-rate house servant, and so on. This was how McKim's enslaved informant already knew he was destined for Alabama while still languishing in Williams' jail. He was the fulfillment of an order. Unlike this unidentified bondman, many of Williams' other prisoners, including the twenty-seven transports from Virginia, had no idea of their final destination, an added source of trepidation as they peered forward in time.[27]

Slaves of the Upper South almost universally dreaded sale, unless they toiled under the watchful eyes of a particularly cruel and brutal master. One correspondent writing from Washington, D.C., in 1834 witnessed the "brisk" traffic in slaves out of the nation's capital. The overwhelming majority of them were headed to the Lower South, likely to work in the cotton fields spreading westward across the region. Bondpeople "were generally opposed to going south," reported the correspondent. "All regard slavery in most parts of Maryland and Virginia as mild, compared with Georgia and Louisiana." But it was more than just that. Forcible separation from family and the uprooting from all that was familiar fueled the widespread revulsion to sale. An elderly enslaved man at Robey's pen in Washington listed the specific reasons why he personally objected to removal further southward: "It was a hot climate – the work would be new – slaves fared hard – he and his wife were old, about 60 – they must be driven 600 miles by land – and besides," he reflected, "he wanted to leave his bones in his native State. To endure this was too much." Understanding slaves' shared sentiment against removal, Chesapeake masters added the threat of sale to the Deep South – and to the terrors of the Louisiana cane fields in particular – to their arsenal of disciplinary techniques. Behave or else, they said. But for hundreds of thousands of Chesapeake slaves, sale by their masters to the Deep South was unavoidable. Many other bondpeople experienced compulsory migration with their masters, which, as with sales, carried the same destructive consequences for marital relationships and friendships that crossed the boundaries between neighbors.[28]

The twenty-seven enslaved transports sleeping on the floor of the Yellow House did not possess even the certainty of sale to somewhere in the Lower South. For years, slave traders had purchased Virginia's convict slaves and resold them for profit, typically in Spanish Florida or somewhere in the West Indies, oftentimes, given the deception endemic to the slave trade, to unwitting masters ignorant of the slaves' criminal backgrounds. Presumably Williams' enslaved convicts understood from their defense attorneys or masters that they were to be disposed of outside the United States. Nothing in their past experience could prepare them for such a fate. Most bondpeople, but especially enslaved women, lived spatially circumscribed lives. Limited in their ability to travel freely, they often lacked geographic knowledge of the adjacent county, much less the wider world, enslaved sailors and other workers in the maritime trades excepted. For the enslaved transports of Williams' gang, the future held for them a new home that they may never have heard of or which existed only in the realm of their imaginations. Wallowing in despair, some of the transports may have preferred death to transportation. They may not have known it, but any bondperson who expired in the Yellow House was buried in "a simple pine box" in the makeshift slave cemetery at the corner of Maryland Avenue and Seventh Street.[29]

The transports confined in Williams' slave pen commenced their forced removal by stepping through an unlocked cell door. Solomon Northup was roused from sleep the night he was taken from the Yellow House for the voyage south. "About midnight," he recounted, "the cell door opened." Slave trader James H. Birch and jailer Ebenezer Rodbird "entered, with lanterns in their hands." Birch ordered Northup and about forty enslaved companions "to roll up our blankets without delay, and get ready to go on board the boat." As Northup described it, outside the cell door, "a small passage" led to "a flight of steps" into the outdoor enclosure. "[H]andcuffed and shackeled [sic]," the captives "were conducted into the yard." Birch needed assistance carrying his trunk, so he led Northup through a "covered passage, and up a flight of steps through a side door," to an "upper room" located above the cells. The "whitewashed room, without any carpet on the floor ... seemed a sort of office," Northup remembered, with "a stove, a few old chairs, and a long table, covered with papers." This was probably where William H. Williams worked. What Northup found most striking, however, was a decoration adorning the wall: "a rusty sword" hanging by a window. Birch jolted Northup out of his momentary sense of wonder with a command to help carry the trader's trunk. Using his "unfettered hand" to take one of the two handles, Northup and his captor together exited the front door of the Yellow House into the street. The other prisoners likely departed the compound through "a strongly ironed door" built into the wall of the pen. It opened "into a narrow, covered passage, leading along one side of the house into the street."[30]

Northup's midnight march through the District of Columbia must have felt surreal. "It was a dark night," he recalled. "All was quiet. I could see lights, or the reflection of them, over towards Pennsylvania Avenue, but there was no one . . . to be seen." This was how the traders preferred it. Steering bondpeople down the streets at night avoided a public spectacle as well as the incongruity of chained slaves treading the roads in the capital of a nation founded on the principles of liberty, freedom, and equality. It was so deserted that, for a fleeting instant, Northup pondered flight. "Had I not been hand-cuffed," he asserted, "the attempt would certainly have been made, whatever consequence might have followed." As it was, Ebenezer Rodbird followed at the rear of the parcel of slaves, "carrying a large stick, and hurrying up the children as fast as the little ones could walk. So we passed, hand-cuffed and in silence, through the streets of Washington." Presumably Northup plodded much the same path in the spring of 1841 as the enslaved convicts from Virginia had the previous autumn.[31]

After passing through the "iron gate [that] open[ed] to take in and let out the unfortunate occupants" of Williams' slave fortress, the twenty-seven convict prisoners from Virginia were marched to the riverfront and ferried across the Potomac to Alexandria. Thousands upon thousands of slaves passed through Alexandria in their forced removals from the Upper South. Traders drove some overland from Alexandria, in coffles, to the south and west, but this was a grueling route of perhaps several hundred miles, depending on the destination. A thousand-mile trek to New Orleans took around fifty days by foot. The journey proved taxing to bondpeople's health and, consequently, detrimental to traders' profits. Another option for the transport of bondpeople from Alexandria was the coastwise domestic slave trade. The same legislation from 1807 that forbade US participation in the transatlantic slave trade authorized the shipment of human cargoes by water between American ports.[32]

As early as the 1820s, traders regularly departed the Upper South ports of Baltimore, Alexandria, and Norfolk with captives bound most often for New Orleans but also for other southern port towns such as Mobile and Savannah. In the 1840s, William H. Williams and his associates increasingly deployed slaving vessels out of Baltimore, but before about 1843 were just as likely to send their waterborne cargoes out of Alexandria in the District of Columbia. Slave ships that weighed anchor from that port sailed down the Potomac, into the Chesapeake Bay, and out into the Atlantic. Once in the ocean, slavers headed south, around the tip of Florida, and into the Gulf of Mexico. Turning northwestward, they headed perhaps to Mobile but more likely than not to New Orleans.[33]

William H. Williams and the other leading slave traders of his era participated in the packet trade. Unlike the earlier transient trade, in which vessels remained docked until fully laden with people and cargo, however long that might take, packet ships ran according to fixed, regular schedules. They might be obligated to pull out of port with space still available on board, but the packet trade absorbed those risks by charging higher prices for passengers and freight. As slave trading professionalized from the 1820s into the 1830s, the major traders all adopted the packet principles. In 1836, when William H. Williams & Co. proudly advertised the purchase of two of Armfield, Franklin & Co.'s "splendid New Orleans packets," the nascent firm stated its intent of "running them regularly" between Washington, D.C. and the Crescent City, "leaving each place on the first of each month." Williams cautioned his readers, "Those wishing to ship, had better have their servants at this place a day or two previous to the vessels sailing." There must have been some disruption in service, though, perhaps occasioned by the dissolution of William H. Williams & Co. When Williams again advertised in October 1837, by then as an individual trader, he noted that his vessels, the *Tribune* and *Uncas*, "will commence their regular trips as formerly" to New Orleans. The *Uncas* would next leave port on October 25. "For freight or passage," Washingtonians were instructed to "apply to WILLIAM H. WILLIAMS, Washington City," but residents of Baltimore were to consult either its captain, Nathaniel Boush, at Chase's Wharf or Baltimore merchant and auctioneer William G. Harrison. Apparently Williams' plan for this particular voyage in

1837 was for the *Uncas* to leave Baltimore and then dock briefly at Alexandria en route to New Orleans.[34]

Williams occasionally made such pit-stops between the starting and ending ports of his voyages. In both 1837 and 1839, Captain Boush sailed the *Uncas* from Alexandria for New Orleans, with brief layovers at Norfolk, Virginia, for additional cargo. In 1838, the same vessel pulled out of port at Baltimore and again visited Norfolk before reaching the Crescent City. For packet ships that left their port of origin with available space, stopping for people or cargo to maximize the room on board made sound economic sense. Occasionally, Boush carried the *Uncas* farther out to sea. In April 1840, he made a journey to Barbados and St. Thomas before returning to Norfolk. By June, port authorities in New Orleans cleared the *Uncas* for a more conventional voyage up the Atlantic coast to Baltimore. The brig arrived in the Chesapeake after nineteen days at sea, bearing "molasses, sugar[,] cotton, lead and wheat."[35]

Ships participating in the packet trade were generally brigs or barques with burthens of 180 to 350 tons. The brigs *Tribune* and *Uncas* that William H. Williams bought from Armfield, Franklin, & Co. in 1836 were smaller than the norm, at 161 and 155 tons, respectively. Franklin & Armfield had built the pair of sailing ships for the slave trade. John Armfield described them, along with the firm's third slaver, the brig *Isaac Franklin*, as "vessels of the first class, commanded by experienced and accommodating officers." Under Williams, as under Franklin & Armfield before him, brothers Samuel C. Boush and Nathaniel Boush served as masters, respectively, of the *Tribune* and the *Uncas*. Throughout the 1830s and beyond, the marine intelligence sections of Chesapeake newspapers documented that both vessels regularly sailed from Alexandria with deliveries of slaves and other cargoes for the New Orleans market and returned with an array of merchant goods for Washington, D.C., Baltimore, and the broader Chesapeake region. The day after Christmas 1837, for example, Nathaniel Boush guided the *Uncas* into Baltimore's harbor, bearing a sweet cargo of "sugar and molasses" from New Orleans. He sometimes stopped at Norfolk or Hampton Roads, Virginia, on the return trip as well.[36]

On Friday, October 9, 1840, the *Uncas* left Alexandria on a brief trip upstream to Washington, D.C., presumably for the explicit purpose of picking up the enslaved transports from the Richmond penitentiary and the other bondpeople then imprisoned in the Yellow House. William H. Williams probably thought it less of a hassle to take the ship to the slaves than vice versa. On this occasion, though, the *Uncas* "ran aground about half way between" Alexandria and the nation's capital. While the slaver was hung up in the Potomac, "Steam Boats running as Ferry boats" between the two cities shuttled "the negroes of Williams" from Washington on to Captain Nathaniel Boush's vessel. Once dislodged from the sand and mud, the *Uncas* returned to Alexandria. The convict slaves awaiting transport now numbered twenty men and six women, a total that marked a reduction of one. Arthur, an eighteen-year-old bondman found guilty in 1839 of breaking into a Norfolk store and stealing a variety of weapons and other goods, had already been sold – illegally – in either Virginia or Washington, D.C., for $800, an amount $200 less than Arthur's courtroom valuation but $100 higher than the August 1840 assessment of auctioneer R. H. Dickinson.[37]

Twenty years later, revelations of Arthur's illicit sale revealed previously unknown details of Rudolph Littlejohn's transaction with the commonwealth of Virginia for the convict bondpeople. Littlejohn served merely as the agent working the deal; the actual money for the purchase came from William H. Williams and his fellow Washington, D.C., slave trader and business associate Thomas N. Davis. Over the antebellum decades, Williams and Davis together conducted "many transactions of various kinds and characters." The acquisition of the convict slaves would count as one of them. The staggering sum involved – $12,500 – demanded that the pair pool their collective resources so as not to spread themselves too thin. Two decades after the acquisition of the enslaved criminals, the precise dollar amounts each trader contributed toward the purchase could no longer be recollected with certainty, but they were, in fact, "joint owners" of the slaves for a period of years. Without question, Williams and Davis divvied up the purchase expense, but Davis' entanglement with the convict slaves largely ended there. It was Davis who sold Arthur contrary to law, but that fact would remain secret until 1860. Meanwhile, Williams, who posted the bond guaranteeing the transports'

Manifest of Negroes, Mulattoes, and persons of Colour, taken on board the Brig Uncas *of* Alexandria *whereof* Nathaniel Boush *is Master, burthen.* One hundred fifty-five and 1/95 *Tons, to be transported from the Port of* Alexandria *for the purpose of being sold or disposed of as Slaves, or to be held to service or labor.*

Number of Entry.	NAMES.	SEX.	AGE.	HEIGHT. Feet.	HEIGHT. Inches.	Whether Negro, Mulatto, or Person of Colour.	Owners' or Shipers' Names, and Places of Residence.	Consignees' Names and place of Residence.
1	Albert Smith	male	24	5	7	Dark		
2	Jack Johnson	,,	25	5	9	,,		
3	James Brown	,,	23	5	6	,,		
4	Nelson Nann	,,	37	5	7	,,		
5	John Cooper	,,	20	6	,,	,,		
6	Geo. Devenport	,,	30	5	7	,,		
7	John Johnson	,,	22	5	7	,,		
8	Henry Burgess	,,	21	5	9	,,		
9	Harrison Reed	,,	20	5	8¾	,,		
10	Alfred Taylor	,,	25	6	2	,,		
11	Henry Gordon	,,	21	5	8½	,,		
12	Nelson Judy	,,	30	5	6½	,,		
13	Fill Harris	,,	21	5	5¾	,,		
14	Stephen Lewis	,,	23	5	9	,,		
15	Ned Whelen	,,	22	5	6	,,		
16	Tom Noel	,,	23	5	4½	,,		
17	James Judy	,,	23	5	7½	,,		
18	John Ninkins	,,	24	5	5½	,,		
19	John Carter	,,	28	5	5½	,,		
20	Landon Carter	,,	27	5	8	,,		
21	Malinda Newsom	Female	32	5	4½	,,		
22	Jane Crump	,,	20	5	4½	,,		
23	Nancy Custos	,,	18	5	5½	,,		
24	Charlott Smith	,,	16	4	11	,,		
25	Arena Williamson	,,	33	5	7½	,,		
26	Nancy Smith	,,	35	4	10	Mulatto		

8 Slave manifest of the brig *Uncas*.
Source: nyhs_sc_b-05_f-16_015 [Manifest of the Brig *Uncas*], MS569, Slavery Collection, Series VI: Manifests, 1812–1855, October 9, 1840, New-York Historical Society.

removal from the country, assumed full responsibility over them, commensurate with Virginia law. The remaining twenty-six convict bondpeople composed Williams' gang.[38]

Arthur's premature and unlawful sale by Thomas N. Davis meant that that bondman's name did not appear on the outward slave manifest from Alexandria. (See Figure 8.) The port collector verified the sixty-eight captives who *were* herded aboard the *Uncas*. The law required that the manifest record each bondperson's sex, age, height, and complexion. Although the male convicts from the penitentiary outnumbered the female twenty to six, the sex ratio of the overall shipment was almost even, with thirty-six men and thirty-two women. These numbers made it typical of most of Williams' slaving voyages, which transported just slightly more bondmen than bondwomen. The average age of the unfortunate souls on board was between twenty and twenty-one. At age twenty-two, the typical male captive was three years older than the average woman, at nineteen. By comparison, in the previous two fall journeys of the *Uncas*, the enslaved men on board were four or five years older, on average, than the enslaved women. Among the enslaved prisoners taken from Richmond, the average age was twenty-four, with the typical man only a few months older than the typical woman. Captives always trended young, with most from their latter teens into their twenties. Slave buyers in the Old Southwest wanted healthy and robust bondpeople capable of grueling labor. Only four of the sixty-eight on board the *Uncas* in October 1840 were listed as older than thirty, although bondpeople often magically aged in reverse on slave manifests to bring more money at sale. The two eldest were estimated at fifty. At the opposite end of the age spectrum, nine of the enslaved were younger than thirteen, including infants of only two, three, four, and nine months of age, each accompanied by his or her mother. Only three bondpeople on board exceeded six feet in height, all of them men. Alfred, convicted of attacking the patrol in Fairfax County, towered above them all at six foot two. The overwhelming majority of all slaves Williams shipped were labeled "black" or "dark," including all but one of the enslaved transports. He carried off far fewer slaves deemed "brown," "mulatto," "yellow," or "copper." Aboard the *Uncas* in 1840, sixty-one (90 percent) of the human cargo was classified as "dark," joined by two mixed-race mulattoes and five still lighter-complexioned "yellow" slaves. A sixth "yellow" bondman's name was crossed off the manifest, indicating that he had been taken off the vessel prior to departure, perhaps because he had died, somehow managed to escape, or was sold at the last minute, closer to home.[39]

No eleventh-hour rescue from the slave ship awaited the twenty-six members of Williams' gang, but such miracles did occasionally happen.

Almost a year earlier, William H. Williams had deposited aboard the *Uncas*, also then docked in Alexandria, the twenty-five-year old John Chambers, "dark"; the twenty-year-old, "copper"-colored Catharine Lewis; and the "dark," sixteen-year-old Silas Mosberry, all to be transported and sold. Moments before the *Uncas* departed for New Orleans, however, authorities plucked the three captives off the brig. Although they had been "banished by order of the Court at Baltimore," Maryland, for their crimes, according to a note scribbled on the slave manifest, the three bondpeople were lawfully "enti[t]led to their freedom after a term of Years." Had they set sail, they would almost certainly have remained perpetually enslaved.[40]

On October 9, 1840, the collector at Alexandria, finding nothing out of the ordinary with the manifest, cleared the *Uncas* for departure to Mobile, Alabama. The brig set sail the following day, Saturday October 10. William H. Williams had left Washington, D.C., that morning for Alexandria to board his vessel, piloted once again by Nathaniel Boush and bearing yet another valuable cargo of human beings. The *Uncas* had borne at least one parcel of slaves to the Deep South each fall for years. Slaving voyages typically left the Chesapeake during the fall, winter, or spring months. This particular shipment was unusual in at least two ways, however. First, all of the slaves aboard the *Uncas* belonged to William H. Williams. Usually, multiple slave dealers shared space aboard coastwise slaving vessels, shipping bondpeople to New Orleans, as one observer explained, "in gangs of 15 to 30." That way, in the event of a tragic accident or disaster, such as a shipwreck, hurricane, or onboard contagion of disease, no single trader incurred the loss of an entire load of slaves. Sound economics transformed such caution into custom. Williams himself tended to transport only between ten and forty captives on any one vessel. Almost as frequently, he deposited fewer than ten aboard a given coastwise slaver. Very rarely did he or his associates ever place more than forty bondpeople on any one ship. (See Appendix C.) But in October 1840, all the slaves aboard the *Uncas* belonged to him and his partner behind-the-scenes, Thomas N. Davis. The second reason this voyage was so unusual is that it transported a hybrid cargo. Forty-two of the sixty-eight captives on board were eligible for sale within the United States through the perfectly lawful coastwise slave trade; twenty-six were not. What did Williams think would happen when he landed in Mobile, as the slave manifest said he would, with dozens of convict bondpeople from outside Alabama mixed in with the usual assortment of surplus Chesapeake slaves for sale? Or was Williams simply planning on disposing of all his slaves in Mobile in flagrant disregard of his agreement with the commonwealth of Virginia, assuming that no one would be any the wiser? This would soon become an important question.[41]

The *Uncas* glided out of Alexandria with its involuntary passengers bound for Mobile. Under ideal conditions, with no additional stops, favorable weather, and a little luck, a skillful ship master like Nathaniel Boush could theoretically reach the Gulf Coast of Alabama in as little as two weeks, although three was closer to normal. A return journey from Mobile to the Chesapeake would be faster. Harnessing the swift and powerful currents of the Gulf Stream up the East Coast in December 1837, Captain Boush propelled the *Uncas* from Balize, the maritime outpost at the mouth of the Mississippi River, to Baltimore in just sixteen days. Two years earlier, the *Tribune* reached Hampton Roads, Virginia, from New Orleans in only eleven. But heading to Mobile, Boush would be working against the prevailing ocean currents. The journey with William H. Williams, Rudolph Littlejohn, and the penitentiary transports would take about twenty days.[42]

In its construction, the *Uncas* was similar to its sister ship of almost identical size, the *Tribune*. The same Connecticut shipbuilders con-structed both two-masted sailing vessels by order of Franklin & Armfield. The *Tribune* was two years older, assembled in 1831. At eighty feet long and thirty-three feet, three inches wide, the dimensions of the 161-ton *Tribune* were one foot longer and wider than those of the 155-ton *Uncas*. Both brigs were wider and deeper than transatlantic slavers, which meant they were also slower. Given their intended coastwise slaving purpose, neither vessel required the swiftness to outrun the British patrols intent on intercepting unlawful shipments of African slaves tra-versing the open Atlantic. Both ships contained a partition to segregate their human cargoes by sex. A visitor who toured the *Tribune* in 1834 beheld "[t]he hold ... appropriated to the slaves." The area below deck was "divided into two apartments," one to accommodate a maximum of "eighty women, and the other about one hundred men." Those 180 captives were allotted about thirty-six cubic feet of space apiece, the same volume contained in a six by three by two foot rectangular box. Sleeping quarters consisted of "*two platforms* running the whole length" of the ship, "one raised a few inches" off the floor, "the other half way up to the deck." Each was "about five or six feet deep," reported the correspondent. "On these the slaves lie," crammed uncomfortably together. Overcrowding would have been comparable for the unwilling passengers below the deck of the *Uncas*. Within a month of its completion and September 1833 launch, the $7,250 *Uncas* shipped its inaugural cargo of almost one hundred bondpeople to New Orleans.[43]

Conditions aboard coastwise slavers only worsened as the pace of the waterborne trade accelerated. Early vessels traveling coastwise packed enslaved captives on board with a variety of other, non-human cargoes. The professionalization of the saltwater domestic slave trade meant that ships plying the waters off American shores increasingly transported but one commodity: slaves. With an emphasis on maximum profits, shippers engaged in a practice resembling the tight-packing of slaves common aboard the oceangoing ships of the dreaded Middle Passage that conveyed bondpeople seized in Africa across the Atlantic. The nightmarish hellscape below deck left a deep impression on captive William Walker, one casualty of the coastwise slave trade. Born in Southampton County, Virginia, Walker spent six weeks in the Petersburg slave pen in 1841 before being hustled aboard the *Pelican* for removal to New Orleans. "It would be impossible for any man to draw the faintest idea of the horrible position in which we were placed while on the boat," he related. "It is indescribable. Men, women and children were packed beneath the hatches like cattle." The *Pelican* was a much larger vessel than either the *Tribune* or the *Uncas*, capable of holding three times the number of slaves. "Think of six hundred human beings living six weeks in the hold of a vessel 180 feet long, 40 feet wide and 10 feet high," Walker implored. "There was no air to be had, for the only means of receiving air was by three small grated windows on either side of the boat, two feet long and eight inches wide; and when sea sickness began among us it was surely one of the most horrible places ever visited by a human being." Walker guaranteed that the stench "from that filthy boat was poisonous to breathe." In such cramped quarters and unsanitary conditions, disease could spread rapidly. Solomon Northup expressed alarm over an outbreak of smallpox aboard the *Orleans* during his voyage. But Northup and Walker both survived, as did the overwhelming majority of all bondpeople displaced via the coastwise domestic slave trade. Walker reported that thirty-one slaves did perish aboard the *Pelican* before even reaching the tip of Florida during what became an epic, six-week ordeal to reach New Orleans, temporally the worst-case scenario for coastwise captives. Overall, the waterborne domestic slave trade claimed far fewer lives than did the Middle Passage, but that was primarily because the journey was shorter, not because conditions were substantively better.[44]

William H. Williams prowled the deck of the *Uncas* as the brig sliced through the undulating waters beneath. Little did he realize the flurry of correspondence being penned about him and his unconventional cargo. Weeks before the *Uncas* ever left Alexandria, Virginia governor Thomas Walker Gilmer received an early warning that Williams might attempt to sell the transport slaves from the penitentiary in the South's leading slave market: New Orleans. His informant was his good friend and mayor of Alexandria, Bernard Hooe. The well-known slaver *Uncas,* Hooe explained, "is now at our wharves, and will *probably* sail *about* [the] *15th*" of October. "Her destination is not yet announced," the mayor continued, but he pledged to advise the governor once that knowledge became public: "I will look out for the movements of the Uncas, and give you timely notice when she may leave this Port." Hooe suspected that William H. Williams would claim the *Uncas* was bound for Texas "as a blind" – a piece of disinformation, or diversion – and instead "go *direct to New-Orleans,*" contrary to Virginia law.[45]

Why did Hooe believe this? And what business was it of his? He never explicitly revealed the source of his intelligence that the *Uncas* would not convey the convict bondpeople outside the country. As mayor of Alexandria, perhaps he had overheard whispers at his city's waterfront or received a heads-up from a loyal political ally in the know. But it is impossible to say. Hooe seems to have inserted himself into the matter based on his friendship with Fairfax County slaveholder Dennis Johnston, owner of the banished bondman Alfred and Alfred's brother Spencer, executed more than four months earlier. Hooe had labored extensively with Johnston to earn reprieves for both slaves, but their efforts were only half successful. What Hooe stood to gain from making sure Alfred and the other twenty-five transports got shipped out of the United States is unclear, beyond a general sense of security for Virginia's and the nation's white citizens. Regardless, Hooe kept close tabs on the transports for the governor. He knew in September that they lodged "in Washington in Williams's Jail," for a bondperson in the neighborhood of Alexandria had seen and shaken hands with Alfred and reported the encounter to "some persons here."[46]

Hooe wrote his next missive to Governor Gilmer, marked "Private," on October 12. He informed the executive that the *Uncas* had sailed two days earlier for Mobile, not New Orleans as he had previously supposed, bearing almost seventy slaves. Hooe knew to keep a lookout for its departure. Dennis Johnston had visited Alfred at the Yellow House "about the middle of the ... week" before the brig weighed anchor. Johnston learned from his confiscated bondman that William H. Williams planned "to leave Washington in a few days for the south" and that Alfred and his fellow transports would be aboard. "I have no doubt those slaves are intended for the Southern market in the United States," Hooe declared. He urged Gilmer's vigilance, for the mayor could not rule out the possibility that the vessel "may possibly change her destination, and go to New-Orleans, or to some other southern port in the United States." Hooe implored the governor, thus armed with this information, to "take the necessary steps in the promises to protect, or punish any violation of your laws." As if to underscore the surreptitious nature of his intelligence for the governor, Hooe assured Gilmer, "No person here suspects me of having any communication with you on this subject."[47]

Gilmer instructed Captain William H. Richardson, secretary for the commonwealth of Virginia, to pen letters warning the people of Mobile – and New Orleans, just to be safe – that William H. Williams and his band of enslaved convicts were on the open seas with possible intentions of landing at their ports. Richardson contacted Mobile mayor Edward Hall, Louisiana governor André B. Roman, and the New Orleans commission merchant firm of A. L. Addison & Co., 22 Bank Place, where the secretary's personal friend and former Virginia resident Andrew L. Addison was a partner. Richardson chronicled the series of events that had

unfolded: that Rudolph Littlejohn purchased twenty-seven slaves convicted of capital crimes in Virginia whose sentences had been reprieved
to sale and transportation outside the United States; that slave trader
William H. Williams, who gave bond in the amount of $27,000 as security
that the slaves would be conveyed outside the country, was the "real
purchaser"; and that the brig *Uncas*, under master Nathaniel Boush,
"sailed from the port of Alexandria" on Saturday, October 10, "carrying
about 70 slaves ... including the 27" convicted criminals. Without getting
into the details, Richardson explained that Governor Gilmer had
"received information since the purchase which justifies the belief ...
that an attempt will be made to sell the slaves" contrary to statute, "either
at New Orleans or Mobile." Because it was "incumbent" upon the governor not only to see Virginia's laws "faithfully executed" but also to prevent
"injury ... to any of our sister States," he called upon the people of
Alabama and Louisiana to remain vigilant. The governor "has directed
me to give you this information," Richardson concluded, "and to request
that you will" take "measures" to detect any possible landing of the
Virginia transports on US soil. The secretary appended a list of the
original twenty-seven transports by name, county of conviction, and
crime. He mistakenly included the bondman Arthur among those slaves
aboard the *Uncas*, ignorant of the fact that Thomas N. Davis had already
sold him unlawfully.[48]

Mobile mayor Edward Hall took the communication from Richmond
seriously and promptly contacted the port collector of his city. Alarmed,
the customs agent furnished the full text of Secretary Richardson's letter
to at least one Mobile newspaper for publication, a move Richardson
later condemned as "very ill advised." Suddenly the masses of citizens in
Mobile were aware of the possible danger lurking just off the coast. The
city was abuzz. The "novel importation, expected daily from Alexandria
... is the subject of much conversation and not a little excitement in our
city," reported the *Mobile Journal.* No doubt many people in Mobile and
its environs kept their eyes fixated on the aqueous horizon, gazing out
into the waters of Mobile Bay for signs of the *Uncas* and its threatening,
illicit cargo carving its way through the Gulf of Mexico. Another reaction
prevalent among the public was anxiety. The *Mobile Journal* did not
criticize Virginia's governor for reprieving the convict bondpeople to

sale and transportation. Doing so, the paper understood, fell within "the proper exercise of his duty." Virginia law fully authorized the commutation of death sentences to banishment outside the United States, relieving the commonwealth's "gaols" of "a number of felon negroes." "Where it was expected they should go" did not seem so clear. Maybe "the Coast of Africa, or some of the free labor settlements in South America," speculated the *Journal.* As it stood, these convict slaves – "a set of worse outlaws" than any that could be imagined – were prepped "to be added to our negro population."[49]

Some voices expressed outrage that Virginia would foist its enslaved convicts on others. "How comes the State of Virginia to dispose of her black convicts in this way[?]" inquired the *New Orleans Commercial Bulletin.* The newspaper conceded that Virginia certainly never intended traders to smuggle "these villains" into the United States, but the commonwealth's law did permit sale and transportation abroad. "[W]hat country allows the importation of slaves from the United States, especially the importation of convict slaves?" mused the editor. Who would want them? The *Commercial Bulletin* recognized and was troubled by the hypocrisy of ongoing US complaints about "European nations" dumping their "white paupers" on American shores when, unbeknownst to most US citizens, "one of our most respectable and powerful States, has a law . . . for turning loose upon other nations, ignorant and brutal slaves, convicted of every enormity upon which its own laws pronounce the punishment of death!" For those previously unacquainted with Virginia law, it seemed too much to comprehend.[50]

Letters reached Virginia governor Thomas Walker Gilmer's desk from concerned, exasperated, and curious citizens such as M. W. Garrison, a partner in running Montgomery Hall, an inn in what would become Alabama's capital in another six years. Writing the governor's reply to Garrison, William H. Richardson both defended and explained Gilmer's actions concerning the convict slaves. He opened by clarifying that the governor had "no controul whatever over, or claim upon, the negroes sold to Littlejohn." Lacking any direct, personal interest in them, Gilmer had contacted the mayor of Mobile to pass along information about William H. Williams' supposed "intention" to land in a southern city for the purpose of "prevent[ing] impositions upon the people of the South in the sale of convict slaves to them." Virginia held a stake in the unfolding events as well, however. If Williams, Littlejohn, and the enslaved transports from the penitentiary were detected entering any US port, the governor could prosecute Williams, and the trader's staggering $27,000 bond would be "forfeited" to the commonwealth. Moreover, any of the enslaved transports ever again discovered in Virginia were subject to execution.[51]

Williams and Littlejohn unwittingly sailed toward a community on high alert. A wary, unnerved, and agitated public awaited their appearance off the coast of Mobile. The slave trader and his agent surely anticipated nothing out of the ordinary. They assumed that the port collector in Mobile would re-check the manifest, complete another roll call, and, assuming all was consistent, correct, and orderly, clear the *Uncas* to land and dispose of its human cargo, or at least the non-criminal majority of it. Given the advanced warning of the approach of the *Uncas*, Mayor Edward Hall made certain that his city was prepared. He collaborated with the port collector to make arrangements "for intercepting the vessel before her foul freight can be landed." According to the *Mobile Journal*, on Friday, October 30, almost three weeks after leaving Alexandria, the *Uncas* and its cargo of convict slaves "reached the bar of our bay." Williams and his agent did not receive a hospitable welcome. "On my arrival at Mobile," Littlejohn later complained to Virginia's Governor Gilmer, "I found the people in a great State of Excitement on account of an article that appeared in the public prints saying that I would sell . . . those negroes I purchased from the State of V[irgini]a." A roused and irate public and its public officials would not permit such an outrage. "We do not know exactly what was done by our authorities to get rid of them," recorded the *Mobile Journal* of Williams, Littlejohn, and the enslaved transports, "but we believe that they were prevented from landing here."[52]

An outline of the events that transpired in Mobile slowly came into focus. William H. Williams claimed that he and the convict slaves, contrary to newspaper reports, "landed at Mobile." The slave trader then promptly "called upon the mayor . . . and acquainted him with the destination of the negroes." As Williams explained it, his intent was to carry the transport slaves "to Texas, via New Orleans and [the] Red

River." In Mobile the same time as Williams, S. F. Slatter, a New Orleans-based slave trader headquartered at the corner of Esplanade and Moreau streets, corroborated the bulk of Williams' account. Slatter's recollections differed from Williams' in that Slatter believed his slave-trading counterpart had landed in Mobile before "the Brig Uncas had arrived there with the negroes in question." Quite possibly Williams had taken a skiff to shore while the *Uncas* remained anchored in Mobile Bay with its captives. Whatever the case, Slatter verified that he "saw Mr. Williams in Mobile" in late October 1840 and that Williams had informed him that he planned to take the convict people to Texas – the identical story he related to Mayor Hall.[53]

Was Williams' word credible, or a fiction conjured to mask criminal intentions? Certainly Texas was a foreign country eligible to receive convict slaves, but if Williams was taking the enslaved transports to Texas, why stop at Mobile at all? The Alabama port was an odd place to land for someone journeying to the Lone Star Republic. In 1840, the infrastructure did not yet exist to travel overland from Alabama to Texas with any degree of ease. No rail line yet connected Mobile to New Orleans or to any point farther west. The New Orleans, Mobile & Texas Railroad was not completed for another thirty years, in 1871. Maybe Williams anticipated unloading the forty-two non-convict slaves in Mobile before continuing on his way with the twenty-six transports. As it happened, the trader disposed of not a single one of the slaves from the *Uncas* in Mobile. Rather, Williams explained, "the authorities of that city" granted him "permission . . . to pass them through." The hostile reception to Williams' arrival dictated that he pull his valuable shipment of slaves out of Mobile Bay quickly and find a different location in which to dispose of them.[54]

CHAPTER 4

Mobile to New Orleans

R EPULSED BY AUTHORITIES IN MOBILE, WILLIAM
H. Williams quickly formulated a strategy for exiting the bay
and getting his shipment of slaves to market. It was a prudent course of
action. Wherever the truth of Williams' intentions lay, public perception
maintained that the trader planned to dump his convict slaves on the
unsuspecting people of Mobile, as nothing in Alabama law specifically
prohibited the importation of enslaved convicts. Viewed through the
most sinister possible lens, perhaps Williams had targeted Mobile knowing that Alabama had no lawful restriction against the introduction of
enslaved criminals, but even if the gap in Alabama law precluded the
possibility of legal entanglements for Williams in that state, he still confronted a hostile public whose patience had worn thin. Were he to linger
unwanted, he might have been subjected to the extralegal, vigilante
justice routinely administered in the nineteenth-century South whenever
the public felt wronged by the pace, outcomes, or lack of courtroom
proceedings.[1]

Williams' solution to his conundrum drew upon all of his knowledge
and expertise accumulated over more than a decade of slave trading. He
resolved to move on to New Orleans but, before departing, to divvy up his
shipment into two. On October 31, the day after the arrival of the *Uncas*
in the waters off Mobile, Williams enlisted the services of the steamboat
Roanoke, captained by William J. Duval. Navigating the undulating waters
beneath him, Duval piloted the *Roanoke* alongside the *Uncas*, "some five
miles down the bay," so that the slave trader could offload a portion of his
human cargo. Stepping gingerly from one vessel to the other, the twenty-
six transport slaves boarded the *Roanoke*, while the forty-two other

bondpeople remained aboard the *Uncas*. Was Williams attempting to deceive forewarned, vigilant officials along the Gulf Coast by switching boats, enabling him to clandestinely dispose of the convict slaves undetected?[2]

As Williams surely knew, transferring the transport slaves to a smaller vessel plying the coastal waters relaxed his legal obligation to record the data on his human cargo. Section eight of the 1807 act that terminated the United States' lawful participation in the transatlantic slave trade from Africa or the West Indies expressly stated that the law did "nothing . . . to prohibit the taking on board or transporting on any river, or inland bay of the sea, within the jurisdiction of the United States, any negro, mulatto, or person of color" for sale. The coastwise slave trade internal to the United States might proceed unimpeded, via "any vessel or species of craft whatever." In January 1840, US Secretary of the Treasury Levi Woodbury of New Hampshire pressed Attorney General Henry Gilpin for answers to questions concerning "the coastwise transportation of slaves" and the legal requirement to fill out slave manifests for voyages back and forth between Mobile and New Orleans. Gilpin replied that the "designated route" between the two cities "should be controlled by section 8 of the Act of 1807," which fully authorized the coastwise commerce in slaves "on any river, or inland bay of the sea." The 1807 law, as he interpreted it, "was not intended to regulate the interior transportation of slaves but rather to prevent the continuance of the illicit foreign trade." Practically, this meant that slave traders aboard vessels traversing "internal waterways" were not required to fill out the detailed slave manifests required of voyages on the high seas. Williams used this policy, formalized only months before the October departure of the *Uncas* to Mobile, to his advantage. Absent the old regulations, Williams hired Captain Duval and instructed him to take only "inland passes" from Mobile to New Orleans, sparing himself the need to file the customary slave manifest or to clear the customs house in Mobile. Strictly speaking, Williams complied with the law, but crucial information that might later be used to identify the twenty-six convict slaves upon arrival in another port conveniently went unrecorded.[3]

If Williams hoped to effect the transfer of the convicts with any degree of secrecy, he failed miserably. He and his gang of transports departed

Mobile on October 31, soon after they changed boats. Later that same day, the *Mobile Journal* documented Williams' expulsion from Mobile Bay for a delighted and relieved readership and predicted that the trader would next appear with his peculiar cargo in New Orleans. In its reporting, the *Mobile Daily Commercial Register and Patriot* added greater detail than did its competitor. The October 31 edition alerted the public that the "convict negroes" from the *Uncas* had been hustled "on board the steamboat Roanoke," bound for the Crescent City: "It is intended, we understand, to ship them thence to Texas, where they will be sold, if no obstacle be interposed by the authorities of that republic." The newspaper could only marvel at Virginia's negligence in permitting the "setting loose [of] such a gang of ruffians." It seemed both "remarkable and extrajudicial" for the commonwealth to entrust the compulsory banishment of convict slaves to anyone but "a special agent of the government."[4]

The New Orleans press first called residents' attention to the Williams' gang slaves in a *Picayune* article of October 31 that reported on Mobile mayor Edward Hall's receipt of the letter sent by Virginia governor Thomas Walker Gilmer. Without elaboration, the paper offered the cursory warning, "LOOK OUT FOR THEM!" The assumption then, however, was that the convict slaves would arrive via the Mississippi River aboard Nathaniel Boush's *Uncas*. On November 3, the *Picayune*, citing the *Mobile Chronicle*, again mentioned Williams, Littlejohn, and the projected landing in New Orleans of the convict bondpeople, mistakenly still reported as numbering twenty-seven. The *Mobile Journal* implicitly congratulated itself on performing a valuable public service by exposing Williams' intended journey to New Orleans. "The authorities there are doubtless on their guard," it printed.[5]

Compared with the newspapers of Mobile, the *Picayune*, after its brief, initial expression of alarm, appeared remarkably undisturbed by William H. Williams' predicted arrival. Surely Mobile's newspaper editors found the *Picayune*'s evident nonchalance arresting. But Williams had been a visible and active participant in the New Orleans slave trade for several years. He in fact held diverse business interests in the city. Many slave dealers in the antebellum South, including Williams, owned stores or other merchant ventures. Beginning in February 1837, Williams and George M. Grant entered into a partnership in New Orleans "for conducting the Boot & Shoe business," initially for a limited term slated to end on November 1, 1839. The partners first leased retail space for a store on the lower floor of 62 Camp Street in Faubourg Marigny, but by July 1839 relocated along the same street to 18 Camp. There, they peddled not only footwear from "the best Northern manufacturers" but also glass cases and shelving, among other goods. Williams and Grant renewed their partnership and in September 1843 leased the ground floor of the City Hotel at the corner of Camp and Common. They remained in business until August 1845, when they dissolved their partnership by "mutual consent." But already by late 1840, the slave trader was a well-known figure in New Orleans, enmeshed in the city's business life, so the *Picayune* calmly dismissed the panic conveyed by the Mobile papers: "Mr. Williams is a man of property and respectability, and there seems to be no good reason why his correct dealing should be questioned."[6]

William H. Williams and Rudolph Littlejohn redirected their gaze toward New Orleans, but they parted company in Mobile. While Williams climbed on to the *Roanoke*, Littlejohn either returned to the Chesapeake or stayed aboard the *Uncas* as Nathaniel Boush guided the brig out into the Gulf of Mexico and up the Mississippi River before docking at New Orleans. Boush and Williams had each affixed their names to a fresh slave manifest in Mobile – one that reflected the offloading of the transport slaves. The names of the forty-two bondpeople remaining aboard the *Uncas* perfectly matched those on the outward manifest signed in Alexandria, appearing in precisely the same order. Of the forty-two, thirty-six were classified as "dark," five as "yellow," and one as "mulatto." Sixteen were men and twenty-six women. The female slaves included Milly Bennett and her three-month-old daughter Mary Ann, and Lavenia Crawford and her two-year-old daughter Catharine. Letty Hollingsworth was joined by her children Abram, age two, and Ellen, four months. Mary Hogan was enslaved together with her four-year-old son William and two-month-old infant Martha. A Louisiana law of 1829 mandated that all these children, since they were under the age of ten, could not be sold separately from their mothers. Daniel Ross, age twenty-four, and Stacy Ross, age twenty-one, may have been either siblings or a married couple. The Louisiana slave code did not grant them the similar protections against separation. Most of the souls on board the *Uncas* had already been severed from their loved ones, and all of the bondpeople old enough to comprehend their situation must have dreaded the future as the slave ship slipped into New Orleans on November 3, 1840.[7]

The following morning, the New Orleans press announced the arrival of the *Uncas*. The fates of the forty-two non-convicts formerly held captive with the Williams' gang slaves mirrored those of the thousands who had already passed through New Orleans for sale, ensnared in the Old South's massive geographic redistribution of enslaved wealth. Thanks to southern cotton, New Orleans, the nation's fastest-growing city and third most populous overall, had dethroned New York City in 1834 as the nation's busiest port from which merchants exported goods overseas. But someone physically needed to grow all that cotton, tilling the earth, sowing the seeds, thinning out the maturing plants, chopping weeds from the growing crop, and, at harvest, picking the fluffy balls at a frenzied pace while simultaneously avoiding getting pricked by the razor-sharp dried bolls that cradled the soft, cloud-like, fibrous orbs. By no coincidence, as the cotton frontier spread to the Old Southwest, New Orleans became the single largest slave market in the South. There, many masters preferred strong, young slaves fresh from Virginia, and demand for them was high.[8]

When the customs officer conducted a roll call to verify the accuracy of the slave manifest from Mobile, he found no discrepancies and cleared the *Uncas* to land and unload its latest shipment of Chesapeake slaves. Per custom, upon docking, the bondpeople were quickly transferred into the custody of the receiving slave trader, his agent, or a consignee invited on board. The enslaved cargo of the *Uncas* was consigned to the merchant firm of J. W. Zacharie & Co., 88 Customhouse Street, although who, precisely, retrieved this particular parcel of slaves is not known. Slaves conveyed to New Orleans were then escorted off the boat and frequently confined, as they awaited auction or private sale, in one of the city's many pens, which numbered as high as twenty during the heights of the domestic slave trade in the 1830s and 1850s. The bulk of the slave jails "lin[ed] Gravier and Baronne streets in the city's business district, and Chartres and Esplanade just downriver from the French Quarter," in

Faubourg Marigny. One ex-slave recalled that "[n]early the entire length of Grand street, in New Orleans, on either side, was one solid row of buildings where human beings were incarcerated waiting for a purchaser." From within the walls of the city's multiple slave pens, at the peak of trading season, thousands of bondpeople went up for sale per day.[9]

The enslaved occupants of the New Orleans pens described these prisons and the conditions inside. The pen in which the enslaved John Brown was detained sported "two entrances . . . one for the 'niggers,' the other for visitors and buyers." The accommodations for the captives "consisted of a block of houses" – each three stories tall and "built upon brick pillars or piers" – that together "form[ed] a square, and cover[ed] perhaps an acre of ground." The common "yard of the pen," shared by all the quarters, "was . . . nicely gravelled [*sic*] for the slaves to take exercise in." Windows in the captives' temporary lodgings "overlooked the yard" as well as the adjacent street and were all "heavily barred" to prevent escapes. Brown noted that the pen in which he was imprisoned "was usually full," with "about five hundred" chattel for sale: "The men were separated from the women, and the children from both."[10]

To prepare the slaves for the market, sellers assured that the bondpeople in the pen were fed regularly and amply, their bodies washed, their hair combed, any gray hairs plucked or dyed, and the men shaved, all to produce the most effective and pleasing presentation to persuade prospective buyers. Motivated by market forces, traders tended to those enslaved within New Orleans pens with greater care than when they were jailed in the Chesapeake. Still, nothing could gloss over the cruel realities of selling people and the emotional toll it took on the victims of the trade. As John Brown summarized of his experience in one of the pens, "It was an awfully gloomy place, notwithstanding the bustle that was always going on in it." Although some bondpeople coped with the grief of separation and their anxiety about the future by whiling away their time singing, dancing, "telling funny stories," or praying, others, dejected and morose, succumbed to depression as they reminisced of homes and families lost. Some captives fell victim to epidemics of yellow fever – a disease familiar to New Orleans – while in confinement.[11]

"Amongst other 'nigger speculators' whom I remember bringing in their coffles" to the pen, John Brown recalled, was "Williams from

Washington." William H. Williams carried in "large gangs . . ., frequently filling the pen" with his latest shipment of slaves. Like those who had gone before, the forty-two bondpeople aboard the *Uncas* in October 1840 certainly contributed to the enslaved population of one of the New Orleans slave pens before they were sold. But Williams did not accompany them on the brig's latest voyage from Mobile. He and the twenty-six convict slaves had taken the *Roanoke*. The "light draught, fast running steamer" skimmed across the water and reached Port Pontchartrain, on the southern end of the massive lake north of New Orleans, late on October 31, the same day it had left Mobile and three days before the *Uncas* would reach the Crescent City. The *Roanoke* ran regularly between Mobile and New Orleans, usually departing Mobile on Sunday mornings and Lake Pontchartrain on Wednesday evenings. The steamer never ventured out into the deep Gulf waters during its weekly jaunts but instead hugged the coastline, navigating between the shore and the smattering of islands running parallel to it, some five to ten miles out to sea. After picking up Williams' gang in Mobile Bay, the *Roanoke* conveyed the slave trader and his cargo on its customary route through Grants Pass, between Dauphin Island and the Alabama mainland, then westward across the length of Mississippi Sound, skirting the northern end of Lake Borgne, through the Rigolets, and into Lake Pontchartrain. Steamboats had carried shipments of Williams' captives via this route before; the only difference this time was the criminal history of the slaves on board.[12]

The brief journey from Mobile to Louisiana may have given the Williams' gang slaves their best opportunity to date to meet and engage directly with one another. They would first have assembled at the Virginia State Penitentiary to await sale and transportation, but authorities there ran a structured, regimented institution marked by demanding rules and regulations. As was true of some other penal institutions in the early nineteenth century, the prison in Richmond maintained that solitude was essential to give inmates the opportunity to reflect upon the errors of their ways. State law mandated solitary confinement for a portion of prisoners' sentences, and, for several years, all inmates at the Virginia State Penitentiary spent their first month in isolation. The building itself was designed to house inmates individually, within their own private cells, although as more convicts entered the institution, single occupancy confinement ultimately proved impossible to sustain. Three or four prisoners per cell was more the norm. Nevertheless, guards rigidly enforced a code of silence within the penitentiary. Convicts labored in common workrooms but were not permitted to make a sound. Furthermore, penitentiary officials imposed a sexual divide, separating male from female inmates, making it that much more difficult for the enslaved men and women of Williams' gang to interact. Surely, though, clever prisoners found the means to overcome the oppressive atmosphere, circumvent the rules, defy authority, and communicate with one another in creative, clandestine ways.[13]

The silence that reigned over the Virginia State Penitentiary, not eliminating but surely frustrating attempts at communication, marked but one of the impediments to the Williams' gang slaves becoming acquainted. During both their incarceration at the Yellow House and aboard the *Uncas,* they were interspersed among other bondpeople. Now, chugging aboard the *Roanoke* en route to New Orleans, the enslaved convicts were a cargo unto themselves, no doubt under Williams' watchful gaze but presumably at liberty to speak with those in the same literal and figurative boat.

Perhaps as the *Roanoke* skimmed the shallows just off the Gulf Coast, they conversed with one another in hushed tones about the circumstances that placed them in the clutches of one of Washington's most notorious slave traders. The criminal histories of the Williams' gang slaves were varied. One-third of the twenty-seven purchased out of the Virginia State Penitentiary had committed violent offenses. In addition to Alfred's conviction for assault on the Fairfax County slave patrol, four slaves were found guilty of the attempted murder of Virginia whites. A Spotsylvania County court of oyer and terminer convicted the bondman John Johnson of assaulting and beating a white man with intent to kill during a Christmas Eve highway robbery in 1838. Arriving at the penitentiary only a week before Alfred in May 1840 were the bondman Jim and his enslaved mother-in-law, Arena, tried and convicted in the Southside Virginia county of Greensville for conspiring and plotting to murder a total of five different white people, including the owners of the estate where they lived, Jim's mistress, and Arena's master and overseer. To protest being driven too hard at work and to prevent their being carried farther South, as so many enterprising slaveholders of the time were doing with their enslaved labor forces, the pair ground up "blue bottle glass" in a mortar and pestle and placed the pulverized, powdered material in a pitcher of water for their oppressors to drink. Their plan failed, and they were instead slated for execution until spared by a gubernatorial reprieve to sale and transportation. The last attempted murderer held captive on the *Roanoke* was thirty-eight-year-old Nancy Via, sometimes called Nancy Smith, or simply Nan, of Patrick County, Virginia. She "had stolen a parcel of clothes" from a local white woman and, when confronted about her crime, lured her into the woods, where she had secreted the filched goods. There, Nan choked her white victim into unconsciousness and stripped her naked. When the white woman revived, she wandered the forest disoriented for a time until gaining her bearings and finding aid. With such compelling evidence against the enslaved female attacker, a Patrick County court of oyer and terminer quickly determined Nan's guilt.[14]

Only one of the violent criminals in Williams' gang had committed a sexual offense. The twenty-year-old John, enslaved in Jefferson County, Virginia, the easternmost county of modern-day West Virginia, sandwiched between northern Virginia and Maryland, was charged in November 1838 "with having ravished, or attempted to commit a rape, upon Elizabeth Bateman a white woman," "against her will." He reportedly ambushed the teen as she was walking to school. He leaped out from behind a tree, caught her by the throat, cast her to the ground, and then "pulled up her clothes, and pulled down his." Bateman screamed and fought off her attacker. John abandoned the assault, apparently unsuccessful in accomplishing his goal. In the Old South, whites outraged by the sexual violation of a white woman did not promptly raise a vigilante mob for the purpose of lynching the accused black offender, as so often happened following similar reports after the Civil War and the end of slavery. In the antebellum decades, cases like John's, though disconcerting to the white community, were usually permitted to course their way through the formal legal system. A Jefferson County court of oyer and terminer found John guilty of the attempted rape upon Elizabeth

Batemen and ordered the sheriff to carry out the sentence of death. In early 1839, Governor David Campbell commuted his sentence to sale and transportation.[15]

The other two-thirds of the Williams' gang slaves had been convicted of property crimes. Half of the twenty-six on board the *Roanoke*, steaming toward New Orleans, had initially been sentenced to death merely for theft. The unlawfully sold Arthur, no longer with the group, had also been convicted of burglary, meaning that a narrow majority of the original twenty-seven reprieved for sale and transportation were guilty of nothing more than robbery. Arthur and fellow bondman John Cooper feloniously broke into a Norfolk Borough store on Christmas night 1838 and pilfered "pistols, one box of dice and several dirk knives of the value of Fifty dollars." Both were convicted in Norfolk Hustings Court, sentenced to hang, and then reprieved to sale and transportation. After Arthur's premature sale while still in the Chesapeake, John Cooper journeyed on alone, absent the small comfort of a familiar face aboard either the *Uncas* or, now, the *Roanoke*, as it churned westward through the coastal waters to Louisiana.[16]

Five members of Williams' gang were well acquainted with one another before they had ever entered the penitentiary in Richmond, for they had all been accomplices to the same crime. On the night of May 15, 1839, Phil Harris, John, and Nelson, all of whom belonged to master Samuel Alsop, William Redd's bondman Harrison, and Henry, the legal property of an infant owner, all broke open a locked "Cellar" that served as the "Warehouse and Store house of George W. Rothrock" along Main Street in Fredericksburg, Virginia. The bondmen purloined a haul of "Sundry goods, wares and Merchandize," mostly fabric, bedding, and clothing valued at more than $130. The combination of physical evidence and verbal testimony arrayed against the accused in the Fredericksburg Hustings Court was overwhelming. The magistrates hearing the case found Phil Harris, John, Nelson, Harrison, and Henry all guilty. Only a gubernatorial commutation of sentence spared them from the gallows. Now, as they steamed toward New Orleans, they could not know their fates, but they at least knew each other.[17]

Two other members of Williams' gang were undoubtedly known to one another prior to their arrests, convictions, incarcerations, and transportations. The bondmen Nelson and James, or Jim, both belonged to Blue Ridge Mountain slaveholder Jacob Judy. They, along with a free black man named Lewis Cromwell, were complicit in a burglary on August 19, 1839. That night around 11 p.m., they broke into and entered "the dwelling house of ... John Buchanan," a white man who lived a quarter mile from the Judy estate, along the same road, and under whom Cromwell was apprenticed. The three thieves entered a cellar window and made off with a small walnut chest containing riches belonging to Buchanan and a boarder in his home, the Reverend Alfred A. Eskridge, both of whom were attending a religious camp meeting at the time. Nelson, James, and their free black accomplice pulled off an epic heist. The chest cradled a mother lode that included "a small white bag containing about thirty dollars" as well as "bonds, accounts, deeds, and other papers and about six hundred and fifteen dollars in bank paper ... and in gold and silver and some jewelry." The haul contained a dizzying array of monies then in circulation – not only paper notes from Virginia banks but also Spanish doubloons and silver dollars, Mexican silver dollars, a French silver crown and other francs, and American half eagles, half dollars, and quarters – indicative of the confused state of American currency after the death of the Second Bank of the United States and its efforts to standardize the monetary system.[18]

John Buchanan suspected Jacob Judy's Nelson and James as well as his own apprentice Lewis Cromwell of committing the crime, but they evaded justice for about half a year, until February 1840. After their apprehension in Botetourt County, the slaves revealed the locations of their secreted loot. Buchanan also overheard them one night while the prisoners were being held in the impromptu jail of Buchanan's kitchen. They recounted how they had plotted to rob some man with a "good 'wad' of money." They would then take their spoils "and go out to some of the new countries," presumably in the West, "and buy land and live like gentlemen, and be free." Such were the dreams of enslaved black men of the Old South. The prisoners had identified Buchanan as a likely target, since he lived only a quarter mile from their master, "had plenty of money," and would be away during the upcoming camp meeting. Supplied such overwhelming evidence against both Nelson and James, a Rockbridge County court of oyer and terminer found both guilty of burglary and directed the sheriff to execute them in May. Governor Thomas Walker Gilmer reprieved them for sale and transportation in April, well in advance of their date with the gallows. Aboard the *Roanoke* and facing uncertain futures, it is impossible to know whether they counted themselves lucky.[19]

Among the fourteen Williams' gang slaves charged with non-violent thefts, four had stolen money exclusively, or nearly so. Unlike Nelson and James, another slave convicted of stealing money and now captive on the *Roanoke* probably acted alone. On the evening of December 9, 1839, the Louisa County, Virginia, bondman Stephen opened a window to the store of Ellisville merchants David M. Hunter and John Ellis, clambered in, and robbed it, carrying off "divers silver & copper coins" totaling $4.42 and "a silver watch" worth $15. Taken up in nearby Orange, only two miles away, on suspicion of the crime, Stephen denied that he had physically entered the store, but some careless replies under interrogation entangled him in his own lies. The five justices hearing Stephen's case in January 1840 found him guilty and ordered the sheriff to hang him in March. But, implicitly acknowledging the severity of the mandatory death sentence for the theft of less than $20, at the same time as it handed down the verdict the court also "unanimously recommend[ed]" Stephen "to the Mercy of the Executive." Concurring with the magistrates, forty-two signers of a petition to Governor David Campbell begged "that the punishment ... be commuted from death to transportation." Campbell obliged.[20]

The same outcome awaited King and Queen County, Virginia, bondman George, who in March 1840 stole "eight silver coin[s]," each worth "half a dollar," a one-dollar note from the Farmers Bank of Virginia, and other goods valued at seven dollars. A court of oyer and terminer expressed "no doubt" that George was guilty of the burglary, but because "the property taken was of inconsiderable values," the justices recommended that the executive commute his sentence to transportation. Magistrates across antebellum Virginia commonly attached such addenda to their decisions. Doing so allotted them a level of flexibility denied them by statute alone and effectively conveyed the court's conviction that the punishment to be meted out did not fit the crime. It seemed unconscionable to execute a valuable bondman over a matter of twelve dollars. Justices' brief comments not only laid the foundation for gubernatorial reprieves through which guilty parties might escape the full brunt of the written law, but also supplied a rationale for the executive should he need to defend the decision to reprieve. Upon consideration of the case, Governor Thomas Walker Gilmer consented to the commutation of sentence, and George, too, ended up, in turn, on the *Uncas* and the *Roanoke*.[21]

George shared one feature in common with three other captives being transported on the *Roanoke*: he stole food, clothing, or a combination thereof. In addition to the money, George also made off with "seven pieces of bacon of the value of seven dollars." A staple meat in the southern diet, bacon was a common target of theft from smokehouses across the region. In June 1840, the bondman Ned, owned by Lancaster County slaveholder Dr. William Jones, broke into "the Meat house" and commandeered "twenty three pieces of bacon," worth twenty dollars, belonging to Jones' farm manager, John E. Watts. Ned then delivered the meat "some five or six miles" distant to a white man, perhaps a witting accomplice accustomed to the clandestine receipt of stolen goods from the slave. Watts followed Ned's tracks, confronted the white man, and pried Ned's name out of him, at which point the slave confessed his crime. On June 16, a Lancaster County court of oyer and terminer judged him guilty of burglary and commanded the sheriff to hang him "by the neck until he be dead." Virginia courts sometimes convicted bondpeople who had stolen food simply because they were hungry, but this case smacked of something more sinister and improper. The sheer quantity of bacon hauled away and its furtive delivery in the dark of night suggested as much. Nonetheless, a quick reprieve from Governor Gilmer, dated July 1, prompted Ned's removal to the Virginia State Penitentiary to await sale and transportation.[22]

Like Ned, Henry Burgess, enslaved in Loudoun County, Virginia, purportedly stole food, albeit in much greater variety. According to the prosecutors of his case, Henry forced his way into John Conner's grocery store in early May 1840 and carried away several comestibles, including "half a pound of tea" and "half a bushel of English walnuts." He may well have had a sweet tooth, taking also "several pounds of Brown Sugar," "half a barrell [*sic*] of Ginger Cakes," and "about Ten pounds" of candy. Perhaps to satisfy another craving, he allegedly filched "three Gallons of whiskey," an item popular among the enslaved but one that masters usually dispensed only as an incentive at harvest or on other exceptional occasions, such as a plantation wedding. As a rule, slave owners prohibited alcohol from the quarters as a source of inebriation and other, related troubles. All of the food and drink Henry was accused of appropriating qualified as special in some way, not part of the standard rations masters allotted their slaves. Such items would, at least momentarily, have eased the burdens of bondage and made life just a little more bearable. For probably the same reason, Henry supposedly also stole clothing and fabrics more comfortable and nicer in appearance than the coarse but durable raiment made of "negro cloth" that masters normally dispensed to their bondpeople. Storekeeper John Conner noted that he was missing "a cloth waistcoat worth $3," 3 yards of linen drilling valued at $1.50, "3 yards of summer cloth worth $1.32 and a stock worth a Dollar." Other stolen merchandise included "half a dozen . . . Pen knives," sixteen Jew's harps, paper, and pens. The utility of the knives was evident enough, and the Jew's harps might be played at slave dances or other get-togethers with or without the master's sanction. If committed by a slave, as Conner assumed, the theft of paper and pens indicated that the thief or someone known to him counted among the 5 or 10 percent of slaves who were literate.[23]

The five justices who comprised the Loudoun County court of oyer and terminer hearing Henry's case ruled Henry guilty of robbery and scheduled him to die by hanging in late June. But they also recommended that "the punishment of death in this case ought to be changed into that of sale and transportation owing to the character of the offence, [and] the youth of the offender." With age working in his favor, Henry earned a gubernatorial reprieve on June 2 and a place among more than a dozen other convicted thieves rebuffed from Mobile and bound for New Orleans.[24]

The last of the burglars on the *Roanoke*, Albert, could not have known precisely what he was stealing when he committed his crime. In April 1838, he carried off "a Hair Trunk" – a chest covered in animal hide, with the fur still attached – belonging to John P. Packer of Campbell County. Packer had loaded the trunk into the "boot" of a Richmond-bound stagecoach at Hugh Raine's tavern in Cumberland County. Upon stopping at Richmond's Union Hotel, he discovered it had been taken before the stage had ever departed the inn. Packer immediately informed the agent representing Messrs. Elam and Fluke, operators of the stage, and supplied descriptions of the trunk as well as its contents. Once back in Cumberland, Packer learned that his trunk and most of the articles inside had been recovered. Still missing were "Two Promissory notes[,] one upwards of One thousand Dollars and the other upwards of five hundred Dollars," plus an array of expensive "mens clothing," including "one broad cloth Coat, one pair of pantaloons, one silk Waistcoat, five linen shirts, five linen collars, six linen bosoms and five pair [of] stockings," valued collectively at fifty dollars. Suspicion fell upon Albert when he was spotted wearing "some very fine clothes" unbefitting a bondman. He admitted to Hugh Raine that he had taken the hair trunk from the Lynchburg and Richmond stage and guided his interrogator to the hiding place of his spoils.[25]

Albert, as it turned out, was a serial offender. The bondman confessed to having taken not one but "three different trunks from the Stage at three different times." On April 5, he swiped "one large leather trunk containing one dress black cloth coat, a pair of dark pantaloons and a waistcoat of the value of fifty dollars," all the property of Isaac H. Oliver. Four days later, he snatched John P. Packer's hair trunk, and the following day "a leather trunk," filled with clothing, from a man named Nichols. Albert had probably assembled the finest wardrobe of any bondperson in Cumberland County. But the theft of whites' attire was always problematic for slaves because any time they wore the pilfered garments, their appearance exposed them as criminals. With a pattern of criminal behavior well established, Albert earned swift conviction for the hijacking of Packer's hair trunk. Only the clemency of Governor David Campbell spared him from death at the end of a noose. On August 20, 1838, Albert entered the Virginia State Penitentiary. He spent more time imprisoned there – longer than two years – than any other bondperson purchased by Rudolph Littlejohn in September 1840 with Thomas N. Davis' and William H. Williams' money.[26]

After swiftly traversing the distance from Mobile in less than a day, the *Roanoke* and its cargo of twenty-six enslaved convicts docked at

Milneburg, a village on the southern shore of Lake Pontchartrain, between 6 and 7 p.m. the evening of Saturday, October 31. Samuel H. Page, the surveyor and inspector of customs at Port Pontchartrain, climbed aboard the vessel and cast his eyes upon the captives. He asked if they had been cleared at the customs house in Mobile. Captain William J. Duval informed him that "the boat had taken the inland passage," through Grants Pass. As Inspector Page understood, instructions recently received from Treasury Secretary Levi Woodbury rendered it "unnecessary" for slaves conveyed to New Orleans via that route "to go through any formalities at the Custom house." Satisfied that he had completed his task with due diligence, Page "made no further enquiries," and "[t]he negroes were kept on board all night under a watch." Thanks to Williams' maneuver in Mobile Bay, transferring the convict slaves to the *Roanoke*, he had avoided – evaded? – the need for a slave manifest that would normally have been Page's responsibility to double-check.[27]

At the same time, it becomes difficult to chalk up Williams' move as a clever machination intended to deceive. His forthright verbal admissions of his human cargo's provenance to those he encountered and his attempts to inform authorities in Louisiana of his and his slaves' presence belie the notion that he intended to sell the convict bondpeople in New Orleans, as Mayor Hooe of Alexandria and Governor Gilmer of Virginia suspected. Soon after landing at Port Pontchartrain on Saturday evening, Williams consulted S. F. Slatter of New Orleans, the same slave trader he had seen in Mobile, to determine the best means of "conveyance of the negroes through the City." Williams next attempted to track down New Orleans mayor William Freret to alert him of his arrival at Port Pontchartrain with his unusual cargo and "to obtain from him permission" to pass through, "similar to that which had been granted by the authorities of Mobile." It was Saturday night, so he assumed the city leader would not be in his office. He instead turned up unannounced at the mayor's home. Unsuccessful in his attempt to see the public official, Williams left a note stating that he sought advice "as to the proper means of conveying banished slaves through the City & ... on to Texas, as he wishes not to violate any law or act imprudently in any way whatsoever." He promised to call again at 8:30 a.m. the following day.[28]

Early on Sunday morning, November 1, before heading to the mayor's house, Williams made the trek to consult New Orleans attorney Wheelock S. Upton, either at his home or at his office along Exchange Place in the French Quarter. A New England Yankee by birth and a Harvard graduate, Upton embarked upon his fledgling legal career in 1830s New Orleans. As an outsider, he never could shake native-born southern whites' suspicions that he was a closet abolitionist, although he had no qualms against taking on slave traders as clients. Williams expressed to Upton his concerns over the "convict negroes, whom he . . . was transporting to Texas." He directed the lawyer's attention specifically "to certain editorial remarks" published in the *New Orleans Commercial Bulletin* and other news outlets alleging that he intended to sell his shipment of convict slaves unlawfully in Louisiana. As Upton later recalled, Williams "was fearful that such remarks would lead to some disturbance in the City & perhaps to popular violence against him." The slave dealer requested that the attorney accompany him on his return visit to Mayor Freret's residence, for "he was anxious to see the Mayor & explain his true purposes." "At half past eight," Williams and Upton together journeyed to the mayor's house. Freret had already stepped out, "but . . . left word that he would see Mr. Williams at half past nine." Williams and Upton left and then returned at the appointed time. Again, however, they missed the mayor. His servants explained that he had come home briefly but once again had gone out. Perhaps Freret did not much wish to conduct official business on Sunday morning; he certainly made little effort to accommodate the pair eagerly waiting to see him. By 10 a.m., the waiting visitors were feeling frustrated. Williams and Upton abandoned their hope of seeing Mayor Freret, who seemed intent on going about his schedule, uninterrupted.[29]

Before the pair departed, Upton penned, at Williams' request, a letter to the mayor briefly recounting the history of Williams' gang and "setting forth the intentions & purposes" of his client. Upton explained that Williams "has called twice at your house, anxious to see you," apprehensive that "the City authorities" might suspect "improper conduct . . . meditated on his part, relative to the negroes in his charge." Upton further noted that Williams was complying with and in the process of fulfilling all the conditions of the bond he gave to the commonwealth of

Virginia but that he needed to "pass *through*" Louisiana en route to his final destination in Texas. Williams' intent, Upton continued, was to reach the Republic of Texas "via New Orleans and Red River." He had already met with "no interruption" in Mobile, his counsel exaggerated, and "hoped that none will be [met with] here." With the mayor's permission, Upton concluded, the convict slaves will "be immediately taken from the Steamboat at the Lake end of the Pontchartrain Rail Road," whisked through the city to the Mississippi River, "and put on board a Steamboat" – the *Vicksburg* – "which leaves this morning for Red River." For the last leg of his journey, Williams would transport the slaves over-land to Texas.[30]

Williams returned to the *Roanoke* at Port Pontchartrain. Presuming that his attorney's letter to Mayor Freret would prove sufficient to enable safe passage through New Orleans, he resolved to continue the journey without further delay. Williams explained to agent Samuel H. Page that the slaves "were under his charge & that he was taking them to Texas." The convicts disembarked, doubtless chained, probably toward 11 a.m. Almost immediately, a prospective buyer expressed interest in Williams' cargo. Christian Meyers inquired "if the slaves which he had with him . . . were for sale" because he "wished to purchase a negro girl." Williams politely declined, saying no, "[t]hey were not for sale"; he was carrying them to Texas. A nearby bystander who overheard this conversation confirmed that Williams refused the transaction because he was taking them to the neighboring republic in the West. Williams' story had never once wavered since speaking with authorities in Mobile.[31]

Williams loaded his twenty-six captives from the *Roanoke* on to a train. The lakeside village of Milneburg served as the northern terminus of the Pontchartrain Railroad, New Orleans' first rail line, opened in 1831. The Pontchartrain Railroad used mostly steam and some horse-drawn loco-motives to transfer waterborne cargoes some five or six miles southward from the lake to the Mississippi riverfront, where they could be loaded aboard steamboats heading upriver. Countless merchants and traders used this route routinely, and Williams planned to use it for his cargo of enslaved convicts as well. Williams and his gang reached New Orleans "by the Pontchartrain Railroad cars" on Sunday afternoon, November 1.[32] (See Figure 9.)

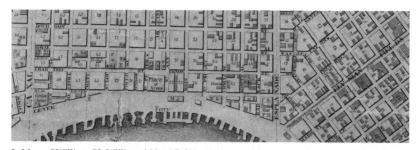

9 Map of William H. Williams' New Orleans.
Source: S. Pinistri, *New Orleans General Guide and Land Intelligence* (1841), map 0072, The Historic New Orleans Collection, Williams Research Center.

If Williams had an active Saturday and Sunday, so too did William Freret, mayor of the Louisiana state capital of New Orleans. On Saturday, October 31, the same day as the *Roanoke* steamed into Port Pontchartrain, commission merchant Andrew L. Addison sought him out to alert him of a letter received at the firm of A. L. Addison & Co. four days earlier, on October 27, "in the ordinary course of mail." It was the missive that William H. Richardson, secretary for the commonwealth of Virginia, had written to give advanced warning of Williams' possible arrival in New Orleans. Even though Richardson had mailed his letter to a personal friend outside of government, Freret considered it "official information" about "the contemplated violation of the laws" of Louisiana. The delay in receiving the message gave him precious little time to act.[33]

Alarmed, the mayor knew he needed to consult Louisiana's state attorney general, Etienne (Stephen) Mazureau. Freret personally made haste, either to Mazureau's office at Exchange Place or to the attorney general's home at 6 Royal Street, to share his intelligence. Mazureau was already aware of William H. Williams and the approaching convict slaves because William H. Richardson had also dispatched a missive identical to the one he sent Addison to Louisiana governor André B. Roman. Roman, in turn, forwarded that letter, which only had to travel within the city, to Mazureau on October 30. The governor gave his attorney general explicit instruction "to take such measures as are warranted by law to prevent these convicts from being admitted in the State & mixed with our slave populations." Mazureau welcomed Freret's arrival. The New Orleans mayor, insisting that he was "credibly informed," recounted for the attorney general how the convict bondpeople had set sail from Alexandria aboard the *Uncas*. For his part, Freret was absolutely convinced that the enslaved convicts were indeed "about to be imported into the State of Louisiana." Listening intently, Mazureau heard confirmation of the same news he had received separately.[34]

Operating under the mistaken assumption that the captives were still being transported on the *Uncas*, the attorney general advised the mayor to keep a lookout for the brig's first "appearance in the Mississippi," probably meaning at the Balize. The island at the river's mouth, notorious for both smuggling and hurricane strikes, boasted a lighthouse and functioned as a port where vessels often landed temporarily to have their paperwork inspected, prior to proceeding on to New Orleans. From Balize, expert local pilots sometimes helped seafaring captains navigate the constantly shifting sands and silt of the Mississippi upriver to the Crescent City. Possibly the *Uncas* would stop there as well, Mazureau speculated. He further directed Mayor Freret to "issue proper warrants," which he did, so that the brig could be searched for the convict slaves and, if found to have them on board, seized for escort into port at New Orleans. Once located, Captain Nathaniel Boush and the enslaved transports would be secured under guard, and Attorney General Mazureau would launch the state's prosecution of William H. Williams for his crime.[35]

With a strategy in place, Freret took his leave. Late that Saturday night, he presumably received Williams' message from earlier in the evening informing him of Williams' intent to visit the mayor the next morning at 8:30. *So the reports were true!*, Freret must have thought. *The slave criminals are already in my city!* Nevertheless, on Sunday, Freret did not take special pains to keep the appointment with Williams. Perhaps the mayor was attending church, or perhaps he was gathering local officials, organizing them, and plotting the defense of New Orleans from the menace that threatened it. Attorney Wheelock Upton's letter deposited at the mayor's house at 10 a.m. surely simplified this task, for in it Upton telegraphed Williams' future movements. The enslaved criminals will "be immediately taken from the Steamboat at the Lake end of the Pontchartrain Rail Road," straight to another steamboat on the Mississippi River. Like a general deploying the troops, Freret stationed city authorities so that they could likely intercept Williams and his parcel of enslaved criminals.

Although sources do not indicate the precise time, one newspaper credited Luc H. Seré, the secretary in the recorder's office of New Orleans' Second Municipality, as the first public official in Louisiana to recognize that Williams and the twenty-six convicts had reached Milneburg. Seré tracked down Third Municipality Recorder George Y. Bright, perhaps at the latter's office at 45 St. Louis Street, to file an affidavit stating that Williams had brought enslaved convicts into the state. Upon receiving this information, Bright surely would have contacted Mayor Freret, if Freret had not already alerted him.[36]

Attuned to the unfolding drama and under orders from the mayor, Bright positioned himself near the depot at the New Orleans end of the Pontchartrain Railroad, joined by slave dealer S. F. Slatter. Bright was unfamiliar with Williams' appearance, but Slatter, having encountered Williams in Mobile only a day or two before, knew the slave trader by sight and could help pick him out from a crowd. Slatter and Bright were engaged in conversation about Williams' convict slaves when the rail cars from the lake arrived at about 11 a.m. Either Slatter saw Williams first and pointed him out to Bright ("there is the negroes & yonder is Mr. Williams too"), or Bright spotted someone he presumed was Williams and then asked Slatter to confirm his identity. The two men began walking toward the train. As they did, "Williams got out of the cars." Slatter introduced Williams and the recorder of the Third Municipality. Bright assumed that the bondpeople the trader had in tow were the exact ones who had inspired such vigilance among officials and the general public in the major ports of the Gulf Coast for the past several days. But he needed verification. "[W]hat slaves are them[?]," Bright inquired, eager to see "if his conjectures were right." Williams observed matter-of-factly that the bondpeople with him were convict slaves from Virginia. Conducting a quick headcount, Bright noticed that one of the reported twenty-seven transports – the illegally sold Arthur – was missing. Responding to Bright's inquiry about the absent bondperson's whereabouts, Williams lied, replying "either that he was sent overland to Texas or that he was dead." Williams then shared the explanation he recited in Mobile, that he was en route to Texas to dispose of the enslaved convicts and "had no design or intent to violate any law." Bright's suspicions confirmed, the recorder informed Williams, "it [is] my duty to arrest them slaves." The trader "made no objection" as Bright ordered Lieutenant Mazerat of the New Orleans Day Police to take custody of Williams' gang. Mazerat conveyed the enslaved convicts to the constable's office at 1 p.m. and then on to confinement in the Watch House.[37]

CHAPTER 5

Legal Troubles

I N THE SUMMER OF 1816, A SLAVEHOLDER FROM NEW YORK resettling in Mississippi stopped at the river town of Donaldsonville, Louisiana, in Ascension Parish, en route to his new plantation home. Among the slaves relocating with him were some convicted felons whom he had purchased out of a New York prison. Word of the enslaved convicts' presence somehow leaked out and generated an uproar among local whites in the Donaldsonville community. The public, it was rumored, would have lynched the Yankee traveler "had he not clandestinely escaped with the slaves in a steamboat" to resume his journey upriver. When the Louisiana state legislature next reconvened, in January 1817, lawmakers promptly passed a statute intended to keep enslaved criminals from abroad from "contaminating our soil or … atmosphere at all." They crafted the law to preclude the possibility of convict bondpeople from outside the state "poisoning the mind[s] or perverting the morals" of Louisiana's "servile population." Several other slaveholding states would eventually follow suit and pass similar legislation.[1]

The rising tide of new settlers to the Old Southwest and the acceleration of the domestic slave trade in the later 1820s and 1830s generated social tension and fears among Louisiana whites for their own safety. The legislature remained sufficiently anxious about troublesome, vicious, or rebellious slaves entering the state that, for two years from 1829 to March 1831, it mandated that traders file a certificate of "good moral character" on behalf of each bondperson over the age of twelve brought into Louisiana. The law obligated two or more freeholders from the same county as the enslaved import and acquainted with him or her "for several years" to declare on oath that the slave carried into the state had neither been convicted of a crime nor demonstrated a propensity to run away from the master. A different section of the same statute forbade the introduction of any bondperson "accused of any conspiracy or insurrection" or who merely resided in the same county where one had occurred. After two years elapsed, slaves who lived in the same county in which a conspiracy or insurrection had been detected but who were neither implicated nor accused of participation in it were again eligible for removal to Louisiana.[2]

In the wake of the Nat Turner revolt of 1831, lawmakers in Louisiana and other states took the extraordinary step of suspending the domestic slave trade altogether, at least temporarily. The ban in Louisiana lasted until 1834. Impediments to and prohibitions of the traffic in black bodies could never have achieved permanence, however, for they would have had to have triumphed over the frenzy of speculation in western land and slaves that reaped ambitious entrepreneurs astounding profits during the flush times of the 1830s. The enormous rewards of slavery's expansion for a select few entailed certain risks for the safety and well-being of all, but that was the necessary price to pay for the prospective economic windfall. To the consternation of those who still felt besieged by unruly bondpeople from distant lands, the law mandating testimonials of slaves' good character ended almost a decade prior to William H. Williams' arrival at New Orleans in 1840. The slave pens of the Chesapeake, many Louisianans fretted, "are filled principally by the vicious, who are sold by their masters on account of bad temper or vices." Williams' shipment of slaves aboard the *Roanoke* in November 1840 only reinforced lingering suspicions that Louisiana had become the dumping ground for undesirable chattel from across the South. Nervous residents could at least take solace in the fact that the act of January 1817, prohibiting the mere introduction of enslaved felons into the state, remained on the books, and authorities resolved to prosecute Williams for violating it, a misdemeanor offense.[3]

That same statute authorized the punishment of the *Roanoke*'s pilot, William J. Duval, for his role in the developing story. Section 4 maintained that "any captain or master" who knowingly "receive[d] on board his ... vessel, boat, flatboat, or pirogue, raft, or other water craft" enslaved convicts for transport into Louisiana was subject to a $500 fine and the forfeiture of "the tackle, apparel and furniture" from his vessel. That the state never prosecuted Duval suggests that authorities understood he was William H. Williams' unwitting accomplice, unaware of the histories of the slaves he conveyed to Port Pontchartrain. Williams may well have withheld that information from him. Maybe he had conscientiously transferred the enslaved convicts on to Duval's steamboat precisely so that its captain could truthfully claim ignorance in a way that Nathaniel Boush of the *Uncas* could not. Freed of any criminal liability, Captain Duval by July 1841 had drawn upon his navigational expertise to take a position with the United States government, plying the Gulf coastal waters in the "fast running US Mail steamboat ANNA CALHOUN." Leaving behind the *Roanoke*, Duval shuttled packages and correspondence back and forth between New Orleans and Mobile, with stops at Pascagoula, Bay St. Louis, Pass Christian, Biloxi, and Mississippi City. If the state of Louisiana resolved to pursue the case surrounding the twenty-six criminal transports from Virginia, the possible punishment would devolve upon William H. Williams alone.[4]

After the arrest, confiscation, and incarceration of Williams' gang on November 1, 1840, the sequence of events that Sunday afternoon becomes muddled. The likeliest possible reconstruction suggests that Recorder George Y. Bright looked around the railroad depot and saw Mayor William Freret at the scene. It is not clear whether they merely acknowledged each other with a nod for a job well done in intercepting and seizing the parcel of enslaved convicts or if they communicated verbally. If the latter, they probably discussed the propriety of Williams' arrest. Bright also spied Joshua Baldwin, Recorder of the Second Municipality, and invited him "to stop up" at his office, as "I thought I might profit by his superior experience." City leaders resolved to prosecute the case against Williams for violating the act of 1817. Probably after consulting with Baldwin, Bright "thought it best to hold Mr. Williams to bail," rather than to incarcerate him while awaiting trial. Mayor Freret recommended the amount: the hefty sum of $30,000. Bright then met with the slave trader and asked him "if he would sign a Statement" acknowledging "that the slaves he had were convict slaves." Williams verbally assented "[w]ithout any hesitation."

Bright quickly drafted the document, but just as Williams placed pen to paper, the recorder dutifully reminded him "that he was not obliged to sign it." Williams had previously "appeared apprehensive of a popular tumult" fomented by residents of New Orleans angered by his importing convict slaves, but Bright's remark seemed to bring home to Williams the reality that the state was going to put him on trial for it.[5]

Any shrewd, responsible slave trader would have had to have been aware of the laws regulating the domestic traffic in bondpeople in all the states where he did business. For elaborate, far-flung enterprises such as Williams', this would have proved no simple matter. The federal government did not regulate many aspects of the internal slave trade; that was mostly a state and municipal prerogative. Presumably, then, Williams was not ignorant of the Louisiana law of 1817 that forbade the introduction of enslaved convicts into the state. If he was, he was woefully negligent in carrying them to New Orleans. But his open and prompt observation at the railroad depot that he was en route to Texas, in 1840 a foreign country open to the receipt of convicted slave felons, suggests he knew the law. He also surely understood that, by 1840, the independent slaveholding republic of Texas was the playground for a slew of unsavory characters, distressed debtors, and other fugitives from the law who, appreciating the Lone Star Republic's lack of an extradition arrangement with the United States, had "G.T.T." (the shorthand abbreviation for "gone to Texas"). There, many migratory masters whose economic aspirations had been dashed at points farther east during the Panic of 1837 or the double-dip depression of 1839 sought a fresh start. The infant government of the independent Texas had condemned the international slave trade, but its weakness and fiscal misery prevented it from quelling the rampant smuggling of slaves into the republic. Moreover, its developing monocrop cotton economy demanded laborers, so slaveholding immigrants from the southern states poured across the US border with their bondpeople in tow before those slaves might be seized to cover their debts back home. From 1837 to 1842 alone, the enslaved population of Texas increased fourfold, to almost 20,000 bondmen, -women, and children. Williams planned for his convicts to contribute to the developing migratory pattern. The trader observed that the route up the Mississippi and Red rivers to Texas was more direct than taking the

Sabine River, then an international boundary, into the interior of East Texas. Were Williams indeed heading to Texas as he claimed, he likely would have found buyers there completely ignorant of the tainted provenance of the slaves he had for sale, and he almost certainly would not have volunteered information about the transports' criminal pasts. Even if Williams proved more forthcoming than most traders in divulging his slaves' histories, buyers in Texas, often desperate to reinvent themselves and to revive shattered economic dreams, may have been relatively less concerned about the slaves' pasts than purchasers elsewhere. Assuming Williams was telling the truth – that he was merely passing through Louisiana, with no intention of disposing of his cargo within the state – he thought himself innocent of any legal infraction.[6]

Still, as the gravity of the situation dawned on him, Williams realized the wisdom of acquiring legal counsel. Stopping short of affixing his signature to Bright's document, Williams requested that he "send for a lawyer." The recorder consented. Attorney John Randolph Grymes arrived to assist his new slave-trading client. A preeminent member of the New Orleans bar, Grymes wielded considerably more clout in the courtroom than did Wheelock Upton, whom Williams had initially consulted upon reaching New Orleans. Grymes' height, elegance, disarming smile, penetrating eyes, and lilting voice carried from his native Virginia all worked to his advantage before judges and juries in New Orleans. The graying hair he sported at age fifty-three suggested that he possessed greater intelligence than his education had actually imparted, but he compensated for that with wit, charm, eloquence, and his naturally sharp mind. Grymes cultivated an image in which he swept into court seemingly unprepared but instinctively grasped how to craft arguments and win cases. As a result, he attracted the wealthiest clients, from whom he commanded exorbitant fees. The charges for his legal services allowed him to live large. Grymes ate the best foods, drank the finest wines, and kept company with the ladies of his choosing. He dueled more than once. His gambling usually took other forms, as he attended cockfights, bet on the horses, played cards at the St. Charles Hotel, and once partied with the Lafitte family of smugglers and pirates he had defended in court. Grymes also shared in the prevailing racism of his times. He was perfectly suited to offer counsel to slave trader William H. Williams.[7]

Grymes immediately made his presence felt, helping get Williams' bail reduced from $30,000 to $13,000, or $500 per enslaved felon. Coming up with the money presented no obstacle. James W. Zacharie, the New Orleans merchant to whom Williams had consigned the shipment of slaves from the *Uncas,* had "long known" the trader and had served "[f]or many years" as "his business Correspondent." Hearing of the proceedings launched against Williams but "unable himself to go to the recorder's Office," Zacharie sent his brother in his stead, with instructions "to sign his name as bail for Mr. Williams *to any amount.*" The $13,000 Zacharie pledged kept Williams out of jail while it served as security that the trader would appear before the Criminal Court of New Orleans' First District in January 1841 for violating the 1817 statute against importing convict slaves.[8]

Williams' slave-trading activities made him no stranger to antebellum southern courtrooms. Across the Old South, slave dealers most commonly ended up in court as defendants in breach of warranty suits. Those in the business of trafficking in black bodies often warranted slaves' mental and physical soundness in the bills of sale that accompanied the transactions, but buyers of slaves knew that some unscrupulous dealers prowling the slave markets of the Old South peddled bondpeople with known illnesses or diseases. They therefore took all the precautions they could to defend their interests and their pocketbooks from such rascals. They inspected potential purchases closely to detect any telltale signs of injury, sickness, disability, or other malady that might hamper productivity or prematurely shorten the slave's useful working life. They stripped bondpeople to scrutinize their bodies minutely and immodestly, poking them, prodding them, and peering into their mouths to divine their states of health from their teeth, just as one might do when purchasing a horse. Buyers asked questions of slaves' skills, talents, aptitudes, abilities, work experience, and histories, a process that also permitted them to discern something of a bondperson's character, attitude, and tractability. Slaves did not always give frank and honest replies, as they, too, visually read the party interested in purchasing them and proffered information that they intended either to encourage or discourage the sale, depending upon their own prognostications for the future under the particular prospective master quizzing them. The cultural dance between slave and potential buyer thus worked in both directions. In spite of it all, sellers and buyers reached mutually agreeable terms and finalized their sales.[9]

Buyers hoped for the best when acquiring new bondpeople, but they did enjoy access to legal recourse after the sale. If bondmen or -women developed fits, a cough, "nigger fever" or "nigger consumption" (neither of which differed remotely in its symptoms compared with the same affliction in whites), or any of a number of other conditions, litigation might ensue. Those purchasers who believed themselves grievously conned could file breach of warranty suits in southern courts of law. This was not an ideal or even preferable solution. Court actions took time and money and came with no guarantees. But for purchasers who felt swindled by the misrepresentations of a professional slave trader or other seller and could not make the sale good through informal channels, the courtroom remained an available option. Southern courts generally adhered to the doctrine of *caveat emptor* (let the buyer beware) for the sales of any commodity *except* slaves. Bondpeople were a unique form of property, in that sellers maintained a distinct advantage in knowledge and information over potential buyers. Therefore, to encourage sales, sellers often gave warranties to reassure buyers. In such cases, vendors of slaves were held financially responsible for the bondpeople post-sale, even for conditions of which the sellers were genuinely ignorant during their period of ownership. In these transactions, the legal burden of making the sale right consistently fell to the seller.[10]

Although the law across the South generally favored slave buyers in cases of contested sales, nowhere was this more true than in Louisiana. Unique among the slaveholding states, Louisiana borrowed wholesale from ancient Roman law the notion of an implied warranty that applied to slave sales, even when buyer and seller made no such explicit agreement. Thus, Louisiana permitted civil suits against vendors of flawed or defective slaves under terms more favorable to deceived or disgruntled buyers than could be found in any other slaveholding state. Louisiana's redhibition law (based on the Roman concept of *redhibitia,* or the annulment of a slave sale), approved by Governor André B. Roman in 1834, made clear the state's "legal presumption in favor of the buyer," whether the exhibited vices related to a slave's body or character. The statute maintained that any "bodily or mental maladies discover[ed]" among Louisiana slaves within three days of sale, or "within fifteen days after the sale" of slaves living in the state for less than eight months, "shall be presumed to have existed" at the time of sale. Compared with consumers of native-born or longer-term resident Louisiana bondpeople, buyers who purchased slaves imported into the state by traders such as William H. Williams therefore gained a temporal window five times longer in which to assess the quality of their human purchases and to detect any hidden defects among them. Buyers were also at liberty to launch "a redhibitory action" against a slave seller based on the bondperson's character flaws. The redhibition law of 1834 declared a slave "a runaway or thief" if the bondperson absconded or stole from the new master "within two months after the sale." In bringing a legal challenge on the basis of a bondperson's alleged propensity to flee or steal, Louisiana buyers were not obligated to establish a longstanding pattern of such misconduct prior to sale. The only restriction imposed upon them was that they could not have compelled the offending bondperson to misbehave. Buyers' negligence, such as the failure to provide reasonable medical care, or abuse, such as through the infliction of "unusual punishments," invalidated the law's protective provision. With that exception, the burden of Louisiana law weighed far more heavily upon sellers. If found guilty of duping buyers, either knowingly or unwittingly, slave traders were ordered to rescind and void the sale, take back the unsound bondperson, and provide a full refund or, alternatively, return a portion of the purchase price.[11]

Louisiana courtrooms played host to frequent redhibition suits in the antebellum decades. Of 1,200 slavery cases argued before the Louisiana Supreme Court, about one-sixth concerned contested slave sales alone. This figure dwarfed the smattering of cases after 1808 concerning the illegal importation of slaves from outside the United States into Louisiana. The legal domestic slave trade kept the state's courts far busier. A majority of all slaves conveyed domestically to Louisiana for sale originated, like Williams' gang, in Virginia. Inevitably purchasers sometimes thought themselves fleeced during these transactions, as hidden or latent physical and mental defects manifested after sale. The legal principle of *caveat venditor* – let the seller beware – woven into the structure of Louisiana slave law made guilty verdicts against traders routine in the state's courts.[12]

The unusually generous legal terms extended to purchasers of enslaved men and women in Louisiana effectively encouraged the thriving trade in the New Orleans slave market. But the law did not ensnare William H. Williams in redhibitionary hassles. He avoided redhibition suits by taking enormous pains to keep his customers reassured and satisfied. Several deals from the mid-1840s illustrate the point. When Williams sold the imported bondman Frank, a thirty-two-year-old blacksmith, to George Otis Hall of A. Ledoux & Co., the parties mutually agreed that, if Frank proved unsatisfactory at his profession during a three-week trial period, Otis "shall have the privilege … to return him" to Williams for a full refund "without any delay or difficulty." The trader regularly backed up his promises, readily negating completed sales for dissatisfied customers. He promised the New Orleans Gas Light and Banking Company in June 1843 that the bondman Robert was "fully guaranteed against the redhibitory vices, maladies and defects prescribed by law." Nine days later, the business must have complained to Williams, for he "[c]ancelled and annulled" the transaction. He also abrogated the sale of the twenty-five-year-old enslaved mother Betsy Ann Dyer and her four children, who ranged in age from infancy to seven. Dr. Samuel White Logan of St. Charles Parish had purchased them on March 16, 1847, paying $1,000 in "ready money" and a promissory note for $250 payable in twelve months. Almost two months later, when Logan returned the five bondpeople, Williams refunded the $1,000 and the note. More than five months after the June 23, 1843, sale of a $550 bondman named Cyrus to West Baton Rouge slaveholder Treville Babin, Williams probably thought the transfer of ownership complete. But on November 30, Babin returned Cyrus for a full refund "as if the [sale] had never been executed." No doubt Williams' accommodating abrogations of sale exposed the trader to the potential for abuse by unscrupulous masters who might effectively gain months and months of enslaved labor for free, but the practice also cultivated a reputation that earned him new customers and brought old ones back.[13]

As an alternative to refunding the purchase price, Williams explicitly welcomed some buyers, if unsatisfied with their purchases, to exchange them for different bondpeople. "This sale," he assured the Jefferson Parish buyer of three $700 bondmen in 1846, "is made under the express condition" that the new owner had "sixty days" in which "to return all or any of the slaves . . . and to take in lieu thereof other slaves at his choice from the stock" then on hand. On December 12, 1843, Williams sold Jacques Chalaron of New Orleans the fourteen-year-old enslaved girl Sarah. Exactly one month later, he agreed to "rescind, abrogate and make null and void" that sale. The same day, Chalaron purchased the nineteen-year-old bondwoman Ann as a replacement for Sarah in a swap that produced no legal drama whatsoever.[14]

Williams also offered protections against certain specified conditions or diseases as a means of alleviating buyers' peculiar concerns and eliminating any reservations or fears that could stymie sales. In 1845, he sold Theodore Soniat Dufossat of Jefferson Parish an enslaved black-smith named Henry, whom he warranted against developing a hernia for one year. The Soniat Dufossat family ranked among the old French aristocracy. If anyone could cope financially with the loss of a slave's labor as a result of illness or injury, it was a Soniat Dufossat. Still, as a savvy consumer, Theodore demanded protections, and even if Henry showed no evidence of a hernia until 364 days after the sale, Williams pledged to take him back, increasing Dufossat's confidence in the transaction. Similarly, when Williams did business with Sosthene Roman of St. James Parish, the trader "particularly guaranteed" the mulatto bond-man whom Roman purchased "against the consumption," the nine-teenth-century term for tuberculosis. Williams thus absorbed the fiscal risk from ailments over which, in reality, he exercised no control. It was just good business.[15]

William H. Williams got dragged into one court action akin to a breach of warranty suit, but it was the seller rather than the buyer who was disappointed with the sale. The case was neither heard in the courts of Louisiana nor fully of Williams' own making. Williams' much younger brother Thomas started working regularly with his slave-trading sibling about 1839, as the junior Williams reached maturity and departed his guardians in Alabama. Even before that, however, in 1836 or 1837, when Thomas was still in his teenage years, William H. Williams called upon his brother sporadically to undertake tasks as an apprentice in the business of slaving. Such reliance on immediate family or other kin was not unusual among successful domestic slave traders of the Old South. The largest slave-trading enterprise of the 1820s, operated by the Woolfolk clan out of Baltimore, included brothers Austin, Samuel Martin, and Joseph Biggers Woolfolk, as well as an uncle named John. Isaac Franklin of Franklin & Armfield employed his nephews James Franklin and James Purvis. Slave-trading partnerships or other business arrangements based on familial relationships and kinship networks engendered greater trust than those forged between mere acquaintances or erstwhile strangers. Slave traders sometimes learned the hard way how easily they could be cheated by a partner in a business they did not yet know well. Family, or at least very close friends, were the most trustworthy associates in a profession rife with deception. Domestic slave traders typically paired up: one kinsman in the Chesapeake bought surplus slaves for shipment to Louisiana, where another family member sold them to a buyer willing to pay the right price. William H. Williams hammered out just such an agreement that made his brother Thomas his agent and representative. William sent enslaved captives aboard vessels such as the *Uncas* to Thomas, who then disposed of them in the New Orleans slave market.[16]

Almost always, the Williams brothers' bookending of the coastwise domestic slave trade between the Chesapeake and New Orleans func-tioned smoothly and successfully for them. One sale gone awry in 1838 marked an exception. In 1837, for reasons known only to him, master William Gray of Norfolk, Virginia, looked to unload his forty-year-old house servant Oliver for maximum profit in the southwestern market. He paid John G. Breshwood, at that time the captain of William H. Williams' slaver *Tribune*, twenty dollars to ship the bondman to New Orleans and to dispose of him once there. Unable to find a buyer, Breshwood trans-ferred Oliver to the Williams siblings to sell.[17]

William H. Williams delivered Oliver to his brother Thomas, an underage "minor" who, at about eighteen years of age, was making some of his first forays into the world of slave trading, and instructed him to convey Gray's house servant and a parcel of other bondpeople to the slave market in Natchez, Mississippi. There, Thomas sold Oliver for $250, substantially below the estimated $600 that William Gray was expecting. The problem was that Oliver had developed dysentery while en route to New Orleans. He had become almost "impossible to sell . . . owing to his being sick and diseased and laboring under an attack of the bowels and other diseases which rendered him at the time worth but little, if any sum whatsoever." A disappointed and frustrated William Gray refused to absorb such a monetary loss and rejected the $250 generated by the sale. After failing to elicit further funds from the slave-trading brothers, he finally instituted a suit against William H. Williams on January 24, 1839, in the amount of the $600 "which ought to have been obtained" from Oliver's sale. The Circuit Superior Court of Law and Chancery for Norfolk County found in favor of the plaintiff, but Gray earned only a pyrrhic victory, awarded merely Oliver's actual sale price of $250, plus 6 percent interest from the date of sale.[18]

Another charge that dogged some slave traders was that of slave stealing. From the 1830s to the Civil War, southern newspapers normally attributed the thefts of bondpeople to subversive Yankee abolitionists lurking in their midst, but sometimes native-born Southerners, especially poor whites, kidnapped slaves to appropriate their labor for their own use, to collect the reward money offered by the bondperson's owner, to profit by reselling the enslaved abductee, or to spite a despised local slaveholder. The Old South's human traffickers also faced occasional charges of stealing slaves when they attempted to sell bondpeople for whom they did not hold proper title. New Orleans slave traders Bernard Kendig and Theophilus Freeman, for example, were both accused of slave stealing during their careers. It was a serious charge. As the most egregious violation of property rights in the slave South, a conviction for slave stealing carried among the harshest possible penalties of any crime. The North and South Carolina legislatures had made it a capital offense, punishable by death, in the colonial era. Other states, including Virginia, Louisiana, and Mississippi, imposed multi-year prison sentences as punishment. Just as William H. Williams seems to have successfully avoided redhibition suits filed by dissatisfied customers in Louisiana, no known evidence survives to suggest he ever stood accused of abducting slaves, either.[19]

Nor was Williams ever directly accused, like others in his line of work, of kidnapping free blacks to carry away for sale in the Deep South. Starting in 1831, Congress raised the punishment for a conviction of kidnapping and selling free black persons out of Washington, D.C., from $800 and five years' incarceration to a much stiffer $5,000 fine and imprisonment for twelve years. These penalties may have been stringent enough to deter a portion of prospective kidnappers, but not all. By the nature of the offense, historians are unable to quantify precisely how prevalent the abduction of free persons of color for sale into slavery was. Certainly the free status of people with dark skin was ever fragile and tenuous, the threat of kidnapping quite real, and stories of illicit sale far from isolated. Rightfully fearful of the possibility of kidnapping, free black people were wise to carry their free papers with them when they traveled in the slave states. This precaution applied equally to northern free blacks venturing south and to southern free blacks traveling outside their home communities where their free status was publicly known. Washington, D.C. law, in fact, required free people of color to carry with them their certificate of freedom, signed by three white people whose signatures attested to their "good" and "sober" character. Any white person walking the roads anywhere in the Old South could accost any black person and demand to see documentation, either a pass from the master that permitted a slave to journey off the plantation or a free black's certificate of freedom.[20]

Yet even when free people of color had their papers in order and in their possession, their status was in constant peril. Unscrupulous slave traders commonly victimized free black people in Baltimore, the District of Columbia, and throughout the Chesapeake, by seizing them, destroying any certificates of freedom on their person, briefly placing them in a slave pen such as the Yellow House, and whisking them away to bondage, either chained as part of a coffle or on board a departing slave ship plying domestic waters to the Deep South. Slave dealers could accomplish this entire process before the victims' families ever realized they had gone missing. Many of those so abducted were free black children, who would not have had any papers on them or even fully understood what was happening.[21]

Slave traders indeed faced accusations of kidnapping perpetually vulnerable free black people. In 1847, Thomas N. Davis, William H. Williams' partner in the purchase of the twenty-seven enslaved convicts out of the Virginia State Penitentiary, reportedly carried off a pair of "free negro boys" with the surname Bristow from Washington, D.C., and offered them "for sale as slaves for life." Authorities in Memphis, Tennessee, intercepted Davis with the "two colored boys in his possession," detained him, and alerted Washington's mayor of the suspected kidnapping. Two justices in the nation's capital gathered testimony that revealed the Bristows had been emancipated "by the will of their former owner" in Alexandria, Virginia, and subsequently bound out to Matthew Thomas, a plasterer in Washington. According to one newspaper report, "Measures were also taken to secure the arrest in Memphis of Thomas Davis." The "negro buyer" and his captives returned to Washington, where the trader was taken up and interrogated about the charge against him. Davis spent one night in jail before posting the bail required for his release. His case was scheduled to go before the upcoming session of the Criminal Court, but trial papers do not survive.[22]

William H. Williams narrowly avoided a lawsuit brought by Solomon Northup, the most famous kidnapped free black man to suffer confinement in the Yellow House. As part of their charade as kind and considerate gentlemen, Northup's abductors in 1841 encouraged him to procure free papers prior to traveling with them into the South. At the time, Northup appreciated their seeming foresight. As a free man living in New York, he would not have thought to do so otherwise. Northup paid the requisite fees for the official documents, tucked them into his pocket, and commenced the journey to Washington. After his duplicitous companions drugged him into unconsciousness and Northup awoke in Williams' private jail, he immediately placed his hand to his pocket, only to discover that his "free papers were ... gone!" Northup's kidnappers had stolen or destroyed the legal proof of his freedom.[23]

After twelve years of bondage in Louisiana, a redeemed Northup arrived in Washington, D.C., on January 17, 1853, on a quest for righteousness. His attempt to pursue legal action against William H. Williams went nowhere, however, for the slave trader "denied having bought or owned the man," admitting only to having kept him in his pen overnight.

Northup's more robust complaint was filed against James H. Birch for having kidnapped him and sold him into slavery. "I took pains to seek him out, to confront him in a court of law," Northup explained, to convey the "burning sense of the wrong he had inflicted upon me, and a desire to bring him to justice." When authorities arrested Birch for kidnapping, the slave trader was, according to Northup's recollections, "much excited, exhibiting the utmost fear and alarm."[24]

Among the witnesses at Birch's trial was Ebenezer Rodbird, an acquaintance of the slave trader's for the past fourteen years and, more importantly, jailer at the Yellow House during Northup's confinement in 1841. Rodbird definitively remembered the free black plaintiff present in the courtroom. Nevertheless, the all-white jury, convinced that Birch genuinely believed he was purchasing a slave rather than a free black man, acquitted the trader of the kidnapping charge. Throughout the proceedings, Solomon Northup uttered not a single word that might have helped secure Birch's conviction. Under Washington, D.C. law, as throughout the South, blacks were prevented from testifying against white defendants.[25]

William H. Williams escaped any formal charges of kidnapping, and the documentary record provides no direct evidence of his intentionally doing so, although through his imprisonment of free blacks in the Yellow House – Solomon Northup most famously – he undeniably benefited indirectly from the practice. As the owner/operator of Washington's most notorious slave jail, Williams faced numerous court challenges brought by black captives at his jail who claimed they were free persons. In February 1848, for example, the free black William Scott filed a petition for his freedom against Williams in the District of Columbia Circuit Court. The court ordered the slave trader to appear the following month to answer the memorial. A decade earlier, in March 1838, a bondman named William Kennedy, known by the alias Candy, also petitioned for his liberty. Kennedy's master, J. Purnell Pendleton of Winchester, Virginia, had allowed the bondman to hire himself out by the month in northern Virginia and in the District of Columbia starting in 1837. With his owner's consent, Kennedy found work at Washington's National Hotel, better known as Gadsby's. John Gadsby had opened his establishment in 1827 at the intersection of Pennsylvania Avenue and Sixth Street. By the late 1830s, John's son William Gadsby and his partner Augustus Newton were running the hotel. Messrs. Newton & Gadsby frequently advertised to hire male and female servants, preferably slaves, to serve as barkeepers, butlers, waiters, dining room attendants, washers, ironers, chambermaids, housekeepers, and the like. Kennedy spent more than a year with the hoteliers, but "for some *alledged* [*sic*] misbehavior" not specifically recounted in the records, he ended up on the opposite side of the National Mall in the "private jail kept by ... William H. Williams for the custody of negroes." Kennedy was not sure if Pendleton or Newton & Gadsby had had him committed, but after languishing in the Yellow House for at least two weeks, the bondman grew anxious that perhaps Pendleton "is about to sell him & has offered him for sale."[26]

Kennedy filed a petition for his freedom based on his interpretation of his master's behavior and his knowledge of the applicable laws. Within the District of Columbia, the institution of slavery was governed by the laws of the state – either Maryland or Virginia – that had ceded the land for the capital. Thus, Maryland law applied to Washington and Georgetown, but Virginia's to Alexandria. Maryland law permitted slave-holders from outside the District, such as J. Purnell Pendleton, to hire their bondpeople to employers living in Washington, pending payment of the applicable annual tax. The statute clarified, however, that "[a] slave" living north of the Potomac "is not entitled to freedom" merely "from being hired to a resident of the District of Columbia for a limited time." In his appeal, Kennedy stressed the allowable duration of the term of hire, claiming that he essentially lived in the District. It was an important distinction. According to Kennedy's petition, Pendleton understood that slaves attracted higher wages in Washington than in northern Virginia and, ideally, would have hired Kennedy "permanently in the city of Washington," were that legally permissible. Maryland law stated, though, that "[a] slave brought from any place" other than "Maryland, into the District of Columbia ... to reside, is entitled to freedom." In his petition, Kennedy argued that his master, in allowing him to hire himself out "by *the month*" in the District of Columbia, fundamentally evaded the intent of the statute "against the importation of slaves to *reside* in

Washington county" permanently. Since, as he saw it, his owner violated the law, Kennedy concluded that he was legally "entitled to his freedom," per the statute. He feared that Pendleton was planning "to sell him to foreign parts" and that "his immediate sale & transportation" out of Washington was a distinct possibility. Therefore, Kennedy's petition sought an injunction from the US Circuit Court to prevent Pendleton, Newton, Gadsby, or William H. Williams from selling him until the court had the opportunity to consider his petition for emancipation. The court granted Kennedy's request and barred his removal from Washington.[27]

If Kennedy and other black people lodged in the Yellow House protested their confinement and clamored for freedom, other inmates languished there as whites sparred over the ownership of them in the Washington, D.C. court system. Given the nature of their profession, slave traders were often swept up in familial dramas surrounding the possession, distribution, or inheritance of enslaved property. In May 1838, for example, John and Mary Mellon filed a bill of complaint in the US Circuit Court for the District of Columbia against William H. Williams to prohibit the conveyance of "a certain negro boy named James" outside the nation's capital. Nine years earlier, John and Mary's father, George Mellon of Alexandria, had deposited James with a white man named Lewis Piles as security for a $30 debt. Such forms of commodification of enslaved bodies were common in the Old South. Slaveholders readily passed bondpeople around, like cash, to settle debts or estates or as collateral for loans. John and Mary Mellon chronicled how their father had passed away while they were still minors. Now of age, they learned that Piles had recently sold the nineteen-year-old bondman to William H. Williams as a slave for life "in violation of all laws . . . and in derogation of the reversionary rights" of George Mellon's two adult children. Mellon's son and daughter objected to the transaction on two grounds. First, their father's $30 debt to Piles had "long since" been paid. Second, their father, as they came to understand, had held the legal title to James only until the bondman reached his twenty-eighth birthday, at which point he would be emancipated. In the meantime, James belonged to them.[28]

The saga of James' eventual freedom predated his birth by about a decade and a half. In 1805, an Alexandria County slaveholder chose to manumit James' mother, a bondwoman named Bet, effective March 31, 1823. He also decreed that her future offspring would each be freed upon attaining the age of twenty-eight. Over the course of her lifetime, Bet fell into the possession of John Gadsby, proprietor of the National Hotel, who later sold her to "one Mr. Piles," an older relation of Lewis, who passed her along, through either sale or gift, to his son-in-law George Mellon. When Mellon utilized James as security for a debt with Lewis Piles, then, he was doing business with his wife's family.[29]

Accusing William H. Williams of knowingly purchasing a slave to whom the seller enjoyed no legal "right or title," the Mellons called for the trader to surrender James from his imprisonment in the Yellow House and for an injunction forbidding either Williams or Piles from taking the bondman outside the court's jurisdiction to sell. As Piles deposed before the court in June, however, he had actually "sold the boy James" not to Williams but to Jesse A. Bynum, a prominent North Carolina congressman, for "three hundred dollars cash." Through his attorneys, Brent & Brent, representing him in court, Williams pleaded ignorance of the whole affair. It was Bynum, he stated, who had placed James in the Yellow House, where the bondman remained in custody. Other than that, Williams explained, he knew "nothing" about the ownership dispute over James, he had "no interest therein," and he should therefore be dismissed from the suit. Williams, it seems, was merely collecting his fee of twenty-five cents per day to keep James secure for the congressman from North Carolina. Probably realizing that their allegation against Williams and Lewis Piles for conspiring to defraud them strained the available evidence, the Mellons settled out-of-court with Jesse Bynum in the fall of 1838. Assuming all went according to the siblings' proposed plan, the Mellons dismissed the suit once Bynum paid them fifty dollars and court costs and executed a bond pledging to liberate James once the bondman turned twenty-eight.[30]

Whereas James presumably gained his freedom through his sched-uled manumission, another black man detained in the Yellow House, James Ash, relied upon the terms of a will as his legal avenue to liberty. In September 1824, slaveholder Maria Anne T. Greenfield of Prince George's County, Maryland – immediately east of Washington,

D.C. – composed her last will and testament. In it, she bequeathed to her nephew and executor, Gerard T. Greenfield, "all my negro slaves" – some twenty in total, including James Ash – provided that "he shall not carry them out of the State of Maryland or sell them to any one." In the event that Gerard Greenfield violated either of these stipulations, his aunt directed that "the said negroes ... be free for life." After Maria died, her nephew took possession of his deceased aunt's bondpeople per the terms of the will, but he found the restrictions imposed upon him "repugnant to the nature of the estate." Gerard Greenfield had long lived in Tennessee, and he had journeyed to Prince George's County, Maryland, merely for the purpose of settling his aunt's affairs. He wished to return to Tennessee with his enslaved inheritance in tow. So he concocted a plot "to obtain a Judicial decision" on the legal questions his aunt's will raised. On December 18, 1839, Greenfield sold James Ash for $700 to William H. Williams, who took custody of the bondman and deposited him in his private jail. After the sale, Greenfield informed Ash what he had done and presented him "an opportunity ... to commence a suit for his freedom." Privy to the terms of the will, and without anything to lose, James Ash willingly conspired with Greenfield to get their case to court. Although they hoped for opposite outcomes, they could cooperate for the time being. Ash filed a petition in the Circuit Court of the District of Columbia the very next day, on December 19, stating that he was entitled to his freedom.[31]

On March 24, 1840, Greenfield and Ash got their day before the US Circuit Court, held in the old Washington City Hall. Chief Judge William Cranch presided over the proceedings. Answering a subpoena to appear before Cranch's court, William H. Williams denied Ash's claims to liberty, but the twelve-man jury impaneled to decide the case levied a judgment in Ash's favor. Under the contract law of Maryland effective at the time Maria Anne T. Greenfield executed her will, slaveholders maintained the right to free slaves, either by deed or by last will and testament, "after any given period of service, or at any particular age, or upon the performance of any condition, or on the event of any contingency." The court recognized no distinction between a will's bequest to a third party and a bequest of freedom to a slave. Slave owners enjoyed

the lawful right to attach whatever conditions they pleased to the distribution of their property, including the emancipation of their bondpeople. According to the Circuit Court, such provisions did not infringe on
the property rights of heirs. Thus, the moment Gerard Greenfield sold
James Ash, the terms of his aunt's will took effect, and the bondman was
liberated. The court ruled Ash free and ordered him discharged from
Williams' private jail.[32]

Displeased with the verdict, Williams' attorney, John Marbury, filed
a writ of error with the US Supreme Court in May 1840. Marbury recognized that the case "involves a question of law, important to the slave
states." The "extensive interest" in the case therefore "render[ed] a final
decision . . . by the Supreme Court of the United States desirable." The
Supreme Court, led by Chief Justice Roger B. Taney since 1836, consented to hear Williams' appeal. The case was originally slated to go
before the court in January 1841, but it was postponed, quite possibly
because, by that time, Williams himself was indisposed in New Orleans,
with his cargo of enslaved convicts.[33]

Representing Williams before the Taney court, Marbury contended
that Maria Anne T. Greenfield's will gave her nephew "an absolute
estate," with no valid limitations placed upon it. Gerard Greenfield
could hold the slaves for life and, assuming he neither removed nor
sold them, could distribute them to his heirs or have them passed on to
his next of kin. Marbury made the argument that, legally, "a restriction
on the right to sell never has been construed into a limitation of the
estate." The conditions of the will, he contended, were in fact "repugnant
to the nature of the estate, and therefore void." Further pressing his
client's cause, Marbury observed, "Negroes, by the laws of Maryland,
are property precisely as money," no less than "funds, or household
effects." Had the terms of the will applied to any other form of property
than slaves, he insisted, they "would have been declared void" as "repugnant" conditions. How could it be any different for a provisional "bequest
of freedom" to a bondman? It would be impossible to implement "without denying to the master that control over the negroes which he is by law
entitled to exercise." As a result, the will must have given Greenfield "the
absolute property in the negroes bequeathed," so his sale of James Ash to
William H. Williams was not subject to challenge.[34]

James Ash's attorney, Joseph H. Bradley, argued otherwise. Maria Anne T. Greenfield's "intent" was "clear," he explained: "She meant to give Gerard a qualified, not an absolute estate." The slaves mentioned in the will were to gain their freedom pending the satisfaction of either of two possible conditions. Gerard was subject to a "conditional limitation of that estate, contingent until the event occurs, but becoming absolute so soon as that has happened." His aunt "meant to aid him, but ... in her own manner, by his taking a qualified estate to be held in Maryland." This was her way of providing "protection" to her slaves, who had "grown up around her" and "to whom she is attached." She left them to her nephew but under terms "controlling the right conferred on Gerard," "qualifying and restraining his power over them." That was the "great primary intent pervading the whole will." His aunt bequeathed to him a "qualified estate," "not intended to be absolute."[35]

Taking another tack, Bradley also pointed out the peculiar character of slaves: they were not "merely property" but also "human beings." Slaves could commit crime, be placed on trial, and convicted of wrongdoing, none of which was true of property alone. As written, the law implied that slaves possessed "a reasoning faculty, a conscience, [and] an immortal spirit." Bondpeople, Bradley argued, should benefit from the duality of their nature because people are "superior to property," and any "question of freedom" must take precedence over "any question of property." "[S]uits for freedom," the lawyer concluded, always "are to be favoured."[36]

Anyone acquainted with the legal absurdities and historical inaccuracies of the Taney court's infamous verdict in the much later *Dred Scott v. Sandford* decision of 1857 would place little confidence in the likelihood of the Supreme Court allowing James Ash his freedom. Delivering the majority opinion in *Dred Scott*, Taney declared in part that black people were not citizens of the United States and never had been, that they therefore had no right to bring cases before the court, and that they had no rights that white men were bound to respect. The political context of the 1850s differed from that of the 1840s, however, and in the early 1840s, when *Williams v. Ash* went before the Supreme Court, Taney, an ex-slaveholder himself, was less committed to the institution of bondage. The Taney court, in short, was not the judicial body it would later become, much to James Ash's advantage.

Writing for the majority, Taney eschewed altogether the issue of slaves' humanity as raised by attorney Joseph Bradley, focusing instead on the specific character of Maria Anne T. Greenfield's will. The chief justice described the bequest to her nephew as "a conditional limitation of freedom to the petitioner [Ash]," one "that . . . took effect the moment he was sold." The Supreme Court thus concurred with the verdict of the US Circuit Court of the District of Columbia and, consequently, affirmed Ash's liberation from bondage. One New York newspaper in 1857 reflected on the sharp juxtaposition of the recent *Dred Scott* decision with the older verdict in *Williams v. Ash.* Though separated by fifteen years in time, both cases involved slaves pursuing emancipation through the courts, but the contrast of the outcomes could not have been more striking. Recollecting the *Williams v. Ash* case in light of Taney's atrocious and wrongheaded *Dred Scott* ruling, the *Albany Evening Journal* scoffed at the nation's highest court when it marveled that, in the previous decade, "a Negro might not only be a party to a suit before the US Supreme Court like any other citizen, but . . . a Slave might go there and recover his Freedom!" Formerly confined in William H. Williams' Yellow House, the James Ash who was the beneficiary of the Supreme Court's decision in March 1842 was probably the forty-four-year-old black laborer of the same name whom a census taker in 1850 found living in Washington, D.C.'s seventh ward as a free man.[37]

In January 1840, five persons of color imprisoned in the Yellow House – Emanuel Price, Maria Course, Israel Brinkley, Peter Butler, and Joseph Armstrong – all claimed that they were free blacks illegally held in William H. Williams' slave jail. Their alleged kidnapper was not Williams himself, however. The first four identified Williams' business associate Thomas N. Davis as the trader who had wrongfully deprived them of their freedom. (Armstrong named a different slave dealer.) Anxious that they would soon be sold into slavery, all five slaves took advantage of the best legal tool at their disposal: they petitioned William Cranch and the US Circuit Court of the District of Columbia for a writ of *habeas corpus.* Predating the Bill of Rights, the privilege of applying for a writ of *habeas corpus* appears in the text of the US Constitution as originally ratified, enshrined in Article I, section 9. A writ of *habeas corpus* is a court order, issued by a judge, instructing an individual accused of unjustly detaining another person to produce the detainee in court for the purpose of explaining the reason for that confinement. Upon hearing the rationale, the court determines whether the detainee remains in custody or is released. Free blacks kidnapped by slave traders and unlawfully incarcerated in public or private jails routinely appealed for writs of *habeas corpus* as the most effective legal avenue for regaining their liberty.[38]

In their collective petition to the Circuit Court, filed January 14, 1840, Armstrong, Butler, Price, and Course identified themselves as "coloured persons" and "Citizens of the state of Delaware," either "entitled to their freedom now" or in the near future as their terms of servitude expired. They neglected to specify who among them was already free versus who anticipated imminent emancipation, but it did not particularly matter. All of them equally had been "forcibly taken" from Delaware, lodged "in the Jail of a certain William H. Williams" in Washington, D.C., and now feared being "removed to some remote part of the southern country," "sold in[to] everlasting servitude," and "deprived of the opportunity of establishing their freedom."[39]

Israel Brinkley's circumstances differed from those of the other four. A man identified as Robert Ball, familiar with the history of the "negro boy," learned that Brinkley was "in the possession and custody of Wm. H. Williams." That should not have been the case, however, for Ball knew for a fact that Judge William Cranch of the D.C. Circuit Court had "discharged" Brinkley in the summer of 1839 "as a free boy." It is not clear how Brinkley ended up in the Yellow House, but on the morning of January 14, Thomas N. Davis retrieved him, Emanuel Price, and Maria Course from Williams' private slave jail, perhaps to hide the wrongfully detained free blacks in advance of their illegal sale. Continuing in Davis' custody, Brinkley pursued a writ of *habeas corpus* so that he might protest his detention in front of the judges of the Circuit Court.[40]

Believing the claims to freedom of all five detainees, US District Attorney for the District of Columbia Francis Scott Key championed their cause and represented them as they sought their writs of *habeas corpus*. After witnessing the bombardment of Fort McHenry during the War of 1812 and penning the lyrics to "The Star-Spangled Banner," Key spent several decades as a prominent, prosperous attorney in Washington, D.C. Presidential candidate Andrew Jackson energized Key politically, and the lawyer would become one of Old Hickory's close confidants and a member of his informal group of advisors dubbed the "kitchen cabinet." Jackson rewarded Key's loyalty in 1833 by appointing him US attorney for the District of Columbia, a post he would hold until 1841. While in that capacity, Key exercised continued sway over the president. In 1836, he was influential in getting Jackson to name Key's brother-in-law and friend Roger B. Taney the fifth Chief Justice of the US Supreme Court.[41]

Vis-à-vis matters of race and slavery, Key proved no less a bundle of contradictions than former president Thomas Jefferson. Born into a slaveholding family, the Georgetown attorney thought slavery evil and the mistreatment slaves suffered appalling, but he still owned four bondpeople in 1840. He himself purchased slaves but abhorred the breakup of enslaved families through sale and expressed his desire to suppress the ongoing smuggling of African slaves into the United States. Key emancipated seven slaves over the course of his life but denounced the abolitionist movement. He instead favored the colonization abroad of free people of color, whom he regarded as inferior to whites, lazy, and socially troublesome. To that end, Key spoke at the founding of the American Colonization Society in December 1816 and served, with Judge William Cranch, on its board of managers. Nevertheless, he also dispensed legal advice *pro bono* to poor free blacks and to slaves seeking emancipation and regularly represented them in court without charge. At various times, he aided free blacks taken up illegally as slaves and helped slaves petition or sue for their freedom. Key served on the legal team that labored – unsuccessfully – for the freedom of the captives taken from aboard the ship *Antelope* when their international slave trafficking case went before the US Supreme Court. Yet if he represented enslaved and free blacks in court, Key did the same for slaveholders as well, defending the institution of slavery, upholding masters' constitutional right to own slaves, and trying antislavery sympathizers who aided fugitives fleeing bondage in the District of Columbia. Equally adept at prosecuting free blacks, slaves, and abolitionists, on one hand, and slave traders and owners on the other, Key left a complicated, mixed record of litigation before the bench that defied easy categorization, yet he still garnered a reputation as the "Nigger Lawyer."[42]

Key thus got to work crafting petitions on his black clients' behalf. For the four Delaware inmates, he pleaded for a "writ of Habeas Corpus directed to ... Wm. H. Williams or the officer who has charge of his Jail" – Ebenezer Rodbird – commanding him to appear in court with the petitioners to explain "the cause of their detention." The same day, Key also filed the request for a writ of *habeas corpus* for Israel Brinkley, "now in custody of Thos N Davis." After William H. Williams informed Key of the news that Davis had pulled not only Israel Brinkley but also Emanuel Price and Maria Course out of the Yellow House, Key submitted a third request for a writ of *habeas corpus*, with the intention of compelling Davis to produce Price and Course in court. Only with the assistance of a court order could any of the five detainees "be discharged from their illegal confinement" and avoid being "carried as slaves for life to the South." Judge William Cranch of the D.C. Circuit Court looked favorably upon all the petitions and issued the writs, although the cases of Joseph Armstrong and Peter Butler thereafter disappear from the documentary record.[43]

The next day, William H. Williams complied with the writ issued him. He appeared before the Circuit Court and deposed that Rodbird, his agent and jailer, informed him on December 31, 1839, that Thomas N. Davis had "placed three negroes in his jail ... for safe-keeping": Brinkley, Price, and Course. Rodbird then reported that, on January 14, 1840, Davis "had called for and taken away" the same three inmates. Williams checked the register of prisoners and verified that "one of the said negroes was booked in the name of Israel." Beyond that, Williams offered little information. He denied holding "any interest of ownership whatever" in the prisoners or knowing the whereabouts of any of the three individuals Davis had retrieved. But he did cooperate and presumably, after testifying, returned to the Yellow House.[44]

Thomas N. Davis did not seem as forthcoming in court as did William H. Williams. He answered the pair of writs the day after he was presented them, although the court found his response unsatisfactory. Davis reported that, on December 31, 1839, he purchased Brinkley, Price, and Course "as slaves for life," paying $1,200 to seller Joseph Woodall, "publickly in the bar room" of Washington, D.C. tavern keeper Thomas Lloyd. Davis secured from Woodall "a bill of sale warranting the title" to them. Woodall, he explained, maintained a good "character" as a man who "might be safely dealt with" and "upon whose word reliance might be placed." When Woodall stated that he had brought Brinkley, Price, and Course from Maryland's Eastern Shore for sale, Davis had no reason to doubt their status as slaves. His testimony aroused the skepticism of the court, however, when he claimed that the three persons of color in question "were removed . . . beyond the district of Columbia before the service of the said writs of habeas corpus . . . and that the said individuals are now beyond [his] control and out of [his] custody."[45]

Representing his black clients whose freedom hung in the balance, Francis Scott Key characterized Davis' answer to the writs of *habeas corpus* as "insufficient and evasive." "It does not deny that the prisoners are in his power, or that he is unable to produce them," he indicated. Moreover, the timing of their extrication from William H. Williams' slave pen, the very same morning of the day that the court granted the writs, struck Key as too suspicious to be mere coincidence. Evidence supplied by a number of witnesses suggested "that Davis had removed the negroes, because he suspected that they would apply for a writ of habeas corpus." Doing so with the express "intent to avoid the expected process of this court," Key added, constituted "an obstruction of justice, and a contempt of court."[46]

The D.C. Circuit Court under Judge Cranch agreed wholeheartedly with Key's assessment of the case. In its decision handed down on January 16, 1840, it concurred that Davis' response to the writs of *habeas corpus* was indeed "evasive and insufficient." The court expected Davis "to produce the bodies of the said negroes," and since he refused to do so, ordered the marshal to take him into custody for contempt. Davis would sit in jail until he surrendered the persons of Emanuel Price and Maria Course. Even had Davis been so inclined, he could not have given over Israel Brinkley to appear physically in court, for Brinkley had absconded after he was taken out of the Yellow House on January 14.[47]

On January 18, the Circuit Court clarified that Davis would be discharged from jail if either he or "any other person for him" produced Emanuel Price and Maria Course for the marshal to take into custody.

Perhaps not coincidentally, the same day, Judge Cranch issued a writ of *habeas corpus* ordering an obscure white man from Alexandria named Elias Legg to bring the captives before the Circuit Court. The implication was that Davis may have deposited Price and Course under Legg's watch as part of his effort to conceal the pair from the law.[48]

No direct evidence of Legg's reply to the writ survives, but two days later, on January 20, Thomas N. Davis presented Emanuel Price and Maria Course to the court, securing his own release from jail. (Israel Brinkley, meanwhile, had been apprehended and jailed in Baltimore.) District Attorney Francis Scott Key submitted new petitions for freedom on behalf of his two clients. Price claimed that "he is [a] free man" whom Davis "unjustly held in bondage." Course asserted that "she is entitled to her freedom," suggesting that she may have been one of the captives from the Yellow House for whom a set emancipation date was approaching. She, too, complained that she was "illegally held in bondage by ... Thomas N. Davis" and prayed the court to "enquire" into her case. Judge Cranch summoned Davis to appear before the D.C. Circuit Court at the appointed date in March 1840 and required him "to enter into recognizance, in the sum of $1,000, that he would not remove the said negroes out of the jurisdiction of this court" prior to the scheduled adjudication of their freedom suits. Davis refused to pay the requisite security, so the court ordered that the "negroes be committed to the marshal ... for safekeeping" until the trial. In March, Price and Course "established their right to freedom, and were discharged," having narrowly escaped slave trader Thomas N. Davis' apparent attempt to kidnap them. Their successful suit demonstrated free blacks' ability to use the courts to avoid becoming the next victims of abduction and illegal sale into slavery.[49]

Just months after helping liberate Emanuel Price and Maria Course from the clutches of Thomas N. Davis, Francis Scott Key aided in the prosecution of two free women of color – Harriet Jones and Lucretia (Letty) Clarke, both of Washington County – for fraud. In a bizarre plot, a presumably white yeoman named William H. Brewster; Jones, his purported wife; and Clarke targeted William H. and Thomas Williams as the objects of a swindle. In October 1839, Brewster and Jones sold Clarke, then masquerading as their bondwoman, to Thomas Williams for $300. About twenty years old at the time and still relatively new to the business of slave trading under his older brother's tutelage and oversight, Thomas had no reason to doubt Clarke's status as a slave and paid the agreed-upon price. Presumably the three conspirators had a plan to pocket the money and still liberate Clarke from the Yellow House before the feigned slave was shipped off to permanent bondage in the Southwest, but court papers do not make their precise scheme clear. No doubt it did not pan out as expected. Although details remain sketchy, William H. Brewster evaded prosecution and probably fled with the trio's ill-gotten gains. Meanwhile, accomplices Harriet Jones and Letty Clarke appeared before the Criminal Court of Washington County, charged with three counts of fraud. A jury found the pair guilty during the March 1840 term, and they were sentenced to "suffer imprisonment and labour in the Penitentiary of the District of Columbia, for the period of two years." Jones and Clarke sought to overturn their conviction before the US Circuit Court for the District of Columbia, where Francis Scott Key fought their appeal. Despite his efforts, Judge William Cranch concurred with the two women of color that their convictions were improper because they did not "obtain the fruit of the fraud." Since Brewster alone had absconded with the Williams brothers' money, Cranch reversed the judgment.[50]

By the time the state of Louisiana confiscated William H. Williams' twenty-six enslaved convicts from the New Orleans railcars on November 1, 1840, the trader was already a hardened veteran of southern courtrooms, having been embroiled in no fewer than half a dozen separate lawsuits pertaining to his profession between 1838 and 1840 alone. A seventh began in October 1840 and unfolded concurrently with the developing story in the Crescent City. This other case occupied the courts not of Louisiana but of Maryland and exposed the shady world of finance that underwrote the domestic slave trade.

CHAPTER 6

The Millington Bank

WHEN THE MOBILE CHRONICLE PUBLISHED IN LATE
October 1840 the Virginia governor's warning about the
possible approach of the *Uncas* and its cargo of convict slaves, editors
speculatively sneered that "[t]he men" involved, "[Rudolph] Littlejohn
and [William H.] Williams, are probably the same who were engaged in
circulating the spurious notes of the 'Commercial Bank of Millington.'"
On October 12, the Commercial Bank of Millington, located on
Maryland's Eastern Shore, had closed its doors for the last time. Bigger-
city papers condescendingly described Millington as "no great shakes of a
place," a trifling, "obscure village ... containing perhaps a store and
blacksmith shop" and "about fifty houses." A stagecoach passed through
three times per week, helping the town forge some commercial ties to
Elkton, to the north, and Baltimore, across Chesapeake Bay. But despite
Millington's generally sleepy countenance, the hamlet had nevertheless
secured in 1836 a state charter for a bank, joining the proliferation of
financial institutions that sprouted after President Andrew Jackson's
attacks killed the centralized, purportedly sinister Second Bank of the
United States. The Millington Bank did not become fully operational
until 1838, when broker Moses Holmes "opened an account" on behalf of
the Commercial Bank of Millington at the Chesapeake Bank of
Baltimore, where its notes could be redeemed. That account closed
later the same year, however, and the Millington Bank continued to
languish, barely surviving the depression of 1839. Throughout this
time, it eked out but "a nominal existence" with little influence outside
the vicinity of Kent County. Its cashier presided over a "large ledger,"
according to one report, "but there were few or no entries made in it."[1]

The small, initially insignificant bank's fortunes rose fantastically and deteriorated just as dramatically after the enigmatic "stranger" William Weed, his brother F. A. Weed, and a third investor, a man identified only as Sherwood from Buffalo, New York – probably the banker Merril B. Sherwood – together purchased the establishment's charter from Moses Holmes in November 1839 for $10,000. The partners then installed F. A. Weed as bank president, reopened the Millington account at the Chesapeake Bank, and adopted "the high pressure principle," embarking upon the reckless printing of bank notes with wanton disregard to the concern's specie reserves, an increasingly common practice absent the regulatory constraints of the Second Bank. The speculative bubble of the 1830s that had burst so spectacularly in the catastrophic Panic of 1837, ushering in widespread bank failures and the ignominious end of the "flush times," might have cautioned the Weeds against the irresponsible issuance of bank notes, but in a climate of national deregulation, in which bank oversight devolved entirely upon overwhelmed state governments, the prospect of realizing immense profits through overly generous lending policies proved too tantalizing. Issuing more paper than banks had specie in the vault backing it up had long been normative, but the practice was now carried to unprecedented extremes. As early as May 1840, the Millington lacked the "funds or coin sufficient to redeem its circulation." By the time the Millington Bank finally exploded in October, joining the Patapsco Savings Fund and a slew of "other defunct shinplaster factories" and "swindling shops" of Baltimore, as much as half a million dollars in Millington money had been dumped into circulation across the United States. Yet when the hapless "people of the neighborhood took possession of the banking house" in Millington to seize "whatever valuable funds they could lay their hands on," they found but $565 lying in the vault. William and F. A. Weed fled Maryland to avoid the public's wrath.[2]

The Weed brothers' speculative ventures in the banking industry rendered them briefly notorious. The *New York Times* in 1840 dubbed the Millington fraud "the greatest shave extant." Like so many others of their shady ilk, the Weeds functioned as agents of capitalist excess in the age of Jackson. Americans placed tremendous trust in specie – the hard currencies of gold and silver – but abhorred the inconvenience of lugging it around in quantity. Thus, despite the universal respect for it, bulky, unwieldy specie remained scarce in actual circulation. Instead, people used paper money – bank-issued notes representing hard money – in their day-to-day economic transactions. In theory, any bank issuing such notes kept in its safe a quantity of specie sufficient for the simultaneous redemption of all the paper money that that institution had in circulation at any one moment in time. The reality proved quite different. Banks' printed issues regularly outpaced their capital on reserve, sometimes, as in the case of so-called "wildcat banks" like the Millington, to outlandish excess. The term "wildcat bank" originally referred only to "institutions founded by unscrupulous financiers in remote areas for the express purpose of making it difficult, if not impossible, for the notes to be exchanged for gold and silver." By 1840, the American public had generalized the phrase to apply to any banking concern whose paper issues vastly exceeded its specie in the vault and, hence, its ability to redeem its notes. By either definition, the Weeds' Millington enterprise qualified as one of the dozens of wildcat banks that sprouted between 1836 and the 1863 passage of the National Bank Act crafted to impose financial order on the reigning chaos. Only a blurry line separated legitimate from illegitimate financial institutions in the age of Jackson, however, so perhaps the progenitors of the Commercial Bank of Millington had originally conceived it in good faith and with the best of intentions. At the same time, the uncertainties of the emerging nineteenth-century American capitalist system supplied ample opportunities for all manner of fraud. In churning out currency with reckless abandon, the Millington wildcat joined thousands of other, relatively more cautious and legitimate institutions in churning out bank notes to meet the country's insatiable demand for credit. Those funds, in turn, facilitated the acquisition of land and slaves, the twin engines that drove the cotton economy and the development of American capitalism.[3]

Slave trader William H. Williams was intimately connected to the Millington concern. On the one hand, antebellum banking institutions such as the Millington lent domestic slave traders like Williams the funds that financed their operations, enabling them to pay ready cash to sellers for bondpeople whom they would later redistribute southwestward to the advancing cotton frontier as well as to the cane fields of Louisiana. On the other hand, the propagation of state-chartered banks in the 1830s demanded start-up capital, and to capitalize these new institutions, banking entrepreneurs sometimes appealed directly to purveyors of human chattel. Calculating, profit-seeking slave dealers such as Williams entertained a wide variety of investment opportunities. With ample monetary resources at their disposal, they might underwrite the very banking ventures that later granted them credit and kept them awash in paper money.[4]

Unscrupulous bankers involved in risky wildcat concerns probably would not have divulged fraudulent intentions when soliciting funds from prospective slave-trading financiers, for the slave dealers would not have wished to alienate themselves from the local slave-selling public. At the same time, traders exhibited no qualms about profiting by economic endeavors that other Americans condemned as morally objectionable and – unflattering popular rhetoric about their profession notwithstanding – suffered little by doing so. Wildcat bankers, in turn, appreciated traders' ability to circulate their dubious notes widely. Whether slave traders carried bank paper dozens of miles away from the issuing institution to purchase bondpeople or stuffed wads of bills in their pockets as they undertook slaving journeys across the country to New Orleans, they delayed that paper's redemption for specie by days, weeks, or even months. Relieved of anxiety over their notes' prompt return, wildcat banks such as the Millington could blissfully continue the irresponsible printing of paper money. At the Commercial Bank of Millington, those who speculated in banks and those who speculated in enslaved black bodies thus developed a close relationship, one at times symbiotic but at other times riven by tension.

Slave traders' occupation inherently demanded expertise in local money markets. Their advertisements consistently promised "cash" for one hundred, three hundred, four hundred, or more "negroes," and they paid in bank notes of various sorts, sometimes bowing to the preferences of the seller for paper from a particular state or even a specific bank. Traders needed access to banks' paper, along with an acute understanding of the relative values of the multifarious bills through which they might complete their transactions. These were paramount to running a successful operation. Headquartered in Washington, D.C., slave dealers and occasional business associates William H. Williams and Thomas N. Davis were as familiar with the currencies in circulation as anyone. That Alexander Lee had made Williams a partner at his Lottery and Exchange Office in the nation's capital in the 1830s suggests that Williams had mastered the evaluation of diverse paper monies and the estimation of the scrip's fluctuating worth.[5]

With a solid understanding of bank notes and the wider financial system in which they circulated, Williams and Davis were both deeply involved in the Millington concern. Each had "exchanged with [William] Weed some thousands of dollars" in support of the Commercial Bank of Millington during its meteoric rise. They were invested in the institution, and the institution invested in them, channeling them the cash they needed. The system could theoretically function in ways mutually beneficial to bankers and slave traders alike, but the death of the Second Bank of the United States and the shockingly careless proliferation of little monitored state-chartered institutions permitted the formation of banking concerns erected on fragile foundations, their metaphorical edifices susceptible to even the slightest financial breeze.[6]

The founders of the Millington Bank sowed the seeds of the establishment's own destruction. Buffalo, New York financier and founder of the Erie County Bank Merril B. Sherwood and two unnamed "others" – probably the Weed brothers – launched the Gallipolis Bank of Ohio in 1839 with $200,000 in capital, including $80,000 in Millington money "as a special deposit . . . not to be put in circulation" but "for the sole purpose of giving credit" to the institution so that it might commence operations. The Millington bills were supposed to sit in the vault and merely help accountants balance the Gallipolis Bank's books. The bank fraudulently put them into circulation, however, and in late August 1840 some $12,000 unexpectedly returned to the Millington Bank for redemption. The Millington paid on the notes, but at great cost. It "exhaust[ed]" its "coin & funds," sending the institution into the suicidal tailspin that ended in its October collapse. Steeped in fraud from its reinvention and in the throes of insolvency, the Millington Bank, in desperation, aggressively printed notes for traders such as Williams and Davis to "broadcast over the land," floating them "as far away from home as possible, so as to prolong the time before they would return for redemption." The longer the notes stayed out, the more paper the bank could print and thereby extend its life.[7]

Some contemporaries expressed serious reservations about the soundness of Millington notes well before the institution collapsed. Alexander Lee, William H. Williams' partner in the exchange office, observed that he knew "nothing of the character of the money except that it was bad." John Corse, who ran an exchange office in Alexandria, declared that "he would have nothing to do with Millington notes, and refused to Exchange" them. Washington, D.C. slave trader James H. Birch, abductor of the free black Solomon Northup, insisted that he "did not consider the Millington money good & never did." Thanks to the institution's suspect reputation, "the only persons" Birch knew of who "circulat[ed] it in large amounts" were Williams and the "negro trader" Thomas N. Davis.[8]

The financial ties between the pair of slave dealers and the Commercial Bank of Millington compelled the traders, as investors, to try and prop up the dying institution once they realized it was in trouble. The best means of doing so was to get its notes into circulation, as far away as possible from sites of redemption in Millington or Baltimore. In late September and early October 1840, only weeks and days before the Millington Bank went under, William H. Williams and his two leading purchasing agents – his younger brother Thomas Williams and Ebenezer Rodbird, jailer at his slave pen – conducted a brisk business, buying up slaves in northern Virginia and southern Maryland with Millington notes. The flurry of purchases with Millington money proved insufficient to resuscitate the dying institution and in fact only generated problems for William H. Williams for a decade to come.[9]

The economic effects of the Millington Bank's failure reverberated locally – in the Chesapeake region – and throughout the nation. Most immediately affected were the citizens of Baltimore and its environs. Area merchants who had previously been paid in Millington notes now found themselves holding money devoid of all value. Customers at times cheated shopkeepers by handing over Millington paper in exchange for merchandise and then bolting out of the store before a careful inspection of the note revealed its worthlessness. Desperate holders of Millington money sought to pawn off their devalued currency on unwitting individuals yet to hear the news of the bank's collapse. As unethical as that was, it reflected the actions of Millington Bank employees themselves. Unnamed representatives – unscrupulous "rogues" – of the "infamous swindling concern" had reportedly approached laborers along the Baltimore & Ohio Railroad about a week before the bank went under. Like other companies of the time, the B & O issued its own scrip with which it paid workers their wages. These shinplasters were always intended to circulate locally, but the Millington agents generated anxiety among the laborers when they claimed that the company notes "would never command specie." They successfully persuaded many railroad workers to exchange their paper for Millington money, a healthy supply of which the bank's boosters not coincidentally happened to have at the ready. Those "poor men" persuaded to swap currencies "soon learned that they had been robbed by these bank swindlers." Dreams of socking away "a few hundred dollars to purchase for themselves small farms in the west, where they could settle with their families and have a home," were dashed. Some lacked the pecuniary resources to afford even their next meal, "having lost all they had saved for the last fifteen months."[10]

Within a month of the Millington explosion, its bills had spread like an economic contagion across the country. (See Figure 10.) "Several hundred dollars" in worthless currency soon surfaced in New York. One informant to the *New York Times* claimed that "$100,000 are afloat in Indiana" and that "Western Pennsylvania is . . . flooded with the same trash." Already in November 1840, newspapers reported "[f]ive dollar notes of the old broken down Commercial Bank of Millington" having appeared in Philadelphia, "altered so as to read 'Commercial Bank of New York.'" These may have been amateurish efforts by holders of Millington paper to salvage the face value of the notes still in their possession, but certainly professional counterfeiters spied opportunity in the Millington meltdown as well. Counterfeiting was a pervasive problem in the antebellum decades, and defunct institutions such as the one in Millington had printed the raw materials for a thriving underground business. Although the bank had died, its notes still circulated. Counterfeiters therefore routinely took the paper from bankrupt

10 An obsolete $5 bank note from the Commercial Bank of Millington, Maryland, 1839. Source: In possession of the author.

concerns to create "altered notes," in which either the name of the bank or its location was modified so that it appeared good, masquerading as the issue of a solvent institution. Beginning in 1840 and for years afterwards, counterfeiters doctored the Millington Bank's notes to disguise their provenance. Alerting their readers to the bogus bills then in circulation, newspapers reported that various forgeries "ingeniously" substituted the word "Millington" on the Commercial Bank's notes – mostly in five- and ten-dollar denominations – with "New York," "Pennsylvania," "Baltimore," "Buffalo," "Albany," "Boston," "Cincinnati," or "Hartford." As the *New York Tribune* observed, the names of "nearly all the Commercial Banks in the Union" graced the counterfeits that originated as Millington notes.[11]

The Millington Bank's insolvency dealt a uniquely devastating blow to the riverine village of Vicksburg, Mississippi, more than a thousand miles to the southwest. The population of Vicksburg had skyrocketed during the flush times, from several hundred residents to, by 1835, some two thousand. Despite the Panic of 1837, the port grew by another 50 percent between 1835 and 1840, to more than three thousand. But amid continued economic struggles in the wake of the painfully slow recovery from the depression, the city council sought out investors in their corporation to finance such projects as the installation of a sewer system and the macadamization of the streets. It therefore dispatched the city financier to Baltimore in 1840 for the purpose of selling city bonds – a first for Vicksburg but routine in other urban areas such as New Orleans – as a means of raising more immediate funds. In August, the agent secured a deal. In exchange for $50,000 in municipal bonds (fifty bonds at $1,000 each) that paid 6 percent interest, he returned to Vicksburg with $45,000 in bank notes and time checks ready for use. Of that tally, Vicksburg's agent had returned from the East with $9,000 in paper promises issued by the Commercial Bank of Millington. Less than two months later, the "little broken swindling Bank in Maryland" had folded. Our "agent appears to have fallen into the hands of sharpers," decried chagrined Vicksburg newspaper editor James Hagan. No doubt, he fumed, the "swindling managers" of the Millington Bank, having hoodwinked their victims, now "laugh at their dupes." Desperate to avoid absorbing such a crippling financial blow, the town of Vicksburg proclaimed a plan of debt repudiation in December 1840, through which it absolved itself of all responsibility for payment on the municipal bonds it had exchanged for the fraudulent Millington money.[12]

In addition to holders of Vicksburg bonds, unsuspecting victims caught holding worthless Millington notes kept court dockets full in the 1840s, particularly in the vicinity of Baltimore. Individuals paid in Millington paper either before the bank crashed or before they knew the bank had crashed pursued recompense in legitimate currencies before the law. Court actions over valid payments dogged not only city merchants but also the slave traders who scoured the Chesapeake in search of bodies to purchase, transport, and resell at higher prices in the Southwest. After the failure of the Commercial Bank of Millington, some of William H. Williams' customers thought it no mere coincidence that, in late September and early October 1840, Williams and the agents he deployed were spreading Millington bank notes profusely throughout Maryland, Virginia, and the District of Columbia.[13]

On October 8, William H. Williams crossed the Potomac to visit Matthias Snyder, Jr., a gold, silver, and bank note broker on Fairfax Street in Alexandria. For months, Williams had been carrying around "a considerable amount" of Millington bank notes to spend on slaves, but now, late in the day, he hoped "to exchange some Millington money for Virginia [money]." As Williams explained it, he "had made some purchases in Alexandria, & he was surprized [sic] to find that people preferred Virginia paper," even though the Millington notes qualified as

"Baltimore funds," redeemable nearby at the Chesapeake Bank of Baltimore. Matthias Snyder's brother John, then minding the exchange office, refused to do business with Williams because "it was after Bank hours." The slave trader departed but returned the following day, on October 9, still laden with Millington bank notes. Again, Williams "proposed to exchange some of the Millington money for Virginia Bank money," the trader reiterating the point that, although the Millington notes "were perfectly good and current ... he had contracted certain debts in Alexandria, where Virginia money was preferred." This was Matthias Snyder's lucky day, Williams further elaborated, because "the Millington Bank paper, was really better than Virginia money, and that it was redeemable at and would be redeemed by the Chesapeake Bank of Baltimore." Aware that "Baltimore funds were then worth a premium over Virginia" and thinking they would yield him a tidy profit, Matthias Snyder made the deal and accepted $680 worth of Millington money at par, giving Williams in exchange $680 in Virginia currency, "including a small draft on North Carolina."[14]

Williams also ventured to another exchange office in Alexandria, run by John Corse, but was rebuffed in his attempt "to pass off Millington Bank paper." Corse may have heard disconcerting intelligence about the institution that Snyder had not, or perhaps his suspicions were raised when Williams presented him a formidable stack of bills, with a face value of some $500 or $600, all of them Millington paper with the exception of a "$100 note of a Baltimore bank" conspicuously placed on top, as if to disguise the dying bills underneath. Whatever the reason, Corse "replied he would have nothing to do with Millington notes, and refused to Exchange."[15]

Snyder, meanwhile, immediately forwarded his newly acquired Millington notes by train to J. I. Cohen, Jr., & Brothers of Baltimore to be credited to his account at the Cohen Bank, as he had done many times in the past. Apparently anticipating the bursting of the Millington bubble, Messrs. Cohen rejected the paper and returned the notes. "We have always looked on the Millington Bank as a doubtful Concern," wrote one correspondent from Baltimore on October 10, "an[d] have never purchased its Notes; there is now no sale for it here and although we have not *actually heard* of its failure, we are satisfied that either [it] has blown up or will very shortly do so. Do not touch the note at any time." Based on this information, one day after Snyder swapped bank notes with Williams, exchange merchants in Alexandria heeded the warning and joined their counterparts in Baltimore in considering Millington money no good. Within a matter of days, the Millington Bank did, in fact, fail, rendering its notes definitively valueless. By then, Williams had already departed Washington, D.C., for Alexandria and set off on his coastwise slaving voyage with twenty-six convict bondpeople to the Southwest, ultimately not returning from New Orleans until 1842. Upon Williams' much-delayed homecoming, Snyder confronted the slave trader, "tendered him the $680 of Millington Bank paper" that he had been holding for two years, "and demanded current money" in exchange. Williams did make such a currency swap with a man named Richards, to whom he had paid $620 in Millington money on October 1, 1840, but on this occasion, Williams "obstinately refused" to deal. Snyder filed suit against him in Alexandria County Circuit Court, seeking to recover damages in the amount of exactly $680.[16]

In the case of *Matthias Snyder, Jr. v. William H. Williams*, argued in early October 1842, Snyder posited that the Commercial Bank of Millington had been unlawful and fraudulent from its inception. Although he could not identify William or F. A. Weed as the masterminds behind the scheme, rumor had it that "certain persons" had "made an arrangement with the Chesapeake Bank of Baltimore" to "redeem a portion of the notes" that the Millington Bank began to print, lending the institution the air of legitimacy. But it was all a fraud. Snyder maintained that the bank had never complied with the terms of its charter from the Maryland legislature, investing into the institution only a minute fraction of the capital procured, and therefore was not "entitle[d] to the privileges granted" by the state. As Snyder related the story, the whole concern was nothing more than an elaborate ruse to deceive the public, involving the Weed brothers and William H. Williams. Snyder alleged a close connection between Williams and the Millington Bank, based on a letter Snyder claimed to have seen, sent from Williams to an unidentified person, probably one of his slave-trading agents in the field. Banks lent slave traders the notes that dealers used to purchase the chattel they later resold. According to Snyder, Williams had deposited "a large amount of

... Millington Bank notes" in the hands of his unnamed accomplice – possibly Thomas N. Davis – and other agents, with instructions either to exchange them for better paper or to "use the same as rapidly as possible" in Maryland or Virginia. Meanwhile, Williams made his own transaction with Snyder, at which time, Snyder claimed, "the Chesapeake Bank of Baltimore had [already] ceased to redeem" Millington paper. Such were the incriminating actions of someone aware of the bank's financially precarious position. Snyder further charged that, in the letter Williams had written, the slave dealer had admitted, "in substance," his ties to the beleaguered bank, acknowledged its "fraudulent" character, and confessed that "robbing the public through it was the most unfortunate act of his life." Believing Williams "cognizant" of the bank's impending collapse at the time of their transaction, he expected the court to order Williams to fork over recompense.[17]

Missing court records prevent us from learning the outcome of Snyder's suit, but if two similar cases are any indication, Williams would have been legally obligated to pay in good bills. On October 9, 1840, the very same day that Williams entered Snyder's exchange office a second time, his younger brother Thomas was more than thirty miles up the Potomac River from Washington, D.C., in the Loudoun County, Virginia, village of Leesburg. There, in a spacious upstairs room at Sinclair's Tavern, Thomas Williams, acting as his brother's agent, purchased from William H. Cassedy an enslaved man named John, a "stout made" but diminutive twenty-year-old, less than five feet tall, with "a slight impediment in his speech." Thomas Williams paid the seller $600, all in Millington money his elder brother had given him. Cassedy wrote out the bill of sale not to Thomas but to the "better known" and more established William H. Williams, perhaps at Thomas' recommendation as a means of encouraging confidence in the sale. Cassedy "replied it made no difference ... he was in a hurry," and completed the transaction. After the sale, Cassedy showed an acquaintance named Denham the "bundle of notes, which he had just received." Upon realizing that it was Millington money, Denham counseled Cassedy to return the paper to Williams "& get Virginia money for them." Already rumors must have spread to at least some Chesapeake residents of the Millington Bank's instability. Acting on the advice, Cassedy sought out Williams at the jail where John had been imprisoned while awaiting sale, but neither trader nor bondman could be found there. Cassedy returned to the tavern clutching the same wad of bills he had before. He never saw Thomas Williams again, for the slave trader had hastily departed with John in tow, destined either for William H. Williams' private jail in Washington, D.C., or for Alexandria, where the brig *Uncas*, fitted out for the coastwise domestic slave trade, awaited, ready to convey the Williams brothers' latest human cargo – including twenty-six enslaved convicts – to the Deep South. But John effected his escape while still in Virginia, "at the junction of the Fredericksburg and Louisa railroad." When master Nathaniel Boush guided the *Uncas* downriver from Alexandria toward the Chesapeake Bay on October 10, the elusive John did not count among the captives on board. Ultimately, though, absconding only postponed the horrible fate he had tried heroically to avoid. John was eventually apprehended in Maryland, jailed, and retrieved by either William H. Williams' lawyer or his jailer, Ebenezer Rodbird. Another slave trader – Thomas Williams could not remember if it was Hope Hull Slatter or George Kephart – carried John to the New Orleans slave market for auction to the highest bidder.[18]

The public cared little about what happened to John, but according to the *Alexandria Gazette*, his sale nevertheless "awakened the liveliest interest in the community." The reason was the payment made in Millington notes. When the Millington Bank explosion just days after the sale left the bills "utterly worthless," William H. Cassedy knew he needed to sue. He filed a complaint with the justice of the peace on December 16 but needed to wait for William H. Williams, whose name was on the bill of sale, to return from his lengthy detention in New Orleans. Soon after he did, Cassedy took the slave trader to the District of Columbia Circuit Court. He hired an attorney named Joseph H. Bradley, the same lawyer who had recently helped free James Ash from the confines of the Yellow House. Up against a familiar adversary in William H. Williams, Bradley contended, first, "that the [Millington Bank] originated in the grossest fraud," and, second, "that [Williams] had good reason to know of the insolvency of the institution at the time of the payment."[19]

Among those summoned to testify was well-known Washington, D.C. slave trader James H. Birch. Birch had been in Leesburg the day Thomas

Williams purchased John; in fact, Birch himself had offered Cassedy a maximum of $500 for his "negro boy." Cassedy declined the offer, insisting that his bondman was worth $600, the precise sum the younger Williams later paid. Particularly damaging to Williams was the testimony of James Lowndes, an officer of the Chesapeake Bank of Baltimore since 1838, the year the Millington first launched operations. Lowndes recounted that William Weed deposited specie at the Chesapeake Bank to permit the redemption there of Millington paper, but the Millington's struggles to maintain sufficient funds were ongoing. The Chesapeake Bank vowed "not [to] redeem" Millington money "beyond the amount of funds left in their hands for that purpose," so it "repeatedly refused to redeem the said notes" whenever the supply of specie to cover them dried up. The bank made this policy clear to "all . . . persons who made enquiry on the subject" and cautioned Baltimore banks, brokers, and merchants to accept Millington notes "on deposit or in their business . . . at their own risk." By early October 1840, Lowndes explained, Millington money merited no "standing or credit in Baltimore." Public confidence in Millington currency withered, and anxious holders of the institution's notes inundated the Chesapeake Bank. Over several days, Lowndes testified, the "great demand for the redemption of said notes" exceeded "$1,000 a day." The Chesapeake Bank soon ceased redemption of Millington notes altogether. Lowndes dated that decision to October 6, although several other sources placed it on the tenth, which seems more likely. The Baltimore bank closed the Millington's account, gathered up more than $100 in Millington notes, "sealed [them] up in an envelope," and returned them to William Weed. Based largely on this narrative of the Millington Bank's tortured path to insolvency, Cassedy claimed damages in the amount of the original $600 purchase price for John, plus interest, from the October 9 date of sale.[20]

William H. Williams' defense pivoted on the health of Millington money at the time of John's purchase. As the *Alexandria Gazette* reported, Millington notes "circulated as current money for several days" after October 9, and correspondence elicited from the Chesapeake Bank's cashier confirmed that Millington notes were not completely "discredited" or "uncurrent" until after October 12. In court, landlord James Sinclair acknowledged that Thomas Williams had "paid . . . his tavern bill in Millington money," and Sinclair "immediately passed it away" in another transaction without any fuss. An officer at the Leesburg Bank had assured him prior to October 9 that his institution was pleased to receive Millington notes. Upon arriving in the Chesapeake from Alabama in 1840, Thomas Williams exchanged his Alabama notes with his brother for Millington paper, "at 12 ½ per cent in favor of the Millington money," receiving 87½ cents for every Alabama dollar he possessed. William H. Williams' attorneys also introduced a parade of witnesses who had happily accepted Millington notes until they read of the bank's failure in the newspapers. Washington, D.C. merchant Peter F. Bacon, John Little, "beef butcher in the Washington Market," and fellow butchers Philip Otterback and John T. Wright all granted Millington money "the same confidence" as that from any other bank and even "preferred it to Virginia notes." In fact, John Little testified, Millington notes were worth a premium in exchanges for Virginia paper, which was discounted in the nation's capital. Of the Millington's bills, Little said, he had "never heard any one refuse them." That businesses and professionals in the District of Columbia held Millington money in such high esteem lent legitimacy to Thomas Williams' purchase of John. "I paid the money to . . . Cassedy *bona fide*, believing it to be good money," Williams insisted. "I had no knowledge that it had been dishonored or would be dishonored." His brother's lawyers argued the same: since William H. Williams "was ignorant of the condition of the bank," Cassedy had been paid "in good faith."[21]

The validity of Millington notes at the time of sale marked one issue debated in court; who officially owned the bondman John as a consequence of the transaction was another. Cassedy filed the lawsuit against William H. Williams because he had written out the bill of sale to him rather than to Thomas. According to witness and exchange office proprietor Alexander Lee, Thomas Williams and Ebenezer Rodbird each acted as agents for William H. Williams in the acquisition of Chesapeake-area bondpeople, and "the business was *all* carried out" in William's name. Lee was "certain" that Williams had informed him as recently as August or September 1840 that Thomas "was purchasing negroes for him." William H. Williams deposited money with Lee, his partner in the exchange office, whenever the slave dealer was absent so that Lee might "pay demands against him for [the] purchase of negroes & other matters." Lee saw Thomas Williams "frequently at my office on his brother[']s business" and "changed money for him. He has come to me repeatedly & got money from me which had been left by his brother . . . to pay for negroes purchased by him." Thomas "never brought any written order"; Lee automatically "dealt with" Thomas as his brother's agent. Slave pen jailer Rodbird shared Lee's understanding of the economic relationship between the Williams siblings. After John absconded, Rodbird explained, Thomas Williams wrote him a letter asking him to place a runaway advertisement in the newspaper, but William H. Williams appended his name to the ad and offered the fifty-dollar reward for his apprehension. Moreover, Thomas "charged William H. Williams with the costs of the arrest of the negro boy . . . without any previous authority" from his brother.[22]

For his part, Thomas Williams claimed to operate as an independent slave trader. Whether this was a statement of fact, the product of a genuine misunderstanding with William H. Williams, or an attempt to confuse the prosecution's case against his brother is not entirely clear, although the ill-defined business relationship between the Williams siblings had already surfaced in 1839 during slaveholder William Gray's attempt to recover the anticipated sale price of $600 for his bondman Oliver. A pattern seemed to emerge whereby the Williams brothers labored to capitalize in the courts from their ambiguous working arrangement. Thomas acknowledged that he had indeed worked as his brother's agent before he "came of age . . . and came to his Estate in the latter part of 1839." Since the spring of 1840, however, he insisted that he had "dealt solely on his own account" and not on behalf of his elder sibling. Thomas Williams believed that, at the time of John's purchase, the only agent purchasing slaves for William H. Williams was Ebenezer Rodbird, who was engaged in manning the jail in early October 1840. Thomas Williams openly admitted to giving Millington money for John, but contended that "he had made the purchase for himself," not for his brother. "I made the contract on my own account & risk," he declared on cross-examination. "My brother did not authorize me to do this, nor did he know that I had put his name to it . . . The proceeds of the sale . . . were received by me for my own use." In fact, Thomas added, as if to underscore his independence, William H. Williams "owed him money" in mid-October 1840, and still did.[23]

The judge's instructions to the jury members stated that if Thomas purchased John with his own money for his own benefit, they were obligated to acquit William H. Williams. If, however, Thomas bought the slave as his brother's agent, and the slave dealers "*knew* or had *good reason* to believe" on the date of the transaction that the Millington Bank "was in failing circumstances," the jury should find in Cassedy's favor. Jurors did not believe that the Millington notes exchanged hands in good faith, and on April 29, 1843, sided with the plaintiff against Williams, in the amount of $575 plus interest from October 9, 1840. Williams' attorneys filed a motion on May 18 to arrest judgment on a number of grounds, including their doubts that the $600 in Millington money Cassedy had produced in court were the same notes Thomas Williams had paid to purchase John from him. Thomas stated in court that he "did not identify the notes" and "put no mark on them so as to identify them." Thus, Williams' lawyers implied that Cassedy was exploiting their client to salvage some value from his dead bills. The court overruled the motion.[24]

Williams lost the last of the three Millington money lawsuits against him as well. On September 25, 1840, his agent Ebenezer Rodbird was in Calvert County, Maryland, buying bondpeople in the Western Shore village of Prince Frederick. Rodbird offered George Wilkinson, the postmaster in nearby Huntingtown, $600 in Millington notes for "a negro man" named Frisby. Wilkinson preferred Maryland notes to those of Virginia, but perhaps because he had already heard disquieting rumors about the health of the Millington Bank, he "objected" to Rodbird's paper. Williams' agent "had no other kind of money with him," however. Uncertain whether to proceed with the transaction, Wilkinson informally consulted Augustus R. Sollers, an attorney who happened to witness the ongoing negotiations, about the wisdom of accepting Millington money. At the time, Sollers had no reason to doubt the soundness of the notes and encouraged Wilkinson to complete the sale. To ease Wilkinson's anxiety, the lawyer proposed that the seller soon go to Baltimore to redeem the Millington notes and, if he discovered that they were "not good," return them to Rodbird for different paper. Rodbird assented, commenting, as another bystander recalled, that "if the money was not good, he would make it good." The observer, Alexander Buckmaster, interjected that Rodbird's employer, William H. Williams, "was a wealthy and an honest man" who would give Wilkinson "other money" if necessary. "[Y]es," Rodbird replied. "[H]e certainly would." Reassured that he would be supplied "other funds" if the Millington money was not "passable" in Baltimore, Wilkinson accepted Rodbird's notes in exchange for Frisby and pledged to see the jailer in Washington the following Monday to deliver the bondman's clothes.[25]

When Wilkinson forwarded the Millington paper to Baltimore, his agent found that he could not deposit it because, by that time, the city was rife with rumors that the Millington Bank had already closed. Bankers in Baltimore recommended that Wilkinson contact Williams immediately to work out a solution to his dilemma. Unable to travel to Washington, D.C., in person as he had planned, Wilkinson penned a letter to Williams on October 18 in which he appealed to the slave trader as "a man of Honor" to give him "no dif[f]iculty" and quickly "see matters settled with other passable funds." Utilizing no shortage of flattery, Wilkinson wrote, "I feel confident from reports of your carracter [sic] and standing you will relieve me without further trouble and expense." The Huntingtown postmaster neglected to mail his missive until October 26, and it arrived at Williams' slave pen three days later.[26]

Williams had departed Washington, D.C., almost three weeks earlier and had, by October 29, almost reached Mobile, so Ebenezer Rodbird, left in charge of the slave pen, took the liberty of opening and reading the letter from Wilkinson. The jailer pondered leaving the response to Williams, but he did not anticipate his employer's return to the capital for several months, in either January or February 1841. Upon further reflection, Rodbird decided to send a prompt reply. In a letter dated October 30, he adopted a defensive posture. He pointed out to Wilkinson that "the bank was not known to have failed in the City of Baltimore up to the 12th of Oct[obe]r," some two and one-half weeks after the sale. He also explained to Wilkinson that, if the postmaster had come to Washington the Monday after the sale – "as you promised" – "you then might of [sic] got from W[illia]ms any other money you wanted." Williams had left Rodbird with "money other than Millington," including ample Virginia notes, had Wilkinson been willing to accept those. "[T]herefore," Rodbird concluded, "I think you wont [*sic*] hold me responsible for any moral obligation that I might of [*sic*] given you at the time of our traiding [*sic*]." In a weak attempt at offering some consolation, the jailer added, "you are not the only one caught with Millington money." Beyond this, Rodbird pledged to "say no more" until Williams' return.[27]

Williams arrived in Washington, D.C., sometime in the latter part of 1842. Wilkinson offered to return the Millington notes to the slave trader, but he refused. Getting no satisfaction, Wilkinson went to the Circuit Court of the District of Columbia in November. The case then disappeared from the dockets for the next seven years, until 1849, by which time George had died and his widow, Priscilla, as executrix of his estate, sued Williams to recover the $600 worth of Millington notes given her husband nine years before, $530 of which her attorney produced in court. Priscilla Wilkinson alleged that William H. Williams served as "an agent" of the Millington Bank "in getting its notes into circulation." The payment to her deceased husband, she charged, was part of an effort "to injure and defraud" him, another victim of the grand Millington swindle.[28]

At trial, the attorneys in *Wilkinson v. Williams* debated what constituted fraud. Priscilla Wilkinson's counsel, John Marbury, the same attorney who had represented William H. Williams nearly a decade earlier in the case against the free black James Ash, cited several court cases in which plaintiffs sued if the notes involved in a transaction turned out to be worthless, as if no money had changed hands at all. "Fraud," countered Williams' attorneys, "consists in intention." The instructions to the jury stated that Williams must be found guilty if he had foreknowledge of the impending Millington collapse and that his agent, Rodbird, gave the money "for the purpose of deceiving and defrauding the public," assuming that George Wilkinson had made an effort, "within a reasonable time," to notify Williams that the notes were bad and had "returned ... or offered to return them." The jury found in favor of Priscilla Wilkinson, but not for the full $600 in Millington money her husband had accepted in 1840; rather, the jury awarded her $530 – the precise amount of obsolete bills Marbury had presented in court – plus interest from the date of sale. According to the ruling, "Where bank notes are taken in payment of goods sold with the understanding that they are to be returned if not current, the seller cannot sue for the price without returning the notes." There was one exception, however. If "the buyer knew the notes were worthless when he made the bargain," the seller need not return them. Since the jury granted Priscilla Wilkinson an award of only the $530, its members must not have believed that Williams consciously committed fraud. Williams' attorneys filed a motion for a new trial but were overruled. For at least a second and probably a third time, Williams' and his agents' use of Millington money in 1840 came back to lighten the slave dealer's pocketbook. But finally, after nine years, Williams could put the Millington fiasco behind him.[29]

Prior to the Millington's demise, William H. Williams conspired with William Weed to hatch another concerted and even more aggressive plot to rescue the ailing Commercial Bank of Millington by attracting a massive influx of capital into the institution. At an unspecified date in the fall of 1840, before the Millington's failure, Williams rendezvoused with fellow slave trader Thomas N. Davis at the railroad depot in Washington, D.C., and persuaded him to meet with "two gentlemen . . . who would propose a . . . scheme" through which Davis "might make a large sum of money." Intrigued, Davis consented to the proposed meeting between the four. Williams and the mysterious "two gentlemen" – Millington bank investor William Weed and co-conspirator Joseph T. Guthrie – pressed Davis to accept $100,000 in Millington notes so that he might dump them, at a discount, into circulation in Washington, D.C., in exchange for other, more valid funds. Even though the other bills would command a premium over Millington paper, Davis would be disposing of increasingly suspect Millington notes in favor of more sound currency that he could then forward to the Eastern Shore to keep the Millington afloat. Reports of this last-ditch effort to save the Millington confirmed that William H. Williams most assuredly knew that the bills he and his agents, Thomas Williams and Ebenezer Rodbird, were using to purchase slaves in the fall of 1840 had been issued by a bank teetering on the brink.[30]

Ultimately, Davis "declined the . . . proposition" because his own growing suspicions of Millington paper made it seem too risky. Slave traders engaged in a sordid commerce, but they were also savvy, calculating businessmen. Although often portrayed as dealing in slaves only temporarily, until they could amass the wealth to purchase a plantation or invest in other ventures, professional slave traders bought and sold enslaved people as they engaged concurrently in a range of other economic pursuits. Some owned a stake in general stores or were merchants in various commercial enterprises. Throughout a good portion of his decades-long career as an active trader, William H. Williams partnered with George M. Grant to sell boots and shoes at 18 Camp Street in New Orleans. Slave dealers willingly backed any number of concerns, but it made sense for Williams and Davis to gravitate toward banking institutions that not only promised to generate revenue but also financed the slave trade itself. Nevertheless, traders' drive for profit and shrewd cost–benefit analyses superseded any loyalty to financiers whose schemes might jeopardize their bottom line. Davis' unwillingness to participate in the latest machinations of William Weed and Joseph T. Guthrie gave Williams pause as well. Suddenly anxious over the proposal, he lost his enthusiasm for the arrangement and likewise withdrew.[31]

Although Williams and Davis terminated their flirtation with the proposition, William Weed and Joseph T. Guthrie, undeterred, forged ahead with their plan to salvage the Commercial Bank of Millington. Paradoxically, the plot they concocted hinged on launching a new bank, the Farmers and Millers Bank of Hagerstown, Maryland. Located about seventy-five miles northwest of Baltimore, Hagerstown in 1840 was a rural outpost of only a few thousand souls. Maryland's country folk had been clamoring for easier access to credit for years, so despite – and in fact, because of – Hagerstown's small size and relatively remote location, the Maryland legislature had incorporated the Farmers and Millers Bank in 1836 to appease lawmakers' rural constituents. The charter mandated the possession of $75,000 in specie, through any combination of gold and silver coin, before the bank could lawfully issue notes or commence operations. William Weed and Joseph T. Guthrie made it their mission to secure the necessary funds, for those monies were crucial to their plans. The pair calculated that they could raise sufficient resources to launch the Hagerstown enterprise and then, given Weed's connections to both institutions, divert a portion of the funds intended to capitalize the new institution for the purpose of propping up the struggling Commercial Bank of Millington.[32]

Slave traders William H. Williams and Thomas N. Davis had rebuffed Weed and Guthrie's pleas to underwrite the Farmers and Millers Bank of Hagerstown and thereby indirectly funnel money into the Millington, but the determined entrepreneurs persevered. Both had a stake in the plan's success. Whereas Weed wanted the Millington Bank to survive, Guthrie was a significant shareholder in the Hagerstown concern. To fund the enterprise, Weed redirected funds that Williams and Davis had previously supplied the Millington to the embryonic Hagerstown venture, without either slave dealer's permission. But Weed's great coup came in securing for the Farmers and Millers Bank two specie certificates totaling $60,000, including one drawn on the Commercial Bank of Millington, to count toward the $75,000 specie requirement. "The Millington Bank at that time was in as good credit as any of the county banks in the State," boasted the *Baltimore Sun*, "their paper being at a discount of only ½ per cent in Philadelphia." In reality, as Weed surely knew, these were phantom funds. Specie certificates stated a bank's willingness to supply the quantity of gold or silver indicated on the paper; they did not guarantee the bank was in actual possession of that specie. And the Millington was not. Nevertheless, banks routinely counted money that was only pledged on paper and not physically present in the vault. In August 1840, the Treasurer of the Western Shore of Maryland dispatched a committee of three commissioners to certify the Farmers and Millers Bank's specie reserves. After consulting the advice of legal counsel, the investigators, satisfied that the specie requirement had been met, handed over the requisite certificate for the bank to go into operation. Counting monetary promises that existed only on paper, the Farmers and Millers Bank opened its doors on September 10, 1840. When the Millington failed a little more than a month later, its specie certificate had already served its function, as qualified assets for the Hagerstown wildcat, and been cast, according to one chronicler, into the metaphorical waste basket. With the Millington's demise, William Weed promptly carried the institution's furniture, locks, and other portable assets to Hagerstown for use in the new facility. Although the bank president in Hagerstown denied "any official connection whatever" between the two establishments, truly the Farmers and Millers Bank was the specious "offspring" of the defunct Millington Bank.[33]

The Millington's spawn institution in Hagerstown fell into crisis soon after its September opening. The Commercial Bank of Millington's failure the next month caused, as the *Baltimore Sun* reported, "wide spread ruin and distress," and the Farmers and Millers Bank could not escape the deleterious effects of its mother's death. Facing financial ruin, Hagerstown bank co-founder, stockholder, and cashier Joseph T. Guthrie consulted Thomas N. Davis. He informed the slave dealer in the spring of 1841 that the Farmers and Millers Bank had, in its first weeks of operation, been "doing well, but when the Millington Bank... failed, the money came in on them very rapidly." It weathered the immediate storm, and by the time he spoke with Davis in 1841, Guthrie insisted that "the prospect was good." Nevertheless, the shifty Guthrie, now absent his absconded partner, William Weed, devised a familiar strategy to relieve the Hagerstown bank from any similar fiscal misery in the future: he aimed to get another bank chartered and operational as quickly as possible. His particular focus was the salt manufacturing center of Kanawha, Virginia (now West Virginia). The "object" of establishing a bank there, Guthrie admitted, "was to keep the Farmers and Millers Bank good." He could certainly marshal funds from the Hagerstown bank to get the Kanawha venture "rightly under way," but he also required "some little specie" for launch. Guthrie confided to Davis that, behind the scenes, the proposed Kanawha concern "*could be broke*," but that was immaterial because "it was *away from home*," more than two hundred miles from his base of operations in Hagerstown.[34]

Guthrie solicited Davis' assistance with his scheme, encouraging him "merely to make exchanges," such that Farmers and Millers Bank notes should not be redeemed "at once or at least for a few days." Float "our notes in Philadelphia and Baltimore," he urged Davis. That would allow the Hagerstown institution "to raise our circulation and credit," because "all the [good] money we can raise together" would fund a "new issue" of Farmers and Millers currency. Davis would take the good notes he received and give them to Guthrie, who, in turn, would use them as collateral to get bank loans to underwrite the Hagerstown enterprise.

In short, Guthrie's plan was to run a bank with borrowed money. To start this process, he gave Davis $1,000 in Farmers and Millers Bank notes to place in circulation.[35]

It was no accident that Guthrie intimated the latest ploy he had formulated to Thomas N. Davis. Both belonged to a mesmerizing kaleidoscope of unscrupulous shysters who prowled the Chesapeake for monetary gain, and just as slave traders relied on bankers to finance the slave trade, bankers sometimes relied on slave traders to finance banking institutions. Guthrie would probably have consulted William H. Williams again as well, but the proprietor of the Yellow House was still in Louisiana, and in the latter half of 1841 was imprisoned in the Orleans Parish jail for illegally importing twenty-six enslaved convicts from Virginia into Louisiana.

CHAPTER 7

State v. Williams

A N ANONYMOUS "FRIEND" OF WILLIAM H. WILLIAMS, quite possibly his purchasing agent Rudolph Littlejohn, informed the New Orleans *Daily Picayune* "that all necessary forms of law in the transportation of the [convict] slaves have been attended to" and that Williams alone, "having taken upon himself all the responsibilities of Littlejohn, ... is now on his way carrying the negroes out of the country." By the time the story appeared in print on November 3, 1840, however, the transport slaves had already been arrested in New Orleans, and William H. Williams faced a court date in the not-too-distant future. After parting ways with Williams in Mobile, Rudolph Littlejohn disappeared from the historical record, with one exception. He surfaced once more, in late November. From the slaving port of Baltimore, Maryland, he penned a letter to Governor Thomas Walker Gilmer of Virginia complaining of the "great State of Excitement" occasioned by his arrival in Alabama, thanks to Secretary William H. Richardson's letter "that appeared in the public prints," warning the people of Mobile "that I would sell or attempt to do so those negroes I purchased from the State of V[irgini]a." An obviously perturbed, if not outraged, Rudolph Littlejohn explained to the executive that that "falsehood ... injured me verry [*sic*] much" – although whether in reputation, pocketbook, or both he did not make clear – and pressed Gilmer to surrender the name of his informant so that Littlejohn might "make things right." Before closing his missive, Littlejohn assured the Virginia executive – in language virtually identical to that of Williams' "friend" who wrote the *Picayune* – "that all ne[ce]ssary forms of law have been strictly attended to as was anticipated when I purchased the slaves" out of the penitentiary. "[B]y this time," the agent concluded, "they are in Texas." Either Littlejohn was not apprised of the enslaved felons' arrest, which is difficult to fathom if he ever read a newspaper, or he lied directly to the governor.[1]

Gilmer next received a letter from a concerned Wheelock S. Upton, the attorney whom William H. Williams consulted soon upon his arrival in New Orleans with the convict bondpeople. Early in December 1840, Upton explained to Gilmer and Richardson that "proceedings have been instituted against William H. Williams by the authorities of Louisiana, in the Criminal Court of New Orleans, and the slaves taken from his possession, and imprisoned." Upton sincerely believed that Williams intended "to comply with the conditions of his bond" with Virginia to convey the enslaved felons out of the United States. "He designed to transport the slaves to Texas," the lawyer explained, and passage through New Orleans "appeared to him to be the safest, cheapest and most expeditious route." Louisiana officials' "interference," however, impeded Williams' progress. They not only subjected Williams "to very heavy and grievous expenses," but also prevented him from complying "with the conditions of his bond to your Commonwealth," "as he, in all honesty and good faith intended."[2]

In addition to stressing Williams' desire to fulfill his agreement with Virginia, Upton also inquired about "the precise object of the communication . . . to Messrs Addison & Co." that warned of the slave trader's possible arrival with the enslaved transports in New Orleans. William H. Williams persuaded himself that the letter "was written solely with the intention of putting the authorities here upon the alert, to detect, prevent and punish any violation of their laws by him," should he actually commit an infraction. Williams could understand and accept that interpretation of the missive, for it merely sought the enforcement of Virginia law. "The authorities at Mobile adopted this construction" of the letter addressed to them, Upton indicated. As a result, in Mobile, Williams "was not . . . disturbed or impeded in his progress." He passed on by, steaming into Lake Pontchartrain, and, from there, riding the rails into New Orleans. In making this argument, Upton overlooked or studiously ignored the fact that the importation of convict slaves was not illegal in Alabama. In contrast, authorities in the Crescent City seemed to construe the Virginia letter "in quite a different light," Upton noted, as "an *official accusation* . . . of an intended infringement of the laws of Louisiana, not as a *notification* that such intention *might* exist." Louisiana's prosecution of Williams marked the unjust persecution of the trader, Upton maintained, "because ... no violation has ever been intended by him for one moment," and the commonwealth of Virginia possessed no evidence of any ill intent. He concluded his letter with an urgent plea that Gilmer and Richardson promptly correct New Orleans officials' "misapprehension of the nature and purpose" of the commonwealth's prior correspondence. Justice demanded a prompt reply, for the date of Williams' first hearing rapidly approached.[3]

As the commonwealth's secretary, William H. Richardson replied to Wheelock Upton on the Virginia governor's behalf. Richardson clarified that the letter had been sent "to prevent the sale of convict slaves from this state in any of the other states, and to detect the parties to the bond given for their transportation out of the United States," should they not fulfill their obligation. Richardson confirmed slave trader William H. Williams' understanding of the correspondence: "No charge is made against those parties" transporting the convict slaves, Richardson concurred. The letter to Messrs. Addison & Co. merely alerted the recipient of intelligence that Governor Gilmer had received about the possibility of their unlawful sale.[4]

Armed with this information, William H. Williams awaited his day before Judge John François Canonge and the Criminal Court of the First District of New Orleans. The sole judge presiding over that court, Canonge grew up in the French port of Marseille but was living in the Caribbean colony of Saint-Domingue when the violent slave revolt that ultimately produced the independent black republic of Haiti forced him to flee to safety in Cuba. Discovered there plotting to wrest the island from Spain and hand it over to Napoleon, Canonge took flight again, seeking refuge with his brothers in Philadelphia. He found his calling in the law and, as he embarked upon his legal career, gravitated toward New Orleans, where familiar French influences and culture remained strong. Canonge's linguistic dexterity made him useful as clerk in the Louisiana House of Representatives, recording conversations in English, French, or a combination thereof. His accomplishments as a noted linguist, orator, and attorney earned him the notice of Governor André B. Roman, who appointed him judge of the Criminal Court that would eventually hear William H. Williams' case. As a later court would observe, the suit against the slave trader "has in it some very peculiar features": one state's law expelled enslaved criminals, and another's prevented them entry.[5]

After a postponement of some weeks, movement in Williams' case began in February 1841. A grand jury impaneled from residents of Plaquemines, Jefferson, and Orleans parishes convened on February 17 and presented a true bill of indictment against Williams, charging him with knowingly "Importing and Bringing Criminal slaves into the State" in violation of the Louisiana law of 1817. The true bill identified a total of only twenty-four enslaved convicts, two fewer than the number Williams conveyed via the railcars into New Orleans. The bondmen Albert and Stephen, both arrested by the day police on November 1, disappeared from the roster of enslaved criminals confiscated from the trader. Through some form of chicanery, Williams may have persuaded Louisiana authorities that the two bondmen were not subject to the 1817 statute, even though they clearly were. At his arraignment on February 27, Williams pleaded not guilty to the charges against him. As his trial commenced, already the case "excited great interest" among an enthralled New Orleans public.[6]

Christian Roselius, nominated by Louisiana governor André B. Roman for attorney general earlier in the month of Williams' arraignment, spearheaded the state's prosecution of the slave dealer. The German-born Roselius had migrated to New Orleans in 1820, at the age of seventeen. With little education or fluency in English, he found work as a printer's apprentice, and through his own self-directed efforts gained command of the language and evolved into a proficient typesetter. After only five years in Louisiana, the immigrant launched his own short-lived magazine on New Orleans' literary and artistic culture. But Roselius was simultaneously reading law and in 1828 gained admittance to the bar. He earned a reputation in the courtroom for studious preparation and in 1840 won election to the state legislature. Upon being named attorney general, however, Roselius resigned his seat in the Louisiana House to take on the first challenge of his new role: to secure a guilty verdict against William H. Williams for importing enslaved convicts into New

Orleans. The attorney general acknowledged that Williams had neither sold nor attempted to sell any of the convict bondpeople he had transported. Still, Roselius explained, when Williams imported his human cargo into Louisiana, "knowing them to have been guilty" of criminal activities in another state, he violated the statute of 1817. Any person so convicted was, by statute, subject to a $500 fine "for every slave he so brings in," plus the forfeiture of those bondpeople to the state. With the facts of the case indisputably established, Williams' guilt seemed so self-evident to the attorney general that, in a moment of hubris, he reportedly summoned "no witnesses" to testify against the defendant, although trial papers indicate that Mayor William Freret of New Orleans, Recorder of the Third Municipality George Y. Bright, and Second Municipality secretary Luc H. Seré were called by the state to testify.[7]

Williams' defense lawyer, John R. Grymes, called an arsenal of witnesses, including Captain William J. Duval of the *Roanoke*; Samuel H. Page, customs inspector at Port Pontchartrain; slave trader S. F. Slatter; and attorney Wheelock S. Upton, among others. They collectively testified to the fact that Williams never denied the criminal backgrounds of the commodified bodies he was transporting. Upton recounted Williams' frank admission of their origin and the trader's strenuous efforts to consult Mayor Freret and enlist his aid. A number of other witnesses also recalled Williams' repeated assertions that he was simply passing through Louisiana en route to Texas.[8]

Witness Seneca Bennet was well acquainted with the New Orleans slave-trading scene. A slave dealer himself, Bennet by 1838 operated a trading house at No. 18 Moreau Street in Faubourg Marigny. In January 1840, he relocated to No. 74 Esplanade, where he pledged to continue "his business of keeping and boarding Slaves that are for sale." The accommodations, he boasted, were "new, clean, and airy, and for convenience and comfort not surpassed by any establishment of the kind in the United States." As at William H. Williams' Yellow House, Bennet boarded slaves at masters' request, although at a pricier rate of 37½ cents per day, a charge Bennet nevertheless claimed took "into consideration the hardness of the times and scarcity of money." Williams' attorney would have been hard pressed to find a witness who understood his client's business any better.[9]

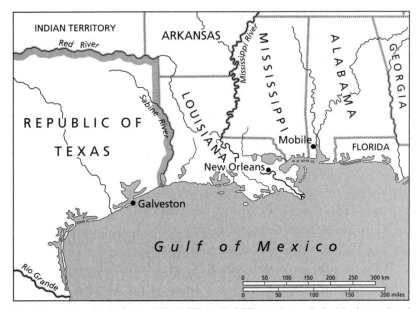

11 The northern Gulf Coast, 1840. William H. Williams first sailed with the enslaved convicts to Mobile, Alabama, before conveying them to New Orleans, allegedly while en route to Texas.

Aiding Williams' cause, Bennet confirmed that slaves bound for Texas routinely passed through New Orleans. (See Figure 11.) Traders and other slave owners forced bondpeople on to steamboats able to overcome the powerful Mississippi currents and then navigate the Red River upstream in a generally northwesterly direction. Some enslaved people, including Solomon Northup, disembarked in Louisiana's Red River Valley to work the plantations there; others were offloaded, chained in coffles, and marched by land to Texas. In the past few weeks, Bennet observed, even since Louisiana had commenced its suit against Williams, "*Mr. Slades negroes* from the *District of Columbia* had been taken by this route." In fact, Bennet thought it "the best and cheapest route for a small lot," such as the twenty-six convict bondpeople Williams was transporting. Bennet explained that he "never knew any [slaves] shipped direct from *Alexandria* or *Virginia* to *Texas*." That route would have been too long, and the port of Galveston too far removed from Texas cotton country. Slaves destined for Texas, he declared, passed through New Orleans, whether they started in the Chesapeake, in South Carolina, or even in nearby

Mobile. New Orleans merchant James W. Zacharie later concurred with the substance of Bennet's testimony. Zacharie, too, knew of slaves "transported from the Atlantic States to Texas by . . . way of New Orleans," for it was "the most direct route." As for William H. Williams specifically, he stated, "the freight of twenty six Slaves" would have been prohibitively costly to "authorize the Charter of a vessel from Alexandria to Texas." No wonder Williams originally put the enslaved convicts aboard the *Uncas* with more than forty other bondpeople not found guilty of crimes. It was smart business. The difference, of course, was that the shipments Bennet and Zacharie described did not include enslaved criminals.[10]

A major point of contention at the trial concerned Williams' intentions. What did he mean to do with the enslaved convicts he carried into New Orleans? John R. Grymes called to the stand Christian Meyers, the man who had asked Williams in Milneburg if his slaves were for sale. Williams rebuffed his offer "to purchase a negro girl," Meyers recollected, since the trader said he was taking the entire lot to Texas. Frederick Barton, a bystander who overheard the conversation between Williams and Meyers, corroborated Williams' refusal to sell. Producing not one but two witnesses who testified that Williams answered in the negative when asked to dispose of a transport slave, Grymes emphasized Williams' intent *not* to break the Louisiana law of 1817. And as Grymes pointed out in his closing, "it is . . . a settled axiom of criminal jurisprudence that the intention forms part of the crime." In contrast, Attorney General Roselius observed that, according to the indictment, intentions were immaterial. Williams indisputably escorted convicted slave felons into the state: end of story. "The indictment does not charge him with the intent of selling them to our citizens, or keeping them here," Roselius pointedly indicated in his closing argument; "there was not a single word relative to . . . intent . . . in the statute" of 1817: "intention . . . formed no part of it."[11]

Closing arguments also revealed the two attorneys' contested interpretations of how best to keep Louisiana safe. Roselius declared William H. Williams' trial one of "paramount importance" and of "vital interest to the people" of Louisiana because it involved "the well being of our citizens and the internal police laws of the State." The legislature, he explained, passed the act of 1817 precisely "to prevent the minds of our servile population from being poisoned by convicted slaves, such as Mr. Williams brought here." Internal security demanded "that the law be rigidly enforced" and Williams convicted. The slave trader's counsel, John R. Grymes, agreed that his client's case "was one of a grave, serious, and important nature," but, he observed, "If the object of the Attorney General was to prevent the State from being contaminated by those convict slaves ... then he was defeating that object." Grymes reminded the jury that the Louisiana law prohibiting the importation of enslaved convicts stated that, upon detection, such slaves would "be seized and sold, for cash, to the highest bidder," meaning that, nonsensically, the very slaves the law meant to exclude from Louisiana could end up living in the state. If jurors returned a verdict against Williams, Grymes cautioned, his criminal cargo "will be sold and remain among us." Therefore, it was incumbent upon the jury to find Williams innocent. He had "already suffered enough" anyway, prevented from leaving New Orleans for the past four months; there was no need to "forever blast and prostrate his prospects in life." Rather, Grymes implored, permit him to fulfill "the conditions of his bond" with the commonwealth of Virginia by "taking the slaves to a foreign country, to Texas." The opposing lawyers thus presented competing yet compelling arguments, both of which resonated in a slaveholding society that valued white security.[12]

The consequence was a hung jury. Four jurors favored Williams' conviction, eight his acquittal. Prior to their deliberations, Judge Canonge instructed them "to decide according to law; but with regard to the intention," for "he always thought there could be no crime but where there was an evil intention." With those conflicting considerations established, the jurors retired to consider the verdict and found themselves at loggerheads. After they spent "a considerable time" sequestered, the sheriff ordered them into court at 6:30 p.m. Jurors explained to the judge that "there was no possibility of their ever agreeing," so Canonge dissolved the jury and discharged its members. Williams was held to bail for a retrial, as his enslaved cargo continued to languish in jail.[13]

Williams' commenced his second trial less than two weeks later, on March 11, in Judge Canonge's courtroom. The state offered no new evidence against him. Attorney General Roselius continued to insist that the agreed-upon facts of the case were sufficient for conviction under the indictment. Roselius instead reminded the newly formed jury of the purpose of the law: to ensure whites' safety from rebellious slaves. Williams' acquittal, he warned, would render the law of 1817 "a dead letter, a nullity." In that event, he said, stoking jurors' fears, Williams could sell "those slaves at public auction"; some of the slaves had their masters' blood on their hands and had revolted against the white people of a sister state. Roselius added that any "notions of sympathy" toward the defendant, based on his "character and respectable standing," had no bearing on the case, and that Williams' intentions "should form no part of their deliberations." John R. Grymes continued to impress upon jurors that Williams held no evil intent in carrying his enslaved cargo into New Orleans, but he also elaborated upon the previous defense of his client. As an American citizen, he declared, Williams had the constitutional right to travel through Louisiana, and because the trader's cargo was not to be sold or kept in Louisiana, he could not be found guilty of "importing or bringing" convict slaves into the state.[14]

The major distinction between Williams' first trial and his second concerned the presiding judge's instructions to the jury. At the initial trial, Canonge allowed the jury to take Williams' intent into account. Upon further contemplation, Canonge found Roselius' arguments hostile to the consideration of intent increasingly convincing. Admitting his former position "erroneous," the judge reversed himself and ordered the new set of jurors at the second trial to reach a decision "without any regard to [Williams'] intention." The editors of the New Orleans *Picayune* expressed shock at Canonge's change of heart and criticized him for it. They characterized Canonge as "a humane and . . . upright Judge, but . . . not infallible nor above errors of judgment." What, they pondered, if he had had a similar change of heart after condemning a convicted murderer to hang? Despite Canonge's revised parameters, again the jury deadlocked. After two and one-half hours of deliberation, the foreman reported to the court "that there was not the most remote probability of their agreeing on a verdict." For a second time in as many attempts to try Williams, Canonge discharged a hung jury.[15]

After two split juries, Williams appeared before Judge Canonge and a new slate of jurors on April 30, 1841, for his third trial. At 3 p.m. the day's proceedings ended, with the court set to reconvene at 10 a.m. the next morning. On May 1, the third jury found the slave trader guilty of the charge against him. Never before had anyone been convicted for violating the Louisiana law of 1817 forbidding the importation of enslaved criminals. No new evidence had been introduced to sway the jurors, and the newspapers regularly complimented the legal acumen of Williams' defense attorney, John R. Grymes. Only the composition of the jury had changed. The seven jurors traceable in the census owned between four and fifteen slaves each, but did not clearly stand out as any different from their predecessors impaneled to hear the case. Unlike them, however, the third jury achieved consensus. Its collective wisdom maintained that upholding the law against importing convict slaves would make Louisiana safer than would letting Williams pass through the state with the criminals in tow.[16]

Within weeks, newspapers across the country – but in the northeastern antislavery press in particular – were reporting the verdict against Williams and the astronomical monetary loss he would suffer as a result. According to one lone report, the jury that found him guilty "petitioned the Governor to remit the fine which the law imposed." If true, André B. Roman paid no heed. The press calculated that the conviction would cost Williams $48,000, a tally composed of the $12,000 purchase price of the convict bondpeople taken out of the Virginia State Penitentiary, the $24,000 in bonds that Williams would have to forfeit to the commonwealth of Virginia for failing to transport the state's enslaved criminals out of the country, and the $12,000 in fines – $500 for each of the twenty-four slaves named in the indictment – due the state of Louisiana per the act of 1817. Newspapers actually underestimated the financial hit Williams stood to absorb. They not only undervalued by $500 the money he initially paid to the Virginia state auditor for the twenty-seven enslaved felons, but also undercounted by three the original number of convicts he had purchased. Recalculating to correct for those errors adds another $3,500 to the press's $48,000 estimate, for a total loss to Williams of $51,500, or about $1.43 million in 2016 dollars. This figure included neither Williams' legal fees for his "eminent counsel" nor the incalculable "trouble or anxiety" the entire affair forced him to bear. The court discharged the slave trader on his own recognizance.[17]

Immediately Grymes busied himself in preparation to move for an arrest of the judgment against Williams based on different – and more substantive – legal grounds than any issues raised during the preceding three trials. On May 5, Grymes returned to Judge Canonge's courtroom to make the filing. He observed that Williams' case was not criminal in nature at all and therefore outside the jurisdiction of the Criminal Court. The penalty Williams faced was "exclusively of a pecuniary nature," and the Criminal Court, Grymes maintained, was "incompetent to pass or render a judgment for the recovery of money." This served as "conclusive proof," he said, "that the State had proceeded erroneously in instituting criminal proceedings against his client." Williams, in short, should have been tried through civil proceedings. Unpersuaded, on May 21 Judge Canonge overruled Grymes' motion for a new trial.[18]

As his July sentencing date approached, William H. Williams cast his net wide in search of support for his cause. Writing from New Orleans, he shared his tale of woe with Virginia's recently inaugurated governor, John Rutherfoord. He explained that he had purchased the twenty-seven transport slaves in September 1840 "in full faith that the highways of all the states in the Union would be free to me to pass over ... for the purpose of complying with the obligation I had entered into with the State of Virginia." Little did he anticipate "any interruption in carrying the law of Virginia into effect," but his "reasonable expectation" had "been most cruelly disappointed." Williams recounted the deep wounds he suffered by Louisiana law: "My person has been arrested, and the slaves seized, by the authorities ... I have been prosecuted with the utmost rigor, and have been condemned to a ruinous fine of Twelve Thousand Dollars." To underscore his real source of distress, he then reiterated that the enslaved convicts had been "taken out of my possession" and "forfeited to the State of Louisiana," even though he was "peac[e]ably and [in] full faith and confidence entering the State of Louisiana with the real and true intention of conducting the slaves, by the most direct route to Texas, in compliance [*sic*] with the obligation I had entered into with Virginia."[19]

Williams supplied Rutherfoord sources documenting his misery. He enclosed a copy of the letter "emanating from the Executive Department of Virginia" – the one warning of Williams' possible arrival – that he blamed for putting him "in this most disastrous position." "[U]pon what foundation" this missive was sent, Williams complained, "I am to this day ignorant." Williams also sent a copy of a letter solicited from Christian Roselius in which the attorney general who prosecuted his case conceded that "no evidence whatever was offered that Mr. Williams either sold or attempted to sell any of those slaves in the State of Louisiana. It was proved, on the contrary, by two witnesses that when asked whether the slaves were for sale Mr. Williams answered in the negative, and said that he was going to Texas with them." The third jury nevertheless convicted the slave trader, and now, Williams explained to Rutherfoord, "I have been . . . cut off from all possible means of executing my contract with the State of Virginia."[20]

As such, Williams thought it his "duty" to communicate with the governor, the highest authority in the commonwealth, "and to invoke your interference." Williams solicited gubernatorial intervention upon his conviction that Virginia "is bound to use her exertions to protect me in the exercise of the right to use the highways of all her sister states, for the purpose of carrying her law into execution." Were the Old Dominion to apply political pressure to Louisiana, the slave trader stood to benefit personally as well, for it would "releive [*sic*] me from the consequences of the prosecution . . . [and] restore my confiscated property." He would furthermore be spared the surrender of the $27,000 penalty for failing "to comply with my engagements to the State of Virginia." Williams ended his missive with a postscript stressing the urgency of the governor's reply.[21]

Rutherfoord's response offered Williams only a single shred of positive news, on the matter of his $27,000 bond with the commonwealth. During Williams' third and final trial before the First District Criminal Court, juror W. W. Caldwell asked lawyer and witness Wheelock S. Upton directly "what effect the proceedings here in Louisiana would have upon that bond." In Upton's professional opinion, "a verdict of guilty here, would at least be *prima facie* evidence in a suit against Williams upon that bond." If Upton were correct, Williams' conviction set the stage for further action initiated by Virginia. Rutherfoord's correspondence implied, however, that the commonwealth was not interested in pursuing the $27,000 in bonds the trader had pledged as his guarantee to carry the convicts out of the United States. Writing on behalf of the governor, commonwealth secretary William H. Richardson reassured the slave trader that the executive letters originally sent to Mobile and New Orleans "contain[ed] no *charge* against you, but were precautionary merely." The proceedings against him had been instituted, "not for a violation of the laws of this State, or any breach of your contract with her, but for an infraction of the laws of Louisiana." Henceforth, in short, Williams' legal troubles would be with Louisiana and Louisiana alone.[22]

Although surely relieved to avoid future entanglements with Virginia, Williams also had his hopes for the commonwealth's assistance on his behalf dashed. Governor Rutherfoord proved "unable to perceive how he could properly interpose" in the affairs of a sister state. Virginia thus absolved itself of further involvement in Williams' case; the slave trader's fate belonged squarely in the hands of Louisiana authorities. "If they can be satisfied of your bona fide intention to carry the slaves out of the United States, and that the facts are as stated in your letter," replied the governor with a hollow measure of assurance, "it is presumed that they, or some of them, are competent to remit the penalties which have been incurred," if the political will to do so existed.[23]

Williams did not need Rutherfoord's advice to seek the mercy of Louisiana officials. He had already penned a petition to Governor André B. Roman "in which he prays to be relieved from the fine and forfeiture to which he has become liable, because they have ... been inflicted on him when there was no intention on his part to violate the laws of Louisiana." Shrewdly, Williams enclosed a copy of the letter in which Attorney General Roselius acknowledged that the slave trader's trials produced "no evidence whatever ... that Mr. Williams either sold or attempted to sell any of those slaves in the State of Louisiana." Roselius' admission confused Governor Roman. "In the Several conversations that I have had with you in relation to this same trial," he wrote the attorney general, "the impression has been left on my mind that you were of opinion that the slaves were introduced by Williams into the State, *with the intention of selling them here* and that he had therefore no claim whatever to the mercy of the Executive." Because Roman now had "to act officially on this subject," he sought clarification from Roselius. Had the attorney general changed his mind? Should Williams "be relieved from the fine and forfeiture which he has incurred"? Roselius' reply does not survive, but it must have been hostile to gubernatorial interference. As he had previously explained, "I took the ground that the mere fact of bringing such slaves into the State, was a violation of the statute; and constituted the offence of which Mr. Williams stood charged. This position was sustained by the Court." Governor Roman did not intervene.[24]

Williams' counsel was persistent, and at sentencing, on July 24, 1841, filed one last-ditch appeal to Judge Canonge. Grymes presented the judge a petition praying for a suspension of the final judgment rendered on May 1 as well as for an appeal to the Louisiana Supreme Court. Canonge denied the requests. The judge indicated – correctly – that, according to Louisiana law, Williams' case was not even eligible for appeal. The state of Louisiana did not permit appeals from the criminal courts until the passage of the Constitution of 1845. In 1841, one could only seek appeals to the state Supreme Court in civil suits. A well-intentioned desire to administer the law fairly among people of all classes supplied the rationale behind this quirk of the Louisiana legal code. As the argument ran, only "the rich man ... can avail himself" of the opportunity to make appeals from criminal courts, since he alone possessed the wealth to pay "lawyers liberally." Through the use of skilled, highly paid attorneys and tactics of delay, the wealthy would avoid punishment, regardless of guilt. The socioeconomically impartial administration of the criminal law thus required the impossibility of appeal to a higher court. The editors of the *Picayune* greeted this line of argumentation with skepticism. The inability to appeal Criminal Court decisions struck them as "an absurdity" and openly recommended its correction. Revision of the law, they contended, would better serve "the ends of humanity and justice," for "better [that] ninety-nine guilty persons should escape punishment than that one innocent man should suffer."[25]

Judge Canonge did not share the *Picayune*'s apparent sympathy for Williams' plight. At sentencing, William H. Williams bore the compulsory forfeiture of his enslaved convicts to the state and incurred a $12,000 penalty for importing them into Louisiana, plus court costs. The slave trader did have available under Louisiana law one alternative to the payment of his hefty fine. A statute from March 1818 held that "every person being adjudged to pay *any fine*, shall, in default of payment or recovery thereof . . . be imprisoned for a period *not exceeding* one year." So, in lieu of paying the exorbitant financial penalty for his offense, Williams exercised his legal prerogative to spend twelve months in the Orleans Parish jail "and keep the $12,000 in his breeches pocket." On July 24, the keeper of a Washington, D.C. slave pen thus commenced his own stint in a Louisiana prison for unlawfully importing convict bond-people into the state. Although Williams naturally groused about the "ruinous fine" his confinement would erase, he almost certainly could have afforded to pay it. At the very least, he could have readily secured a loan on favorable terms from J. W. Zacharie or another affluent business associate. But Williams' firm belief in his own innocence deterred him from paying, as a matter of principle. Distinctly unmoved by Williams' choice to spend a year in a cell rather than part with a substantial sum of money, *The Colored American*, a short-lived African-American newspaper published in New York, observed brusquely, "Good enough for him."[26]

William H. Williams occupied his cell for less than a week before he penned a long letter, dated July 29, with a salutation directed to Judge John François Canonge of the First District Criminal Court. From the confines of the Orleans Parish prison, Williams claimed to write of his own accord, without the assistance of counsel. Whatever plans the slave dealer had concocted to combat his confinement required information, so he asked Canonge for complete, written records of his trial proceedings. "If the time of your Honor should be too much occupied, to make out a record with your own hand," and "it will better suit your convenience," obliged Williams, "I will myself draft it, and ask for your certificate that it is substantially correct." The judge presumably declined to accommodate any manner of Williams' request, for starting on July 31 and lasting into September, the incarcerated slave trader, either by letter or through surrogates, gathered the testimonial evidence from his days spent in Canonge's courtroom. Two witnesses verified their testimony before Associate Judge of the City Court A. Laneuville on July 31.

Customs inspector Samuel H. Page followed suit, with Associate Judge Thomas N. Morgan, on August 2. Two days later, James W. Zacharie recollected his testimony, a copy of which he filed with Judge O. P. Jackson on October 4. Slave trader and witness Seneca Bennet certified a written account of his testimony from the Criminal Court with Judge Laneuville on September 27. Recorder George Y. Bright refused Williams' plea "to draw up the substance of his testimony before the Jury," so the slave trader took it upon himself to undertake the task. He also abstracted to the best of his recollection the sworn statements of two other witnesses, including Sheriff Ursin Bouligny. W. C. Duncan, a member of the jury in Williams' third trial, affirmed and signed off on the correctness of Williams' three transcriptions. Twice, on September 24 and then again on November 23, Williams took the written evidence he had assembled and delivered it – somehow appearing in person, despite still serving his term in prison – for deposit with New Orleans notary Carlile Pollock. Pursuant to Williams' wishes, Pollock recorded the documents in his notarial register, thus preserving a detailed record of the slave trader's trials. What plan had Williams formulated? And how did painstakingly preserved documentation figure into his calculations?[27]

Although Williams most immediately directed his July 29 missive to Judge Canonge, he requested that the *New Orleans Commercial Bulletin* publish it for all to see that very day. Williams had two objects in mind. First, Williams explained, he wanted "to set my conduct in its true light before the public." In the public discourse of the antebellum South, proslavery propagandists described slave traders as outcasts, disreputable and despised social pariahs rendered offensive by their shrewd and ruthless dealing, callousness to human suffering, and the brutality of their ways. Thus, in slaveholders' minds, buying bondpeople from degraded, stigmatized slave traders transmogrified such acquisitions into elevated acts of salvation, as purchasers rescued the enslaved from dealers' terrible grasp. From the opposite perspective, enslaved people, as the victims of human trafficking, unsurprisingly also viewed slave trading as "a disreputable calling." Yet blanket condemnations of slave traders as a group oversimplified matters and strayed from dealers' lived social reality. Certainly some traders were more disreputable than others, but for the most part they were wealthy, prominent men who, despite their occupation, enjoyed the respect and standing of whites in their communities, enough sometimes to get elected to political office. For this reason, it made sense when the New Orleans *Picayune* seemed remarkably unfazed by Williams' arrival in New Orleans with a shipment of convict slaves. He "is a man of property and respectability," the newspaper printed. There was "no good reason why his correct dealing should be questioned," for he had been operating in the city, as his associate James W. Zacharie testified, "[f]or many years." Having "long known Mr. Williams," Zacharie confidently characterized Williams as "a high minded honorable man." Williams felt compelled to protect his finely honed reputation. Exposing the facts of his case for public consumption, he explained, would "shield my character (which I am proud to say has ever stood unsullied) from any imputation of intentional wrong": "[I]f I have violated a law, it has been through an honest misconception of its meaning."[28]

Williams' public recounting of his uniquely unfortunate legal circumstances not only aimed to preserve his reputation in New Orleans' business circles and among the slave-buying public at large, but also to renew his previously rejected plea for aid from the commonwealth of Virginia. He explicitly stated his desire for "the Legislature of my native State" to read about his plight, evaluate "the results flowing from one of the laws of their State, and extend to me such relief . . . as their wisdom and equity may suggest." Williams was arrested while merely attempting to fulfill his end of an "official contract" with Virginia governor Thomas Walker Gilmer. As a result, he explained, "I am fully impressed with the belief, that Virginia, though she has been unable to shield my person from imprisonment, will yet do all in her power to repair the wrong which has been done."[29]

Williams' open letter, self-serving as it was, reiterated the familiar argument that the trader was taking his cargo of enslaved criminals to Texas. After having contracted with Virginia, "under a heavy penalty, to remove convicts from her limits beyond the territory of the United States," Williams explained, he determined that "[t]he most convenient, and to my view the only practicable high road" to Texas "lay through Louisiana." "*I was on the route*" to Texas when I was arrested, Williams emphasized, and his trial produced "no tittle of evidence" to the contrary. These remarks added little to Williams' previous statements and did nothing to account for dropping anchor in Mobile Bay before moving on to New Orleans.[30]

The trader then offered something new and revealing that reframes our understanding of his transfer of the enslaved convicts from the *Uncas* to the steamboat *Roanoke*. That maneuver had significance beyond avoiding the completion of a slave manifest. Reaching New Orleans via the so-called inland waterways, hugging the coastline from Mobile and entering Lake Pontchartrain, would frustrate any British attempt to interfere with his mission and make his convict slaves less susceptible to foreign interception. "I May be wrong," Williams reasoned, "but it was my belief that the transportation of slaves by sea from this country to a foreign country would subject both vessel and cargo to liability of seizure by British cruzers [*sic*]." Great Britain had passed a law in 1833 that commenced the abolition of slavery throughout almost the entirety of its empire and patrolled the Atlantic basin more aggressively than any other nation to suppress the African slave trade and slave smuggling. As Williams fully understood, he was, in the most basic sense, partaking in the international traffic in human beings. The United States had outlawed its participation in the international slave trade from January 1, 1808, and in 1820 declared it a form of piracy punishable by death. Thus, in directing slave traders such as William H. Williams to carry enslaved convicts outside the United States, the laws of the commonwealth of Virginia authorized the commission of a federal crime. Williams' errand for the Old Dominion technically violated prohibitions against the international slave trade and made him a pirate under US law, and if captured, he could be executed. With stakes so high, Williams feared being intercepted by British patrols on the high seas. To protect himself and "avoid such exposure" on his planned journey from Alexandria to Mobile, Williams obtained a federal coasting license for the *Uncas* under the terms of a congressional act of 1793. Worst case scenario, if a British vessel caught the slave ship and seized Williams' captives, he could then invoke the power of the US government on his behalf. Williams suggested that congressional intervention was still not out of the question to rescue him from the injustice he continued to endure. He was arrested, convicted, and punished in Louisiana, he argued, while "acting as the agent of Virginia" and performing his obligation under a contract with that commonwealth. "If the laws of Virginia conflict with the laws of this State, and an honest citizen is crushed between them," insisted Williams, obviously referring to himself, "as an American, I have too much regard for the integrity and the power of Congress, to believe that her support will not be extended should I fail to find it elsewhere." Certainly the US Constitution explicitly granted Congress the authority to regulate both foreign and domestic commerce, but for now, at least, Williams restricted his "appeals to the authorities of Virginia for protection and redress."[31]

Adding insult to injury, the state of Louisiana soon commandeered two of William H. Williams' enslaved transports to pay court costs. Albert and Stephen, both convicted of theft in Virginia, shipped to Louisiana, and arrested in New Orleans with the two dozen other slaves from the *Roanoke*, had been incarcerated in the Orleans Parish prison but did not count among those mentioned in the indictment against the slave trader. Louisiana would target these two bondmen to recoup the costs of trying Williams. On August 5, 1841, Judge Canonge issued an order holding Williams responsible for paying courtroom expenses totaling $1,785.31. A week later, Sheriff of the First District Criminal Court and Orleans Parish prison keeper Ursin Bouligny informed Williams, then sitting in jail, that the trader had a three-day window in which to pay up. If his bill remained unpaid at that time, Canonge authorized the sheriff to seize $1,785.31 worth of Williams' "personal estate" in Orleans Parish, excluding slaves, if possible. Only as a last resort could Bouligny appropriate the "real estate and slaves" in Williams' possession as of July 24. By the time the sheriff conversed with Williams on August 12, he had apparently had no luck in locating other assets belonging to the trader and had therefore seized Albert and Stephen, whom he would soon advertise to sell to offset Williams' debt to the state. The Virginia magistrates who had convicted Albert and Stephen valued them, together, at $1,800. If all went according to plan, the pair's sale would supply just enough money to cover the state's costs for Williams' prosecution. We do not know if Albert and Stephen ever had occasion to speak to their one-time captor, William H. Williams, but for a period of at least several weeks, their terms in the Orleans Parish prison overlapped, making slaver and enslaved more nearly equal than they had ever been before.[32]

In August 1841, as his slave-trading client languished in a jail cell, an undaunted John R. Grymes continued his labors on Williams' behalf. Claiming that Williams was "illegally imprisoned and detained" in the Orleans Parish jail, Grymes petitioned Judge Charles Maurian of the Parish Court of the City and Parish of Orleans for a writ of *habeas corpus* so that the trader might be discharged to get another opportunity to plead his case before the judge. On August 26, Maurian assented to the request and ordered prison keeper Ursin Bouligny to produce Williams in court on Saturday the 28th at 10 a.m. Bouligny, who had himself purchased a slave from Williams since the state initiated legal proceedings against him for importing the transports from Virginia, pledged to have the captive slave dealer in court as instructed.[33]

Grymes and Attorney General Roselius rehashed for Judge Maurian many of the same arguments Canonge had heard in the spring. The *Picayune*, a Williams ally throughout his ordeal, complimented Grymes' arguments as "replete with sound reasoning and strongly supported by legal authority." Williams' counsel contended that the case against the slave trader did not fall "within the scope" of the Criminal Court's jurisdiction and that the trial proceedings were "therefore null and void, or at least informal." Moreover, he argued in a new twist, Williams' resulting incarceration was illegal. Louisiana law permitted detention for only up to twelve months for the nonpayment of a fine, but Judge Canonge's orders to Sheriff Bouligny stated that Williams "be kept in safe custody . . . till he pay," an unlawful "stretch of power beyond the judge's prerogative," tantamount to "perpetual imprisonment." Representing the state, Roselius reminded Judge Maurian that decisions from civil courts could be appealed, but those from the criminal courts could not. As such, the "judiciary power" of the First District Criminal Court "was supreme," subject to no appellate challenge.[34]

After a few days of deliberation, Judge Maurian issued his opinion. He concurred with the attorney general that his court did not have the judicial authority to evaluate or overrule the "the action[s] or decisions of the Criminal Court." He also took special pains to dispute the notion that Williams was confined illegally. The 1817 law against importing

enslaved criminals mandated imprisonment until payment of the fine
was made, however long that might be, but the state legislature eliminated the possibility of "perpetual imprisonment" the following year
when it limited incarceration for nonpayment of a fine to a "period not
exceeding one year." As it stood, Williams would make a mockery of
Louisiana law if he was fined, failed to pay that fine, and was then
permitted simply to walk away. Maurian reminded Grymes that his
slave-trading client maintained the ability to shorten his sentence at
will: "If at any time during the year the fine is either *paid* by the party
condemned, or *recovered* out of his property, he is entitled to his liberty."
Unless or until that happened, though, Williams "must await the expiration of one year." State law precluded "an indefinite commitment," but
"[t]he prisoner alone can avail himself of the alternative either to pay the
fine, or to stay in jail for the *limited* period of one year." Maurian's
decision was firm: the relevant laws on the books were clear, the court
that convicted Williams was legitimate, and there was nothing irregular
about the proceedings against him. Pending the payment of his fine,
Williams would sit in jail for up to the year allowed by law.[35]

A lull in William H. Williams' saga followed, but in late 1841, his lawyer,
John R. Grymes, joined fellow Bourbon Street resident Randall Hunt, an
attorney at 12 Exchange Place, to launch a new offensive. Together the
co-counselors made a motion before the Louisiana State Supreme Court
for a writ of *mandamus* that would force an appeal of what they saw as the
erroneous judgment handed down by Judge Canonge of the First District
Criminal Court. Higher courts may use writs of *mandamus* to demand that
an inferior court fulfill its responsibilities or remedy an abuse or mis-
carriage of justice: this was William H. Williams' legal team's new strategy.
Attorney General Christian Roselius again denied the right to appeal a
case from the Criminal Court. By now, the significant constitutional
issues raised by Williams' case had captured the Supreme Court's attention, and a lively debate ensued among the justices. The high court
granted the requested writ of *mandamus* and ordered Judge Canonge to
allow Williams an appeal. On February 5, 1842, Grymes and Williams
together appeared before the judge to pray that he conform to the terms
of the writ. Canonge initially refused to comply. He stood by his original

decision and argued against any appeal because, according to Louisiana law, there was no appellate court for criminal cases. The judge stated explicitly that he did not acknowledge the Supreme Court as superior to his own, and any valid writ of *mandamus*, he said, must be issued by a court "unequivocally the Superior of the one to whom it is directed." "Had . . . I erred when I refused the appeal," confessed Canonge, "I would unhesitatingly have yielded to their Superior Judgments," but the Supreme Court justices had supplied him no evidence "that I was laboring under a mistake." As much as he "regretted any collision of opinion" with them, he explained, his convictions remained "unshaken," and "he was bound by a sense of duty to adhere to his opinion and refuse to obey the call of the Supreme Court."[36]

The high court justices, eager to hear Williams' case, were not amused. On February 7, they therefore authorized the Orleans Parish sheriff to arrest and imprison Judge Canonge for contempt if he persisted in his refusal to submit to the writ of *mandamus*. Only after the Supreme Court threatened the judge with incarceration did Canonge begrudgingly relent and forward the papers of the trial. He complied with the writ only under duress. Canonge did not suddenly concur with the Supreme Court's position, but he did fear the consequences of dragging a Criminal Court judge "from his Bench into the walls of a prison." Beyond the obvious inconvenience to himself, which he neglected to mention, Canonge expressed apprehension that his imprisonment would "have the effect of weakening . . . the dignity and respect" of the post he occupied. Furthermore, his confinement would halt the Criminal Court's proceedings, prevent "public business" from being "dispatched regularly and speedily," "create confusion," and ultimately "bring our institutions into disrepute." And so Canonge yielded to the Supreme Court's wishes. Attorney General Roselius filed a motion to send the papers back down and dismiss Williams' latest appeal, but it failed. Over Roselius' continued protests that Williams' case "was of a purely criminal character, and beyond the appellate jursidiction," the Louisiana State Supreme Court insisted on a new trial. At last, Williams would get his appeal to the state's final arbiter of the law. The slave trader put up a $3,000 bond, with James W. Zacharie as his security, to assure the justices of the high court that he would appear before them in March.[37]

The Louisiana State Supreme Court heard arguments from both sides in the spring of 1842. Williams' lawyers, Grymes and Hunt, insisted that the previous judgment against their client was "illegal and erroneous." "[T]he whole proceedings," they charged, were "irregular and void," "a mixture of civil and criminal jurisprudence, inconsistent, repugnant, and contrary to law." At heart, they argued, the case against the slave trader was an action of debt, to recover "a fine or pecuniary penalty" from Williams, and any such matter should have been tried in the civil rather than in the criminal courts. If Williams' trial was indeed civil in nature, he was therefore entitled under existing Louisiana law to an appeal, and the Supreme Court was at liberty "to set aside the verdict of Judge Canonge" of the Criminal Court.[38] Attorney General Roselius argued that Williams' was "strictly a criminal case" and moved to dismiss the slave trader's appeal because the Supreme Court lacked "appellate jurisdiction in criminal cases." The legislative act of 1817 under which Williams was tried made "the introduction of slaves convicted of certain crimes" into Louisiana an indictable offense properly tried before the criminal courts.[39]

The Supreme Court's deliberations on the case extended into the summer. In the middle of June, New Orleans newspapers speculated that the court would view the attorney general's argument favorably and find against Williams. The slave trader continued to bide his time in the Orleans Parish jail, although his year's confinement as an alternative to paying the $12,000 fine was drawing to a close. After a delay of more than two months, at last the court handed down its verdict on July 5.[40]

Judge François-Xavier Martin delivered the majority opinion. At eighty years of age in 1842, the French-born Martin was an eminent jurist who honed his knowledge of both the English language and the law while living in North Carolina. In 1809, President James Madison named him a federal judge for the Mississippi Territory. The following year, a transfer took him to the Orleans Territory, where his equal mastery of French and the law came in handy. After Louisiana entered the Union, Martin became the state's first attorney general and in 1815 earned an appointment to the state Supreme Court. There he remained for more than three decades, with his elevation to presiding judge coming in 1836. Two years later, blindness set in, but he soldiered on dutifully at the bench, an unmarried eccentric and a miser but also a respected legal mind.[41]

In his ruling, Martin restricted himself to the narrow question of the Supreme Court's jurisdiction over appeals from the criminal courts. He acknowledged that Louisiana's constitution was vague. Article 4, section 2 stated plainly enough that the Supreme Court maintained only appellate jurisdiction – that cases could not originate before that body. The meaning of the subsequent clause was far more ambiguous. According to the state constitution, the Supreme Court's "jurisdiction shall extend to all civil cases, when the matter in dispute shall exceed the sum of three hundred dollars." Was that to suggest the court's appellate powers were limited exclusively to that financial subset of all civil suits, or did the language imply that such jurisdiction in civil cases was *in addition to* jurisdiction in criminal cases? As Martin observed of the state constitution, "No mention is made ... of appeals in criminal cases" at all. The judge therefore turned for clarification to the Louisiana legislature, which in 1832 passed a law that granted jurisdiction to the Criminal Court of the First District over "all suits and prosecutions on penal statutes, and all suits and prosecutions instituted in behalf of the State for any violation of a public law, reserving to the parties the right of appeal to the Supreme Court, in all cases in which an appeal is allowed by law." Williams' case did concern both a violation of "penal statute" – one that imposed a fine or penalty – and a "violation of a public law." By either standard, then, the law of 1832 made Williams eligible to appeal his case to the Supreme Court, even though the attorney general had prosecuted him criminally.[42]

Furthermore, Martin continued, if the state wished to recover the penalty as outlined in the act of 1817, the attorney general should have instituted an action of debt – a civil suit – against Williams. Indicting him criminally was the improper course to take under Louisiana law. Doing so, however, did not fundamentally alter the character of the case, and the state constitution clearly bestowed the Supreme Court appellate power in civil suits with more than $300 at stake. Williams' $12,000 fine certainly qualified, entitling him to an appeal before the state's highest court. The Criminal Court's judgment against the slave trader, Martin concluded, "ought to be reversed." Justices Alonzo Morphy, Edward

Simon, and Rice Garland concurred with Martin in the 4–1 decision in Williams' favor.[43]

The lone dissenting voice from the bench against Williams belonged to Supreme Court Justice Henry Bullard. Bullard was a Massachusetts native, his mother from the same Adams family that produced two of the nation's first six presidents. He completed a pair of degrees at Harvard and demonstrated a particular knack for languages. Multilingual, he exercised equally strong command of English, French, Spanish, German, and Italian. After some unsuccessful military exploits in Mexican Texas in 1813, Bullard settled in Natchitoches, Louisiana, where he opened a law office. His linguistic talents helped ingratiate him with some of the leading families of his adopted state, and his education, culture, mellifluous voice, and handsome looks all carried him far. Twice named a district judge in the 1820s, he represented Louisiana in the US House of Representatives from 1831 to 1834, stepping down only to accept an appointment to the state Supreme Court.[44]

Bullard could certainly comprehend Chief Justice Martin's argument but still viewed William H. Williams' transgression as fundamentally criminal in nature. "The argument that this is essentially a civil case, although the proceeding is by [criminal] indictment, is ingeniously carried out," he conceded, "and appears at first plausible." True, he acknowledged, contravention of the law of 1817 was "punishable only by fine," but, he added, "I am yet to learn that the character of a law depends upon its sanction." For Bullard, it made no sense to define an offense as criminal or not contingent upon the punishment meted out by law. "[I]f murder were made punishable by fine alone," he reasoned, "it would not be less a crime." Likewise, importing slave criminals marked "an offense against the State," indictable in the Criminal Court, despite the solely pecuniary punishment attached to the statute. Bullard explained that the law of 1817 that Williams purportedly violated "was intended to prevent ... a great public evil" that imperiled "the public safety." Declaring it "essentially immoral knowingly to let loose convicted felons upon a christian [*sic*] community," Bullard saw Williams' offense as criminal and the "criminal proceeding" against him, launched by Attorney General Roselius, as appropriate. Because Louisiana law did not grant the Supreme Court jurisdiction over Criminal Court appeals,

Bullard concluded, "we can afford no relief." Although Bullard agreed with Roselius that Williams' appeal should be dismissed, he was the only justice so convinced. The outcome of the case appeared favorable to the slave trader, for the moment.[45]

The Louisiana Supreme Court decision of early July 1842 likely shaved a few weeks off Williams' year of confinement in the Orleans Parish prison. Having spent almost twelve months "brood[ing] over his trying misfortune," he emerged from jail a free man. He was $12,000 richer than he otherwise would have been had he not opted for imprisonment, but the conditions of confinement had taken a toll on his health, and he still lacked "his property forfeited to the State." Though his conviction for importing enslaved criminals had been overturned, the transports from Virginia would remain in state custody, for Williams' legal battles were not yet over. Attorney General Christian Roselius proved just as dogged in prosecuting Williams as John R. Grymes had been in defending him. Roselius applied for a re-hearing before the Louisiana Supreme Court to get Williams' successful appeal of the Criminal Court decision dismissed.[46]

CHAPTER 8

Slave Trading in "Hard Times"

W HEN WILLIAM H. WILLIAMS DEPARTED ALEXANDRIA on October 10, 1840, he anticipated a return to the District of Columbia sometime in January or February 1841, pending the sale of the twenty-six enslaved convicts and the forty-two other bondpeople aboard the *Uncas*. In his absence, and at his direction, purchasing agent Ebenezer Rodbird, who had been in the field, scouting out available Chesapeake slaves to buy on his employer's behalf, "took charge" of the Yellow House. It was Rodbird – "the keeper Radburn" – whom Solomon Northup recalled having charge of Williams' private jail in the spring of 1841 when the free black man from New York suddenly found himself enchained in a basement dungeon.[1]

Williams' legal entanglements in Louisiana postponed his homecoming and dictated a reconfiguration of his business operations. While the trader was indisposed in New Orleans, Rodbird lived at Williams' "place of business in Washington, & acted there as his agent," but at some point in 1841 surrendered the duties of jailer, presumably at Williams' explicit behest, to Joshua Staples. A Virginia native and Williams' agent, Staples in December 1841 began using his name publicly to recruit Chesapeake masters' surplus slaves for Williams. In an advertisement that appeared several times per week for more than a year, Staples expressed a desire "to purchase immediately a number of Negroes, for which he will pay the highest cash price," urging sellers to visit the Yellow House "at the corner of 7th street and Maryland avenue." Precisely when Staples took over as jailer is unclear. Rodbird recollected that the transition came in January 1841, but Solomon Northup's narrative suggests that it occurred sometime after the spring.[2]

The most significant restructuring came as William H. Williams commenced his nearly year-long detention in the Orleans Parish prison in July 1841. Ebenezer Rodbird recalled that his boss sent him – in the summer or fall, he could not remember – a written "order to deliver up all" of Williams' "money & property to . . . Thomas Williams." By 1841, the younger Williams brother, only about twenty-two years old, had already gained at least four years' experience in the slave-trading business, watching, learning, and absorbing all he could under his elder sibling's tutelage. Thomas Williams had proven a trusted confidant and increasingly took on the responsibilities of managing the New Orleans end of William H. Williams' slave-trading enterprise, freeing up the senior Williams to spend more time in the Chesapeake buying and imprisoning enslaved men and women for sale in the Deep South. William's own incarceration in July 1841 left a gaping hole on the Chesapeake side of the business. He therefore made the most logical decision under the circumstances. William H. Williams would direct operations in New Orleans, inasmuch as was possible from the confines of his cell, and dispatch his brother Thomas, a more knowledgeable and competent trader than ever, to Washington, D.C., to manage his affairs there. "I took [over] the jail in 1841," Thomas affirmed. It was, not coincidentally, in the month of July that Thomas Williams took up residence in the Yellow House and announced in the newspapers that he "can at all times be found at William H. Williams's establishment, [at the] corner of 7th street and Maryland avenue," ready "to give the highest prices for likely negroes" for "the New Orleans market." Like his brother before him, Thomas Williams also offered masters the convenience of boarding slaves "for safe keeping . . . at the low rate of 25 cents per day." During William H. Williams' absence and throughout much of the remainder of the decade, the slave trader's underlings, led by Thomas Williams, carried on profitably in his stead. It was Thomas Williams whose name appeared in most of the advertisements for the Yellow House up through 1846. After October 1840, his older brother did not see Washington again "until upwards of two years had elapsed."[3]

Thomas Williams took over his brother's Washington, D.C. operations at an inauspicious moment for those who trafficked professionally in enslaved bodies. For domestic slave traders to realize any financial gains, they needed to sell bondpeople in the Deep South for substantially more than they paid for them in the Chesapeake. The differential offset the expenses traders incurred in jailing, transporting, maintaining, and then prepping the slaves prior to sale. Covering these costs and still coming out ahead had grown more challenging after the Panic of 1837. With the economic collapse, cotton prices plummeted. By 1842, they had dropped by more than half compared with their pre-depression highs. Prior to the 1850s, slave prices fluctuated in lock-step with cotton prices, so with cotton prices remaining low until the middle of the decade, slave prices followed suit. From their peak before the crash, sale prices for slaves dropped by one-half to two-thirds, bottoming out in 1844. The precipitous downturn in slaves' market value dramatically reduced the profitability of slave trading, forcing some dealers out of the business altogether. These were "hard times."[4]

It was not a fortuitous stretch in the nation's economic life when Thomas Williams assumed greater responsibility for the family business, but he was prepared for the task. He had been among the consignees in New Orleans to whom William H. Williams had shipped enslaved cargoes from Alexandria aboard the *Uncas* in November 1838 and 1839. Thomas had also received a similar shipment sent by Ebenezer Rodbird on the brig *Architect* in March 1840. Based on extant slave manifests documenting the human traffic between the Chesapeake and New Orleans, Thomas Williams and Rodbird almost wholly took over William H. Williams' slave exporting business out of Washington, D.C., suggesting that their employer's widely publicized legal fiasco may have indeed tarnished his finely honed reputation as a slave trader. After the debacle in New Orleans, Thomas Williams and Rodbird dispatched slaving vessels from the Chesapeake under their names, with slave manifests listing one or the other of them, rather than William H. Williams, as the shipper. They clearly stood in as his proxy not only during the period of his confinement in the Orleans Parish jail but for the remainder of the decade of the 1840s. Thomas Williams and Rodbird also virtually abandoned the nearby port of Alexandria, almost as though William H. Williams' business was no longer welcome there in light of his scandal. In a sample of thirty-two slaving voyages from 1843 to 1850, the Williams brothers and Rodbird sent slaves out of Alexandria only twice, or

6.25 percent of the time. They much more frequently used Baltimore as their preferred site of departure. Twenty-five of the thirty-two shipments (78 percent) originated in the Maryland port. Although Baltimore lacked the convenience of Alexandria, located just across the Potomac from Washington, D.C., it was still readily accessible from the Yellow House by either foot or rail.[5] (See Appendix B.)

The enslaved men and women whom Thomas Williams and Ebenezer Rodbird forcibly relocated to New Orleans did not differ in any meaningful way from those who had gone before, when William H. Williams directed operations. Although scholarship has shown that about two-thirds of the black laborers imported into New Orleans were male, a fact correlated with the physical demands of Louisiana sugar production, William H. Williams habitually sent captive men and women in roughly equitable numbers. He, and then his brother and Rodbird after him, shipped for sale only slightly more bondmen than bond-women; the sex ratio was consistently about even. As had always been the case, the slaves they sent to the Deep South trended young. The average age of the captives on any given voyage ranged from the late teens to early twenties, although the typical bondman was marginally older than the average female slave on board, usually by one to four years.[6] (See Appendix C.)

Unlike most official, written records documenting the institution of bondage in the United States, slave manifests listed bondpeople by both first and last names, which permits us to discern potential relationships among the captives on board the same vessel. Some manifests listed all the enslaved men first, followed by all the enslaved women, obscuring possible spousal bonds. Others listed the partners composing apparent couples consecutively. Most bondmen and -women sold in New Orleans commenced the tragic new chapter of their life isolated from loved ones, without the support of a wife, husband, or other family member, but manifests of the Williams brothers' and Ebenezer Rodbird's slaving voyages show some exceptions. Rodbird carried Jim and Nancy Roberson, ages thirty and twenty-eight, respectively, to New Orleans aboard the *Elizabeth* in 1848 with an "Infant Babe." The following month, an apparent family of three arrived intact on the *Union*, also shipped by Rodbird. Other slave ship manifests hint that siblings, such as possible brothers George and William Mason, separated by only two years of age, or sisters Mary, Susan, and Sarah Brooks, ages eighteen, fifteen, and thirteen, respectively, offered one another some modicum of comfort during the terrifying coastwise journey to New Orleans. With the slave auction looming, however, they could not be assured that they would remain together for much longer.[7]

One notable feature of the Williams enterprise's human cargoes was the frequency with which enslaved mothers appeared on slave manifests together with at least one child. Children enumerated in the manifests always appeared on the line immediately below that of their mothers. As a result, it is easy to tell that William H. Williams shipped the twenty-five-year-old Dorcas Hawkins aboard the *Uncas* to New Orleans in 1839 with her son Lewis, age three, and daughter Sarah, two. In a majority of the sample voyages from 1843 to 1850, the Williamses or Ebenezer Rodbird shipped enslaved mothers and their children jointly. Nancy Rankins sailed involuntarily aboard the *Colonel Howard* in 1844, but she took some consolation in the fact that she had not been torn from her children, Matilda, aged five, William, three, and George, two months, who clung to her side during their shared journey. When Thomas Williams transported Bettyann Dyer to New Orleans via the *General Pinckney* in 1847, she had her daughters Mary and Lucy, three and two years old, respectively, with her, as well as her "Two Infant Twins." Several slave vessels conveyed multiple enslaved mothers and their infants in a single shipment. The living and breathing cargoes aboard the *Victorine* in 1845 and the *Kirkwood* in 1847 each included three different bondwomen still united with their infants and children.[8]

Although one scholar calculated that 93 percent of all bondwomen of childbearing age sold in New Orleans were auctioned off without children, those female slaves shipped to Louisiana together with their children supplied Washington, D.C. traders evidence backing their own self-proclaimed efforts to conscientiously preserve enslaved families. Such pronouncements, however disingenuous, served to deflect and refute abolitionists' repeated, accurate charges that traders ruthlessly severed Chesapeake slaves' family ties, separating parents from children and husbands from wives. For traders, however, sometimes keeping families together represented sound business.

Some buyers did subscribe to the belief that bondpeople with familial attachments on the home plantation would prove less troublesome and less likely to run away than those without, and so would purchase enslaved couples or parents with their children. At the same time, some of slave dealers' well-known, callous practices earned legislative rebuke and compelled Louisiana lawmakers to enact certain minimal standards of decency to govern the trade. An act of 1829, for example, forbade the introduction or sale of enslaved children, ten years of age or younger, without their mothers, "if living." Anyone – slave dealers included – who separated such a mother and child for the purposes of sale faced fines of $1,000–2,000 and imprisonment from six months to a year. Additionally, the state of Louisiana itself would confiscate and sell the bondpersons in question. The law thus afforded at least the youngest victims of the domestic slave trade a modicum of protection. Those infants born into bondage aboard ships en route from the Chesapeake likewise could not be lawfully separated from their mothers for a decade. For slave traders, though, such births still came as a welcome financial boon and no doubt figured into their initial calculations to purchase pregnant bond-women. Enslaved newborns not only put a little extra money in slave dealers' pockets but also amply demonstrated bondwomen's fecundity, an important factor in determining their value at market.[9]

Effective April 1, 1829, Louisiana law mandated that "an authentic act of every sale" of a bondperson more than twelve years old be executed before a notary public or parish judge. These bills of sale filed with one of the dozens of notaries public operating in antebellum New Orleans supply a wealth of information about slave sales in the city. A random sample based on the sales of 244 bondpeople orchestrated by either William H. or Thomas Williams over the sixteen years from 1837 to 1852, inclusive, shows seven enslaved women sold with a child, including Louisa and "an Infant not named"; the "griff woman" Nancy Barnes and "her son named Wesley," age six; and Milly Boman and her fourteen-month-old boy named Edwin. Louisa, Nancy, and Milly all embarked upon a new chapter of their lives, owned by strangers in an unfamiliar land, each with a youngster depending on them for maternal love, care, and support.[10]

The bills of sale also reveal information about the enslaved people's ages. In the sample of 244 individuals sold, only twelve were listed as thirty years old or more, with only two in their forties, by which age typical slaves were physically broken down, well past their prime, and, in a word, old. At the opposite end of the spectrum, the Williams brothers sold slaves who were three and four months old and younger (along with their mothers). Seventy-five percent of the captive laborers in the sample sales ranged in age from sixteen to twenty-five, robust and healthy slaves at peak strength, physicality, and reproductive capabilities.

Geographically, the buyers of the Williams brothers' slaves came from near and far to do business. Almost half of the sample bondpeople's purchasers (46 percent) lived in New Orleans, a finding consistent with other studies of the city's slave trade. Five of every eight (62.5 percent) of the Williamses' customers from the sample lived in either New Orleans, neighboring Jefferson Parish, or nearby St. James Parish, straddling the Mississippi River not far upstream. Approximately 93 percent of the sample slaves sold by the Williams brothers went to owners in one of nineteen Louisiana parishes, almost all of which were either due south of the state of Mississippi – in the Florida parishes, the eastern portion of Acadiana, or the environs surrounding New Orleans – or adjacent to the Mississippi River. The Williamses sold some bondpeople to Tensas, Concordia, and West Feliciana parishes, all of which watched the Mississippi flow by and ranked as the three leading producers of cotton in the state by 1850. The slaves sold to such parishes as Ascension, Assumption, Iberville, Plaquemines, St. James, and St. Mary likely toiled in sugar production. The Williams brothers did business with slave buyers from outside Louisiana as well, hailing from the states of Alabama, Arkansas, and especially Mississippi. Still, 36 percent of the slaves in the sample of 244 were sold to buyers living right in New Orleans. Another 12 percent apiece went to Jefferson and St. James parishes, followed by 6 percent taken to Assumption Parish. No other individual parish absorbed more than about 4 percent of the total.[11]

Though based in Washington, D.C., Thomas Williams had begun to sell substantial numbers of slaves in Louisiana on his brother's behalf starting about 1839. That year, in one of his more lucrative sales, he transferred ownership of three enslaved men – Lindsey, George, and

Addison, all "recently introduced into this State" – to Horace Boardman Rose of Franklin County, Arkansas, for $1,100 each, or $3,300, no small sum for a twenty-year-old slave-trading novice. Only the month before, he sold the bondwoman Frances to a buyer in St. Bernard Parish after "having bought [her] in the district of Columbia, and imported her on board the brig Ancas [*Uncas*]." Thomas Williams also purchased Amy, in Maryland, and then found a buyer for her in St. James Parish in January 1840. After the senior Williams brother ushered his shipment of convict slaves into New Orleans on November 1, 1840, he continued to dispose of various bondpeople in Louisiana as he awaited trial. On February 6, 1841, only a week and a half before the first jury assembled to hear his case, William H. Williams closed a blockbuster deal, swapping five bondmen – Washington, William, Frisby, Charles, and James – to Alfred Penn and John Freeland of New Orleans for a total of $4,175. But by May 1841, the very month the third jury convicted Williams of the unlawful importation of enslaved convicts, Thomas already assumed a dramatically more pronounced role in his brother's business affairs. By that point, Thomas had journeyed aboard a slaving vessel to New Orleans and attached his name to an increasing number of bills of sale, including all of those from a database of sample sales transacted during William H. Williams' year in confinement from July 1841 to July 1842. After 1841, William did not affix his name to any of the bills of sale in the sample until 1843.[12]

With Thomas conducting much of the day-to-day operations in both Washington, D.C., and New Orleans during 1841 and 1842, William H. Williams' business suffered no discernible decline due to personnel issues. The economy continued to lag, but Thomas Williams had accumulated enough experience to navigate rough times. His elder brother no doubt instructed him in the slave trader's ways, in the techniques of attracting clients and keeping them satisfied and coming back for future purchases. In February 1841, Thomas Williams auctioned off Tamer, "a negress twenty two years old, field hand, [and] somewhat of a cook," at the City Exchange. In 1842, he sold Maria, "a good Washer, Ironer & Cook" from Virginia, to a buyer from Ascension Parish. A few months later, he disposed of, "at public auction at the St. Louis Exchange," a "Mulatto Girl slave for life" named Miranda, "a seamstress, Lady's

Maid, house servant and fair Washer and Ironer." To reassure wavering purchasers, Williams sold these bondwomen, as he did other slaves, "fully guaranteed against the redhibitory vices, maladies and defects prescribed by law."[13]

The Williams brothers also happily exchanged slaves for customers wanting someone or something different from their enslaved labor forces. Joseph Moncla of Avoyelles Parish, for instance, inherited Mary, a twenty-five-year-old "griffoune" valued at $700, following the death of her master. For whatever reason, Moncla did not find her a suitable addition to his holdings, so he swapped her for three slaves William H. Williams had imported from the Chesapeake: the twenty-eight-year-old bondwoman Letty and her two children – Abram, four, and Ellen, ten months – worth a collective $1,100. Moncla paid "the sum of Four hundred Dollars in ready money" to make up the difference in price. Accommodating clients such as Moncla generated goodwill and enhanced the likelihood of his consulting the Williamses when it next came time to buy another slave.[14]

To mollify customers discontented with their purchases, William taught Thomas the wisdom of negating previously completed sales as a means of avoiding litigation and fostering smooth relations with the slave-buying public. Thirteen days after Thomas sold Henry Leche of St. John the Baptist Parish a bondman named Peter, he nullified the sale at Leche's request. Thomas conceded to partial abrogations of sale as well. In February 1841, he sold Vincent David Walsh of West Feliciana Parish two bondwomen: Molly, age twenty, worth $715, and Celia, seventeen, valued at $700. Walsh paid Williams in two separate bank drafts, the one for $700 payable in ten days, and the other for $715 payable in thirty days. Almost two weeks later, Walsh, dissatisfied with Celia, returned her. Fortunately for him, Williams had not yet taken the $700 payment for Celia to the bank. The two men agreed to "abrogate & make null & void" Celia's sale, and Williams returned Walsh's draft.[15]

To cultivate positive relations with his clientele, Williams generously accommodated returns and exchanges, almost to a fault. In May 1841, he sold the bondman Jack to Louis Deshields of Lafourche Interior Parish for $860. A full eight months later, after harvest season, Deshields returned him for a full refund. Deshields thus accrued two-thirds of a year of Jack's labor for free, without absorbing a dollar's worth of depreciation. There may indeed have been times when buyers took advantage of slave traders' interest in satisfying their customers. In this case, at least, the same day he brought Jack back, whether out of a sense of obligation or actual need, Deshields did purchase a different bondman held by Williams, a fifteen-year-old mulatto named Adam, for $700.[16]

With time and experience, Thomas Williams' business acumen sharpened, and he developed a comprehensive understanding of slaveholding's power in the capitalist economic system in which southern slavery thrived. Already by age twenty, he knew firsthand slaves' ability to function in direct and immediate ways as monetary instruments. In 1839, Williams took out a $400 loan from André Tivollier of New Orleans, signing a promissory note stating that he would pay back his creditor in six months. In working out the terms of the agreement, Williams used "a certain negro man slave named Jerry, aged about Fifty years," whom he had acquired only the week before, as collateral, by mortgaging the bondman. Even if Tivollier should transfer Williams' promissory note to someone else, the holder could feel confident that he would get paid, for Jerry's market value met or exceeded the amount of the loan.[17]

Thomas Williams' own customers sometimes availed themselves of the same economic wizardry of slave mortgages when they bought from him. Whereas slave dealers paid cash when they acquired Chesapeake bondpeople as fodder for the domestic slave trade, they often sold those same captive laborers for some combination of paper money, promissory notes, and various other credit arrangements. Rarely paying in specie, buyers instead took advantage of the other, more economically sophisticated options at their disposal. And they often did not pay the full price for their enslaved purchases up front. During the flush times of the mid-1830s, slave traders sometimes gave buyers as long as fifteen months to pay in full. By the hard times of the early 1840s, generosity to that extent had waned. Nevertheless, Thomas Williams' customers frequently negotiated bargains with him that gave them a grace period of half a year in which to produce the necessary funds to finalize the sale. Slave mortgages played an important role in this process. A number of buyers would "mortgage and specially hypothecate" the slaves they bought in favor of Williams as assurance that the purchasers' promissory notes would be punctually paid at maturity. Jeremiah Melbourne Rhodes of New Orleans, for instance, bought three bondmen from Williams for $2,450. He paid $2,000 on the date of sale and furnished a promissory note for the balance, due in six months. Agreements such as these were accompanied by buyers' promises "not to sell, alienate, or encumber" those same slaves upon whom the mortgage was placed. The mortgaging of slaves was so commonplace that the required paperwork documenting slave sales often specified that "there is no mortgage . . . recorded against" the bondperson or -persons involved, indicating to buyers that no one would later make a claim to another's costly slave. In one transaction of 1841, Thomas Williams guaranteed the purchaser of "Patsey alias Louise" that the bondwoman was free "of all troubles, liens, mortgages, evictions, alienations and all other incumbrances and maladies prescribed by law."[18]

As Williams' activities demonstrated, even in grim economic times when slave prices were depressed, bondpeople retained some value and could be leveraged in useful ways. For that very reason, bank speculator Joseph T. Guthrie could offer both sympathy and assurance to the Williams brothers' fellow D.C. slave trader Thomas N. Davis after a disappointing, atypically early-season slaving voyage to New Orleans. "I was sorry you did not meet with better success" in selling slaves, wrote Guthrie in 1841. "Your negroes must sell, sooner or later, and where a person is obliged to keep stock on hand, they are the best investment." Economic downturns might test traders' faith in enslaved commodities, but it would not be broken.[19]

To the contrary, the financial world's decline in 1837, which might have unleashed an overabundance of fiscal caution, only promoted further speculative ventures and risky economic behaviors. Thomas Williams took his chances in the realm of slave trading, in 1842 purchasing from Auguste Reggio of Plaquemines Parish five bondmen, including a pair of fugitives named Enoch and John. "It is . . . understood that . . . Enoch and John are sold as runaway slaves & are now absent," stated the agreement. "[T]he purchaser is well aware." Nevertheless, Thomas Williams willingly paid $650 apiece for two absconded slaves he might never see. Williams wagered, however, that they would be apprehended and fetch a far more handsome price in the New Orleans slave market than what he paid for them. A pervasive spirit of speculation fueled the domestic slave trade generally: the entire business was premised on the belief that dealers like the Williamses could buy low in the Chesapeake and sell high in the Deep South. Thomas Williams' bargain with Reggio took his peculiar form of gambling to the next level.[20]

If Thomas Williams and his brother's cadre of other employees in the slaving business all shared in its profits (diminished as they were in the early 1840s), they also got a taste of the legal battles their profession invited. Joshua Staples, William H. Williams' appointee as the new jailer at the Yellow House, was soon ensnared in difficulties that would normally have bogged down Williams himself. Staples' position as jailer placed him squarely in the crossfire of others' drama. At the center of one controversy stood the bondwoman Betsey Chapman. On September 2, 1840, her owner, Sarah Boarman, sold Chapman to Lydia H. Slack of Washington County, D.C. By their arrangement, Slack agreed to pay $150 for Chapman in monthly installments of $25. At that point, Chapman understood, she would gain her freedom. Lydia Slack and her husband, John, however, made only one payment of $25 before they deposited Chapman in William H. Williams' Yellow House, "under the direction of Joshua Staples." By its reputation, the bondwoman knew well that the nondescript compound "is a private jail for the reception of all Slaves who are sold or intended to be sold to negro traders," and she rightfully feared that "she will be immediately removed" from Washington for sale. Therefore, at the end of June 1842 – as William H. Williams neared the end of his confinement in New Orleans – and with the aid of the law firm of Brent & Brent, Chapman filed a bill with Judge William Cranch and the Circuit Court of the District of Columbia in which she explained that the Slacks were depriving her of her impending liberty and attempting "to make her a slave for Life." Fearing immediate removal, she pleaded for the court to issue an injunction so "that they do not sell or remove her from the District of Columbia" or dispose of her to a local buyer. Finally, Chapman asked to be "relieve[d]" of her imprisonment and returned to her former mistress, Sarah Boarman.[21]

For her part, Boarman rallied to the bondwoman's support. One $25 installment notwithstanding, she stated, the Slacks "have not paid one cent" toward Chapman's purchase because, as Boarman claimed, they are "totally insolvent" and "have not the means to pay." Lydia Slack was simply attempting to "defraud" her. Therefore, Boarman wrote, the sale of Chapman to Slack should be invalidated, the bill of sale cancelled, and the bondwoman released from the Yellow House and restored to her possession. In a last grasp for judicial sympathy, Boarman added that Chapman's "health is suffering" while idling in Williams' slave pen.[22]

In late January 1843, the Circuit Court ruled that Betsey Chapman be released from Williams' private jail to prevent any improper sale but, at the insistence of the Slacks, directed that she be "committed to the custody of the Marshal" of Washington, D.C., for safekeeping "until the further order of the Court." There she remained longer than anyone anticipated. In late May 1843, Joshua Staples "disclaim[ed] all title" to Chapman. He explained that the Slacks had committed her "to the private jail of Thomas Williams," for whom he merely served as jailer. He had no direct or immediate interest in the case, he insisted. Two days later, Sarah Boarman filed a bill with the court, pleading for Chapman's release. On June 7, the Circuit Court ordered that Chapman "be relieved from prison," conditioned upon the Slacks, within the next ten days, executing a bond for her "with good & sufficient security" in the amount of $1,000. Alternatively, "in default of their doing so," Sarah Boarman "might give the bond" and take custody of Chapman. Both parties agreed to these terms, but neither took responsibility for Chapman or "availed themselves of this order, probably on account of the fees" – 34 cents per day – "due to the marshal for the imprisonment of the slave." And so Betsey Chapman sat, lingering in jail as the years passed. In March 1845, Sarah Boarman disclaimed her interest in the bondwoman and opted to "withdraw all proceedings in the case ... as I never considered her my property further than for Mr. Slack to comply with his contract as to the money due to me."[23]

A little more than a year later, in April 1846, John H. Slack sent a similar letter to his attorney. "I am sick to the soul of all suits," he stated. "I want to begin my life anew as respects litigation." Slack did express serious concerns, however, over his household's safety should Betsey Chapman be set at liberty. He vividly imagined the possible consequences of her release after years of confinement, during which she had ample time to seethe over her unfair plight. Fearing her simmering emotions might get the better of her, Slack sought some assurance that "the poor colored woman" was "reformed in her disposition ... & kept so she may not wreak her vengeance, for I believe she cherishes the spirit of vengeance on me or my innocent family, if suffered to go at large." In a defense of his own manly responsibility not only to protect but to provide, Slack also took the opportunity to rebut Sarah Boarman's claim that he had only made one payment on Chapman. "[T]he statements that I was unable & unwilling to pay for her are all false," he declared. "I can prove I sent the first installment" and that Boarman refused the second and third. In fact, he continued, "I ... proposed to give up the slave if they would pay back the money & they would not. I then offered to give her & the money if they would indemnify me from all liability for her support. [T]hey refused. I then sent her to the pen for sale. The court know the rest of the unpleasant history." The Circuit Court accepted Slack's letter, like Boarman's thirteen months earlier, "as disclaiming all interest and abandoning the case."[24]

The remaining obstacle to Betsey Chapman's liberation was not John or Lydia Slack, Sarah Boarman, or Joshua Staples, but the Washington city marshal. He continued to insist upon the payment of his fees for keeping Chapman in jail the previous several years, and no one accepted responsibility for settling up the account with him. The marshal therefore detained the bondwoman "as security for his fees." At last the Circuit Court intervened to end the impasse. On January 17, 1848, after almost exactly five years in the Washington public jail, the court ordered "that the Injunction be dissolved & the commitment be rescinded." Chapman walked free after spending 1,816 days in incarceration. At 34 cents per day, her confinement cost the marshal $617.44, plus another dollar in fees for her commitment and release.[25]

Like Betsey Chapman, other slaves in the early and mid-1840s sought out injunctions to escape the Yellow House. Barney Montgomery was "a lad about twelve or fourteen years old" in 1824, the property of Martha P. Graham, living near Dumfries, Virginia, in Prince William County. In the spring of 1824, Graham, a weaver, relocated to Washington, D.C. – Georgetown, to be precise – while Barney stayed behind, "hired out" to various slaveholders until he joined her at a later date. When Graham died almost two decades later, Montgomery fell into the possession of John R. Bronaugh, who placed the bondman in William H. Williams' slave pen. With his longtime mistress's demise and his transfer to jail, Barney Montgomery filed a freedom suit. The slave laws of Maryland governed slavery and slaveholding in the parts of the District of Columbia north of the Potomac River, and according to one legislative act of 1802, "A slave brought from any place except Maryland, into the District of Columbia, more than a year after his master, and sold, or to be sold, or to reside, is entitled to freedom." (The law did not apply to or interfere with the conduct of domestic slave traders such as the Williamses, based in Washington.) On the basis of this statute and his prolonged delay in leaving Virginia to reunite with his mistress in Georgetown, Barney Montgomery took his case before the US Circuit Court in March 1843. The court found against him, for his former neighbors from Prince William County recalled that the "colored man" left for Washington, D. C., in 1824, shortly after Graham's departure, and not more than a year later, as required by law. Montgomery's motion for a new trial was overruled.[26]

Montgomery appealed to the court again, in the summer of 1843. By then, John R. Bronaugh had confined him "in the private jail of William A. [sic] Williams & Thomas Williams who are traders in slaves." Montgomery pleaded for another appearance before the court, at its upcoming August session, because he had gathered new testimony in support of his cause. Susan Wright, "a respectable white woman" from the old neighborhood "and a credible witness" whom Montgomery had not realized was still alive, had been located, and she was willing to appear before a justice of the peace and file an affidavit that the bondman had lingered in Prince William County about fifteen months after his mistress moved to Washington County. Montgomery could thus renew his drive for freedom, because he now had proof that he had been physically separated from his owner three months longer than allowed by Maryland and D.C. law. This new information bolstered Montgomery's case significantly and boded well for him should he be granted a re-hearing. In his appeal, Montgomery stressed the urgency of his case and requested an injunction against his captors, for "he fears that he will be sold into parts beyond the jurisdiction of the court" before it met again, rendering him "unable to make his application to the court & strike out" the former judgment against him. Judge William Cranch granted the injunction on July 8, preventing John R. Bronaugh, William H. Williams, and Thomas Williams "from removing, or suffering, or permitting" Montgomery's removal outside the court's jurisdiction. The bondman would get another day in court.[27]

Like Barney Montgomery, James Becket in 1845 begged the Circuit Court of the District of Columbia for intervention. Becket's journey to the court began decades earlier, before he was even born, when his mother's master made out his last will and testament in November 1815. John Chew of Prince George's County, Maryland, freed one bondman immediately in his will but gradually emancipated his other slaves, staggering their liberations over many years. Specified bondwomen named in the will would be set free in five, seven, eight, and nine years. The balance of Chew's slaves, plus the currently living and future children of all of them, would be emancipated upon attaining thirty years of age. Becket's mother, Elizabeth, counted among the bond-women freed eight years after 1815. Born about 1819, Becket would have learned, probably from his free black mother, that he would gain his freedom, too, come 1849.[28]

After John Chew's death, the Clarke family inherited James Becket. The widow Agnes Clarke of Montgomery County, Maryland, became Becket's new owner, but he obtained her permission to live in Washington, D.C., "hiring himself and paying his wages from time to time," either to her or to her agent. Becket found the arrangement tolerable but naturally looked with anticipation toward his thirtieth birth-day. In 1845, however, "one William Glover, claiming to act by the authority" of mistress Agnes Clarke, took the twenty-six-year-old Becket into custody "and closely confined him in the private slave jail of one Thomas Williams, a dealer in slaves for exportation." With emancipation tantalizingly near, Becket felt understandable panic when he heard that "Glover has given out publicly" that Becket was "a slave for life, & that he is for sale as such." Fearing that he would, in fact, be "sold for life, into foreign parts, and so be utterly deprived of his rights under the will" of John Chew, Becket petitioned the Circuit Court for aid in avoiding that fate. All the evidence bore out Becket's story, and Judge Cranch filed the requested injunction on August 28. Directed at both Thomas Williams and agent Ebenezer Rodbird, it "prohibited and strictly enjoined [them] from removing ... Becket beyond the jurisdication of the ... Circuit Court."[29]

Although William H. Williams' slave-trading operations survived the "hard times," his legal troubles cast a long shadow that could not help but interfere with his focus on business. After two hung juries, a conviction for illegally importing enslaved criminals, and the overturning of that verdict by the Louisiana Supreme Court, Williams appeared to have weathered the lawsuit against him. But Attorney General Christian Roselius was eager to re-litigate the case. He successfully applied for a rehearing before the state Supreme Court that would drag out Williams' prosecution another two years.

The Louisiana Supreme Court revisited Williams' importation of convict slaves in the spring of 1844. This time, Attorney General Roselius set aside the question, central in the 1842 trial, of whether the Supreme Court could exercise appellate powers over Criminal Court rulings. He instead refocused attention on the language of the 1817 slave importation law that Williams had allegedly violated. To date, Roselius explained, all parties involved in Williams' case had "taken for granted, that nothing but a penal action is given by the act of 1817" and that "penal actions are civil suits." But how, precisely, does one define "penal action"? According to Roselius, "It is a suit brought for the recovery of a pecuniary penalty for the commission or omission of an act in violation of a penal statute, in virtue of a special provision in the law authorizing the plaintiff *to sue for it.*" Under no circumstances could there be a "penal action ... unless the authority *to sue* ... or *to recover*" the fine is "expressly given by the statute on which the action is founded." Echoing Justice Henry Bullard's dissent from the first Supreme Court trial, Roselius noted that the punishment appended to an unlawful act did not determine whether it was a crime or misdemeanor, on one hand, or a penal action on the other. Louisiana law enumerated a number of offenses punishable only by fine but that were nonetheless criminal. In Louisiana, the one state that did not adhere to the common law, the legislature explicitly identified those relatively "few penal actions, or actions on penal statutes" in the language of the law. The 1817 prohibition against importing slave convicts was not one of them. "No authority is given in the act of 1817," Roselius declared, "either to the State, or to a common informer, to sue for the recovery of the fine or forfeiture," and "I contend, that ... [t]here is no penal action unless the right to sue for and recover the penalty be given by the statute." Without such a provision, the act of 1817 must establish "a crime or misdemeanor" properly heard before the Criminal Courts, from which there was no appeal.[30]

Yet again, John R. Grymes and Randall Hunt represented William H. Williams. In defense of their client, they revisited the previous case that appeared before the Louisiana Supreme Court and invoked the arguments of Judge François-Xavier Martin's majority opinion from almost two years earlier. The 1817 act was "purely penal," imposing "nothing but a certain, definite, fixed pecuniary penalty." Williams, then, should properly have been subject to a civil suit from which he could appeal to the Supreme Court. Grymes and Hunt then proceeded to challenge Roselius' premise that there could be no "penal action" or civil suit unless a given law expressly granted the authority to sue for or recover a penalty. "Wherever a statute prohibits a thing, as being an immediate offence against the public good in general, under a certain penalty," they argued, "the statute is a penal statute," and the proper avenue for recovering that penalty is "in a court of revenue, and not by indictment." Any time Louisiana law attached only "a pecuniary penalty" to an offense, the proper legal recourse was "a civil action" rather than a criminal indictment, unless the statute stated otherwise. The law of 1817 did not explicitly allow for a criminal indictment, so Williams' case was "in no just sense a criminal proceeding."[31]

The Louisiana Supreme Court rendered its final verdict on the case of William H. Williams on April 8, 1844. By a 3–2 margin, it found in favor of the state and against the slave trader. Judges Martin and Rice Garland remained steadfast in their support of the arguments of Williams' counsel. Henry Bullard heard nothing to sway him toward Williams, and he was joined in the newly aligned court majority by justices Alonzo Morphy and Edward Simon, both of whom, upon further reflection, reached different conclusions from those in the first Supreme Court decision.[32]

Judge Morphy had been born in Charleston, South Carolina, in 1798 but moved to Louisiana in his youth. After being admitted to the bar in 1819, he practiced law on Toulouse Street in New Orleans. His career carried him to the Louisiana statehouse in 1825 and to the office of state attorney general prior to his appointment in 1839 to the Supreme Court. Morphy found Attorney General Roselius' arguments convincing: "If a statute imposing a fine does not authorize its recovery by action of debt, bill, plaint, or information of debt, but merely denounces such fine or penalty to be paid by the offender on conviction," Roselius stated, "the law is properly a criminal one, and the offender must be prosecuted" criminally. By that standard, Morphy agreed, "The act of 1817 is criminal law. It contains no provision for the recovery of the fine by suit; its language excludes the idea of a civil proceeding, as it imposes the fine upon the conviction of the offender." Moreover, Morphy indicated, Louisiana law allowed the substitution of up to one year's confinement in jail as an alternative to paying the fine. As he explained, the fine could therefore not be construed as "a mere civil debt" because "under our present laws no imprisonment [for debt] exists." Legally, the fine must have been the consequence of a criminal conviction.[33]

Like Morphy, Judge Florent Edouard "Edward" Simon, a native of Belgium and the first of four generations of Louisiana jurists, concurred with the newly constituted majority opinion. To his admitted surprise, Simon, a member of the Supreme Court since 1840, likewise reached the conclusion promoted by Attorney General Roselius that the legislative intent behind the law of 1817 was "to create a crime or misdemeanor punishable criminally." The state's prosecution of William H. Williams in the Criminal Court was therefore legitimate, and the slave trader had no grounds for appeal from that court. Siding with the state, the Louisiana Supreme Court granted Roselius' motion to dismiss Williams' case.[34]

Had the state's prosecution of William H. Williams reached the state Supreme Court after 1844, the outcome might well have gone in the slave trader's favor. One significant change in the revised Louisiana Constitution of 1845 was that it permitted appeals of criminal cases to the Supreme Court. Moreover, the court's composition would have been entirely different. The Constitutional Convention abolished the existing state Supreme Court on March 19, 1846, and promptly reconstituted it with an entirely new slate of judges. None of the five justices who heard Williams' case was welcomed back.

By the time his courtroom odyssey concluded in 1844, William H. Williams had long since served out his year's imprisonment in the Orleans Parish jail as punishment for his crime. He emerged from prison an injured man, he later said, physically sick and with "the odium of a convicted felon attached to his otherwise fair name." Upon gaining his release, Williams quickly resumed the business of slave dealing. As suggested by slaves' bills of sale filed with a host of notaries public, from 1843 to 1847, he spent the overwhelming preponderance of his time in New Orleans. From his office on Esplanade Street, the "negro trader" raked in thousands of dollars from the sales of hundreds of enslaved men and women. Some transactions were monetarily small: Williams sold the eleven-year-old Albert to Joseph Salvant of Plaquemines Parish in May 1844 for a mere $75. Others involved enormous sums totaling several thousand dollars. But Williams' accumulating profits did little to tamp down his sense of loss and the impression that he had been unfairly maligned, his reputation damaged. Thoughts of the convict bondpeople forfeited to the state of Louisiana never strayed far from his mind, and he determined to get them back, if it was the last thing he did.[35]

CHAPTER 9

Politics of the Slave Pen

BORN INTO POVERTY IN THE SMALL VILLAGE OF Farmington, New Hampshire, in 1812, Jeremiah Jones Colbath grew up with little. When he reached the age of ten, his shiftless, drunken father apprenticed him to a neighboring farmer for whom young Jeremiah toiled, with few opportunities for formal schooling, for the next eleven years. The lad's unfortunate circumstances nurtured within him a drive and ambition utterly foreign to his father. During his apprenticeship, upon his own initiative, Jeremiah voraciously consumed his master's books and others he could borrow, and at the age of nineteen he swore off alcohol in an implicit rejection of his father's intemperate ways. His twenty-first birthday in 1833 brought liberation. Estranged from his family, Jeremiah petitioned the state legislature to cast off the name his parents had given him at birth. The newly rechristened Henry Wilson left Farmington behind, walking the hundred miles to the Boston area. In Natick, Massachusetts, he took up the shoemaker's trade, a humble occupation but one that produced a product in high demand. Self-motivated to a fault, the striving cobbler worked so incessantly and aggressively, albeit carelessly, churning out for market shoes of dubious quality, that his labors took a toll on his health. Taking time to relax and recuperate from a pulmonary ailment, Wilson traveled to the nation's capital of Washington, D.C., in May 1836.[1]

It was a transformative journey that permanently altered the trajectory of the twenty-four-year-old Henry Wilson's life. "I didn't know anybody in Washington, and nobody had any reason to know me," he later recounted, but what the naïve, wide-eyed Wilson saw made a profound impression. Crossing on to the Island, he gazed upon "the infamous

Williams slave pen, and ... the poor people marched down to the river-side and shipped off to the 'far South.'" He also witnessed "men and women, in chains, put upon the auction block for the crime of possessing 'a skin darker than his own,' and sold to hopeless slavery." As a consequence of these spectacles, Wilson stated, "I pledged myself to liberty." He "thought deeply and sadly of the horrors and aggressions of slavery, its inhuman cruelties, its traffic in the souls and bodies of men, its deliberate trampling upon the political as well as social rights of the nation, and from that day forth the settled purpose of his heart was to make war upon slavery." The young man returned "to Massachusetts, filled with pity for the hapless bondman, and with defiance to his oppressor." His interest in politics intensified, Wilson was elected to the Massachusetts legislature at age twenty-eight and occupied a seat in the statehouse from 1841 to 1852. He also edited the Free-Soil *Boston Republican* newspaper from 1848 to 1851 before moving on to serve in the US Senate from 1855 to 1873. Though not as vociferous, eloquent, or flamboyant as his Massachusetts senatorial colleague Charles Sumner, whose 1856 Crime against Kansas speech prompted the infamous bludgeoning administered by the cane-toting representative Preston Brooks of South Carolina, Wilson reliably pursued slavery's demise. The Yellow House directly contributed to the education of Henry Wilson, the poor farm boy and shoemaker who resigned his Senate seat to become Ulysses S. Grant's vice president.[2]

William H. Williams' slave jail at the corner of Maryland Avenue and Seventh Street garnered frequent mention by observant contemporaries. Shrouded as it was "behind leafy trees" that obscured it somewhat from the public gaze of passersby, the looming hulk of the slave pen was nevertheless unavoidable. "It is a house by which all must go in order to reach the building of the Smithsonian Institution," remarked Mississippi senator and museum regent Jefferson Davis in 1850. Davis' eventual Civil War adversary noticed Williams' private prison as well. Abraham Lincoln remarked that, during his brief stint in Congress, he could see, "from the windows of the capitol, a sort of negro-livery stable, where droves of negroes were collected, temporarily kept, and finally taken to Southern markets, precisely like droves of horses."[3]

The troubling proximity of the slave prison to the US Capitol building earned repeated notice in the abolitionist press and by travelers struck by the incongruity of the juxtaposition. As Henry Wilson put it when he first reached Washington, D.C., "I saw slavery beneath the shadow of the flag that waved over the Capitol." Abolitionist J. Miller McKim described the relative locations of the US Congress and the Yellow House as an "abomination." The slave jail sat "within a short distance of the stars and stripes of the capitol," he complained with righteous indignation. Approximately five generous city blocks separated the two structures, or "about half a mile," estimated one newspaper correspondent. Solomon Northup reported that, "looking down from [the] commanding height" of Capitol Hill, congressmen and visitors alike could peer westward and readily identify the Yellow House "within plain sight ... A slave pen within the very shadow of the Capitol!" Touring the Capitol in 1850, traveler Fredrika Bremer confirmed that Williams' slave jail "may be seen from it," "[i]n full view."[4]

The sight of slave traders marching bondpeople in coffles through Washington, D.C., ranked as one of the most stinging visual images of the paradox that was American slavery. Enslaved people plodded along in chains "through the Capital of a nation, whose theory of government, we were told, rests on the foundation of man's inalienable right to life, LIBERTY, and the pursuit of happiness!" Solomon Northup exclaimed. "Let it be known to the citizens of America," declared one abolitionist society in the presidential election year of 1840, "that at the very time when the procession which contained the President of the United States and his cabinet was marching in triumph to the Capitol, another kind of procession was marching another way." That second parade was no raucous celebration. It was solemn rather than festive, for it "consisted of coloured human beings, *handcuffed in pairs*, and driven along by ... a man on horseback!"[5]

African Americans passing through the nation's capital in the antebellum decades well understood the fundamental, underlying absurdity of the enslaved condition in an alleged land of freedom. Free black sailor George Henry, upon reaching the Washington Navy Yard in the 1830s, was permitted to "go up to see the Capitol, the centre of this so called free country." Although unable to partake of all the nation's fruits, Henry "longed to see" the home of the national government. En route, "under the hill of the building," he recalled, "we heard ... screaming and crying"

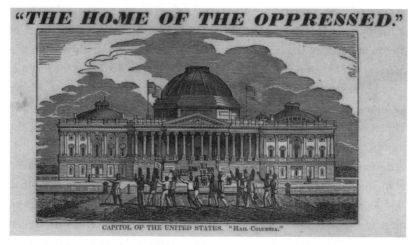

"THE HOME OF THE OPPRESSED."

CAPITOL OF THE UNITED STATES. "HAIL COLUMBIA."

12 A slave coffle passes the US Capitol.
Source: "The Home of the Oppressed"/"Hail Columbia," *Slave Market of America* (New York: American Anti-Slavery Society, 1836), Broadside Collection, portfolio 118, no. 26c, Library of Congress, Rare Book and Special Collections Division, Washington, D.C.

emanating from some unknown source in the distance. Continuing on, he and his companions encountered "about two hundred men and women chained together, two and two," some "as fair as the sun ever shone upon." They explained to Henry that they were trudging to Alexandria for transport to New Orleans and sale. At that moment, Henry recounted,

> When I saw that virtue was to be sacrificed to the highest bidder I said . . . "Away with your pretended free America, it is all a sham in my eye." It was then and there I took an oath against slavery . . . that I would never go to Washington [again], unless I went with an army to take her or burn her down.

Two decades before Henry came face-to-face with the ugly reality of the Washington, D.C. slave trade, a "drove of manacled coloured people" passed the Capitol as several congressmen congregated outside on the street. In a poignant and daring act of social criticism, one member of the coffle raised his enchained arms to the sky and serenaded the gentlemen lawmakers with an ironic rendition of the patriotic song and unofficial national anthem, "Hail Columbia! Happy Land." (See Figure 12.) The unmistakable mockery evident in the bondman's performance may have brought the soloist a fleeting moment of catharsis as he condemned the cruel irony of his situation.[6]

Frequent complaints of slaves' visibility in the nation's capital forced a modification in traders' practices over time. The offensive sight of slave coffles paraded through Washington's streets became less common. In 1849, a Washington correspondent for the *New York Tribune* reported that thirty or forty bondpeople arrived in the capital from Baltimore, bound for Williams' slave jail. "Seven or ten years ago," he wrote, "They would have been driven in irons," by foot, "up the great Federal Avenue to Seventh street . . . Now they are quietly put into *seven hacks*" and wheeled by horse-drawn coach to the Yellow House. In 1850, Mississippi senator Jefferson Davis, who first arrived in Washington to assume national office in 1845, denied having ever set eyes on manacled slaves herded by traders through the city, a recurring scene so vividly described by previous visitors to the District.[7]

The abolitionist press widely publicized a litany of dramatic, sorrowful, and terrible tales that exposed the brutal realities of slavery, a few of which directly condemned Williams' pen. "If ever you have been to Washington, you have probably noticed a large yellow house which stands about a mile from the avenue, near the Potomac," reported a correspondent of the Lowell, Massachusetts, *Journal.* "That is the slave prison; it is owned by a celebrated slave trader, who has made a large fortune by following his hellish traffic." Inside the Yellow House, he continued, languished "a colored man . . . whom his master hired to the government to fight in Florida, against the Indians. The poor fellow did the fighting, while his master drew the pay. He is now petitioning the government for freedom and a pension." In the meantime, he remained in Williams' "jail until the question is decided."[8]

An anonymous "Member of Congress," later identified as antislavery Whig representative Seth M. Gates of New York, in 1842 related another tragic tale from the "gloomy walls" of the Yellow House. Gates described an unnamed "smart and active female slave" deposited in Williams' private prison for sale in the southern market, who, the evening prior to her scheduled departure from Washington, "darted past her keeper," broke jail, "and ran for her life." She headed south-west down Maryland Avenue, straight toward the Long Bridge that spanned the Potomac and led to the portion of the District ceded by Virginia. "It [was] not a great distance from the prison to the long bridge," Gates observed, and on the opposite side of the river lay the Custis estate and its "extensive forests and woodlands" where the fugitive could hide.[9]

The bondwoman's flight took the keeper of Williams' jail, Joshua Staples, by surprise. By the time he secured the other enslaved prisoners and set off in pursuit, the fleeing bondwoman had a sizeable head start. Also working in her favor, "no bloodhounds were at hand" to track her, and the late hour meant that "horses could not readily be obtained for the chase." Staples and a small band of men at his immediate disposal would have to overtake her on foot. Although they "raised the hue and cry on her pathway" to summon the public's aid, the absconded slave breezed past the bewildered citizens of Washington who streamed out of their homes, struggling to comprehend the cause of all the commo-tion along the avenue. Realizing the scene unfolding before their eyes, some residents prayed for the fugitive's successful escape, while others joined "the motley mass in pursuit," too late to meaningfully impede her progress. Fleet of foot and with everything to lose, the bondwoman put still more distance between her and her would-be captors. In this contest of "speed and endurance, between the slave and the slave catchers," the runaway was winning. She reached the end of Maryland Avenue and made it on to the Long Bridge. All the "poor hunted female" needed to do was cross the three-fourths of a mile expanse of the Long Bridge to secrete herself in the Custis woods. Yet just as Staples and his men set foot on the bridge, they caught sight of three white men at the opposite end, "slowly advancing from the Virginia side." Staples called out to them to seize the runaway slave. Dutifully, they arranged themselves three abreast, blocking the width of the narrow bridge. The unidentified bondwoman "looked wildly and anxiously around, to see if there was no other hope of escape," but her prospects for success had suddenly evaporated. As her pursuers rapidly approached, their "noisy shout[s]" and threats filling the air, she lost the last shreds of hope that spurred her flight from the Yellow House. The woman then "vaulted over the railing of the bridge," plunged into "the deep loamy water of the Potomac," and sank "forever beneath the waves of the river." Apparently concerned that the dramatic tale of the bondwoman's demise may have sounded apocryphal, Gates insisted that several other members of Congress could attest to the veracity of the story he shared. The suicide, he concluded, demonstrated "the unconquerable love of liberty the heart of the slave may inherit" and offered "a fresh admonition to the slave dealer, of the cruelty and enormity of his crimes."[10]

Gates reserved his harshest scorn for Joshua Staples, whom William H. Williams, sitting in the Orleans Parish prison, had installed as jailer at the Yellow House only the year before the bondwoman's self-destruction. "This shameless human flesh dealer," wrote Gates in his anonymous rebuke, "has the use of a *private slave prison*, standing midway between the Capitol and the President's House, in the city of Washington, on the lowlands below Gadsby's." There, Staples "secures the poor heart-broken captives that he purchases." Any Washington, D.C. master "who[,] from losses at the gaming table or race course, from extravagance, improvidence, or other cause," wanted to dispose of one or more slaves knew to do so by "*secret sale* to Mr. Joshua Staples." Gates unleashed a religiously inspired condemnation of all slave traders for their wicked and "damnable traffick" and, in a final moralizing flourish, urged Staples and all who "persist in buying and selling the bodies and souls of thy fellow-men, after being warned of the tendency and cruelty of thy villainous trade," to repent at the risk of sacrificing their eternal salvation in heaven.[11]

Slave traders did not much fret over their souls and even mocked those critical of them. In 1841, an English abolitionist and traveler to Washington, D.C., after visiting the US Senate, "drove to a slave-dealer's establishment, near at hand, and within sight of the *Capitol*," no doubt William H. Williams' slave prison. There, he "looked in upon a group of human beings herded together like cattle for the market, within an enclosure of high brick walls surrounding the jail." Inside the Yellow House, the informant cast his eyes upon "portraits and caricatures of abolitionists" hanging on the walls of the slave trader's office. The derisive artwork ridiculed renowned Irish antislavery agitator Daniel

O'Connell; American-born abolitionist Arthur Tappan, founder of both the American Anti-Slavery Society and the American and Foreign Anti-Slavery Society; and former US president John Quincy Adams, not an abolitionist per se but long an antislavery gadfly in the House of Representatives. "The young man in charge of the establishment" – probably Joshua Staples, at the time of the visit – "began to explain them, for our amusement," the traveler recalled. Upon learning that his guest was an abolitionist, Staples turned sheepish, "uneasy," and eager to see him on his way.[12]

Slave dealers bolder than Staples directly rebutted their critics, whether Yankee abolitionists or southern slaveholders themselves. Despite the social reality that most slave traders were wealthy, respected businessmen and even community leaders engaged in an entirely lawful occupation, after the rise of radical abolitionism in the early 1830s, slave owners deflected responsibility for the sin of slave ownership by scapegoating the dealers who peddled human commodities. Time and again, masters proclaimed that the dishonest, disreputable, and reviled "nigger trader" was to blame for the scourge of slavery. "We despise the slave-trader," declared one D.C. slaveholder. "Throughout all the South he is a marked man. The *gentleman* does not shake hands with . . . the . . . 'Negro-buyer.'" Kentucky-born lawyer and one-term Illinois congressman Abraham Lincoln understood the discourse and parroted it back to an audience in 1854. "[Y]ou have amongst you, a sneaking individual, of the class of native tyrants, known as the 'SLAVE-DEALER,'" he told them:

> He watches your necessities, and crawls up to buy your slave, at a speculating price. If you cannot help it, you sell to him; but if you can help it, you drive him from your door. You despise him utterly. You do not recognize him as a friend, or even as an honest man. Your children must not play with his; they may rollick freely with the little negroes, but not with the "slave-dealers" children. If you are obliged to deal with him, you try to get through the job without so much as touching him. It is common with you to join hands with the men you meet; but with the slave dealer you avoid the ceremony – instinctively shrinking from the snaky contact. If he grows rich and retires from business, you still remember him, and still keep up the ban of non-intercourse upon him and his family.

Mississippi senator and slaveholder Jefferson Davis carried the argument one step further. Slave dealers, he declared, "are usually northern men, who come among us but are not of us." The problem in all of this was that the truthfulness of the rhetoric did not match its ubiquity.[13]

Richard Hildreth wrote in his antislavery novel, *The White Slave; or, Memoirs of a Fugitive*, that practically every slaveholder "pretends to look with a certain contempt on the trader to whom he sells them" and "of whom he buys them," yet "in what respect the slave traders are less respectable than the slave raisers, or the slave buyers, I am unable to see." Certainly slave traders such as the Williams brothers acknowledged no dishonor or embarrassment in their occupation. They advertised their services and wants in the public papers and upon request shamelessly took abolitionists on guided tours of their incarceration facilities. One correspondent observed in 1849 that "Col. WILLIAMS" – likely William H. – "looks and talks like a kind-hearted, benevolent man." In conversation, Williams "argue[d] that his vocation as a dealer in human chattels is no more cruel or disreputable than working slaves on plantations, and buying or selling them as caprice or wants might dictate." The amused visitor wrote incredulously, "He eased his conscience of the damning sin by comparison!" It was a tried and true defense. Eight years earlier, a "young man" in charge of Williams' jail, probably Joshua Staples, informed English abolitionist Joseph Sturge "that he knew of no reasons for condemning slave-traders, which did not equally apply to slave-holders." The remark struck the traveler as valid. "You will bear in mind," Sturge recorded, "that this was said within view of the capitol, where slave-holders control your national legislation, and within a few minutes' walk of that mansion where a slave-holder," John Tyler of Virginia, "sits in the presidential chair." As a result, the abolitionist continued facetiously, "the humble slave-dealer of the district should feel himself in honourable company, and really regard his occupation as one of respectability and public utility."[14]

The presence of William H. Williams' slave jail in Washington, D.C., supplied ample fodder for abolitionist critiques of slavery and the slave trade in the nation's capital and lent urgency to appeals for their termination there. But how to achieve such lofty goals? And who would lead the effort? Who could display the requisite strength and courage and moral fortitude to stand on principle against the evils of human bondage? Thousands upon thousands of American citizens believed that perhaps such an individual could be found somewhere in the halls of Congress.[15]

The District of Columbia had been purposefully created from slave territory. No less significant a founder than George Washington preferred a southern home for the nation's new capital, a location where southern traditions would be respected and the institution of bondage insulated from challenge. And so the District was conjured out of the slaveholding states of Maryland and Virginia, the federal city arising from mosquito-infested swampland. Although southern slaveholders assumed the site of the capital would dissuade agitators from pressing antislavery causes and encourage acceptance of the institution there, some who recognized the incongruity of slavery in the District spoke out. In January 1802, the grand jury for Alexandria County, within the District of Columbia, presented Congress with a statement of grievance about the disgrace of buying and selling bondmen and -women in the new national capital. A proposal in January 1805 to gradually emancipate children born on or after July 4 of that year to enslaved mothers whose masters resided in the District of Columbia failed in Congress by a vote of 47–65. By the early nineteenth century, the revolutionary era's momentum in the direction of freedom had stalled.[16]

Yet despite the waning enthusiasm for extending freedom's blessings to slaves, in spring 1816, Virginia representative John Randolph of Roanoke made a motion "to inquire into the existence of an inhuman and illegal traffic in slaves, carried on, in, and through the District of Columbia" and to report on the propriety of implementing measures to end it. Article 1, section 8 of the US Constitution empowered Congress to exercise exclusive legislative authority over the District "in all Cases whatsoever," but that provision posed an immediate threat to southern congressmen's slaveholding constituents. The United States' legal participation in the transatlantic slave trade had formally ended in 1808, so, to meet their labor demands, states wedded to slavery necessarily relied on the redistribution of the country's existing enslaved workforce via the domestic slave trade. As a result, already by 1816, many southern congressmen viewed any proposition "to prevent the internal trade in slaves" as "an idea well calculated to produce excitement and alarm in the slave-holding States."[17]

Nevertheless, petitions from across the country, begging Congress to grapple with the institution of slavery in the national capital, trickled in throughout the 1820s. A few even originated in southern, slaveholding states. In 1822, Congress received a memorial from the Manumission Society of Tennessee, requesting that slaves born in the District of Columbia be freed upon attaining a certain age. The House of Representatives referred the request to a committee, where it died. In 1826, the House Committee on the District of Columbia voted down another effort to gradually abolish slavery in the capital and restrain the slave trade within its boundaries.[18]

During his two terms in Congress spanning 1825 to 1829, Representative Charles Miner of Pennsylvania emerged as the most persistent, early congressional champion for the eradication of the D.C. slave trade. Slave dealers had made Washington "their headquarters for carrying on the domestic slave trade," he informed his colleagues. "This traffic, and the views it exhibits ... are as offensive to the people of the District as they are unjust in themselves, and impolitic in us to countenance." Miner reviewed the history of attempts to rescind the slave trade in the nation's capital and then collated and presented the full range of arguments against it. Slave dealers made extensive use of the public jails to house their chattel and also erected their own private prisons, "those secret repositories of misery," for the same purpose. Traders kidnapped and unlawfully enslaved free blacks, carried away into lifetime bondage slaves scheduled to become free, and drove desperate slaves to kill or maim themselves "from anguish and despair" at the prospect of forced relocation and sale away from family and friends. The D.C. slave trade inflicted a host of injustices upon the black population, but it also exerted detrimental consequences upon whites and the nation as a whole. The spectacle of manacled slaves trudging sullenly through the streets of Washington was offensive to the "moral sensibility of its citizens" and injurious to public morals as the masses became anesthetized to the brutality of it all. Furthermore, the slave trade damaged the US reputation abroad. The US government, Miner explained, stood for "[j]ustice and equal rights" rather than despotism, yet foreign guests – the panoply of ambassadors, dignitaries, and diplomats from across the globe – congregated in the nation's capital, only to witness shocking, shameful scenes of slave coffles paraded through the streets. It was a national embarrassment incongruent with American values. The honorable thing for Congress to do was act, Miner concluded, and the time for Congress to act was now. Otherwise, he cautioned his colleagues, "Your silence gives sanction to the trade." The House of Representatives agreed to consider Miner's motion by a vote of 104–70, but southern opposition prevented the passage of any legislation hostile to the commerce in black bodies.[19]

The emergence of a radical abolitionist movement in the late 1820s and early 1830s accelerated the pace at which petitions calling for legislation to restrict slavery and the slave trade in Washington, D.C., reached Congress. Memorials arrived from Massachusetts, New York, Ohio, and other northern states. Indicating "the gross inconsistency of the theory and practice of our Government," one representative from Pennsylvania presented seven petitions totaling more than one thousand signatures from those who favored a ban on slavery and the slave trade in the District of Columbia.[20]

Many of the politically active signatories of these petitions bound for Congress were women who, though unable to vote, still voiced their informed opinions. As subordinated members of American society, denied many basic rights, antebellum-era women could sympathize with the plight of slaves in ways that most white men could not, and the well-known traffic in slaves in the nation's capital captured their attention. In late 1831, Quaker abolitionist Lucretia Mott and 2,311 "other female citizens of the city of Philadelphia and its vicinity" sent a memorial to abolish the slave trade in Washington, D.C. The House of Representatives also received, in 1835, petitions "signed by eight hundred ladies" from New York and another from "172 females," among others, "praying for the abolition of slavery and the slave trade in the District of Columbia." The next year, a Vermont congressman presented similar petitions from "one hundred females of Cornwall," Vermont, and an additional 426 women from surrounding Addison County. Female petitioners' words at times took their male congressional representatives by surprise. When two antislavery petitions arrived from Ohio – one just from women – in January 1836, future president James Buchanan, in his brief stint as US senator from Pennsylvania, observed that "the memorial from the softer sex contains as much matter of offence, insult, and vituperation, applicable to all the slaveholding portions of their fellow-citizens, as could possibly have been put into a paper of the same compass." Buchanan found it unbecoming. He disapproved of the women's bold language and criticized their "fanaticism," remarking, "They have unsexed themselves."[21]

Representative John Quincy Adams of Massachusetts, unique among former presidents in returning to the House after stepping down as commander-in-chief, submitted more petitions in favor of the abolition of slavery and the slave trade in the District of Columbia than did any other congressman. Soon after his return to the House chamber in 1831, Adams presented a batch of fifteen such memorials, not from his own constituents in Massachusetts but from individuals in Pennsylvania who entrusted him with their written sentiments. In January 1836, Adams offered the House a similar petition from four hundred citizens of Indiana and Westmoreland counties, also in the Keystone State.[22]

From 1835 to 1836, what was once a trickle and then a steady stream of petitions against the D.C. slave trade became a raging torrent. In 1835, the American Anti-Slavery Society launched a mass mailing campaign that sent thousands of abolitionist pamphlets to the South, enraging slaveholders, who responded by burning the incendiary literature and stepping up their vigilance in detecting possible abolitionist agents in their midst. Abolitionists then redoubled their efforts to persuade Congress through a flood of petitions requesting the destruction of the slave trade in Washington, D.C. One estimate placed the total number of signatures over the two-year span from 1835 to 1836 at 34,000. Memorials concerning slavery in the District of Columbia composed a sizeable majority of all petitions submitted to Congress in the second half of the 1830s. Yet in a nation of approximately 15 million people, signers represented less than one-quarter of 1 percent of all Americans. Proslavery defenders took comfort in the fact that, however vocal they were, abolitionists were miniscule in their numbers, with little public support. "The whole number of abolition petitioners scarcely exceeded thirty thousand," observed Representative Henry Laurens Pinckney of South Carolina, adding dismissively that "one half ... were females, and it was confidently believed that a considerable number of the remainder were children." As he saw it, none of their signatures really mattered.[23]

Still, southern congressmen vehemently resented the deluge of incoming petitions. Most practically, the onslaught of memorials from out-of-the-way places such as Belmont County, Ohio, and some two dozen more from the town of Utica and Oneida County, New York, robbed inordinate quantities of time on the floor that they would rather spend debating other issues. More pointedly, southern senators and representatives believed the petitions an affront to their constituents, their traditional way of life, and their states. Among the arguments political leaders from the South invoked in the 1830s to ignore calls for Congress to interfere with slavery in Washington, D.C., was the fact that almost all of the petitions originated in the North and "came from persons not interested personally in the question of negro slavery." Moreover, "[c]onsidering that the District of Columbia is composed of cessions of territory made to the United States by the [slaveholding] States of Virginia and Maryland," reported one House committee in 1831, nothing should be done "until the wisdom of State Governments shall have devised some practicable means of eradicating or diminishing the evil of slavery." Any action on Congress's part would violate Virginia's and Maryland's implied faith that slavery would be legal in the lands they donated to the District. In addition, members of Congress recognized that any liberation of slaves in the nation's capital would transform Washington into a haven for runaways from the adjoining states, thereby endangering the security of area masters' right to their enslaved property. Until Virginia and Maryland developed their own plans to deal with bondage, the committee concluded, "it would be unwise and impolitic, if not unjust . . . for Congress to interfere in a subject of such delicacy and importance as is the relation between master and slave." By 1836, as the abolitionist petition drive gained increasing momentum, southern representatives more readily denied that Congress exercised lawful jurisdiction over slavery in the District at all. Recognizing that congressional tampering with slavery in Washington set a precedent to meddle with slavery in the western territories, and possibly even in the states, southern congressmen simply rejected altogether the notion that Congress possessed the constitutional authority to legislate on the matter. To do so, they cautioned, would insult the slaveholding states and jeopardize the survival of the Union. One southern congressman who adhered to these views was Representative Rice Garland, who in just a few years would be sitting on the Louisiana Supreme Court to deliberate William H. Williams' fate after importing enslaved criminals into New Orleans.[24]

The House of Representatives, where the Three-Fifths Compromise from 1787 magnified the South's political voice by counting slaves, though ineligible to vote, as 60 percent of a free person for purposes of representation, opted to stifle debate over slavery rather than confront the divisive issue head-on. By the so-called "gag rule" of 1836, any petitions to the House on the subject of slavery were received and automatically tabled, precluding their reading, discussion, or printing. Watching from the gallery the day the "gag rule" first passed was convalescing shoemaker Henry Wilson, visiting Washington from Massachusetts. From his vantage point, he recollected, "I ... saw the slave masters 'laying on the table' the petition[s] of the Christian men and women of the country against the abominable traffic in human beings." Because it was a resolution and not a standing rule, the gag rule required renewal each legislative session to remain in force. A majority in the House voted to continue it during subsequent congresses, and its 1840 iteration grew more onerous than ever. According to the "21st rule" approved that year, "No petition, memorial, resolution, or other paper praying the abolition of slavery in the District of Columbia, or any State or Territory, or the slave trade between the States or Territories of the United States in which it now exists, shall be received by this House, or entertained in any way whatever." The harsh new gag rule did not allow for even the receipt of antislavery memorials. "To receive these petitions would imply the power to grant their prayers," explained a Georgia representative. As he and his southern colleagues maintained, "Congress has no such power. Hence the absurdity of their reception." As in the House, antislavery petitions in the 1830s had thrown the Senate into a dither, but after extensive debate that legislative body adopted a policy less stringent than the House's gag rule, if not much different in net effect. These attempts to silence opponents of slavery and the slave trade in the District of Columbia did not produce the intended outcome, however. To the contrary, energized abolitionists flooded Congress with more antislavery petitions than ever, some with several thousand signatures, in the optimistic hope that they might be heard.[25]

For years, Massachusetts' elder statesman John Quincy Adams led the charge to overturn the gag rule in the House. Although no abolitionist, Adams upheld antislavery petitioners' First Amendment rights to speak freely and express their grievances to their government. Despite southern representatives' hostility to those opinions, memorialists still deserved an airing on the House floor, Adams insisted. Marshaling his unparalleled knowledge of parliamentary procedure and its arcane loopholes, acquired through a lifetime of public service in his nation's government, Adams' wily tactics and crafty ploys made slavery a frequent topic of conversation in the House, in spite of the gag rule. In 1837, Adams "presented a petition from one hundred and fifty women, [the] wives and daughters of his immediate constituents, praying for the abolition of slavery in the District of Columbia." Soon thereafter, he submitted before the House "the petition of nine ladies of Fredericksburg," Virginia, "to put a stop to the slave trade" in the capital. Because the women lived in a slaveholding state, he assiduously avoided identifying them by name out of fear for their personal safety. Adams barely escaped censure when, perhaps too cleverly, he "attempt[ed] to introduce ... a petition from slaves, for the abolition of slavery in the District of Columbia." Appalled House colleagues proposed a resolution stating that Adams "committed an outrage on the rights and feelings of a large portion of the people of this Union; a flagrant contempt on the dignity of this House; and, by extending to slaves a privilege only belonging to freemen, directly invite[d] the slave population to insurrection." Adams survived the temporary outrage and persisted in his labors. In 1838, he offered for the House's consideration some 350 petitions bearing a total of between 34,000 and 35,000 names. The next year, he revealed to his colleagues that "he had received a mass of letters threatening him with assassination" for attempting to introduce petitions banning slavery or the slave trade. Despite the intimidation, Adams drew upon his uncanny knack for besting his congressional adversaries to chip away at the gag rule. It took him eight years to achieve its demise: members of the House finally voted to overturn the measure in December 1844.[26]

That same year, 1844, also brought the United States its fifteenth presidential election campaign season. Slave pens such as the one belonging to William H. Williams had seen many commanders-in-chief come and go uneventfully, but in 1844 the politics of the slave pen injected themselves into the national contest for president, at least for local voters in and near the nation's capital. That year, slavery infiltrated mainstream presidential politics to an unprecedented degree, affecting the candidate selection process and the political debates between the two competing major parties, the Democrats and the Whigs. When the Democratic convention opened in Baltimore, former president Martin Van Buren, who served as the heir to Andrew Jackson from 1837 to 1841, appeared the obvious choice to secure the nomination once again. On the first ballot, however, Democratic challengers Lewis Cass of Michigan, Richard M. Johnson of Kentucky, and James Buchanan of Pennsylvania collectively denied the ex-president the requisite two-thirds majority vote. In subsequent rounds of balloting, Van Buren's support waned as Cass' grew, but Cass could not attain the needed two-thirds vote either. James Knox Polk received his first vote on the eighth round of balloting and quickly emerged as the Democrats' compromise candidate, winning the nomination on the ninth ballot. As one anonymous Democratic contemporary explained, Polk gained preference over frontrunner Van Buren "because he was from [the] slave holding state" of North Carolina (though a legislator in Tennessee) and, more importantly, because he was "positively and absolutely" sympathetic to the "unconditional and immediate annexation" of the slaveholding republic of Texas into the United States. American political observers unanimously understood that, whenever Texas entered the Union, it would augment the tally of slave states. Polk ran for president with vice presidential nominee George M. Dallas of Pennsylvania on an avowedly expansionist platform that would usher slaveholding Texas, as well as other parts of the North American continent, into the Union and shun federal interference with slavery. Polk squared off against three-time presidential nominee Henry Clay, the Whig former senator from Kentucky. Clay announced his opposition to

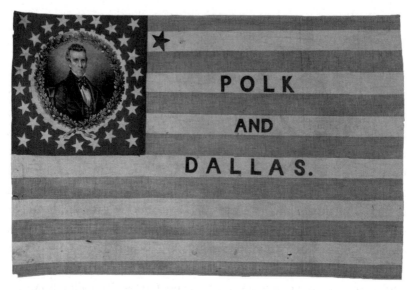

13 A Polk and Dallas flag from the presidential election of 1844.
Source: The Mark R. and Rosalind E. Shenkman Collection, Shenkman Capital, 461 Fifth Avenue, 22nd floor, New York, N.Y.

the annexation of Texas, which he calculated could earn him antislavery votes in the North despite his status as a slaveholder himself.[27]

In mid-October 1844, Thomas Williams, presiding over the Yellow House while his brother fought court battles in Louisiana, sparked controversy when he hoisted a flag above the Yellow House with the names of the Democratic ticket of Polk and Dallas inscribed on it. (See Figure 13.) In the last month of the 1844 presidential election, the Polk and Dallas flag that rippled in the wind over the Yellow House became a touchstone for political division. It set off a newspaper war in which the Whig and Democratic presses each labored to impose the onus of the political banner's placement over Williams' slave pen on to their political opponents.[28]

The kerfuffle over the Polk and Dallas flag demonstrated its potency as a symbol of political identity. It began with a report from a correspondent in Washington, D.C., to the *New York American*, stating that "a tall pole surmounted with a large and handsome flag, bearing in the largest letters the names of 'POLK and DALLAS,'" had been erected inside "the '*jail*' or '*pen*'" where the city's "negro traders put their negroes, until they get enough to ship to the south." Picking up the story, the editor of an obscure Massachusetts newspaper, the Boston *Daily Tribune*, criticized proprietor Thomas Williams for spending his ill-gotten profits from the domestic slave trade to promote the Democratic ticket, whose expansionist platform, most especially the anticipated annexation of slaveholding Texas, would render the Williams brothers' business still "more extensive and prosperous." The editorial concluded with a reprint of Thomas Williams' advertisement in Washington's *National Intelligencer* directing sellers "of negroes for the New Orleans market" to visit him "at my establishment, [at the] corner of Seventh street and Maryland avenue." Other New England newspapers chimed in on the story as well, denouncing Williams' political activism on behalf of the Democrats as "disgust[ing]."[29]

The *National Intelligencer*, Washington's hometown paper and the leading organ of the Whig Party, was thus not responsible for initiating what became yet another political spat with its cross-town rival, the Democratic *Washington Globe*. *Intelligencer* editors Joseph Gales and William Winston Seaton at first remained above the developing fray, making little comment beyond confirming that a Polk and Dallas banner had indeed "been raised and kept daily flying" by a "citizen" – unnamed in their column – "who deals in the purchase and sale of slaves" and who kept "the depôt for that trade." Other than that, Gales and Seaton deemed the Polk and Dallas flag worthy of "no remark, because the citizen who raised it had as unquestionable a right as any other person ... to express his preference for the Democratic candidate for the Presidency." Nevertheless, the northern press's reporting on the flag had already captured the public's attention and thrust the Yellow House into the American political discourse as the election drew near.[30]

John C. Rives, co-publisher with Francis P. Blair of the Democratic mouthpiece, the *Washington Globe*, was only vaguely familiar with Thomas Williams and never had any inkling of the slave trader's alleged Democratic affiliation until the *Boston Tribune* article labeled him. Seeking verification, Rives inquired of prominent local Democrats in Washington if they could corroborate the claim. They could not. As a Democrat himself, the editor sought to place some distance between his party's presidential ticket and the operator of the city's slave pen.

Although, individually, slave dealers such as Thomas Williams were prosperous and respectable men rather than social outcasts, collectively they still attracted broad censure in public conversation. Any association in voters' minds between Rives' Democrats and the Washington slave jailer flying the Polk and Dallas flag could damage the party's prospects in the November election, certainly locally and perhaps even farther afield.[31]

With an eye toward the political consequences should the Democrats become too closely associated with slavery, Rives corresponded with his friend C. G. Greene, editor of the *Boston Post*, to dispute the meaning of the banner waving over the slave pen. Rives' basic argument was that, despite hoisting the Polk and Dallas flag, slave trader Thomas Williams was, in fact, a Whig. First, he noted, Williams advertised for slaves in the *National Intelligencer*, the District's Whig paper. The Democratic *Globe*, by contrast, refused to publish advertisements from slave dealers. As proof, Rives shared one anecdote in which trader Hope Hull Slatter of Baltimore mailed the editor twenty dollars to print an ad for slaves, but Rives sent the money back. Perhaps "Williams was aware of this," Rives speculated, for he "never asked us to insert his advertisement." Second, Rives swore that "I saw [Thomas Williams] marching in a whig procession about two months ago," down Pennsylvania Avenue. The editor had known Williams as a slave dealer for years but was not a close acquaintance. He was therefore somewhat surprised when Williams initiated a brief conversation with him as the slave trader passed by during the parade. Not long after, when Rives ambled the mile from his home to the Yellow House to gaze upon the alleged Polk and Dallas flag with his own eyes, he encountered the "negro trader" again. Rives spoke of the parade, but Williams denied participating in it until the editor reminded him of their chat. At that point, the slave trader paused and replied dismissively "that he was marching with them for curiosity or for fun." Rives, however, claimed that Williams' Whiggery was heartfelt and genuine. Third, turning to the details of the newspaper account of the flag over the pen, Rives clarified that Williams' slave jail had "no pole in the 'centre' of the 'pen' . . . where the negroes are kept," as had been alleged. The pole in question was some "fifty or sixty feet from it," erected there by Thomas's older brother, William H. Williams, a Whig in 1840 but purportedly not a supporter of Clay in 1844. In this active presidential election season, the

Globe editor continued, having a flagpole near the slave jail was unexceptional. Most "houses or 'pens' in this city . . . have . . . a whig or democratic pole within sixty feet of them." Simply put, Thomas Williams' proximity to a Polk and Dallas flag did not make him a Democrat.[32]

Finally, Rives asserted that "the *negro traders are betting on Clay.*" Affluent men of business routinely wagered on the outcomes of elections, typically putting money on their preferred candidates, although occasionally prosperous men seeking sport and quick profits took a more mercenary approach and gambled on the candidate they believed would win, regardless of political ideology. Back in 1840, slave dealer Hope Hull Slatter of Baltimore, a Democrat who operated the slave jail on Pratt Street, remained true to party nominee Martin Van Buren, but his allegiance cost him a purported $11,000 betting against Whig challenger William Henry Harrison. Meanwhile, in Washington, D.C., Harrison's victory lined the pockets of Yellow House owner William H. Williams, at the time a Whig who bet loyally on the log cabin, hard cider candidate. By 1844, the elder Williams brother had switched parties, and Rives heard that he "had made some small bet of Polk and Dallas," which the editor "considered . . . a good sign" for the Democrats' prospects, for Williams "is a shrewd man, *who bets to win.*" William H. Williams excepted, Rives perceived that the slave traders on the whole were backing the Whigs. Rives' Democratic partner at the *Globe* office and one-time member of former president Andrew Jackson's kitchen cabinet, Francis P. Blair, bet $10,000 on the upcoming election with a pair of Richmond slave traders supporting the Whig candidate, Clay. Taking into account all of the assembled evidence, Rives concluded that Thomas Williams was a partisan with an "intimate association with whig[g]ery." "[T]his slave-dealer and flag-raiser has always been one of their own coon whigs," Rives announced in the columns of the *Globe*, invoking the masked mammalian mascot of the Whig Party. Williams' Whig convictions alone could explain how, in his conversation with Rives, the slave trader "appeared to know all about" northern newspapers' allegation of his Democratic loyalties "and not to care" about the revelation. With conspiratorial flair, the *Globe* editor reckoned the flying of the Polk and Dallas flag near the Yellow House a clever Whig hoax designed to undermine the Democratic Party in advance of the election.[33]

As the Democrat Rives postulated, elevating a Polk and Dallas flag that cast a shadow on Williams' slave pen was part of an elaborate Whig plot to attract northern antislavery voters to the Whig Party's slaveholding presidential candidate, Henry Clay. The national press widely publicized news of the Clay campaign actively courting the antislavery vote, despite ex-slaveholder James G. Birney's return in 1844 for a second presidential run on the Liberty Party abolitionist ticket. Strategically, the Clay campaign pinned its hopes for victory on northern votes, and Rives maintained that the placing of the Democratic flag above the slave pen supplied the Whigs a deceitful piece of ammunition to use in their electioneering efforts. "This appears to me to be the deepest laid, the most diabolical and nefarious scheme that I have yet seen concocted, to injure Col. Polk, and get votes for Mr. Clay," he carped.[34]

George Watterston, the corresponding secretary of the Washington City Clay Club, wrote what Rives described as a "secret circular" to two Whig surrogates campaigning on Clay's behalf in the North. The Watterston letter dwelled heavily on the Yellow House, over which the Polk and Dallas flag fluttered. The Washington "Slave Jail, or 'Negro Pen,' as it is called," Watterston began, was "the property of a man named Williams, (partner of the man who was recently fined and imprisoned in New Orleans for importing into Louisiana ... slaves who had been convicted of criminal offences.)" In actuality, William H. Williams owned the establishment, but the public often conflated him and his brother. For the Whigs' purposes, it frankly did not matter. The proprietor, Watterston continued, "is exclusively a negro trader; that is his vocation," and he "engaged so largely" in that occupation "as to require him to *own* a jail, and the vessels in which his living cargoes are transported southward."[35]

Watterston pointed out the sudden public visibility of Williams' slave pen in the autumn of 1844. He conceded that the Yellow House had previously been "as unobtrusive as such a place ought to be": "Strangers might have passed the place unnoticing or merely wondering what misanthrope could have planned and inhabited so gloomy a dwelling." Of course, citizens of the District of Columbia were aware of its existence, and, Watterston maintained, even "regretted" its presence, but "they reconciled themselves" to it, unable to devise any remedy for slavery in their midst. With the approaching election, the Whig correspondent detected a change. "*Now,*" Watterston complained, "this slave depot, this mockery of the Capitol, within full sight of which it stands," had "grown insolent in hope of extended trade" in slaves and projected profits contingent upon the annexation of Texas into the Union. The foreign country of Texas that William H. Williams repeatedly identified in 1840 as the intended destination for his shipment of enslaved criminals could, under the prospective Democratic administration of James Knox Polk and George M. Dallas, achieve statehood and receive not merely trifling numbers of convicted felons but untold thousands of surplus Chesapeake slaves. Put another way, an outlawed international slave trade could, through the medium of the ballot box and the sorcery of the Electoral College, metamorphose into a lawful domestic slave trade remunerative for dealers such as the Williams brothers. And so, Watterston groused, the operator of the slave jail boldly "dared . . . to rear a tall staff above the walls of its cells, and to append thereto the *slavetrader's banner*, bearing, in most conspicuous letters, the names of 'POLK and DALLAS.'"[36]

"Of course these names!" Watterston jeered. It made absolute sense. Williams was "a clear-sighted man of business" who "has already grown rich in his trade." He naturally "desires . . . and strives for the success of that party whose policy will enable him to grow richer." Without question, Democratic candidates "*Polk and Dallas* are his *protection.*" Watterston also revealed that Williams, unlike the Richmond slave traders mentioned by Rives and unbeknownst to the *Globe* editor, had "bet very largely . . . upon the success of his candidates" Polk and Dallas, to the tune of "[s]everal thousands" of dollars. Williams "*does* spend money freely" to promote the Democratic ticket, Watterston announced, but those expenditures counted as "investments." Make no mistake, he criticized: "*The identical dollars, profits of his loathsome traffic, are active electioneering dollars for Polk & Dallas and Texas.*"[37]

Watterston trusted that Clay's Whig operatives in the North could use the waving of the Polk and Dallas flag above Williams' slave pen to foment righteous outrage among abolitionist and moderately antislavery voters. Though at first glance a trifling thing, he stated, the story served as an index "of the character of our [Democratic] opponents' cause, and the degrading alliances by which it is supported." Williams' slave pen boasted "a thriving business." Only days before Watterston penned his missive, "a 'gang' ... of sixty were marched out from its cells to the wharf, for shipment to New Orleans, via Alexandria." However common such scenes in the District of Columbia were, Watterston observed, "Even *we* ... are indignant" that "this *Negro-buyer* should have dared, as he has done," to hang "*his own peculiar banner ... upon the same staff*" as "*the flag of our common country*" – that he "should presume to flaunt its banner to the common gaze." Watterston urged Clay's campaigners to impress upon every northern voter that, "by voting for James K. Polk, or for *any other man* than Henry Clay" – an unmistakable nod to third-party abolitionist candidate and possible spoiler, James G. Birney – "he is directly, or indirectly, participating in an insult to his country's flag, *extending the limits of slavery* ... and ... put[ting] dollars in the pockets of" slave traders. Northern voters should not want to "be instrumental in perpetuating this revolting slave traffic," Watterston predicted, for the chained captives marched out of the slave jail did not join "their keepers in huzzas for *Polk and Dallas*."[38]

To discredit the Democratic candidates' critics, John C. Rives of the *Globe* unleashed an *ad hominem* attack upon Whig secretary Watterston. Rives marveled at the irony of Whig "coons seeking abolition votes for Henry Clay." Not only was Watterston "himself a slaveholder," Rives pointed out, but he also made "more out of them than ever Williams did, and much less honestly." Watterston served as the official Librarian of Congress from 1815 to 1829. He lost his position when newly inaugurated president Andrew Jackson dismissed him as part of a spoils system purge of officeholders who had opposed his candidacy. But while still serving as the Librarian of Congress, Rives charged, Watterston "had the unconscionable avidity" to spend $700 of the government's money annually to hire one of his own slaves as a messenger. Rives estimated that this sum was about five times too generous, given the going rates of the time. Yet this was the man accusing slave traders of turning their profits into "active electioneering dollars" for Polk and Dallas. Rives' indignation was palpable. "Williams, the slave-dealer, whose pen has the Polk and Dallas flag in its vicinity – who marches in the whig processions, and is hail-fellow-well-met with the coons, wherever he meets them," the *Globe* publisher insisted, cynically raised the flag simply to supply a talking point with which the Whigs could smear the Democrats during the campaign season, thereby "currying favor with the abolitionists" of the North. Truly, Rives concluded, the Whigs were "unscrupulous adversaries."[39]

The *Globe*'s denials that the Democrats kept "a slave mart" in the nation's capital continued the following day. In addition to repeating arguments from his previous columns, Rives related new evidence he found pertinent – evidence that the Whigs were intimately linked to the institution of slavery and should therefore make no political headway among northern abolitionist voters in the upcoming election. First, according to an unnamed "friend," each of the "six or eight notorious slave traders" in Washington, D.C., was "an active, zealous Clay man." Second, Whigs on the city council, including president W. W. Seaton, co-editor of the *National Intelligencer,* and member George Watterston, the secretary of the Clay Club, had been responsible for passing laws that imposed "almost insurmountable obstacle[s]" to emancipate bondpeople in the District, one of which required each manumitted slave to supply a $1,000 bond annually, backed by five "responsible freeholders," to guarantee his "good and orderly conduct." The alternatives for free blacks in the District were banishment or imprisonment in the workhouse. Rives pondered publicly as to who benefited from the expulsion of free people of color from the nation's capital. One answer was slaveholders such as George Watterston, with bondpeople to rent out. Through the economic law of supply and demand, a decline in the number of free black laborers would increase the rents owners fetched for their hired slaves. Another answer was slave traders, because obstacles erected to manumission would push some masters simply to sell their surplus bondpeople rather than liberate them. To bolster the case that the Whigs were no allies of the abolitionists, Rives also printed a letter from Washington attorney Charles S. Wallach, who verified that the slaveholding Watterston, only months ago, had sold one enslaved woman, whose emancipation date loomed, into permanent bondage in the South, "separating her from her husband" – a free black man – and "two small children" in the process. Given such close ties to the institution of slavery, Rives contended, the Whigs' effort to attract abolitionist votes for Clay by saddling the Democrats with ownership of Williams' slave pen was nothing but a "conspiracy" and "a concocted contrivance among the coons."[40]

In response, the Whig *National Intelligencer* printed a letter from an anonymous but "well known," respectable Washington "gentleman," "whose word no man would doubt." As it turned out, however, in his missive to the *Intelligencer*, the gentleman inadvertently confused Thomas Williams, who then presided over the Yellow House, with his brother William H. Williams, the actual owner of the private slave jail. The unnamed correspondent was incredulous that anyone would charge "Mr. Williams" – meaning William H. Williams – with colluding "with other Whigs" to wave "the [Polk and Dallas] flag for political purposes." Although William H. Williams was formerly a Whig, the informant admitted, "The abandonment of the Whig party by Mr. Williams in 1842, and his reasons for so doing, are facts notorious to his friends in this city." The letter to the *Intelligencer* explained that Williams' political conversion hinged not on national issues but on personal affairs: he had been prosecuted in Louisiana for the illegal importation of slaves and forced to forfeit those slaves and to submit to "a heavy pecuniary penalty or long imprisonment." According to the informant's information, the slave trader blamed Louisiana Whig officials such as Governor André B. Roman and Attorneys General Stephen Mazureau and Christian Roselius for pursuing the legal case against him. Out of resentment and spite, Williams abandoned the Whig Party and vowed to "do every thing in his power to defeat the election of Mr. Clay." So for the past two years, the unidentified gentleman summarized, William H. Williams had been "a member of the Locofoco party" (by the mid-1840s the Whigs' pejorative nickname for all Democrats). He flew the Democrats' flag, in short, for the simple reason that he was a Democrat.[41]

Unwilling to admit political kinship with a slave dealer flying the Polk and Dallas flag, John C. Rives of the Democratic *Globe* wanted to get to the bottom of the discrepancy between his reporting and that in the Whig *Intelligencer* over the slave pen proprietor's political allegiances. On October 31, 1844, Rives and co-editor Francis P. Blair dispatched *Globe* reporter William W. Curran to the *Intelligencer* office to request the name of that paper's anonymous source who identified "Williams" as a Democrat. W. W. Seaton replied that the author was Richard Wallach, the brother of lawyer Charles S. Wallach, who had sent the testimonial condemning George Watterston to the *Globe*. Curran tracked down

Richard Wallach for an interview. Wallach explained that he had written the *Intelligencer* in reference to William H. Williams because he understood that William H. was the Williams brother who actually owned the slave jail; Thomas was merely his agent. The *Globe*, however, had consistently reported Thomas Williams as running the Yellow House, which he was then doing while his brother was bogged down in Louisiana courtrooms. It was indeed "THOMAS WILLIAMS," not William H. Williams, crowed the *Globe* triumphantly, who advertised for slaves in the *National Intelligencer*, who marched in the Whig procession, who kept the slave depot, who hoisted the Polk and Dallas flag, and whom Watterston claimed was a Democrat. Rather than chalking up the confusion to a simple misunderstanding, the *Globe* congratulated itself for exposing the *Intelligencer*'s "whole tissue of deception," as if Richard Wallach had conjured William H. Williams as a scapegoat "to mislead the public." Furthermore, reported the Democratic rag, Richard's brother Charles once overheard Thomas Williams verbally confess his commitment to Whiggery.[42]

The *Globe* also renewed its vituperation directed at Clay Club secretary George Watterston. Revelations from Charles Wallach's letter unmasked him as the true slaveholding monster he was, the editors implied. They pointed out Watterston's hypocrisy for feigning distress and mortification at the sight of a Democratic flag flying above "a negro prison" when he "was himself engaged in the very traffic he shed crocodile tears over" and was "himself the evil genius remorselessly perpetrating the inhumanity he affected to deplore." The totality of the assembled evidence persuaded the *Globe*'s Democratic editors that the Whigs had implemented an "imposture," "a subterfuge . . . to blind the public eye." Through "the fraudulent appropriation of a Polk and Dallas flag" flying proudly over a notorious slave depot, deceitful Whig operatives had colluded with fellow Whig and slave dealer Thomas Williams to besmirch and "disgrace" the Democratic Party only weeks before the presidential election.[43]

In light of the *Globe*'s reporting, Richard Wallach wrote the *National Intelligencer* to clear any aspersions that may have been cast upon his character and good name. "I . . . deny that Mr. Thomas Williams is either the owner of the premises where the negro depot or jail is kept, or that it was he that raised or caused to be raised the Polk and Dallas flag over the premises," he reiterated. But of his politics, "I know nothing." William H. Williams, however, Wallach could say with certainty, was indeed "a Locofoco." That he "has betted largely on the election of Polk and Dallas, is notorious." Only a few days earlier, the elder Williams brother informed Wallach by mail that "he had given five dollars" to Washington Democrats "for the purpose of raising another Polk and Dallas flag in the neighborhood of . . . City Hall." Perhaps, then, it was William H. Williams, from afar, who had ordered the Democratic banner elevated above the Yellow House compound, on the flagpole he had erected.[44]

At that point, the daily exchange of barbs between Washington's two leading partisan newspapers concluded, at least with respect to the contentious political banner. The true identity of the controversial flag raiser remains as much a mystery as Thomas Williams' genuine political affinities, although self-interest and the principle of Occam's razor would equally dictate that, like his elder brother, Thomas, too, was more likely a Democrat than a covert Whig operative. Whatever the reality, in the last days before presidential voting began, the fuss over the flag took on a life of its own in newspapers from Massachusetts to New York to Virginia. Editors from many corners of the nation reproduced in full or summarized the original text of the printed stories of the Polk and Dallas flag flying over Williams' slave pen.

The debate raged even as balloting began. Congress did not codify into law the uniform date for presidential elections – the first Tuesday following the first Monday in November – until 1845, so voting in 1844 lasted from November 1 to December 4. As voters headed to the polls, the Democratic press continued to identify Thomas Williams as a Whig and decried the detestable "course of Electioneering" that sought an "unhallowed Coalition" between southern Whigs and northern abolitionists for Henry Clay. As the Democratic *Albany Argus* saw it, the Whigs had committed an "infamous fraud" in hoisting a Polk and Dallas banner over the slave pen. By contrast, Whig papers insisted that Williams was a Democrat expressing his legitimate political preferences. "[A]re we to be lied out of the election?" bemoaned a Whig correspondent to the Boston *Atlas*. "[W]hoever denies that this negro dealer

Williams ... is a Loco Foco, asserts an untruth." The same reporter thought Thomas Williams too "ultra in his support of the [Democratic] party" ever to masquerade as a Whig in good conscience. He further opined that Williams, though a "negro dealer" financially invested "in bets on Polk's election," would not be so depraved and desperate for money as to represent himself as a loathsome Whig just to increase his odds of winning.[45]

Speculation over who would claim victory consumed the country for weeks as voting continued. Already by mid-November 1844, the abolition-ists conceded the defeat of their third-party candidate, James G. Birney. Although he improved his electoral performance ninefold compared with his run in 1840, he still garnered little more than 60,000 votes. "It is certain that one of the two notorious slaveholders" – Polk or Clay – "has been elected," wailed the abolitionist *Cincinnati Herald*. "It is not a matter of the smallest consequence ... which of these two anti-republican, anti-democratic candidates have succeeded." Most contemporary political observers attached greater import to the election's outcome. Were political experience the barometer for success, Clay would have won handily. But his stance in opposition to Texas annexation damaged his chances with southern voters, who saw his position as antithetical to slavery's westward expansion. In a close contest in which only 38,000 popular votes separated winner from loser, Clay's strategy to compensate for lost southern votes with antislavery votes in the North failed. John C. Rives of the *Washington Globe* had predicted as much back in October, noting that abolitionist voters, by refusing to unite behind the Whig nominee, "risk[ed] ... assist-ing in the elevation of Polk and Dallas." James G. Birney of the Liberty Party, in fact, siphoned off enough votes from Clay in the crucial state of New York to tip the election to Polk and seal the Democratic victory. The bondman Louis Hughes, ensnared by the domestic slave trade and march-ing overland from Virginia to the cotton frontier of Mississippi when news of the election result spread, witnessed "every white man ... yelling, 'Hurrah for Polk and Dallas!'" Though curious, Hughes did not inquire into the cause or meaning of their celebration, for he did not wish to be whipped for "impertinence."[46]

CHAPTER 10

Brothers

I N THE MID-1840s, WILLIAM H. WILLIAMS' VARIOUS AND
wide-ranging economic machinations ensnared him tangentially in
others' courtroom dramas, but these relatively minor suits into which he
was dragged in no way compared to his crushing loss before the
Louisiana Supreme Court. That was the case that gained the greatest
notoriety and personally stung most deeply. On a more positive note, the
improving national economy, finally emerging in 1845 from the residual
funk of the Panic of 1837, afforded Williams some consolation. The
annexation of Texas into the Union in late December widened the
market for bondpeople in the eastern portion of the new state, and rising
cotton prices after 1845 lent further impetus to Williams' business. The
formerly thriving trade of the "flush times," between the Chesapeake and
New Orleans, was slowly returning. The quantity of surviving slave manifests from Williams' voyages and the pronounced jump in the number of
slave sales in 1845 testified to the economic recovery underway. For
William H. Williams, the accelerated pace of the domestic slave trade
that coincided with the revitalized economy meant a growing reliance
upon his younger brother Thomas, who coordinated the family business
in whichever city William was not.[1]

By 1843, William H. Williams had exited prison and resumed actively
trading in New Orleans, where he lived the bulk of the next four years. In
about half of his sales, he sold slaves individually, but about as often, he
vended multiple slaves, sometimes in sizeable lots, in a single purchase.
Florent and Septime Fortier of St. James Parish bought ten bondmen
from Williams in January 1846 for $725 each. In 1845, Williams sold
another ten slaves to Joseph Dufossat, Sr., of Jefferson Parish for $5,450

and seven to Theodore Soniat Dufossat, also of Jefferson Parish, for $4,975. Francois Melicour Bienvenu of St. Bernard Parish paid Williams a less impressive $1,200 for four bondmen in March 1847. Many other buyers acquired two or three slaves at a time.[2]

With the restoration of a more robust economy, slave trading was becoming more lucrative again in the mid-1840s, but a state-imposed tax did take a miniscule cut from the sale of each bondperson. In March 1842, while still in the throes of the economic downturn, the Louisiana legislature passed "An act to increase the revenue of the State," which included a $5 tax on each slave sold. Thus, when Williams sold the ten slaves to Joseph Dufossat, Sr., in February 1845, he paid $50 in head taxes. This amounted to less than a 1 percent tax on that particular sale. Given prevailing slave prices of the time, the tax typically ran at about 1 percent, plus or minus one or two tenths. Amid an improving economic outlook and rejuvenated domestic slave trade, on March 10, 1845, Louisiana lawmakers reduced the state tax on slaves to $3 per bondperson sold.[3]

While William H. Williams conducted business operations in New Orleans, his brother Thomas handled the supply side in Washington, D.C. Arriving in the nation's capital in July 1841, Thomas Williams accompanied at least one coastwise slaving vessel to New Orleans during his brother's confinement in the Orleans Parish prison, but he then returned to Washington in 1842, probably once William gained his release from jail. Thomas spent the next several years in the District, becoming a firsthand witness to and source of controversy during the tumultuous presidential election of 1844. He remained in the capital until 1847. Sometime that summer, William H. Williams decided to return to the nation's capital. He and his younger brother would swap places in the coastal slaving network that conveyed bondpeople from the Chesapeake to New Orleans.

To coordinate the family business over such vast distances, the Williams siblings must have communicated extensively by mail and tele-graph, although none of their correspondence survives. In 1847, William wished to see Thomas in person. The pair may have convened regularly to discuss business, perhaps as often as annually, most likely during the slave trade's summer off-season, but the patterns of names attached to slave bills of sale in New Orleans cannot confirm that. William H. Williams made a return trip to Washington in 1847, possibly – thanks to lawsuits and the demands of work. Whether he saw Thomas in New Orleans prior to his departure or upon his arrival in Washington, we do not know, but it may have been the first time he saw his brother face-to-face in perhaps as many as five years. Either way, the Williamses would have made certain not to miss each other aboard passing ships slicing through the water, headed in opposite directions.

During absences from New Orleans, William H. Williams sometimes appointed Edward Barnett his "authorized agent" and proxy. Located on Conti Street, Barnett served as Williams' preferred notary public to finalize his slave sales. From 1838, when first appointed notary by Louisiana governor Edward D. White, to the end of 1850, Barnett alone notarized more than 260 separate transactions – mostly sales (94 percent) but also small numbers of abrogations (4 percent) and exchanges (2 percent) – between the Williams brothers and their clients. Altogether, Barnett figured in almost half (47 percent) of all the known slave deals the Williamses made in New Orleans. Unless he was on a leave of absence, Barnett reliably handled a distinct plurality of all the brothers' slave-trading paperwork. He had clearly earned their loyalty and trust. When William H. Williams left New Orleans in 1847, he may have again counted upon Barnett to manage his affairs until Thomas Williams arrived to take charge.[4]

Though ordered to New Orleans by his elder brother in 1847, Thomas Williams had been engaged in an active commerce in slaves out of Washington, D.C. Prior to his departure, he maintained "six agents out in the country buying ... negroes." Between May 31 and September 14, the off-season for the coastwise domestic slave trade to the Old Southwest, Williams sold more than one hundred bondpeople, or better than one per day. Seventeen went to Richmond, Virginia trader Silas Omohundro alone, who anticipated disposing of them at still higher prices than he paid. That, after all, was the game.[5]

In May and June, Thomas Williams corresponded frequently with auctioneer R. H. Dickinson, located on Franklin Street in Richmond. His letters to Dickinson documented the routine, day-to-day operations of the Williams brothers' domestic slave-trading enterprise as well as Thomas' private musings on the supply of enslaved bodies and the current market for enslaved workers. On May 26, 1847, Thomas pledged to "send over some negroes very soon" for Dickinson to sell, observing that "good negroes are scarce and hard to buy." Curious about the latest from the Richmond slave market, he also queried the auctioneer, "How are families selling[?]" Williams was particularly interested in the going rates for "a woman & child, & a woman and 3 to 5 children."[6]

In early June, Williams was not fully pleased with the prices for which a recent shipment of slaves was selling. "Nancey Jane & Elizabeth sold" to Silas Omohundro "for about what I calculated," he explained, "but ... Douglass & Edgar sold below my calculation." Disappointed, Williams urged Dickinson to "do the best you can with the balance of them." Still, Williams continued to direct additional slaves for sale to the auctioneer. Within days, the trader informed Dickinson, "I send you some good negroes.... I expect to send over some more stock in 4 or 5 days." In fact, Williams wrote, "you may look for negroes from me pretty often."[7]

Less than a week later, Williams seemed less enthusiastic about his latest crop of bondmen and -women. Believing them less valuable than prior shipments, he urged Dickinson "to do the best you can with [them]." Despite Williams' misgivings about this particular human cargo, he felt compelled to pass them on to the auctioneer for sale, for the competition in the slave traffic was fierce. "If I don't continue to buy and send over, other Traders will buy & send them over, and they will go into the market at any rate," he explained. As Thomas reasoned, if the slaves were going to be sold, he might as well be the one to profit from them. A short time later, Williams instructed Dickinson to "keep possession of the [enslaved] men until I send you other negroes to sell," promising to pay the necessary expenses to maintain them prior to sale. He anticipated that more bondpeople would arrive in Richmond the following week. In the meantime, Williams desperately sought out "good No. 1 men" to satisfy market demand. During the summer of 1847, Williams was paying "$750 for No 1 men" and "$575 for No 1 women" age seventeen to twenty-one, but, he confessed, "they are scarce at these prices." Nevertheless, as promised, the slave dealer soon sent additional bondpeople to Dickinson. Williams assessed them with the cold, calculating callousness required of his trade. "The woman with the yellow girl & boy, is well qualified and ought to sell well," he predicted, but "the little Black boy has a large navel, [so] do the best you can with him. I will send over two or 3 women with one child each in a couple of days," he added. "I have all my agents in the country buying." But Williams' ideal enslaved quarry proved elusive, he confided in a postscript: "I want black good sound strong negro men, fair men," he stated. They "are the sort to buy" if he expected to make real money.[8]

The quest for profits required not only good product but also good information. Like any slave trader, Thomas Williams craved market intelligence, for if he could divine future slave supplies and prices he could better determine the optimal time to sell. "Write me fully on the receipt of [my letter]," Williams urged Dickinson, about "how you think your market will range from the 1st to the 15th [of] July. If your market will justify it, I will send you over some 40 to 60 and perhaps 75 negroes" before July 15. Williams also intimated his future plans, noting, "I am determined to buy 150 or more [bondpeople] to the 1st Sept." Rest assured, the slave trader told the auctioneer, "If you will keep me well advised of your market, I will send over every negro I can buy & make $10, to $15, on."[9]

Williams forwarded to Dickinson in Richmond a substantial shipment of bondmen and -women on June 30. These included "some good negroes," according to Williams' estimation: "I send a strictly no. 1 woman, 19, Sarah & child, and I calculate to get $625 to $650 for her." Additionally, he wrote, "I send over a No. 1 brown skin girl 18, Elizabeth, which I think will bring $600." A third enslaved woman – "a girl 17 to 18" – was "in the family way." Having paid $570 for the pregnant bondwoman, Williams wished Dickinson "to do the best you can for me with her." Among the enslaved men Williams shipped at the same time were Tom, age twenty-four, who cost the slave trader $625; Henry, thirty, for whom he paid $550; and Bill, twenty-four or twenty-five years old, acquired for $625. Tom's eventual sale price of $650 and Henry's, for $625, earned Williams profits of $25 and $75, respectively, minus expenses. Sarah and her child fetched $720, exceeding the slave trader's expectations by some $70–95, but Williams of course welcomed errant prognostications when they worked to his favor.[10]

Profit was paramount, as revealed by one story Thomas Williams shared with Dickinson. Williams bought an enslaved family from "a gentleman at his own price" and, in conformity with the seller's instructions, "sent them out of the city" of Washington. The master's wife, however, wanted them returned to the District so that she might free them and permit the bondwoman "to live as a *wife* to a *Mexican,* who is the father of her two youngest children." Williams claimed a willingness to oblige the mistress's wishes, but he also insisted that "I am not disposed to take one cent less than they are worth, in order to have them brought here." The bondwoman, Williams explained, was valuable. She "is qualified certain, [a] first rate washer & ironer & cook, and I warrant her to be such." He predicted with confidence that "a good paddling" in advance of her auction would induce comportment on her part that "will make her bring a good price, which I want" for her and her children. The implication was that Williams would happily sell the bondwoman, despite her recent mistress's pleas, if the price was right. That the white woman intended to "*set free*" the enslaved family may have contributed to Williams' reluctance to yield to her preference, for slaveholders commonly characterized free blacks as lazy ne'er-do-wells or criminals. Their presence also sent the message to enslaved men and women that people with dark skin need not be held in bondage.[11]

By October 1847, Thomas Williams left Washington, D.C., behind for New Orleans, where he occupied his brother's office at No. 18 Esplanade, a street swarming with competitors in the slave trade. Late in the month, Williams' slave-dealing colleague Ebenezer Rodbird shipped him twenty-seven bondpeople, including three infants, out of Baltimore aboard the slaving barque *Kirkwood,* one of many such cargoes Williams would receive from 1847 to 1850. (See Appendix B.) By November 1847, Thomas Williams' name replaced that of his brother on slaves' bills of sales recorded by New Orleans' notaries public. Field hands, house servants, enslaved blacksmiths, carpenters, and more passed from Thomas Williams' clutches to new masters in New Orleans, surrounding Louisiana parishes, and points more distant still.[12]

Soon after his arrival in New Orleans, Thomas Williams completed one of the single largest transactions he or his brother ever made. They sold eleven slaves for a combined total of $9,150 cash to the partnership of Kock & McCall, operators of the Bayou Lafourche Plantation, a sprawling sugar estate in Assumption Parish. Working out of an office at 22 Bank Place in New Orleans, Charles Kock, joined by his associate Evan Jones McCall of Donaldsonville, Louisiana, had previously bought individual bondpeople from William H. Williams, but the quantity and dollar value of their purchases rose with Thomas. In 1848, the firm paid $8,800 "in ready and current money" for a dozen more bondpeople. Kock and McCall must have been satisfied customers, for they kept returning to Williams to meet their labor demands. They paid $1,550 for two additional slaves in February 1849 and another $800 for a "mulatto girl" the following month. The firm of Kock & McCall represented Thomas Williams' single most important client from 1847 to its dissolution in 1850.[13]

With the improved economic climate of the late 1840s, Williams made several sales for thousands upon thousands of dollars. On January 1, 1848, he sold John Armfield, then serving as an executor of his deceased former partner Isaac Franklin's estate, "[t]en male slaves" worth $8,000, for use on Franklin's Loango plantation along the Mississippi River. Later that same month, Paulin Joseph Fleytas of Plaquemines Parish bought four of Williams' bondpeople at auction for $2,625. Williams sold three slaves to buyer Naoma Hagerty of Catahoula Parish and another three to Florent and Septime Fortier of St. James Parish, in separate transactions that each totaled well in excess of $2,000. Henry McCall of Ascension Parish paid $3,500 cash for five bondwomen in 1848, Sosthene Roman of St. James Parish $4,200 for five bondmen the next year, and New Orleans' William Frederic Mason $3,500 for five enslaved women the year after that.[14]

Thomas Williams' customers ran the spectrum of free Louisianans but betrayed readily discernible patterns. Almost all of his buyers were men, but women such as Elizabeth Charles of New Orleans, known to some as Mrs. Victor Jourdain, and Naoma Hagerty made purchases in their own right and under their own names. Almost all of Williams' clients were white, but he also sold individual slaves to Winny Uell and Sarah Gaines, both free women of color. Gaines purchased a "mulatto boy named John, aged about four years," for the bargain price of $100, less than half the cost of other children whom Williams sold at the time. It is possible that Thomas Williams was the boy's father. He had owned the youngster's enslaved mother, Elizabeth Dorsey, although we do not know for how long. Had he purchased her recently for shipment to New Orleans, like any other bondperson? Or had he been her master long enough to father her four-year-old child in an act of sexual coercion or rape? Either way, Dorsey passed away at the age of thirty-two, leaving her young, mixed-race son motherless, a de facto orphan. Curiously, when Williams sold John to Gaines, the terms of the transaction proved unique. The bill of sale stipulated, as an "express and formal Condition," that the free black woman who would become John's adoptive mother pay, "at her own Cost and expense and without compensation whatever" from Williams, to take the required, lawful steps to emancipate the boy "as soon as he will become of age or sooner if she should think [it] proper." John's sale thus laid the groundwork for his freedom, even as it perhaps separated him from the white father who disavowed the boy's paternity.[15]

Thomas Williams' most nationally prominent client was Mexican-American War hero and East Baton Rouge Parish plantation owner General Zachary Taylor. In June 1848, Williams sold Taylor two bondmen, Henry and Daniel, for $1,500, via his son Richard Taylor. A week later, Old Rough and Ready became the Whig Party's nominee for president. General Taylor went on to win the presidency that November.[16]

The summer of 1848 brought the seasonal downturn in the New Orleans slave trade. Sometime in July or August, Thomas Williams took the opportunity to shuttle back temporarily to Washington, D.C. On August 19, he sent Richmond auctioneer R. H. Dickinson "some good stock, which I think will sell well." Williams cheerily urged Dickinson to prepare them for sale, "to have them fixed up right, and sell them privately [or] at auction, as in your judgment they will do best"; however, he added, for unspecified reasons, "I do not wish the yellow man John sold," nor, for the time being, a bondman named Nathan, "brought back from New Orleans this summer," in a reversal of the usual direction of the domestic slave trade. Finally, Williams solicited Dickinson's expert opinion on the latest shipment: "Let me know by

Telegraph what you think of the boys or girls, and how they will sell." The autumn slave-trading season carried Williams, probably accompanying a cargo of enslaved property, back to New Orleans, where he orchestrated in early November the sales of three Virginia-born bondmen to Jeremiah Melbourne Rhodes and another sizeable parcel of slaves to sugar masters Kock & McCall.[17]

Williams offered his clients accommodating payment options. Whereas the wealthiest of purchasers, such as Kock & McCall, could fork over thousands of dollars in cash, most buyers did not possess sufficient quantities of "ready money" to pay up front and in full. Some made partial payments in cash and used credit to pay off the remainder over time. When Plaquemines Parish master Paulin Joseph Fleytas purchased four slaves from Williams, he paid $875 in cash, with the balance on a promissory note due in four months at the going rate of 8 percent annual interest. Still other purchasers relied wholly on credit arrangements. Williams released the bondman Henry to buyer Moses Eastman in exchange for a promissory note of $900 "made payable One year after date, with interest thereon, at the rate of Eight per centum per annum from date until final payment." Williams held a mortgage on the enslaved man until Eastman paid for Henry in full. In the meantime, Eastman vowed "not to sell, alienate nor encumber" the slave that did not yet belong to him outright. In November 1849, while advertising "six very likely Girls, ten to twelve years of age," in the New Orleans papers, Williams stated that they "will be sold for cash, or on credit of one year, for approved paper."[18]

Like his older brother and mentor William H. Williams, Thomas went to great lengths to assure his customers' satisfaction in their dealings with him. He "fully guaranteed" the overwhelming majority of all the bondpeople he sold "against the redhibitory vices, maladies, and defects prescribed by law," regardless of whether the buyer was General Zachary Taylor or someone less prominent. Larger, more expensive purchases, however, by the extraordinarily well-to-do merited Williams' extra special treatment. Offering generous terms to buyers such as sugar producers Kock & McCall, whose extensive labor demands could give the trader ample business from one year to the next, helped him retain the partnership as a repeat customer. Time and again, Williams granted Kock & McCall a four-month window in which to return slaves they purchased from him, no questions asked. When Charles Kock acquired the bondman Henry Gordon in 1848, Williams allotted a still more generous "one year" from the date of sale in which to return him, replete with "the privilege of so doing without assigning any cause whatever." Kock received the same deal the next year when he bought the "mulatto boy" James Wilson.[19]

When preferred customers returned bondpeople sold with Williams' special guarantee, they maintained the option to exchange them for other slaves from the selection the trader had available or to receive a full refund of the purchase price. In November 1847, Kock & McCall returned a "negro man, named Len Humphreys, aged about Twenty two years," who had been purchased from William H. Williams eleven months earlier, in December 1846. Thomas Williams upheld his brother's bargain and swapped Humphreys for the bondman Alfred Bland, also twenty-two. The exchange left a balance of $75 in Williams' favor, which Kock & McCall paid him in cash to make up the difference. The next year, Williams "cede[d], transfer[red] and grant[ed] in exchange unto the said Charles Kock and Evan Jones McCall ... a certain negro woman named Mary Ann Davis, aged about Eighteen years," in return for the twenty-year-old Tamer, whom he had sold them about forty days earlier but who had not satisfied her purchasers. Since the parties involved valued both bondwomen at $650, no money changed hands. The transaction was merely a substitution of one slave for the other.[20]

On other occasions, Williams cancelled previously made sales altogether. On November 7, 1848, Kock & McCall paid $650 apiece for the bondwomen Milly and Mary, and a little more than three months later, on February 13, 1849, purchased the bondman Sam Jones for $900. Exactly one month after buying Sam Jones, Kock & McCall returned all three slaves to Williams. Buyer and seller "mutually agreed and determined to cancel, annul and rescind" each of the sales, and Williams refunded the $2,200 that Kock & McCall had paid. Williams was not so forgiving with all of his slave-buying clients. Seeking a bondman with specialized skills, Florent and Septime Fortier purchased the enslaved

Horace Ware in early 1850. The slave dealer granted them "the right to cancel this sale," but only "within fifteen days," should he fail "to be a first rate blacksmith" as Williams had claimed. Edward Barnett notarized several abrogations of sale for Thomas Williams. The trader willingly nullified the November 1847 sale of the bondman John to Jean Marie Desplats of Jefferson Parish, for example, as well as a January 1848 sale to a different buyer of the twenty-three-year-old bondwoman Charlotte and her infant.[21]

As accommodating as Thomas Williams was in catering to his slave-buying clients, he could not entirely escape the redhibition suits that plagued many human traffickers in Louisiana. His first brush with the state's redhibition laws came in 1840. Thomas Kellar of St. Landry Parish complained to Judge Charles Maurian of the Orleans Parish Court on May 23 that, precisely one year earlier, he had paid "one Thomas Williams a resident of Washington City" $1,050 for the bondman Morris, whom the young slave trader declared "free from the redhibitory diseases." Kellar claimed that Morris had an "incurable disease of the heart or of some other organ which renders himself entirely incapable of doing the ordinary labour & work of a plantation & renders him useless." The disgruntled purchaser expressed a willingness to return the slave, pending receipt of a full refund. But by the end of 1840, authorities in New Orleans reported that Williams "could not be found after diligent search." He may have been in Washington, D.C., or back home in Alabama. The dispensation of the case is unknown.[22]

In another, better-documented case, New Orleans merchants Thomas McLellan and John Kelty jointly purchased two bondmen from Williams on November 15, 1849. The sale, notarized by Edward Barnett, "warranted [them] . . . free from all the vices and maladies provided against by law." McLellan and Kelty set one of the bondmen, George Emmy, whom Williams had imported into Louisiana almost eight months earlier, to work as a fireman on the steam towboat *Louis Philippe*. On the morning of November 22, just one week after he was purchased, Emmy did not report to work, complaining of chest pains. The engineer rubbed Emmy with mustard and "put his feet in warm water," but since the *Louis Philippe* was anchored at the Southwest Pass, en route from New Orleans to the Balize at the time the bondman showed his first symptoms, no other medical aid was available. By 11 a.m., Emmy was dead, the victim of an apparent heart attack.[23]

McLellan and Kelty believed themselves swindled. They alleged that George Emmy was afflicted with a mortal condition of the heart at the time of purchase and that Thomas Williams had "fraudulently concealed" the bondman's physical defect. They asked the trader to rescind the sale and to return Emmy's $700 purchase price, since "the negro must have died of some old or chronic disease." Williams refused, arguing that there was no way for him to have been aware of the bondman's condition. McLellan and Kelty therefore filed suit against Williams, charging that he had deceptively hidden Emmy's "redhibitory malady."[24]

Louisiana's Third District Court heard the case. Williams' counsel denied that anything was wrong with George Emmy at the time of sale, and even a physician who had examined both of McLellan and Kelty's purchases for insurance purposes testified that "they appeared to be stout, healthy negroes." Judge Thomas H. Kennedy handed down the court's judgment. The bondman's disease manifested within fifteen days of sale, as required by Louisiana law, but other factors worked against McLellan and Kelty's claim. For starters, their complaint failed to identify Emmy's fatal disease by name and gave no description sufficient for an accurate diagnosis. No one ascertained the precise cause of death. As such, it was impossible to determine if it was curable. Emmy's illness, Kennedy observed, "was as violent as it was sudden[,] demanding the promptest and most energetic treatment." Yet no doctor saw or attended to the bondman because his location was too remote. Had Emmy been in New Orleans, and no physician summoned, explained the judge, McLellan and Kelty's suit would have been dismissed immediately, on account of buyer negligence. But in this case, no doctor was called because none was available while anchored out on the water. The question at law therefore devolved upon how to properly treat a redhibition case under those circumstances. Judge Kennedy found in Thomas Williams' favor. He concluded that the slave trader could not be held legally responsible for George Emmy's death, for "[t]he vendor does not take the risk of the service in which the slave sold may be employed." There was no fundamental difference, in other words, "between not calling a physician when one could be had," and working a slave at a remote location in which no physician "could be had for him."[25]

McLellan and Kelty filed an appeal to the Louisiana Supreme Court in October 1855. Their attorney claimed, with the verification of one witness, that Thomas Williams had at one point admitted liability for the deceased bondman and pledged reimbursement for him. The slave trader then reneged on the promise. More substantively, the lawyer continued, his clients should not "be cut off from all relief, because *it so happened*" that George Emmy's fatal disease, of which McLellan and Kelty "were ignorant," manifested itself and developed "at [a] time and place" in which "no physician could be had." The "absence of medical aid," he contended, was "accidental" and "no fault" of the bondman's owners. The Louisiana Supreme Court concurred that McLellan and Kelty had not intentionally neglected Emmy's care but rejected the thrust of their lawyer's arguments. Siding fully with the rationale from Judge Kennedy, the Supreme Court affirmed the Third District Court's verdict. Thomas Williams could not be held culpable for George Emmy's demise because he could not control where his employers worked him. McLellan and Kelty's redhibition suit failed; Williams paid them nothing.[26]

A mere two days before George Emmy's death in November 1849, Thomas Williams announced that he had "just received at No. 18 Esplanade street, a choice lot" of one hundred "Virginia and Maryland NEGROES," including "Field Hands, Home Servants, Coachmen, Cooks, Washers and Ironers, Seamstresses, and Mechanics," with additional shipments slated to arrive in New Orleans throughout the slave-trading season. He and his brother had, over the course of about a decade and a half, and in spite of their many collisions with the law, nurtured an immensely profitable coastwise slaving enterprise that linked the capital city and the Crescent City. Slave trading was, for most dealers, a lucrative profession, with routine, healthy profit margins of around 20 percent or more. Theophilus Freeman, a slave trafficker active in the New Orleans and Natchez markets, managed to buck the trend and descend into insolvency in the early 1840s, but no similar misfortune befell the Williams brothers. Without specifying which sibling, the abolitionist newspaper *The Liberator* reported in 1850 that "Williams, the

Washington slave-dealer, boasts that he has cleared *thirty thousand dollars,* within the last few months, by the traffic in human flesh."[27]

Back in Washington, D.C., William H. Williams stumbled into more legal trouble. In 1848, he became embroiled in another allegation of kidnapping, this time of a black waiter in the capital named Henry Wilson. At the time, Wilson was in the process of slowly purchasing his freedom from an unidentified white woman who lived at the Navy Yard, a widow described unflatteringly in the abolitionist press as an "old Jezebel" and "vixen." He owed her only sixty more dollars on his contract when, callously disregarding the arrangement with her bondman, she sold him to Williams for $550. One Friday evening in January, three "base ruffians" in Williams' employ assembled to collect his latest purchase. The thugs entered the Washington boardinghouse where Wilson worked, seized him, gagged him, bound him in irons, and, at gunpoint, whisked him away. Wilson's free black wife, Sylvia, a former servant of President William Henry Harrison and now a maid at the same boarding- house, witnessed the abduction in horror. Distraught and desperate, she turned immediately for help to one of the boarders residing at the establishment, a Free-Soil Ohio congressman and vocal abolitionist named Joshua R. Giddings. Giddings regarded the Wilsons highly and promptly took action. He and Pennsylvania representative Abraham R. McIlvaine walked to Williams' slave jail at Seventh and Maryland in an attempt to retrieve Sylvia's husband. The formidable structure's "gloomy walls," bathed in faint moonlight, "retained all the horrid bar- barity of the darker ages," Giddings mused. Inside the Yellow House, he found two of Williams' agents sitting by a fire, "smoking segars." "The negur has gone," they informed the Ohio representative. "We took him immediately on board ship at Alexandria, and he has sailed for New Orleans."[28]

Rebuffed by Williams' underlings but not convinced by their tale, Giddings did not abandon his exertions on behalf of the kidnapped Wilson and his anxious and "inconsolable" wife. After filing for a writ of *habeas corpus,* he took to the House floor to relate Wilson's ordeal. Giddings recounted for his colleagues how "three armed persons, engaged in the internal slave trade," hustled Wilson off "into one of the slave prisons of this city" and, from there, to "the slave market at New Orleans." As he was a waiter in Washington, many congressmen were familiar with the bondman of whom Giddings spoke, but, according to one abolitionist's report, "a majority had no sympathy, no heart." Giddings also consulted Wilson's former owner, but the woman "was indifferent, stern, and immovable in her avariciousness." She had determined to sell the bondman and stood by her decision. A return trip to Williams' slave jail also produced no results, yielding only a recitation of information on Wilson that Giddings had already been told. Exhausting all other avenues of aid for the abducted bondman, the congressman "laid the case in all its hideous enormity before Duff Green," a prominent Washington journalist and, not coincidentally, owner of the boarding-house from which Wilson had been snatched. Green "immediately investigated the matter and volunteered his assistance."[29]

Acting as intermediary, Green wrote William H. Williams, stating forcefully that "Henry is entitled to his freedom on the payment of a small balance due on his contract" and that his defenders "are resolved to enforce his claim to freedom." Green requested the return of the bondman. Williams had already sent Wilson to Richmond, so, on the same day he received Green's missive, he replied that he could not "give a definate [sic] answer" until he sent a telegraph to the Virginia capital to find out "what the boy could be had back at, as he is in the Hands of annother [sic] person. I will venture to say," Williams added, that "for $700 he can be had at this time," but he awaited further intelligence on the Richmond slave market before giving "a positive answer." Williams fully intended to profit from his purchase of Henry Wilson, the bondman's peculiar situation be damned. But Williams met his match in Duff Green, who had anticipated Williams' recalcitrance. "Under such circumstances," his letter warned the slave dealer, "you cannot receive more than the money you paid." Intending to brook no nonsense from Williams, Green insinuated his next steps, if necessary. "How far it may become the duty of the district attorney to enquire into this matter is not for us now to say," he wrote. "All that we now require and all that we at this time propose is the liberation or restitution of the boy. If this be not done immediately, we will take efficient measures to compel his return and do all that is in our power to prevent the recurrence of a similar outrage."[30]

Finding Green's letter "offensive," Williams turned it over to his lawyer, Richard Wallach, who assumed authority over all communications between his client and Green, a situation Green himself preferred. The journalist and boardinghouse owner informed Wallach in no uncertain terms "that the boy can recover his freedom in any court in any of the southern states." Green went on to propose an arrangement through which, in exchange for Henry Wilson's prompt return, Williams' purchase price would be "restored to him" as a matter of justice. "What he has paid as expenses," however, Green qualified, "for the purpose of removing the negro beyond the jurisdiction of the Court, has been paid in his own wrong, and he can have no just claim upon Henry or the public on that account." Green encouraged Wallach to advise his client to accept the bargain he outlined, for it would behoove his public image if "his conduct" demonstrated "that at the time he sent the boy out of the district he did not know that he was entitled to his freedom." Presumably at his attorney's urging, perhaps combined with reflection upon his own self-interests, Williams begrudgingly caved. He agreed to return Henry Wilson for the purchase price he paid and not a penny more. Thanks to pressure from Joshua Giddings and threats of a lawsuit, Wilson's former owner agreed to repay the slave dealer the money from her bondman's sale. The "old woman" groused, however, that she had already spent $130 of the proceeds. Therefore, to finalize the deal, Giddings took up a collection from among his antislavery allies in Congress and, through a number of $5 donations, raised in "some twenty or thirty minutes" the funds required to make up for the woman's monetary deficit and compensate the slave trader in full. An additional $60 gathered from the congressmen went to Henry Wilson's owner to secure the bondman's freedom. Working together, Green and Giddings brokered a deal in which the kidnapped waiter simultaneously gained his release from a slave trader's clutches and from bondage itself. In gratitude and triumph, he reunited with his relieved and overjoyed wife, Sylvia, in February, lawfully drawn-up free papers in hand.[31]

Extralegally hounded into surrendering Henry Wilson and absorbing the cost of the bondman's maintenance and transportation to and from Richmond, William H. Williams surely felt the sting of defeat yet again. At the same time, the loss of a single slave whose purchase price was reimbursed seemed trivial compared with the trader's other main concern. Though physically in Washington, Williams never allowed his mind to stray far from the valuable shipment of convict slaves confiscated from him in Louisiana. If anything, the coerced return of Henry Wilson only heightened Williams' resolve to get the enslaved criminals back.

CHAPTER 11

The Louisiana State Penitentiary

W HAT OF THE ENSLAVED CONVICTS WHOM William H. Williams transported into Louisiana? Immediately upon their arrest on Sunday afternoon, November 1, 1840, the New Orleans Day Police deposited Williams' gang in the Watch House at city hall. Afterwards, they were transferred to the recently completed Orleans Parish prison for safekeeping as William H. Williams' case began its trek through the Criminal Court of the First District. According to the act of 1817 under which Williams was prosecuted, pending the conviction of anyone who "imported or brought" enslaved felons into Louisiana, the convict bondpeople shall "be seized and sold, for cash, to the highest bidder, after fifteen days notice of time and place of sale." Defying common sense, the sloppily constructed and hastily passed law thus specified that the very enslaved criminals whom legislators intended to exclude from Louisiana were ordered auctioned off within the state. Williams' attorney, John R. Grymes, noted the irony: "If the object . . . was to prevent the State from being contaminated by . . . convict slaves," the law was self-defeating, for "they will be sold and remain among us."[1]

In July 1841, within days of Williams' sentencing for violating the act of 1817, the New Orleans press publicly contemplated the fate of the convict slaves. The law clearly specified that they would be forfeited to the state and sold, observed the *Commercial Bulletin*, but it "does not specify *at what time after conviction* they are to be advertised for sale." This was an important omission in the law because, while the white masses of Louisiana citizens preferred not to have two dozen enslaved criminals foisted among them by their government, they needed time to determine precisely what to do with the felons. At "the advice and consent" of Governor André B. Roman and Attorney General Christian Roselius, the Criminal Court ordered Williams' gang "to be retained in jail" until the next meeting of the legislature. Lawmakers would then get the opportunity to remedy the longstanding oversight made while crafting the 1817 statute.[2]

Governor Roman apprised the Louisiana legislature of the situation in a message to the Senate and House of Representatives, meeting in the capital of New Orleans on December 13, 1841. "Twenty four slaves convicted in Virginia of heinous crimes, but whose punishment had been commuted to being carried out of the limits of the United States, were imported & seized in this city," he told the two chambers. The law stipulated that the confiscated slaves should be sold, with "the price divided between the state & the informer" who alerted the authorities of the violation. In William H. Williams' case, the informer should have been the Virginia governor or the Alexandria mayor, for they had been responsible for the missive sounding the alarm over Williams' possible arrival in New Orleans. But Louisiana officials did not consider either Virginia official a proper informant worthy of reward. Thus, Roman continued, "As there was no informer in this case, the slaves belong entirely to the state; and the attorney general has by my advice, postponed the sale until after the meeting of the Legislature."[3]

Governor Roman then got to the heart of the matter. The legislature in 1817 made an inadvertent error in drawing up the law, he explained. It was obviously a mistake "that convict slaves whose importation is prohibited under the penalty of fine and confiscation, should after this importation be sold in the state, and thus cause the very evil from which it was the object of the law to protect our fellow citizens." Never before, however, had anyone been found guilty of violating the act of 1817. Thanks to William H. Williams, the contradiction embedded within the statute had been exposed. As the governor viewed it, the slave trader's unlawful importation "now presented" lawmakers the "opportunity ... to correct" the "evil effects" of the existing statute by enacting a supplemental measure to close the loophole. Specifically, Roman recommended that Williams' gang and "all such others as may hereafter be imported and seized under similar circumstances ... be employed for life, under strict guard upon the public works of the State." If "the whole amount of the fines and forfeitures" from William H. Williams accrued to the state, as the executive desired, the government was going to take full advantage. Williams' economic loss was to become Louisiana's financial gain.[4]

Per the governor's instruction, the legislature quickly passed a bill, approved in 1842, placing the twenty-four members of Williams' gang "under the control of the president and board of public works." As Williams' appeals wound their way through the court system for the next two years, the convict slaves confiscated from the trader remained constantly under the guard of their new master, the state of Louisiana. Taken out of the Orleans Parish prison, the bondpeople labored, in chains, on the public works, by 1843 under the direction of the state engineer. Their use on the public works before the Civil War presaged Louisiana's use of black male prisoners on the chain gangs of the post-bellum years, yet the state's appropriation of the black convict labor irritated some antebellum Louisiana whites. On the eve of the final state Supreme Court verdict against Williams in April 1844, the New Orleans *Courier* groused, "For about four years the State has retained within its limits slaves that by law are not permitted to remain." The newspaper thought it hypocritical that the state government had taken advantage of Williams' gang. Louisiana "present[ed] to the civilized world the most singular spectacle of a sovereign state punishing a citizen for violating her laws," the editor complained, "when she violates the same ordinance, and reaps profit" from it. And already, the *Courier* added, without supplying names or a number, "Some of the slaves have died while in the possession of the State." As Williams' courtroom drama continued to play out, the state failed to compensate the trader for either the convict bondpeople who expired or "for the labor of the others" who continued to toil away under the state engineer. The *Courier* regarded the treatment of Williams as shameful and the whole situation a disgrace to the "honor and dignity" of Louisiana. Yet the Supreme Court's final ruling against Williams in April 1844 ensured that his gang of enslaved convicts would remain state property. Having arrived in New Orleans via sale out of the Virginia State Penitentiary, Williams' transports would soon become acquainted with a similar incarceration facility in Louisiana.[5]

The late eighteenth and early nineteenth century witnessed the construction of the first penitentiaries in the United States. Although the reformist impulse that inspired early American penal institutions is more commonly associated with the North, most southern states also erected penitentiaries during the same era. Kentucky built its state prison in 1794, only four years after Pennsylvania opened the nation's first such institution. Virginia followed suit in 1800, then Maryland (1812), Georgia (1817), Tennessee (1831), Missouri (1836), Mississippi (1840), Arkansas (1841), Alabama (1842), and Texas (1849). Among southern, slaveholding states, only the two Carolinas and Florida lacked a state penitentiary by the outbreak of the Civil War. Louisiana joined the wave of penitentiary building in 1832 when its legislature authorized construction of a state penitentiary in Baton Rouge. It opened for the reception of prisoners three years later. The almost three decades during which Louisiana locked up enslaved convicts in a biracial state penitentiary testified to the fact that, although unorthodox, the incarceration of bondmen and bondwomen was not incompatible with the institution of slavery. Yet the imprisonment of slaves also presented challenges to penitentiary administration. Slaves' presence prompted disputes over the proper work for them to perform as well as over the social organization behind prison walls.[6]

Harsh conditions greeted all inmates, white or black, arriving at the new state penitentiary from the New Orleans city jail in 1835. Convicts donned the prison uniform, consisting of "a coarse cotton jacket and trowsers, coarsely plaited straw hat, and a pair of brogans." Prison guards then deposited them in a cramped, individual cell, just three and one-half feet wide and seven feet deep, secured by an iron door, ill ventilated, and unheated in winter time. There, inmates slept "upon mattresses on the floor." A concern over "dollars and cents" meant "scanty" rations and a menu guaranteed to whet no prisoner's appetite. For years, each inmate ate for supper "a tub of soft soapish looking mush and molasses" unceremoniously dumped "in a tin plate to be eaten in his cell," in the dark and alone. Refractory inmates of all races, colors, and complexions confronted the possibility of whipping for misbehavior.[7]

By the law of 1832 establishing the prison, all convicts were "condemned to hard labor." Inspired by the Auburn plan of penitentiary administration, the act read that prisoners "shall labor diligently, and in silence." A supplementary law in 1837 forbade inmates from working outside penitentiary walls, except when making deliveries or running other errands for the institution. Within the prison, male convicts in the late 1830s and early 1840s labored in the prison brickyard and garden and at an array of other tasks, as shoemakers, tailors, spinners and weavers, carpenters, wheelwrights, cabinet makers, coopers, turners, painters, saddle and harness makers, blacksmiths, gunsmiths, cigar makers, carters, corn grinders, cooks, bakers, waiters, and hospital attendants. The relatively few female prisoners within the Louisiana State Penitentiary engaged in tasks traditionally gendered feminine and deemed culturally appropriate for their sex. A male guard kept watch over the half dozen or so women "employed washing & mending" in the prison laundry. That inmates in Louisiana's penitentiary worked during their period of incarceration made the institution typical among antebellum prisons.[8]

In the early 1840s, the work regimen changed dramatically, but only for the black male convicts working in the penitentiary. Louisiana had long been in need of laborers for internal improvement projects throughout the state. Late in 1841, Governor André B. Roman observed that "[t]he men of colour condemned to hard labor [in the penitentiary] ... could also during the term of their sentence be advantageously transferred to our public works." Starting in 1842, Louisiana law decreed that "all the colored male convicts now in the penitentiary, sentenced to hard labor, shall be transferred" outside the prison to labor for the good of the community. Additionally, those henceforth found guilty of crimes but whose death sentences were "commuted by the Governor and Senate to hard labor for life or for [a period of] years" would similarly be sent to the public works as an alternative to prison.[9]

The removal of enslaved and free black male prisoners to the public works provided essential labor as it alleviated in some measure the economic pressure that their products, sold at a prison store across the street from the penitentiary, placed on local Baton Rouge merchants. For years, irate business owners in the city had complained that the products of convict labor – an unpaid, captive workforce behind penitentiary walls – represented unfair "competition with the labor and industry of the resident mechanics of the State." Fears of cheap, affordable prison goods offered locally for sale "produced excitement and discussion" in many states, North and South, where convicts were put to work. In 1844, the Louisiana legislature banned the production of commodities inside the penitentiary that vied at market with those from local merchants, mandating that "no mechanical business shall be pursued for profit which may come in competition with the citizen-mechanics of Baton Rouge." The restriction applied to "carpenter's work, blacksmith's work, [and] any other mechanical work" formerly completed in the penitentiary. To the extent that black convicts performed these labors, their transfer to the public works would reduce the quantity of goods made in the penitentiary.[10]

Presumably joining the convicts from the Louisiana State Penitentiary on the public works, as the governor had directed, were the Williams' gang slaves, plucked from the Orleans Parish jail. Under the direction of the state engineer, they and dozens of other enslaved and free black male inmates toiled at internal improvement projects, primarily road construction, for the next few years. They faced no shortage of work. In 1843, the legislature instructed "the State Engineer ... to employ the colored convicts in completing the road from Baton Rouge to Clinton," in East Feliciana Parish. The next year, they worked on several roads in the vicinity of Grosse Tête, one linking Vidalia and Harrisonburg, and another in St. James Parish. Louisiana's recently inaugurated governor, Alexandre Mouton, practically beamed with satisfaction in early 1844 when he declared that "[t]he black and colored convicts have, with great propriety, been removed from the Penitentiary by the Legislature" and set to work for the public benefit.[11]

Louisiana authorities pondered employing enslaved and free black prisoners' labor on internal improvement projects other than road-building. In 1844, Governor Mouton proposed using black convict labor for "the clearing and draining of the swamps" around New

Orleans to create a healthier and more comfortable city. As the governor explained, "It is a work on which these convicts might be employed with great advantage; and thus repair, in some degree, the damage they have done to the community." He recommended that the cities of New Orleans and Lafayette each plan "for the maintenance, clothing and guarding [of] the black and colored convicts, and their employment in clearing and draining the swamps within their limits, or other municipal works." The *Baton Rouge Gazette* championed another project in which enslaved prisoners would "clear out the Bayou Fontaine." Williams' gang may have performed these dangerous and unhealthy labors in Louisiana's swamps and bayous in 1844, although no evidence can definitively confirm it.[12]

The Louisiana legislature understood the overwhelming demand for internal improvements but sought to minimize the state's expenses. Beyond directing the state engineer where to work the enslaved and free black convicts and appropriating money to arm the guards with muskets, Louisiana sought to wash its hands of the expenses that black convict labor entailed. Legislative directives to the state engineer drowned in contingencies. Black prisoners could only build the road to Clinton, for example, on the condition "that the inhabitants furnish guards and buildings for the safe keeping of said convicts ... pay their expenses of transportation to this point, and furnish provisions for the force there employed."[13]

Some local communities anxious over black convicts laboring in their midst objected to their presence and openly expressed their disdain, despite the uses to which they were put. The 1842 law permitting enslaved and free black prisoners to labor on the public works reserved for Louisiana parishes the right to prevent criminals from toiling within their boundaries. "[C]olored convicts" would not be employed in any parish "without first obtaining the consent of the police jury," so any parish disinclined to the use of black convict labor need only make sure that the police jury "inform the governor of such unwillingness." Some Louisiana residents feared that black prisoners working in public might pilfer from nearby homes or have "corrupting communication with their slaves." To allay these concerns, the state engineer assured citizens "that working in chains, these convicts can be easily worked with a small guard." In East Baton Rouge Parish, the editor of the *Baton Rouge Gazette* advocated the employment of enslaved and free black inmates on at least an experimental basis. When the East Baton Rouge police jury convened, it granted its consent, but its endorsement stipulated that any projects must "be done at the expense and charge of the State" – problematic, given the state's strained finances – and "that the strictest discipline be observed towards said negroes and convicts ... to prevent their interference or intercourse with the slaves of the neighboring plantations."[14]

If local communities sometimes resisted the employment of black convict labor in their neighborhoods, developments at the Louisiana State Penitentiary itself would soon pull some of the inmates laboring on the public works back to prison in Baton Rouge. In 1839, Louisiana's penitentiary committee had recommended erecting an establishment for "the manufacture of coarse cotton and woollen [*sic*] cloths" within the facility, an idea fully endorsed by Governor Roman. The state struggled to fund the undertaking optimally, however, frustrating advocates of the plan. The factory became a reality but never realized the anticipated profits. In 1843, the Committee on the Penitentiary proposed expanding the operation so that it might "be a source of considerable revenue to the State" rather than "a drain on the treasury, as it has been heretofore." Finances were so bad at the penitentiary that the House of Representatives admitted with embarrassment in early 1843 that "the officers and the guards" at the institution had "received nothing in the way of compensation" for nearly a year. Finally cutting its losses, the legislature in 1844 entered into a five-year lease of the prison and its occupants to the private firm of McHatton, Pratt, & Co., making the state a pioneer in the practice of convict leasing.[15]

Leasing proved a popular avenue through which antebellum southern states abrogated responsibility over their penitentiaries. A few southern states successfully implemented industrial programs within their prisons and earned a profit. Georgia prisoners built railroad cars, while Mississippi in 1849 constructed a prison cotton factory. The Maryland Penitentiary also became a lucrative manufacturing center, producing textiles, "[c]ombs and brushes, nails, bags, brooms and hats." These were the exceptions, however. Consistent profitability eluded most antebellum penitentiaries under state direction. Failing to become self-supporting, the state prisons of not only Louisiana but also Kentucky, Missouri, Alabama, and Texas all leased convicts to private enterprises before the Civil War. The lease system permitted states to make money through their agreements with private companies. Through leasing, Kentucky's penitentiary became the single most profitable incarceration facility in the United States. Louisiana's penitentiary likewise became a source of revenue once private enterprise took over. Ultimately, the state legislature relied on lessees to manage the penitentiary and maintain its prisoners virtually uninterrupted from 1844 to 1901.[16]

According to their agreement with the state, penitentiary lessees James A. McHatton and William Pratt would employ Louisiana convicts "chiefly in the manufacture of coarse cotton and woolen cloths, of negro shoes, and of cotton bagging and rope from hemp," in addition to inmates' customary labors in the prison brickyard. The advent of the leasing system in Louisiana thus had a profound effect on the state's enslaved and free black prisoners. The privatization of penitentiary operations and the language of the lease demanded the redistribution of the state's black convict laborers and a reorientation of the work they did, away from internal improvement projects on the state's roads and waterways and toward industries within the penitentiary walls. For the state engineer and other white authorities, the transition was welcome. "The experiment of working the colored convicts, on the public roads, seems entirely to have disappointed public expectation," explained the penitentiary report of 1844: "the civil engineer" in charge of the black inmates had recommended "that some other disposition be made of them, as the cost of the present system exceeds the value of their labor."[17]

When McHatton, Pratt assumed control of the penitentiary on October 12, 1844, it took charge of a total of 176 prisoners already inside the prison, transferred from the state into their possession. Only six of that number were black, and of those, all were women. A legislative enactment of 1845 called "for the return of the colored convicts to the Penitentiary" to labor under the direction of the lessees. The retrieval of enslaved and free black inmates from the public works increased their numbers inside the penitentiary dramatically. From October 1844, when

McHatton, Pratt took over, to 1851, the number of black men in the facility rose from zero to sixty-two. Throughout the 1850s and into the 1860s, African-American prisoners consistently made up almost one-third of the penitentiary population. Of the black inmates, about 85 percent were male, put to work in the cotton factory and at other industrial pursuits.[18]

Some members of Williams' gang apparently eluded deposit in the state prison. They continued on as before, farmed out to various work sites across Louisiana. Laboring under "several authorities," they were reportedly "employed upon her rivers in removing snags" and probably numbered among the "State hands" working Louisiana's bayous and canals. State engineers' reports documented the dangers inherent to their labor on the public works. In little more than half a year in 1849, "five of the State hands" – perhaps even one or more of William H. Williams' transports – died. Not listed by name, "two were drowned" in the murky waters in which they toiled, while another "two were accidentally killed" on the job. As the state engineer rationalized, "our work is of such a character that accidents . . . will sometimes occur, even with the most prudent superintendents." A fifth convict laborer succumbed to "a chronic disease." The unhealthiness of Louisiana's marshes and swamps exposed enslaved and free black workers to cholera, dysentery, typhoid fever, and other waterborne illnesses and produced "an usual amount of sickness" among them. The Williams' gang slaves who labored outside the penitentiary were not necessarily better off than those inside; their labor merely differed. Newspapers reported that, starting in 1847, some of the convict slaves from Virginia participated in the construction of the statehouse at the new state capital of Baton Rouge.[19]

Pursuant to the legislative decree of 1845, ten members of Williams' gang took up involuntary residence within the Louisiana State Penitentiary on March 13. They included six of the original twenty-one bondmen and four of the original six bondwomen purchased in Richmond. Together, they represented about 4 percent of the more than two hundred known slaves sentenced to hard labor at the prison between 1835 and 1862. This small group of slaves endured the singular misfortune of incarceration in the penitentiaries of two different southern states. Suffering from "double bonds," shackled literally and metaphorically by both the institution of slavery and imprisonment in the penitentiary, the enslaved inmates truly were, as one historian of slave law put it, "twice condemned."[20]

The vast majority – about two-thirds – of all inmates in antebellum southern prisons were not enslaved or free black people but white men. African Americans in bondage rarely spent time in antebellum southern penitentiaries. When bondpeople committed crimes, masters typically dispensed justice on their own, without resort to formal legal channels. Plantation law held sway in all but the most extraordinary cases. With the whip at the ready, masters could punish slaves without depriving themselves of a misbehaving bondperson's labor during a period of confinement. Nevertheless, slaves might be imprisoned briefly in local public jails or workhouses if convicted of various crimes in the southern court system or if apprehended as a runaway. Masters might make use of those same facilities to punish troublesome slaves privately or, if needed, to store them securely. Bondpeople might also spend brief stints in city or county jails while they awaited trial, sale at auction, or, after conviction for a capital crime, a date with the gallows. In all of these cases, slaves usually measured their terms of incarceration in days or weeks. Even that was too long for most slaveholders. Local jails were notoriously overcrowded, damp, and disease-ridden. The deplorable conditions inside endangered inmates' health and imperiled their lives. Consequently, most masters preferred keeping their valuable slaves out of jail.[21]

If relatively few bondpeople saw the inside of a local jail, they almost never entered a state penitentiary. As one former Mississippi bondman explained, "you niver heard tell uf a slave bein' sent ter de pen" during bondage. Slaves understood that penitentiaries were "for the white folks when they did wrong." One ex-bondwoman in Texas summarized the situation bluntly: "When niggers done sumpin dey wasnt sposed to dey just give dem a real good whipping and dat was all der was to hit."[22]

In many ways, it made little sense to imprison slaves in the penitentiary. Slavery itself already functioned as an institution of social control. Depositing bondpeople in prison was therefore redundant. Many southern whites hardly considered incarceration an appropriate punishment anyway, for it provided slaves a reprieve from the routines of the cane and cotton fields and other varieties of plantation labor. For masters invested in human property, a bondperson serving time in an incarceration facility neither produced for the southern agricultural regime nor profited the slaveholder. Finally, the incarceration of bond-people was incompatible with how southern whites viewed slaves, a degraded segment of society with "no rights to respect, no civic virtue or character to restore, no freedom to abridge."[23]

Nevertheless, the penitentiary was not entirely unknown to slaves in a few states of the antebellum South. For a brief period, Maryland and Arkansas both accepted enslaved prisoners.[24] Maryland sentenced slaves to the penitentiary from its opening in 1812 until 1819, receiving some sixty slaves during those years. A revised state law thereafter required the transportation out of state of any slave convicted of a serious crime and not sentenced to hang.[25] Arkansas permitted the imprisonment in the state penitentiary of slaves convicted of second degree murder and manslaughter, but few slaves actually served time before the legislature eliminated that penalty in 1858. Virginia courts did not sentence slaves directly to confinement in the penitentiary, but as Williams' gang demon-strated, the Virginia state prison did house on a temporary basis con-victed bondmen and -women awaiting sale and transportation out of the United States. Those individuals typically spent only months to a year or so in the penitentiary before a slave trader such as William H. Williams picked them up for relocation and sale. After 1819, Louisiana stood alone in punishing enslaved criminals with prolonged prison sentences, usually for life. No other southern state could match it in either the frequency with which it incarcerated bondpeople or the duration of their terms of imprisonment. The ten members of Williams' gang introduced into the Louisiana State Penitentiary in Baton Rouge would go on to become some of the longest-serving felons, black or white, in antebellum US prison history.[26]

We know the names of ten members of Williams' gang imprisoned in the Louisiana State Penitentiary. They included the enslaved bacon thief Ned of Lancaster County, Virginia, and Phil Harris, one of the five bondmen convicted of burgling a store in Fredericksburg. Probably three other transports who ended up in Louisiana's state prison in Baton Rouge were named John. One was John Johnson of Spotsylvania

County, found guilty of an assault upon a white man during an attempted robbery. To differentiate himself from his fellow inmates named John, another went by the name of Jack Johnson. It was probably a third John from among the Williams' gang slaves who nicknamed himself King. The bondman King may have been John Carter, one of Phil Harris' partners in crime in the Fredericksburg robbery.[27]

Two of Williams' gang – Thomas Jarrett, or Tom, of Louisa County, and the bondwoman Malinda, of Southampton County – stood out from the others who entered the Louisiana State Penitentiary in 1845. Each had been found guilty of the murder, not of a master, patroller, or other white person, but of a fellow slave. Both incidents offered a glimpse of life in the slave quarters gone wrong. Tom hurled a heavy iron pot at the head of a bondman named Davy, fracturing his skull and producing an "inflammation . . . of the brain," which ultimately led to Davy's death. The bondwoman Malinda, meanwhile, killed another slave while defending herself from a sexual assault by an enslaved man. In January 1840, the bondman Allen, owned by the same master as Malinda, made her uncomfortable through his repeated, uninvited touching. According to the testimony of an eyewitness, Allen approached Malinda and "laid his arm on her shoulder" but was met with rebuke. Malinda "told him to get away" and threatened to "stick the knife in him" if he refused. Allen persisted in his harassment, and in the tussle that followed, Malinda nicked Allen's jacket and inflicted a minor cut upon his arm. Later the same day, when the relentless Allen pressed his body against hers, sandwiching her between him and a post, Malinda fatally stabbed him in the chest. A court of oyer and terminer sentenced her to death for her crime but also "recommend[ed] to the Executive to commute the punishment ... to Transportation" because the magistrates took into account the circumstances of her case and viewed her sympathetically. No claim of self-defense would have carried weight with the justices had her victim been a white man, but they believed Malinda within her rights to protect herself from a bondman's unwanted sexual advances. Since both their victims were other slaves, Virginia courts viewed severe punishment short of execution as appropriate for both Tom and Malinda.[28]

The final three slaves of Williams' gang committed to the Louisiana State Penitentiary were all convicted arsonists. With but one exception –

the bondman Landon from Prince William County – all of the enslaved arsonists whom Williams conveyed to Louisiana were women. Southern courts held female slaves responsible for most of the arsons committed in the region. Setting fire to a structure took stealth, cunning, and a little know-how, rather than physical strength. In this way, arson resembled poisoning as a crime that bondwomen were relatively more likely to attempt compared with more violent offenses. The crime avoided direct confrontation yet sent a distinct message to the owner of the property consumed in flame. Arson's victims were harmed not in body but in spirit and pocketbook, their valuable dwelling, outbuilding, or other inanimate property destroyed. For the perpetrator, starting a blaze required only a motivating grievance, an opportunity, and a source of fire. For slaves in the Old South, none of these ingredients was in short supply. The three enslaved female arsonists in Williams' gang – the young bondwomen Jane of Spotsylvania County, Charlotte of Clarke County, and Nancy of Accomack County – all ended up in the Louisiana State Penitentiary.[29]

Ned, Phil Harris, John Johnson, Jack Johnson, King, Thomas Jarrett, Malinda, Jane, Charlotte, and Nancy: all of them entered the state prison in Baton Rouge on March 13, 1845. Like slavery itself, prison life was oppressive, exploitive, and centered on work. Antebellum penitentiaries North and South routinely prioritized the extraction of labor from inmates at the expense of reforming them. Enslaved prisoners in Louisiana, such as those from Williams' gang, were never candidates for rehabilitation at all. About 85 percent of them were imprisoned for life and required no preparation for reincorporation into society. Forfeited to the state, the Williams transports, too, faced indefinite incarceration. For them, the penitentiary marked a more or less permanent repository, one that offered the convict slaves no hope for redemption. Their time in the state prison would be spent as cogs in the penitentiary's productive machinery, under the direction of lessees driven to achieve maximum profitability. In accordance with the McHatton, Pratt, & Co. lease, "a large portion of the convicts," including both black and white men, were "employed in the cotton factory." In 1849, Messrs. Armfield and Hayes, executors for the deceased slave trader Isaac Franklin, bought osnaburg – coarse, plain fabric appropriate for slaves' attire –produced by convict labor inside the Louisiana State Penitentiary from McHatton, Pratt. In 1855, Governor Paul O. Hébert proudly proclaimed the "ninety-five negroes in the Penitentiary ... as efficient laborers as may be found on any plantation in this State." Of the ninety-nine men of color in prison the following year, approximately 60 percent worked in the brickyard, 40 percent in the factory and other pursuits. The seventeen enslaved female inmates in 1856, including the four from Williams' gang, may still have been restricted to "washing, &c.," although it is possible that they sometimes labored in the cotton factory as well.[30]

Williams' gang and the other bondpeople condemned to compulsory and usually lifelong labor in the Louisiana State Penitentiary endured trying conditions. Annual prison reports, gubernatorial and state auditor's records, and newspapers allow us to peer behind prison walls and catch a glimpse of the estimated two hundred enslaved inmates who lived, worked, and sometimes died under the watch of penitentiary officials. The presence of the transports from Virginia and the other enslaved prisoners complicated the administration of the penitentiary. How to employ, secure, and manage slave convicts remained enduring questions for prison officials throughout the antebellum era.[31]

Most of the enslaved inmates at the penitentiary had been born in Louisiana, although the state only narrowly edged out slave-exporting Virginia as the most common birthplace of the convict slaves housed there – a testament to the magnitude of the domestic slave trade to the Old Southwest. By 1860, slaves composed 47 percent of Louisiana's total population, but enslaved and free blacks together made up only 31 percent of the penitentiary's prisoners that year. Statistically, then, black prisoners were underrepresented as a proportion of the total inmate population in the antebellum era. Convictions for murder or arson most often landed enslaved inmates in the penitentiary. Because the overwhelming majority of enslaved prisoners had received life sentences, several in fact served for decades, toiling away, in turn, for the state and then the lessees.[32]

The prisoners inhabited a structure built of brick and consisting of three stories. By 1851, the board of directors observed with concern "the crowded state of the Prison and increased number of Convicts" owing to the rising quantity of black male prisoners. The total number of inmates, 249, exceeded the 240 cells within the facility. The board expressed its alarm, because they considered it "unsafe and unwise to confine during the night more than one in the same *cell*," for "huddling" criminals concocted "deeds of darkness and plans for escape." The lessees made unspecified "[t]emporary arrangements . . . for the surplus number," but conceded that the stopgap measures were "neither *convenient, comfortable, or secure*." The Louisiana legislature passed an act in 1852 to build two hundred additional cells, construction that would eventually alleviate the overcrowding. The pre-Civil War prisoner population peaked in 1856 at 356, a figure that included 116 slaves.[33]

Investigators attributed the overcrowding at the institution to the accumulating numbers of enslaved prisoners in the penitentiary. A Joint Committee studying the facility in 1854 took note of "the large number of slaves confined" there and averred that, henceforth, "slaves convicted of crimes ought not . . . be sent" there. Moreover, those already incarcerated inside "ought to be removed . . . because confinement is to them no adequate punishment, but in many cases is actually preferred to their former condition." This was a stunning admission, but for enslaved criminals spared the legendary horrors of Louisiana's sugar cane fields, the committee's suspicion may have held some merit. As an alternative to imprisonment, the Joint Committee proposed a return to labor on the public works. It was not the first body to make the same suggestion. The *Minority Report of the Committee on the Penitentiary* had raised the possibility in 1852, contending, despite prior experience to the contrary, that the "the negro convicts . . . might be advantageously employed on the works of internal improvement." The new state engineer agreed. He declared with confidence that convict slaves performed double the work "at one-quarter of the cost of white labor." To reassure Louisiana whites anxious about enslaved convicts working in public, the *Minority Report* stressed that the prisoners "would not be much more at large, in such employ-ment, than they are at present." The Joint Committee of 1854 similarly insisted that slaves "might be employed to advantage on the public works of the State, if properly guarded and confined so as to prevent them from having any intercourse whatever with other slaves." Although the committee respected the legal rights of the private firm operating the pen, acknowledging that "the slaves already there cannot be withdrawn without the consent of the lessees until the termination of the lease," Harvey Richardson and W. B. Philips, respective chairs of the Senate and House Committees on the Penitentiary, recommended the passage of "a law abolishing imprisonment of slaves in the Penitentiary as a punishment for crime" and the creation of an adequate substitute for confinement. As late as 1860, Governor Robert C. Wickliffe echoed their call, complaining that the many slaves sent "to the State Prison for offenses slight and trivial" clogged the penitentiary. Nothing came of their suggestions, and Williams' gang and the other enslaved prisoners continued to labor in the prison textile mill and brickyard on the penitentiary grounds.[34]

Lessees of the penitentiary did make it common practice by the mid-1850s, however, "to send the negro prisoners" outside the prison walls for small tasks essential to running the institution, such as gathering water. They also dispatched black inmates "to a neighboring forest for the purpose of cutting wood for the use of the prison." Perhaps that policy permitted some of Williams' gang to breathe somewhat freer air momentarily, but the practice reportedly "led to evil consequences; [and] complaints were made." Some observers believed allowing enslaved inmates to exit the prison grounds on various, purposeful errands undermined the intent of the penitentiary. They generally looked anxiously upon enslaved convicts dressed in prison garb sent outside the penitentiary to work in public. Consequently, in 1857, the state legislature mandated that "no convict shall be employed without the walls of the Penitentiary."[35]

The new legal restriction against slaves working outside the penitentiary hamstrung prison operations and imposed an unnecessary financial burden on the latest lessees, McHatton, Pike, & Co. They had made it common practice to dispatch enslaved prisoners to the Mississippi River "to haul water . . . to supply our engines." The change in the law mandated that, in lieu of using slaves, the lessees hire outsiders "at high wages." The Board of Control reported that the penitentiary spent some $4,000 to do the same task that enslaved prisoners had formerly completed at no additional expense. To the business-savvy lessees, such a practice made little sense when "we have negro convicts, who, accompanied with a proper guard, could have performed the labor at a great saving of cost." McHatton, Pike also complained of a city-wide labor shortage that frequently "render[ed] it impossible to obtain a sufficient number of laborers to do the work required outside of the walls." In June 1857, an emergency compelled the lessees to flout the law unapologetically. They took "part of the negro convicts out to discharge two boats of coal we had purchased," they explained, "as we could not, at any price, have obtained a sufficient number of laborers to unload the boats, and should have probably lost boats and coal, had we not employed a part of the negro convicts to unload them."[36]

When the penitentiary hired outside laborers, many of whom were black, the penitentiary's Board of Control fretted over "the constant contact and intercourse that must inevitably take place between the prisoners and those thus employed." "[I]n spite of the strictest vigilance exercised by the officers," guards proved unsuccessful "in preventing the introduction of contraband articles: such as whisky, secreted in loads of cotton brought to the prison, correspondence from outside persons, etc.," "thereby seriously infracting the discipline of the prison." McHatton, Pike maintained that they could use convict labor "with far less injurious effects to the prisoners and prison discipline, than is now produced by having negroes from without the prison employed within the enclosures, and in constant intercourse with the prisoners." The Board of Control recognized the catch-22 the prison faced:

> We have but to choose between two evils. We must have outside negroes employed within the walls of the prison, thereby placing them in contact with the prisoners, to the great danger of discipline, or we must allow the prison negroes to do the hauling of the prison under guard, thereby inflicting a slight wound on the objects of the Penitentiary system.

Acknowledging it was "impossible ... to prevent improper intercourse" even "with the strictest vigilance," the board and the lessees preferred the latter option. They appealed to the legislature to modify the law "as to allow the negro prisoners to do the hauling and labor to and from the river and within the limits of the corporation." The state refused to act, however, prompting renewed pleas from the Board of Control the next year.[37]

Penitentiary officials openly admitted that security at the Louisiana State Penitentiary was imperfect. Prisoners' shackles certainly hindered their ability to flee. As the New Orleans *Picayune* reported in 1840, "Each of the convicts wears an iron ring round the right leg, to which is attached an iron chain that reaches to the waist, and is there fastened by a belt that extends round the body." As a deterrent to escape attempts, guards also had at their disposal muskets, broadswords, and pistols. Yet while formidable walls surrounded most of the penitentiary, a portion of the prison grounds was enclosed only "by a picket fence." This most vulnerable point along the penitentiary's perimeter was adjacent to the "brick-yard and garden," locations where the enslaved prisoners frequently labored. At least one slave was known to have fled "when employed in making bricks." As late as 1858, lessees McHatton, Pike & Co. were still commenting upon "the necessity of enclosing with a brick wall the grounds of the Prison."[38]

Within the penitentiary, the racial segregation of the prisoners represented the ideal for prison management to strive for. In 1841, Governor André B. Roman expressed the commonly held view among whites that "the mixing" of "[t]he men of colour condemned to hard labor ... with the white convicts in the Penitentiary" stood "in opposition to our institutions." Roman had supported the transfer of black convicts to the public works partly as a means to achieve a more rigid separation of the races. A Joint Committee on the penitentiary in 1844 recommended at the time of the initial lease to McHatton, Pratt & Co. "the propriety" of working black prisoners "separate and apart from the white convicts," language that appeared verbatim in the law bestowing the lease. The separation of the races was not easily implemented, however. The lessees "deem[ed] it impracticable by the present arrangement of work shops and yard" and insisted "that it cannot be effected without a change ... in [blacks'] employment" or to the lessees' contract with the state. They grossly disregarded the legislative prescription that "[a]ll colored Convicts ... be worked separate and apart from the white Convicts."[39]

The degree of racial segregation inside the penitentiary gradually increased as the antebellum years wore on. Initially, for example,

Louisiana's prisoners consumed their rations in isolation, in their cells, but at some point, black and white prisoners began eating in an integrated setting. By 1857, the construction of a new dining hall exclusively for the white prisoners separated the races at meal time. Louisiana's "negro convicts" ate together in a building separate from the white prisoners. A correspondent from a Baton Rouge newspaper described the segregated dining facilities as "the best improvement yet made in prison discipline."[40]

Penitentiary officials also eventually made special accommodations for separating female from male inmates. In 1856, the lessees constructed new "apartments for female prisoners," a building "deemed indispensably necessary, as there were no adequate accommodations for female convicts." Because so few white women served sentences in the penitentiary, enslaved women such as Malinda, Jane, Charlotte, and Nancy must have been the primary inhabitants of the new structure. A newspaper correspondent confirmed the next year that "the females have a substantial building to themselves, and are never brought in contact with the men."[41]

Yet the segregation by sex could not have been perfect throughout the antebellum decades, for several imprisoned bondwomen bore offspring more than nine months after their incarceration began. Among the four female slaves seized from William H. Williams, the convicted arsonist Charlotte gave birth in prison to three children – John, Mary Ann, and Harriet – by January 1855. The identity and race of the father or fathers are unknown, the circumstances surrounding conception uncertain. With both black and white men among the prison population, enslaved women may have willingly participated, in spite of vigilant officials, in loving relationships or clandestine affairs with fellow prisoners. At least as likely, female convicts proved captive, convenient, and vulnerable targets for the unwanted advances of sex-deprived inmates, coercive white guards, or other penitentiary authorities who wielded power over them. Bondwomen across the South confronted the daily prospect of rape, and that possibility within the penitentiary would only have made an already miserable situation that much more nightmarish for the enslaved female inmates. Or perhaps the relatively few bondwomen in prison exploited their carnal leverage to extract various favors from those in charge or from inmates able to smuggle in goods from the outside. Given the range of possible encounters, Charlotte's son and daughters may have been the products of consensual acts, forced sex, coercion, or some combination thereof.[42]

A Louisiana law of 1848, unique among the slaveholding states, declared that children born to enslaved female prisoners confined in the penitentiary would be appropriated from the bondwoman's master and surrendered to the state. The act of 1829 forbidding the sale of children under the age of ten away from their mothers still applied, however, so to conform with the law, penitentiary officials kept mother and child together in prison until the youngster reached his or her tenth birthday. Upon attaining the requisite age, the child was seized as state property and auctioned off by the East Baton Rouge Parish sheriff to the highest bidder, with the proceeds of the sale going to "the free school fund." In short, sons and daughters in bondage, severed from their enslaved and imprisoned mothers, helped finance the education of Louisiana's white schoolchildren. Altogether, about a dozen enslaved children were born in the penitentiary and sold away from convict bondwomen. Prison "officials, administrators, and employees" often purchased them, suggesting that they may have been the fathers.[43]

For enslaved children under ten, incarcerated in the penitentiary but technically not inmates, aging afforded an automatic, if emotionally and psychologically traumatizing, exit from state prison. Most enslaved prisoners could not so predictably evade their confinement and had little hope of ever leaving. Small numbers received gubernatorial pardons or discharges for serving out their time. A few others escaped, while some achieved liberation only through death. The last generation of enslaved inmate in the Louisiana State Penitentiary, however, achieved its release in the crucible of war. During the Civil War, the penitentiary played a crucial role in the southern war effort as an important supplier of Confederate clothing. The penitentiary lessees handed the institution, its cotton factory, and its inmates over to the state of Louisiana in April 1862 to "take charge of and manage it for the benefit of the army." The very next month, Union forces seized Baton Rouge, converged on the penitentiary, assumed control of it, and camped on its grounds. The penitentiary's contribution to the Confederate cause came to a sudden end. Confederate soldiers attempted to retake Baton Rouge in August 1862 and for a brief period regained "part possession of the penitentiary" before northern troops successfully repelled them. Union forces held the penitentiary, reduced by battle to ruins, for the remainder of the war and emancipated the inmates still captive there. Only months later, on January 1, 1863, President Abraham Lincoln's Emancipation Proclamation freed any bondperson living in East Baton Rouge Parish and in all but thirteen Louisiana parishes. For the enslaved convicts still housed in the penitentiary, the Civil War enacted a double liberation, freeing them from both the Louisiana state prison and bondage itself. But William H. Williams' transport slaves missed the Jubilee at the penitentiary, because by the outbreak of the Civil War, they were no longer there.[44]

CHAPTER 12

Closure

I N NOVEMBER 1844, THE NATIONAL CALAMITY OF THE civil War was almost seventeen years into the future, less an immediate threat than a bogeyman occasionally raised by partisans for political effect. The more pressing issue was the ongoing presidential election. With two weeks of voting to go, the *Cincinnati Herald* castigated slave trader and Polk and Dallas flag-waver Thomas Williams as a "wretch" and the "devil's deputy." He "carries on his infernal trade, within sight of the Capitol, under a license granted him under the authority of Congress for *four hundred dollars!*" sneered the editor. "His *establishment* is a *gloomy* Jail, in which men, women, and children ... are imprisoned, chained, and beaten ... at the will of the negro trader." The *Herald* reported that, only five weeks earlier, Williams had marched "a company of sixty persons ... from the cells of this horrible private prison to the wharf" along the Potomac and placed them aboard one of his "vessels constantly engaged in transporting his miserable victims to market" in the Deep South. "[H]ow much longer shall our nation's capital continue to be desecrated and polluted by the vilest and most detestable abominations of slavery and slave trading?" asked William Lloyd Garrison's *Liberator* with customary fervor. "[H]ave we no national pride? No ... national honor? No regard to the world's opinion? ... [A]re we dead to shame?" Constitutionally, change in the laws of the District of Columbia must originate with the elected leaders serving on Capitol Hill, overlooking the Yellow House. As the *Cincinnati Herald* understood, "[T]he awful responsibility" for the domestic slave trade devolved "upon the Congress of the United States ... as fully as [it did] upon the slave dealer himself."[1]

After the presidential election as well as before, Congress was inundated with pleas to abolish slavery and the slave trade in the District of Columbia. With the gag rule lifted, the House of Representatives no longer automatically tabled the petitions sent to it. After reading the memorials, the House determined their fate on a case-by-case basis. As in the past, however, congressmen frequently voted to table the measures. Petitions from Washington County, New York, in 1845, from 211 citizens of Jay County, Indiana, in 1847, and others were still often neglected, shunned for their divisive content rather than passed on to committee. But the issue refused to die. As a result of war with Mexico, the United States in 1848 acquired a vast territory between Texas and the Pacific Ocean in which the status of slavery must be decided. This emerged as the most pressing political question of the time. The issue of the slave trade in the nation's capital would soon become wrapped up in these broader considerations of slavery in the West, and increasingly requests for the wholesale extinction of slavery in the territories accompanied the memorials praying for abolition of at least the slave trade in Washington, D.C. The debates over these issues built to a crescendo in 1850.[2]

After sharing in Congress the story of the abducted black waiter Henry Wilson in January 1848, Free-Soil representative Joshua R. Giddings of Ohio called for the creation of a select committee to investigate the case and to determine the propriety of abolishing the slave trade in the District. Alternatively, he proposed, the committee should ponder the removal of the nation's capital to a free state, a suggestion that resurfaced sporadically over the next two years. As with so many motions before his, the House voted to lay Giddings' on the table, albeit by the narrow margin of 94–88. Undeterred, the representative from Ohio made the slave trade in Washington a persistent topic for discussion in the House.[3]

During his brief, one-term stint in that same chamber, fellow Ohio congressman John Crowell frequently agitated on the issue as well. "The practice of buying and selling men, women, and children, at public sale, like cattle, horses, and mules, is looked upon by many persons who are not familiar with the customs of slaveholding communities, with unmingled abhorrence and detestation," Crowell declared in July 1848. "And nothing is so well fitted to awaken and perpetuate sectional feelings and prejudice, and alienate the affections of the people, as the traffic in slaves, as it is now carried on at the seat of the General Government." No less than the transatlantic slave trade, the internal trade was filled with "cruelty" and "terrific horrors." "It may not be quite as shocking to humanity as some scenes exhibited in the Middle Passage," Crowell averred, but "the difference is too slight to waste any time in defining it." Slave jailers "shut out the light of day, and conceal their enormities from the public gaze," the Ohio congressman declared. What must be "the condition of the manacled and wretched inmates" inside? Crowell explicitly expressed his personal curiosity about "one of these secret prisons, near the Smithsonian Institute ... and in full view of this Capitol" – a clear gesture to William H. Williams' Yellow House. How ironic, he said, that "the stripes and stars ... float so proudly over it."[4]

If the internal workings of the slave pen remained veiled from Congress's view, public spectacles and atrocities on the streets of Washington, D.C. – all directly tied to the institution of slavery – were plain for all to see. For two consecutive evenings in April 1848, immediately following the failed waterborne escape attempt of almost eighty fugitive slaves from the District of Columbia aboard the schooner *Pearl*, a violent, anti-abolitionist mob congregated on Seventh Street. According to reports, slave dealers from Alexandria, Annapolis, Baltimore, Richmond, and Washington "led on, excited, and encouraged" the rabble. Sources identified slave trader Hope Hull Slatter of Baltimore as among the participants in the tumult, but neglected to mention William H. or Thomas Williams as complicit in the unrest. That the clamor erupted on Seventh Street, however (the street adjacent to the Yellow House), meant that whichever Williams brother was in town at the time could have readily joined the assembled mob.[5]

Also in 1848, "three ruffians from Alexandria" brazenly kidnapped a free black man "on Pennsylvania avenue, ... in the presence of several members of [the] House [of Representatives]," and whisked him off to a slave pen in Alexandria. Fortunately for him, legal counsel, paid for through "funds raised by the members of Congress," restored the man's liberty before it was too late. All too often, lamented Representative Crowell, "Free men have been seized ... and confined in these secret prisons, by lawless wretches engaged in the slave-trade, and sold into perpetual bondage." Such was presumably the fate of one "honest and industrious colored woman" in May 1850. The enslaved mother of six, "employed as a cook . . . near the Capitol," had been slowly accumulating the funds to purchase her freedom when a pair of constables accosted her and ordered her to the slave jail. When she walked too slowly to suit her captors and resisted their efforts to speed her along, they struck her in the head with a cane, bound her hands and feet, "rudely thrust [her] into a hack, and . . . hurried off to Williams's slave pen."[6]

As the abolitionist press relentlessly recounted these and other shocking and offensive scenes, northern members of the House of Representatives grew more serious about enacting a law against the slave trade in the District of Columbia. Article I, section 8 of the US Constitution explicitly bestowed upon Congress the authority to "exercise exclusive Legislation" over the District "in all Cases whatsoever." This plain language appeared so unequivocal as to erase all doubt of Congress's right to outlaw the D.C. slave trade, at least as far as the North was concerned. Yet the possibility of restriction sparked heated resistance among House members from the South. When one resolution to draw up a bill that would prohibit slave sales in the District passed by a vote of 98–88, a representative from South Carolina threatened a walkout of "every southern member."[7]

One concern, even among some northern lawmakers, was that the House respect the wishes of Washington, D.C. residents, since they did not have a representative of their own in Congress. In late December 1848, Representative Charles Stuart of Michigan declared that "every principle of right, of justice, and of morality" demanded that the people of the District be consulted on the matter. The following month, the City Council of Washington supplied the House a petition "praying [for] the abolition of the slave trade in the District of Columbia" or, alternatively, the authority for local authorities in Washington and Georgetown to take that step themselves. By the end of January 1849, the House Committee on the District of Columbia "reported a bill to prohibit the introduction of slaves into the District of Columbia as merchandise, or for sale or hire," beginning August 1, but legislative wrangling stalled it out for the remainder of the year. Inertia set in, lasting well into 1850.

When, in late May of that year, Representative John Crowell of Ohio asked to introduce "A bill to abolish the slave trade in the District of Columbia," his colleagues in the House voted not to receive it.[8]

Any proposal to terminate the "nuisance" and "outrage" of the slave trade in the nation's capital would affect all five or six dealers still active in the District. William H. Williams' friend and former associate Thomas N. Davis, for example, was still advertising in the city papers. "I want to purchase $1,000 worth of Family Servants, such as man and wife, with their children," he announced in May 1850, along with instructions to call upon him "at King's Hotel" on Pennsylvania Avenue, "between 3d and 4½ streets." But the abolition of the slave trade would have a uniquely devastating impact on William H. Williams' business. The mayor of Washington, D.C. – probably Whig editor W. W. Seaton of the *National Intelligencer* but possibly his successor, Walter Lenox – informed Senator Henry Clay of Kentucky that there was "perhaps but one" slave jail still operating in the nation's capital in 1850, "with slaves continually in it" and "constantly for sale": Williams' Yellow House. In 1846, the retrocession to Virginia of all portions of the District of Columbia south of the Potomac reduced the size of the nation's capital from one hundred square miles to about sixty-nine. The restoration of land to the Old Dominion meant that any legislation abolishing the D.C. slave trade would not threaten the slave pens of Alexandria at all. Traders headquartered there could freely continue to pursue their grim commerce unimpeded, regardless of what might come. Any measure to outlaw the slave trade in Washington, D.C., therefore targeted William H. Williams' livelihood more profoundly than that of any other trader in the area. That fact did not bother Henry Clay. "I have never visited one of these depots," he confessed, but they "are nothing more nor less than private jails, subject to no inspection of public authority, under the exclusive control of those who erect them." Inside, "the owner of the jail" was law, imposing "police regulations" over the enslaved prisoners as he saw fit. No southern proslavery radical despite owning slaves himself, Clay found the traffic in bondpeople in the nation's capital abhorrent and objectionable. Like his colleagues in Congress from the North, he "shared in the horror at this slave trade" and agreed that it brought "some degree of odium on the District."[9]

Clay thus shepherded a bill abolishing the D.C. slave trade through the Senate. That legislative body, like the House of Representatives, had long received memorials asking as much. As the Washington City Council petitioned the House in January 1849, the Senate received a similar petition from citizens of Washington requesting the abolition of the slave trade. That memorial was directed for consideration to the Senate Committee on the District of Columbia. Genuine movement on the matter did not come until early 1850, however, by which time the D.C. slave trade joined a constellation of other pressing and contentious issues all related to slavery: the admission of California to the Union, the fate of slavery in southwestern lands appropriated from Mexico, the boundary of Texas, and the return of fugitive slaves to their masters. Without solutions to these questions, cracks already evident in the edifice of Union would only widen. In his last great act of statesmanship before his death, Henry Clay emerged as the architect of the Compromise of 1850, a series of laws passed individually rather than as a collective, omnibus bill, to ensure their passage. When voted upon as a whole, the measures failed, since they offered something to offend each section of the Union and every member of Congress. Deconstructed into its constituent parts, the disaggregated provisions of the compromise could pass. As a result of this process, California entered the Union in 1850 as a free state. The Utah and New Mexico territories were organized according to the principle of popular sovereignty, which allowed voters living in those territories to determine by ballot the future of slavery there. Texas surrendered claims to western lands in exchange for a US government agreement to assume the former Republic's debts, and a new, more aggressively enforced Fugitive Slave Act went into effect. The last, unpassed component of the Compromise of 1850 remaining on the legislative agenda was the abolition of the slave trade in the District of Columbia.[10]

Charged with crafting the Compromise of 1850, the Senate's Committee of Thirteen, chaired by Clay himself, developed a brief, succinct proposal for outlawing the D.C. slave trade. The first section stated that "it shall not be lawful to bring into the District of Columbia any slave whatever for the purpose of being sold, or for the purpose of being placed in depot, to be subsequently transported to any other State or place to be sold as merchandise." Any slave so introduced into the capital "shall thereupon become liberated and free." The second section of the proposal granted "the cities of Washington and Georgetown" the authority "to abate, break up, and abolish any depot or place of confinement of slaves brought into the said District as merchandise," contrary to law. Clay explicitly spelled out to the Senate the precise parameters of the bill. It forbade "the introduction within the District of slaves from adjoining slave States, and their being placed in depot here ... for subsequent transportation to different markets by land or water," most notably Mobile and New Orleans. "The bill does not propose to interfere in the slightest degree with the right of one inhabitant of the District to sell a slave to another inhabitant of the District," he clarified, "nor does it interfere with the right on the part of the inhabitant of the District to go out of it and purchase for his own use a slave, and to bring the slave within the District for his own use." No, Clay conceded, "A slave cannot be brought within this place for sale and be ... sold," but slave traders and slaveholders "may go to the distance of five miles and purchase one, and bring him here." It struck the Kentucky senator as but a trifling "inconvenience" to "go somewhere else" so nearby – either Virginia or Maryland – to make the purchase.[11]

Senators opposed to legislating against the D.C. slave trade justified their stance in different ways. Many focused on constitutional issues. Some acknowledged that Congress enjoyed the right of "exclusive legislation" over the District, but observed that that constitutional provision did not equate to "a grant of absolute power." Limits did exist, they insisted: Congress was powerless to prohibit the sale of slaves – or any other commodity – within the nation's capital. Other senators outright denied Congress's constitutional authority to interfere with slavery in the District at all. Many viewed the abolition of the slave trade with suspicion, as an "entering wedge" in a broader assault upon the interstate slave trade and upon slavery as an institution. Some southern senators openly speculated that the bill to abolish the slave trade in the District of Columbia "hazard[ed] the existence of the Union" and would ultimately lead to its dissolution. Senator and Committee of

Thirteen member Willie P. Mangum of North Carolina determined not to vote to end the D.C. slave trade because he did not want to "wade through the blood knee-deep of the whole South, and over the wreck of this Union."[12]

Some southern senators contended that, while Congress possessed legislative power over the District of Columbia, the circumstances of the District's creation mandated special consideration and deference to the states that ceded their territory for it. Maryland and Virginia each contributed land for the national capital. Both were slave states that assumed that slavery would face no restrictions within the District. The retrocession of Alexandria back to Virginia in 1846 meant that, by 1850, "an implied obligation" existed only with Maryland. As the only remaining donor of territory for the national capital, argued southern senators, Maryland ought to be consulted prior to acting upon slavery in the District. To do otherwise "would be contrary to conscience, to good faith, and to the implied obligation."[13]

This line of argumentation was easily disputed. First, upon accepting the land cession from Maryland, Congress assumed jurisdiction over it and full responsibility to legislate for it. Congress adopted Maryland slave law for parts of the District north of the Potomac, but Maryland did not exercise continuing or concurrent sovereignty over it. Complicating the southern argument further, the Maryland legislature had already outlawed the introduction of slaves into the state for sale. As Henry Clay noted, the Committee of Thirteen's bill was thus "a mere adoption of the law of Maryland." Inquired one congressman pointedly, "Why should southern men endure here what they will not tolerate in their own States?" Why should Congress, invested with the power of making exclusive legislation for the District, not exercise that same prerogative?[14]

Compared with his senatorial colleagues from the South, Mississippi's Jefferson Davis took one unique tack in criticizing the bill to end the slave trade in Washington, D.C. His remarks drifted to William H. Williams' slave jail itself. "The depôt is a comfortable looking house," declared Davis, minimizing the emotional terror and physical horror that slaves experienced inside. "Rather a boarding-house in its aspect than a prison." With a "spacious yard" and a "growth of poplar trees" surrounding it, Davis concluded cheerily, Williams' private pen "look[ed] as little like a jail as any residence in the city of Washington." More practically, the senator stressed the important function the facility served. The slaveholding traveler, accompanied by his servants, "lodges them in jail for safe keeping" throughout the duration of his stay, he noted. It would be inhumane to deprive the paternalistic master, so invested in the care of his enslaved property, of this enormous convenience. Yet chair Henry Clay seemed adamant that the bill reported from the Committee of Thirteen "will break up the depôt and the private jail in which the slaves are kept." The very "object" was to abolish "the depots themselves." Senator Thomas Pratt of Maryland understood the bill differently. As he saw it, the slave trade bill did not outlaw slave depots per se; it only forbade slave traders and other sellers from placing into pens bond-people whom they "intended to carry ... elsewhere, to be sold as merchandise." Thus, by Pratt's reasoning, Davis labored under a misapprehension. Like many of his southern colleagues, however, Davis retorted that a master ought to be able to sell his enslaved property wherever and whenever he pleased.[15]

Other opponents of the Committee of Thirteen's bill objected to its punishment: the liberation of slaves carried to the District of Columbia for sale. That provision deprived masters of their property and, more-over, threatened to increase the number of free black people in Washington, D.C., which many whites already considered alarmingly high. Most whites regarded free people of color as a troublesome nui-sance, so the prospect of augmenting that population was not greeted with enthusiasm. Henry Clay defended the forfeiture clause on two grounds. First, legally, seized contraband merchandise was always for-feited, so it should be no different when the commodity in question was a slave. Second, emancipation as a penalty for violating the law, Clay predicted, would increase the statute's efficacy. On one hand, most masters would not dare bring slaves to Washington, D.C., for sale, know-ing those bondpeople could be confiscated and freed. On the other hand, slaves taken to the capital for sale would have a strong motivation to pursue their freedom in court. Emancipation, Clay reminded his colleagues, was not a goal of the proposed law but rather the conse-quence for breaking it. The senator believed that, as constructed, the bill offered an effective deterrent to the slave trade in the District.[16]

Clay fully intended for the bill emerging from the Committee of Thirteen, narrowly focused on the suppression of the D.C. slave trade, to pass the Senate without amendment. In the context of the Compromise of 1850, he saw the measure as the northern counterpoint to the Fugitive Slave Act, which had been passed for the sole benefit of southern slaveholders. As one northern senator concurred, abolishing the slave trade in the capital lent "symmetry" to the grand design. As Clay further understood, "when we go a hundred miles ... to the North" of Washington, D.C., "the enormity of the slave trade here is the leading theme of conversation." Northerners thought the issue "more calculated to agitate and excite ... than almost any other subject," explained the Kentucky senator. Tamping down political passions demanded the slave trade's abolition in the capital, the one and only purpose of the bill before the Senate.[17]

Despite Clay's aim, amendments arose in the Senate chamber. Opposed to the existing bill, Senator James Mason of Virginia moved to gut it by striking out the entirety of its original language. These efforts were rejected, 30–18 and 31–17, on separate votes for each of its two sections. New York senator William H. Seward went the opposite direction with his radical proposal to alter the bill so that it liberated all bondpeople in the District of Columbia and provided compensation to masters of emancipated slaves. That amendment never stood a realistic chance of adoption; the Senate rejected it by the resounding vote of 45–5. Other recommended amendments added rules against aiding runaway slaves and further regulations of free black people. In the end, however, the Senate voted against revising the original bill, 26–16. Henry Clay successfully guided the Committee of Thirteen's bill, unscathed, through to a final vote. A last-minute adjustment made the bill effective January 1, 1851, pending final passage.[18]

Congress approved the bill to suppress the slave trade in Washington, D.C., on September 20, 1850. It comfortably passed the House without amendment by a vote of 124–47 and the Senate by a 33–19 margin, with all opposition predictably coming from Maryland, Virginia, and the other slaveholding states. Mississippi senator Jefferson Davis acknowledged the slave-trade bill as "the last of the great measures of the 'omnibus'" that together composed the Compromise of 1850, but it did not matter. A staunch opponent of the bill from the outset, he could not support it. In fact, another lawmaker observed, only seventeen of the sixty senators in total voted yea on all features of the Compromise: the admission of California, popular sovereignty for the Utah and New Mexico territories, the Texas boundary question, the Fugitive Slave Act, *and* the suppression of the slave trade in Washington, D.C. Four of those seventeen – senators Jesse Bright of Indiana, Lewis Cass of Michigan, James Cooper of Pennsylvania, and Daniel Dickinson of New York – had served on the Committee of Thirteen that crafted the legislation to abolish the slave trade in the District. Only Henry Clay's division of the Compromise of 1850 into its constituent parts enabled the laws' passage. Members of Congress afterwards partook in copious self-congratulations for their legislative feat. The last of the compromise measures to pass, the bill to abolish slavery in the capital "harmonizes with the kind feelings of most of this Chamber," reflected one senator, "drawing as to a common centre the good feeling both of the North and the South." Engineer of the compromise Henry Clay concurred. Collectively, he predicted with satisfaction, the compromise measures would "restore ... concord and harmony throughout the country."[19]

In August 1850, only six weeks before Congress approved the destruction of the D.C. slave trade, a census taker found William H. Williams living in Washington's Seventh Ward. He listed his occupation as "Slave dealer," a designation not so openly acknowledged on other traders' census returns. Williams maintained active operations throughout 1850 as Congress deliberated the future of slave trading in the District of Columbia, but talk of ending the slave trade there damaged his slave-trading enterprise well before Congress enacted the final measure into law. Congressional debates over all features of the Compromise of 1850 appeared in print and stimulated widespread public dialogue. Between reading about unfolding events themselves and, more commonly, overhearing bits and pieces of whites' conversations, the free black and enslaved populations of Washington, D.C., could hardly have remained ignorant of the rumblings of change afoot. The ongoing discussions over the termination of the D.C. slave trade throughout 1850 may well have emboldened bondpeople's efforts to evade Williams' clutches.[20]

Under normal circumstances, Williams aided in the apprehension and detention of runaway slaves. If given information as to the whereabouts of fugitives, the slave trader would sometimes capture and then store them until the master either retrieved them or sold them as punishment for attempted flight. But in 1850, Williams placed at least two newspaper advertisements for five fugitive slaves who had evaded his grasp. The slave trader ran a tight jail and had hardly ever needed to announce runaways in the preceding fifteen years. That suddenly changed while congressmen contemplated the abolition of the slave trade. In May 1850, Williams offered a $400 reward: $100 apiece for twenty-six-year-old James; twenty-five-year-old Sam, with "one front tooth out"; the dark, twenty-year-old George; and the ailing Gusta, described as "ruptured." In August, Williams again sought public assistance, this time in the recovery of "my MAN JOE," a six-foot-tall but "spare made" twenty-six-year-old black slave recently purchased from Dr. T. W. Smith of Upperville, Fauquier County, Virginia. Joe absconded near Fredericksburg and was heading, according to Williams' prognostications, for Pennsylvania by way of Winchester, Virginia, "as he has a grandmother and other relations residing in that place." Neither runaway ad mentioned whether the escapees had fled while in transit to Williams' Washington slave pen or from the Yellow House itself.[21]

The law that eradicated the slave trade in Washington, D.C., dealt William H. Williams' business an inescapable, final, and fatal blow. Although the statute did not technically forbid the keeping of slave pens outright, private jails such as Williams' earned profits primarily by warehousing slaves destined for sale, not by providing incarceration services for traveling slaveholders visiting the capital. By the time the prohibition of the slave trade became law on January 1, 1851, some Washington slave dealers had relocated across the Potomac to Alexandria. Because that city's retrocession to the commonwealth of Virginia in 1846 spared it from the effects of the 1850 congressional action against the slave trade, Alexandria absorbed Washington's share of the traffic and remained a thriving slave depot throughout the coming decade. Its location attracted the likes of Solomon Northup's captor, James H. Birch, who assumed control of the former Franklin &

Armfield slave pen, but no evidence suggests that William H. Williams similarly crossed the river to Alexandria.[22]

During its last year of active use, Williams' slave jail merited a visit from Swedish feminist writer Fredrika Bremer, then undertaking an extensive American tour. She marveled at how closely situated Washington's infamous slave pen was to the Capitol, but noted that the "gray house" (it had apparently been painted a less conspicuous hue prior to 1850), "the prison-house of the innocent, hides itself behind leafy trees." Upon reaching the pen, Bremer met "the slave-keeper, a good-tempered, talkative, but evidently ... coarse man" not identified by name – perhaps Ebenezer Rodbird or Joshua Staples – at a "little grated door." He spoke to his guests candidly about slave pen management, observing with a devilish smile that the inmates "would be unruly enough if they were not afraid of a flogging." "[T[he negro people, both men and women, must be ruled by the whip," he insisted with a perverse laugh. The keeper, Bremer remarked, "seemed pleased to show us his power and authority."[23]

While at Williams' slave pen, a female traveling companion of Bremer's wished to purchase "a negro boy as a servant." The women cast eyes upon several "little negro children ... sitting or leaping about" on the grassy area inside the enclosure of the pen, but they learned from the keeper that "no slave was allowed to be sold here for the present." This would not have been due to any legal restriction yet, but rather to Williams' own market calculations. Slaves brought substantially more money at auction in the Southwest than in the Chesapeake, so it made economic sense not to part with them in in-person, local sales in Washington. Bremer's slave-keeping host explained that the children then in the pen "were kept here for a short time to fatten" before heading "to the slave-market down South, to be sold" at higher prices. Rebuffed in her attempt to purchase, Bremer's friend departed empty-handed, having gazed upon some of the last enslaved people incarcerated inside Williams' private jail.[24]

A bondman named Lewis Ferguson would have counted among the final slaves William H. Williams ever sold in Washington, D.C., proper. Ferguson was a fifty-five-year-old, "copper colored" man about five feet seven inches tall as well as "a drunkard." His age and intemperate habits

would have rendered him unsuitable for the southern market and therefore not worth the expense of transportation to New Orleans. On
January 24, 1850, Williams let the relatively more disposable bondman
go. Local buyer Thomas Murphy paid the trader a modest $390 for him.[25]

No fanfare or public announcement accompanied the closure of
William H. Williams' private prison, but one day in late 1850 or soon
thereafter it wrapped up operations in conformity with the law. The D.
C. Department of Corrections Runaway Slave Book shows that, from
1849 to 1850, William H. Williams, acting as agent for various slaveholders, retrieved twenty-five bondpeople from the D.C. Slave Jail, run
by the city, presumably for transfer to his own pen. Nineteen of the
twenty-five had been held merely for "safekeeping" while their owners
did business in Washington. That Williams' jail undercut the government's prices for the identical service perhaps explains the inmates'
relocation. The other slaves whom Williams took into custody had been
committed as runaways. Perhaps, upon the masters' instructions, the
slave trader would sell some of these bondpeople to the Deep South as
a punishment for their perceived wrongdoing. Williams retrieved his
last bondperson from the D.C. Slave Jail on November 13, 1850.
Stephen, as he was named, could not have spent long inside Williams'
compound. The slave dealer may have attempted to maintain his facility
after January 1, 1851, strictly by imprisoning apprehended fugitives and
housing slaves for safekeeping, but the preponderance of his income
derived from peddling the black bodies incarcerated inside the pen.
According to one secondhand source, "after the abolition of the slave
trade had ceased to make [the jail] profitable," Williams sold the facility. The unnamed gentleman who purchased it saw for himself the site's
artifacts of horror and torment. Touring the property, he discovered
stout staples, driven into "the walls of the out-house and of the room
adjoining the kitchen," to which Williams' enslaved prisoners had been
shackled. The facility purportedly had a long history of slave incarceration that predated Williams. Former congressman Abraham Lincoln
remarked in 1854, probably with some exaggeration, that the slave pen
operated by Williams "had been openly maintained for fifty years." The
congressional act of September 20, 1850, guaranteed that its iron gate
clanged shut for the last time.[26]

"[T]he 'slave pens' at Washington were a cause for irritation to the immaculate eyes of certain Northern Abolitionists!" sneered the proslavery southern press. "[T]he fanatics ... could not be satisfied with the Union while the 'slave pens' were tolerated in the city of Washington." Congressional extermination of the slave trade in the District of Columbia altered the very landscape of the nation's capital. In 1854, former shoemaker turned Massachusetts politician Henry Wilson returned to Washington, D.C. "I went to the spot where stood Williams's slave pen," he said, the very place "where, eighteen years ago, I saw men, women and children chained together for the Southern market," a powerful and transformative scene that propelled him into the world of antislavery politics. By 1854, though, the slave jail – that reprehensible site of misery and terror – had vanished, torn down within just a few years of the slave trade's demise in the District. The "pen had passed away," Wilson recorded, "and flowers were blooming where the slave once sighed." A sign advertised "Flowers for sale and bo[u]quets made 'to order.'" An enterprising businessman still utilized the former site of Williams' slave pen, but this one engaged in an infinitely more pleasant trade. The ugliest humanity had to offer had yielded to beauty, an auspicious sign for Wilson and his fellow abolitionists: "I hope but a few years more shall pass until every spot wherever the groans of human bondage are heard shall be a garden in which the blossoms of freedom shall make glad the eye, and the accents of hope delight the ear."[27]

With the shuttering of the Yellow House, the careers of those persons involved in the acquisition, imprisonment, and transport of the Williams' gang slaves went in different directions. By 1850, Rudolph Littlejohn, the enigmatic agent who finalized the purchase of the enslaved convicts from the commonwealth of Virginia, was no longer trading in slaves but rather a forty-two-year-old engineer living with his wife, Julia, in a Clarke County, Virginia hotel, not far west of Washington, D.C.[28] William H. Williams' former jailer and agent Ebenezer Rodbird shipped slaves in his own name throughout the 1840s and into 1850 to whichever Williams brother resided in New Orleans at the time. Born in England and just slightly younger than his employer, he died in November 1861, the owner of multiple plots of land in Washington, D.C.[29] Williams' other known jailer, Joshua Staples, had relocated to the cotton frontier by the time the Yellow House was about to close. He and his wife, Mariah, had a dozen children before 1865, born either in the state of Mississippi or in Chambers or St. Clair County, Alabama. Staples never acquired more than a modest estate.[30] Achieving vastly greater financial success, Nathaniel Boush, captain of the brig *Uncas*, which carried the Williams' gang slaves as far as Mobile, maintained a long career as a mariner. Born around 1811 to a seafaring family firmly tethered to Norfolk, Virginia, and the greater Chesapeake, he piloted several other slaving vessels after his tenure with the *Uncas* ended. By the later 1850s, the seasoned sailor left the seafaring trade behind and embarked upon a new, related career as ship chandler and grocer on King Street in Alexandria, Virginia. He became a leading figure in the Alexandria business community and at the time of his death in 1873 possessed an estate valued at almost $400,000 in 2016 dollars.[31]

William H. Williams appears to have largely exited the domestic slave trade with the closure of the Yellow House. Just as the timing of his entry into the business of human trafficking meant that he missed much of the domestic slave trade's most spectacularly profitable years in the 1830s, his departure from the trade meant that he lost out on its resurgence in the 1850s to heights not seen since the flush times. In the decade before the Civil War, traders carried an additional quarter million bondmen and bondwomen to the Old Southwest to toil in cotton and cane. Williams was no longer a major player in this renewed, brisk pace of business.[32]

His brother Thomas, however, did partake in the financial windfall of the 1850s economic boom. Until 1853, Thomas Williams maintained a slave-trading business at 18 Esplanade in New Orleans, although the number of bills of sale bearing his signature plummeted after 1850. In 1852, Williams sold faithful customer Charles Kock the six-year-old mulatto girl Rachel, the daughter of a slave whom the purchaser already owned, but for the most part, either the slave dealer was leaving it to employees to complete the paperwork, or he was not selling nearly as many bondpeople as in the past. Competition in the New Orleans slave market was stiff. By the 1850s, dozens of private slave jails lined Gravier and Baronne streets, with other slave traders on Moreau and Esplanade. Thomas Williams may have extracted himself from the slave trade for other reasons. Perhaps, basking in the successes of his long career, he was succumbing to the siren song of home and family or surrendering to a nagging desire to take up other pursuits. Whatever the reason, in the early 1850s, he was consciously downsizing his New Orleans operations. By 1854, he no longer appeared in New Orleans city directories at all.[33]

Frequently in the early 1850s, Thomas Williams returned to his childhood home of Macon County, Alabama, the repository for an extensive clan of Williamses, most of the adults having migrated from the Carolinas or Georgia. While back in Alabama, Thomas, whether intentionally or in spite of himself, found love. On December 30, 1851, he married Amelia Malvilla (or Marilla, or Marvilla) Gibson of neighboring Tallapoosa County. As much as sixteen years Thomas' junior, Malvilla, as she was usually referred to in the records, had been born in Georgia sometime between 1833 and 1836, probably the daughter of Benjamin Gibson, a slaveholder residing in Tallapoosa County by 1850. Likely sometime in 1854, the newlywed Williams couple relocated southwestward, to Butler County, Alabama. Thomas Williams, like Isaac Franklin, Rice Ballard, and other successful slave traders before him, began to set aside the hectic, turbulent, and semi-transient life of the slave trader to embrace the refined and domesticated trappings of the gentleman planter.[34]

On their sprawling plantation in Butler County, near Starlington post office, Thomas and Malvilla Williams started a family. They soon had two children of their own, daughters Mary, born about 1855, and Anna, who arrived three years later. The Williamses also briefly assumed legal guardianship, on May 14, 1855, of two minor girls, sisters named Sarah and Margaret Daniel, about seventeen and sixteen years old, respectively. Five years before, the girls had been living in the household of David C. Daniel, a prosperous, sixty-year-old farmer in Macon County who had migrated to Alabama from Virginia. He was also likely the girls' grandfather. With his death, the Daniel sisters, rapidly approaching adulthood and marriage, required a guardian for just a couple of years. Thomas Williams stepped in to help. Perhaps the deceased Daniel had been a friend or neighbor. Maybe the Daniel and Williams clans had even known each other back in the Old Dominion. Or perhaps Thomas, who had himself once lived under a guardian in Montgomery County prior to joining his older brother in the slave trade, was simply paying it forward.[35]

By 1855, Thomas Williams certainly enjoyed the means with which to feed two additional mouths. He possessed exorbitant wealth. The will he drafted in Macon County in 1854 bequeathed "a large Estate" to his "beloved wife" Malvilla, who, along with her father, Benjamin Gibson, served as executor. Census records in 1860 showed that Thomas Williams owned $20,000 in real estate and $100,000 in personal estate. He employed an overseer to monitor the forty-four slaves he owned, all of whom lived in one of eight slave cabins on his property. Williams' enslaved workforce trended young, with all seventeen of his male slaves aged six to twelve. Of his twenty-seven female slaves, eleven were between six months and six years old, with two in their teenage years and another five in their twenties. The forward-looking Thomas Williams was anticipating a bright and prosperous future, one built on young, strong black backs and the reproductive power of fertile young bondwomen.[36]

Although Williams was making the transition to Alabama Black Belt planter, he could never escape New Orleans' orbit. Although he may have sent his cotton crop to market in Mobile rather than in New Orleans, he continued to dabble as a slave trader in the South's largest slave market. In 1858, Williams sold "a first rate Blacksmith" for $2,000 to a master in Concordia Parish, Louisiana. Chances are he went to New Orleans whenever he needed to augment his personal enslaved labor force as well. In 1857, Williams also began a new but related career as a cotton factor in the Crescent City. Cotton factors of New Orleans, sometimes called commission merchants, worked closely with cotton-producing planters. As one scholar succinctly explained, they helped sell slaveholders' cotton and then "used the proceeds to provide planters with what they needed, such as food and clothes for their slaves, and everything they wanted." Using their business connections, cotton factors also "solicited credit from merchants and bankers" to extend to their slaveholding clientele. They "made their living by charging either a flat rate" for their services "or a percentage on every transaction made on behalf of planters." Williams may have originally conceived of embarking upon work as a commission merchant as a means of capitalizing upon the economic wave of the 1850s, but he did not begin his new duties until November 1857, by which time a financial panic had struck. He perhaps saw his latest occupation as a hedge against economic uncertainty, a means to augment his income and protect the wealth that he had already accumulated.[37]

On November 2, 1857, Thomas Williams joined partners William T. Scott and A. J. Bateman in the newly christened commission merchant firm of Scott, Williams & Co., located at 157 Gravier Street. Both hailing from the town of Jefferson, in East Texas, Scott, "a large planter, well off," with "g[oo]d connect[ion]s & influence," and Bateman, his thirty-five-year-old clerk, had teamed up in the New Orleans cotton factorage business less than a year earlier. Bateman managed W. T. Scott & Co.'s concerns from their office at 46 Union Street. The addition of Thomas Williams to the partnership brought the company a wealth of expertise in the New Orleans market as well as a new name and address.[38]

Launched in the 1840s, R. G. Dun & Company, the United States' first credit reporting agency and precursor to Dun & Bradstreet, initially expressed uncertainty about Scott, Williams & Co. Its brief commentary in November 1857 assessing the creditworthiness of the new firm remarked that William T. Scott, a "Planter in Harrison Co[unty,] Texas ... is a Director of the Pacific Road Co.," while the recently welcomed partner, Thomas Williams, was a Macon County, Alabama, native, a married man in his thirties, and a planter of "means, & of consid[erable] influence" in his home state. The R. G. Dun agent apparently did not pursue Williams' personal business history deeply, for he mischaracterized the longtime slave trader as unknown in New Orleans, which could hardly have been the case. His evaluation stated that Scott and Williams "as yet ... are very little known here ... respecting their means & position." Because Scott, Williams & Co.'s predecessor, W. T. Scott & Co., "commenced [operations] late" in 1856, "& their business was small," and since the fall of 1857 "will be their 1st full season," gauging the new firm's likelihood of success proved challenging. By March 1858, an updated R. G. Dun entry expressed cautious optimism toward Scott, Williams & Co. They "[h]ave means," wrote the credit reporting agent. Business was moderate, with "[g]ood prospects for a fair & increasing bus[iness]."[39]

Scott, Williams & Co. could not escape the fact, however, that it formed at an inopportune economic moment. Amid the stubborn, depressed financial climate of 1858, the partnership moved to a new physical location at 10 Union Street, but the R. G. Dun report of July hinted at troubling signs for the partners' future. "Tis said they are too anxious to secure bus[iness] and issue their paper too lavishly," the agent divulged. That was the widespread rumor in the business community, at any rate. Nevertheless, he continued, "Their cr[edit] has been and now is, fair to good."[40]

May 1, 1859, brought significant changes to New Orleans' business landscape. The previous March, the state legislature had passed an act, signed into law by Governor Robert C. Wickliffe, "to prevent persons from transacting business under fictitious names." Lawmakers made it a misdemeanor offense, punishable by a fine of as much as $1,000, for a company in Louisiana to conduct "business in the name of a partner not interested in his firm." As a result, more than a dozen companies in New Orleans re-organized and re-named themselves to avoid unlawfully leveraging the identity of an individual not directly involved in their operations. A small number of companies disbanded entirely. On May 1, the partnership of Scott, Williams & Co. announced its immediate termination as well, although not for the purpose of conforming with the recently passed law. The New Orleans papers reported that Scott, Williams & Co. "dissolved by limitation," indicating that Scott, Williams, and Bateman had agreed to partner for only a predetermined amount of time. Concluding operations on May 1, the partnership had been in business for precisely eighteen months.[41]

With his partners failing to renew their arrangement, Thomas Williams took it upon himself to "settle up the business of the firm ... in liquidation" and continue "the Cotton Factorage and Commission business in his own name, for his own account." After the announcement of Scott, Williams & Co.'s closing, R. G. Dun doubled down on its early indications of concern, reporting that the partnership had not been "consid[ere]d very good." It then critiqued each partner individually: "Scott was a Planter" with little "if any means in the concern," and "Bateman did not am[oun]t to much, except as a working p[artne]r. Tho[ma]s Williams alone ranks as fair only." The credit agency reported on August 1, 1859, that Williams' new business had declined in the three months since the prior partnership dissolved. It rated Thomas Williams' solo operation as "fair" at best.[42]

By early 1860, however, the fortunes of the former Scott, Williams & Co. dramatically improved. The turnaround coincided with a revived national economy emerging from recession, but R. G. Dun generously bestowed much of the credit on Thomas Williams himself. In addition to reporting on businesses' assets and creditworthiness, R. G. Dun agents often critiqued the "personal habits and moral character" of individual businessmen. The January 1860 report on Thomas Williams found no fault with either. He "[i]s a Cotton Planter" who "[r]aises from 250 to 300 Bales of Cott[o]n yearly," it read. His "respectability & moral char[acter]" were beyond reproach. Brimming with effusive praise, it further described Williams as "one of the best bus[iness] men in the City." The report added with some understatement that Williams, worth an esti-mated $200,000, was "consid[ered] g[oo]d for all his bills." His establish-ment, concluded the R. G. Dun report, "Ranks no 1 among the Cotton Houses" of New Orleans.[43]

Williams' successful reincarnation of Scott, Williams & Co. under his own name compelled the R. G. Dun report to reinvent the defunct partnership's past and to some degree retroactively repair a reputation the credit reporting agency had formerly besmirched. The Dun agent's freshest entry in his register frankly acknowledged the difference. Whereas in May 1859 the "concern was not consid[ere]d very good," on January 28, 1860, he described Scott, Williams & Co. as "a firm who did their bus[iness] noiselessly, quietly, & without much intercourse with Brokers & Merchants, & it has been only lately that their real position as men of business & standing commanded the public attention." Thomas Williams, the agent added, was "their succes-sor" and the implied driving force behind his cotton house's recent success.[44]

At the same time, Williams carried the burden of the financial bag-gage left behind by Scott, Williams & Co. In early April 1860, "a reliable source" informed the Dun reporter that Williams' "House is under pro-test" by its previous iteration's creditors, "& will in all probability suspend operations for the present." In 1860, Thomas Williams stepped back from the cotton factorage game he had entered in November 1857. As he had promised to do when Scott, Williams & Co. folded and he took over the business, he would now "wind it up." "Some of the protested paper still has cred[it]," the R. G. Dun agent reported in October, but he also hastily added that it "will ultimately be paid." His confidence derived from knowledge of Williams and his esteemed reputation. Apparently having returned to his Black Belt plantation, Thomas Williams, the credit agency observed, "lives in Alabama & is a man of wealth & will ultimately pay all the liabilities of the old firm." The last entry for him was dated January 18, 1861. The repayment of Scott, Williams & Co.'s lingering but not overwhelming debts notwithstanding, Williams put his lives as both professional slave trader and commission merchant behind him.[45]

The year 1861 would prove as calamitous for the Thomas Williams household as it did for the nation as a whole. The first shots of a four-year Civil War between the North and the slaveholding South rang out at Fort Sumter, South Carolina, on April 12. Perhaps not coincidentally, back in Alabama a twenty-eight-year-old "negro man" named Charles, Williams' enslaved property, ran away, possibly inspired to make a bid for freedom. It was not yet to be. Apprehended in nearby Montgomery County, Charles sat in jail on April 26, dreading retrieval by his master and a return to plantation bondage. Thomas Williams would personally profit from Charles' labor for only another six months or so, however, for on November 10, the former slave trader died, in his early forties, of unknown causes. Although the Civil War raged, and dozens of Thomas Williamses from Alabama fought for the Confederacy, the Butler County plantation owner likely did not breathe his last on the battlefield. In November, the war was young, and sufficient volunteers still filled soldiers' ranks. The Confederate government had not yet instituted the draft or summoned men of Thomas Williams' age to duty. Had Williams lived deeper into the war, he would have become eligible for service, but his fantastic wealth would have enabled him to hire a substitute to serve in his stead, at least until the Confederate government overturned that policy to appease those who pointed out the socioeconomic unfairness of it all. Moreover, a man of Williams' prominence would have entered Confederate service at a high rank.

The Thomas Williamses of Alabama fighting in gray consisted almost entirely of privates.[46]

Thomas' final parting left behind his wife, Malvilla, and "two minor children" – his daughters Mary, age six, and Anna, age three. Economically, the deceased slave trader ably provided for his surviving family. The inventory and appraisement of Williams' estate showed that he held in bondage at least six full or partial enslaved families. It listed forty-two slaves worth a collective $28,900, a 440-acre plantation, almost fifty bales of cotton at various stages of processing, several horses, dozens of head of livestock, a buggy, and a carriage. The total value of slaves, land, and personal property tallied nearly $37,000. In addition, many individuals, mainly from Louisiana, Mississippi, and the cotton-growing region of Texas, owed debts to Williams totaling the massive sum of almost $80,000. Altogether, Thomas Williams had amassed assets worth $116,624.82. By modern standards, he was a millionaire three times over. But his immense fortune could not buy longevity.[47]

Thomas Williams' affluence did, however, relieve his wife of the economic pressure to remarry in haste. The widowed Amelia Williams, as the census listed Malvilla in 1870, appeared as the head of her own household, a farmer with $6,000 in real estate. Two children kept her company. One was her and Thomas' older daughter, Mary, now fifteen. But the other was not their younger girl, Anna, perhaps a casualty of child mortality. At the time her husband passed, Malvilla Williams was either pregnant or at least suspected herself so, for she had remarked while settling Thomas's affairs that "a posthumous child may yet be born." Indeed, in 1870, the slave trader's widow dwelled in a household that included a young son, a boy poignantly named Thomas, after the father he never knew.[48]

CHAPTER 13

Perseverance

W ILLIAM H. WILLIAMS NEVER RECONCILED HIMSELF to the final verdict against him issued by Louisiana's highest court. Although the confiscation of the enslaved criminals from Virginia had not broken him fiscally or precipitated complete financial ruin, he still suffered an extraordinary pecuniary loss. He resented the fact that Louisiana authorities had seized a valuable shipment of transport slaves whose sale should have lined his pockets but who instead now labored profitably for the state. Those bondmen and -women appeared in the wrong column of his ledger books. Moreover, Williams' temporary withdrawal from active slave trading suggests that he incurred at least some damage to his previously unsullied reputation in the business. The slave dealer sincerely believed that he had been maltreated and wrongly convicted under Louisiana law, and the whole episode, culminating in an outcome unfavorable to his interests, gnawed at him incessantly. As owner of Washington, D.C.'s most notorious slave prison and one of the most prominent human traffickers of his day, Williams was a man who habitually and brutally victimized others. With the tables turned, the experience of victimhood consumed him, overwhelming his thoughts. He refused to accept defeat and, as a white man of privilege, enjoyed access to the legal tools to undo it. He could never recover the lost year of his life spent in the Orleans Parish prison, but he could still try to get the forfeited slaves returned. Lingering in New Orleans throughout much of the 1840s, Williams embarked upon a protracted protest of the Louisiana Supreme Court's decision. When Congress effectively shuttered the Yellow House in 1850, reducing his professional responsibilities and liberating his time, he redoubled his efforts to remedy what he saw as

298

a case of justice gone awry. When Williams exhausted all possible courtroom solutions to his personal calamity, the slave trader next turned to
the Louisiana legislature for redress.

William H. Williams' personal quest for justice initially targeted
just two of the twenty-six convict bondpeople forfeited to the state.
On May 21, 1841, three weeks after his indictment before the First
District Criminal Court, Williams made a bold maneuver: he
attempted to sell a pair of convict bondmen he had conveyed to
New Orleans, named Albert and Stephen, for $800 each. Although
the two had been found guilty of theft back in Virginia, Williams had
miraculously duped authorities in Louisiana into thinking that they
did "not com[e] within the provisions of the act of 1817." The state
nevertheless confiscated and imprisoned them alongside the twenty-
four members of Williams' gang officially identified in the indictment. It was an unusual sale. The enslaved men were not in the
trader's possession at the time he sold them, making his claim to
them tenuous. For that reason, Williams violated his standard business practice and disposed of Albert and Stephen "without any guarantee whatever." His trusted friend and most reliable notary public
Edward Barnett documented the sale and filed all the proper paperwork in this unconventional transaction that belied all of the protests
of a man who, in ongoing trials, was denying any intention of ever
selling enslaved criminals in Louisiana. If that *had* been true, as
Williams consistently claimed, it certainly no longer reflected reality.
But since he had already somehow hoodwinked the state into thinking that Albert and Stephen were not convict slaves, the sale would
not undermine his case before the law.[1]

Among the most intriguing aspects of the sale was the buyer, a young
man from Virginia who considered Chambers County, Alabama, his
home: Joshua Staples. Only nineteen or twenty years old in 1841, this
was the same Joshua Staples who had assumed the role of jailer at the
Yellow House earlier in the year, once it became clear that Williams' legal
morass in Louisiana would prevent his return to Washington, D.C., any
time soon. But the third week of May 1841, Staples suddenly surfaced in
New Orleans bearing $1,600 with which to purchase Albert and Stephen.
Staples agreed to retrieve the pair – "then detained in prison without any

legal cause," according to a defiant Williams' bill of sale – from jail. The bill of sale also stipulated that Staples then "carry them out of the Country of the United States within a reasonable time." If Albert and Stephen were not convicted criminals, as Williams had told state authorities, it made little sense for him to specify in the bill of sale that the buyer agree to terms that complied with the trader's original bond with Virginia. Even as Williams denied Albert's and Stephen's criminal pasts in communications with the state, he was consciously trying to fulfill his original obligation with the commonwealth, knowing the possible financial repercussions to himself should he fail to meet it. And of course Williams craved the money that Albert and Stephen made flesh. The peculiar sale of Albert and Stephen in May 1841 rings of an experiment Williams was conducting. If he could successfully sell two of the convict bondpeople, perhaps he could sell the others as well. Given that the youthful Staples was not wealthy (and never would be), it is quite possible that Williams, after ordering him to New Orleans, supplied or secured for Staples the funds for the transaction. Through Staples, Williams may have paid for Albert and Stephen with his own money so that the jailer could extract the slaves from Louisiana's grasp, carry them to Texas in Williams' stead, and profit from the sale. It was tantamount to money laundering, but with slaves. If the scheme to evade the fiscal consequences of Virginia law worked, perhaps Williams could repeat the process with the other transports.[2]

Ursin Bouligny, Jr., frustrated whatever design Williams and Staples had concocted. Appointed sheriff of the Criminal Court of New Orleans by his prominent father-in-law, Louisiana governor André B. Roman, Bouligny refused to surrender the enslaved bodies of Albert and Stephen to Staples to complete the purchase. In fact, pursuant to the instructions of Judge John François Canonge of the First District Criminal Court, Bouligny seized the exact same pair of bondmen in August 1841 to pay Louisiana's costs for prosecuting Williams' case. The choice to appropriate Albert and Stephen was no coincidence. Mathematically, the two slaves' collective value roughly matched the state's expenses. In addition, Williams had denied their criminal pasts, so the pair would not be attached to Williams' continued appeals in the court system. Six months after the sale to Staples was completed on paper, Bouligny still denied Staples possession of the two bondmen. Consequently, in November, Staples filed suit against the sheriff for failing to turn over his lawfully acquired property. Williams' jailer was suing for either possession of the bondmen or a refund of the $1,600 purchase price, plus $360 in damages for half a year's lost labor "at the rate of 30 Dollars per month," per slave. Staples' case was set to go before a jury.[3]

Attorney General Christian Roselius, who had already secured a guilty verdict against William H. Williams in late July 1841 and continued to represent the state during the slave dealer's appeals, defended Bouligny in court against the trader's employee. Roselius successfully got the jury discharged from the trial by filing an exception in February 1842. The attorney general stated that the two bondmen under dispute "were actively & at the time [Staples] purchased them" in Bouligny's custody in his capacity as sheriff of the Criminal Court. After Williams' conviction, Bouligny also detained the slaves in accordance with a writ of *fieri facias* issued by the First District Criminal Court. Writs of *fi. fa.*, as they are often abbreviated, permit sheriffs such as Ursin Bouligny to seize property or assets from someone, like Williams, against whom a judgment has been rendered. A Louisiana law of 1805 unequivocally authorized the state to confiscate the goods and chattels of those convicted of crimes, for the purpose of reimbursing "the expenses incurred in their prosecution and conviction," so Bouligny operated entirely within the confines of the law. Even if the sheriff had been personally inclined to release Albert and Stephen to Staples, "he could not have permitted them to go," Roselius explained. Finally, concluded the attorney general, Staples did not pursue the proper channels in attempting to gain possession of the slaves. As the attorney general explained, any "party who claims the ownership of property seized is bound to apply" for redress, not to the sheriff who did the seizing, but "to the Court from which the order of seizure issued." Staples should have petitioned Judge Canonge of the Criminal Court. His claim should have been directed "against the party at whose suit the seizure was made," which in this case was the state of Louisiana itself. Given the bizarre circumstances surrounding the suit against Williams, Roselius denied that Staples was even eligible to sue the state. After reviewing these arguments, in late April 1842 Judge Charles Maurian of the Orleans Parish Court sustained the attorney general's exception. Bouligny was under no legal obligation to surrender the pair of slaves.[4]

Within days, Joshua Staples filed an appeal to gain "possession of his slaves illegally detained" by Bouligny "under color of his office." His case finally reached the Louisiana Supreme Court in 1845. There, the ancient sage François-Xavier Martin handed down the court's opinion. Judge Martin wholly concurred with Attorney General Roselius' legal reasoning and the recommended lawful path that Staples should have taken. Assessing the chronology of the evidence, Martin correctly noted that the bondmen Albert and Stephen had initially been committed to Bouligny's custody "as part of a gang introduced into the state contrary to law by William H. Williams." This occurred in November 1840, several months before the First District Criminal Court issued the writ of *fi. fa.* in July 1841, when it passed down the judgment in Williams' case. Yet Williams had sold the slaves to Staples on May 21, exactly three weeks after the third jury found him guilty of illegally importing the enslaved convicts into Louisiana. Even a blind jurist like Martin could clearly see that the transaction "shows an intention of evading the law" and a desire to profit from the sale of bondpeople Williams no longer owned. Martin affirmed the judgment of the Parish Court. Neither Staples nor Williams would gain possession of Albert and Stephen. The state retained possession, but rather than put the two bondmen on the auction block instead set them to labor "upon the public works." While toiling under state custody, both of them died.[5]

After 1845, William H. Williams circumvented Louisiana's court system by appealing directly to the state legislature. In an era of small, personal government, aggrieved citizens often asked lawmakers for private acts of relief, and Williams regularly filed legislative petitions praying that Louisiana's elected leaders right the wrong he believed he had suffered when the state confiscated his shipment of convict slaves. Williams submitted his first known request for financial relief in 1847 to a legislature that now met in the new state capital of Baton Rouge. The Louisiana House of Representatives referred his memorial to a special committee for consideration. On April 24, B. G. Fonteneau gave the minority report of that committee. Upon "close examination of all the documents,"

Fonteneau reached "the conclusion that ... William H. Williams is not entitled to relief." He gave two reasons in support of his position. First, he explained, based on the evidence from the trial, the jury's verdict against the trader seemed "just and correct ... and in strict conformity to the act of 1817 upon which the prosecution was based." Second, Fonteneau believed that tampering with the verdict would mark an unconstitutional and "improper interference with the judiciary department." Such action would be a "violation" and "a dangerous assumption of power" on the part of the legislature, "well calculated to disorganize our whole system of government, subverting the well settled order of things, and bringing into disrepute and disrespect the decisions of our tribunals."[6]

On Monday, April 26, the Louisiana House took up the committee majority's proposed "Act for the relief of William H. Williams." The Committee of the Whole, consisting of all members of the House meeting under different procedural rules, received the bill. Its original text does not survive, but after its second reading one lawmaker proposed an amendment stating that Williams should be awarded an "amount of money sufficient to pay for the services and labor which the State has received by employing [the] said slaves on her public works." Under this proposal, the governor would order the delivery of the convict slaves to Williams within thirty days, contingent upon the trader's willingness to execute a bond, as he had done with Virginia, to remove the transports "beyond the limits of this State." Another lawmaker, hostile to the idea, made a motion to lay the amendment on the table. Upon a call for the yeas and nays, legislators voted 39–14 to suspend consideration of the amendment. Almost three-quarters of Louisiana House members objected to aiding Williams in the way it described. One of the lawmakers most vehemently opposed to the measure then made a motion to lay the same bill on the table "indefinitely" – basically not to discuss it at all for the foreseeable future, if ever. That motion carried the sentiment against helping Williams too far, however, and it was voted down 38–26. More discussion ensued. On May 3, the House read the "act for the relief of W. H. Williams" a third time but, on motion, laid it on the table. Williams' petition was denied.[7]

Williams submitted another petition for relief in early 1850. Representative John C. Larue introduced it to the House on

February 25, and it was referred to the Committee on Propositions and Grievances. On March 1, that committee reported back a bill "for the relief of William H. Williams," and on motion three days later it appeared before the Committee of the Whole. The House "took up the Bill for a second reading" and, on motion, made it "the special order for Friday, March 8th." The bill then mysteriously vanished from the House record until March 19, when Representative Larue withdrew Williams' petition. Although scattered voices spoke approvingly of Williams' requests, his memorials could not earn enough votes in either 1847 or 1850.[8]

The slave trader refused to give up. The Louisiana House next considered another of his petitions in February 1852. This time, it went to the Judiciary Committee, where Williams found a devoted ally in representative and committee chair J. G. Sever. Although the majority on the committee "reported adversely" to Williams' plea "for compensation for 26 slaves forfeited to the State," Sever was "deeply impressed with the injustice done to Williams" and declared on February 27 that "even handed justice demands" he be reimbursed. Sever took Williams at his word, that he had introduced the enslaved convicts into Louisiana only while "passing them through the State into the Republic of Texas." Evidence presented at his trial and later verified by prosecuting attorney Christian Roselius proved that the trader "had no intention of disposing of any of the slaves" within Louisiana. For Sever, the attorney general's certificate "fully exonerates Williams" of wrongdoing. He expressed "grave and serious doubt" that "the mere passing through the territory of the State with convict slaves in transitu for a foreign country" constituted a violation of the 1817 statute. It seemed to him that the slave dealer had been convicted only by the strictest possible reading of the law, "a mere technical infraction" devoid of any "evil or criminal intention against the State."[9]

Moreover, Sever added, when Williams was forced to surrender the convict slaves, he did not enjoy the benefit of a genuine appellate process. Prior to Louisiana's adoption of the Constitution of 1845, "there was by law, no appeal allowable from the Criminal Court of New Orleans," Sever indicated, "and hence no opportunity has ever been afforded to Williams to have the judgment revised by another and higher tribunal . . .

[H]e has therefore been left, without remedy or redress for the wrongs he has suffered at the hands of the State." In making this claim to his House colleagues, Sever overlooked the fact that, despite the law (as we saw in Chapter 7), the Louisiana Supreme Court had taken special pains to hear Williams' case, even threatening Judge Canonge with imprisonment if he persisted in withholding the paperwork from the slave trader's trial. But it remained true that Williams' case did not appear before the Supreme Court as the result of any established, conventional route. His ultimate conviction, to Sever, was therefore not "just."[10]

Williams, Sever continued, suffered tremendously as a result of the verdict against him. He not only endured a year's worth of "loathesome [sic] imprisonment" "in the city prison of New Orleans," but also absorbed a "very heavy" financial loss. Adding up the values of the twenty-four confiscated slaves, their combined labor in service to the state, plus Albert and Stephen, the representative calculated that, altogether, the state of Louisiana had deprived Williams of "the sum of $27,000 at the lowest estimate," or about $844,000 in 2016 dollars. And that figure did not include "the payment of the costs of the prosecution."[11]

The Judiciary Committee's minority report concluded that Williams was entitled to recompense. Because Louisiana had unfairly attacked "a respectable citizen of a sister State" "with merciless and vindictive rigour," Representative Sever declared, "justice demands that Williams should be relieved from the oppression and wrongs under which he has so long suffered." The proper way "to cancel the wrong unjustly inflicted" was to reimburse the slave trader for his losses. Sever telegraphed his intention "to bring in a bill providing compensation to W. H. Williams … for the sum of thirteen thousand dollars," enough for him to recoup almost half of what Sever figured he was owed.[12]

On March 1, 1852, the House took up the latest bill to provide Williams financial relief. As Sever had forewarned, it pledged the trader "$13,000 for the negroes confiscated to the State in 1840." The House decided to make it the "order of the day" for Thursday, March 4. The Committee of the Whole convened that day as scheduled to consider the bill. After four hours of unrecorded debate, the House rejected it. The next day, a representative in the House "asked and obtained leave to withdraw the bill" for Williams' relief.[13]

Yet, in an abrupt about-face, the Louisiana legislature approved a different act in Williams' favor just two weeks later. Lawmakers granted Williams "or his legal representatives" permission to apply for the return of the "slaves seized by and forfeited to the State." The terms were straightforward. Pending Williams' executing a bond with the governor to remove the convict slaves from the jurisdiction of Louisiana immediately, the "several authorities now in possession" of them would be "required to deliver" the frustrated trader all of the enslaved criminals "now living," plus their "increase" – the emotionless euphemism for the children born since 1840 to any of the half dozen enslaved female members of Williams' gang. The law, approved by Governor Joseph Walker on March 18, explicitly stated that it "be considered an act of clemency," absolving Williams of any and all wrongdoing in introducing the slaves into Louisiana. A weary legislature inserted a final clause within the measure that stipulated Williams could make "no further demands . . . on the State" in the future. Louisiana officials thus allowed Williams' longstanding claims to the enslaved criminals.[14]

But the slave dealer stunned Louisiana authorities when he rejected the state's offer. He explained that the 1852 act of relief bound him to remove the enslaved transports from Louisiana, but with the annexation of Texas in 1845, "there was no other State or Government" to which he could carry them. Slavery still lingered on in other nations or colonies of the western hemisphere, but they were neither convenient nor, given restrictions against the international slave trade, safe for Williams to access. Nor were they eager to absorb the United States' criminal bond-people. But on top of all that, Williams had made a career out of his penchant for speculation. He gambled with black bodies professionally. It is easy to imagine that, just as he weighed the risks of transporting convicts in 1852, he also looked to maximize his rewards. He thought he could get a still better deal out of the state of Louisiana.[15]

Relentlessly, Williams' continued to file petitions with the legislature. On April 16, 1853, the House's Committee on Claims declared itself "satisfied of the justice of the prayer of the petitioner" and crafted yet another "act for the relief of William H. Williams." It allotted him a grand total of $15,000 in damages "as . . . compensation for the wrong he has suffered." Hearkening back to the evidence from Williams' courtroom trials, the committee was impressed that the slave dealer had made "no secret" about the character or provenance of the convict slaves, promptly notified the mayor upon his reaching New Orleans, consistently stated "his intended destination," and refused to sell the criminals even when afforded the opportunity. If Williams "ever had such intention" to sell them within the state, the committee concluded, "he had abandoned it on his arrival" in New Orleans, and never made any such dastardly attempt. Williams was simply executing the obligation he had made to Virginia when he brought the slaves through Louisiana while "in transit" to the Republic of Texas. Acknowledging the trader's right to traverse the state with his property, the committee considered it "an act of usurpation and injustice" on the part of Louisiana to have impeded his travels and seized and imprisoned his slaves.[16]

Two days later, another member of the Committee on Claims issued a strong dissent. He "examined all the facts of the case" and found them "materially the same as those upon which the action of the last General Assembly was based." Barring the introduction of "additional proof, calculated to excite the sympathies," he did not deem it "proper" to revisit Williams' memorial "after so recent an examination" by the same legislative body. Nothing new was presented to sway "the judgment of the members of this House." Williams, in short, was wasting the lawmakers' time. And a significant number of representatives were still unconvinced that the slave trader was as innocent as he claimed. Until Williams could produce evidence to erase "in the public mind" all "doubt" of his intention to pass quietly through Louisiana with the convict slaves, the state could not hope to "deal with him in that spirit of liberality which one free from suspicion has a right to demand." Even this critic of compensation, however, believed Williams' fiction that the two bondmen Albert and Stephen were not convicted criminals and thus "were never legally in possession of the State." He therefore conceded that the slave dealer should be paid for the state's use of them, "with interest from 1840."[17]

The House made the "act for the relief of William H. Williams . . . the special order of the day" for Tuesday, April 19. Sensing the tide turning against Williams, a member of the Committee on Claims in favor of aid to the slave trader made a motion to postpone further consideration of the measure until Saturday, giving him much needed time to drum up support for relief. When that motion failed, another House member moved to lay the bill on the table, a recommendation approved by a vote of 36–22. The House was not feeling as munificent in 1853 as it had the previous year. Some representatives were obviously perturbed by Williams' repeated, bothersome requests and perhaps even miffed by his refusal to accept their generous offer from the year before. Williams must have wondered if he had overplayed his hand. Rebuffed for the time being, his quest for the reimbursement he felt he deserved would have to await a future legislative session.[18]

As William H. Williams continued to press his case for reimbursement in the mid-1850s, two other lawsuits also occupied his mind. One was a suit he filed against the defunct Washington, D.C. firm of Selden, Withers & Co., a "private banking-house" formed in October 1850. The original partners in the concern were William Selden and Robert W. Latham, both of Washington, and John Withers and Lawrence P. Bayne, each from Alexandria. Selden sold his interest in the partnership in June 1852, to G. W. Carlyle Whiting of Washington, while Latham largely withdrew from the firm at the end of May 1854, despite maintaining some small interest in it. By November 1854, John Withers was the real name and face behind the company and the Exchange Bank that he operated "on the west side of Seventh street, between Louisiana avenue and D street north." Approaching eighty years old by 1854, Withers was listed as a "Retired Merchant" in the census of 1850, but he remained far more active and economically engaged in the community than the governmental form indicated, despite his advancing age.[19]

John Withers' business interests had made him obscene sums of money by the standards of the time. Not only a banker, he actively invested in real estate, purchasing multiple properties fronting Pennsylvania Avenue and collecting rents from tenants. Among his many entrepreneurial endeavors, in August 1854 he also helped found and incorporate the National Hotel Company of Washington, D.C. Weighing Withers' extensive and visible business ventures, public rumor maintained that he was a millionaire, probably an exaggerated estimate. Nevertheless, one Washington paper confidently regarded him as "a man of great wealth – worth, at least, $600,000 in bona fide property" – almost $16.7 million in 2016 dollars. With greater modesty, Withers "never . . . claimed to be worth over $300,000." Specific figures aside, his affluence enabled widespread philanthropic activity. His donations of tens of thousands of dollars at a time to Columbian College, the predecessor to George Washington University, made him the institution's leading benefactor. Newspapers credited Withers with almost single-handedly rescuing the school from the "burden of debts" and relieving it of its "pecuniary embarrassments."[20]

The year 1854 brought far more turmoil than the elderly Withers could have anticipated. Amid the throes of a recession that began late the year before, in November "the money dealers of Baltimore" refused to redeem the notes of Selden, Withers & Co.'s Exchange Bank. Rumors of the Exchange Bank's insolvency and impending failure unnerved the public, and confidence in the establishment plummeted. The resulting run on the bank turned fears into reality. Despite D.C. newspapers' initial proclamations of the bank's health and assurances that the "men of means" who ran it held "assets . . . at least $300,000 above and beyond any and all liabilities of the concern," the crowds of "note-holders and depositors" who simultaneously descended upon the institution quickly depleted its liquid resources. On November 24, the House of Selden, Withers & Co. expired. The partners issued a public statement expressing their "warmest gratitude" to the public for its "generous indulgence" during this "painful step" and pledged to deal with claimants "in a just and impartial spirit."[21]

The public's magnanimity toward the failed concern soon evaporated. In late November, the partners of the Exchange Bank appointed two trustees to distribute its assets to creditors: William Bayne, Alexandria merchant and brother of the firm's Lawrence P. Bayne; and John A. English, "a competent business man" and nephew to John Withers. English and Bayne were "invested with [the] power to adjust and settle" Selden, Withers & Co.'s debts at "their discretion." The deed of trust prioritized the order of payments that they would make, beginning with the two trustees' expenses. Next came the redemption of $190,000 worth of Virginia and Tennessee Railroad bonds and finally the redemption of the Exchange Bank's paper notes. "The deed of trust executed by Messrs. Selden, Withers & Co. astonishes the public," the press reported. Some questioned the selection of the trustees, which smacked of nepotism, a word whose etymology could be traced to the Latin word for nephew – John A. English's precise relationship to partner John Withers. Moreover, the masses could not help but notice that they ranked third in the list for reimbursement. This caused serious concerns. How far would Selden, Withers & Co.'s assets go? Would there be any money left for run-of-the-mill depositors? No one charged John Withers with any malfeasance in the collapse of the Exchange Bank, and in fact, to cover the concern's creditors, he personally sacrificed some $200,000 of private property he owned in St. Louis, Missouri. But he and his partners needed time to sift through all the claims for payment and to make the necessary arrangements to cover the firm's liabilities. As days turned into weeks and weeks into months, apprehensions that the financial spigot would soon run dry sparked a flurry of lawsuits as anxious depositors in the Exchange Bank scrambled to recover their money.[22]

William H. Williams joined the parade of plaintiffs filing lawsuits as a consequence of the Exchange Bank's collapse. He appeared in the Alexandria County, Virginia, Clerk of Court's office on January 1, 1855, to initiate his complaint. Williams was suing Selden, Withers & Co.'s four partners, in assumpsit, for $2,757.18 he had on account with the Exchange Bank. Three months later, on April 2, the slave trader united with several other complainants to launch a separate suit against John Withers; Withers' nephew, John A. English; two additional members of the Withers family; Columbian College, Withers' preferred recipient of charitable donations; and one other defendant. The plaintiffs in this case sought "to annul and vacate" the deed that empowered John A. English to serve as trustee for his uncle's firm.[23]

On January 11, 1855, just ten days after William H. Williams first filed suit to recoup money from Withers, a man named William Gil went before a Louisiana judge in pursuit of compensation from the slave trader, for "professional services rendered." This case stemmed directly from the enslaved transports Williams introduced into Louisiana. Williams was frustrated both by the "defect of the laws" that had left him without satisfaction in the courtroom and by Louisiana lawmakers' early rejections of his requests for recompense. But he was not the only one affected by the events that transpired. Washington, D.C. slave dealer

Thomas N. Davis, who had partnered with Williams in the purchase of the slave transports, felt the economic blow as well. Davis therefore enlisted, on March 13, 1850, the aid of three attorneys – William Gil, A. M. Dunn, and J. C. Patterson (and after Patterson's death, A. S. Herron) – to represent the slave traders' interests before the legislature. In the event the lawyers lobbied successfully on their clients' behalf, Davis pledged to pay them a collective $1,500, no small sum but well worth it were he and Williams indemnified for the loss of the enslaved convicts seized by the state. Gil explained that he and his colleagues labored "diligently and effectually" for Williams and Davis, circulating unspecified "documents" among lawmakers. Yet, after the Louisiana legislature offered Williams a generous compensation package in 1852 (the one the trader refused), neither he nor Davis made good on the promissory note, despite Gil's "amicable demand[s]." And so on January 11, Gil petitioned Judge William B. Robertson of the Sixth Judicial District Court in East Baton Rouge Parish for an order enabling Gil to recover his third of the $1,500 due the attorneys, plus interest and court costs. Judge Robertson sent Williams and Davis copies of Gil's petition along with separate letters summoning each trader either to appear at the sheriff's office in East Baton Rouge Parish and comply with Gil's demands or to submit a written response to Gil's memorial. Since both of the accused debtors then resided out of state, in the nation's capital, Robertson appointed attorney J. M. McCutcheon to represent them *in absentia*. On February 20, 1855, McCutcheon filed paperwork suggesting that Williams and Davis acknowledged their obligation but that they both denied Gil had met the condition for payment. The case would go to trial in March 1856.[24]

As Williams' case against Withers and Gil's case against Williams and Davis coursed concurrently through the respective court systems of Virginia and Louisiana, Williams appealed once again to the Louisiana legislature for a private act of relief. This time, his memorial headed to the House Judiciary Committee, which, after "a patient and ... attentive investigation," issued an extensive report in 1855. Upon a thorough review of the facts of the case, the committee concluded "that the Act of 1817 ... is not applicable to a person simply passing through the State of Louisiana with convicted slaves" and, therefore, "the sentence of the court ... was not sanctioned by law." The committee understood the rationale of the 1817 statute against "the importation of convicted slaves," "the sole object" of which was "to keep the slaves of this State pure," uncontaminated by "foreign convicts of their own cast and color." But the committee also insisted that the criminal justice system consider the intention of the white person who accompanied the convict slaves. It stated that the law was never designed "to strike at the natural right of transit," whereby masters might pass through the state unimpeded, with their property in tow. Certainly by the mid-1850s, proslavery apologists of all stripes had made the sanctity of slaveholders' property rights a fixture in their defense of slavery as an institution and of masters' right to carry their chattel into new western territories. Rising to meet the challenge of increasingly emboldened abolitionists ready to restrict owners' ability to resettle with their slaves in places such as Kansas, southern ideologues' political defense of slavery's expansion routinely invoked the Constitution's Fifth Amendment protections against governmental assaults on property without due process. Politically and culturally by the 1850s, it had become unconscionable for a southern state to deny a master such as William H. Williams ownership of his slaves. As such, the Judiciary Committee charged that Louisiana had "illegally and unjustly deprived [Williams] of his property."[25]

The committee next turned its attention from the law to the sentence imposed upon the slave trader. It determined that the penalty, "whereby the convicted slaves were forfeited and turned over to the State of Louisiana[,] was not sanctioned by law." The act of 1817 specified that enslaved convicts illegally imported into Louisiana "shall be siezed [*sic*] and sold at public auction," not commandeered by the state to use as its property, as it had done. By this line of argument, too, it again seemed to the committee "a self evident proposition" that Williams had "been unjustly deprived of his property," which "has without law or equity gone into the hands of the State."[26]

If Louisiana held no legitimate claim to the transport slaves, reported the committee, the legislature must "right the wrong committed" by granting Williams relief. Insisting on the propriety of compensating

Williams, the committee recommended "ascertaining the value of the negroes confiscated by the State" and paying the slave trader that amount, plus 8 percent interest from the November 1, 1840, date of seizure. The committee advised, however, that the convicted bondpeople "remain ... property of the State," since Williams "cannot remove the slaves to another State, without subjecting himself to further arrest and trial." In essence, the Judiciary Committee was requesting that the state of Louisiana purchase the enslaved criminals from Williams retroactively from the day he first carried them into New Orleans.[27]

Per the Judiciary Committee's report, on March 12, 1855, representatives in the House began a debate to determine precisely how much to offer in payment for the Williams' gang slaves. A proposal to grant him a budget-busting $45,000 was quickly laid on the table by the lopsided vote of 59–16. A substitute figure of $15,000 fared better. The attempt to set that bill aside failed, 28–46. One representative then offered a substitute bill that, rather than make a cash payment, would restore to William H. Williams the enslaved convicts seized by the state, "with the privilege of disposing of them either within" Louisiana or outside of it, at the slave trader's discretion. This arresting concession to Williams marked an admission of fault by the state. Granting Williams the option to lawfully sell the convict slaves from Virginia on Louisiana soil also fundamentally undermined the intent of the 1817 statute under which the trader had been prosecuted fifteen years earlier. Nevertheless, representatives in the House approved the substitute bill, 50–23. Legislative action then shifted to the Senate. On March 14, one proposed amendment to the House bill, not detailed in the records, failed. So did a motion to lay the bill on the table, 7–14. Put to a vote, the House bill passed the Senate, 13–10. The next day, at the final vote in the House, the measure passed by a tally of 46–26. After toiling for years to gain relief, William H. Williams had won, even gaining the right to sell the slaves where he wished. This time, he accepted the offer.[28]

While it would seem that Williams' legislative victory in March 1855 would have made him giddy with excitement over the imminent return of his slaves, he was still not fully satisfied with the terms he had received and therefore made one final plea to the Louisiana legislature. On January 23, 1856, the state approved a supplementary act that again authorized him to recover the convict slaves he had been forced to forfeit and granted him "full permission to keep or to sell or dispose of the said slaves within the limits of the State," as he chose. Additionally, the law of January 23 restored two features of the 1852 act for relief that Williams had previously rejected. The act of 1856 reinstated Williams' lawful right to the "issue" born to the enslaved women of Williams' gang who had been appropriated by the state and bestowed "clemency" upon Williams, legislatively absolving him of the crime he had committed sixteen years earlier. Williams, in short, got everything he wanted. A surely fatigued legislature, weary of the slave trader's constant petitions over the past decade, acquiesced to all of Williams' demands, couched as they were in the respectful language of requests. But the lawmakers' generosity came with one advantage to themselves: the 1856 act for Williams' relief stipulated that he make "no further demands . . . upon the State on account of [the] said slaves." Speaker of the House John M. Sandidge, President of the Senate Robert C. Wickliffe, and Governor Paul O. Hébert all signed the final document.[29]

William H. Williams' legislative victories had consequences for his other active courtroom battles. Two months after Louisiana legislators agreed to return the transport slaves to him to sell, the slave dealer uncharacteristically abandoned his "suit to annul & vacate" the deed of trust from John Withers to the banker's nephew, John A. English. It is not clear if Williams ever recouped his $2,757.18 from Selden, Withers & Co.'s failed Exchange Bank of Washington, D.C., but by the time the slave dealer's lawyer dismissed the case in May 1855, the anticipated return of the convict slaves made the sum he had lost when the bank went under appear relatively smaller than it had before.[30]

Williams' success with the Louisiana legislature also shaped his counsel's defense strategy in the lawsuit initiated by attorney William Gil, for non-payment of legal services. When that case began in January 1855, Williams' lawyer J. M. McCutcheon argued that, since his client had not yet recovered the enslaved felons, Gil had failed to meet the conditions for payment. Some time later, McCutcheon further pleaded that Williams had never authorized Thomas N. Davis to enter him as a party to the contract with Gil and the other two attorneys. He had a point.

Williams had never affixed his signature to that document, even if its purpose was to reclaim convict bondpeople whom the pair of slave traders had teamed up to buy. Then came January 1856 and the dramatic improvement in Williams' legal fortunes. Now that the Louisiana legislature authorized the slave trader's bodily recovery of his cargo of convict slaves, his attorney would be hard-pressed to contend that Gil had not satisfied the condition embedded in Thomas N. Davis' promissory note. J. M. McCutcheon needed to revise his approach to the case. On February 21, 1856, just one month after the last act for Williams' relief was approved, McCutcheon unveiled a new tactic, filing an exception stating that "the condition of the obligation [in the contract between Davis and Gil] is *contra bonos mores*" – against good morals. When Williams and Davis' trial began, in March 1856, Judge William B. Robertson of the Sixth Judicial District Court quickly pointed out the inconsistency of the defense attorney's successive pleadings, but excused the irregularities because McCutcheon was court-appointed to represent absent clients.[31]

Robertson then handed down his judgment in the case of *Gil v. Williams & Davis*. First, he agreed with McCutcheon that the suit against Williams must be dismissed because nothing in the case record demonstrably proved that Davis was authorized to include Williams in the disputed contract with the three attorneys. Neither the legislative act of 1852 for Williams' relief nor that of 1856 mentioned Davis at all; their benefits accrued to Williams alone. The working relationship between Williams and Davis was never teased out, made explicit, or proven. Second, Judge Robertson failed to comprehend how Gil could conceivably demonstrate that his efforts were directly responsible for the legislative enactments in Williams' favor. "What particular members did he influence to vote for the act?" Robertson inquired rhetorically. Some lawmakers, he postulated, were probably predisposed to vote for Williams' relief anyway, without extracurricular persuasion. It was therefore incumbent upon Gil to show conclusively that he persuaded legislators otherwise disinclined "to vote for the passage of the law." Only then could he prove that he fulfilled the terms of the contract entered into with Davis. Given the impossibility of securing such evidence, Robertson concluded, "the Court must presume that the Legislative body ... acted from disinterested motives, for the good of the State or from motives of clemency as asserted in the acts, uninfluenced and unbiassed [*sic*] by interested parties or Lobby members."[32]

Third and most decisively, Judge Robertson ruled on the plea that the contract between the trio of attorneys and Davis was *contra bonos mores*. Citing established legal precedents, Robertson explained that contracts that were fundamentally immoral or harmful to the public order were not enforceable at law. "[W]hat," Robertson asked, "can be more contrary to good morals than a malign influence brought to bear upon the Legislative body of the State to effect the passage of a law from private motives alone[?]" Lawmakers, he insisted, "ought to be left free and untrammeled to decide for the true interests of the State," independent of pernicious outside influences. Hapless legislators could never know for certain whether a citizen impressing a particular viewpoint upon them acted out of "private and interested motives or for the good of the public." Worse still for Robertson, Gil and his colleagues violated all definitions of propriety when they agreed to attempt to sway lawmakers for pay. The judge could hardly contain his outrage over the injection of money into the political process. "I cannot conceive any thing that would have a more immoral influence upon the Legislation of the State," he declared, "than to permit parties to be paid avowedly to obtain the passage of a particular act." Were filthy lucre permitted to corrupt the voters' elected representatives, "the only safeguard for the purity of our legislation is overthrown." His heated condemnation of political lobbying (normative if still reviled in our time) complete, Robertson dismissed Gil's suit against the pair of slave traders.[33]

After the District Court's verdict against his client in March 1856, William Gil's attorney, J. J. Burk, promptly filed a motion for a new trial. He not only disputed Robertson's finding that the original contract was *contra bonos mores* but also cited pertinent new evidence that "he could not with due diligence have obtained before." In a sworn affidavit, Gil explained that he had located Robert E. McHatton, a Louisiana State Penitentiary clerk and likely younger brother of lessee James A. McHatton, whom he claimed could establish the tie between William H. Williams, Thomas N. Davis, and the convict slaves mentioned in the acts of the legislature. If Williams' connection to and arrangement with Davis, as signatory of the contract with Gil and the other two attorneys, could be proven, Williams would be responsible for reimbursing the plaintiff. The appeal in *Gil v. Williams & Davis* headed to the Louisiana Supreme Court, an institution with which Williams was no stranger.[34]

In March 1857, the Supreme Court affirmed the District Court's decision and denied Gil the remuneration he sought. Concurring with Judge Robertson's prior ruling that Gil was suing for an obligation "founded on an illicit cause," Justice Henry M. Spofford delivered the court's opinion. He expressed some confusion as to why Thomas N. Davis alone signed the contract with the three lawyers when, first, the document identified both Davis and Williams as claimants of the convict slaves, and second, all of the eventual benefits of the Louisiana legislature's acts of 1852 and 1856 accrued solely to Williams. Quickly setting those puzzling matters aside, Spofford highlighted the fact that the contract with Thomas N. Davis stipulated that Gil's compensation was contingent upon the legislative outcome of his efforts. "If the scheme fails, the lawyer is to get nothing, no matter how great his labor," Spofford summarized; "if it succeeds, he ... partake[s] of the bounty." This was the crux of the problem: "law, public order and good morals strike all such contracts with nullity." The Louisiana Supreme Court disregarded the question of whether Gil had actually employed "improper influences," nor did it impute that he had. By general principle alone, Spofford explained, the law "opposes the beginnings of evil" and "shuts the door against temptation." By their very nature, contingent contracts bred corruption and promoted "the use of sinister influences." Were people of means permitted to craft bargains with lawyers to procure a desired result and "profit jointly" from "legislative generosity at the public expense," they would "seduce legislators from ... their duty" as elected representatives. With such nefarious effects on the political system, Spofford and the Louisiana Supreme Court ruled the contract between Gil and Davis "contrary to good morals" – *contra bonos mores* – and therefore unenforceable. The court denied the attorney compensation because it considered any payment for services rendered for the purpose of swaying the legislature morally repugnant. To whatever degree Gil had aided Williams' effort to obtain relief, he ultimately offered the slave trader his services *pro bono*.[35]

The Supreme Court's March 1857 ruling in *Gil v. Williams* came just one month after the surviving slave transports from Virginia were pardoned and released from the Louisiana State Penitentiary after twelve years' confinement there. Restoration of the convict slaves to William H. Williams had proceeded apace. Robert C. Wickliffe, inaugurated Louisiana's governor only a week after serving as president of the state Senate during the passage of the 1856 act for Williams' relief, pardoned the ten slaves "[k]nown as the Williams Negroes" and discharged them from the pen on February 7, 1857. The official tally did not count Charlotte's three children whom she had conceived and birthed while in prison, but per the act of relief, Williams was awarded them as well. As of January 1855, the total of thirteen enslaved persons were valued at $8,300. The enslaved transports had spent almost a dozen years as inmates of the penitentiary and had toiled under the watchful eyes of the state of Louisiana for sixteen. For the men and women of Williams' gang, exiting prison marked a perverse form of liberation: the governor's order ended their incarceration, but they were escorted directly into the custody of Thomas Williams, brother and agent of the very trader who had marched them aboard a slave ship almost seventeen years earlier. As the bondpeople tramped outside the state prison, surely in chains, they left approximately one hundred other black (and well over two hundred white) inmates behind its walls. The members of Williams' gang confronted a future filled with different forms of imprisonment. But at that point, their specific stories become virtually untraceable.[36]

William H. Williams retrieved a small number of other convict slaves due him by legislative enactment as well. A few of the enslaved criminals had been confined in institutions other than the Louisiana State Penitentiary, although details about them are sketchy. Neither the slaves nor these additional incarceration facilities are identified by name in surviving records. We may only say with confidence that Louisiana surrendered to Williams a grand total of "sixteen negroes." Fellow slave trader Thomas N. Davis variously recollected their total value at

$12,000 and $20,000. By the act of relief that restored them to Williams, and in spite of the 1817 act under which Williams had originally been convicted, all of the slaves were eligible for resale within Louisiana and the state's dreaded sugar cane fields. Threats of sale to the harsh environment of Louisiana's swamplands had long been used by masters in the Upper South to impose discipline upon intransigent, troublesome bondpeople. The specter of sale there had become ingrained in slaves' minds, contributing raw material for their nightmares. Now, surely, for some of Williams' gang, it would become a reality. Williams "disposed of [the convicts] at private sale," and then they vanished into Louisiana's miasmic mists.[37]

More than sixteen years after Williams herded his shipment of captive felons off the *Roanoke* and on to the train cars that carried them into New Orleans, the slave trader's legal troubles appeared over at last, his unsettled business interests in Louisiana resolved. Williams had "been in attendance upon the Legislature ... year after year seeking ... relief," and his persistence finally paid off. With the aid of the legislature, he righted the wrong he believed he suffered and recovered the enslaved property stolen by the state. He proceeded to sell those bondmen, bondwomen, and their "issue" for thousands of dollars and, with the aid of the Louisiana court system, evaded payment to the lawyers who navigated the legislative process on his behalf.[38]

The vindication that Williams must have derived from the Louisiana legislature's acts of 1855 and 1856 proved fleeting. Little more than a year after reclaiming the enslaved transports from Virginia, he died, on April 18, 1858, at his home in Washington, D.C., on the corner of B and Eighth streets. Williams was fifty-six years old, having celebrated his birthday just forty-eight hours earlier. If as spiteful as they had every right to be, the enslaved transports whom Williams plucked from the penitentiary in Richmond might have been gratified to learn that, in a roundabout way, they contributed to their captor's death. Upon his initial conviction for importing the convict bondpeople, the parsimonious slave trader opted for a year's imprisonment as a preferable alternative to paying the $12,000 fine. But he emerged from the Orleans Parish prison in 1842 a damaged man, "his health impaired." The Louisiana House of Representatives in 1855 confirmed the deleterious effects of incarceration upon Williams' body. Imprisonment "most seriously . . . impair[ed] his health," declared Judiciary Committee chair Thomas Green Davidson. His report explicitly telegraphed Williams' imminent demise. "[H]e is aged and infirm," Davidson wrote, predicting that, "in all probability before the next meeting of the Legislature he will have paid the debt which frail humanity owes to nature." Williams' detention in the Orleans Parish jail would, Davidson confidently believed, "hasten the period which will seperate [sic] him from the things of time and carry him to the grave, on the very edge of which he is now standing." Because the slave trader appeared on the verge of death already by 1855, Davidson appealed to his House colleagues' sense of manliness and honor when he urged them to "without delay grant . . . him that relief and justice which he in his dying moments asks, not so much for himself as his dependent family" back in Washington, D.C. Yet if Williams anticipated that his successful recovery of the convict slaves would be an unequivocal blessing for his wife and daughters, he was sorely mistaken. After his death, the legal dilemmas the enslaved criminals generated didn't disappear; they merely transferred to his loved ones.[39]

CHAPTER 14

Violet

W ILLIAM H. WILLIAMS' DEATH IN 1858 FAILED TO liberate his family from the legal morass into which he had sunk. Although he had reclaimed and sold the cargo of Virginia convicts, courtroom hassles over them persisted, and the deceased slave dealer bequeathed his troubles to the young woman whom he had widowed, Violet Milburn Williams.

Remarkably little is known of William H. Williams' private life. Slave trading was a young man's profession that required extensive travel. As such, the occupation was not conducive to domestic attachments or families gathered peaceably around the hearth. Many slave dealers remained single or married only late in life, as their slaving careers drew to a close. Williams fell into the latter category, not uniting in matrimony until the age of forty-five. This did not imply that he remained celibate. The slave trade supplied plenty of opportunities for forced sex and the rape of female captives. "[T]he slave-pen is only another name for a brothel," scoffed former bondman John Brown, and the site of "some of the most frightful scenes of immorality and vice." Slave traders routinely helped themselves to the pleasures of enslaved women's bodies. As one bondman at a Washington, D.C. slave pen acknowledged delicately in 1834, "the white gentlemen, the . . . dealers, come in every night" to the female quarters and "staid till . . . breakfast." Escaped slave Moses Roper confirmed that traders "often sleep with the best looking female slaves among them." They preyed particularly upon the so-called "fancy girls," the light-skinned bondwomen who most aroused their lust. Traders imposed their salacious will upon those cursed by beauty, tastelessly joked and boasted among themselves of their sexual conquests, and then fetched handsome prices at market for many of their victims, from smitten buyers with identically lascivious desires.[1]

William H. Williams cannot be definitively shown to have indulged in sexual relations with his female prisoners, but it would have been out of the ordinary had he not. Opportunities abounded within the Yellow House. During Fredrika Bremer's 1850 tour of the slave jail, the unnamed keeper could not help but boast openly about his "very splendid" merchandise. One "young girl," he said, whose owners had treated her as their own daughter and "brought [her] up in all respects 'like a lady;' . . . could embroider and play on the piano, and dress like a lady, and read, and write, and dance." But, he continued, the white family felt that "her mind had grown too high for her" station. To subdue her pride and restore her humility, they decided to sell her. The unfortunate young woman who so enchanted Williams' jailer bore all the hallmarks of a "fancy girl," destined for sale to an affluent white man appreciative of her talents, achievements, and more. The temptations within the Yellow House probably did occasionally prove too great for Williams to resist.[2]

In 1840, the year he set out from Alexandria with his load of convict slaves, Williams, then thirty-eight years old, lived with a white woman in her thirties and a white girl aged fifteen to nineteen. Such a household structure would usually indicate a husband, wife, and daughter, or perhaps a couple and their servant girl. If they were Williams' immediate family, other surviving sources cannot confirm that. It is possible that Williams was cohabiting with the widow and eldest daughter of George Milburn, his business acquaintance and possible friend who had died two years before, the result of a savage beating on the city streets of Washington. Williams' busy work schedule – roving the countryside for slaves, managing his private prison, taking slaving voyages to New Orleans – left him precious little time for courtship. Convenience, then, perhaps drew his eye to someone familiar – not his contemporary, the widow Margaret Milburn, but her stepdaughter and George Milburn's youngest girl, Violet, eleven years old in 1840. William H. Williams and Violet Alice Milburn wed eight years later, on February 8, 1848. Williams would soon be forty-six; she was eighteen. The groom was slightly older than his stepmother-in-law. In 1850, he lived in Margaret Milburn's household in Washington's Seventh Ward, along with his now twenty-year-old wife; their first child, a newborn daughter named Olivia Alice; Violet's older sisters Margaret A. Milburn and Mary Ann Hinton; and Mary Ann's daughter, Violet, named for the girl's aunt.[3]

Financially, Violet Williams married well. Already by 1840, William H. Williams owned "one female bob tail sorrel horse," a "celebrated trotter"; another "Sorrel mare," with a "hind leg injured"; "one bay horse" named Curley; a wagon; a cart; and harnesses. His household goods included a bedstead, quilt, blankets, sheets, and bureau for the bedroom, a three-piece dining set, and "one writing desk & a lot of books (36 in number)." Altogether, the value of his personal property totaled almost $850. As time passed, the trader's wealth only grew. In 1850, he owned thirteen slaves – eight male and five female – ranging in age from five to forty. Three of them accompanied Williams on a journey to Richmond in 1852. Customarily the trader went to the Virginia capital for business, but this trip must have been for pleasure. Joining him at the Exchange Hotel were his wife Violet, their daughter Olivia, and the latest addition to the family, another girl, named Fannie Jane. Two more girls came shortly thereafter: Elizabeth H. ("Lizzie") Williams was born around 1853 and her younger sister, Margaret Agnes ("Maggie"), two years later. William H. Williams thus left four daughters under the age of ten when he passed in April 1858.[4]

Violet Williams attended to all of the minutiae that came with her husband's passing. She paid Glenwood Cemetery $85 for the lot, $8 for a vault, and $3 for digging a grave, less a $2.12 discount for paying in cash. Other expenses included $50 for a coffin and case, $5 for a hearse, $2.50 each for the use of twenty-five hacks in the funeral procession, and $5 for a "brest plate." One physician charged her $165 for William H. Williams' medical care dating back to January 1858, while another billed her $10 for a visit in April. In July, A. Gaddess Steam Marble Works of Baltimore sent the widow an invoice for $500 for her husband's lavish monument erected in the cemetery.[5]

The bills streamed in, but Violet Williams was able to pay them. Her husband left behind a massive estate, although carelessly he died intestate, an inexcusable error of omission for a man whose imprisonment from 1841 to 1842 had taken a notable toll on his health and who had appeared on the verge of death to Louisiana lawmakers three years earlier. Had Williams bothered to write a will, enumerating his possessions one by one would have proved a time-consuming chore. Williams owned several full and partial lots of land in the nation's capital. An inventory of the slave trader's personal property taken within two weeks of his death included a mahogany secretary, a mirror, chairs, sofa, mahogany tables, rugs, carpets, vases, chandeliers, a $15 refrigerator, stoves, clock, looking glasses, china, silver plates and tea pots, forks, spoons, mugs, eighteen wine glasses, china pitchers, walnut and mahogany wardrobes, mattresses, bedding, bedsteads, four horse carts, five mules, three horses, a wagon, carriages, and $1,625 in tobacco, all of which together was valued at $3,751. This tally, though impressive, paled compared with his primary source of wealth: slaves. His holdings had increased dramatically from the thirteen listed in the 1850 census, to a total of fifty-seven, including more than a dozen children. Although Williams owned four "very old" slaves and another "not in [his] wright [sic] mind," none of whom were of much monetary value, he had other individual bondmen worth as much as $1,000. Appraisers put his bondpeople's total value at $28,425, or about $836,000 in 2016 money. Combined with his non-slave property, Williams possessed almost enough wealth to qualify as a modern-day millionaire.[6]

In the absence of a will, the Orphans Court of Washington County appointed Violet Williams the administrator of her deceased husband's estate. It would fall to her to wrap up the slave dealer's business concerns. Accordingly, the same month that Williams died, his widow placed an advertisement in the local newspaper alerting "[a]ll persons having claims against" the trader to come forth within the next full year, up until April 24, 1859. Within that window of time, Violet's neighbor John N. Trook sued her in the D.C. Circuit Court for $518 in damages to his "flowers and shrubbery" as she took "possession of land" upon which he was a tenant. Trook complained that she had not given him "due time to remove his property" prior to his eviction, but he lost his suit. The Orphans Court also ordered that Violet Williams auction off many of her husband's slaves, the cash from which would help dispose of the debts he owed. In December, the widow informed the public of the impending sale of "Forty Likely Negroes" from her husband's estate, at Hughesville, in Charles County, Maryland, since by law slaves could no longer be sold within the District of Columbia. Violet Williams paid $1.25 for "printing Handbills" advertising the looming "Sale of Negroes." Between travel expenses, jail fees, and doctor bills, it cost her in excess of an additional $350 to dispose of other of William H. Williams' slaves in Richmond, Virginia. Although she had much to do, Violet capably settled her husband's affairs.[7]

Widowed before the age of thirty, Violet Williams soon gained a suitor in John B. Abell, a prosperous farmer no more than ten years her senior, from St. Mary's County, Maryland, southeast of Washington. Abell's first wife had passed in 1857, leaving him with four motherless children. Only six months after her death, slave trader William H. Williams expired. Having thus both recently lost a spouse, Abell and Violet Williams decided to marry in 1859. By 1860, they were living together in Washington, D.C.'s, Seventh Ward. Their bustling household included a combined eight children – two boys and six girls – between the ages of four and eleven. The Abell and Williams kids matched almost perfectly in age, with two seven-, nine-, and eleven-year-olds in the house. The youngest girls were close in age, at four and five. John and Violet Abell would later up their total number of children to eleven, contributing three additional family members of their own creation – all girls.[8]

The newly constituted couple boasted ample pecuniary assets. John B. Abell brought to the marriage real estate and personal property each valued at $20,000. Violet Abell retained $12,000 in real estate and $18,000 in personal estate, all held by her "as Guardian for the children of W. H. Williams." After selling off dozens of her first husband's slaves soon after his death, by 1860 she held in trust for his four daughters a total of fourteen bondpeople. These included four male and ten female slaves. Other than one forty-year-old bondwoman, none was over the age of twenty-one. Half a dozen ranged from twelve to eighteen years old. Four others were from four to nine, plus an additional pair of one-month-olds, presumably twins. Violet hired out six of her bondpeople, including one to her brother Thomas Milburn and another to her stepmother, Margaret Milburn. Eight of Violet's slaves were black in complexion; the remaining six were mulattoes, a twenty-one-year-old man and five girls from seven to sixteen. Had William H. Williams fathered any of these mixed-race slaves? It is impossible to say, but by 1860, all six of Violet Abell's mulatto bondpeople had run off, "Fugitives from the State." Perhaps Williams' death and the slaves' fears of possible sale had motivated them to flee.[9]

The loss of the mulatto runaways may have prompted Violet Abell to revisit her slave-trading first husband's long-time dispute with the state of Louisiana over his 1840 shipment of enslaved criminals from Virginia. Maybe her new spouse encouraged it. Or perhaps the rising tensions wrought by the unfolding secession crisis and what retrospect reveals was the coming of the Civil War made her concerned for her biological daughters' economic future. Whatever the cause, in February 1861, William H. Williams' heirs embarked upon a quixotic effort to extract further remuneration from the Louisiana legislature. Less than a week after the formation of the Confederate States of America, many of the same lawmakers who just the month before had voted Louisiana out of the Union received a petition, the precise text of which does not survive, from Williams' family. The House dutifully referred the memorial to the Judiciary Committee, which punted the matter to the Committee on Propositions and Grievances. Before the end of February, the latter committee rebuffed the petition. Recalling that Louisiana lawmakers had previously inserted a clause into the 1856 act for Williams' relief denying the ability to make "further demands . . . upon the State on account of" the convict slaves, it reported back "unfavorably."[10]

The Civil War rendered uncertain the fate of slaveholding in the District of Columbia for the likes of Violet Abell. Abolitionists had been agitating for Congress to eradicate slavery in Washington for decades. Soon after the passage of the Compromise of 1850 terminated the slave trade in the District as part of an effort to ease mounting sectional tensions over slavery, one congressman sought a separate vote to abolish the institution altogether in the capital. A representative critical of the measure believed "the bill . . . introduced for a mischievous purpose, and for no good." Yet throughout the 1850s, northern petitions to Congress continued to filter in, unabated, seeking a final overthrow of bondage in the District.[11]

The secession of eleven southern, slaveholding states from December 1860 to June 1861, the withdrawal or expulsion of southern congressional delegates from Congress, and the commencement of the Civil War in April 1861 all lent momentum to the drive to end slavery in Washington, D.C. In December 1861, the House of Representatives produced a bill to abolish the institution and instructed Secretary of the Interior Caleb B. Smith "to furnish . . . information as to the number of slaves now [held], or resident within the District of Columbia, and of their estimated value." Meanwhile, in the Senate, former shoemaker Henry Wilson, offended decades earlier by the sight of William H. Williams' slave pen, took great pleasure in introducing a bill "for the release of certain persons . . . held to service or labor in the District of Columbia."[12]

Congressional debates highlighted some longstanding strains of thought concerning how any hypothetical program of abolition should proceed. Whereas members of Congress from slaveholding border states that had not seceded believed that respect for masters' property rights demanded the pairing of emancipation with compensation, others objected to the reimbursement of slaveholders as a reward for wrongdoing. Compensation implicitly validated the loathsome principle that masters laid lawful claim to their bondpeople. As one senator observed, genuine justice should bestow any forthcoming federal monies not on slave owners but on the slaves who would be liberated. More practically, compensation entailed expenses that would exacerbate the budgetary stresses already manifest during wartime. Another issue that surfaced was that of colonization, the transportation of freed slaves outside the boundaries of the United States. Echoing arguments more than a half century old, congressmen from slaveholding border states recommended that colonization accompany emancipation to spare whites from the perceived horrors of a substantial free black population in their presence. Other voices criticized plans for colonization as prohibitively costly, while more socially progressive politicians upheld the right of freedpeople to remain in the land of their birth.[13]

The final bill that emerged from Congress on April 12, 1862, passed the Senate by a vote of 29–14 and the House, 92–38. It freed "all persons held to service or labor within the District of Columbia by reason of

14 Former slaves in Washington, D.C., commemorate the fourth anniversary of their emancipation.
Source: F. Dielman, "Celebration of the Abolition of Slavery in the District of Columbia by the Colored People, in Washington, April 19, 1866," *Harper's Weekly*, May 12, 1866.

African descent." (See Figure 14.) It granted D.C. masters ninety days in which to affirm their loyalty to the Union and to apply for compensation for their forfeited slaves, limited to an average of $300 per bondperson. (Disloyal slaveholders were ineligible to receive the plan's financial perks.) The bill authorized the president to appoint three commissioners from the District to investigate the validity of slaveholders' claims prior to payment. Congress appropriated a total of $1 million to reimburse Washington slave owners. It furthermore allotted an additional $100,000 "to aid in the colonization and settlement of such free persons of African descent now residing in said District ... as may desire to emigrate to the Republics of Hayti or Liberia, or such other country beyond the limits of the United States," although no individual could receive more than $100 to voluntarily depart. The colonization provision eased the concerns of border state congressmen who feared an inevitable war of racial extermination between whites and freed blacks, or who anticipated that the mass of freedpeople would become idle paupers or criminals. Colonization, declared one senator from a slaveholding state, represented "philanthropy to the negro race and . . . justice to the white race."[14]

Whereas a more racially radical bill would have freed District slaves without compensation to masters or funding for colonization, the more moderate proposal, designed to attract votes from slaveholding border state congressmen, seemed custom-made for President Abraham Lincoln's signature. Although lawmakers in the Capitol had for decades hotly debated whether Congress could tamper with the institution of slavery in Washington, D.C., Lincoln explained that "I . . . never doubted the constitutional authority of Congress to abolish slavery in this District." He had said so explicitly as early as 1837. For Lincoln, that was never the question. At the same time, however, he had long tied abolition to the principles of compensated emancipation and colonization. As a Whig congressman in the House of Representatives in 1848, he expressed his preference for compensated emancipation should slavery be abolished in the capital. The next year, he advanced a proposition to gradually free "all children born of slave mothers, within [the] District, on or after the first day of January," 1850. Under his plan, slave owners would support and educate their bondpeople up to a certain but unspecified age, at which time the slaves would become free and the master reimbursed by the government. Almost a decade later, Lincoln was vying for a US Senate seat from Illinois. In a debate with his opponent Stephen Douglas in the Mississippi River town of Quincy, Lincoln reiterated his belief that the abolition of slavery in Washington, D.C., should be contingent upon "compensating the unwilling owners" whose slaves were set at liberty.[15]

Lincoln also stubbornly championed a sincere belief in the wisdom of colonization. He embraced the idea of sending former slaves to distant lands, albeit on a voluntary rather than compulsory basis, as early as 1852. The throes of the Civil War only reinforced his commitment to colonization. Politically, as president, Lincoln desperately needed to keep the slaveholding border states of Maryland, Kentucky, and Missouri from defecting to the Confederacy, and those states adamantly opposed any swelling of their free black populations. Colonization supplied a theoretical solution. Socially, too, Lincoln's understanding of race relations fed his support for colonization. As he would bluntly explain to one black delegation, "You and we are different races . . . Whether it is right or wrong I need not discuss, but this physical difference is a great disadvantage to us both, as . . . your race suffer very greatly . . . by living among us, while ours suffer from your presence." Therefore, he concluded, "we should be separated," for whether enslaved or not, "you are . . . far removed from being placed on an equality with the white race." Lincoln eyed the Chiriquí region of Panama as a particularly desirable destination for former slaves. Thus, when the president signed the District of Columbia Emancipation Act into law on April 16, 1862, he remarked, "I am gratified that the two principles of compensation and colonization are both recognized and practically applied" in the law.[16]

Never before had the US government emancipated slaves directly. All previous formal liberations of bondpeople had resulted from state constitutions, state laws, or individual owners' private acts of manumission. Slaves in the District of Columbia were the first emancipated by federal statute. President Lincoln's better-known Emancipation Proclamation of January 1, 1863, freeing slaves in those southern regions still actively in rebellion, would not go into effect for another nine and one-half months. Liberation in the District was also unique in that no other masters anywhere within the United States would be compensated for the loss of their enslaved laborers. After the Civil War ended in the Union's favor, the masses of Confederate slaveholders would not partake of any similar compensated emancipation program. When the Thirteenth Amendment eradicated American slavery altogether in December 1865, slave owners were not reimbursed for their bondpeople made free.[17]

Per the Emancipation Act, Lincoln appointed a three-man board of commissioners to field written petitions for compensation from District masters. Owners submitted lists of their slaves' names that identified each by sex, color, age, and height, gave brief descriptions of their duties, and indicated their monetary values. Beginning on April 28, the commissioners met four days per week to review and evaluate the validity of the claims. By publishing in the Washington, D.C. newspapers lists of slaveholding petitioners, their slaves' names, and their respective values as claimed by their owners, the commissioners elicited the public's aid in exposing and preventing fraud. Evaluating slaves' market value proved a challenging task for several reasons. Slave prices had declined precipitously after Abraham Lincoln's election in 1860 and had not stabilized because Civil War chaos disrupted the routine functioning of slave-trading networks over land and by sea. That the very future of slavery itself remained uncertain only added to the volatility of the slave market. Confronting these difficulties, the commissioners enlisted the aid of Baltimore slave trader Bernard M. Campbell, operator of that city's Pratt Street slave pen. As an outsider unfamiliar with the residents of the District, he would be impartial in his assessments of owners' claims. Yet he was also knowledgeable, with many years of experience in the slaving business. It was a desirable combination of characteristics. Campbell cautioned the commissioners that the collective real value of the Districts' slaves would far outpace the $1 million appropriation approved by the US government.[18]

Although Violet Abell maintained a residence on Virginia Avenue in Washington, D.C., near Seventh Street, she sent her request for compensation in late May 1862 from Baltimore. Abell's accounted for one of the 966 total petitions filed with the board of commissioners under the terms of the Emancipation Act of April 16. Her enslaved workforce had been significantly reduced from the fourteen she owned in 1860, for in 1862 she claimed compensation for only five bondpeople discharged from service. Perhaps some of the half dozen mulatto runaways from 1860 had escaped permanently; she may already have sold others. Violet's claim to reimbursement for the five servants amounted to less than two-tenths of 1 percent of the 3,100 total bondpeople reported to the board. After supplying the mandatory affirmation of her loyalty to the United States, her petition explained that she came into possession of the slaves in April 1858 when the Orphans Court appointed her administrator of the estate of her late husband, William H. Williams. Violet Abell counted as one of only four masters who submitted paperwork alleging ownership of individual slaves worth $2,000, the highest price any slave owner declared. In addition to her $2,000 twenty-year-old mulatto blacksmith Adam Bell, Abell claimed John Brent, a twenty-four-year-old mulatto "coachman and house servant" ($1,800); Joseph Davis, a "dark copper color[ed] ... stout and well made ... valuable house servant" of seventeen ($1,400); John Jackson, a "healthy and active ... house servant," age thirteen ($1,300); and a pregnant, forty-year-old bondwoman and cook named Maria Douglass ($1,000).[19]

Abell described her five bondpeople as "very useful and serviceable," each free of "any defects or infirmities either morally[,] mentally or bodily" and a source of "heavy revenue derived . . . [from] their hire." Still, she would have been hopelessly optimistic to think that she would receive anything close to their total valuation of $7,500. The Emancipation Act limited compensation to an average of just $300 per slave. As a result, some individual slaves were valued higher than that; others lower. Violet Abell counted among the more fortunate masters. The board of commissioners paid her $2,387.10 for the five bondpeople she claimed, allotting $613.20 for John Brent, $569.40 for Adam Bell, $547.50 for Joseph Davis, and $394.20 for John Jackson, but a below-average $262.80 for the lone bondwoman among them, Maria Douglass. Altogether, the three commissioners spent $993,406.35 in compensating masters for the slaves liberated in the District of Columbia. Although they spent almost the entire $1 million appropriated them by Congress, the process left the majority of District slaveholders, who were opposed to the Emancipation Act from its inception, feeling shortchanged and embittered.[20]

On May 2, 1862, precisely twenty-seven days before Violet Abell filed her petition for compensation, Senator Charles Sumner gave "notice that I shall . . . introduce a bill to abolish the coastwise traffic in slaves," which was still authorized by the same act of 1807 that outlawed US participation in the transatlantic slave trade. Sumner announced his intention to "remove" the "disgraceful statute . . . from the statute-book." It took more than two years for him to achieve his object, but on July 2, 1864, Congress – devoid of members who had deserted for the Confederacy – dealt the final blow to the saltwater domestic slave trade that had made William H. Williams and his heirs wealthy. It repealed the sections of the 1807 law that countenanced and regulated the waterborne traffic and declared that "the coastwise slave-trade is prohibited forever." By that point, the exercise was largely symbolic. The Civil War had effectively ended the coastal trade, shutting it down in the port of Baltimore already in May 1861. Baltimore trader Bernard Campbell, who appraised the emancipated slaves in Washington, D.C., only managed to stay in business by boarding suspected runaways and slaves whose masters feared losing them to the Union if not imprisoned and under guard. But amid the chaos of wartime, bondpeople in Campbell's Pratt Street slave pen revolted, necessitating the arrival of police to subdue the riot. In late July 1863, Union troops liberated the last fifty-six captives from Campbell's slave jail.[21]

The Civil War would also have dramatically affected the surviving convict slaves whom Williams H. Williams had transported to Louisiana in 1840. President Lincoln's Emancipation Proclamation, effective January 1, 1863, did not apply to New Orleans or to several Louisiana parishes already under Union control, so, depending upon where the masters lived who purchased members of Williams' gang, many, if not all, of the enslaved criminals likely remained in bondage until the ratification of the Thirteenth Amendment in December 1865. Three male members of Williams' gang, however – James Brown, John Cooper, and Jack Johnson – shared names with soldiers serving together in the 7th Regiment of the Louisiana Infantry (Colored). Brown, Cooper, and Johnson were common enough names, so the trio of US Colored Troops may not have been the one-time transports. But it is satisfying to imagine the bondmen taking up arms against the system of slavery that had long imprisoned them, sometimes behind bars and at other times not.[22]

Several of the Williams' gang slaves may have lingered in Louisiana after emancipation. The 1870 census reveals the names of many black men and women who were both born in Virginia and of the appropriate age to have formerly composed part of Williams' human cargo, yet multiple James Browns, John Carters, John Johnsons, Nancy Smiths, and Alfred Taylors make it impossible to know for certain. Moreover, female members of Williams' gang may have married and changed their surnames, rendering them virtually impossible to trace. Although we cannot definitively track any of the Virginia transports into the postwar era, two possibilities seem the most likely, both of whom shared the name of US Colored Troops in the 7th Louisiana. One was John Cooper, a fifty-year-old black man and farm laborer living in St. John the Baptist Parish with his wife, America. The other was Jack Johnson, a cooper of fifty-five, who lived in St. Mary Parish with a native Louisiana woman named Elizabeth, age thirty-six and presumably his wife. She kept house, while a thirteen-year-old boy named Ben attended school. If indeed Jack Johnson's son, he would have been born in 1857, the same year that the Williams' gang slaves left the Louisiana penitentiary in February.[23]

When William H. Williams' slave pen closed around 1850, his friend and on-and-off-again slave-trading colleague Thomas N. Davis was living and doing business out of King's Hotel in Washington. A Chesapeake native, Davis was, at the age of fifty, just marginally older than Williams. Like his slave-dealing contemporary, Davis shuttled back and forth between Washington, D.C., and New Orleans and had his own frequent encounters with the law. His machinations would ultimately ensnare Williams' widow and send her to court as well. Davis, who, with William H. Williams, had jointly purchased the twenty-seven enslaved convicts from Virginia in 1840, re-emerged almost two decades later in the Williams saga, thanks to an agreement he made with a man named Allison Nailor of Washington, D.C. Nailor may have been the same individual identified by the elderly former bondwoman Susan Keys as the slave trader who, in the mid- to late 1830s, "put [her] on the block at the age of eleven or twelve" and sold her "to her masters in Virginia." In 1839, a different "coloured woman," Hannah Stewart, filed a petition with the D.C. Circuit Court because, though "entitled to freedom," she was "unjustly held in bondage by Allison Nailor," who claimed her as a slave. Trader William H. Williams had faced many similar allegations during his slaving career.[24]

Compared with Williams, however, Allison Nailor at best dabbled in slave dealing as an occasional speculator rather than as a professional. His primary businesses were real estate and transportation. By 1846, he ran a livery stable on E Street in Washington, between 13½ and 14th streets. The 1850 census listed him as a prosperous, forty-one-year-old coach maker who owned an impressive $100,000 in real estate. Nailor had proven a scrappy competitor as he rose to affluence. In 1841, he was "indicted for riotously attacking a cab" belonging to the rival transportation firm of Kimmell & Walker and for "an assault and battery upon Samuel Wright, driver of the said cab." The Washington City Criminal Court found him guilty on both counts. Altogether, Nailor racked up $100 in fines for the incident, although the satisfaction he derived from the pummeling and the message it sent may have seemed worth the cost. The next year, he filed a lawsuit that resulted in the seizure and sale of "one hackney carriage" from another likely competitor. Nailor had done the same thing in 1838, using the law to deprive a man of "1 hack, 2 dark-gray horses and harness." By 1845, Nailor employed a fleet of omnibus drivers to shuttle clients about Washington, D.C., and two years later agitated for a "certain modification of the laws in relation to omnibuses" that would benefit his business. By all accounts, Nailor was a ruthless promoter of his economic interests. As his contemporaries explained, "He was shrewd and active in business, and had the capacity for making money and accumulating property." His success was readily apparent. Buildings were named in his honor, and in 1858, he boasted of a brand new livery stable at the corner of Thirteenth Street and Pennsylvania Avenue.[25]

He also claimed ownership of significant numbers of bondpeople. Some of them, however, were discontented enough to run away. In November 1843, a "woman owned by Mr. Allison Naylor" counted among the "[t]en colored persons" apprehended in advance of an apparent mass escape attempt frustrated before the slaves decamped from Washington, D.C. for Canada. Another bondperson, "my negro man JOHN, who calls himself John Tasset," fled from Nailor's estate in Montgomery County, Maryland, in early 1849, perhaps to visit his wife in Prince George's County or to make for a free state. Despite those few slaves who may have absconded, Nailor still owned consistently around twenty bondpeople from 1850 to 1860, between his holdings in Montgomery County and in Washington, D.C. When emancipation came to the District in 1862, however, Nailor filed petitions to gain compensation for just six bondpeople in total, including Lewis, who was a "first-rate coach painter," violin player, and band leader. The board of commissioners disallowed two of his claims because, as Nailor openly acknowledged, he had purchased the pair of mulatto boys from their mother to serve him only until they reached age twenty-one. Since they were "free born," Nailor could not claim them under the D.C. Emancipation Act. Although the coach maker submitted paperwork showing a combined value of $5,400 for six slaves, he received compensation in the amount of $1,620.60 for four.[26]

Precisely how Allison Nailor first came to know Thomas N. Davis is unclear. Both were commercial men in the nation's capital who actively

engaged their local politicians. As a coach maker and livery stable operator, Nailor took keen interest in the grading and paving of the city streets
and in municipal water mains near his place of business. He and Davis
both filed separate petitions with Washington's Board of Common
Council at about the same time in 1846. At some point, Davis also
borrowed a sum of money from the wealthy Nailor, although he could
not recollect precisely how much. Davis' indebtedness may have
prompted him to strike a speculative bargain with his creditor, one with
long-term legal implications for William H. Williams' widow, Violet.[27]

In 1847, Thomas N. Davis transferred to Allison Nailor in writing his
ownership stake in the slave transports from Virginia, then long out of his
or Williams' possession, and some of whom were confined in the
Louisiana State Penitentiary. "I do hereby assign all of my right, title,
claim and interest" in the "negroes purchased by William H. Williams and
Thomas Davis" to Nailor, declared the agreement, dated November 12.
The arrangement listed by name each of the twenty-seven enslaved convicts purchased out of the Virginia penitentiary and the total of $12,500
paid to the commonwealth for them. By the terms of the deal, should
Williams successfully reclaim the enslaved prisoners and sell them, that
share of the "value received" formerly due Davis would instead be redirected to Nailor. Davis signed his name in the presence of witness John
Hands, Jr., who added his signature as well. William H. Williams was not
a party to the contract, but with the bargain complete, Allison Nailor,
accompanied by his brother Dickerson Nailor, "notified Williams of the
assignment." In reply, the slave dealer allegedly "promised to pay one-
half of the value of the negroes" to the Washington coach maker, if and
when the trader ever got them returned and sold. Under the scenario
Nailor envisioned, once Williams "should receive the money" from the
enslaved convicts' sale, the trader would forward Nailor's portion to
him.[28]

To explain what happened next, Davis must have either forgotten his
arrangement with Nailor, dismissed it as legally nonbinding, or
attempted a willful double-cross of the Washington coach maker. In
1850, three years after assigning his interest in Williams' gang to Nailor,
Davis hired William Gil and two other attorneys to seek redress from the
Louisiana legislature for those very same slaves. He would have had no

motive to do so unless he believed he continued to hold a stake in them. "Davis told me that he did not recollect making any transfer to Nailor," explained Thomas Williams, "and if he did, it was a sham." So Davis continued to claim "interest in any reimbursement which may be made by the Legislature of Louisiana" for the convict slaves forfeited to the state. As Davis admitted, however, "There was a difference of opinion" with William H. Williams, "touching my interest or right . . . in the negroes." The exact "extent of that interest has been contested," probably as a result of the time and money that Williams had invested in his attempts to re-secure the enslaved criminals from the Louisiana State Penitentiary. The two slave traders therefore crafted a "compromise." On February 24, 1855, paperwork made out in East Baton Rouge Parish, Louisiana, documented an arrangement through which Williams agreed to pay Davis $4,000 "to close finally and forever all the interest that the said Thomas N. Davis" had in the Virginia transports "and to settle and pay all other claims that . . . Davis may have" had upon Williams, "resulting from this or any other transaction whatever." Under the terms of their bargain, Williams would pay Davis $950 in cash and then give him the balance of $3,050 "only when the State of Louisiana shall, through her Legislature pass any Bill for the relief of William H. Williams in compensation for [the] said negroes." While consenting to this, Davis also "transfer[red], deliver[ed], and set over" to Williams "any and all right, title or interest he may have, had, or has" to the enslaved prisoners and "acquit[ted,] deliver[ed] and release[d]" Williams "from any and all [other] claims." Davis and Williams both affixed their signatures to the contract before two witnesses, one of whom was the twenty-nine-year-old, Kentucky-born clerk of the Louisiana State Penitentiary, Robert E. McHatton. Davis later recalled that the document he and Williams signed "covered the entire settlement of all our differences in money matters."[29]

Initially, the terms of their agreement played out accordingly. Davis recalled that he received Williams' initial payment of $950 on or about April 1, 1856, although it was probably a year earlier than Davis' recollection. (His memory was often off by a year.) Later in 1855, Williams must also have attempted to pay the remaining $3,050 he owed Davis, for it was in July of that year that Davis issued a public caution in the New Orleans

Picayune "against trading in or purchasing a certain obligation, made in my favor by William H. Williams, for three thousand and fifty dollars," which Davis, in turn, had assigned to John M. E. Sharp. Something – we do not know precisely what – had gone awry with that $3,050 transaction. As a result, Davis consulted New Orleans attorneys J. Redman Coxe and Gustave A. Breaux in late 1856 to collect the same sum from Williams. Breaux knew Davis well, for slave traders were generally on close terms with their lawyers. Although Williams had not yet taken delivery of the enslaved prisoners, the Louisiana legislature had passed the private act of relief in his favor the previous January and had agreed to turn over the confiscated slaves to him. Davis thus felt it was time for his associate to pay up per their February 1855 agreement. As Breaux remembered, "Davis claimed no interest in the said slaves beyond the [remaining] payment" of $3,050 he was owed. Lawyerly nudging coaxed Williams to remit the balance due Davis to Coxe & Breaux in either 1857 or early 1858, shortly before Williams' death.[30]

Through the D.C.-area newspapers, Allison Nailor had long tracked the convoluted history of the Williams' gang slaves. When the state of Louisiana turned over the prisoners to Williams' custody in 1857, Nailor knew it. He must have been delighted that his speculative investment in the convict slaves was about to pay off, a full decade after cutting the deal with Thomas N. Davis. But his share of the profits from the enslaved convicts' sale was not forthcoming. Perhaps Nailor even heard rumors that Williams had paid Davis rather than him, a galling insult and outrage. Nailor may well have already been planning a lawsuit against Williams when the one-time proprietor of the Yellow House passed away. Death presented no obstacle to Nailor's pursuit of litigation. Williams had not been interred in Glenwood Cemetery for long when Nailor, in June 1858, instituted a suit against the widow and administrator, Violet Williams, to recover the debt her deceased husband owed him. What followed was an epic and revelatory series of trials that would end before the US Supreme Court in 1869, eleven years after Williams' demise and four years after the Civil War and slavery's nationwide destruction.[31]

The exact dollar amount Allison Nailor sought is unclear. Some newspapers reported that he went to court "to recover one-half ($12,500) of the sum for which certain negroes were sold by Wm. H. Williams," implying that the convict slaves had attracted a combined $25,000 at market. But these publications mistakenly conflated the price Williams and Thomas N. Davis had paid the commonwealth of Virginia for the enslaved inmates in 1840 with the dollar value pursued by Nailor years later. By 1857, most of the surviving transports would have been well into their thirties. Because "they were some seventeen years older than when received from the State of Virginia," Thomas Williams explained, "they had depreciated in value." Nevertheless, court records revealed that Williams sold the captives restored to him "for a large sum," vaguely placed at "several thousand dollars." Thomas deposed that, after the enslaved convicts' delivery to him in 1857, they collectively "sold for between eight or nine thousand dollars," but "I can not state the exact Sum." If at the low end of this estimate, the $4,000 Williams gave Davis represented precisely one-half of the profits from the convicts' sale: the half that Nailor claimed belonged to him, along with interest dating from his 1847 agreement with Davis.[32]

In the case of *Nailor v. Williams*, decided by the Circuit Court in October 1862, the plaintiff fared poorly. The depositions of Thomas Williams and Thomas N. Davis, both taken in 1860, obliterated Nailor's claims to part-ownership of the Williams' gang slaves. Thomas Williams conceded that he did not know whether his departed brother had purchased the convicts out of the Virginia State Penitentiary "alone or by him and Thomas N. Davis jointly," but, he insisted, "I know that they were in the possession of William H. Williams and introduced in the State of Louisiana as his individual property, and that he claimed to be the sole owner of them" at the time the authorities confiscated them from him. Thomas Williams questioned how Nailor, whom he had known "for about twenty years," could have acquired a financial stake in Williams' gang in 1847: "throughout the whole year," he explained, "the title to the negroes was vested in the State of Louisiana," the consequence of extensive "Judicial proceedings." Therefore, "neither William H. Williams nor any other person had any claim whatsoever" to the enslaved inmates, "except upon the bounty of the State of Louisiana." Nothing altered this state of things "until the passage of the Act in 1856 and the delivery of said negroes in 1857."[33]

The conclusion was clear. Nailor, Thomas Williams declared, "had no interest in said slaves or claim for relief so far as I know." Nailor had not partaken in the effort to procure relief from the Louisiana legislature, nor had he "contribute[d] any thing" to that end, either "in money or personal exertion, so far as I know. I never even heard of his doing so." By contrast, Williams was aware of four "different settlements" between his brother and Thomas N. Davis from 1852 to 1857. Thomas Williams, in fact, noted that he, personally, had made the final payment of $3,050 to Davis' attorneys, Coxe & Breaux, who had actually "instituted suit in the District Court of East Baton Rouge [Parish]." Williams, in short, knew nothing of any "assignment to Nailor." "I never heard of it" at all, he stated, until the spring of 1859.[34]

Thomas N. Davis echoed the same key points. "The negroes" at the time of the agreement, he emphasized, were "in the possession of the State of Louisiana," and physically "the negroes were in Louisiana. The State of Louisiana claimed them." When the state offered William H. Williams relief in 1856, "Al[l]ison Nailor had no interest in those negroes, nor any claim whatever that I know of." In Davis' telling, only he and William H. Williams had "attended" to applications for relief, a process that "involved considerable expenditure of time and money. Mr. Nailor did not contribute anything."[35]

The Circuit Court acknowledged some nagging doubts about the specific details of the 1840 arrangement between Williams and Davis, "owing to the long lapse of time" since the traders had acquired the convict slaves from Virginia and the inability of surviving witnesses to recollect with confidence, twenty-two years after the fact, the precise terms of their agreement. The court thus spelled out to jurors the issues for them to consider. Most fundamentally, were Williams and Davis at some point the "joint owners" of the "negroes recovered from the penitentiary" in Baton Rouge in 1857? If so, had Davis' "interest become vested in Nailor"? If so, had Williams been apprised of the assignment? For Nailor's claim to have any legal merit, the court explained, Williams would have had to have "had actual notice of the transfer ... from Davis to Nailor." By such notice, Davis' title would have been "extinguished" and "supplanted" by the plaintiff's and Williams obliged to "respect that title in his subsequent treatment of the property, and . . . the money derived from it." Finally, if Nailor's suit was legitimate, jurors needed to determine, "What is the amount of the accountability?" Nailor placed the figure at, bare minimum, the $4,000 Williams had already paid to Davis, plus interest. But as witnesses for Williams' widow argued, the profits from the 1857 sale of the convicts retrieved from the Louisiana State Penitentiary had been "all consumed in the costs incurred through litigation and the wear and tear of 17 years." The court showed some sympathy on this matter. It acknowledged that "Williams appeared to be nominally the sole proprietor of these slaves after they left this District" and acted as if he was. He alone paid for their transportation to New Orleans. He alone incurred the expense of "defending the title to these slaves against confiscation." And "after the powers of New Orleans (with or without authority)" seized and forcibly detained them, Williams led the charge to get them back. "Whoever jointly owned that property with Williams," in other words, had thrust the burden of the work upon him and him alone to protect their interests. The court therefore believed Williams "entitled to a reimbursement for any expenses legitimately incurred in defending the title to these slaves." Thomas Williams deposed that his brother's efforts to claim relief from the Louisiana legislature absorbed an estimated $3,000–5,000 in legal fees. All of these costs, the court insisted, must rightfully be deducted from any possible award to the plaintiff Nailor. "Your duty," it instructed the jury, "is to ascertain, and unfortunately from indefinite data to a large extent, what the expense was." If William H. Williams "in his lifetime converted this property and realized out of it more money than he consumed in the process of" getting it back, his estate owed Nailor money, assuming that Williams "had notice of the transfer of that interest."[36]

Perhaps because the jurors believed Williams had not been informed of the assignment from Davis to Nailor or, more likely, because they thought his profits from the convict slaves had all been eaten up in legal fees, after deliberations they found against Allison Nailor's claim. The attorneys of the re-wed Violet Abell, herself busily navigating the turmoil and confusion of wartime and the emancipation of slaves in Washington, D.C., successfully defended her first husband's estate and preserved it for his four children. In early 1865, the Orphans Court named Saturday, February 4, as the date "for the final settlement and distribution of the personal estate" of William H. Williams. A public announcement in the newspaper invited the last of Williams' creditors to attend the Orphans Court that day to collect their lawful portions of his available assets. But if Violet Abell believed the legal headaches concerning her first husband's shipment of convict slaves were over, she was sorely mistaken. Allison Nailor extended his suit past the Orphans Court's deadline, past the April 1865 close of the Civil War, and past the December ratification of the Thirteenth Amendment abolishing slavery.[37]

Emancipation probably hurt Allison Nailor's pocketbook more than Violet Abell's. Violet Williams had sold most of her husband's slaves shortly after his death, a year prior to the start of southern secession. She and Nailor received compensation for almost the same small number of bondpeople living in Washington, D.C., but when liberation arrived, Nailor owned many more chattel still enslaved on his Montgomery County, Maryland, estate. No government reimbursed him for the loss of those bondpeople. Those financial losses may have pressed him to renew his case against Williams' widow.

Nailor had long protested the original verdict against him as contrary both to the evidence and to the law. He disputed the Circuit Court judge's instructions to the jury. As his attorneys explained, "the Jury was told it was competent to . . . allow" Violet Abell "to charge the cost & expense of getting the negroes to Louisiana," however much the jury "might find that to be," and deduct that from any possible award to the plaintiff. Nailor's lawyers objected because "there was no evidence before the Jury" concerning "the amount of such cost & expense" and no indication of how Davis and Williams had divided those expenses "at the time of the shipment . . . south." In addition, Nailor's lawyers contended, the Circuit Court erred in allowing the jury to "find that there was no notice [given] to W. H. Williams of the assignment made by Davis" to Nailor. Nailor took affront. He insisted that he had informed Williams of the transfer of the slaves and that Williams understood the arrangement. John Hands' signature proved the assignment in 1847 genuine, he stated, and witness Dickerson Nailor testified before the Circuit Court that Williams assented to it. On cross-examination, Violet Abell's defense attorneys asked Dickerson Nailor if, in 1847, either he or Allison Nailor was "engaged in trading in negroes." Nailor's counsel objected, but the court overruled the objections. In filing for an appeal, his attorneys took exception to the question. They submitted that the court erred in allowing it because the inquiry was not germane to the case. All that mattered was whether Williams had received notice of the assignment from Davis to Nailor and whether he had made the alleged promise to their client: Nailor's business dealings (which sometimes did include slave trading, with Dickerson Nailor's assistance) were "not in the slightest manner" relevant to the trial and "thr[e]w no light upon the issues." Moreover, the buying and selling of slaves in Washington, D.C., and throughout the country was perfectly legal in 1847. The question was therefore inadmissible, nothing more than a clever attempt to impeach Nailor's character and "to raise a prejudice" against him because he "might have dealt in slaves." Likewise, Nailor's attorneys filed an exception by stating that it was inadmissible to impugn "the credit or respectability" of witness Dickerson Nailor "by interrogating him as to the character of his business, when that business has no reference to the subject matter of the suit, and can in no manner elucidate the issue." Based on these arguments, Allison Nailor's suit was reinstated in March 1867. He would get a new trial and a fresh chance to prove his claim.[38]

Nailor's latest effort to secure payment for his alleged share of Williams' gang was undeniably odd. The case originated almost three decades before, in the depths of American slavery. Yet a court would now adjudicate it two years after emancipation. With slavery now lawfully purged from the land, Nailor's suit had become an anachronism. The "great subject" of slavery that long plagued the nation "has come here to plague us" at the bench, reported one of the judges who heard Nailor's complaint. But, he added, mercifully "w[e] are pretty well assured . . . that it will be about the last case of the kind." Nailor's resolve would guarantee slavery's lingering presence in an American courtroom. In 1867, his appeal went before the Supreme Court of the District of Columbia, a judicial body established by Congress in 1863 as a substitute for the old Circuit Court. In 1867 it consisted of three justices and a chief justice, all four of whom had been nominated by Abraham Lincoln and confirmed as the Civil War raged.[39]

During a special term of the court, presided over by Chief Justice David Kellogg Cartter in late March, Nailor again lost his bid for Violet Abell's money. About a month later, on April 29, a still-dissatisfied Nailor entered a motion for a new trial, but Cartter overruled him. Nailor immediately filed an appeal to the same court *en banc.* Any plaintiff disappointed with a verdict handed down by the Supreme Court of the District of Columbia meeting in special term could appeal to the general term, when three of the court's justices composed the bench. Abram Baldwin Olin, Andrew Wylie, and George Purnell Fisher assembled to hear Nailor's appeal in May 1867 but again ruled against him. Nailor's lawyers promptly filed an application for a writ of error to the United States Supreme Court.[40]

Less than a week later, Allison Nailor got an assist from the highest authority. On May 15, President Andrew Johnson sent the justices of the Supreme Court of the District of Columbia a serious message. He informed them that, as far as he could ascertain, "a manifest error hath happened, to the great damage of ... Allison Nailor." If his impression was correct, he wanted to remedy the situation and provide Nailor "full and speedy justice." Johnson "commanded" that the justices "render your seal, distinctly and openly, to send the record and proceedings" of Nailor's case forward to the US Supreme Court by the time that body convened again in December. Johnson's relationship to Allison Nailor and his motive for helping are not clear, but the month before the Democratic president sent the missive, Allison Nailor, Jr., was elected secretary of Washington, D.C.'s Second Ward Democrats. He may have called in a political favor for his father. Fellow Democrat Andrew Johnson's order to the Supreme Court of the District of Columbia arguably violated the separation of powers between branches of government, but if so, it presaged a larger pattern of behavior. In another ten months, the presidential overextension of executive authority in a separate matter would get Andrew Johnson impeached.[41]

In December 1868, more than a decade after William H. Williams' death, his widow's accounts were still being "filed and approved" in the Orphans Court, and, per President Johnson's instruction, Nailor's case against her finally progressed on appeal to the US Supreme Court. Chief Justice Salmon P. Chase presided over that judicial body, but Associate

Justice Samuel Freeman Miller delivered the opinion. The fundamental issue at stake pertained to Nailor's exceptions to the questions asked in court about his or Dickerson Nailor's slave dealing. The lower court had permitted replies to them (although the responses were not recorded in the trial record). Miller began the court's decision with a hypothetical counterpoint to Nailor's case. "If a question is asked of a witness on the stand, the answer to which is pertinent and legal testimony, and the court refuses to permit the witness to answer," an appellate court would correct that error, because the court's "refusal ... to permit the answer to be given" injured one of the parties at law. "But where a question is asked which is illegal only because it may elicit improper testimony," Miller continued, "and the court permits it to be answered against the objection of the other party, the injury done the party" is contingent, based on the answer. So, "if the witness knows nothing of the matter to which he is interrogated, or if his answer is favorable to the objecting party, it works him no injury." If, in contrast, the testimony did cause injury, "he can show it by making the answer a part of the bill of exceptions" to the verdict. If the injured party failed to take that step, "there is no error of which a revising court can take notice." For that reason, Miller concluded, and because his fellow justices identified "nothing" in Nailor's bills of exception to suggest that "the questions themselves" were unreasonable or that the lower court failed to exercise sufficient "discretion" during cross-examination, the Supreme Court could find "no error" in the bills of exception. On November 1, 1869, the high court affirmed the previous decisions against Nailor and in favor of William H. Williams' widow. Twenty-nine years to the day that William H. Williams entered New Orleans with the transport slaves from Virginia, the Supreme Court's ruling at last exorcised the legal ghosts that haunted Violet Abell. Williams' profession generated constant lawsuits in life and, as it turned out, in death, but now, with this final, posthumous victory at law, his heirs could reap the full fruits of his repugnant trade.[42]

The final chapter of William H. Williams' legal odyssey did not end happily for Allison Nailor. Still, by 1869, he had amassed real estate in Washington, D.C., and in Montgomery County, Maryland, worth about $150,000, the equivalent of more than $2.6 million in 2016. For decades, he had bought and sold land, kept his livery stable, and farmed. But the façade of prosperity cloaked seedy business practices and a scandalous personal life. Many of his properties he reportedly rented out as "houses of ill fame" or as grog shops for the "retail of spirituous liquors." Nailor himself imbibed too freely. By at least 1854, observers noted, he had begun to lead "a dissolute and intemperate life."[43]

In 1869, the sixty-year-old real estate tycoon took up with a twenty-one-year-old woman named Catherine Conley. Whether she seduced him with her charms, or he attracted her with his money and standing, or a little of each, in November or December, soon after Nailor lost his US Supreme Court case against Violet Abell, he abandoned his wife and family, moved in with Conley, "and lived with her in concubinage until his death" in January 1879. Their adulterous relationship produced two children: an "infant son" named Willie Earnest and a daughter named Mary Edna, the latter of whom died at the age of two. Nailor executed two deeds of trust in the 1870s to bestow parcels of property upon each of them once they reached maturity. Nailor's first family, shocked by his indecent, "illegal and criminal intercourse" with Conley, sought recourse at the law. His wife, Rachel Nailor, his son Washington T. Nailor, and his married daughters Lizzie Trimble and Frances Clarke went to court to prevent the family patriarch from squandering their inheritance on his lover and illegitimate children.[44]

Nailor's wife, adult children, and other witnesses painted in court a portrait of a besotted man wholly surrendered to dissipation. The fifty-year resident of Washington, D.C., and prominent figure in the community had, "from a long course of dissolute and intemperate habits," become "demented," "insane," and, most importantly, "mentally incapable . . . of transacting business," such as making deeds. A parade of dozens of witnesses called by the family testified to Nailor's drunkenness. Some "never saw him sober," others "never saw him sober but once," and still others "seldom saw him when not intoxicated." His "habitually intemperate" ways were bad enough, but the family also charged that Catharine Conley had committed fraud by using her feminine wiles to exercise "undue influence" over the aging Nailor. Whether drunk or sober, Nailor was, "[i]n all conditions . . . perverse, willful, obstinate, and defiant of public opinion." Shamelessly, according to reports, he took great pride in his ability to provide financially for his illegitimate children and "often boasted to his friends and acquaintances" about it. His relationship with Conley was satisfying, certainly for him and possibly also for her, although her voice remains silent in the records. Seven years after Nailor's death, the law issued its final opinion in 1886. The "great preponderance of evidence" showed Nailor, "though in feeble health," competent to execute the deeds under dispute. His young mistress and their son would indeed partake in a portion of Nailor's immense fortune, just as he intended. Nailor's failure to secure a share of the Williams' gang profits thus did little to dampen the selfish happiness of his twilight years.[45]

Violet Abell's triumph over Allison Nailor at the US Supreme Court came at a dark period of her life. In 1869 and 1870, she was ensnared in several other lawsuits, at least two of which appeared before the Supreme Court of the District of Columbia. More serious still, her sister Margaret A. Amidon passed away on December 3, 1869. Born to George and Alice Milburn in 1827, she was two years older than Violet. Margaret A. Milburn established herself as a well-respected educator at the Fourth District Female Grammar School in Washington, D.C. No despised schoolmarm, she graciously accepted in 1864 a Christmas gift of "a fine set of table castors" from her grateful students. Thirteen months after her death, current and former "pupils of the Fourth District Schools gave a grand concert, at Lincoln Hall, to aid in erecting a monument in memory of" their favorite teacher. The school also began the tradition of awarding the Amidon medal to the female student voted by "her teacher and schoolmates to be most distinguished for 'amiability and scholarship.'" Margaret Milburn Amidon left a legacy far more worthy of pride and admiration than did her brother-in-law, William H. Williams, her near neighbor in Glenwood Cemetery.[46]

The former Violet Williams and her second husband, John Abell, resided in Washington's Seventh Ward in 1870. Although each brought their own children to the marriage, they continued to enlarge the family, adding Flora in 1860, Violet L. in 1867, and Lucy in 1871. By 1875, the blended Abell clan relocated to Baltimore, but three years later, John Abell ran successfully for register of wills in St. Mary's County, Maryland. In 1880, the family lived in Leonardtown. John, Violet, and the three daughters they created together lived in a household that also included a pair of nineteen-year-old black servants, Nannie Waley and William Douglas, the latter of whom may have been the son of Violet's one-time enslaved cook Maria Douglass. For Violet Abell and other well-off whites who had long forcibly extracted labor from slaves, the presence of African-American domestics would have lent a semblance of normalcy to their post-Civil War, topsy-turvy world lawfully deprived of bondpeople.[47]

John Abell breathed his last in July 1886, nine years before Violet died of tuberculosis in 1895. Violet outlived her slave-trading first husband, William H. Williams, by thirty-seven years. She saw her and Williams' four daughters all reach adulthood, marry, and bear her grandchildren. Olivia Alice Williams wed William N. Dalton, "a prosperous shoe merchant" of Washington, D.C. Curiously, her slave-trading father and George M. Grant had also sold shoes in New Orleans decades earlier. In 1880, Olivia Williams Dalton lived on Virginia Avenue, right next door to her younger sister and William H. Williams' second daughter, Fannie. Fannie Williams married William H. Beall, a grocer on Louisiana Avenue near Seventh Street. They lived for a time in Prince George's County, Maryland, where Beall worked as a merchandise broker, before returning to Washington, D.C. Beall's unexpected death in 1901 due to suspected complications from asthma widowed Fannie, who spent the rest of her life living with an unmarried daughter, a clerk, in rented dwellings in the nation's capital. The longest lived of William H. Williams' children, Fannie Beall died in 1931 at the age of eighty. Her younger sister Lizzie Williams married Eugene K. Stewart, a wood and coal dealer in 1880 and, by 1900, a shoe salesman, perhaps employed by William N. Dalton. The youngest daughter of William H. and Violet Williams was Maggie. She wed John B. Riley, a man whose occupation as horse dealer bore some resemblance to her father's profession. All four of William H. Williams' daughters had sons who shared a name with their slave-dealing grandfather. As a young man in 1895, William H. Riley, one of Maggie's sons, served as a pallbearer at his grandmother Violet Abell's funeral. He helped bear her casket to her final resting place in Glenwood Cemetery, next to her first husband, William H. Williams. William H. Riley went on to spend a long career as a shipping clerk prior to his death in 1966. It is not certain that he ever knew his grandfather was involved in a form of shipping as well.[48]

William H. Williams' daughters did not stray far from home over the course of their lives. When Olivia Dalton and Fannie Beall lived adjacent to one another on the Island, they were a mere block and a half or so from the former site of the Yellow House. But South Washington was no residential paradise for them. In 1879, the two sisters and their husbands filed a $5,000 lawsuit against the Baltimore & Potomac Railroad Company. They "repeatedly complained" about "the blocking of Virginia avenue, between Sixth and Seventh streets, by freight cars." The railroad used the tracks near their homes to park, to link and unlink train cars, and to load and unload cargoes. Annoyed and frustrated, the sisters grumbled that their street had become "a general depot for discharging freight." It was not the first time people had felt outrage over the "depot" that was Washington, D.C. Decades before, abolitionists had attacked their father for the slave depot he kept in the nation's capital. But unlike the railroad, William H. Williams' business was no simple nuisance, the cargoes he transported no typical freight.[49]

The Legal Legacy of the Domestic Slave Trade

O N JUNE 7, 1839, A CHARLES CITY COUNTY, VIRGINIA, court unanimously found John, "a negro man slave the property of the late Benskin Hopkins," guilty of the homicide of James Carradus, "a white man." The next day, the court reconvened for sentencing, and John learned his fate: in little more than a month, he was to "be hanged by the neck till he be dead." Yet John, even if he was no saint, was certainly not the killer. Ample evidence indicated that the true murderer was a white man who had since absconded from Charles City County and who remained on the lam. The proceedings underscored the difficulties enslaved blacks such as John confronted in antebellum southern courts of law. Although some scholars have stressed the procedural fairness of slave cases before the bar, emphasizing the facts that bondpeople did gain access to trials and were not often the victims of vigilante justice in the pre-Civil War South, *Commonwealth v. John* numbers among the countless cases over the centuries in which black defendants could expect harsh and unfair treatment in their journeys through the criminal justice system.[1]

Taken before the Charles City County court of oyer and terminer, John appeared before a slate of five "Gentlemen Justices." All of them were not only white men but also prominent slaveholders. When the census taker arrived in Charles City County the year after John's trial, the "poorest" of the justices owned a dozen slaves, the wealthiest, sixty-eight. Three qualified as "planters," owning twenty or more bondpeople, and a fourth owned nineteen, just one short of the necessary threshold for planter status. Altogether, the adjudicating body claimed ownership of 180 bondmen and -women, an average of thirty-six per justice.[2]

Any trained defense attorney would certainly have spotted the holes in the case against John. Testimony revealed that the bondman, though gratified with Carradus' demise, did not commit the murder and was at best an accomplice to the crime. The scenario outlined in the court record was this: in mid-November 1838, James Carradus, a landowner with holdings both in Charles City County and in neighboring New Kent County, was at a landing along the Chickahominy River that separated the two counties, with a bondman named Squire, who, like the accused slave John, belonged to a deceased man named Benskin Hopkins. Together Carradus and Squire were "mending a Seine," a type of net used to gather fish out of the area's many waterways. As they toiled, Squire spotted Benskin Hopkins the younger, the son of the bondmen's departed owner, peering out of a nearby thicket, gun drawn and pointed at Carradus. With a motion of his hand, Hopkins silently waved Squire away from his intended target and fired. "Carradus fell dead," Squire reported. The slave instinctively fled, but Hopkins "called him back" and threatened to shoot him, too, if he did not help dispose of the corpse. Squire dutifully returned to join Hopkins and the bondman John, who lived at the same residence as Hopkins and was apparently at his side when he pulled the trigger. The three together wrapped up Carradus' remains "in an old Seine" and carried them "into the marsh" for an unceremonious burial in the mud.[3]

Pleasant, an enslaved man employed by Carradus, had heard the report of a gun while crossing the Chickahominy at about sunset. He redirected his canoe and paddled over to investigate the sound of muffled voices drifting over the marsh, drawing near enough to hear "distinctly" the bondman John encourage his partners in crime to "ram [Carradus'] head in the mud." John's animus toward Carradus was unmistakable. "[D]amn him," the slave snarled, "he flashed a gun at me once." Further testimony revealed that Carradus had hired John two years earlier, in 1837, an arrangement that proved contentious. John reportedly "behaved badly," running away "several times," perhaps provoking Carradus to snap his gun at the slave. John did not commit the murder, but he was present, still harbored lingering resentment toward Carradus, and took macabre satisfaction in desecrating the body. As John explained, Carradus, now dead, "will never trouble any one again." The morning after the murder, Pleasant discovered Squire at the landing, cleaning up blood, and upon inquiry learned that it was Carradus whom Benskin Hopkins had shot. A week later, Pleasant, probably overcome by a troubled conscience, divulged his knowledge of the crime to a white man who may have been the one eventually responsible for initiating legal action. Benskin Hopkins and John each expressed outrage that Pleasant had betrayed their "secret."[4]

As the conspiracy of silence unraveled, newspapers filled in the details. Initially, when Carradus "mysteriously disappeared" in November 1838, his family presumed that he had drowned in the Chickahominy. Revelations of foul play prompted an exhaustive search of the marsh for "the Coat, hat & body of Carradus." John and Squire guided authorities to the spot where they had deposited the corpse and its accoutrements, but they recovered only the buckshot-ridden coat and hat later produced in court. Dragging for the body turned up nothing, for Hopkins, newspapers reported, had relocated Carradus' remains "to some more secret spot," lending support to the bondman John's declaration to a fellow slave that "they will never find him." Carradus' bones may still lie undiscovered somewhere in the Chickahominy marshes.[5]

Authorities did arrest Benskin Hopkins and charge him with Carradus' murder. While the particular motive for the crime is unknown, Carradus had a history of interactions with the Hopkins family. Carradus was a neighbor to the senior Hopkins, a witness when Hopkins drew up his will in 1834, and the man who married Hopkins' widow, Mildred. That Carradus was the younger Benskin's stepfather suggests the possibility of some familial drama, emotional or financial, lurking behind the incident. Many questions remain, however, since Hopkins fled from justice before he stood trial. The Charles City County court had scheduled him to appear and answer to the charge against him on June 7, 1839, the same day the justices heard John's case, but by that time, he had absconded, never to be seen again.[6]

The bondman John alone would bear the punishment for James Carradus' murder. But as the five magistrates hearing his case found him guilty and sentenced him to the gallows, they also identified him "as an object for transportation." The "Gentleman Justices" valued John at $900 to be paid to the Hopkins estate and forwarded the transcript of the case to Governor David Campbell, who spared John the noose and instead reprieved him on June 17, 1839, to sale and transportation.[7]

Like other Virginia slaves whose sentences were commuted to banishment, John was conveyed to the state penitentiary in Richmond to await purchase by a trader willing to carry him out of the country. Through the customary bidding process, John, after languishing in prison for more than a year, fell into the possession of William H. Williams, in September 1840. The bondman joined the twenty-six other enslaved felons conveyed to Washington, D.C., to spend the next month in the Yellow House in advance of their fateful journeys aboard the *Uncas* and the *Roanoke* to the bustling commercial center of New Orleans. After Crescent City authorities seized Williams' cargo of enslaved convicts, John was incarcerated and, in 1845 – quite possibly under the name Jack Johnson – transferred with nine others to the Louisiana State Penitentiary to toil at hard labor for the state.[8]

Two southern states' judicial systems radically shaped the course of John's life, even though it was abundantly clear that he did not pull the trigger. As a mere accomplice (albeit perhaps a willing one) and spectator to the murder of a white man, John became legally responsible for a death that could not go unanswered. The racial dynamics at play meant that someone must be punished. The law could show little leniency because the social dangers were too great, and thanks to Benskin Hopkins' timely escape into the historical mists, John ended up as the only person penalized for the fatal shooting. He and many others among the twenty-seven enslaved convicts of Williams' gang were convicted on flimsy or circumstantial evidence.

When viewed through a panoramic historical lens, the outcome of *Commonwealth v. John* hardly seems surprising. It was neither the first nor the last instance of racial injustice before the law. One does not need to be a Black Lives Matter activist or sympathizer or a person of color to attest to this. Any casual consumer of history or of twenty-first-century news must recognize the undeniable inequalities built in to the US justice system. Wrongful convictions such as John's are not historical aberrations but rather part of a longstanding pattern that continues to the present time, not only in the South but throughout the country. After a Greensville County, Virginia court of oyer and terminer convicted the bondwoman Arena in 1840 for attempting to administer poison, thirty-one white petitioners on her behalf stated frankly that "a person of another color" – that is, a white person – "would not have been condemned on the evidence" supplied in court. That blunt admission to Governor Thomas Walker Gilmer in May 1840 – repeated in countless other antebellum pleas for gubernatorial clemency – applies equally well to many cases in modern times. Exoneration data reveal the extent to which people of color are still wrongfully convicted despite weak evidence against them. The Innocence Project reported the findings of one study of 297 exonerations resulting from DNA testing. Minorities collectively received roughly 70 percent of those exonerations; blacks alone, 63 percent. News outlets in March 2017 widely reported the results of a National Registry of Exonerations analysis of 1,900 exonerations in the United States from 1989 to October 2016. Although African Americans composed only 13 percent of the US population, the study showed that they represented 47 percent of the "innocent defendants wrongfully convicted of crimes and later exonerated." The report collected data on erroneous convictions for three specific types of crime: murder, sexual assaults, and drug offenses. Racial disparities were evident within each category.[9]

If American law has treated black defendants unfairly in the courtroom for centuries, the propensity to incarcerate them disproportionately and for prolonged terms is a relatively more recent phenomenon that first emerged in the immediate post-Civil War years. Most enslaved people did not spend time imprisoned. Generally in the Old South, slaveholders *were* the law on their plantations. When bondpeople committed crimes, masters themselves typically punished slaves without reliance upon formal legal channels. Since slave owners wanted their bondpeople at work, producing wealth, rather than idle, they usually avoided detaining slaves, instead preferring whipping as the standard punishment for real or perceived wrongdoing. Occasionally slaveholders in the American South confined troublesome bondpeople by chaining them temporarily in irons in private plantation prisons or improvised dungeons under the main dwelling house or in a barn or outbuilding. Some locked unruly or poorly behaved slaves in a hot box or sweatbox out in the open, under the beating sun. Confinement, though, was more common if slaves' crimes entered the court system. Enslaved convicts might be imprisoned briefly in local public jails or workhouses, but if so, they usually measured their terms of incarceration in days or weeks, not years. Bondpeople might occupy local jails while they awaited trial or sale at auction. In addition, enslaved convicts slated for execution remained confined in city or county jail until their fateful date with the gallows arrived. More frequently than rural slaveholders, urban masters sometimes utilized local jails for their own purposes, placing slaves there for safekeeping or to punish recaptured runaways or other difficult bondpeople. Local jails, however, were notoriously overcrowded, damp, and dangerous to the health of valuable chattel. Most masters preferred keeping their slaves out of them.

Excepting a small number of bondwomen housed in the Louisiana State Penitentiary in excess of twenty years, no slaves in antebellum US history remained imprisoned longer than did those of Williams' gang. The enslaved men and women transported from Richmond to New Orleans were unique in the range of incarceration facilities they inhabited. They spent time, successively, in public county and city jails of Virginia, the Virginia State Penitentiary, the Yellow House in Washington, D.C., the Orleans Parish prison, and various other Louisiana institutions, including, for some, the state penitentiary in Baton Rouge. With the exception of William H. Williams' private jail, designed specifically to accommodate slaves, whites in the antebellum era outnumbered blacks detained in all of these facilities.[10]

This would change after the Civil War and the eradication of race-based slavery. After the Civil War, an influx of black prisoners transformed southern prisons from institutions dominated by white inmates to repositories for African-American men. Whereas during slavery, masters handled most crimes privately, without resort to the law, emancipation transformed minor offenses such as petty theft into crimes against the state worthy of rigorous prosecution. In the absence of slavery, imprisonment emerged as a means of controlling freedmen as well as small numbers of freedwomen. Consequently, prison populations across the South became disproportionately African-American. Already by 1866, for example, a majority of all prisoners in the Virginia State Penitentiary were black, a first in the commonwealth's history. In

Louisiana, two-thirds of the inmates in the state penitentiary in 1860 were white; eight years later, two-thirds were black. The same pattern repeated itself in other southern states. Across the postwar South, prisons witnessed dramatic rises in the numbers of black inmates and increases in their percentage of all people in confinement.[11]

Denied continued access to the institutional constraints of blacks' enslavement, southern whites found imprisonment a useful tool for the social control of black men in particular, whom they would put to work to compensate for the loss of their slaves. The rapidly growing and overwhelmingly black postwar prison population soon exceeded the capacity of penitentiaries and local jails damaged or destroyed in the war to accommodate them. Many southern states therefore launched or expanded upon existing convict lease systems in which individual landholders or private enterprises rented out prisoners' labor. Although initially conceived in some states as a temporary expedient to alleviate overcrowding, by 1880 the convict lease system evolved into an entrenched part of the criminal justice system in all former Confederate states. Convict leasing decentralized the punishment of criminals by moving inmates outside the penitentiary to work for private companies or individuals who had contracted to use convict labor. In exchange, lessees assumed from the state the responsibility to feed, clothe, shelter, and guard the inmates. The system functioned well for all but the prisoners. States earned revenue through the leases, while lessees reaped the profits produced through a reliable supply of comparatively cheap, low-cost laborers who could be driven to work harder than those who were free. Black prisoners lived in convict camps as they performed jobs that whites refused to do at the wage employers were willing to pay. Convicts labored in plantation cotton fields, on railroads, in sawmills, and in coal mines. In Louisiana, they built levees along the Mississippi River and drained swamps. Although a few white convicts were also leased out, the overwhelming preponderance of all of the prisoners swept up by convict leasing were black men. (In such states as Virginia, only African-American inmates were eligible for leasing.) The profits they generated incentivized southern courtrooms to convict black defendants as a means of perpetuating the system. Laboring without compensation and subject to physical punishment, the black convicts leased out truly lived under "slavery by another name." For southern whites accustomed to the presence of slavery, the convict lease system represented the next step in the evolution of compulsory labor.[12]

Mounting criticisms of the abuses inherent in post-Civil War convict lease systems eventually sparked reform, and they were gradually abandoned, state by state, in the first three decades of the twentieth century. Still, other forms of convict labor persisted or emerged, including both chain gangs who slaved away on the public roads and prison farms such as Mississippi's Parchman Farm or Louisiana's notorious Angola Prison, situated in West Feliciana Parish on the former plantation of slave trader Isaac Franklin. Angola supplanted the old Louisiana State Penitentiary in Baton Rouge, where ten of the Williams' gang slaves had been held for twelve years. That institution closed in 1918 after more than eight decades of use.

Today, the state of Louisiana, the pioneer in antebellum-era convict leasing, continues to benefit from the labor of its prisoners, much like it did from the members of Williams' gang. The state has ample human resources to exploit. The United States incarcerates more of its people than any other nation in the world. Although boasting less than 5 percent of the global population, it is home to almost 25 percent of the world's inmates. In 2014, US prisons held more than 2.2 million people, or one in every 145 Americans, and no state in the Union incarcerates its people at a higher rate than does Louisiana. If the United States ranks first among all nations in jailing its people, and if Louisiana is first among the fifty states, then Louisiana stands as the global leader in incarcerations per capita. In 2014, Louisiana imprisoned more than 38,000 individuals, or 816 people per 100,000 in its population, substantially more than Russia (492), China (119), France (100), or Germany (78). Data from 2015 showed that Louisiana's incarceration rate decreased from 816 to 776 per 100,000 residents. Among Louisiana adults, one in every eighty-six was in jail. Despite the decline, with an incarceration rate still more than twice the US average of 385 prisoners per 100,000 people, Louisiana maintained its title as "world's prison capital."[13]

Historically, Louisiana has not always held that ignominious distinction. In 1965, the state ranked thirteenth of the fifty in incarcerations, with 109 prisoners per 100,000 people. By 1986, Louisiana rose to fifth place, with 322 inmates per 100,000. The trend worsened from there. The state took third in 1990, with 427 prisoners per 100,000. The last decade of the twentieth century witnessed the most significant jump, carrying Louisiana to second in incarcerations, at 801 per 100,000. In the twenty-first century, Louisiana secured the top spot. The state's incarceration rate had increased sufficiently to outpace that of Iran by a factor of five. It was thirteen times higher than China's and twenty times higher than Germany's. The Associated Press reported the grim statistic that, since the late 1970s, the number of inmates in Louisiana "has grown 30 times faster than the state's population."[14]

The notable increase in Louisiana incarcerations over time, particularly since about 1980, is *not* due to an increase in violent crime. Nationally, the rate of violent crime in 2015 was only about half of what it was at its peaks in 1980 and in the early 1990s. By 2014, the US murder rate had declined by more than half since 1993 and had declined each year since 2006. Murder rates in 2014 were the lowest on record, dating back to 1960. But even as violent crime rates have been significantly reduced, the US prison population has exploded, doubling since 1991. If violent crime does not account for the dramatic rise in the number of incarcerated Americans, it must be nonviolent crime, in part, that it responsible. This is as true in Louisiana as anywhere in the United States. As reported by the Associated Press, "81 percent of admissions to prison in Louisiana in 2015 were for nonviolent crime." The top ten crimes for which people in Louisiana are incarcerated are all nonviolent. Five of the top ten are drug-related offenses, with simple drug possession the most common. Nationally, too, "more than 46 percent of all inmates in federal prison as of March 2016" sat in their cells for convictions on drug charges.[15]

The emergence of a private, for-profit prison system has also contributed to Louisiana's burgeoning prison population. As of 2014, 8 percent of all US prisoners were "held in privately-owned prisons . . . run by corporations,. . . beholden to investors and . . . in the business of making profits." Under this system, speculators finance the construction of private prisons, typically in economically depressed rural areas, and local sheriffs keep them well stocked in inmates, not only by arresting alleged criminals in their jurisdictions to face trial, conviction, and imprisonment, but also by accepting surplus prisoners from the state or from overflowing facilities in other locales, for which the prison receives payments. The for-profit, private prison industry, thoroughly entrenched in Louisiana and prevalent in other southern states as well, realizes astronomical profits. In 2015, the GEO Group, the largest private corrections corporation, reaped $1.84 billion in revenue. The Corrections Corporation of America (CCA) followed closely behind at $1.79 billion. Both organizations, one expert explains, work with Federal Prisons Industries, Inc., "a government-owned corporation, also known as UNICOR, that serves as a contractor for prison labor," to put prisoners to work at some economically advantageous enterprise. Toiling for virtually no pay – 23 cents to $1.15 per hour – convicts produce goods from which private prisons and their parent corporations reap the profits. UNICOR reported in 2015 that it paid total wages of $33,538, combined, to all the laboring inmates it supplied. From those prisoners' efforts, UNICOR raked in $558 million in revenue. Collectively, private prisons constitute a $5 billion industry.[16]

If the inmates themselves are the engines driving the economic machine, private prisons must maintain sufficient quantities of prisoners to sustain the institutions' profitability. Under this business model, "[l]ocking up as many people as possible for as long as possible" enables private prisons to maximally exploit inmate labor and make such facilities as lucrative as possible. To that end, the "prison-industrial complex" relies overwhelmingly on African-American labor. Although blacks compose only 13 percent of the total US population, African-American men alone make up 37 percent of the male inmates across the country. In 2014, 2.7 percent of all black men – compared with 0.5 percent of white men – were sentenced to at least a year in a state or federal incarceration facility. Overall, African Americans are five times more likely than whites to serve time in prison, most likely for convictions on drug offenses. The war on drugs, launched in the 1980s, has disproportionately targeted minority communities and people of color. For drug offenses alone, blacks are imprisoned at rates ten times higher than for whites. The centrality of black labor to the prison-industrial complex holds true for Louisiana as it does for other states. According to one report, "About 5,000 black men from New Orleans" alone "are doing state prison time, compared with 400 white men from the city." Of "black men from New Orleans, one in 14 is behind bars." Moreover, "one in seven is either in prison, on parole or on probation." The prison-industrial complex cannot permit prisoner levels to drop too low without jeopardizing the bottom line, and Louisiana's court system has proven itself up to the challenge of supplying the requisite number of inmates, many of whom are recidivists. The Associated Press reports that "[o]ne in three people return to prison in Louisiana within three years of release," and within five years, "about half of the state's ex-convicts end up behind bars again." As one writer put it, "it's not a justice system, it's a business."[17]

However morally or ethically objectionable the business model, private, for-profit prisons are perfectly lawful. The Thirteenth Amendment to the US Constitution, ratified in December 1865, prohibited slavery or involuntary servitude "except as a punishment for crime whereof the party shall have been duly convicted." In other words, for convicts held in US prisons, slavery remains legal. The prison-industrial complex has not reintroduced slavery as it was known prior to its post-Civil War abolition, but, as many commentators have observed, it has created something akin to it. A small elite acquires wealth through the exertions of a captive and miserable labor force, one that, racially, is overwhelmingly black. This system of quasi-slavery is furthermore most prevalent in southern states: Louisiana, the former slaveholding Indian Territory now called Oklahoma, Alabama, Arkansas, and Mississippi. "It's not *quite* slavery, but it's close," wrote one investigator. "American slavery has returned with a new name." Another describes Louisiana's prison-industrial complex as the reincarnation of the nineteenth- and early twentieth-century convict lease system, while lawyer and civil rights advocate Michelle Alexander describes the mass incarceration of black Americans as a new form of Jim Crow-style oppression. A biased American criminal justice system sends one-third of all black people in the United States to prison at some point in their lives. Alexander describes such large-scale imprisonment of blacks as a new form of social control based on race, one that perpetuates the legal system of segregation enforced in the Jim Crow South. Her point is hard to contest.[18]

Accounting for fewer than 10 percent of the 2.3 million inmates incarcerated in the United States today, private prisons cannot shoulder the full burden of, or even take majority responsibility for, the modern-day phenomenon of mass incarceration in the United States. Rather, they mark merely the most recent innovation in a long pattern of black oppression that originated with the institution of slavery itself. Historians often think of slavery and imprisonment as sequential forms of racial and social control, with the eradication of bondage necessitating the creation of new, innovative institutional forms to perpetuate black subjugation. But as the story of Williams' gang reveals, slavery and black incarceration arose in concert and readily co-existed. The antebellum criminal justice system heard slaves' cases, punished those who were convicted, and often put them to work, a precursor to the carceral state of today. Carceral power has taken many different forms over time, but they all maintain a tradition of putting blacks (and other people of color) to work for someone else's benefit. Slavery, convict leasing, chain gangs, prison farms, mass incarceration, and the modern for-profit prison system all occupy space on a shared, thematically linked historical timeline. America laid centuries ago the racial foundation that undergirds the prison-industrial complex of today.[19]

The forces of capitalism have long enabled the drive to profit from black bodies in the United States. Many incarceration facilities in our own time are speculative ventures that depend upon an adequate supply of black workers. Officials transfer inmates from one penal institution to another to meet labor demands and make money through the appropriation of captive labor. In the basic contours of its operation, the system smacks of the antebellum slave trade in which William H. Williams participated. Williams, too, redistributed black labor to where it was most needed. The domestic slave trade conveyed more than one hundred thousand bondpeople for sale to New Orleans alone. Taking bondpeople gathered from throughout the Chesapeake, William H. Williams and his brother Thomas acquired vast fortunes through the traffic in enslaved laborers. Their countless customers then enriched themselves by the wealth extracted from their captives' toil.

In the late nineteenth century, decades after federal action terminated Williams' slave-trading operations in the District of Columbia, Washington's slave-trading past entered the hazy realm of historical memory. Some white residents looked back upon the years of bondage with nostalgia. In 1883, an elderly storekeeper located "only a block or so away from the site" of a former slave jail fondly reminisced about the "wonderful stories . . . told about the old Washington slave-pen." According to one local newspaper in 1891, "Many an old resident has paused while hunting skylarks and snipe in the neighborhood of the Centre Market" to summon recollections from the neglected recesses of the mind of "the dusky lines of slaves moving south by way of the Long Bridge to the plaintive music of quaint old hymns, with hands bound together by twos from the slave-pens of Marse Williams." As the twentieth century approached, the Yellow House had not passed into lore or become wholly the stuff of legend, but Washington whites had already stripped it of the horrors encountered by those captives who passed in and out of its gates.[20]

In a creative re-writing of Washington's history, at least some city residents voiced vehement denials of the capital's role in the slave trade. As one District white recorded in 1897, "Ninety-nine hundredths of the people of Washington" still "think . . . that there were slave pens on every square." He took umbrage with their recollections and disputed the historical fact that the District was indeed "a veritable hotbed of slave traders," dismissing such a notion as "wide of the truth." The chronicler conceded that "[t]here were a few 'nigger' jails here, the principal one being near B and 8th streets" – Williams' Yellow House – but rejected the notion that "any considerable dealing in human flesh" took place. Willful misremembrance among whites, consistent with the Lost Cause and a defensive, parochial pride, had begun to set in. Several elderly inhabitants of the nation's capital by the turn of the century erased the city's slaveholding past altogether. They claimed that they "never saw a 'gang in chains driven through the streets.'" They described the "clanking chains, shuffling and weary limbs, downcast eyes, and the pitiful hopelessness of the bondman on his way to the southern cane and cotton field" as foreign to their gaze, even as they painted a verbal portrait of the somber scene with uncanny accuracy. One old-timer betrayed the collective thrust of white reminiscences, however, when he added that the only slaves "I ever heard of as having been sold out of the District . . . deserve[d] it."[21]

Even while slavery still thrived in Washington, one "dingy group of buildings with a brick wall around them," formerly used as a pen, was "tumbling into ruin" from neglect and "disuse." Williams' slave pen would not slowly erode away in a similar fashion. With the end of the slave trade in the District, Washington's slave pens were transformed, repurposed, or replaced. Originally erected among a grove of locust trees on a city block that for years had been planted in flora, the Yellow House had conquered nature. After the facility closed, the site quickly reverted to a garden from which a man named Hughes sold flowers up until the Civil War. Urban development would soon claim the location once again. By 1902, reported one city paper, "[t]he old slave pen on 8th street southwest below B street" had "long since [been] covered with dwellings." In an ironic twist, by 1899 a different former D.C. slave prison became the site of a black church. Other incarceration facilities came to less glorious ends. "[S]ome of the old slave pens which have fallen into decay," even those "within the very shadows of the Capitol," reported the *Washington Post* in 1924, "are used now for the storage of rubbish and ashes." It was only a matter of time before the remains of all Washington slave jails vanished from the capital's landscape. Within the first few decades of the twentieth century, as the last firsthand observers of the pens departed this earth, the memory of them faded as well.[22]

But the forgotten slave pens of Washington, D.C., merit rediscovery. In our own time, a different form of the slave trade persists, funneling prisoners, disproportionately black in their numbers, to institutions that deploy their labor for financial gain. As with the slave trade, prisons engage in a form of economic speculation grounded in African-American bodies and the shipment of captive workforces to locations where the demand for labor is high. The modern-day exploitation of black inmates' labor remains a thriving business in which the law has again been complicit. Steel bars of the prison-industrial complex have replaced the clanking iron chains of the slave coffle, but now as then, black captives remain similarly shackled.

The Williams' Gang Slaves

Bondperson	Age[a]	Height	Color	County	Crime	Date entered Virginia pen	Owner	Valuation ($)
Men								
Albert Smith	23–24	5'7"	dark	Cumberland	burglary	8/20/1838	Moses A. Smith	950
Arthur Carr/Carey	16–18	n/a	n/a	Norfolk	burglary	3/2/1839	Virginia Carey	1,000
John Cooper	14–20	6'0"	dark	Norfolk	burglary	3/2/1839	Dennis Dawley	800
Landon Carter	27–35	5'8"	dark	Prince William	arson	3/25/1839	William Bowen	900
John [Henkins?]	20–34	5'5½"	dark	Jefferson	attempted rape	3/26/1839	Humphrey Keyes	700
John Johnson[b]	20–30	5'7"	dark	Spotsylvania	attempted murder	5/13/1839	Mrs. Christian Bankhead	1,000
Thomas/Tom Jarrett/Noel	23–24	5'7½"	dark	Buckingham	murder	6/12/1839	Thomas G. Noel	700
Harrison Redd	19–20	5'8½"	dark	Fredericksburg	burglary	6/14/1839	William Redd	1,000
Henry Gordon/Godard	20–21	5'8½"	dark	Fredericksburg	burglary	6/14/1839	John/Philip Crutchfield	1,000
John Carter	28–42	5'5½"	dark	Fredericksburg	burglary	6/14/1839	Samuel Alsop	900
Nelson Nann	27–30	5'7"	dark	Fredericksburg	burglary	6/14/1839	Samuel Alsop	900
Phil Harris	20–36	5'5½"	dark	Fredericksburg	burglary	6/14/1839	Samuel Alsop	1,500
John/Jack Johnson	23–40	5'2"	dark	Charles City	murder	6/20/1839	Benskin Hopkins	900
Stephen Lewis/Green	22–23	5'3"	dark	Louisa	burglary	2/4/1840	Martha A. Johnson	850
George Devinport	30–35	5'7"	dark	King and Queen	burglary	4/8/1840	John Mann	550
Nelson Harris/Judy	30–45	5'6½"	dark	Rockbridge	burglary	4/14/1840	Jacob Judy	250
James/Jim Judy	23	5'7½"	dark	Rockbridge	burglary	4/14/1840	Jacob Judy	750
James/Jim Brown	23	5'6"	dark	Greensville	attempted murder	5/14/1840	Susan Shepherd	700
Alfred Taylor	25–29	6'2"	dark	Fairfax	conspiracy & insurrection	5/21/1840	Dennis Johnston	900
Henry Burgess	21	5'9"	dark	Loudoun	burglary	6/15/1840	Townsend McVeigh	530
Ned Whiten	22–25	5'6"	dark	Lancaster	burglary	7/3/1840	William Jones	600

Women	Age[a]	Height	Color	County	Crime	Date	Claimant	Value
Jane Crump	15–20	5'4½"	dark	Spotsylvania	arson	10/27/1838	John Crump	700
Nancy Custis	16–20	5'3½"	dark	Accomack	arson	3/2/1839	H. B. Custis	700
Malinda Newsom	20–22	5'4½"	dark	Southampton	murder	3/5/1840	Thomas Newsom	450
Charlotte Smith	16–18	4'11"	dark	Clarke	arson	4/15/1840	Eliza Pine	500
Arena Williamson	33–40	5'7½"	dark	Greensville	attempted murder	5/14/1840	Martha Madell	375
Nan/Nancy Smith/Via	33–38	4'10"	mulatto	Patrick	attempted murder	7/15/1840	Elizabeth Via	380

[a] When the enslaved prisoners' ages were not consistent across the records, a range of ages appears.

[b] Italicized names indicate those enslaved criminals incarcerated in the Louisiana State Penitentiary from 1845 to 1857.

Sources: "A List of Slaves and Free persons of color received into the Penitentiary of Virginia for sale and transportation from the 25th June 1816 to the 1st February 1842," Auditor of Public Accounts, Condemned Blacks Executed or Transported, Records – Condemned Slaves, Court Orders, and Valuations, 1858–1865, Misc. Reel 2555, Frames 996–997, LVA; Outward Slave Manifest, Alexandria, October 9, 1840 (*Uncas*), New-York Historical Society, MS569, Slavery Collection, nyhs_sc_b-05_f-16_015–001, http://cdm16694.contentdm.oclc.org/cdm/compoundobject/collection/p15052coll5/id/24223/rec/6 (accessed February 25, 2015); Report of the Day Police, November 1, 1840, New Orleans (La.) Third Municipality Guard, Mayor's Book, 1838–1850, vol. 2, p. 200, 89–214, TKD205 M, NOPL; *Nailor v. Williams* (1869), Records of the United States Supreme Court, Box 624, Case File #5032, NA.

Sample Slaving Voyages of William H. Williams and his Associates (N=46)

Date	Type of vessel	Ship name	Burthen (tons)	Master	Port of departure	Port of arrival	Shipper/owner
Feb. 4, 1828	brig	Ajax	126	Robert H. Banks	Norfolk	New Orleans	William H. Williams, to James B. Diggs
Mar. 5, 1828	schooner	Maria Ann	85	L. Crocker	Mobile	New Orleans	William H. Williams
Apr. 30, 1828	steamboat	Fair Star	n/a	Swiler	New Orleans	Mobile	William H. Williams
Oct. 18, 1828	n/a	Jefferson	434	Thomas J. Ivy	Norfolk	New Orleans	William H. Williams, to James B. Diggs
Dec. 1, 1836	brig	Tribune	161	Samuel C. Boush	Georgetown	New Orleans	William H. Williams, to Edward Williams
May 4, 1837	steamboat	Ouachita	160	Samuel B. Griffin	Mobile	Pontchartrain	William H. Williams
Nov. 3, 1838	brig	Uncas	n/a	Nathaniel Boush	Alexandria	New Orleans	William H. Williams, to Thomas Williams, Messrs. Durrive & LeBlanc, Messrs. J. H. Leverich & Co., Messrs. Campronica & Gerand
Apr. 9, 1839	brig	Edwin	133	Henry Fitzgerald	Baltimore	Savannah	Thomas N. Davis, to John Boston
Nov. 19, 1839	brig	Uncas	155	Nathaniel Boush	Alexandria	New Orleans	William H. Williams, to A. N. Wallis & Co., N. Boush, James F. Purvis, William G. Slade, Thomas Williams, Samuel F. Richards
Nov./Dec. 1839	steamboat	Seabrook	n/a	n/a	Savannah	Jacksonville	Thomas N. Davis
Mar. 27, 1840	brig	Architect	114	S. A. Gray	Baltimore	New Orleans	Ebenezer Rodbird, to Thomas Williams
Apr. 7, 1840	steamboat	Forrester	n/a	E. W[illegible]	Savannah	Jacksonville	Thomas N. Davis
Nov. 4, 1840	brig	Uncas	154	Nathaniel Boush	Mobile	New Orleans	William H. Williams
Nov. 28, 1840	n/a	Katharine Jackson	n/a	n/a	n/a	New Orleans	Ebenezer Rodbird, to William H. Williams
Nov. 4, 1843	n/a	Alexandria	491	Charles W. Turner	Alexandria	New Orleans	Ebenezer Rodbird, to William H. Williams, Robert Daily
Dec. 20, 1843	n/a	Pioneer	523	John C. Grissom	Alexandria	New Orleans	Thomas Williams, to William H. Williams

Date	Type	Vessel	Tons	Master	From	To	Owner/Shipper
Nov. 21, 1844	barque	Colonel Howard	332	Samuel H.G. Prentiss	Baltimore	New Orleans	William H. Williams, owner; William Harker, shipper
Dec. 20, 1844	brig	Victorine	239	J. B. Tanner	Baltimore	New Orleans	Thomas Williams, shipper, to William H. Williams
Feb. 18, 1845	barque	Nancy W. Jackson Stevens	346	J. J. Stevens	Baltimore	New Orleans	Ebenezer Rodbird, shipper
Mar. 1, 1845	brig	Victorine	239	Thomas D. Davis	Baltimore	New Orleans	Ebenezer Rodbird, shipper
Mar. 22, 1845	barque	Home	377	W. J. Watts	Baltimore	New Orleans	Ebenezer Rodbird, shipper
Apr. 15, 1845	brig	Kirkwood	211	John F. Haynie	Baltimore	New Orleans	Ebenezer Rodbird, shipper
May 14, 1845	brig	Victorine	239	Thomas D. Davis	Baltimore	New Orleans	Ebenezer Rodbird, shipper, to William H. Williams
Nov. 29, 1845	brig	St. Mary	188	R. D. White	Baltimore	New Orleans	Thomas Williams, shipper
Dec. 1, 1845	brig	Jno. A. Lancaster	159	Jesse Loveland	Richmond	New Orleans	William H. Williams
Jan. 14, 1846	brig	Kirkwood	211	John F. Haynie	Baltimore	New Orleans	William H. Williams
Feb. 11, 1846	brig	Architect	n/a	Gray	New Orleans	Baltimore	William H. Williams
Feb. 21, 1846	brig	General Pinckney	194	George Hobbs	Baltimore	New Orleans	Ebenezer Rodbird, shipper
Oct. 28, 1846	barque	Hermitage	317	John H. Fry	Baltimore	New Orleans	Thomas Williams
Dec. 31, 1846	brig	Victorine	239	George Hobbs	Baltimore	New Orleans	Ebenezer Rodbird, shipper, to William H. Williams, Horatio Harbin
Jan. 19, 1847	brig	General Pinckney	194	J. R. Gale	Baltimore	New Orleans	Thomas Williams
Feb. 16, 1847	brig	Zoe	196	William Phillips	Baltimore	New Orleans	Thomas Williams
Mar. 27, 1847	barque	Phoenix	244	Nathaniel Boush	Baltimore	New Orleans	Ebenezer Rodbird
Oct. 18, 1847	barque	Bachelor	277	Hiram Horton	Richmond	New Orleans	Thomas Williams
Oct. 26, 1847	barque	Kirkwood	343	Hugh Martin	Baltimore	New Orleans	Ebenezer Rodbird, to Thomas Williams
Nov. 11, 1847	brig	Osprey	236	Gibbons	Baltimore	New Orleans	Ebenezer Rodbird, shipper
Nov. 17, 1847	barque	Phoenix	240	Nathaniel Boush	Richmond	New Orleans	Thomas Williams
May 13, 1848	brig	Union	180	Edward Hooper	Baltimore	New Orleans	William H. Williams
Oct. 9, 1848	brig	Union	180	Edward Hooper	Baltimore	New Orleans	Thomas Williams
Oct. 28, 1848	schooner	Henry A. Barling	161	Haynie	Baltimore	New Orleans	William S. Campbell, to Thomas Williams
Nov. 18, 1848	barque	Elizabeth	230	Alexander Jones	Baltimore	New Orleans	Ebenezer Rodbird, shipper, to Thomas Williams

(continued)

Date	Type of vessel	Ship name	Burthen (tons)	Master	Port of departure	Port of arrival	Shipper/ owner
Dec. 16, 1848	brig	*Union*	180	Edward Hooper	Baltimore	New Orleans	Ebenezer Rodbird, shipper, to Thomas Williams
May 1, 1849	n/a	*California*	n/a	Reynolds	Mobile	New Orleans	William H. Williams
Nov. 17, 1849	brig	*Union*	180	John H. Goodmanson	Baltimore	New Orleans	Ebenezer Rodbird, to Thomas Williams
Jan. 21, 1850	barque	*Southerner*	338	Edward Hooper	Baltimore	New Orleans	Ebenezer Rodbird, to Thomas Williams
Nov. 28, 1850	n/a	*Narragansett*	420	Edmonds	Baltimore	New Orleans	William H. Williams

APPENDIX C

Slave Data from Sample Slaving Voyages (N=46)

Ship	# Male slaves	Age range, male slaves	Average age, male slaves	# Female slaves	Age range, female slaves	Average age, female slaves	Total # slaves[a]	Age range	Average age
Ajax	6	1-25	16.0	3	12-18	15.7	10[b]	1-25	15.9
Maria Ann	0	-	-	1	19	19.0	1	19	19.0
Fair Star	1	1	1.0	2	12-14	13.0	3	1-14	9.0
Jefferson	7	15-23	19.9	3	16-17	16.3	10	15-23	18.8
Tribune	19	16-25	21.1	11	15-20	17.4	30	15-25	19.7
Ouachita	1	24	24.0	0	-	-	1	24	24.0
Uncas	24	15-30	20.9	23	11-30	18.7	47	11-30	20.0
Edwin	7	19-26	23.1	2	19-45	32.0	9	19-45	25.1
Uncas	25	3-30	21.6	24	6 mos.-29	16.7	49[c]	6 mos.-30	19.2
Seabrook	8	17-26	22.1	2	19-45	32.0	10	17-45	24.3
Architect	8	11-32	22.5	4	18-20	18.8	12[c]	11-32	21.3
Forrester	8	15-57	25.5	2	10-16	13.0	10	10-57	23.0
Uncas	16	2-50	18.8	26	2 mos.-50	17.1	42	2 mos.-50	17.8
Katharine Jackson	1	20	20.0	0	-	-	1	20	20.0
Alexandria	19	9-30	21.4	24	1 mo.-28	17.4	43	1 mo.-30	19.2
Pioneer	5	9-18	13.2	2	15-17	16.0	7	9-18	14.0
Colonel Howard	12	2 mos.-40	15.5	10	2-40	19.8	22	2 mos.-40	17.4
Victorine	5	11-26	20.4	3	8 mos.-26	15.6	8	8 mos.-26	17.3
Nancy W. Stevens	3	14-20	18.0	3	4-25	16.7	6	4-25	17.6
Victorine	5	3-35	18.8	17	infant[3d]-24	13.2	22	infant-35	14.5
Home	10	18-45	25.5	12	3-35	20.1	22	3-45	20.7
Kirkwood	17	19-50	24.9	6	20-30	23.5	23	19-50	24.5

(continued)

Ship	# Male slaves	Age range, male slaves	Average age, male slaves	# Female slaves	Age range, female slaves	Average age, female slaves	Total # slaves[a]	Age range	Average age
Victorine	12	infant[d]-25	16.3	11	12-48	20.8	23	infant-48	18.5
St. Mary	11	10-30	22.8	10	infant[d]-48	20.6	21[e]	infant-48	21.6
Jno. A. Lancaster	1	30	30.0	1	35	35.0	4[f]	30-35	32.5
Kirkwood	3	19-23	20.7	0	-	-	3	19-23	20.7
Architect	4	17-35	26.8	1	23	23.0	5	17-35	26.0
General Pinckney	5	16-22	19.6	7	14-30	18.4	13[g]	10 mos.-30	17.5
Hermitage	10	21-28	23.4	10	18-22	19.7	20	18-28	21.6
Victorine	22	8-32	20.4	22	6-30	16.4	45[h]	6-32	18.4
General Pinckney	9	11-38	18.7	14	2-40	16.6	25[i]	2-40	17.4
Zoe	12	8-30	18.6	5	10-20	15.4	18[b]	8-30	17.6
Phoenix	6	17-24	20.8	5	11-20	15.4	11	11-24	18.4
Bachelor	1	24	24.0	0	-	-	1	24	24.0
Kirkwood	16	20 mos.-26	20.9	10	4 mos.-28	18.4	27[j]	3 mos.-28	19.2
Osprey	1	16	16.0	4	15-35	25.8	5	15-35	23.8
Phoenix	1	15	15.0	1	17	17.0	3[b]	15-17	16.0
Union	3	23-45	30.3	3	18-40	27.7	6	18-45	29.0
Union	30	20 mos.-33	21.3	17	8-25	16.2	57[k]	20 mos.-33	19.5
Henry A. Barling	3	20-33	27.0	5	15-22	17.8	8	15-33	21.3
Elizabeth	8	6-30	17.6	7	infant-28	16[d]	16[i]	infant-30	16.9
Union	24	15 mos.-26	19.7	11	10-28	18.0	35	15 mos.-28	19.2
California	1	4	4.0	3	11-32	20.0	4	4-32	16.0
Union	11	infant-22	17.4	7[l]	13-23	17.0	18	infant-23	17.2

Southerner	10	18-23	20.6	6	17-23	19.5	16	17-23	20.2
Narragansett	6	4-28	13.8	4	3-24	14.0	10	3-28	13.9
Total	417			344			782		
Average	9.07			7.32			17		

[a] Vessels often carried slaves belonging to different owners and consigned to different individuals. The total number of slaves conveyed on a given voyage typically exceeds the number indicated in the table, which counts only those bondpeople transported by William H. Williams or his associates.

[b] Total includes one infant or child for whom no data is given.

[c] One child was born in transit, adding to the total listed.

[d] Infants identified by sex have been given the maximum age of one for the purpose of these calculations.

[e] No age was listed for four total captives.

[f] Total includes two children for whom no data is given.

[g] Total includes one ten-month-old infant for whom no data is given.

[h] Total includes one infant four months old.

[i] Total includes twin infants for whom no data is given.

[j] Total includes one infant for whom no sex is given.

[k] Total includes ten additional slaves for whom the data was illegible in the manifest.

[l] Total includes one woman for whom no age is given.

Notes

INTRODUCTION: THE SLAVE DEPOT OF WASHINGTON, D.C.

1. Glenwood Cemetery Records, Washington, D.C., 1854 to 2013, plat book, vol. C, p. 64; Records of the District Courts of the United States, Old Series Case Files, 1801–1878, Entry 115, Box 114, Folder 3969, NA.
2. Chris Simkins, "US Government Recognizes Site of Former Slave Prison," VOA News, January 11, 2017, www.voanews.com/a/us-government-recognizes-site-former-slave-prison/3673046.html (accessed January 19, 2017).
3. Zeba Blay, "Why Michelle Obama's 'I Live in a House Built by Slaves' Quote Is Vital," *Huffington Post,* July 26, 2016, www.huffingtonpost.com/entry/why-michelle-obamas-i-li ve-in-a-house-built-by-slaves-quote-is-vital_us_57976fbce4b02d5d5ed2dbeb (accessed January 19, 2018); Julie Hirschfeld Davis, "Yes, Slaves Did Help Build the White House," *New York Times,* July 26, 2016, www.nytimes.com/2016/07/27/us/politics/mic helle-obama-white-house-slavery.html; Tingba Muhammad, "The Congo of America: The Slave Trade of Washington, D.C.," www.finalcall.com/artman/publish//prin ter_9038.shtml (accessed August 12, 2014); Jesse J. Holland, *Black Men Built the Capital: Discovering African-American History in and around Washington, D.C.* (Guilford, Conn.: Globe Pequot Press, 2007). Important works documenting this new history of slaves' roles in US history include Sharon Ann Murphy, "Securing Human Property: Slavery, Life Insurance, and Industrialization in the Upper South," *Journal of the Early Republic* 25 (Winter 2005): 615–652; Bonnie Martin, "Slavery's Invisible Engine: Mortgaging Human Property," *Journal of Southern History* 76 (November 2010): 817–866; Walter Johnson, *River of Dark Dreams: Slavery and Empire in the Cotton Kingdom* (Cambridge, Mass.: Belknap Press of Harvard University Press, 2013); Edward E. Baptist, *The Half Has Never Been Told: Slavery and the Making of American Capitalism* (New York: Basic Books, 2014); Sven Beckert, *Empire of Cotton: A Global History* (New York: Vintage, 2015); Calvin Schermerhorn, *The Business of Slavery and the Rise of American Capitalism, 1815–1860* (New Haven: Yale University Press, 2015); Sven Beckert and Seth Rockman, eds., *Slavery's Capitalism* (Philadelphia: University of Pennsylvania Press, 2016); Craig Steven Wilder, *Ebony and Ivy: Race, Slavery, and the Troubled History of America's Universities* (New York: Bloomsbury, 2013); Jennifer Oast, *Institutional Slavery: Slaveholding Churches,*

Schools, Colleges, and Businesses in Virginia, 1680–1860 (New York: Cambridge University Press, 2016); Alfred L. Brophy, *University, Court, and Slave: Pro-Slavery Thought in Southern Colleges and Courts and the Coming of Civil War* (New York: Oxford University Press, 2016).

4. Calvin Schermerhorn, "The Coastwise Slave Trade and a Mercantile Community of Interest," in *Slavery's Capitalism*, ed. Sven Beckert and Seth Rockman (Philadelphia: University of Pennsylvania Press, 2016), 210–211. On the transition from the international to the domestic slave trade, see Adam Rothman, "The Domestication of the Slave Trade in the United States," in *The Chattel Principle: Internal Slave Trades in the Americas*, ed. Walter Johnson (New Haven: Yale University Press, 2004), 32–54.

5. Baptist, *The Half Has Never Been Told*, 173, 175, 179; William Jay, *A View of the Action of the Federal Government, in Behalf of Slavery* (Utica, NY: J. C. Jackson, 1844), 41 (first through third quotations); *The Emancipator*, October 18, 1838; Edward Ingersoll, comp., *A Digest of the Laws of the United States of America, from March 4th, 1789, to May 15th, 1820* (Philadelphia: James Maxwell, 1821), 799–800; Schermerhorn, "Coastwise Slave Trade," 216.

6. Baptist, *The Half Has Never Been Told*, 84; William Calderhead, "The Role of the Professional Slave Trader in a Slave Economy: Austin Woolfolk, a Case Study," *Civil War History* 23 (September 1977), 197, 200–201; Steven Deyle, *Carry Me Back: The Domestic Slave Trade in American Life* (New York: Oxford University Press, 2005), 98, 315n14.

7. Frederic Bancroft, *Slave Trading in the Old South*, introduction by Michael Tadman (1931; Columbia: University of South Carolina Press, 1996), 45; Herman Freudenberger and Jonathan B. Pritchett, "The Domestic United States Slave Trade: New Evidence," *Journal of Interdisciplinary History* 21 (Winter 1991), 459; Baptist, *The Half Has Never Been Told*, 193–194; Schermerhorn, "Coastwise Slave Trade," 211; Mary Beth Corrigan, "Imaginary Cruelties?: A History of the Slave Trade in Washington, D.C.," *Washington History* 13 (Fall/Winter 2001/2002), 7; Jay, *View of the Action*, 36; House of Representatives, *Register of Debates*, 23rd Cong., 2d sess., 1133 (quotation); Executive Committee of the American Anti-Slavery Society, *Slavery and the Internal Slave Trade in the United States of North America; Being Replies to Questions Transmitted by the Committee of the British and Foreign Anti-slavery Society, for the Abolition of Slavery and the Slave Trade throughout the World* (London: Thomas Ward, 1841), 205, 207–208; *Daily National Intelligencer* (Washington, D.C.), September 7, 1840.

8. *Washington Times*, September 29, 1895; Charles Noble, "Memories of Washington before the Civil War," *Washington Post*, January 31, 1926; Worthington G. Snethen, *The Black Code of the District of Columbia in Force September 1st, 1848* (New York: William Harned, 1848), 43 (first quotation); *The Emancipator*, October 18, 1838 (second quotation). Other references to the $400 annual fee may be found in House of Representatives, *Register of Debates*, 23rd Cong., 2d sess., 1134; Jay, *View of the Action*, 40; William Wells Brown, *A Description of William Wells Brown's Original Panoramic Views of the Scenes in the Life of an American Slave, from his Birth in Slavery to his Death or his Escape to his First Home of Freedom on British Soil* (London: Charles Gilpin, 1849), 12; Deyle, *Carry Me Back*, 157, 198.

9. House of Representatives, *Register of Debates*, 23rd Cong., 2d sess., 1134 (first and second quotations); *The Emancipator*, October 18, 1838 (third through sixth quotations).

10. David L. Child, *The Despotism of Freedom; or the Tyranny and Cruelty of American Republican Slave-Masters, Shown To Be The Worst in the World; in a Speech, Delivered at the First Anniversary of the New England Anti-Slavery Society, 1833* (Boston: Boston Young Men's Anti-Slavery Association, 1833), 51 (first quotation), 14 (second and third quotations); Brown, *A Description of William Wells Brown's Original Panoramic Views*, 9; House of Representatives, *Register of Debates*, 23rd Cong., 2d sess., 1134 (fourth quotation). See also *The Liberator* (Boston), March 31, 1843.

11. House of Representatives, *Register of Debates*, 19th Cong., 2d sess., 564 (first and second quotations); House of Representatives, *Register of Debates*, 20th Cong., 2d sess., 178 (third and fourth quotations).

12. Freudenberger and Pritchett, "The Domestic United States Slave Trade," 463, 465; Baptist, *The Half Has Never Been Told*, 175; Wendell Holmes Stephenson, *Isaac Franklin: Slave Trader and Planter of the Old South* (Baton Rouge: Louisiana State University Press, 1938), 52; Schermerhorn, "Coastwise Slave Trade," 216, 209 (quotation), 217; Walter Johnson, *Soul by Soul: Life inside the Antebellum Slave Market* (Cambridge, Mass.: Harvard University Press, 1999).

13. Johnson, *River of Dark Dreams*, 2, 403, 84; Baptist, *The Half Has Never Been Told*, xxiii, 2, 175, 256; Erin M. Greenwald and Joshua D. Rothman, "New Orleans Should Acknowledge its Lead Role in the Slave Trade," NOLA.com, February 19, 2016, www .nola.com/opinions/index.ssf/2016/02/new_orleans_history_slave_trad.html (accessed February 20, 2016); Schermerhorn, "Coastwise Slave Trade," 223, 211; Andrew J. Torget, *Seeds of Empire: Cotton, Slavery, and the Transformation of the Texas Borderlands, 1800–1850* (Chapel Hill: University of North Carolina Press, 2015), 157 (quotation); Vernon Valentine Palmer, *Through the Codes Darkly: Slave Law and Civil Law in Louisiana* (Clark, N.J.: The Lawbook Exchange, 2012), 159; Calvin Schermerhorn, "Slave Trading in a Republic of Credit: Financial Architecture of the US Slave Market, 1815–1840," *Slavery and Abolition* 36, no. 4 (2015), 586, 597; Steven Deyle, "Rethinking the Slave Trade: Slave Traders and the Market Revolution in the South," in *The Old South's Modern Worlds: Slavery, Region, and Nation in the Age of Progress*, ed. L. Diane Barnes, Brian Schoen, and Frank Towers (New York: Oxford University Press, 2011), 105; Joshua D. Rothman, "The Contours of Cotton Capitalism: Speculation, Slavery, and Economic Panic in Mississippi, 1832–1841," in *Slavery's Capitalism*, ed. Sven Beckert and Seth Rockman (Philadelphia: University of Pennsylvania Press, 2016), 127.

14. *Mobile Journal*, reprinted in *Pensacola Gazette*, November 7, 1840; *Daily Picayune* (New Orleans), February 28, 1841; *Times-Picayune* (New Orleans), October 31, 1840. The precise number of slaves Williams sold during his career is impossible to determine from surviving records, but notarized sales from New Orleans alone reveal close to one thousand.

15. Works devoted to specific slave traders include Wendell Holmes Stephenson, *Isaac Franklin: Slave Trader and Planter of the Old South* (Baton Rouge: Louisiana State University Press, 1938); Isabell Howell, "John Armfield, Slave-trader," *Tennessee Historical Quarterly* 2 (March 1943): 3–29; Richard Tansey, "Bernard Kendig and the

New Orleans Slave Trade," *Louisiana History* 23 (Spring 1982): 159–178; Kari J. Winter, *The American Dreams of John B. Prentis, Slave Trader* (Athens: University of Georgia Press, 2011); Daniel L. Schafer, *Zephaniah Kingsley Jr. and the Atlantic World: Slave Trader, Plantation Owner, Emancipator* (Gainesville: University Press of Florida, 2013); Hank Trent, *The Secret Life of Bacon Tait, a White Slave Trader Married to a Free Woman of Color* (Baton Rouge: Louisiana State University Press, 2017). Works that mention William H. Williams, however briefly, include Bancroft, *Slave Trading in the Old South,* 274–275; Judith Kelleher Schafer, "The Long Arm of the Law: Slavery and the Supreme Court in Antebellum Louisiana, 1809–1862" (Ph.D. diss., Tulane University, 1985), 411n42; Philip J. Schwarz, *Twice Condemned: Slaves and the Criminal Laws of Virginia, 1705–1865* (Baton Rouge: Louisiana State University Press, 1988), 28n42; Judith Kelleher Schafer, *Slavery, the Civil Law, and the Supreme Court of Louisiana* (Baton Rouge: Louisiana State University Press, 1994), 163n20, 164n21; Stanley Harrold, *Subversives: Antislavery Community in Washington, D.C., 1828–1865* (Baton Rouge: Louisiana State University Press, 2003), 54, 104, 108–111, 209; Deyle, *Carry Me Back,* 121; Philip J. Schwarz, *Slave Laws in Virginia* (Athens: University of Georgia Press, 2010), 97–98, 111, 214nn2-3; Tom Calarco, et al., *Places of the Underground Railroad: A Geographical Guide* (Santa Barbara, Calif.: Greenwood, 2011), 350; Jefferson Morley, *Snow-Storm in August: Washington City, Francis Scott Key, and the Forgotten Race Riot of 1835* (New York: Nan A. Talese/Doubleday, 2012), 12; Kenneth J. Winkle, *Lincoln's Citadel: The Civil War in Washington, D.C.* (New York: Norton, 2013), 15–16; Marc Leepson, *What So Proudly We Hailed: Francis Scott Key, a Life* (New York: Palgrave Macmillan, 2014), 17; Jeff Forret, *Slave against Slave: Plantation Violence in the Old South* (Baton Rouge: Louisiana State University Press, 2015), 138, 142–143; Schermerhorn, *Business of Slavery,* 156, 170; Padraig Riley, *Slavery and the Democratic Conscience: Political Life in Jeffersonian America* (Philadelphia: University of Pennsylvania Press, 2016), 126; Trent, *Secret Life of Bacon Tait,* 88. Schafer, *Slavery, the Civil Law, and the Supreme Court of Louisiana,* 163n20, contains four errors in a single footnote: (1) Williams purchased twenty-seven enslaved convicts, not twenty-four; (2) his jail sentence was an alternative to the fine, not a penalty to endure until he paid it; (3) the Louisiana Supreme Court found in his favor in 1842 and did not rule against him, as Schafer states, in both 1842 and 1844; and (4) the slaves were indeed sold in Louisiana, but the proceeds went to Williams and not the state and the informer.

16. The first significant look at the domestic slave trade after the original publication of Frederic Bancroft's *Slave Trading in the Old South* in 1931 was Michael Tadman, *Speculators and Slaves: Masters, Traders, and Slaves in the Old South* (Madison: University of Wisconsin Press, 1989). More than a decade passed before the appearance of a quick succession of works on the topic. Those included Walter Johnson, *Soul by Soul: Life inside the Antebellum Slave Market* (Cambridge, Mass.: Harvard University Press, 1999); Robert H. Gudmestad, *A Troublesome Commerce: The Transformation of the Interstate Slave Trade* (Baton Rouge: Louisiana State University Press, 2003); Walter Johnson, ed., *The Chattel Principle: Internal Slave Trades in the Americas* (New Haven: Yale University Press, 2004); Deyle, *Carry Me Back;* David L. Lightner, *Slavery and the Commerce Power: How the Struggle*

against the Interstate Slave Trade Led to the Civil War (New Haven: Yale University Press, 2006). On the domestic slave trade's role in the emergence of American capitalism, see Johnson, *River of Dark Dreams*; Baptist, *The Half Has Never Been Told*; Beckert, *Empire of Cotton*; Schermerhorn, *The Business of Slavery*; Beckert and Rockman, eds., *Slavery's Capitalism.*

17. On the Middle Passage, see, for example, Marcus Rediker, *The Slave Ship: A Human History* (New York: Viking, 2007); Stephanie E. Smallwood, *Saltwater Slavery: A Middle Passage from Africa to American Diaspora* (Cambridge, Mass.: Harvard University Press, 2007); Sowande' M. Mustakeem, *Slavery at Sea: Terror, Sex, and Sickness in the Middle Passage* (Urbana: University of Illinois Press, 2016); Sean M. Kelley, *The Voyage of the Slave Ship Hare: A Journey into Captivity from Sierra Leone to South Carolina* (Chapel Hill: University of North Carolina Press, 2016). For courtroom battles inspired by transatlantic slavers, see, among other works, Jonathan M. Bright, *Dark Places of the Earth: The Voyage of the Slave Ship Antelope* (New York: Liveright, 2015); Marcus Rediker, *The Amistad Rebellion: An Atlantic Odyssey of Slavery and Freedom* (New York: Viking, 2012). See also Sylviane A. Diouf, *Dreams of Africa in Alabama: The Slave Ship Clotilda and the Story of the Last Africans Brought to America* (New York: Oxford University Press, 2007).

18. *Edenton Gazette* (N.C.), March 16, 1831; *Newbern Spectator* (N.C.), April 4, 1834; Schermerhorn, *Business of Slavery*, 182; Jay, *View of the Action*, 26; Ralph Clayton, *Cash for Blood: The Baltimore to New Orleans Domestic Slave Trade* (Westminster, Md.: Heritage Books, 2007), 71–73; Schermerhorn, "Coastwise Slave Trade," 221; Arthur T. Downey, *The Creole Affair: The Slave Rebellion that Led the US and Great Britain to the Brink of War* (Lanham, Md.: Rowman and Littlefield, 2014); Phillip Troutman, "Grapevine in the Slave Market: African American Geopolitical Literacy and the 1841 *Creole* Revolt," in *The Chattel Principle: Internal Slave Trades in the Americas*, ed. Walter Johnson (New Haven: Yale University Press, 2004), 203–233. In one famous maritime incident, almost eighty fugitives, aided by white accomplices, attempted their escape from slavery in 1848 aboard the schooner *Pearl*. They set out from Washington, D.C., and down the Potomac River, but uncooperative weather frustrated their progress. The vessel was soon overtaken and directed back to Washington. The slaves were returned to their owners, and a pair of white men spent four years in jail for their complicity in the affair. President Millard Fillmore pardoned them. See Josephine F. Pacheco, *The Pearl: A Failed Slave Escape on the Potomac* (Chapel Hill: University of North Carolina Press, 2005); Mary Kay Ricks, *Escape on the Pearl* (New York: HarperCollins, 2007).

19. *Acts Passed at the First Session of the Ninth Legislature of the State of Louisiana; Begun and Held in the City of New-Orleans, on Monday, the Eighth Day of December, in the Year of Our Lord One Thousand Eight Hundred and Twenty Eight, and of the Independence of the United States of America, the Fifty-Second* (New Orleans: John Gibson, 1829), 40; Baptist, *The Half Has Never Been Told*, 173; Jeff Adelson, "Notarial Archives Tell Story of New Orleans in Thousands of Historic Documents," *New Orleans Advocate*, www.theneworleansadvocate.com/news/13 664438–123/notarial-... (accessed October 22, 2015).

20. Isabell Howell, "John Armfield, Slave-trader," *Tennessee Historical Quarterly* 2 (March 1943), 19; Maria R. Montalvo, "The Slavers' Archive: Enslaved People, Power, and the Production of the Past in the Antebellum Courtroom" (Ph.D. diss., Rice University,

2018); Jenny B. Wahl, "The Jurisprudence of American Slave Sales," *Journal of Economic History* 56 (March 1996), 143, 144; Baptist, *The Half Has Never Been Told,* 245; Schermerhorn, "Slave Trading in a Republic of Credit," 597.

21. *The Emancipator,* October 18, 1838.

22. *Evening Star* (Washington, D.C.), August 23, 1854; *Baltimore Sun,* April 2, 1855; *Baltimore Sun,* May 28, 1855; *Philadelphia Inquirer,* March 23, 1848; *Richmond Dispatch* (Va.), July 20, 1852; William Y. Lewis, vol. 4, act no. 165, NONA; Inward Slave Manifest, New Orleans, April 28, 1822 (*Susan*), NARA M1895, reel 2, image 276; Ralph Clayton, *Cash for Blood: The Baltimore to New Orleans Domestic Slave Trade* (Westminster, Md.: Heritage Books, 2007), 451, 452, 453, 455, 467, 481, 490. *Nailor v. Williams* (1862), Records of the US District Court for the District of Columbia, Case Papers, 1802–1863, Civil Trial #38, Box 999, Folder 1, NA, identifies William H. Williams as "a citizen of . . . Maryland."

23. *The State v. William H. Williams* (1842, 1844), Supreme Court of Louisiana, 7 Rob. (LA) 252, 1844 WL 1414 (La.). As Louisiana's Judge Alonzo Morphy explained, "We have in this State no common law offences punishable with fine and imprisonment; with us, all crimes and misdemeanors must be created by statute, and can only be punished in the manner provided for by law. If the Legislature merely prohibits an act without annexing a punishment for doing it, no one is punishable for having done the act." Newspapers excepted, the earliest known published account of Williams' courtroom battles in New Orleans is found in Gustavus Schmidt, ed., "Trial of William H. Williams, before the Criminal Court of New-Orleans," *Louisiana Law Journal* 1 (May 1841): 151–153, https://babel.hathitrust.org/cgi/pt?id=uc1.b4001703;view=1up;seq=7 (accessed October 17, 2017).

24. *The Emancipator,* October 18, 1838 (first through third quotations); Baptist, *The Half Has Never Been Told,* 2, in a chapter tellingly titled, "Feet"; Bancroft, *Slave Trading in the Old South,* 57–58 (fourth quotation). The quotation about the jail may refer to either William H. Williams' Yellow House or another slave jail directly across the street from it.

CHAPTER 1: AN AMBUSH

1. *Commonwealth v. Alfred & Spencer* (1840), Executive Papers, Thomas Walker Gilmer, Box 4 (Oversized), Folder 1, LVA; R. C. Mason to Thomas W. Gilmer, April 24, 1840, Executive Papers, Thomas Walker Gilmer, Box 1, Folder 6, LVA. On the weapons used, see Deposition of George Mason to James Millan, May 7, 1840, Executive Papers, Thomas Walker Gilmer, Box 1, Folder 6, LVA; Deposition of Richard C. Mason to James Millan, Executive Papers, Thomas Walker Gilmer, Box 1, Folder 6, LVA. On slave patrols, see Sally E. Hadden, *Slave Patrols: Law and Violence in Virginia and the Carolinas* (Cambridge, Mass.: Harvard University Press, 2001).

2. *Commonwealth v. Alfred & Spencer* (all quotations except the second); Deposition of George Mason; *Alexandria Gazette* (Alexandria, D.C.), March 5, 1840 (second quotation). On illicit dances and their significance to slaves, see Stephanie M. H. Camp, *Closer to Freedom: Enslaved Women and Everyday Resistance in the Plantation South* (Chapel Hill: University of North Carolina Press, 2004).

3. *Commonwealth v. Alfred & Spencer.*

4. *Commonwealth v. Alfred & Spencer; Alexandria Gazette*, March 5, 1840. Samuel Catts is the only Catts who appears in Fairfax County, Virginia, census records for 1840. See Sixth Census of the United States, 1840, Fairfax County, Virginia, NAMS M-704, reel 558, page 153.

5. *Commonwealth v. Alfred & Spencer.*

6. *Commonwealth v. Alfred & Spencer.*

7. *Commonwealth v. Alfred & Spencer.*

8. *Commonwealth v. Alfred & Spencer.*

9. Jeff Forret, *Slave against Slave: Plantation Violence in the Old South* (Baton Rouge: Louisiana State University Press, 2015), 113–114; *Commonwealth v. Alfred & Spencer,* Sixth Census of the United States, 1840, Fairfax County, Virginia, NAMS M-704, reel 558, page 171; B. Hooe to Thomas W. Gilmer, May 17, 1840, Executive Papers, Thomas Walker Gilmer, Box 1, Folder 6, LVA.

10. *Commonwealth v. Alfred & Spencer* (1840). See also *Alexandria Gazette*, March 16, 1840.

11. Forret, *Slave against Slave*, 130–134; Joseph Tate, *Digest of the Laws of Virginia, which are of a Permanent Character and General Operation; Illustrated by Judicial Decisions; to which is Added, an Index of the Names of the Cases in the Virginia Reporters*, 2nd ed. (Richmond: Smith and Palmer, 1841), 274 (quotations); "A List of Slaves and Free persons of color received into the Penitentiary of Virginia for sale and transportation from the 25th June 1816 to the 1st February 1842," Auditor of Public Accounts, Condemned Blacks Executed or Transported, Records – Condemned Slaves, Court Orders, and Valuations, 1858–1865, Misc. Reel 2555, Frame 996, LVA; Auditor of Public Accounts, Slaves Transported or Executed, 1833–1846, Misc. Reel 2555, Frame 1015, LVA.

12. Forret, *Slave against Slave*, 10; Steven Deyle, *Carry Me Back: The Domestic Slave Trade in American Life* (New York: Oxford University Press, 2005), 50, 305n19; Philip J. Schwarz, *Slave Laws in Virginia* (Athens: University of Georgia Press, 2010), 105.

13. Deposition of George Mason (first and second quotations); Deposition of Richard C. Mason (third quotation).

14. Deposition of George Mason (first through third quotations); Deposition of Richard C. Mason (fourth through ninth quotations); William H. Chichester to George Mason, April 22, 1840, Executive Papers, Thomas Walker Gilmer, Box 1, Folder 6, LVA. See also G. Mason and R. C. Mason to Thomas W. Gilmer, n.d., Executive Papers, Thomas Walker Gilmer, Box 1, Folder 6, LVA.

15. G. Mason and R. C. Mason to Thomas W. Gilmer. See also William Brent Jr. to Richard C. Mason, March 4, 1840, Executive Papers, Thomas Walker Gilmer, Box 1, Folder 6, LVA.

16. G. Mason and R. C. Mason to Thomas W. Gilmer (first and fifth quotations); Richard C. Mason to John M. Patton, April 29, 1840, Executive Papers, Thomas Walker Gilmer, Box 1, Folder 6, LVA (second and third quotations); Richard C. Mason to John M. Patton, April 29, 1840, Executive Papers, Thomas Walker Gilmer, Box 1, Folder 6, LVA (fourth quotation). On Nat Turner and the Southampton Insurrection, see Kenneth S. Greenberg, *Nat Turner: A Slave Rebellion in History and Memory* (New York: Oxford University Press, 2003); David F. Allmendinger, Jr., *Nat*

Turner and the Rising in Southampton County (Baltimore: Johns Hopkins University Press, 2014); Patrick H. Breen, *The Land Shall Be Deluged in Blood: A New History of the Nat Turner Revolt* (New York: Oxford University Press, 2015).

17. William Brent Jr. to Richard C. Mason (first and second quotations); G. Mason and R. C. Mason to Thomas W. Gilmer (third quotation); Deposition of Richard C. Mason.

18. G. Mason and R. C. Mason to Thomas W. Gilmer (first and second quotations); William M. McCarty to George Mason, March 25, 1840, Executive Papers, Thomas Walker Gilmer, Box 1, Folder 6, LVA (third through fifth quotations).

19. William Brent Jr. to Richard C. Mason (first, second, and eighth quotations); G. Mason and R. C. Mason to Thomas W. Gilmer (third, fifth through seventh, ninth, twelfth, thirteen, and sixteenth quotations); William M. McCarty to George Mason (fourth quotation); R. C. Mason to Thomas W. Gilmer, recd April 24, 1840, Executive Papers, Thomas Walker Gilmer (tenth, eleventh, and fourteenth quotations); Deposition of Richard C. Mason (fifteenth and seventeenth quotations).

20. Dennis Johnston to George Mason and Richard C. Mason, March 30, 1840, Executive Papers, Thomas Walker Gilmer, Box 1, Folder 6, LVA; B. Hooe to George Mason, March 21, 1840, Executive Papers, Thomas Walker Gilmer, Box 1, Folder 6, LVA; Fred R. Carper to Dennis Johnston, March 25, 1840, Executive Papers, Thomas Walker Gilmer, Box 1, Folder 6, LVA; John Gunnell to Dennis Johnston, March 25, 1840, Executive Papers, Thomas Walker Gilmer, Box 1, Folder 6, LVA. A member of the Associated Survivors of the War of 1812 of the District of Columbia, Bernard Hooe after 1840 served as register of wills for Alexandria County, a justice of the peace for Alexandria County, and Chief Clerk of the Pension Bureau. He died in 1869.

21. G. Mason to David Campbell, March 17, 1840, Executive Papers, Thomas Walker Gilmer, Box 1, Folder 6, LVA (first quotation); G. Mason and R. C. Mason to B. Hooe and Dennis Johnston, March 19, 1840, Executive Papers, Thomas Walker Gilmer, Box 1, Folder 6, LVA; B. Hooe to George Mason (second quotation); G. Mason and R. C. Mason to Thomas W. Gilmer; G. Mason to Silas Burke, March 27, 1840, Executive Papers, Thomas Walker Gilmer, Box 1, Folder 6, LVA (third and fourth quotations).

22. Silas Burke to George Mason, April 4, 1840, Executive Papers, Thomas Walker Gilmer, Box 1, Folder 6, LVA; Petition, Executive Papers, Thomas Walker Gilmer, Box 1, Folder 6, LVA.

23. Memorial of Henry Fairfax, E. Jones, J. B. Hunter, Wm. H. Chichester, John Millan, and Silas Burke, March 30, 1840, Executive Papers, Thomas Walker Gilmer, Box 1, Folder 6, LVA. For biblical accounts of the criminals executed alongside Jesus, see the Gospels of Matthew 27:38; Mark 15:27; Luke 23:32–33; John 19:18.

24. Memorial of Henry Fairfax, E. Jones, J.B. Hunter, Wm. H. Chichester, John Millan, and Silas Burke (quotations); *Commonwealth v. Alfred & Spencer.* Bernard Hooe sent a private letter to Governor Gilmer expressing the same sentiments. See Bernard Hooe to Thomas W. Gilmer, April 3, 1840, Executive Papers, Thomas Walker Gilmer, Box 1, Folder 6, LVA.

25. Petition, April 10, 1840, Executive Papers, Thomas Walker Gilmer, Box 1, Folder 6, LVA; Petitions, Executive Papers, Thomas Walker Gilmer, Box 1, Folder 6, LVA (first

through fourth quotations); Bernard Hooe to Thomas W. Gilmer, April 3, 1840 (fifth quotation); S. M. Ball to Thomas W. Gilmer, April 23, 1840, Executive Papers, Thomas Walker Gilmer, Box 1, Folder 6, LVA; G. Mason and R. C. Mason to Thomas W. Gilmer.

26. S. M. Ball to Thomas W. Gilmer; *Alexandria Gazette,* April 28, 1840 (first quotation); Deposition of George Mason (second through seventh quotations); Deposition of Richard C. Mason.

27. R. C. Mason to Jno. M. Patton, May 4, 1840, Executive Papers, Thomas Walker Gilmer, Box 1, Folder 6, LVA; Thomas L. Orr to Thomas W. Gilmer, April 27, 1840, Executive Papers, Thomas Walker Gilmer, Box 1, Folder 6, LVA (first quotation); Thomas H. Jones to George Mason, May 8, 1840, Executive Papers, Thomas Walker Gilmer, Box 1, Folder 6, LVA (second through fourth quotations); Petition of remonstrance of the citizens of Fairfax County to Thomas W. Gilmer, May 8, 1840, Executive Papers, Thomas Walker Gilmer, Box 1, Folder 6, LVA (fifth quotation).

28. B. Hooe to Thomas W. Gilmer, May 17, 1840.

29. William Brent Jr. to Richard C. Mason (first quotation); S. M. Ball to Thomas W. Gilmer (second and third quotations).

30. Dennis Johnston to Thomas W. Gilmer, May 18, 1840, Executive Papers, Thomas Walker Gilmer, Box 1, Folder 6, LVA (quotations); Auditor of Public Accounts, Slaves Transported or Executed, 1833–1846, Misc. Reel 2555, Frame 1015, LVA. Justices valued Spencer at $850.

CHAPTER 2: THE YELLOW HOUSE

1. Solomon Northup, *Twelve Years a Slave,* ed. Sue Eakin and Joseph Logsdon (Baton Rouge: Louisiana State University Press, 1996), 21. On Northup's description of the slave pen, see Sam Worley, "Solomon Northup and the Sly Philosophy of the Slave Pen," *Callaloo* 20 (Winter 1997), 251.

2. Northup, *Twelve Years a Slave,* 23, 21; *The Liberator* (Boston), August 9, 1834; Ralph Clayton, *Cash for Blood: The Baltimore to New Orleans Domestic Slave Trade* (Westminster, Md.: Heritage Books, 2007), 56; *Daily National Intelligencer* (Washington, D.C.), April 5, 1836 (quotations); *Washington Globe,* November 7, 1836; *New York Times,* January 20, 1853.

3. *Daily National Intelligencer,* April 19, 1858; Manuscript Census Returns, Seventh Census of the United States, 1850, Washington Ward 7, Washington, District of Columbia, Schedule 1, Free Population, NAMS M-432, reel 57, page 119A; Tom Bartholow, email message to author, April 15, 2017; ancestry.com, www.ancestry.com/family-tree/person/tree/21218476/person/1211672109/facts. Lizzie Stewart's death record lists her father's birthplace as Charlottesville, Albemarle County, Virginia, whereas Fannie Beall's death certificate identifies it as Mississippi, but this contradicts the census record of 1850 compiled during Williams' lifetime. *Charles Carter v. Admx of Henry Williams* (1813), Albemarle County Chancery Record 1813–031, case 563–55, LVA.

4. Inward Slave Manifest, New Orleans, February 4, 1828 (*Ajax*), NARA M1895, reel 5, image 198; Inward Slave Manifest, New Orleans, March 5, 1828 (*Maria Ann*), NARA M1895, reel 5, image 217, which lists Williams' residence as Montgomery; Outward

Slave Manifest, New Orleans, April 30, 1828 (*Fair Star*), NARA M1895, reel 19, image 78; Inward Slave Manifest, New Orleans, October 18, 1828 (*Jefferson*), NARA M1895, reel 5, image 739; Edward Barnett, vol. 64, act 502, 1857, NONA; *Times-Picayune* (New Orleans), November 14, 1857; *Cassedy v. Williams* (1843), Records of the US District Court for the District of Columbia, Case Papers, 1802–1863, Civil Trial #98, Box 663, NA. Manuscript Census Returns, Fifth Census of the United States, 1830, Montgomery County, Alabama, NAMS M-19, reel 2, page 198, shows the possible household in which Thomas lived, if he resided with a family member sharing the Williams name.

5. Michael Tadman, "The Hidden History of Slave Trading in Antebellum South Carolina: John Springs III and Other 'Gentlemen Dealing in Slaves'," *South Carolina Historical Magazine* 97 (January 1996), 16; Michael Tadman, "The Reputation of the Slave Trader in Southern History and the Social Memory of the South," *American Nineteenth Century History* 8 (September 2007), 252; *Daily National Intelligencer*, June 16, 1835 (quotation); *The Liberator*, August 9, 1834; *Daily National Intelligencer*, April 5, 1836; Steven Deyle, "Rethinking the Slave Trade: Slave Traders and the Market Revolution in the South," in *The Old South's Modern Worlds: Slavery, Region, and Nation in the Age of Progress*, ed. L. Diane Barnes, Brian Schoen, and Frank Towers (New York: Oxford University Press, 2011), 108, 118n16; *Washington Globe*, November 7, 1836.

6. *Daily National Intelligencer*, June 16, 1835 (first and second quotations); *Daily National Intelligencer*, April 5, 1836 (third through fifth quotations); E. A. Cohen & Co., *For 1834. A Full Directory, for Washington City, Georgetown, and Alexandria* (Washington City: Wm. Greer, 1834), 58, 33, unpaginated advertisement for A. Lee's Lottery and Exchange Office.

7. Clayton, *Cash for Blood*, ch. 4; Frederic Bancroft, *Slave Trading in the Old South*, introduction by Michael Tadman (1931; Columbia: University of South Carolina Press, 1996), 53, 56 (first quotation); Stephen Mihm, *A Nation of Counterfeiters: Capitalists, Con Men, and the Making of the United States* (Cambridge, Mass.: Harvard University Press, 2007), 236; Cohen, *Full Directory, for Washington City*, n.p. (second quotation); *Baltimore Sun*, October 28, 1847; *Cassedy v. Williams*.

8. Edward E. Baptist, *The Half Has Never Been Told: Slavery and the Making of American Capitalism* (New York: Basic Books, 2014), 239; Joshua D. Rothman, *Flush Times and Fever Dreams: A Story of Capitalism and Slavery in the Age of Jackson* (Athens: University of Georgia Press, 2012), 174, 178, 195. Jessica M. Lepler, *The Many Panics of 1837: People, Politics, and the Creation of a Transatlantic Financial Crisis* (New York: Cambridge University Press, 2013), 8, recognized "the hazy moral line between illegitimate gambles and legitimate investments" in antebellum America.

9. *Ex parte Milburn*, 34 US 704 (1835) (first quotation); *Daily National Intelligencer*, August 29, 1838; James Croggon, "In Old Washington," *Evening Star* (Washington, D. C.), October 17, 1908; *National Intelligencer*, quoted in *New York Spectator*, August 31, 1838; *Baltimore Sun*, August 29, 1838; *Irish World and American Industrial Liberator* (New York), September 14, 1895 (second quotation). On faro banks, see Ann Fabian, *Card Sharps and Bucket Shops: Gambling in Nineteenth-Century America* (New York: Routledge, 1999), 21–22; Rothman, *Flush Times*, 184–185, 203.

10. *Daily National Intelligencer,* July 20, 1836 (first through third quotations); *Washington Globe,* November 7, 1836 (fourth quotation); Inward Slave Manifest, New Orleans, December 1, 1836 (*Tribune*), NARA M1895, reel 7, images 1243–1248; *Washington Globe,* April 6, 1837 (fifth quotation); *Baltimore Sun,* October 28, 1847; *Daily National Intelligencer,* September 25, 1837 (sixth through eighth quotations). See also *Washington Globe,* November 7, 1836. Slave trader George Kephart, an agent of Franklin & Armfield, took over Franklin & Armfield's jail on Duke Street in Alexandria and bought their third slaving vessel, the brig *Isaac Franklin.* See Bancroft, *Slave Trading in the Old South,* 65. On the history of the *Tribune,* see Calvin Schermerhorn, *The Business of Slavery and the Rise of American Capitalism, 1815–1860* (New Haven: Yale University Press, 2015), 138–139.

11. *Daily National Intelligencer,* December 7, 1837 (first and second quotations); *Daily National Intelligencer,* September 25, 1837 (third and fourth quotations); Walter C. Clephane, "The Local Aspect of Slavery in the District of Columbia," *Records of the Columbia Historical Society, Washington, D.C.* 3 (1900), 240; Bancroft, *Slave Trading in the Old South,* 59–60.

12. Scott Reynolds Nelson, *A Nation of Deadbeats: An Uncommon History of America's Financial Disasters* (New York: Knopf, 2012), ch. 6; Baptist, *The Half Has Never Been Told,* 231; Alasdair Roberts, *America's First Great Depression: Economic Crisis and Political Disorder after the Panic of 1837* (Ithaca: Cornell University Press, 2012), 34.

13. Baptist, *The Half Has Never Been Told,* 232, 233, 244–245, 249, 253, 254, 269, 270; Roberts, *America's First Great Depression,* 31, 33–34; Joshua D. Rothman, "The Contours of Cotton Capitalism: Speculation, Slavery, and Economic Panic in Mississippi, 1832–1841," in *Slavery's Capitalism,* ed. Sven Beckert and Seth Rockman (Philadelphia: University of Pennsylvania Press, 2016), 123–124, 125.

14. Baptist, *The Half Has Never Been Told,* 252; Roberts, *America's First Great Depression,* 32, 33; Rothman, "Contours of Cotton Capitalism," 126–127, 130; Calvin Schermerhorn, "Slave Trading in a Republic of Credit: Financial Architecture of the US Slave Market, 1815–1840," *Slavery and Abolition* 36, no. 4 (2015), 596. Andrew J. Torget, *Seeds of Empire: Cotton, Slavery, and the Transformation of the Texas Borderlands, 1800–1850* (Chapel Hill: University of North Carolina Press, 2015), 212, observes that "English textile mills consumed 592 million pounds of raw cotton during 1840 alone, more than half the world's available supply."

15. Baptist, *The Half Has Never Been Told,* 252, 270; Rothman, *Flush Times,* 184; Walter Johnson, *River of Dark Dreams: Slavery and Empire in the Cotton Kingdom* (Cambridge, Mass.: Belknap Press of Harvard University Press, 2013), 271; Roberts, *America's First Great Depression,* 39; Rothman, "Contours of Cotton Capitalism," 136.

16. Peter Temin, *The Jacksonian Economy* (New York: Norton, 1969); Howard Bodenhorn, *State Banking in Early America: A New Economic History* (New York: Oxford University Press, 2003), 320n80; Roberts, *America's First Great Depression,* 35, 37, 42; Lepler, *Many Panics;* Rothman, "Contours of Cotton Capitalism," 136.

17. Schermerhorn, "Slave Trading in a Republic of Credit," 586, 597; Rothman, *Flush Times,* 296; Baptist, *The Half Has Never Been Told,* 280.

18. *Daily National Intelligencer,* August 23, 1838 (first through third quotations); *Daily National Intelligencer,* July 27, 1839 (fourth through sixth quotations); Jefferson Morley, *Snow-Storm in August: Washington City, Francis Scott Key, and the Forgotten Race Riot of 1835* (New York: Nan A. Talese and Doubleday, 2012), 17 (seventh and eighth quotations); Inward Slave Manifest, New Orleans, November 19, 1839 (*Uncas*), NARA M1895, reel 8, images 517–521; *Daily National Intelligencer,* September 7, 1840 (ninth quotation).

19. Clayton, *Cash for Blood,* 57, 84; Clephane, "Local Aspect of Slavery," 240, 57 (first quotation); *Daily National Intelligencer,* August 23, 1838 (second quotation); *Daily National Intelligencer,* July 20, 1836 (third quotation); *Daily National Intelligencer,* September 25, 1837; Joseph Sturge, *A Visit to the United States in 1841* (1842; New York: Augustus M. Kelley, 1969), 83, 89 (fourth and fifth quotations), 89–90 (tenth quotation), 84 (eleventh and twelfth quotations); Beasley, Jones & Wood Slave Trade Account Book, 1835–1851, Lunenburg County, reel 410, LVA (sixth quotation); Greg Crawford, "To Be Sold: Beasley, Jones, and Wood – Virginia Slave Traders," *Out of the Box: Notes from the Archives @ the Library of Virginia,* www.virginiamemory.com/blogs/out_of_the_box/2014/10/15/to-be-sold-beasley-jones-and-wood-virginia-slave-traders/ (accessed March 24, 2018); *Daily National Intelligencer,* July 27, 1839 (seventh and ninth quotations); *Washington Globe,* November 7, 1836; *The Colored American* (New York), March 3, 1838 (eighth quotation); Tingba Muhammad, "The Congo of America: The Slave Trade of Washington, D.C.," www.finalcall.com/artman/publish//printer_9038.shtml (accessed August 12, 2014).

20. Baptist, *The Half Has Never Been Told,* 184; Clayton, *Cash for Blood,* 18, 57 (third and fourth quotations); Hank Trent, *The Secret Life of Bacon Tait, a White Slave Trader Married to a Free Woman of Color* (Baton Rouge: Louisiana State University Press, 2017), 1, 2, 3, 65, 93; Northup, *Twelve Years a Slave,* 42; Thomas L. Johnson, *Twenty-Eight Years a Slave or the Story of My Life in Three Continents* (Bournemouth: W. Math & Sons, 1909), 11–12; Louis Hughes, *Thirty Years a Slave. From Bondage to Freedom. The Institution of Slavery as Seen on the Plantation and in the Home of the Planter* (Milwaukee: South Side Printing Company, 1897), 7; Rev. William Troy, *Hair-Breadth Escape from Slavery to Freedom* (Manchester, UK: W. Bremner, 1861), 29; Thomas S. Gaines, ed., *Buried Alive (Behind Prison Walls) for a Quarter of a Century: Life of William Walker* (Saginaw, Mich.: Friedman & Hynan, 1892), 9; *The Rev. J. W. Loguen, as a Slave and as a Freeman. A Narrative of Real Life* (Syracuse, N.Y.: J. G. K. Truair & Co., 1859), 73; J. Winston Coleman, Jr., "Lexington's Slave Dealers and their Southern Trade," *Filson Club History Quarterly* 12 (January 1938), 11; Isaac Johnson, *Slavery Days in Old Kentucky. A True Story of a Father Who Sold His Wife and Four Children. By One of the Children,* http://docsouth.unc.edu/neh/johnson/johnson.html (accessed June 1, 2017), 22 (first quotation), 21; George P. Rawick, ed., *The American Slave: A Composite Autobiography, Supplement, Series 1, vol. X, pt. 5: Mississippi* (Westport, Conn.: Greenwood Press, 1977), 2057 (second quotation); Walter Johnson, *Soul by Soul: Life Inside the Antebellum Slave Market* (Cambridge, Mass.: Harvard University Press, 1999).

21. Hughes, *Thirty Years a Slave,* 8–9; Wm. Wells Brown, *My Southern Home: or, the South and its People* (Boston: A. G. Brown & Co., 1880), 116, 112 (fifth and sixth quotations);

Richard Hildreth, *The White Slave; or, Memoirs of a Fugitive* (Boston: Tappan and Whitemore, 1852), 329 (first and second quotations); George P. Rawick, ed., *The American Slave: A Composite Autobiography, vol. XI: Missouri* (Westport, Conn.: Greenwood, 1975), 215 (third and fourth quotations); *Narrative of the Life of J. D. Green, a Runaway Slave, from Kentucky, Containing an Account of his Three Escapes, in 1839, 1846, and 1848* (Huddersfield, UK: Henry Fielding, 1864), 28 (seventh and eighth quotations), 28; Rawick, *Supplement, Series 1, vol. X, pt. 5 Mississippi*, 2057 (ninth and tenth quotations); Johnson, *Slavery Days in Old Kentucky*, 22. On the "soundness" of slaves, see Sharla M. Fett, *Working Cures: Healing, Health, and Power on Southern Slave Plantations* (Chapel Hill: University of North Carolina Press, 2002), ch. 1. On the culture of the slave market, see Johnson, *Soul by Soul.*

22. Rawick, *Supplement, Series 1, vol. VIII, pt. 3 Mississippi*, 1280; Trent, *Secret Life of Bacon Tait*, 46; Steven Deyle, *Carry Me Back: The Domestic Slave Trade in American Life* (New York: Oxford University Press, 2005), 98–99.

23. Mary Beth Corrigan, "Imaginary Cruelties? A History of the Slave Trade in Washington, D.C.," *Washington History* 13 (Fall/Winter 2001/2002), 24, 14; *The Liberator*, August 9, 1834 (first quotation); Bancroft, *Slave Trading in the Old South*, 54; Clephane, "Local Aspect of Slavery," 238–239; E. S. Abdy, *Journal of a Residence and Tour in the United States of North America, from April, 1833, to October, 1834*, vol. II (London: John Murray, 1835), 96 (second through fourth quotations), 97 (fifth through seventh quotations). Unlike Corrigan, Bancroft, *Slave Trading in the Old South*, 53, observed, "Private slave-jails for public use were never numerous in the District of Columbia."

24. *The Colored American*, March 3, 1838 (first quotation); Bancroft, *Slave Trading in the Old South*, 56; *The Liberator*, March 31, 1843 (second and third quotations).

25. Northup, *Twelve Years a Slave*, 22 (first, third through eighth, and sixteenth quotations), 22–23 (fifteenth quotation); *Cleveland Herald*, April 14, 1849 (second and ninth quotations); Clephane, "Local Aspect of Slavery," 239, 239–240 (tenth quotation), 240 (eleventh quotation); *The Colored American*, March 3, 1838 (twelfth quotation); *Daily National Intelligencer*, July 27, 1839 (thirteenth and fourteenth quotations); Bancroft, *Slave Trading in the Old South*, 56–57; Tingba Muhammad, "The Congo of America: The Slave Trade of Washington, D.C.," www.finalcall.com/artman/publish//printer_9038 .shtml (accessed August 12, 2014); "Williams' Private Jail (Slave Pen)," *Histories of the National Mall*, Roy Rosenzweig Center for History and New Media, George Mason University, http://mallhistory.org/items/show/45 (accessed April 26, 2017); Southwest Neighborhood Assembly, www.swdc.org/neighborhood/funfacts_commer ce_center.htm (accessed August 12, 2014).

The Yellow House no longer stands, and the identifying streets around it have been reconfigured. In today's Washington, D.C., it was located just south of the Smithsonian's Hirshhorn Museum, at the present site of the Federal Aviation Administration Drug Abatement Division building. See Alison T. Mann, "Slavery Exacts an Impossible Price: John Quincy Adams and the Dorcas Allen Case, Washington, D.C." (Ph.D. diss., University of New Hampshire, 2010), 147n21; Tingba Apidta, *The Hidden History of Washington, D.C.: A Guide for Black Folks*

(Washington, D.C.: The Reclamation Project, 1998), 17–18; T. Logan Metesh, "The Ambling Historian: In the Shadow of D.C.'s Slave Pens," November 25, 2013, blog, http://amblinghistorian.blogspot.com/2013/11/in-shadow-of-dcs-slave-pens.html (accessed August 12, 2014).

26. *The Colored American,* March 3, 1838.

27. *New York Times,* January 20, 1853 (first quotation); Northup, *Twelve Years a Slave,* 22 (second through fourth quotations), 21. Other descriptions of slave jails may be found in Kari J. Winter, *The American Dreams of John B. Prentis, Slave Trader* (Athens: University of Georgia Press, 2011), 99–101. Prentis ran a slave jail in Richmond, Virginia.

28. Northup, *Twelve Years a Slave,* 21–22 (first quotation), 245; *New York Times,* January 20, 1853; *Cassedy v. Williams* (second and third quotations); Manuscript Census Returns, Seventh Census of the United States, 1850, Washington Ward 7, Washington, District of Columbia, Schedule 1, Free Population, NAMS M-432, reel 57, page 117A; Manuscript Census Returns, Eighth Census of the United States, 1860, Washington Ward 4, Washington, District of Columbia, Schedule 1, Free Population, NAMS M-653, reel 103, page 330; *Wilkinson v. Williams* (1850), Records of the US District Court for the District of Columbia, Case Papers, 1802–1863, Civil Trial #15, Box 739, Folder 15, NA (fourth quotation); *Wilkinson v. Williams* (1850), 2 Hay. & Haz. 1, 29 F. Cas. 1270 (fifth and sixth quotations). Further evidence of Rodbird's position as agent for William H. Williams comes from Alexander Lee's testimony in *Wilkinson v. Williams;* and from Inward Slave Manifest, New Orleans, March 27, 1840 (*Architect*), NARA M1895, reel 8, image 740. For a Rodbird family squabble over property in Washington, D.C., see *Rodbird v. Rodbird* (1837), no. 11,988, 5 Cranch C.C. 125, 20 F. Cas. 1083, 5 D.C. 125.

29. Northup, *Twelve Years a Slave,* 23 (first through fifth quotations), 25 (sixth through eighth quotations), 26 (ninth and tenth quotations), 27 (eleventh quotation). See also *New York Times,* January 20, 1853.

30. Northup, *Twelve Years a Slave,* 28 (first and second quotations); *The Colored American,* March 3, 1838 (third through fifth quotations); Corrigan, "Imaginary Cruelties?," 5 (sixth quotation).

CHAPTER 3: SALE AND TRANSPORTATION

1. Ralph Clayton, *Cash for Blood: The Baltimore to New Orleans Domestic Slave Trade* (Westminster, Md.: Heritage Books, 2007), 54, 67; Outward Slave Manifest, Alexandria, October 9, 1840 (*Uncas*), New-York Historical Society, MS569, Slavery Collection, nyhs_sc_b-05_f-16_015–001, http://cdm16694.contentdm.oclc.org/cdm/compoundob ject/collection/p15052coll5/id/24223/rec/6 (accessed February 25, 2015) (quotations). Section 9 of the Congressional law of March 2, 1807, required slave manifests "specifying the name and sex of each person, their age and stature, as near as may be, and the class to which they respectively belong, whether negro, mulatto, or person or color, with the name and place of residence of every owner or shipper of the same." The manifests were to be "deliver[ed] . . . to the collector of the port, if there be one, otherwise to the surveyor, before whom the captain, master, or commander, together with the owner,

or shipper, shall severally swear or affirm, to the best of their knowledge and belief, that the persons therein specified were not imported or brought into the United States from and after the first day of January" 1808. See Edward Ingersoll, comp.,*A Digest of the Laws of the United States of America, from March 4th, 1789, to May 15th, 1820* (Philadelphia: James Maxwell, 1821), 800. Clayton, *Cash for Blood,* 19, mentions one case from Baltimore in which "the Customs Officer checked the ship's manifest" and "learned that a number of the slaves were convicts from the Baltimore jail." They were "refused clearance for Charleston," apparently not having the proper authorizations.

2. "A List of Slaves and Free persons of color received into the Penitentiary of Virginia for sale and transportation from the 25th June 1816 to the 1st February 1842," Auditor of Public Accounts, Condemned Blacks Executed or Transported, Records – Condemned Slaves, Court Orders, and Valuations, 1858–1865, Misc. Reel 2555, Frame 996-997, LVA; Taja-Nia Y. Henderson, "Crucibles of Discontent: Penal Practice in the Shadow of Slavery, Virginia, 1796–1865" (Ph.D. diss., New York University, 2013), 240.

3. Henderson, "Crucibles of Discontent," 178–181, 184, 202–203, 222; "A statement of the number of Deaths, with the causes thereof, &c., which have occurred in the Penitentiary of Virginia from the 1st December 1839, to the 30th November 1840," Executive Papers, Thomas Walker Gilmer, Box 3, Folder 1, LVA (quotation).

4. Jeff Forret, *Slave against Slave: Plantation Violence in the Old South* (Baton Rouge: Louisiana State University Press, 2015), 138, 141. For one example of a private sale, see Arthur M. Bowen to David Campbell, July 20, 1838, Executive Papers, David Campbell, Box 4, Folder 1, LVA; David Campbell to John Rutherfoord, September 12, 1838, Executive Papers, David Campbell, Box 4, Folder 5, LVA; Nathaniel Matthews to the Lieut. Governor & Council of Va., August 10, 1838, Executive Papers, David Campbell, Box 4, Folder 3, LVA.

5. Auditor of Public Accounts, Condemned Blacks Executed or Transported, Records – Condemned Slaves, Court Orders, and Valuations, 1858–1865, Misc. Reel 2555, Frames 1003, 1005, 1007, 1009, 1011, 1013, 1015, 1017, 1019, LVA; List of slaves, September 5, 1840, Executive Papers, Thomas Walker Gilmer, Box 2, Folder 4, LVA; Walter Johnson, *Soul by Soul: Life inside the Antebellum Slave Market* (Cambridge, Mass.: Harvard University Press, 1999).

6. Executive Papers, David Campbell, Box 4, Folder 2, LVA; James G. Lindsey to the governor and Executive Council, undated [sometime between April and mid-May 1840], Executive Papers, Thomas Walker Gilmer, Box 1, Folder 3, LVA.

7. Auditor of Public Accounts, Condemned Blacks Executed or Transported, Records – Condemned Slaves, Court Orders, and Valuations, 1858–1865, Misc. Reel 2555, Frames 1009, 1011, LVA; Robert Lumpkin to governor, May 22, 1840, Executive Papers, Thomas Walker Gilmer, Box 1, Folder 7, LVA (quotations); "A List of Slaves and Free persons of color received into the Penitentiary of Virginia for sale and transportation from the 25th June 1816 to the 1st February 1842," Auditor of Public Accounts, Condemned Blacks Executed or Transported, Records – Condemned Slaves, Court Orders, and Valuations, 1858–1865, Misc. Reel 2555, Frame 996, LVA.

8. J. W. Coleman to the Governor & Council of the State of Va., August 29, 1840, Executive Papers, Thomas Walker Gilmer, Box 2, Folder 3, LVA (quotations); "List of Slaves," 997.

9. *National Intelligencer* (Washington, D.C.), March 5, 1838, quoted in Walter C. Clephane, "The Local Aspect of Slavery in the District of Columbia," *Records of the Columbia Historical Society, Washington, D.C.* 3 (1900), 235 (first and second quotations); *National Intelligencer,* February 5, 1839 (third through sixth quotations); Thomas N. Davis to the governor, August 29, 1840, Executive Papers, Thomas Walker Gilmer, Box 2, Folder 3, LVA.

10. Nathaniel Matthews to the Governor & Counsil [*sic*] of the State of Va., August 31, 1840, Executive Papers, Thomas Walker Gilmer, Box 2, Folder 3, LVA.

11. Manuscript Census Returns, Seventh Census of the United States, 1850, Clarke County, Virginia, Schedule 1, Free Population, NAMS M-432, reel 940, page 209B; B. Hooe to Thomas W. Gilmer, September 24, 1840, Executive Papers, Thomas Walker Gilmer, Box 2, Folder 5, LVA (first quotation); Rudolph Littlejohn to Messrs. Templeman & Dickinson, August 4, 1840, Executive Papers, Thomas Walker Gilmer, Box 2, Folder 4, LVA (all other quotations); Rudolph Littejohn to Messrs. Templeman & Dickinson, August 20, 1840, Executive Papers, Thomas Walker Gilmer, Box 2, Folder 3, LVA. Littlejohn did not appear in the 1840 or the 1860 census.

12. R. H. Dickinson to the governor, August 16, 1840, Executive Papers, Thomas Walker Gilmer, Box 2, Folder 4, LVA (first quotation); R. H. Dickinson to the governor, September 1, 1840, Executive Papers, Thomas Walker Gilmer, Box 2, Folder 4, LVA (second and third quotations).

13. "A statement of the number of Deaths, with the causes thereof, &c., which have occurred in the Penitentiary of Virginia from the 1st December 1839 to the 30th November 1840," Executive Papers, Thomas Walker Gilmer, Box 3, Folder 1, LVA; R. H. Dickinson to governor, August 16, 1840 (first and fourth through sixth quotations); Thomas N. Davis to the governor (second, third, and seventh quotations).

14. R. H. Dickinson to the governor, September 1, 1840 (quotations); List of slaves, September 5, 1840; R. H. Dickinson to the governor, August 16, 1840.

15. List of slaves, September 5, 1840 (first and second quotations); Council Journal, April 1, 1840, to March 30, 1841, Misc. Reel 2996, p. 74, LVA. Jacob appeared on the lists of Thomas N. Davis to the governor and of R. H. Dickinson to the governor, August 16, 1840; C. S. Morgan to Gov. Gilmer, September 8, 1840, Executive Papers, Thomas Walker Gilmer, Box 2, Folder 4, LVA; "Statement of the number of Deaths" (third quotation).

16. List of slaves, September 5, 1840 (first quotation); Charles S. Morgan to William H. Richardson, September 7, 1840, Executive Papers, Thomas Walker Gilmer, Box 2, Folder 4, LVA (second quotation).

17. R. H. Dickinson to the governor, September 4, 1840, Executive Papers, Thomas Walker Gilmer, Box 2, Folder 4, LVA.

18. R. H. Dickinson to the governor, September 4, 1840; R. H. Dickinson to the Governor & Council of the State of Va., September 14, 1840, Executive Papers, Thomas Walker Gilmer, Box 2, Folder 4, LVA (quotations).

19. Auditor of Public Accounts, Condemned Blacks Executed or Transported, Records – Condemned Slaves, Court Orders, and Valuations, 1858–1865, Misc. Reel 2555, Frame

1019, LVA. The math in the penitentiary records is off by $10. See also Forret, *Slave against Slave*, 143.

20. Rudolph Littlejohn, bond for the purchase and transport of condemned slaves, September 15, 1840, Office of the Governor, Contracts, 1806–1865, Misc. Reel 1648, p. 179, LVA; Affidavit of William H. Williams, September 12, 1840, Executive Papers, Thomas Walker Gilmer, Box 2, Folder 4, LVA (first quotation); Affidavit of Isham Puckett, September 12, 1840, Executive Papers, Thomas Walker Gilmer, Box 2, Folder 4, LVA (second quotation); R. H. Dickinson to the governor, September 4, 1840; A. W. Morton, receipt, September 15, 1840, Executive Papers, Thomas Walker Gilmer, Box 2, Folder 4, LVA.

21. "A List of Slaves and Free persons of color received into the Penitentiary of Virginia for sale and transportation from the 25th June 1816 to the 1st February 1842," Auditor of Public Accounts, Condemned Blacks Executed or Transported, Records – Condemned Slaves, Court Orders, and Valuations, 1858–1865, Misc. Reel 2555, Frame 996, LVA.

22. *Cassedy v. Williams* (1843), Records of the US District Court for the District of Columbia, Case Papers, 1802–1863, Civil Trial #98, Box 663, NA. The missing pages of the ledger book became a source of controversy at a later trial involving William H. Williams. Had the pages been consciously removed to obliterate evidence of Williams' business? To argue as much impugns sinister motives to Williams and his agents. Rodbird recollected neither the contents of the missing pages nor how they had come to disappear from the ledger book. Make no mistake, though: "Rodbird kept it," insisted another of Williams' agents. At the same time, the ledger book "was lying open in the room," where "the children could get at it." In this telling, childhood mischief might easily explain the months of entries conveniently lost the day before Rodbird would have to testify in court about slaves whose names appeared on those pages.

23. *Cleveland Herald* (Ohio), April 14, 1849 (first and third quotations); *The Colored American* (New York), March 3, 1838 (second, fourth, fifth, and eighth through tenth quotations); Solomon Northup, *Twelve Years a Slave*, ed. Sue Eakin and Joseph Logsdon (Baton Rouge: Louisiana State University Press, 1996), 27 (sixth and seventh quotations), 29.

24. *The Colored American*, March 3, 1838 (first through seventh quotations); Northup, *Twelve Years a Slave*, 26–27 (eighth quotation).

25. *The Colored American*, March 3, 1838.

26. *Cleveland Herald* (Ohio), April 14, 1849.

27. *The Colored American*, March 3, 1838.

28. *The Liberator* (Boston), November 15, 1834

29. James Croggon, "In Old Washington," *Evening Star* (Washington, D.C.), October 17, 1908.

30. Northup, *Twelve Years a Slave*, 33 (first through fourth quotations), 22 (fifth, sixth, fifteenth, and sixteenth quotations), 34 (eighth through fourteenth quotations); *New York Times*, January 20, 1853 (seventh quotation).

31. Northup, *Twelve Years a Slave*, 34.

32. *Cleveland Herald*, April 14, 1849 (quotation); Frederic Bancroft, *Slave Trading in the Old South*, introduction by Michael Tadman (1931; Columbia: University of South Carolina

Press, 1996), 49; Herman Freudenberger and Jonathan B. Pritchett, "The Domestic United States Slave Trade: New Evidence," *Journal of Interdisciplinary History* 21 (Winter 1991), 472, 474; Ingersoll, *Digest of the Laws*, 799.

33. Clayton, *Cash for Blood*, 45, 81, 101, 103, 109, 123.

34. Walter Johnson, *River of Dark Dreams: Slavery and Empire in the Cotton Kingdom* (Cambridge, Mass.: Belknap Press of Harvard University Press, 2013), 100; *Washington Globe*, November 7, 1836 (first through fourth quotations); *Daily National Intelligencer* (Washington, D.C.), October 21, 1837 (fifth through seventh quotations); *Baltimore Gazette and Daily Advertiser*, October 17, 1837. In late 1838, Williams alerted the public that the *Uncas* would sail on January 1, 1839. He directed those interested in "freight or passage" to "inquire of the Captain," Boush, "on board," or at Williams' office on Seventh Street in Washington. See *Daily National Intelligencer*, December 22, 1838.

35. *Times-Picayune* (New Orleans), March 7, 1837; Inward Slave Manifest, New Orleans, November 19, 1839 (*Uncas*), NARA M1895, reel 8, image 521; *Times-Picayune*, April 25, 1838; *Alexandria Gazette* (Va.), April 13, 1840; *Baltimore Sun*, June 30, 1840, July 13, 1840 (quotation).

36. Clayton, *Cash for Blood*, 49, 125, 54; Inward Slave Manifest, New Orleans, December 1, 1836 (*Tribune*), NARA M1895, reel 7, image 1243; *National Intelligencer*, February 10, 1836 (first quotation); Charles H. Wesley, "Manifests of Slave Shipments along the Waterways, 1808–1864," *Journal of Negro History* 27 (April 1942), 173; *Baltimore Gazette and Daily Advertiser*, July 20, 1836, December 26, 1837 (second quotation), February 15, 1836, February 22, 1836.

37. B. Hooe to Thomas W. Gilmer, October 12, 1840, Executive Papers, Thomas Walker Gilmer, Box 2, Folder 6, LVA (quotation); Thomas N. Davis to the governor, August 29, 1840, Executive Papers, Thomas Walker Gilmer, Box 2, Folder 3, LVA; *Commonwealth v. John & Arthur* (1839), Executive Papers, David Campbell, Box 5, Folder 4, LVA; *Nailor v. Williams* (1862), Records of the US District Court for the District of Columbia, Case Papers, 1802–1863, Civil Trial #38, Box 999, Folder 1, NA; *Nailor v. Williams* (1868), Records of the United States Supreme Court, Case File #5032, Box 624, NA; "List of Slaves," 996; R. H. Dickinson, "Valuation of 29 Negroes (convicts) now confined in the Penitentiary for transportation beyond the limits of the US," August 16, 1840, Executive Papers, Thomas Walker Gilmer, Box 2, Folder 4, LVA.

38. B. Hooe to Thomas W. Gilmer, September 24, 1840; *Nailor v. Williams* (1862), Records of the US District Court for the District of Columbia, Case Papers, 1802–1863, Civil Trial #38, Box 999, Folder 1 (first quotation), Folder 2 (second quotation), NA.

39. Ingersoll, *Digest of the Laws*, 800; Clayton, *Cash for Blood*, 67; Outward Slave Manifest, Alexandria, October 9, 1840 (*Uncas*); Outward Slave Manifest, Alexandria, November 3, 1838 (*Uncas*), New-York Historical Society, MS569, Slavery Collection, nyhs_sc_b-05_f-16_020-001, http://cdm16694.contentdm.oclc.org/cdm/compoun dobject/collection/p15052coll5/id/24235/rec/5 (accessed February 25, 2015); Outward Slave Manifest, Alexandria, November 19, 1839 (*Uncas*), New-York Historical Society, MS569, Slavery Collection, nyhs_sc_b-05_f-16_021-001, http://cd m16694.contentdm.oclc.org/cdm/compoundobject/collection/p15052coll5/id/24

240/rec/4 (accessed February 25, 2015). The oldest bondperson identified in the set of slave manifests examined for this study was the fifty-seven-year-old "yellow" enslaved man George Williams shipped by Thomas N. Davis from Savannah, Georgia, to Jacksonville, Florida. See Outward Slave Manifest, Savannah, April 7, 1840 (*Forrester*), US, Southeast Coastwise Inward and Outward Slave Manifests, 1790–1860, image 150.

40. Inward Slave Manifest, New Orleans, November 19, 1839 (*Uncas*), NARA M1895, reel 8, image 519.

41. Outward Slave Manifest, Alexandria, October 9, 1840 (*Uncas*); Clayton, *Cash for Blood*, 45, 67; *Alexandria Gazette*, October 12, 1840; testimony of Ebenezer Rodbird, in *Wilkinson v. Williams* (1850), Records of the US District Court for the District of Columbia, Case Papers, 1802–1863, Civil Trial #15, Box 739, Folder 15, NA; testimony of Ebenezer Rodbird, in *Cassedy v. Williams* (1843), Records of the US District Court for the District of Columbia, Case Papers, 1802–1863, Civil Trial #98, Box 663, NA; *Cleveland Herald* (Ohio), April 14, 1849 (quotation).

42. Clayton, *Cash for Blood*, 46, 622–623; *Baltimore Gazette and Daily Advertiser*, December 26, 1837, November 7, 1835. Whites in Washington, D.C., seeking passage to Mobile in 1840 but not wanting to take a boat the entire way, could sail to Augusta, Georgia, and there take advantage of the Alligator Line, a series of rail lines, stagecoaches, and steamers that would convey them to Mobile. The Alligator Line departed Augusta for the Alabama port town every Tuesday, Thursday, and Saturday on a trek that took four days. See *Daily National Intelligencer*, May 9, 1840.

43. Calvin Schermerhorn, *The Business of Slavery and the Rise of American Capitalism, 1815–1860* (New Haven: Yale University Press, 2015), 138–139, 142–143; William Jay, *An Inquiry into the Character and Tendency of the American Colonization, and American Anti-Slavery Societies* (New York: Leavitt, Lord & Co., 1835), 154 (quotations).

44. Calvin Schermerhorn, "The Coastwise Slave Trade and a Mercantile Community of Interest," in *Slavery's Capitalism*, ed. Sven Beckert and Seth Rockman (Philadelphia: University of Pennsylvania Press, 2016), 221; Thomas S. Gaines, ed., *Buried Alive (Behind Prison Walls) for a Quarter of a Century: Life of William Walker* (Saginaw, Mich.: Friedman & Hynan, 1892), 10 (first through fourth quotations), 11 (fifth quotation); Northup, *Twelve Years a Slave*, 46; Clayton, *Cash for Blood*, 623, 47; Isabel Howell, "John Armfield, Slave-trader," *Tennessee Historical Quarterly* 2 (March 1943), 21. The slave manifests for William H. Williams and his associates' voyages reveal few slave deaths. In December 1848, for example, Ebenezer Rodbird shipped a load of enslaved men and women to Thomas Williams aboard the brig *Union*. The twenty-four-year-old Felix Sancen died en route from Baltimore to New Orleans. See Inward Slave Manifest, New Orleans, December 16, 1848 (*Union*), NARA M1895, reel 12, image 249.

45. B. Hooe to Thomas W. Gilmer, September 24, 1840.

46. B. Hooe to Thomas W. Gilmer, September 24, 1840.

47. B. Hooe to Thomas W. Gilmer, October 12, 1840.

48. Affidavit of Andrew L. Addison, Executive Papers, John Rutherfoord, Box 1, Folder 5, LVA; *True American* (New Orleans), April 18, 1839; William H. Richardson to Messrs. A. L. Addison & Co., October 17, 1840, Virginia Governor's Papers, Executive Letter

Book, David Campbell to William Smith, June 10, 1839 to April 29, 1848, Misc. Reel 3014, Frame 121, LVA (quotations); William H. Richardson to Messrs. A. L. Addison & Co., October 17, 1840, Executive Papers, John Rutherfoord, Box 1, Folder 5, LVA; *Mobile Journal* (Ala.), reprinted in *Pensacola Gazette* (Fla.), November 7, 1840. A. L. Addison & Co. was located at 22 Bank Place, New Orleans, and maintained a warehouse on Natchez Street. See *True American* (New Orleans), April 18, 1839; *Times-Picayune*, May 17, 1845.

49. Wm. H. Richardson to M. W. Garrison, November 17, 1840, Virginia Governor's Papers, Executive Letter Book, David Campbell to William Smith, June 10, 1839 to April 29, 1848, Misc. Reel 3014, Frame 127, LVA (first quotation); *Mobile Journal,* reprinted in *Pensacola Gazette,* November 7, 1840 (all other quotations). See also *Mobile Chronicle* (Ala.), reprinted in *New Orleans Commercial Bulletin,* October 31, 1840.

50. *New Orleans Commercial Bulletin,* November 2, 1840.

51. *Times-Picayune,* September 18, 1840; Wm. H. Richardson to M. W. Garrison.

52. Clayton, *Cash for Blood,* 67–68; *Mobile Chronicle,* reprinted in *New Orleans Commercial Bulletin,* October 31, 1840 (first quotation); *Mobile Journal,* October 31, reprinted in *Commercial Advertiser* (New York), November 9, 1840 (second, fifth, and sixth quotations); R. Littlejohn to Gov. Gilmer, November 26, 1840, Executive Papers, Thomas Walker Gilmer, Box 2, Folder 10, LVA (third and fourth quotations). See also *Mobile Journal,* reprinted in *Pensacola Gazette,* November 7, 1840; *New Orleans Commercial Bulletin,* November 2, 1840; *Alexandria Gazette,* November 12, 1840.

53. Memorial of William H. Williams, *Report of the Judiciary Committee on the Memorial of W. H. Williams* (New Orleans: n.p., 1855) (first quotation); Wheelock S. Upton to Wm. Freret, November 1, 1841, Carlile Pollock, vol. 64, act no. 261, Record of Documents at the request of William H. Williams, November 23, 1841, NONA (second and third quotations); *Times-Picayune,* March 25, 1841, November 24, 1842; Document C, Affidavit of S. F. Slatter, [1841], Carlile Pollock, vol. 64, act no. 261, NONA (fourth and fifth quotations); *Daily Picayune,* February 28, 1841.

54. Memorial of William H. Williams (quotation); Legislature, House, Committee on Judiciary, *Report of the Judiciary Committee on the Memorial of W. H. Williams* (New Orleans: n.p., 1855), 1.

CHAPTER 4: MOBILE TO NEW ORLEANS

1. *Mobile Chronicle,* reprinted in *New Orleans Commercial Bulletin,* October 31, 1840; John G. Akin, comp., *A Digest of the Laws of the State of Alabama* (Philadelphia: Alexander Towar, 1833), 391; *Mobile Daily Commercial Register and Patriot* (Ala.), October 31, 1840. See also *Mobile Journal,* reprinted in *Pensacola Gazette,* November 7, 1840.

2. *Daily Picayune* (New Orleans), February 28, 1841.

3. Edward Ingersoll, comp., *A Digest of the Laws of the United States of America, from March 4th, 1789, to May 15th, 1820* (Philadelphia: James Maxwell, 1821), 799 (first, second, and sixth quotations); Charles H. Wesley, "Manifests of Slave Shipments along the Waterways, 1808–1864," *Journal of Negro History* 27 (April 1942), 170–172 (third through

NOTES TO PAGES 89–90

fifth quotations 171, seventh and eighth quotations 172); Affidavit of S. H. Page, August 2, 1841, Carlile Pollock, vol. 64, act no. 227, NONA (ninth quotation).

4. *Mobile Journal*, October 31, 1840, reprinted in *New Orleans Commercial Bulletin*, November 2, 1840, *Commercial Advertiser* (New York), November 9, 1840, and *Alexandria Gazette* (Va.), November 12, 1840; *Mobile Daily Commercial Register and Patriot*, October 31, 1840 (quotations).

5. *Times-Picayune* (New Orleans), October 31, 1840 (first quotation); *Mobile Journal*, October 31, 1840, reprinted in *New Orleans Commercial Bulletin*, November 2, 1840, *Commercial Advertiser*, November 9, 1840, and *Alexandria Gazette*, November 12, 1840 (second quotation).

6. Michael Tadman, *Speculators and Slaves: Masters, Traders, and Slaves in the Old South* (Madison: University of Wisconsin Press, 1989), 47; Michael Tadman, "The Hidden History of Slave Trading in Antebellum South Carolina: John Springs III and Other 'Gentlemen Dealing in Slaves'," *South Carolina Historical Magazine* 97 (January 1996), 19–20; Michael Tadman, "The Reputation of the Slave Trader in Southern History and the Social Memory of the South," *American Nineteenth Century History* 8 (September 2007), 260, 262; Steven Deyle, "Rethinking the Slave Trade: Slave Traders and the Market Revolution in the South," in *The Old South's Modern Worlds: Slavery, Region, and Nation in the Age of Progress*, ed. L. Diane Barnes, Brian Schoen, and Frank Towers (New York: Oxford University Press, 2011), 105; Partnership, William H. Williams & George M. Grant, March 4, 1837, Adolphe Mazureau, vol. 16, pages 345–346, NONA (first quotation 345); *Gibson's Guide and Directory of the State of Louisiana, and the Cities of New Orleans & Lafayette* (New Orleans: John Gibson, 1838), 214; Property lease, June 9, 1837, William Christy, vol. 30, page 31, NONA; *Times-Picayune*, July 18, 1839, August 29, 1845 (second and third quotations), November 20, 1839; *New-Orleans Directory for 1842* (New Orleans: Pitts & Clarke, 1842), 422; *New-Orleans Annual and Commercial Directory, for 1843* (New Orleans: Justin L. Sollée, 1842), 341, 342; *Times-Picayune*, November 9, 1842, August 8, 1843; Property lease, September 1843, Adolphe Mazureau, vol. 28, act no. 67, NONA; *Times-Picayune*, November 6 and 20, 1845, May 30, 1846, October 16, 1847; *Daily Picayune*, November 3, 1840 (fourth quotation).

William H. Williams' boot and shoe selling partnership landed him in court, but not nearly as often as did the slave trade. A dispute with Caleb S. Benedict of New Canaan, Connecticut, and the partnership of Benedict, Bradley & Co. over an unpaid debt, first heard in the New Orleans Commercial Court, reached the Louisiana State Supreme Court in 1843. See *Caleb S. Benedict v. William H. Williams and another* (1843), Supreme Court of Louisiana, 4 Rob. (LA) 392, 1843 La. LEXIS 124, 1843 WL 1419 (La.); Mortgage, William Christy, vol. 47, page 723, NONA; Mortgage, November 28, 1843, Carlile Pollock, vol. 66, act no. 222, NONA; Mortgage, December 26, 1843, Greenbury R. Stringer, vol. 1, act no. 140, NONA. In 1845, Ezra Benedict and Roswald Benedict of the New Canaan, Connecticut, firm of Benedict & Co., sued Williams & Grant for another unpaid debt. See *E. Benedict & Co. v. Williams & Grant* (1845), Case #6929, Commercial Court, NOPL. Each of these lawsuits ended favorably for the Benedicts.

I initially doubted that the William H. Williams of Williams & Grant was, in fact, the Washington, D.C. slave trader, but notary public Carlile Pollock, cited above, identified "William Hendrick Williams, of Washington City," by both full name and residence.

7. Outward Slave Manifest, Alexandria, October 9, 1840 (*Uncas*), New-York Historical Society, MS569, Slavery Collection, nyhs_sc_b-05_f-16_015–001, http://cdm16694 .contentdm.oclc.org/cdm/compoundobject/collection/p15052coll5/id/24223/rec/6 (accessed February 25, 2015); Inward Slave Manifest, New Orleans, November 4, 1840 (*Uncas*), NARA M1895, reel 8, images 770-772; *Acts Passed at the First Session of the Ninth Legislature of the State of Louisiana; Begun and Held in the City of New-Orleans, on Monday, the Eighth Day of December, in the Year of Our Lord One Thousand Eight Hundred and Twenty Eight, and of the Independence of the United States of America, the Fifty-Second* (New Orleans: John Gibson, 1829), 48; *Louisiana Courier* (New Orleans), November 4, 1840. According to Section 15 of the 1829 law, "no slave child, or children, ten years of age, or under, shall be introduced into this state, unaccompanied by his, her, or their mother, if living." It was incumbent upon the person selling any enslaved youth without their mothers to prove that the mothers were, in fact, deceased. See also Herman Freudenberger and Jonathan B. Pritchett, "The Domestic United States Slave Trade: New Evidence," *Journal of Interdisciplinary History* 21 (Winter 1991), 454; Judith Kelleher Schafer, *Slavery, the Civil Law, and the Supreme Court of Louisiana* (Baton Rouge: Louisiana State University Press, 1994), 165. Slave traders needed to prove that unaccompanied young children taken in the trade were indeed orphans. Otherwise, they faced fines of $1,000–2,000 and imprisonment for six months to one year.

8. *Louisiana Courier*, November 4, 1840; Jessica M. Lepler, *The Many Panics of 1837: People, Politics, and the Creation of a Transatlantic Financial Crisis* (New York: Cambridge University Press, 2013), 13; Joshua D. Rothman, "The Contours of Cotton Capitalism: Speculation, Slavery, and Economic Panic in Mississippi, 1832–1841," in *Slavery's Capitalism*, ed. Sven Beckert and Seth Rockman (Philadelphia: University of Pennsylvania Press, 2016), 127; Walter Johnson, *River of Dark Dreams: Slavery and Empire in the Cotton Kingdom* (Cambridge, Mass.: Belknap Press of Harvard University Press, 2013), 86; Frederic Bancroft, *Slave Trading in the Old South*, introduction by Michael Tadman·(1931; Columbia: University of South Carolina Press, 1996), 315.

9. Ralph Clayton, *Cash for Blood: The Baltimore to New Orleans Domestic Slave Trade* (Westminster, Md.: Heritage Books, 2007), 43, 67–68, 134; *Louisiana Courier*, November 4, 1840; *Gibson's Guide and Directory of the State of Louisiana, and the Cities of New Orleans & Lafayette* (New Orleans: John Gibson, 1838), 219; Johnson, *River of Dark Dreams*, 86 (quotation); Thomas S. Gaines, ed., *Buried Alive (Behind Prison Walls) for a Quarter of a Century: Life of William Walker* (Saginaw, Mich.: Friedman & Hynan, 1892), 11.

10. L. A. Chamerovzow, ed., *Slave Life in Georgia: A Narrative of the Life, Sufferings, and Escape of John Brown, a Fugitive Slave, Now in England* (London: n.p., 1855), 110 (first through sixth quotations), 111 (seventh through eleventh quotations). See also Solomon Northup, *Twelve Years a Slave*, ed. Sue Eakin and Joseph Logsdon (Baton Rouge: Louisiana State University Press, 1996), 50.

11. Chamerovzow, *Slave Life in Georgia*, 111 (first quotation), 112; Gaines, *Buried Alive*, 11 (second quotation).

12. Chamerovzow, *Slave Life in Georgia*, 114 (first through third quotations); *Times-Picayune*, October 24, 1840 (fourth quotation); Affidavit of S. H. Page; *Louisiana Courier*, November 4, 1840; *Daily Picayune*, February 28, 1841; Outward Slave Manifest, Mobile, May 4, 1837 (*Ouachita*), US, Southeast Coastwise Inward and Outward Slave Manifests, 1790–1860, image 271.

13. Taja-Nia Y. Henderson, "Crucibles of Discontent: Penal Practice in the Shadow of Slavery, Virginia, 1796–1865" (Ph.D. diss., New York University, 2013), 175, 176, 200, 202, 221, 223.

14. *Commonwealth v. John* (1839), Executive Papers, David Campbell, Box 6, Folder 2, LVA; *Commonwealth v. Jim* (1840), Executive Papers, Thomas Walker Gilmer, Box 1, Folder 5, LVA; *Commonwealth v. Arena* (1840), Executive Papers, Thomas Walker Gilmer, Box 1, Folder 5, LVA (first quotation); *Commonwealth v. Nan (Nancy Via)* (1840), Executive Papers, Thomas Walker Gilmer, Box 1, Folder 9, LVA (second quotation).

15. *Commonwealth v. Negro John* (1839), Executive Papers, David Campbell, Box 5, Folder 4, LVA; Martha Hodes, *White Women, Black Men: Illicit Sex in the Nineteenth-Century South* (New Haven: Yale University Press, 1997); Diane Miller Sommerville, "The Rape Myth in the Old South Reconsidered," *Journal of Southern History* 61 (August 1995): 481–518; "A List of Slaves and Free persons of color received into the Penitentiary of Virginia for sale and transportation from the 25th June 1816 to the 1st February 1842," Auditor of Public Accounts, Condemned Blacks Executed or Transported, Records – Condemned Slaves, Court Orders, and Valuations, 1858–1865, Misc. Reel 2555, Frame 996, LVA.

16. *Commonwealth v. John & Arthur* (1839), Executive Papers, David Campbell, Box 5, Folder 4, LVA.

17. *Commonwealth v. Phil, John, Harrison, Nelson & Henry* (1839), Executive Papers, David Campbell, Box 6, Folder 2, LVA.

18. *Commonwealth v. Nelson* (1840), Executive Papers, David Campbell, Box 8, Folder 1, LVA.

19. *Commonwealth v. James* (1840), Executive Papers, David Campbell, Box 8, Folder 1, LVA; *Commonwealth v. Nelson* (quotations). As a free black man, Lewis Cromwell did not appear before the same court, although John Buchanan testified in James' case that, when Cromwell learned that he had unwittingly stolen from Reverend Eskridge, "a horror came over his conscience for stealing the preacher's money and that he had not rested day nor night, from that time . . . [H]e would have no peace until he would tell all about it." Upon confessing his crime, "he felt at rest and they [the authorities] might do as they pleased with him." See *Commonwealth v. James*.

20. *Commonwealth v. Stephen* (1840), Executive Papers, David Campbell, Box 7, Folder 7, LVA.

21. *Commonwealth v. George* (1840), Executive Papers, David Campbell, Box 8, Folder 2, LVA.

22. *Commonwealth v. George* (first quotation); *Commonwealth v. Ned* (1840), Executive Papers, Thomas Walker Gilmer, Box 1, Folder 9, LVA (second through fifth quotations); Auditor of Public Accounts, Condemned Blacks Executed or Transported, Records – Condemned Slaves, Court Orders, and Valuations, 1833–1845, Misc. Reel 2553, Frames 612, 611, LVA.

23. *Commonwealth v. Negro Henry* (1840), Executive Papers, Thomas Walker Gilmer, Box 1, Folder 5, LVA; Janet Duitsman Cornelius, *When I Can Read My Title Clear: Literacy, Slavery, and Religion in the Antebellum South* (Columbia: University of South Carolina Press, 1991), 8–9.

24. *Commonwealth v. Negro Henry*.

25. *Commonwealth v. Albert* (1838), Executive Papers, David Campbell, Box 4, Folder 2, LVA.

26. *Commonwealth v. Albert* (quotations); "List of Slaves," 996.

27. Affidavit of S. H. Page. Wesley, "Manifests," 171, observes that slaveholders traveling in the opposite direction, "from Port Pontchartrain by Lake Borgne and Pascagoula Bay to Mobile," were also no longer compelled to fill out slave manifests.

28. Document C, Affidavit of S. F. Slatter [1841], Carlile Pollock, vol. 64, act no. 261, NONA (first quotation); Legislature, House, Committee on Judiciary, *Report of the Judiciary Committee on the Memorial of W. H. Williams* (New Orleans: n.p., 1855), 1–2 (second and third quotations); Document B, Affidavit of Wheelock S. Upton, Carlile Pollock, vol. 64, act no. 261, NONA; Document E, William H. Williams' recollections of George Y. Bright's testimony, November 23, 1841, Carlile Pollock, vol. 64, act no. 261, NONA (fourth quotation).

29. Document B (quotations); *New-Orleans Directory, for 1841* (New Orleans: J. L. Sollee, 1840), 185; John Bailey, *The Lost German Slave Girl: The Extraordinary True Story of Sally Miller and her Fight for Freedom in Old New Orleans* (New York: Grove Press, 2003), 89.

30. Document B (first quotation); Document A, Wheelock S. Upton to William Freret, November 1, 1841, Carlile Pollock, vol. 64, act no. 261, NONA (second through eleventh quotations); Wheelock S. Upton to Thomas W. Gilmer or Wm. H. Richardson, December 5, 1840, Executive Papers, Thomas Walker Gilmer, Box 3, Folder 1, LVA.

31. Affidavit of S. H. Page (first quotation); Affidavit of Christian Meyers, July 30, 1841, Carlile Pollock, vol. 64, act no. 227, NONA (second through fourth quotations); Affidavit of Frederick Barton, July 31, 1841, Carlile Pollock, vol. 64, act no. 227, NONA.

32. *Daily Picayune*, February 28, 1841. In a matter of months, Solomon Northup would ride the same rail line as the Williams' gang slaves. See Northup, *Twelve Years a Slave*, 244. Today, the University of New Orleans campus is located on the site of the former Milneburg. The Pontchartrain Railroad ran down the center of modern-day Elysian Fields Avenue.

33. Affidavit of Andrew L. Addison, October 31, 1840, Executive Papers, John Rutherfoord, Box 1, Folder 5, LVA (quotations); *State v. William H. Williams*, no. 4671, Supreme Court of Louisiana, UNO. Addison died of cholera on Sunday, November 7, 1852, at the age of fifty-six. See *Times-Picayune*, November 9, 1852. New Orleans remained Louisiana's state capital until 1849.

34. *New-Orleans Directory, for 1841*, 129; Gov. A. B. Roman to Stephen Mazureau, October 30, 1840, State of Louisiana, Messages & Proclamations of the Governor, 1837–1842, p. 267, LSA (first quotation); Affidavit of Stephen Mazureau, October 31, 1840, Executive Papers, John Rutherfoord, Box 1, Folder 5, LVA (second and third quotations). Another version of this story suggests that Attorney General Mazureau, having

already received the letter from Virginia via Governor Roman, appeared before Mayor Freret "and declared that he is credibly informed and does verily believe that sundry slaves … are about to be imported into the State of Louisiana." See *State v. William H. Williams*, no. 4671, Supreme Court of Louisiana, UNO.

35. Affidavit of Stephen Mazureau (quotations); Hank Trent, *The Secret Life of Bacon Tait, a White Slave Trader Married to a Free Woman of Color* (Baton Rouge: Louisiana State University Press, 2017), 47; AfriGeneas, "A Partial Transcription of Inward Slave Manifests, Port of New Orleans, Record Group 36, United States Customs Service, Collector of Customs at New Orleans," Background, www.afrigeneas.com/slavedata/background.html (accessed August 6, 2017); *Williams v. Louisiana*, no. 14157, Orleans Parish Court, NOLA. For more than a century, Balize had been repeatedly destroyed by storms, rebuilt, and even relocated. After 1860, its extreme vulnerability to hurricanes forced the abandonment of the settlement.

36. *National Era* (Washington, D.C.), February 10, 1853; Gov. E. D. White to Senate, January 28, 1839, State of Louisiana, Messages & Proclamations of the Governor, 1837–1842, p. 130, LSA; *True American* (New Orleans), April 18, 1837. Newspapers occasionally seemed to confuse L. H. Seré and Emile Lasère (variously spelled Lassere and LaSere), a one-time nominee for New Orleans city auctioneer who in 1840 served as deputy sheriff of the New Orleans Commercial Court. Subsequent court records identify Luc H. Seré as a witness in the trial of William H. Williams.

37. Document C; *Daily Picayune*, February 28, 1841 (fourth and sixth quotations); Document E (first through third, fifth, seventh, and eighth quotations); Report of the Day Police, November 1, 1840, New Orleans (La.) Third Municipality Guard, Mayor's Book, 1838–1850, vol. 2, p. 200, 89–214, TKD205M, NOPL.

CHAPTER 5: LEGAL TROUBLES

1. *Daily Picayune* (New Orleans), March 12, 1841 (quotations); Steven Deyle, *Carry Me Back: The Domestic Slave Trade in American Life* (New York: Oxford University Press, 2005), 52. Section 1 of the act of 1817 stated that "no slave shall be imported or brought into this state, who shall have been convicted of the crimes of murder, rape, arson, manslaughter, attempt to murder, burglary, or having raised, or attempted to raise an insurrection among the slaves in any state of the Union or elsewhere." See *Acts Passed at the First Session of the Third Legislature of the State of Louisiana, Begun and Held in the City of New-Orleans on Monday the Eighteenth Day of November, in the Year of Our Lord One Thousand Eight Hundred and Sixteen, and of the Independence of the United States of America the Fortieth* (New Orleans: J. C. De St. Romes, 1817), 44.

2. Michael Tadman, "The Reputation of the Slave Trader in Southern History and the Social Memory of the South," *American Nineteenth Century History* 8 (September 2007), 252, 255, 256; Herman Freudenberger and Jonathan B. Pritchett, "The Domestic United States Slave Trade: New Evidence," *Journal of Interdisciplinary History* 21 (Winter 1991), 447, 448; Winfield H. Collins, *The Domestic Slave Trade of the Southern States* (1904; reprint, Port Washington, N.Y.: Kennikat Press, 1969), 47; *Acts Passed at the First Session of the Ninth*

Legislature of the State of Louisiana; Begun and Held in the City of New-Orleans, on Monday, the Eighth Day of December, in the Year of Our Lord One Thousand Eight Hundred and Twenty Eight, and of the Independence of the United States of America, the Fifty-Second (New Orleans: John Gibson, 1829), 38–40 (first quotation), 38 (second quotation), 48 (third quotation); Edward E. Baptist, *The Half Has Never Been Told: Slavery and the Making of American Capitalism* (New York: Basic Books, 2014), 175. The law went into effect April 1, 1829. Section 1 directed that the certificates of good character must also include "the name, age, sex, and as near as possible, the size, marks, and color" (p. 38) of the bondpeople brought into Louisiana, the name of the place of purchase, and the names of the sellers. Section 2 further stated that "the Clerk of some court of record" (p. 40) in the county from which the slaves had been purchased verify the identity and "good character" (p. 40) of the freeholders attesting to the slaves' good character. According to Section 6, failure to comply with the provisions of the act meant that violators faced harsh financial penalties of $1,000–2,000, imprisonment of between six months and one year, and the forfeiture of the "illegally introduced" slaves (p. 44). The slaves would then be sold at auction by the parish sheriff. Section 13 made it unlawful "for any person . . . to introduce . . . any slave or slaves who shall have been accused of any conspiracy or insurrection, or who had resided in any county of any state or territory of the United States during the time of any conspiracy or insurrection in such county." The penalty for breaking this portion of the law was a fine of $1,000–5,000 and imprisonment of between one and five years (p. 48). An act approved March 24, 1831, repealed the first through eighth, tenth through twelfth, seventeenth, and eighteenth sections of the 1829 act relative to the introduction of slaves in this state. See *Acts Passed at the First Session of the Tenth Legislature of the State of Louisiana. Begun at Donaldsonville, on Monday the Third Day of January, One Thousand Eight Hundred and Thirty-One, and of the Independence of the United States of America the Fifty-Fourth, and Adjourned to, and Held in the City of New-Orleans, on the Eighth of January* (New Orleans: John Gibson, 1831), 78. Joshua D. Rothman, "The Contours of Cotton Capitalism: Speculation, Slavery, and Economic Panic in Mississippi, 1832–1841," in *Slavery's Capitalism*, ed. Sven Beckert and Seth Rockman (Philadelphia: University of Pennsylvania Press, 2016), 132, observes that the state of Mississippi also required a certificate of good character for imported slaves.

3. Collins, *Domestic Slave Trade*, 47; Wendell Holmes Stephenson, *Isaac Franklin: Slave Trader and Planter of the Old South* (Baton Rouge: Louisiana State University Press, 1938), 76; Robert H. Gudmestad, *A Troublesome Commerce: The Transformation of the Interstate Slave Trade* (Baton Rouge: Louisiana State University Press, 2003), 102–117; Tadman, "Reputation of the Slave Trader," 254; *Acts Passed at the Extra Session of the Tenth Legislature of the State of Louisiana. Begun and Held in the City of New Orleans, on Monday the Fourteenth Day of November, A.D. One Thousand Eight Hundred and Thirty One* (New Orleans: John Gibson, 1831), 4 (unnumbered); Baptist, *The Half Has Never Been Told*, 208; *Cleveland Herald* (Ohio), April 14, 1849 (quotation); *Daily Picayune*, March 12, 1841. The law allowed masters emigrating to Louisiana to take their slaves with them, assuming that the owners were settling within the state and "that the slaves were not purchased in the states of Mississippi, or Alabama, or in the Territory of Arkansas, or in Florida" (p. 4). They

also needed to file paperwork in their parish of residence and make oath identifying the slaves and pledging that they were for their own use. Penalties for violating the act included fines of $500–1,000 per slave and "imprisonment till fine and costs be paid" (p. 4). Slaves conveyed unlawfully into Louisiana were "entitled to their freedom" and turned over to the governor, who was empowered to transport them out of the state (p. 6). Section 4 further prohibited masters who introduced slaves into the state from selling them in the next five years. Governor André B. Roman signed several revisions of the Louisiana slave code into law on March 26, 1833. See *Acts Passed at the First Session of the Eleventh Legislature of the State of Louisiana, Begun and Held in the City of New Orleans, the Seventh Day of January, Eighteen Hundred and Thirty Three* (New Orleans: Jerome Bayon, 1833), 81. An amendment approved on April 2, 1832, added Tennessee, Kentucky, and Missouri to the list of states from which slaves could not be imported. See *Acts Passed at the Third Session of the Tenth Legislature of the State of Louisiana, Begun and Held in the City of New-Orleans, on Monday the Second Day of January, in the Year of Our Lord, One Thousand Eight Hundred and Thirty-Two, and of the Independence of the United States of America, the Fifty-Sixth* (New Orleans: Stroud & Pew, 1832), 140. Louisiana formally repealed the prohibition against importation in 1834. See A. A. Taylor, "The Movement of Negroes from the East to the Gulf States from 1830 to 1850," *Journal of Negro History* 8 (October 1923), 375. As one legal scholar has noted, "all southern states, except Arkansas, Florida, and Texas, passed antebellum laws that prohibited the introduction of slaves into their borders." See Andrew Fede, "Legal Protection for Slave Buyers in the US South: A Caveat Concerning *Caveat Emptor*," *American Journal of Legal History* 31 (October 1987), 351. Like Louisiana, Mississippi, in its revised state constitution of 1832, also "outlawed the interstate slave trade altogether," although that provision was unpopular and widely ignored. See Rothman, "Contours of Cotton Capitalism," 132–133.

4. *Acts Passed at the First Session of the Third Legislature of the State of Louisiana*, 46 (first through third quotations); *Times-Picayune* (New Orleans), July 9, 1841 (fourth quotation).

5. Document E, William H. Williams' recollections of George Y. Bright's testimony, November 23, 1841, Carlile Pollock, vol. 64, act no. 261, NONA.

6. *Daily Picayune*, February 28, 1841; *National Era*, February 10, 1853; Walter Johnson, *River of Dark Dreams: Slavery and Empire in the Cotton Kingdom* (Cambridge, Mass.: Belknap Press of Harvard University Press, 2013), 282; Joshua D. Rothman, *Flush Times and Fever Dreams: A Story of Capitalism and Slavery in the Age of Jackson* (Athens: University of Georgia Press, 2012), 49, 279, 296; Andrew J. Torget, *Seeds of Empire: Cotton, Slavery, and the Transformation of the Texas Borderlands, 1800–1850* (Chapel Hill: University of North Carolina Press, 2015), 170, 193, 212, 216; Jessica M. Lepler, *The Many Panics of 1837: People, Politics, and the Creation of a Transatlantic Financial Crisis* (New York: Cambridge University Press, 2013), 137; Calvin Schermerhorn, "Slave Trading in a Republic of Credit: Financial Architecture of the US Slave Market, 1815–1840," *Slavery and Abolition* 36, no. 4 (2015), 598, memorably described the migration to Texas as a "stampede of deadbeats."

7. Document E (quotation); John Bailey, *The Lost German Slave Girl: The Extraordinary True Story of Sally Miller and her Fight for Freedom in Old New Orleans* (New York: Grove Press, 2003), 124–127, 130, 254.

8. Document D, Affidavit of J. W. Zacharie [1841], Carlile Pollock, vol. 64, act no. 261, NONA; *State v. Williams* (1842, 1844), no. 4671, 7 Rob. 252.

9. Judith Kelleher Schafer, *Slavery, the Civil Law, and the Supreme Court of Louisiana* (Baton Rouge: Louisiana State University Press, 1994), 162; J. Winston Coleman, Jr., "Lexington's Slave Dealers and their Southern Trade," *Filson Club History Quarterly* 12 (January 1938), 20, 13; Walter Johnson, *Soul by Soul: Life inside the Antebellum Slave Market* (Cambridge, Mass.: Harvard University Press, 1999); Dea H. Boster, "'I Made up my Mind to Act Both Deaf and Dumb': Displays of Disability and Slave Resistance in the Antebellum American South," in *Disability and Passing: Blurring the Lines of Identity*, ed. Jeffrey A. Brune and Daniel J. Wilson (Philadelphia: Temple University Press, 2013), 83.

10. Coleman, "Lexington's Slave Dealers," 13–14; Frederic Bancroft, *Slave Trading in the Old South*, introduction by Michael Tadman (1931; Columbia: University of South Carolina Press, 1996), 106; Rothman, "Contours of Cotton Capitalism," 132; Jenny B. Wahl, "The Jurisprudence of American Slave Sales," *Journal of Economic History* 56 (March 1996), 144, 146, 148, 149; Fede, "Legal Protection," 327, 336.

11. Wahl, "Jurisprudence," 156, 157; *Acts Passed at the Second Session of the Eleventh Legislature of the State of Louisiana, Begun and Held in the City of New-Orleans, the Ninth Day of December, Eighteen Hundred and Thirty-Three* (New Orleans: Jerome Bayon, 1834), 7 (quotations); Richard Tansey, "Bernard Kendig and the New Orleans Slave Trade," *Louisiana History* 23 (1982), 173; Judith K. Schafer, "'Guaranteed against the Vices and Maladies Prescribed by Law': Consumer Protection, the Law of Slave Sales, and the Supreme Court in Antebellum Louisiana," *American Journal of Legal History* 31 (October 1987), 309, 310, 308. Vernon Valentine Palmer observes that the Spanish law under which Louisiana functioned from 1762 to 1802 favored sellers in cases of contested slave sales: "A seller under Spanish law could not be forced to take back the slave from the buyer unless he had actual knowledge of the slave's defect at the time of the sale." The 1834 redhibition law reflected the influence and practices of the French, who governed Louisiana from 1682 to 1762 and again briefly prior to the United States' acquisition of the Louisiana Purchase in 1803. French law "held the seller strictly accountable for latent defects, regardless of his ignorance of their existence." Palmer also notes that Louisiana and the two Carolinas were the only three slaveholding states who protected buyers through implied warranties. See Vernon Valentine Palmer, *Through the Codes Darkly: Slave Law and Civil Law in Louisiana* (Clark, N.J.: The Lawbook Exchange, 2012), 158.

12. Palmer, *Through the Codes Darkly*, 158n46, 159; Schafer, *Slavery, the Civil Law, and the Supreme Court*, 153, 158, 162, 140–142; Tansey, "Bernard Kendig," 172.

13. Palmer, *Through the Codes Darkly*, 159; Adolphe Mazureau, 1845, vol. 30, act no. 149, NONA (first and second quotations); William Christy, 1843, vol. 47, p. 722, NONA (third and fourth quotations); Edward Barnett, 1847, vol. 38, act no. 771½, NONA (fifth quotation); Edward Barnett, 1843, vol. 23, act no. 279, June 23, 1843, NONA; Edward Barnett, 1843, vol. 23, act no. 364, NONA (sixth quotation).

14. Theodore Guyol, 1846, vol. 3, act no. 12, NONA (first through fourth quotations); Edward Barnett, 1844, vol. 24, act no. 21, NONA (fifth quotation); Edward Barnett, 1844, vol. 24, act no. 19, NONA.

15. Theodore Guyol, 1845, vol. 1, act no. 338, NONA; Theodore Guyol, 1845, vol. 1, act no. 377, NONA (quotations); James D. Hardy, Jr., "A Slave Sale in Antebellum New Orleans," *Southern Studies* 23 (Fall 1984), 307.

16. *Cassedy v. Williams* (1843), Records of the US District Court for the District of Columbia, Case Papers, 1802–1863, Civil Trial #98, Box 663, NA; *William Gray v. William H. Williams, etc.* (1840), Chancery Causes, Chesapeake/Norfolk County, Folder 80, LVA, www.lva.virginia.gov/chancery/case_detail.asp?CFN=902-1840-009 (accessed July 14, 2017); Edward J. Balleisen, *Navigating Failure: Bankruptcy and Commercial Society in Antebellum America* (Chapel Hill: University of North Carolina Press, 2001), 14, 17; Calvin Schermerhorn, "Slave Trading in a Republic of Credit: Financial Architecture of the US Slave Market, 1815–1840," *Slavery and Abolition* 36, no. 4 (2015), 589–590; Calvin Schermerhorn, "The Coastwise Slave Trade and a Mercantile Community of Interest," in *Slavery's Capitalism*, ed. Sven Beckert and Seth Rockman (Philadelphia: University of Pennsylvania Press, 2016), 220; Calvin Schermerhorn, *The Business of Slavery and the Rise of American Capitalism, 1815–1860* (New Haven: Yale University Press, 2015), 126–127; Ralph Clayton, *Cash for Blood: The Baltimore to New Orleans Domestic Slave Trade* (Westminster, Md.: Heritage Books, 2007), 57; Baptist, *The Half Has Never Been Told*, 179, 183; Deyle, *Carry Me Back*, 104; Hank Trent, *The Secret Life of Bacon Tait, a White Slave Trader Married to a Free Woman of Color* (Baton Rouge: Louisiana State University Press, 2017), 46, 52, 53.

17. *William Gray v. William H. Williams, etc.* (quotations); *Newbern Sentinel* (N.C.), December 19, 1829; *Fayetteville Weekly Observer* (N.C.), December 27, 1826.

18. *William Gray v. William H. Williams, etc.* A Thomas Williams of New Orleans was a co-partner in the firm of Richards, Williams & Co. that dissolved on December 3, 1835. Thereafter Williams and John Kellar continued the iron foundry business on their own, but their partnership ended with an ugly dissolution that invited a series of court cases. Nothing in those court records indicates that this Thomas Williams was the brother of slave trader William H. Williams. Thomas Williams would only have been about sixteen years old in 1835, too young to serve as a named partner in a business. See *New Orleans Commercial Bulletin*, December 5, 1835.

19. Jeff Forret, *Race Relations at the Margins: Slaves and Poor Whites in the Antebellum Southern Countryside* (Baton Rouge: Louisiana State University Press, 2006), 143–148; Tansey, "Bernard Kendig," 172, 174; *Mississippi Free Trader* (Natchez), October 12, 1850; *The Liberator* (Boston), October 25, 1840; *Times-Picayune*, January 19, 1845; *Times-Picayune*, June 13, 1843.

20. William T. Laprade, "The Domestic Slave Trade in the District of Columbia," *Journal of Negro History* 11 (January 1926), 19; Mary Beth Corrigan, "Imaginary Cruelties?: A History of the Slave Trade in Washington, D.C.," *Washington History* 13 (Fall/Winter 2001/2002), 11; Mary Tremain, *Slavery in the District of Columbia: The Policy of Congress and the Struggle for Abolition* (1892; reprint, New York: Negro Universities Press, 1969), 49; Carol Wilson, *Freedom at Risk: The Kidnapping of Free Blacks in America, 1780–1865* (Lexington: University Press of Kentucky, 1994), 9, 107, 117; House of Representatives, *Register of Debates*, 20th Cong., 2d sess., 176; Marc Leepson, *What So Proudly We Hailed: Francis Scott Key, a Life*

(New York: Palgrave Macmillan, 2014), 19 (quotations); M. Sammy Miller, "Patty Cannon: Murderer and Kidnapper of Free Blacks: A Review of the Evidence," *Maryland Historical Magazine* 72 (Fall 1977), 419; Todd A. Herring, "Kidnapped and Sold in Natchez: The Ordeal of Aaron Cooper, a Free Black Man," *Journal of Mississippi History* 60 (December 1998), 341, 346; William Wells Brown, *A Description of William Wells Brown's Original Panoramic Views of the Scenes in the Life of an American Slave, from His Birth in Slavery to His Death or His Escape to His First Home of Freedom on British Soil* (London: Charles Gilpin, 1849), 9, 10; Walter C. Clephane, "The Local Aspect of Slavery in the District of Columbia," *Records of the Columbia Historical Society, Washington, D.C.* 3 (1900), 241.

21. Corrigan, "Imaginary Cruelties?," 11; Ralph Clayton, *Cash for Blood: The Baltimore to New Orleans Domestic Slave Trade* (Westminster, Md.: Heritage Books, 2007), 35, 38–41.

22. Tansey, "Bernard Kendig," 172, 174; Coleman, "Lexington's Slave Dealers," 14–15; *Baltimore Sun*, November 2, 1847 (first quotation); *Daily National Intelligencer* (Washington, D.C.), October 2, 1847 (second and fourth through sixth quotations), September 28, 1847 (third quotation). In 1822, Austin Woolfolk was implicated, indirectly, in an attempted kidnapping of a free black man. See Clayton, *Cash for Blood*, 62.

23. Solomon Northup, *Twelve Years a Slave*, ed. Sue Eakin and Joseph Logsdon (Baton Rouge: Louisiana State University Press, 1996), 32, 38; Corrigan, "Imaginary Cruelties?," 11.

24. *Ashtabula Sentinel* (Ohio), January 27, 1853 (first quotation); Northup, *Twelve Years a Slave*, 244–251 [249 (second quotation), 251 (third quotation), 244 (fourth quotation)].

25. Northup, *Twelve Years a Slave*, 244–251.

26. *William Scott v. William H. Williams*, Summons of William H. Williams, O Say Can You See: Early Washington, D.C., Law & Family, http://earlywashingtondc.org/doc/oscys .case.0239.001 (accessed July 5, 2016); RSPP, PAR#20483805, Series 2, Washington, D.C. (quotations); Petition of William Kennedy, alias Candy, March 23, 1838, Records of the US Circuit Court for the District of Columbia, Chancery Dockets and Rules Case Files, 1804–1863, Rules 3, no. 478, Box 110, NA; Streets of Washington, "The National Hotel," www.streetsofwashington.com/2009/11/national-hotel.html; *Daily National Intelligencer*, March 1, 1830; *Evening Star* (Washington, D.C.), November 6, 1902; *Daily National Intelligencer*, November 16, 1840, August 9, 1838; *Baltimore Sun*, February 23, 1839. Trent, *Secret Life of Bacon Tait*, 88, implied that the Williams brothers made trafficking in free blacks a "lucrative scheme." On freedom suits, see Anne Twitty, *Before Dred Scott: Slavery and Legal Culture in the American Confluence, 1787–1857* (New York: Cambridge University Press, 2016); Kelly M. Kennington, *In the Shadow of Dred Scott: St. Louis Freedom Suits and the Legal Culture of Slavery in Antebellum America* (Athens: University of Georgia Press, 2017).

27. Corrigan, "Imaginary Cruelties?," 8; M. Thompson, *Abstract of the Laws of the District of Columbia*, 3d ed. (Washington, D.C.: W. M. Morrison & Co., 1855), 19, 18 (first through third, fifth, and sixth quotations); RSPP, PAR#20483805 (fourth and seventh through eleventh quotations). Maryland law imposed a $20 per year tax per enslaved man between eighteen and forty-five years of age, $12 for each male slave aged twelve to eighteen, and $2 per bondwoman aged fifteen to forty-five. Non-residents' failure to pay the tax in

advance resulted in $20 fines per slave for both the owner and the hirer. The outcome of the case is not known.

28. *John Mellon et al. v. Bynum, Piles, & Williams* (1838), Records of the US Circuit Court for the District of Columbia, Chancery Dockets and Rules Case Files, 1804–1863, Rules 3, no. 481, Box 110, NA; Sharon Ann Murphy, "Securing Human Property: Slavery, Life Insurance, and Industrialization in the Upper South," *Journal of the Early Republic* 25 (Winter 2005): 615–652; Bonnie Martin, "Slavery's Invisible Engine: Mortgaging Human Property," *Journal of Southern History* 76 (November 2010): 817–866; Karen Ryder, "'To Realize Money Facilities': Slave Life Insurance, the Slave Trade, and Credit in the Old South," in *New Directions in Slavery Studies: Commodification, Community, and Comparison*, ed. Jeff Forret and Christine E. Sears (Baton Rouge: Louisiana State University Press, 2015), 53–71. See also RSPP, PAR#20483804, Series 2, Washington, D.C. For a Richmond slave trader involved in a trust dispute, see Trent, *Secret Life of Bacon Tait*, 129.

29. *John Mellon et al. v. Bynum, Piles, & Williams.*

30. *John Mellon et al. v. Bynum, Piles, & Williams.*

31. *James Ash v. William H. Williams* (1840), Records of the US District Court for the District of Columbia, Case Papers, 1802–1863, Civil Appearances #25, Box 617, NA; *William H. Williams v. James Ash* (1843), Supreme Court of the United States, 42 US 1, 11 L. Ed. 25, 1843 US LEXIS 281, 1 How 1 (first through third quotations); *Williams v. Ash*, Records of the United States Supreme Court, Case File #2183, Box 232, NA (fourth through sixth quotations).

32. Leepson, *What So Proudly We Hailed*, 141, 142; *William H. Williams v. James Ash* (quotation); *Williams v. Ash*. The pertinent law in force was the Maryland Act of Assembly, 1809, ch. 171.

33. *Williams v. Ash.*

34. *William H. Williams v. James Ash.*

35. *William H. Williams v. James Ash.*

36. *William H. Williams v. James Ash.* On the duality of slaves as persons and property, see Mark V. Tushnet, *The American Law of Slavery, 1810–1860: Considerations of Humanity and Interest* (Princeton: Princeton University Press, 1981).

37. *William H. Williams v. James Ash* (first quotation); *Albany Evening Journal* (N.Y.), April 7, 1857 (second quotation); Manuscript Census Returns, Seventh Census of the United States, 1850, Washington Ward 7, Washington, District of Columbia, Schedule 1, Free Population, NAMS M-432, reel 57, page 108A.

38. Chris Naylor, "'You Have the Body': Habeas Corpus Case Records of the US Circuit Court for the District of Columbia, 1820–1863," *Prologue: The Journal of the National Archives* 37 (Fall 2005): 54, 56, 58; Damani Davis, "Slavery and Emancipation in the Nation's Capital," *Prologue: The Journal of the National Archives* 42 (Spring 2010), 57; Clephane, "Local Aspect of Slavery," 235.

39. Petition of Joseph Armstrong & others, January 14, 1840, Records of the United States District Court, Segregated Habeas Corpus Records, NA. See also RSPP, PAR#20484002, Series 2, Washington, D.C.

40. Petition of Israel Brinkley, January 14, 1840, Records of the United States District Court, Segregated Habeas Corpus Records, NA. See also RSPP, PAR#20484006, Series 2, Washington, D.C.

41. Jefferson Morley, *Snow-Storm in August: Washington City, Francis Scott Key, and the Forgotten Race Riot of 1835* (New York: Nan A. Talese/Doubleday, 2012), 44, 68, 207, 208; Steve Vogel, *Through the Perilous Fight: Six Weeks that Saved the Nation* (New York: Random House, 2013), 406–407, 411; Leepson, *What So Proudly We Hailed*, xi, xii, 160, 193.

42. Sixth Census of the United States, 1840, Washington, D.C., NAMS M-704, reel 35, page 99; Morley, *Snow-Storm in August*, 30, 40, 41, 80, 218; Vogel, *Through the Perilous Fight*, 407, 410, 411; Leepson, *What So Proudly We Hailed*, xi, xii, xiii, 25, 26 (quotation), 76, 77, 78, 82–83, 96, 101, 103–105, 125, 142, 159, 177–184, 192; Clephane, "Local Aspect of Slavery," 236.

43. Petition of Joseph Armstrong & others (first, second, fourth, and fifth quotations); Petition of Israel Brinkley (third quotation); Petition of Wm. Burrows, Emanuel Price, & Maria Course, January 14, 1840, RSPP, PAR #20484008, Series 2, Washington, D.C. William Burrows was another black man held captive in William H. Williams' private jail but seeking a writ of *habeas corpus*. His case is not well documented.

44. Deposition of William H. Williams, January 15, 1840, RSPP, PAR#20484006.

45. Deposition of Thomas N. Davis, January 15, 1840, RSPP, PAR#20484006. See also *United States v. Davis* (1839), no. 14,926, 5 Cranch C.C. 622, 25 F.Cas. 775, 5 D.C. 622, Circuit Court, District of Columbia.

46. *United States v. Davis.*

47. *United States v. Davis.*

48. *United States v. Davis* (quotation); Petition of Wm. Burrows, Emanuel Price, & Maria Course, RSPP, PAR#20484008.

49. *Emanuel Price v. Thomas N. Davis*, Petition for Freedom, January 20, 1840, O Say Can You See: Early Washington, D.C., Law & Family, http://earlywashingtondc.org/doc/oscys .case.0126.001 (accessed July 5, 2016) (first and second quotations); Petition of Susan [*sic*] Course, January 20, 1840, RSPP, PAR#20484007 (third through fifth quotations); *Emanuel Price v. Thomas N. Davis*, Summons of Thomas N. Davis, January 20, 1840, O Say Can You See: Early Washington, D.C., Law & Family, http://earlywashingtondc.org/ doc/oscys.case.0126.002 (accessed July 5, 2016); *Susan* [*sic*] *Course v. Thomas N. Davis*, Summons of Thomas N. Davis, January 20, 1840, O Say Can You See: Early Washington, D.C., Law & Family, http://earlywashingtondc.org/doc/oscys.case.0207.001 (accessed July 5, 2016); *United States v. Davis* (sixth through eighth quotations); Herring, "Kidnapped and Sold," 342, 352. On free blacks' use of antebellum courtrooms, see Martha S. Jones, *Birthright Citizens: A History of Race and Rights in Antebellum America* (New York: Cambridge University Press, 2018), esp. ch. 7.

50. *Jones et al. v. United States* (1840), Records of the US District Court for the District of Columbia, Case Papers, 1802–1863, Civil Trial #313, Box 620, NA (first quotation); *The Liberator*, November 29, 1839; *Jones et al. v. United States* (1840), 5 Cranch C.C. 647, 13 F.Cas. 1035, 5 D.C. 647, No. 7499, Circuit Court, District of Columbia (second quotation).

CHAPTER 6: THE MILLINGTON BANK

1. *Mobile Chronicle,* October 26, 1840, reprinted in *Commercial Advertiser* (New York), November 9, 1840 (first and second quotations); *Times-Picayune* (New Orleans), December 5, 1840 (third, fifth, and seventh through ninth quotations); *Vicksburg Tri-Weekly Sentinel* (Miss.), September 30, 1840 (fourth quotation); Edward E. Baptist, *The Half Has Never Been Told: Slavery and the Making of American Capitalism* (New York: Basic Books, 2014), 254; Stephen Mihm, "Follow the Money: The Return of Finance in the Early Republic," *Journal of the Early Republic* 36 (Winter 2016), 784; *Cassedy v. Williams* (1843), Records of the US District Court for the District of Columbia, Case Papers, 1802–1863, Civil Trial #98, Box 663, NA (sixth quotation).

   Commercial banks, such as the one in Millington, Maryland, were not savings banks. As historian Ann Fabian describes them, savings banks were the opposite of commercial banks – a moral antidote to the pervasive gambling of the era. Unlike commercial banks, savings banks promoted the values of honesty, frugality, and industry. Philosophically, they were philanthropic institutions designed to help the poor by aiding them slowly and steadily accumulate wealth that otherwise might have been frittered away in gambling sprees or wasted on frivolous or unseemly activities. Savings banks did not issue their own funds and therefore did not compete, per se, with commercial banks. They "compete[d] instead with purveyors of vice, with tavern keepers, with lottery and policy dealers, with gambling-house proprietors, and with friends and relations who lent and borrowed among themselves." See Ann Fabian, *Card Sharps and Bucket Shops: Gambling in Nineteenth-Century America* (New York: Routledge, 1999), 49–53 (quotation 50).

2. *Cassedy v. Williams* (first quotation); *Times-Picayune,* December 5, 1840 (second quotation); Joshua D. Rothman, *Flush Times and Fever Dreams: A Story of Capitalism and Slavery in the Age of Jackson* (Athens: University of Georgia Press, 2012) (third quotation); Joshua D. Rothman, "The Contours of Cotton Capitalism: Speculation, Slavery, and Economic Panic in Mississippi, 1832–1841," in *Slavery's Capitalism,* ed. Sven Beckert and Seth Rockman (Philadelphia: University of Pennsylvania Press, 2016), 138; Stephen Mihm, *A Nation of Counterfeiters: Capitalists, Con Men, and the Making of the United States* (Cambridge, Mass.: Harvard University Press, 2007), 9; Baptist, *The Half Has Never Been Told,* 230; Jessica M. Lepler, *The Many Panics of 1837: People, Politics, and the Creation of a Transatlantic Financial Crisis* (New York: Cambridge University Press, 2013), 15–23; *Wilkinson v. Williams* (1850), Records of the US District Court for the District of Columbia, Case Papers, 1802–1863, Civil Trial #15, Box 739, Folder 15, NA (fourth quotation); *Boston Post,* October 20, 1840 (fifth quotation); *Vicksburg Tri-Weekly Sentinel,* September 30, 1840 (sixth quotation); *Times-Picayune,* December 3, 1840 (seventh and eighth quotations). According to a more conservative estimate, when the Millington Bank "blew up" under then-president J. C. H. Ellis, it had notes of some $100,000 in circulation, with about "$3,780 is specie & good notes on hand." See *Cassedy v. Williams.* For the broader history of banking in Maryland, see Howard Bodenhorn, *State Banking in Early America: A New Economic History* (New York: Oxford University Press, 2003), 123–124, 135, 137–140.

Joshua R. Greenberg defines shinplasters as unregulated, legally questionable paper notes that functioned as money. Real rather than counterfeit, they were used in local or regional money markets. In the late 1830s and early 1840s, the meaning of "shinplaster" evolved to include any note, legal or not, in which the public placed no confidence. See Joshua R. Greenberg, "The Era of Shinplasters: Making Sense of Unregulated Paper Money," in *Capitalism by Gaslight: Illuminating the Economy of Nineteenth-Century America*, ed. Brian P. Luskey and Wendy A. Woloson (Philadelphia: University of Pennsylvania Press, 2015), 55–56, 73.

3. *New York Times* quoted in *Louisiana Courier* (New Orleans), November 12, 1840 (first quotation); Walter Johnson, *River of Dark Dreams: Slavery and Empire in the Cotton Kingdom* (Cambridge, Mass.: Belknap Press of Harvard University Press, 2013), 43; Rothman, "Contours of Cotton Capitalism," 128–129; Mihm, "Follow the Money," 795, 797; Baptist, *The Half Has Never Been Told*, 229; Mihm, *Nation of Counterfeiters*, 8 (second and third quotations), 186, 239; William H. Distillin, *Bank Note Reporters and Counterfeit Detectors, 1826–1866* (New York: American Numismatic Society, 1949), 59. Recent works on the relationship between slavery and capitalism include Johnson, *River of Dark Dreams*; Baptist, *The Half Has Never Been Told*; Sven Beckert, *Empire of Cotton: A Global History* (New York: Vintage, 2015); Calvin Schermerhorn, *The Business of Slavery and the Rise of American Capitalism, 1815–1860* (New Haven: Yale University Press, 2015).

4. Calvin Schermerhorn, "Slave Trading in a Republic of Credit: Financial Architecture of the US Slave Market, 1815–1840," *Slavery and Abolition* 36, no. 4 (2015), 586; Steven Deyle, "Rethinking the Slave Trade: Slave Traders and the Market Revolution in the South," in *The Old South's Modern Worlds: Slavery, Region, and Nation in the Age of Progress*, ed. L. Diane Barnes, Brian Schoen, and Frank Towers (New York: Oxford University Press, 2011), 105, 111; Mihm, "Follow the Money," 783; Michael Tadman, *Speculators and Slaves: Masters, Traders, and Slaves in the Old South* (Madison: University of Wisconsin Press, 1989, 1996), ch. 7. Deyle, "Rethinking the Slave Trade," 106, makes passing reference to traders' involvement with antebellum banks, but the work presented here offers more detail as well as a direct, albeit incomplete, answer to Mihm's query, "Who provided the capital for banks to get off the ground?" See Mihm, "Follow the Money," 795.

5. Deyle, "Rethinking the Slave Trade," 112–113; *Daily National Intelligencer* (Washington, D.C.), April 5, 1836; E. A. Cohen & Co., *For 1834. A Full Directory, for Washington City, Georgetown, and Alexandria* (Washington City: Wm. Greer, 1834), 58, 33, unpaginated advertisement for A. Lee's Lottery and Exchange Office.

6. *Report of the Select Committee Appointed to Investigate the Affairs of the Farmers and Millers Bank of Hagerstown* (Annapolis, Md.: Geo. & Wm. Johnston, 1843), 19.

7. *Nashville Union* (Tenn.), August 30, 1841; John Jay Knox, *A History of Banking in the United States* (New York: B. Rhodes & Co., 1903), 678 (first quotation); *Wilkinson v. Williams* (second through fifth quotations); Thomas J. C. Williams, *A History of Washington County, Maryland, from the Earliest Settlements to the Present Time*, vol. I (Hagerstown, Md.: n.p., 1906; reprint, Salem, Mass.: Higginson Book Company, 1990), 239 (sixth and seventh quotations).

8. *Cassedy v. Williams.*

9. *Matthias Snyder, Jr. v. William H. Williams* (1842), Alexandria County Circuit Court, in *Baltimore Sun*, October 11, 1842; *Cassedy v. Williams; Wilkinson v. Williams.*

10. *Baltimore Sun*, November 18, 1841; Sharon Ann Murphy, *Other People's Money: How Banking Worked in the Early American Republic* (Baltimore: Johns Hopkins University Press, 2017), 62; *Baltimore Sun*, October 27, 1840 (quotations); Greenberg, "Era of Shinplasters," 53; *Vicksburg Tri-Weekly Sentinel*, November 13, 1840. A different account described the victims of the fraud as "poor Irish and Dutch" laborers on a canal in Maryland. See *Vicksburg Tri-Weekly Sentinel*, January 5, 1841. Both incidents may have been true. It was the consensus of the newspaper reporting that Millington shinplasters were "principally in the hands of the poorer classes" who "lost all they had in the world." See *State Capitol Gazette* (Harrisburg, Penn.), December 19, 1840.

11. *New York Times* quoted in *Louisiana Courier*, November 12, 1840 (first through third quotations); *Baltimore Sun*, November 16, 1840 (fourth and fifth quotations); Mihm, *Nation of Counterfeiters*, 6, 8, 239, 288–292; *Baltimore Sun*, December 3, 1840; *Public Ledger* (Philadelphia), February 11, 1841; *State Capitol Gazette*, March 10, 1841; *Sunbury American*, (Penn.), March 20, 1841; *Baltimore Sun*, July 13, 1841 (sixth quotation); *Brooklyn Daily Eagle* (N.Y.), October 27, 1841; *Baltimore Sun*, January 4, May 24, 1842, January 12, 1843; *New York Tribune*, March 27, 1843; *Baltimore Sun*, June 23, 1843; *New York Tribune*, November 2, 1842 (seventh quotation).

12. John Hebron Moore, *The Emergence of the Cotton Kingdom in the Old Southwest: Mississippi, 1770–1860* (Baton Rouge: Louisiana State University Press, 1988), 195; Lepler, *Many Panics*, 24; *Vicksburg Tri-Weekly Sentinel*, November 4, 1840; *Vicksburg Daily Whig* (Miss.), December 23, 1840; *Vicksburg Tri-Weekly Sentinel*, September 28, 1840 (first, third, and fourth quotations), October 2, 1840 (second quotation); Scott Reynolds Nelson, *A Nation of Deadbeats: An Uncommon History of America's Financial Disasters* (New York: Knopf, 2012), 124; *Vicksburg Daily Whig*, December 23, 1840, January 8, 1841.

13. *The Constitutionalist* (Vicksburg, Miss.), June 12, 1844; *Baltimore Sun*, October 23, October 26, 1840, November 18, 1841, February 25, 1842; *Boston Post*, March 29, 1842; Deyle, "Rethinking the Slave Trade," 112–113; *Baltimore Sun*, October 11, 1842.

14. *Alexandria Gazette* (Va.), November 7, 1840; *Wilkinson v. Williams* (first quotation); *Cassedy v. Williams* (second through fifth and ninth quotations); *Baltimore Sun*, October 11, 1842 (sixth through eighth and tenth quotations).

15. *Alexandria Gazette*, November 9, 1840; Manuscript Census Returns, Sixth Census of the United States, 1840, Alexandria County, District of Columbia, Schedule 1, Free Population, NAMS M-704, reel 35, page 218; *Baltimore Sun*, October 11, 1842 (first quotation); *Cassedy v. Williams* (second and third quotations).

16. *Cassedy v. Williams* (first and second quotations); *Baltimore Sun*, October 11, 1842 (third through fifth quotations). In his testimony at the later but related trial of *Cassedy v. Williams*, John Snyder misremembered the amount exchanged as $475 rather than $680.

17. *Baltimore Sun*, October 11, 1842. Matthias Snyder died in February 1850. See *Baltimore Sun*, February 19, 1850.

18. *Daily National Intelligencer*, October 15, 1840 (first, second, and seventh quotations); *Wilkinson v. Williams; Cassedy v. Williams* (third through sixth quotations); *Alexandria Gazette*, October 12, 1840. The *Alexandria Gazette*, May 2, 1843, incorrectly reported the purchase price as $550, but $600 appears in the court record. The tavern in 1840 likely belonged to roughly forty-three-year-old landlord James Sinclair of Leesburg. The twenty-four people, many of them unrelated, living in his household in 1850 suggest that he probably owned the same tavern ten years earlier, when the transaction between Cassedy and Williams took place. See Manuscript Census Returns, Seventh Census of the United States, 1850, Loudoun County, Virginia, Schedule 1, Free Population, NAMS M-432, reel 957, page 355B. There is some disagreement in the primary sources over the date of departure of the *Uncas*, but the *Alexandria Gazette* clearly indicated that the "Brig Uncas, B[o]ush," set sail on October 10 from the Port of Alexandria, destined for Mobile.

19. *Alexandria Gazette*, May 2, 1843.

20. *Cassedy v. Williams*. The more plausible date of October 10 comes from *Wilkinson v. Williams*; and *Baltimore Sun*, November 5, 1849. According to the trial records from *Wilkinson v. Williams*, "notes of [the] said Bank of Millington never had any substantial credit among the mercantile community, but after same circulated generally without any discount," they gained greater public acceptance.

21. *Alexandria Gazette*, May, 2, 1843 (first, thirteenth, and fourteenth quotations); *Cassedy v. Williams* (second through twelfth quotations). Jefferson Morley, *Snow-Storm in August: Washington City, Francis Scott Key, and the Forgotten Race Riot of 1835* (New York: Nan A. Talese/Doubleday, 2012), 17, identified "at least ten butchers" in Centre Market in the mid-1830s.

22. *Cassedy v. Williams* (quotations); *Daily National Intelligencer*, October 15, 1840.

23. *Cassedy v. Williams*.

24. *Cassedy v. Williams* (quotations); *Alexandria Gazette*, May 2, 1843; *Cassedy v. Williams* (1843), 1 Hay. & Haz. 151, 5 F.Cas. 272. News of the verdict circulated widely, in such publications as the *Augusta Chronicle* (Ga.), May 8, 1843.

25. *Baltimore Sun*, November 5, 1849 (first quotation); *Wilkinson v. Williams* (all other quotations).

26. *Wilkinson v. Williams*.

27. *Wilkinson v. Williams*.

28. *Wilkinson v. Williams; Baltimore Sun*, November 5, 1849 (first and second quotations); *Wilkinson v. Williams* (1850), 2 Hay. & Haz. 1, 29 F. Cas. 1270 (third quotation).

29. *Wilkinson v. Williams* (1850), 2 Hay. & Haz. 1, 29 F. Cas. 1270.

30. *Wilkinson v. Williams* (quotations); *Report of the Select Committee*, 19. Although it cannot be absolutely certain, these two disparate sources appear to discuss the exact same meeting.

31. *Wilkinson v. Williams* (quotation); Steven Deyle, *Carry Me Back: The Domestic Slave Trade in American Life* (New York: Oxford University Press, 2005), 120–123; Tadman, *Speculators and Slaves*, 47; Michael Tadman, "The Reputation of the Slave Trader in Southern History and the Social Memory of the South," *American Nineteenth Century*

History 8 (September 2007), 260, 262; Deyle, "Rethinking the Slave Trade," 105; *Gibson's Guide and Directory of the State of Louisiana, and the Cities of New Orleans & Lafayette* (New Orleans: John Gibson, 1838), 214; *New-Orleans Directory for 1842* (New Orleans: Pitts & Clarke, 1842), 422; *Times-Picayune*, November 9, 1842; *New-Orleans Annual and Commercial Directory, for 1843* (New Orleans: Justin L. Sollée, 1842), 341–342; Carlile Pollock, vol. 66, act no. 222, November 28, 1843, NONA; *Times-Picayune*, August 28, 1845.

32. Bodenhorn, *State Banking in Early America*, 139–140; Williams, *History of Washington County*, 239; "Report of the Select Committee Appointed to Investigate the Affairs of the Farmers and Millers Bank of Hagerstown," *Baltimore Sun*, February 6, 1843; *Report of the Select Committee*, 19.

33. *Baltimore Sun*, February 11, 1843 (first and second quotations); *Report of the Select Committee*, 14 (third quotation), 19, 31, 49, 56; Williams, *History of Washington County*, 239; Rothman, "Contours of Cotton Capitalism," 128–129; "Report of the Select Committee," *Baltimore Sun*, February 6, 1843 (fourth quotation).

34. "Report of the Select Committee," *Baltimore Sun*, February 6, 1843.

35. *Report of the Select Committee*, 64 (first, second, and fourth quotations), 65 (third, fifth, and sixth quotations), 12, 20. For more of the story, see Jeff Forret, "'How Deeply They Weed into the Pockets': Slave Traders, Bank Speculators, and the Anatomy of a Chesapeake Wildcat, 1840–1843," *Journal of the Early Republic* 39 (Winter 2019).

CHAPTER 7: *STATE V. WILLIAMS*

1. *Daily Picayune* (New Orleans), November 3, 1840 (first through third and ninth quotations); R. Littlejohn to Gov. Gilmer, November 26, 1840, Executive Papers, Thomas Walker Gilmer, Box 2, Folder 10, LVA (fourth through eighth and tenth through twelfth quotations). No evidence suggests that Thomas Walker Gilmer replied or disclosed his informant's identity. Alexandria mayor Bernard Hooe's role in manufacturing the slave traders' debacle would remain a secret.

2. Wheelock S. Upton to Thomas W. Gilmer or Wm. H. Richardson, December 5, 1840, Executive Papers, Thomas Walker Gilmer, Box 3, Folder 1, LVA.

3. Wheelock S. Upton to Thomas W. Gilmer or Wm. H. Richardson.

4. Wm. H. Richardson to Wheelock S. Upton, December 17, 1840, Virginia Governor's Papers, Executive Letter Book, p. 128, Misc. Reel 3014, LVA.

5. *State v. William H. Williams*, no. 4671, Supreme Court of Louisiana, UNO; Grace King, *Creole Families of New Orleans* (New York: Macmillan, 1921), 393–394; *Nailor v. Williams* (1862), Records of the US District Court for the District of Columbia, Case Papers, 1802–1863, Civil Trial #38, Box 999, Folder 2, NA (quotation).

6. *State v. William H. Williams*, no. 4671 (first quotation); *The State v. William H. Williams* (1842, 1844), Supreme Court of Louisiana, 7 Rob. (LA) 252, 1844 WL 1414 (La.); Report of the Day Police, November 1, 1840, New Orleans (La.) Third Municipality Guard, Mayor's Book, 1838–1850, vol. 2, p. 200, 89–214, TKD205M, NOPL; *Daily Picayune*, February 28, 1841 (second quotation).

7. State of Louisiana, Messages & Proclamations of the Governor, 1837–1842, P86-94, 6483A-1-P, pp. 311, 313, LSA; John Bailey, *The Lost German Slave Girl: The Extraordinary True Story of Sally Miller and her Fight for Freedom in Old New Orleans* (New York: Grove Press, 2003), 90, 111–112; *The State v. William H. Williams* (1842, 1844), Supreme Court of Louisiana, 7 Rob. (LA) 252, 1844 WL 1414 (La.); *National Era* (Washington, D.C.), February 10, 1853; *Daily Picayune*, February 28, 1841 (quotations).

8. *State v. William H. Williams*, no. 4671; *Daily Picayune*, February 28, 1841; Document B, Affidavit of Wheelock S. Upton, Carlile Pollock, vol. 64, act no. 261, NONA.

9. *Times-Picayune* (New Orleans), May 27, 1838; *True American* (New Orleans), April 18, 1839; *Times-Picayune*, January 14, 1840 (quotations). The *New-Orleans Directory for 1842* (New Orleans: Pitts & Clarke, 1842), 30, locates Bennet on Esplanade between Moreau and Casa Calvo streets.

10. Document F, Affidavit of Seneca Bennet, Carlile Pollock, vol. 64, act no. 261, NONA (first through third quotations); Document D, Affidavit of J. W. Zacharie, Carlile Pollock, vol. 64, act no. 261, NONA (fourth through seventh quotations).

11. Affidavit of Christian Meyers, July 30, 1841, Carlile Pollock, vol. 64, act no. 227, NONA (first quotation); Affidavit of Frederick Barton, July 31, 1841, Carlile Pollock, vol. 64, act no. 227, NONA; *The State v. William H. Williams* (1842, 1844), Supreme Court of Louisiana, 7 Rob. (LA) 252, 1844 WL 1414 (La.); *Daily Picayune*, February 28, 1841 (second through fifth quotations).

12. *Daily Picayune*, February 28, 1841 (first through seventh and ninth through thirteenth quotations); *Acts Passed at the First Session of the Third Legislature of the State of Louisiana, Begun and Held in the City of New-Orleans on Monday the Eighteenth Day of November, in the Year of Our Lord One Thousand Eight Hundred and Sixteen, and of the Independence of the United States of America the Fortieth* (New Orleans: J. C. De St. Romes, 1817), 44 (eighth quotation).

13. *Times Picayune*, March 11, 1841; *Daily Picayune*, February 28, 1841 (quotations). The list of jurors is available in *State v. William H. Williams*, no. 4671; or *Nailor v. Williams* (1869), Records of the United States Supreme Court, Case File #5032, Box 624, NA. Only a few of them could be definitively identified in the census taken the year prior to the trial.

14. *Daily Picayune*, March 12, 1841. For the composition of the jury, see *State v. William H. Williams*, no. 4671; or *Nailor v. Williams*.

15. *Daily Picayune*, March 12, 1841 (first, second, and fourth quotations); *Times-Picayune*, March 13, 1841 (third quotation).

16. *Daily Picayune*, April 27, 1841; *New Orleans Commercial Bulletin*, July 26, 1841; *Daily National Intelligencer* (Washington, D.C.), May 13, 1841; *State v. William H. Williams*, no. 4671.

17. *New Orleans Commercial Bulletin*, July 29, 1841; *Daily National Intelligencer*, May 13, 1841; Auditor of Public Accounts, Condemned Blacks Executed or Transported, Records – Condemned Slaves, Court Orders, and Valuations, 1858–1865, Misc. Reel 2555, Frame 1019, LVA; *New Orleans Commercial Bulletin*, July 26, 1841 (quotations); *State v. William H. Williams*, no. 4671. Sample newspapers that reported on the case included the *New-York Tribune*, May 14, 1841; *Albany Evening Journal* (N.Y.), May 15, 1841; *Newark Daily*

Advertiser (N.J.), May 15, 1841; *Centinel of Freedom* (Newark, N.J.), May 18, 1841; *Portland Advertiser* (Maine), May 18, 1841; *Boston Weekly Messenger,* May 19, 1841; *Cabinet* (Schenectady, N.Y.), May 25, 1841; *Hampshire Gazette* (Northampton, Mass.), May 26, 1841; *Barre Gazette* (Mass.), May 28, 1841; *Pennsylvania Inquirer* (Philadelphia), June 15, 1841; *Bridgeton Chronicle* (N.J.), June 19, 1841.

18. *Daily Picayune,* May 22, 1841. See also *State v. William H. Williams,* no. 4671; *Nailor v. Williams.*

19. William H. Williams to John Rutherfoord, July 3, 1841, Executive Papers, John Rutherfoord, Box 1, Folder 5, LVA.

20. William H. Williams to John Rutherfoord (first through fourth and sixth quotations); C. Roselius to John R. Grymes, June 11, 1841, Carlile Pollock, vol. 64, act no. 227, NONA (fifth quotation). The Roselius letter was reprinted twelve years later in the African-American newspaper *National Era,* February 10, 1853.

21. William H. Williams to John Rutherfoord.

22. *Nailor v. Williams;* Document B, Affidavit of Wheelock S. Upton, Carlile Pollock, vol. 64, act no. 261, NONA (first and second quotations); William H. Richardson to William H. Williams, July 23, 1841, Virginia Governor's Papers, Executive Letter Book, p. 182, Misc. Reel 3014, LVA (third and fourth quotations).

23. William H. Richardson to William H. Williams.

24. A. B. Roman to C. Roselius, July 10, 1841, State of Louisiana, Messages & Proclamations of the Governor, 1837–1842, P86-94, 6483A-1-P, p. 353, LSA (first and third through sixth quotations); C. Roselius to John R. Grymes (second and seventh quotations).

25. *The State v. William H. Williams* (1842, 1844), Supreme Court of Louisiana, 7 Rob. (LA) 252, 1844 WL 1414 (La.); Judith Kelleher Schafer, *Slavery, the Civil Law, and the Supreme Court of Louisiana* (Baton Rouge: Louisiana State University Press, 1994), xii; *Times-Picayune,* March 13, 1841 (quotations).

26. *New Orleans Commercial Bulletin,* July 27, 1841 (first quotation); *Daily Picayune,* July 25, 1841 (second quotation); William H. Williams to John Rutherfoord (third quotation); *The Colored American* (New York), October 9, 1841 (fourth quotation). The *Picayune* article was reprinted verbatim in such publications as the *Augusta Chronicle* (Ga.), July 31, 1841; *Commercial Advertiser* (New York), August 4, 1841; *New-York Spectator,* August 7, 1841. The reporting of the *New Orleans Bee* and the *New Orleans Bulletin* was reprinted, in full or abbreviated form, in such publications as the *Pennsylvania Inquirer and Daily Courier* (Philadelphia), August 4, 1841; *Daily National Intelligencer,* August 4, 1841; *Newark Daily Advertiser,* August 4, 1841; *Alexandria Gazette* (Va.), August 5, 1841; *Boston Post,* August 5, 1841; *Hampshire Gazette,* August 10, 1841; *Centinel of Freedom,* August 10, 1841; *Gloucester Telegraph* (Mass.), August 11, 1841.

27. *New Orleans Commercial Bulletin,* July 29, 1841 (first through third quotations); Document E, William H. Williams' recollections of George Y. Bright's testimony, November 23, 1841, Carlile Pollock, vol. 64, act no. 261, NONA (fourth quotation); Carlile Pollock, vol. 64, act no. 227, September 24, 1841, NONA; Carlile Pollock, vol. 64, act no. 261, November 23, 1841, NONA.

28. *New Orleans Commercial Bulletin,* July 29, 1841 (first, eighth, and ninth quotations); Frederic Bancroft, *Slave Trading in the Old South,* introduction by Michael Tadman (1931; Columbia: University of South Carolina Press, 1996), 367; Robert Evans, Jr., "Some Economic Aspects of the Domestic Slave Trade, 1830–1860," *Southern Economic Journal* 27 (April 1961), 329; J. Winston Coleman, Jr., "Lexington's Slave Dealers and their Southern Trade," *Filson Club History Quarterly* 12 (January 1938), 22; Solomon Northup, *Twelve Years a Slave,* ed. Sue Eakin and Joseph Logsdon (Baton Rouge: Louisiana State University Press, 1996), 40 (second quotation); Hank Trent, *The Secret Life of Bacon Tait, a White Slave Trader Married to a Free Woman of Color* (Baton Rouge: Louisiana State University Press, 2017), 97, 98, 127; Michael Tadman, *Speculators and Slaves: Masters, Traders, and Slaves in the Old South* (Madison: University of Wisconsin Press, 1989), 179, 192–200, 207; Michael Tadman, "The Hidden History of Slave Trading in Antebellum South Carolina: John Springs III and Other 'Gentlemen Dealing in Slaves'," *South Carolina Historical Magazine* 97 (January 1996), 8, 16, 19; Michael Tadman, "The Reputation of the Slave Trader in Southern History and the Social Memory of the South," *American Nineteenth Century History* 8 (September 2007), 247, 251, 264; *Daily Picayune,* November 3, 1840 (third and fourth quotations); Document D, Affidavit of J.W. Zacharie [1841], Carlile Pollock, vol. 64, act no. 261, NONA (fifth through seventh quotations).

29. *New Orleans Commercial Bulletin,* July 29, 1841.

30. Ibid.

31. *New Orleans Commercial Bulletin,* July 29, 1841 (first through sixth quotations); Craig B. Hollander, "Underground on the High Seas: Commerce, Character, and Complicity in the Illegal Slave Trade," in *Capitalism by Gaslight: Illuminating the Economy of Nineteenth-Century America,* ed. Brian P. Luskey and Wendy A. Woloson (Philadelphia: University of Pennsylvania Press, 2015), 127–149; James Kent, *Commentaries on American Law,* vol. I (New York: O. Halsted, 1826), 408; *National Gazette* (Philadelphia), August 12, 1841 (seventh quotation), reprinted in the *Boston Courier,* August 16, 1841, and *Connecticut Courant* (Hartford), August 21, 1841, among other newspapers. "An act for enrolling and licensing ships and vessels to be employed in the coasting trade and fisheries, and for regulating the same" passed on February 18, 1793.

32. Journal of the House of Representatives of the State of Louisiana, First Session – First Legislature, April 16, 1853, p. 182; *Nailor v. Williams* (quotations); *Williams v. Louisiana,* no. 4157, Orleans Parish Court, NOLA; "A List of Slaves and Free persons of color received into the Penitentiary of Virginia for sale and transportation from the 25th June 1816 to the 1st February 1842," Auditor of Public Accounts, Condemned Blacks Executed or Transported, Records – Condemned Slaves, Court Orders, and Valuations, 1858–1865, Misc. Reel 2555, Frame 996, LVA. The House Journal states erroneously that the two bondmen seized from Williams had been carried legally into Louisiana. The summary report of April 16, 1853, contains several factual errors.

33. *Williams v. Louisiana* (quotation); *Daily Picayune,* August 29, 1841; Document E, Affidavit of Ursin Bouligny [1841], Carlile Pollock, vol. 64, act no. 261, NONA.

34. *Daily Picayune,* August 29, 1841.

35. *Daily Picayune*, August 29, 1841; *Times-Picayune*, September 2, 1841 (first quotation); *Williams v. Louisiana* (second through seventh quotations). Judge Maurian's ruling appeared in such newspapers as the *Public Ledger* (Philadelphia), September 21, 1841; *National Gazette* (Philadelphia), September 23, 1841; *New-York Tribune*, September 23, 1841; *Alexandria Gazette*, September 24, 1841; *Daily Atlas* (Boston), September 24, 1841; *Centinel of Freedom*, September 28, 1841; *Albany Argus* (N.Y.), September 28, 1841; *Pittsfield Sun* (Mass.) September 30, 1841; *Daily Missouri Republican* (St. Louis), October 1, 1841.

36. *New-Orleans Directory, for 1841* (New Orleans: J. L. Sollee, 1840), 88; *New-Orleans Directory for 1842* (New Orleans: Pitts & Clarke, 1842), 204; *The State v. William H. Williams* (1842, 1844), Supreme Court of Louisiana, 7 Rob. (LA) 252, 1844 WL 1414 (La.); *Daily Picayune*, January 4, 1842; Criminal Court of the First District (Orleans Parish), Minute Book, vol. 4, February 5 (first through fourth and sixth quotations), NOPL; *Times-Picayune*, February 8, 1842 (fifth and seventh quotations), April 19, 1842. The *Times-Picayune* article of February 8, 1842, also appeared verbatim in the February 14 edition.

37. Criminal Court of the First District (Orleans Parish), Minute Book, vol. 4, February 8 (first through sixth quotations) and 12, 1842, NOPL; *Times-Picayune*, April 19, 1842 (seventh quotation).

38. *Times-Picayune*, April 19, 1842 (first, second, fourth, and sixth quotations); *The State v. William H. Williams* (1842, 1844), Supreme Court of Louisiana, 7 Rob. (LA) 252, 1844 WL 1414 (La.) (third and fifth quotations). Randall Hunt commented that the right to appeal was "a great constitutional right" that, regardless of current legal interpretation in Louisiana, should not "be restricted to civil cases." Recovering fines or financial penalties in civil suits is a feature of the common law. Louisiana, however, was not a common law state. As Hunt acknowledged, "we have no common law offences in Louisiana. All crimes and offences against our law, are created and punished by statute."

39. *Times-Picayune*, April 19, 1842 (first quotation); *The State v. William H. Williams* (1842, 1844), Supreme Court of Louisiana, 7 Rob. (LA) 252, 1844 WL 1414 (La.) (second and third quotations).

40. *Daily Picayune*, June 16, 1842; *Times-Picayune*, July 1 and 6, 1842.

41. Dumas Malone, ed., *Dictionary of American Biography*, vol. XII (New York: Charles Scribner's Sons, 1933), 335–336.

42. *The State v. William H. Williams* (1842, 1844), Supreme Court of Louisiana, 7 Rob. (LA) 252, 1844 WL 1414 (La.).

43. *The State v. William H. Williams* (1842, 1844), Supreme Court of Louisiana, 7 Rob. (LA) 252, 1844 WL 1414 (La.); See also *Times-Picayune*, July 6, 1842. The account related here corrects some misinformation that the Supreme Court case of 1842 affirmed the judgment of the Criminal Court against Williams. This could not have been true, or there would never have been a second case before the Supreme Court. See Schafer, *Slavery, the Civil Law, and the Supreme Court of Louisiana*, 163n20.

Born in Lynchburg, Virginia, about 1795, Rice Garland practiced law in Opelousas, Louisiana. As a Whig, he filled the vacancy left in the US House of Representatives when

Henry Bullard joined the Louisiana Supreme Court. Garland served in that capacity until 1840, when he followed in Bullard's footsteps to that judicial body. Garland was the most recent addition to the state Supreme Court at the time of William H. Williams' trial. See Louisiana Historical Association, "Dictionary of Louisiana Biography," http://lahistory.org/site24.php (accessed October 17, 2017). Brief biographies of Alonzo Morphy and Edward Simon appear in Chapter 8.

44. Allen Johnson, ed., *Dictionary of American Biography*, vol. III (New York: Charles Scribner's Sons, 1957), 254–255.

45. *The State v. William H. Williams* (1842, 1844), Supreme Court of Louisiana, 7 Rob. (LA) 252, 1844 WL 1414 (La.).

46. Legislature, House, Committee on Judiciary, *Report of the Judiciary Committee on the Memorial of W. H. Williams* (New Orleans: n.p., 1855), 2.

CHAPTER 8: SLAVE TRADING IN "HARD TIMES"

1. E. Rodbird to George Wilkinson, October 30, 1840, in *Wilkinson v. Williams* (1850), Records of the US District Court for the District of Columbia, Case Papers, 1802–1863, Civil Trial #15, Box 739, Folder 15, NA; *Cassedy v. Williams* (1843), Records of the US District Court for the District of Columbia, Case Papers, 1802–1863, Civil Trial #98, Box 663, NA (first quotation); Solomon Northup, *Twelve Years a Slave*, ed. Sue Eakin and Joseph Logsdon (Baton Rouge: Louisiana State University Press, 1996), 29 (second quotation).

2. *Wilkinson v. Williams* (first quotation); Manuscript Census Returns, Seventh Census of the United States, 1850, District 19, Chambers County, Alabama, Schedule 1, Free Population, NAMS M-432, reel 2, page 274A; *Daily National Intelligencer*, December 30, 1841 (second and third quotations); *Cassedy v. Williams*. Joshua Staples made a poor purchase in 1841, buying "a negro man named JOHN BELL . . . from Doctor Peregrine Warfield," under the misguided impression that the bondman was "sound." In August, Staples alerted the public that he would soon unload the defective Bell at the auction house of Dyer & Wright, which sold, among sundry other commodities, enslaved people. See *Daily National Intelligencer* (Washington, D.C.), August 21, 1841.

3. *Cassedy v. Williams* (first through third quotations); *Daily National Intelligencer*, July 8, 1841 (fourth through sixth quotations); *Georgetown Advocate* (D.C.), July 22, 1841 (seventh quotation); *Daily National Intelligencer*, January 2, 1846; *Wilkinson v. Williams* (eighth quotation). Thomas Williams placed a different advertisement for "fifty Negroes" in the *Daily National Intelligencer*, March 8, 1843.

4. Hank Trent, *The Secret Life of Bacon Tait, a White Slave Trader Married to a Free Woman of Color* (Baton Rouge: Louisiana State University Press, 2017), 47, 102, 130; Andrew J. Torget, *Seeds of Empire: Cotton, Slavery, and the Transformation of the Texas Borderlands, 1800–1850* (Chapel Hill: University of North Carolina Press, 2015), 211; A. A. Taylor, "The Movement of Negroes from the East to the Gulf States from 1830 to 1850," *Journal of Negro History* 8 (October 1923), 376, 377; Joshua D. Rothman, "The Contours of Cotton Capitalism: Speculation, Slavery, and Economic Panic in Mississippi, 1832–1841," in

Slavery's Capitalism, ed. Sven Beckert and Seth Rockman (Philadelphia: University of Pennsylvania Press, 2016), 138; quotation from Alasdair Roberts, *America's First Great Depression: Economic Crisis and Political Disorder after the Panic of 1837* (Ithaca: Cornell University Press, 2012), 21.

5. Outward Slave Manifest, Alexandria, November 3, 1838 (*Uncas*), New-York Historical Society, MS569, Slavery Collection, nyhs_sc_b-05_f-16_020–001, http://cdm16694 .contentdm.oclc.org/cdm/compoundobject/collection/p15052coll5/id/24235/rec/5 (accessed February 25, 2015); Outward Slave Manifest, Alexandria, November 19, 1839 (*Uncas*), New-York Historical Society, MS569, Slavery Collection, nyhs_sc_b-05_f-16_021- 001, http://cdm16694.contentdm.oclc.org/cdm/compoundobject/collection/p15052c oll5/id/24240/rec/4 (accessed February 25, 2015); Inward Slave Manifest, New Orleans, March 27, 1840 (*Architect*), NARA M1895, reel 8, image 739.

6. Edward E. Baptist, *The Half Has Never Been Told: Slavery and the Making of American Capitalism* (New York: Basic Books, 2014), 183; Herman Freudenberger and Jonathan B. Pritchett, "The Domestic United States Slave Trade: New Evidence," *Journal of Interdisciplinary History* 21 (Winter 1991), 451.

7. Baptist, *The Half Has Never Been Told*, 183; Inward Slave Manifest, New Orleans, November 18, 1848 (*Elizabeth*), NARA M1895, reel 12, image 187 (quotation); Inward Slave Manifest, New Orleans, December 16, 1848 (*Union*), NARA M1895, reel 12, image 249; Inward Slave Manifest, New Orleans, October 26, 1847 (*Kirkwood*), NARA M1895, reel 11, image 1115; Inward Slave Manifest, New Orleans, March 27, 1847 (*Phoenix*), NARA M1895, reel 11, image 881.

8. Inward Slave Manifest, New Orleans, November 19, 1839 (*Uncas*), NARA M1895, reel 8, image 517; Inward Slave Manifest, New Orleans, November 21, 1844 (*Colonel Howard*), NARA M1895, reel 10, image 278; Inward Slave Manifest, New Orleans, January 19, 1847 (*General Pinckney*), NARA M1895, reel 11, image 739 (quotation); Inward Slave Manifest, New Orleans, March 1, 1845 (*Victorine*), NARA M1895, reel 10, image 386; Inward Slave Manifest, New Orleans, October 26, 1847 (*Kirkwood*), NARA M1895, reel 11, image 1115.

9. Baptist, *The Half Has Never Been Told*, 183; E. A. Andrews, *Slavery and the Domestic Slave-Trade in the United States* (Boston: Light & Stearns, 1836), 139; William T. Laprade, "The Domestic Slave Trade in the District of Columbia," *Journal of Negro History* 11 (January 1926), 32; Frederic Bancroft, *Slave Trading in the Old South*, introduction by Michael Tadman (1931; Columbia: University of South Carolina Press, 1996), 63, 64; Freudenberger and Pritchett, "The Domestic United States Slave Trade," 455; *Acts Passed at the First Session of the Ninth Legislature of the State of Louisiana; Begun and Held in the City of New-Orleans, on Monday, the Eighth Day of December, in the Year of Our Lord One Thousand Eight Hundred and Twenty Eight, and of the Independence of the United States of America, the Fifty-Second* (New Orleans: John Gibson, 1829), 48 (quotation), 44. Section 15 stated that "no slave child, or children, ten years of age, or under, shall be introduced into this state, unaccompanied by his, her, or their mother, if living." Section 16 stated that, "if any person or persons shall sell the mother of any slave child or children, under the age of ten years separate from said child or children, or shall, the mother living, sell any slave child or children, of ten years of age, or under, separate from said mother," that

individual or those individuals would face fines of $1,000–2,000 and "imprisonment of not less than six months, nor more than one year, and shall moreover forfeit the slave or slaves so illegally introduced or brought into the state." Those slaves "shall be publicly sold, after a notice of twenty days, by the Sheriff of the Parish where such forfeiture may have been pronounced, one fourth of the nett [*sic*] proceeds of which shall be to the use of the informer, and the remainder to the use of the state." Inward Slave Manifest, New Orleans, November 19, 1839 (*Uncas*), NARA M1895, reel 8, image 519, listed "One infant Child Born on Board the vessel on the passage to the Port," while Inward Slave Manifest, New Orleans, March 27, 1840 (*Architect*), NARA M1895, reel 8, image 739, noted that eighteen-year-old captive bondwoman "Eliza Nicholson has an infant born on the passage."

10. *Acts Passed at the First Session of the Ninth Legislature of the State of Louisiana*, 40 (first quotation); Bill of sale, Louisa and child, December 22, 1846, Greenbury R. Stringer, vol. 8, act no. 465, NONA (second quotation); Bill of sale, Nancy Barnes and Wesley, February 28, 1848, Lucien Hermann, vol. 17, act no. 106, NONA (third and fourth quotations); Bill of sale, Milly and Edwin, March 2, 1849, Theodore Guyol, vol. 12, act no. 148, NONA.

11. Richard Tansey, "Bernard Kendig and the New Orleans Slave Trade," *Louisiana History* 23 (Spring 1982), 166, found that New Orleans slave trader Bernard Kendig sold a majority of his slaves in the 1850s to in-town buyers. Freudenberger and Pritchett, "The Domestic United States Slave Trade," 461, stated that "almost half (49.8 percent) of the slaves sold to Louisiana residents [in 1830] were sold to residents of New Orleans." My analysis of the Williams brothers bridges the chronological gap between these two studies and arrives at similar results. The 62.5 percent figure for New Orleans, Jefferson Parish, and St. James Parish is also consistent with Fredenberger and Pritchett's finding for the 1830s that buyers in New Orleans and Jefferson Parish combined to account for 61.5 percent of sales. J. D. B. DeBow, *The Seventh Census of the United States: 1850* (Washington, D.C.: Robert Armstrong, 1853), 484, 486.

12. Bill of sale, Lindsey, George, and Addison, April 5, 1839, William Y. Lewis, vol. 6, act no. 444, NONA (first quotation); Bill of sale, Frances, March 12, 1839, Theodore Seghers, vol. 31, act no. 182, NONA (second quotation); Bill of sale, Amy, January 27, 1840, Felix Grima, vol. 28, act no. 51, NONA; Bill of sale, Washington, William, Frisby, Charles, and James, February 6, 1841, Felix Grima, vol. 33, act no. 53, NONA.

13. Bill of sale, Tamer, February 13, 1841, Felix Grima, vol. 33, act no. 59, NONA (first quotation); Bill of sale, Maria, March 5, 1842, William Y. Lewis, vol. 14, act no. 193, NONA (second quotation); Bill of sale, Miranda, June 11, 1842, Lucien Hermann, vol. 4, act no. 176, NONA (third through fifth quotations); Bill of sale, Mary Ann, April 6, 1839, William Christy, vol. 35, p. 51, NONA (sixth quotation).

14. Exchange of slaves, 1840, Edward Barnett, vol. 13, act no. 726, NONA. As with Joseph Moncla, William H. Williams made an exchange with Mary Emily Amis as well. Williams gave her a twenty-two-year-old bondwoman named Fanny, mutually valued at $700, and another $50 in cash in exchange for "a certain Negro Woman, Slave for life, named Molly, aged about thirty five years, and her child, Anna, aged about eight years, Valued

by the said parties at Seven Hundred and fifty Dollars." See William Christy, vol. 56, p. 41, NONA.

15. Bill of sale, Peter, April 7, 1840, Edward Barnett, vol. 11, act no. 276, NONA; Abrogation of sale, Peter, April 20, 1840, Edward Barnett, vol. 11, act no. 322, NONA; Bill of sale, Molly and Celia, February 12, 1841, Edward Barnett, vol. 14, act no. 113, NONA; Abrogation of sale, Celia, February 25, 1841, Edward Barnett, vol. 14, act no. 165, NONA (quotation).

16. Abrogation of sale, Jack, January 10, 1842, Edward Barnett, vol. 19, act no. 23, NONA; Bill of sale, Adam, January 10, 1842, Edward Barnett, vol. 19, act no. 22, NONA.

17. Mortgage of slave, Thomas Williams, April 6, 1839, William Y. Lewis, vol. 6, act no. 412, NONA. On the mortgaging of enslaved property, see Bonnie Martin, "Slavery's Invisible Engine: Mortgaging Human Property," *Journal of Southern History* 76 (November 2010): 817–866.

18. Calvin Schermerhorn, "Slave Trading in a Republic of Credit: Financial Architecture of the US Slave Market, 1815–1840," *Slavery and Abolition* 36, no. 4 (2015), 587, 588; Rothman, "Contours of Cotton Capitalism," 131; Bill of sale, Tom, Culwell, and Sam, November 13, 1848, Hilary Breton Cenas, vol. 41, p. 103, NONA (first and second quotations); Bill of sale, Sarah, July 3, 1844, Louis T. Caire, vol. 95, act no. 378, NONA (third quotation); Bill of sale, Patsey alias Louise, February 1, 1841, Louis T. Caire, vol. 79, act no. 48, NONA (fourth and fifth quotations). To hypothecate meant to "mortgage without surrendering title." See Schermerhorn, "Slave Trading in a Republic of Credit," 592.

19. Joseph T. Guthrie to Thomas N. Davis, September 6, 1841, in *Report of the Select Committee Appointed to Investigate the Affairs of the Farmers and Millers Bank of Hagerstown* (Annapolis, Md.: Geo. & Wm. Johnston, 1843), 64.

20. Bill of sale, Jackson, Luke, John, Enoch, and Abram/Abraham, March 10, 1842, Adolphe Mazureau, vol. 25, p. 282, NONA.

21. *Betsey Chapman v. John and Lydia Slack and Joshua Staples* (1842), Records of the US Circuit Court for the District of Columbia, Chancery Dockets and Rules Case Files, 1804–1863, Rules 4, no. 225, Box 126, NA. See also RSPP, PAR#20484206, Washington, D.C.

22. *Betsey Chapman v. John and Lydia Slack and Joshua Staples.*

23. Ibid.

24. Ibid.

25. Ibid

26. *Barny Montgomery v. Bronaugh et al.* (1843), Records of the US Circuit Court for the District of Columbia, Chancery Dockets and Rules Case Files, 1804–1863, Rules 4, no. 280, NA (first, second, and fourth quotations); M. Thompson, *Abstract of the Laws of the District of Columbia*, 3d ed. (Washington, D.C.: W. M. Morrison & Co., 1855), 18 (third quotation). I have opted to use the more conventional spelling of "Barney" in the text. The name appears in the court records both with and without the "e." See also RSPP, PAR#20484304, Washington, D.C.

27. *Barny Montgomery v. Bronaugh et al.* The outcome of the case is unclear.

28. *James Becket v. William Glover, Thomas Williams, & Agnes Clarke* (1845), Records of the US Circuit Court for the District of Columbia, Chancery Dockets and Rules Case Files, 1804–1863, Rules 4, no. 382, NA.

29. Ibid.

30. *The State v. William H. Williams*, Supreme Court of Louisiana (1842, 1844), 7 Rob. (LA) 279, 1844 WL 1415 (La.).

31. Ibid.

32. Ibid. Papers across the country reported on the outcome of the trial. See, for example, *Spectator* (New York), April 20, 1844; *Daily Atlas* (Boston), April 20, 1844; *Boston Courier*, April 22, 1844; *Washington Reporter* (Pa.), May 4, 1844.

33. Louisiana Historical Association, "Dictionary of Louisiana Biography," https://lahistory .org/resources/dictionary-louisiana-biography/dictionary-louisiana-biography-m/ (accessed November 18, 2017); *The State v. William H. Williams*, Supreme Court of Louisiana (1842, 1844), 7 Rob. (LA) 279, 1844 WL 1415 (La.) (quotations). Alonzo Morphy was the father of chess champion Paul Morphy.

34. *The State v. William H. Williams*, Supreme Court of Louisiana (1842, 1844), 7 Rob. (LA) 279, 1844 WL 1415 (La.).

35. Legislature, House, Committee on Judiciary, *Report of the Judiciary Committee on the Memorial of W. H. Williams* (New Orleans: n.p., 1855), 2 (first quotation); *New Orleans Annual and Commercial Register for 1846* (New Orleans: E. A. Michel & Co., 1845), 582 (second quotation); Act of Sale of Slave "Albert" to Joseph Salvant, 1844, Edward Barnett, notary, Folder 5, Salvant and Veillon Family Papers, The Historic New Orleans Collection, New Orleans, La.; Bill of sale, Thomas Isby, Isaac Turbon, Dick Mason, James Thomas, George Williams, Frank Jennings, William Cock, George Washington, James Baker, and Thomas Briscoe, January 24, 1846, Theodore Guyol, vol. 3, act no 20, NONA; Bill of sale, Henry, Davis, Mose, Vinson, Nace, Cilus, Matilday, Charlotte, Mary, and Ann, February 11, 1845, Louis T. Caire, vol. 97, act no. 44, NONA; Bill of sale, William, Spencer, Robertson, Prince, Bill, William Duval, and Henry, June 26, 1845, Theodore Guyol, vol. 1, act no. 338, NONA.

CHAPTER 9: POLITICS OF THE SLAVE PEN

1. Richard H. Abbott, *Cobbler in Congress: The Life of Henry Wilson, 1812–1875* (Lexington: University Press of Kentucky, 1972), 1–8, 11; Elias Nason and Thomas Russell, *The Life and Public Services of Henry Wilson, Late Vice-President of the United States* (Boston: B. B. Russell, 1876), 17–21, 29–32; Ernest A. McKay, *Henry Wilson: Practical Radical: A Portrait of a Politician* (Port Washington, N.Y.: Kennikat Press, 1971), 6–12, 14–15; Alfred F. Young, *The Shoemaker and the Tea Party: Memory and the American Revolution* (Boston: Beacon, 1999), 14–15, 19.

2. *National Republican* (Washington, D.C.), July 5, 1865 (first and second quotations); *Philadelphia Inquirer*, June 7, 1872 (third and fifth quotations); *The Liberator* (Boston), June 25, 1855 (fourth quotation); National Lincoln Monument Association, *Celebration by the Colored People's Educational Monument Association in Memory of Abraham Lincoln, on the*

Fourth of July, 1865, in the Presidential Grounds, Washington, D.C. (Washington, D.C.: McGill & Witherow, 1865), 28 (sixth quotation); *Evening Star* (Washington, D.C.), June 7, 1872.

3. Walter C. Clephane, "The Local Aspect of Slavery in the District of Columbia," *Records of the Columbia Historical Society, Washington, D.C.* 3 (1900), 240; Fredrika Bremer, *The Homes of the New World; Impressions of America*, vol. I, trans. Mary Howitt (New York: Harper & Brothers, 1853), 492 (first quotation); Appendix, *Congressional Globe*, 31st Cong., 1st sess., 1642 (second quotation); Roy P. Basler, ed., *The Collected Works of Abraham Lincoln*, vol. II2 (New Brunswick, N.J.: Rutgers University Press, 1953), 253 (third quotation). See also Mark Auslander, "Enslaved Labor and Building the Smithsonian: Reading the Stones," *Southern Spaces: A Journal about Real and Imagined Space and Places of the US South and Their Global Connections*, https://southernspaces.org/2012/enslaved-labor-and-building-smithsonian-reading-stones (accessed November 28, 2017).

4. Nason and Russell, *The Life and Public Services of Henry Wilson*, 31 (first quotation); *The Colored American* (New York), March 3, 1838 (second and third quotations); *Cleveland Herald*, April 14, 1849 (fourth and eighth quotations); Solomon Northup, *Twelve Years a Slave*, ed. Sue Eakin and Joseph Logsdon (Baton Rouge: Louisiana State University Press, 1996), 23 (fifth and sixth quotations); Bremer, *Homes of the New World*, vol. I, 492 (seventh quotation).

5. Northup, *Twelve Years a Slave*, 34 (first quotation); Executive Committee of the American Anti-Slavery Society, *Slavery and the Internal Slave Trade in the United States of North America; Being Replies to Questions Transmitted by the Committee of the British and Foreign Anti-slavery Society, for the Abolition of Slavery and the Slave Trade Throughout the World* (London: Thomas Ward, 1841), 207 (second through fourth quotations).

6. George Henry, *Life of George Henry. Together with a Brief History of the Colored People in America* (Providence: H. I. Gould & Co., 1894), 17 (first through seventh quotations); Jesse Torrey, *A Portraiture of Domestic Slavery, in the United States* (Philadelphia: The Author, 1817), 40 (eighth and ninth quotations).

7. *The Liberator*, August 3, 1849 (quotations); Appendix, *Congressional Globe*, 31st Cong., 1st sess., 1642.

8. *The Liberator*, March 31, 1843.

9. *New York Evangelist*, September 8, 1842. The *Cleveland American* of October 17, 1844, identified Seth M. Gates as the mystery correspondent to the *Evangelist*.

10. *New York Evangelist*, September 8, 1842.

11. Ibid.

12. Joseph Sturge, *A Visit to the United States in 1841* (1842; New York: Augustus M. Kelley, 1969), 83 (first and third through sixth quotations), 89 (second quotation).

13. Steven Deyle, "Rethinking the Slave Trade: Slave Traders and the Market Revolution in the South," in *The Old South's Modern Worlds: Slavery, Region, and Nation in the Age of Progress*, ed. L. Diane Barnes, Brian Schoen, and Frank Towers (New York: Oxford University Press, 2011), 115, 106–107; Edward E. Baptist, *The Half Has Never Been Told: Slavery and the Making of American Capitalism* (New York: Basic Books, 2014), 239; Charles Noble, "Memories of Washington before the Civil War," *Washington Post*,

January 31, 1926 (first quotation); Frederic Bancroft, *Slave Trading in the Old South*, introduction by Michael Tadman (1931; Columbia: University of South Carolina Press, 1996), 365, 368, 369, 375, 378; Letter of George Watterston, October 19, 1844, reprinted in *Washington Globe*, October 29, 1844 (second and third quotations); Manuscript Census Returns, Sixth Census of the United States, 1840, Washington, D.C., NAMS M-19, reel 35, page 106; Roy P. Basler, ed., *The Collected Works of Abraham Lincoln*, vol. II (New Brunswick, N.J.: Rutgers University Press, 1953), 264 (fourth and fifth quotations); Appendix, *Congressional Globe*, 31st Cong., 1st sess., 1642 (sixth and seventh quotations).

14. Richard Hildreth, *The White Slave; or, Memoirs of a Fugitive* (Boston: Tappan and Whitemore, 1852), 329 (first through third quotations); Bancroft, *Slave Trading in the Old South*, 371; *Cleveland Herald* (Ohio), April 14, 1849 (fourth through seventh quotations); Sturge, *A Visit to the United States in 1841*, 90 (eighth through thirteenth quotations).

15. Executive Committee, *Slavery and the Internal Slave Trade*, 207.

16. Garry Wills, "Seat of Bondage," *American Heritage* 54 (December 2003), 58, 62; House of Representatives, *Register of Debates*, 20th Cong., 2d sess., 177; House of Representatives, *Annals of Congress*, 8th Cong., 2d. sess., 995. On congressional agitation against the slave trade in the District of Columbia, see Mary Tremain, *Slavery in the District of Columbia: The Policy of Congress and the Struggle for Abolition* (1892; reprint, New York: Negro Universities Press, 1969), 58–98.

17. House of Representatives, *Register of Debates*, 20th Cong., 2d sess., 178 (first quotation); US Constitution, Article I, section 8 (second quotation); House of Representatives, *Register of Debates*, 19th Cong., 2d sess., 564 (third quotation), 564–565 (fourth quotation). On John Randolph, see Robert H. Gudmestad, *A Troublesome Commerce: The Transformation of the Interstate Slave Trade* (Baton Rouge: Louisiana State University Press, 2003), 35–39; David L. Lightner, *Slavery and the Commerce Power: How the Struggle against the Interstate Slave Trade Led to the Civil War* (New Haven: Yale University Press, 2006), 47–48.

18. House of Representatives, *Annals of Congress*, 7th Cong., 1st sess., 709; *House Journal*, May 13, 1826, 560.

19. House of Representatives, *Register of Debates*, 20th Cong., 2d sess., 166 (first quotation), 167 (fourth quotation); House of Representatives, *Register of Debates*, 20th Cong., 2d sess., 178 (second, third, fifth, and seventh quotations), 179 (sixth quotation).

20. *House Journal*, February 4, 1833, 267; House of Representatives, *Register of Debates*, 22nd Cong., 2d sess., 1584 (quotation).

21. Elizabeth R. Varon, *We Mean to Be Counted: White Women and Politics in Antebellum Virginia* (Chapel Hill: University of North Carolina Press, 1998); *House Journal*, December 29, 1831, 121 (first quotation); House of Representatives, *Register of Debates*, 23rd Cong., 2d sess., 1131 (second quotation); House of Representatives, *Register of Debates*, 24th Cong., 1st sess., 1961 (third and fourth quotations); House of Representatives, *Congressional Globe*, 24th Cong., 1st sess., 116 (fifth quotation); Senate, *Register of Debates*, 24th Cong., 1st sess., 186 (sixth through eighth quotations).

22. House of Representatives, *Register of Debates*, 22nd Cong., 1st sess., 1425; House of Representatives, *Congressional Globe*, 24th Cong., 1st sess., 137. For the latest on John Quincy Adams on this subject, see Peter Charles Hoffer, *John Quincy Adams and the Gag Rule, 1835–1850* (Baltimore: Johns Hopkins University Press, 2017).

23. William L. Van Deburg, "Henry Clay, the Right of Petition, and Slavery in the Nation's Capital," *Register of the Kentucky Historical Society* 68 (April 1970), 132; Mary Beth Corrigan, "Imaginary Cruelties?: A History of the Slave Trade in Washington, D.C.," *Washington History* 13 (Fall/Winter 2001/2002), 24; House of Representatives, *Register of Debates*, 24th Cong., 1st sess., 3757 (quotations).

24. Senate, *Congressional Globe*, 24th Cong., 1st sess., 68; House of Representatives, *Congressional Globe*, 24th Cong., 1st sess., 273; House of Representatives, *Register of Debates*, 22nd Cong., 2d sess., 1585 (first quotation); House of Representatives, *Register of Debates*, 22nd Cong., 1st sess., 1425 (second through fourth quotations); Senate, *Register of Debates*, 24th Cong., 1st sess., 73, 84; House of Representatives, *Congressional Globe*, 26th Cong., 1st sess., 89.

25. *Evening Star*, June 7, 1872; *National Republican* (Washington, D.C.), July 5, 1865 (first quotation); *The United States Magazine and Democratic Review*, vol. 7 (Washington, D.C.: S. D. Langtree, 1840), 328 (second quotation); Appendix, *Congressional Globe*, 26th Cong., 1st sess., 821 (third and fourth quotations); Senate, *Register of Debates*, 24th Cong., 1st sess., 186. On the Senate's attempts to balance the right of the petitioners without ultimately dealing with slavery issues, see Van Deburg, "Henry Clay," 133, 134, 137, 139.

26. House of Representatives, *Register of Debates*, 22nd Cong., 2d sess., 1585; House of Representatives, *Congressional Globe*, 24th Cong., 2d sess., 79 (first quotation); House of Representatives, *Register of Debates*, 24th Cong., 2d sess., 1587 (second and third quotations), 1593 (fourth and fifth quotations); House of Representatives, *Congressional Globe*, 25th Cong., 2d sess., 180 (sixth quotation); House of Representatives, *Congressional Globe*, 25th Cong., 3d sess., 130 (seventh quotation).

27. William A. Degregorio, *The Complete Book of US Presidents*, 4th ed. (New York: Barricade, 1993), 167; clipping from the *Albany Argus* (N.Y.), 1844, Harmanus Bleecker Papers, New York State Library, Albany (quotations).

28. Thomas Hylland Eriksen, "Some Questions about Flags," in *Flag, Nation and Symbolism in Europe and America*, ed. Thomas Hylland Eriksen and Richard Jenkins (New York: Routledge, 2007), 1, 3–5, 7–8, 13; David L. Child, *The Despotism of Freedom; or the Tyranny and Cruelty of American Republican Slave-Masters, Shown to Be the Worst in the World; in a Speech, Delivered at the First Anniversary of the New England Anti-Slavery Society, 1833* (Boston: Boston Young Men's Anti-Slavery Association, for the Diffusion of Truth, 1833), 14; Maurie D. McInnis, "The Auction," *To Be Sold: Virginia and the American Slave Trade*, www.virginiamemory.com/online-exhibitions/exhibits/show/to-be-sold/eyre-crowe/the-auction (accessed December 13, 2017). Antebellum auctioneers would customarily hang a red flag at the site of an upcoming slave auction.

29. *Boston Post*, October 29, 1844. In conversation with co-editor John C. Rives of the *Washington Globe*, Thomas Williams attributed the *Boston Tribune* report of his Democratic political affiliation to a letter written by a mysterious man named Banks, an

alleged accomplice, arrested in Erie County, New York, of Philo N. Rust in the December 1843 robbery from Pomeroy's Express of a trunk containing $400,000, taken off the steamboat *Utica*. The trunk was later recovered, with almost all the money still in it. See *Albany Argus*, November 5, 1844; *Boston Traveler*, December 19, 1843; *Commercial Advertiser* (N.Y.), January 8, 1844; *Baltimore Sun*, January 9, 1844; *Jacksonville Republican* (Ala.), January 10, 1844; *Brooklyn Evening Star* (N.Y.), January 13, 1844.

30. *Daily National Intelligencer* (Washington, D.C.), October 24, 1844.

31. *Albany Argus*, November 5, 1844.

32. John C. Rives to Col. C. G. Greene, *Boston Post*, October 29, 1844. For a slightly different account by Rives, see *Albany Argus*, November 5, 1844. Born in Virginia and raised in Kentucky, John C. Rives took great pains to distance not only his party but also himself from the institution of slavery, minimizing his complicity with the peculiar institution. Documenting his personal interactions with slaves, he proclaimed himself "a better abolitionist than nine-tenths" of those who wore that label. He claimed to favor slavery's demise but feared that it would result in the dissolution of the Union and leave people of color still worse off than under bondage. See *Boston Post*, October 29, 1844 (quotations); *Albany Argus*, November 5, 1844.

33. John C. Rives to Col. C. G. Greene, *Boston Post*, October 29, 1844 (first, seventh, and eighth quotations); *Daily Atlas* (Boston), November 2, 1844; *Albany Argus*, November 5, 1844 (second through fourth quotations); *Washington Globe*, October 29, 1844 (fifth and sixth quotations).

34. *Washington Globe*, October 29, 1844; *Albany Argus*, November 5, 1844 (quotation).

35. Letter of George Watterston, October 19, 1844, reprinted in *Washington Globe*, October 29, 1844.

36. Ibid.

37. Ibid.; *Albany Argus*, November 5, 1844.

38. Letter of George Watterston, October 19, 1844, reprinted in *Washington Globe*, October 29, 1844.

39. *Washington Globe*, October 29, 1844. See also *Albany Argus*, November 5, 1844.

40. *Washington Globe*, October 30, 1844.

41. *Daily National Intelligencer*, October 31, 1844. The letter was dated October 30.

42. *Washington Globe*, October 31, 1844.

43. *Washington Globe*, October 31, 1844.

44. *Daily National Intelligencer*, November 1, 1844.

45. *Evening Post* (New York), October 31, 1844; *Richmond Enquirer* (Va.), November 1, 1844 (first and second quotations); *Evening Post*, November 2, 1844; *Albany Argus*, November 5, 1844 (third quotation); *Daily Atlas*, November 2, 1844 (fourth through ninth quotations).

46. Degregorio, *Complete Book of US Presidents*, 167–168; *Cincinnati Herald*, reprinted in *Christian Citizen* (Worcester, Mass.), November 23, 1844 (first through third quotations); *Boston Post*, October 29, 1844 (fourth quotation); Louis Hughes, *Thirty Years a Slave. From Bondage to Freedom. The Institution of Slavery as Seen on the Plantation and in the Home of the Planter* (Milwaukee: South Side Printing Company, 1897), 13 (fifth and sixth quotations).

CHAPTER 10: BROTHERS

1. *Waller v. Adams* (1845), Circuit Court of the District of Columbia, County of Washington, 1 Hay. & Haz. 218, 29 F.Cas. 91, No. 17,107; *Waller v. Adams* (1845), Records of the US District Court for the District of Columbia, Case Papers, 1802–1863, Civil Trial #132, Box 688, NA; Calvin Schermerhorn, "Slave Trading in a Republic of Credit: Financial Architecture of the US Slave Market, 1815–1840," *Slavery and Abolition* 36, no. 4 (2015), 587, 598.

2. George W. Nelson, Slave Bills of Sale, Mss. A00-385, BECHSA; Bill of sale, Thomas Isby, Isaac Turbon, Dick Mason, James Thomas, George Williams, Frank Jennings, William Cock, George Washington, James Baker, and Thomas Briscoe, January 24, 1846, Theodore Guyol, vol. 3, act no 20, NONA; Bill of sale, Henry, Davis, Mose, Vinson, Nace, Cilus, Matilday, Charlotte, Mary, and Ann, February 11, 1845, Louis T. Caire, vol. 97, act no. 44, NONA; Bill of sale, William, Spencer, Robertson, Prince, Bill, William Duval, and Henry, June 26, 1845, Theodore Guyol, vol. 1, act no. 338, NONA; Bill of sale, Patrick, George, George Kimbo, Sam Kimbo, March 4, 1847, Octave DeArmas, vol. 40, act no. 45, NONA.

3. Bill of sale, Sarah, July 3, 1844, Louis T. Caire, vol. 95, act no. 378, NONA (quotation); Bill of sale, Henry, Davis, Mose, Vinson, Nace, Cilus, Matilday, Charlotte, Mary, and Ann, February 11, 1845, Louis T. Caire, vol. 97, act no. 44, NONA; Bill of sale, Fanny, June 8, 1846, Theodore Guyol, vol. 4, act no. 282, NONA; Bill of sale, Butler Jackson, May 15, 1847, Louis T. Caire, vol. 106A, act no. 186, NONA.

4. *The Jeffersonian* (New Orleans), August 6, 1846 (quotation); *New-Orleans Directory, for 1841* (New Orleans: J. L. Sollee, 1840), 12; State of Louisiana, Messages & Proclamations of the Governor, 1837–1842, P86-94, 6483A-1-P, p. 84, 249, 348, 355, LSA; *Daily Picayune* (New Orleans), March 3, 1841, January 26, 1845, June 22, 1847, September 17, 1848, April 10, 1850, October 22, 1852, March 20, 1853.

5. Thomas Williams to R. H. Dickinson & Brother, June 9, 1847, R. H. Dickinson & Brother Correspondence, Box 1, Folder 3, AAS (quotation); R. H. Dickinson & Brother Daybook, 1846–1849, AAS.

6. *Richmond Dispatch* (Va.), March 3, 1853; Charles B. Dew, *The Making of a Racist: A Southerner Reflects on Family, History, and the Slave Trade* (Charlottesville: University of Virginia Press, 2016), ch. 5; Thomas Williams to R. H. Dickinson & Brother, May 26, 1847, R. H. Dickinson & Brother Correspondence, Box 1, Folder 3, AAS (quotations).

7. Thomas Williams to R. H. Dickinson & Brother, June 3, 1847, R. H. Dickinson & Brother Correspondence, Box 1, Folder 3, AAS (first through fourth quotations); quoted in Dew, *Making of a Racist*, 109 (fifth quotation); Thomas Williams to R. H. Dickinson, June 9, 1847 (sixth quotation).

8. Thomas Williams to R. H. Dickinson, June 14, 1847, R. H. Dickinson & Brother Correspondence, Box 1, Folder 3, AAS (first and second quotations); Thomas Williams to R. H. Dickinson, June 18, 1847, R. H. Dickinson & Brother Correspondence, Box 1, Folder 4, AAS (third and fourth quotations); Thomas Williams to R. H. Dickinson, June 30, 1847, R. H. Dickinson & Brother Correspondence, Box 1, Folder 4, AAS (fifth through seventh quotations); Thomas Williams to R. H. Dickinson, June 22, 1847, R. H. Dickinson & Brother Correspondence, Box 1, Folder 4 (eighth through twelfth quotations).

9. Thomas Williams to R. H. Dickinson, June 28, 1847, R. H. Dickinson & Brother Correspondence, Box 1, Folder 4, AAS.

10. Thomas Williams to R. H. Dickinson, June 30, 1847.

11. Thomas Williams to R. H. Dickinson, June 28, 1847.

12. *Cohen's New Orleans and Lafayette Directory, Including Carrollton, Freeport, Algiers, Gretna and M'Donogh, for 1850* (New Orleans: Delta, 1849), 172; Ralph Clayton, *Cash for Blood: The Baltimore to New Orleans Domestic Slave Trade* (Westminster, Md.: Heritage Books, 2007), 57; Inward Slave Manifest, New Orleans, October 26, 1847 (*Kirkwood*), NARA M1895, reel 11, image 1115. Earlier in the decade, the *New-Orleans Directory for 1842* (New Orleans: Pitts & Clarke, 1842), 422, listed Thomas Williams at 13 Moreau Street. Thomas Williams was primarily working in Washington, D.C., at that time, but may have kept this Moreau Street office in New Orleans as well. The corner of Moreau and Esplanade marked the epicenter of the New Orleans slave trade. See Clayton, *Cash for Blood*, 57.

13. Bill of sale, Jacob Doeres, Frank Campbell, Isaac Wassy, Jim Sly, Simon Bynaters, John Dyson, Elijah White, Washington Morehand, Joe Dyer, Frank Chun, and Harriet Butler, November 9, 1847, Lucien Hermann, vol. 16, act no. 581, NONA; *Daily Delta* (New Orleans), March 10, 1850; *Cohen's New Orleans and Lafayette Directory*, 101; *Baltimore Sun*, July 2, 1839; Bill of sale, Maria Bruce, January 20, 1847, Lucien Hermann, vol. 14, act no. 30, NONA; Bill of sale, Charles, April 3, 1847, Lucien Hermann, vol. 15, act no. 208, NONA; Bill of sale, David, Anzy, Lewis, Joe, Rogers, Lucy, Milly, Ellen, Tamer, Sarah, Catherine, and Mary, November 7, 1848, Lucien Hermann, vol. 19, act no. 567, NONA (first quotation); Bill of sale, Sam Jones and Frances Spence, February 13, 1849, Lucien Hermann, vol. 20, act no. 67, NONA; Bill of sale, March 13, 1849, Lucien Hermann, vol. 20, act no. 108, NONA (second quotation); *Times-Picayune* (New Orleans), May 2, 1850.

14. Wendell Holmes Stephenson, *Isaac Franklin: Slave Trader and Planter of the Old South* (Baton Rouge: Louisiana State University Press, 1938), 222 (quotation); Bill of sale, Jack, Elijah, Moses, and Harriet, January 20, 1848, Theodore Guyol, vol. 9, act no. 35, NONA; Bill of sale, Frances, Mary, and Louisa, February 15, 1848, Lucien Hermann, vol. 17, act no. 83, NONA; Bill of sale, Charles Henry, Nace Fowler, and Isaac Gray, February 29, 1848, Theodore Guyol, vol. 9, act no. 138, NONA; Bill of sale, Charlotte Hodge, Ellen Borrie, Susan Gilbert, Harriett Smith, and Sophia Generals, March 22, 1848, Lucien Hermann, vol. 17, act no. 151, NONA; Bill of sale, Robert Harris, George Mason, William Paine, George Wilson, and Nace Young, December 29, 1849, Theodore Guyol, vol. 14, act no. 742, NONA; Bill of sale, Rebecca, Maria, Lydia Ann, Catherine, and Matilda, March 25, 1850, Hilary Breton Cenas, vol. 45, page 713, NONA. Slave trader Isaac Franklin died in 1846 in West Feliciana Parish, Louisiana.

15. Bill of sale, Harriet, November 3, 1849, Amedee Ducatel, vol. 41, act no. 468, NONA; Bill of sale, Frances, Mary, and Louisa, February 15, 1848, Lucien Hermann, vol. 17, act no. 83, NONA; Bill of sale, Kitty, May 9, 1848, William Christy, vol. 59, page 509, NONA; Bill of sale, John, December 28, 1849, Lucien Hermann, vol. 21, act no. 484, NONA (quotations).

16. Bill of sale, Henry and Daniel, June 1, 1848, William Christy, vol. 60, page 567, NONA.

17. Thomas Williams to R. H. Dickinson, August 19, 1848, R. H. Dickinson & Brother Correspondence, Box 1, Folder 5, AAS; Bill of sale, Tom, Culwell, and Sam, November 13, 1848, Hilary Breton Cenas, vol. 41, page 101, NONA; Bill of sale, David, Anzy, Lewis, Joe, Rogers, Lucy, Milly, Ellen, Tamer, Sarah, Catherine, and Mary, November 7, 1848, Lucien Hermann, vol. 19, act no. 567, NONA.

18. Bill of sale, Jacob Doeres, Frank Campbell, Isaac Wassy, Jim Sly, Simon Bynaters, John Dyson, Elijah White, Washington Morehand, Joe Dyer, Frank Chun, and Harriet Butler, November 9, 1847, Lucien Hermann, vol. 16, act no. 581, NONA; Bill of sale, Charles Henry, Nace Fowler, and Isaac Gray, February 29, 1848, Theodore Guyol, vol. 9, act no. 138, NONA (first quotation); Bill of sale, Jack, Elijah, Moses, and Harriet, January 20, 1848, Theodore Guyol, vol. 9, act no. 35, NONA; Bill of sale, Henry, November 30, 1849, Hilary Breton Cenas, vol. 43, pages 630 (second quotation), 631 (third quotation); *Daily Picayune*, November 20, 1849 (fourth and fifth quotations).

19. Bill of sale, Henry and Daniel, June 1, 1848, William Christy, vol. 60, page 567, NONA (first and second quotations); Bill of sale, Jacob Doeres, Frank Campbell, Isaac Wassy, Jim Sly, Simon Bynaters, John Dyson, Elijah White, Washington Morehand, Joe Dyer, Frank Chun, and Harriet Butler, November 9, 1847, Lucien Hermann, vol. 16, act no. 581, NONA; Bill of sale, Charles, April 3, 1847, Lucien Hermann, vol. 15, act no. 208, NONA; Bill of sale, David, Anzy, Lewis, Joe, Rogers, Lucy, Milly, Ellen, Tamer, Sarah, Catherine, and Mary, November 7, 1848, Lucien Hermann, vol. 19, act no. 567, NONA; Bill of sale, Henry Gordon, December 2, 1848, Lucien Hermann, vol. 19, act no. 597, NONA (third and fourth quotations); Bill of sale, James Wilson, February 13, 1849, Lucien Hermann, vol. 20, act no. 68 (fifth quotation).

20. Bill of sale, Charlotte Hodge, Ellen Borrie, Susan Gilbert, Harriett Smith, and Sophia Generals, March 22, 1848, Lucien Hermann, vol. 17, act no. 151, NONA; Bill of sale, Henry Gordon, December 2, 1848, Lucien Hermann, vol. 19, act no. 597, NONA; Exchange of slaves, November 24, 1847, Lucien Hermann, vol. 16, act no. 606, NONA (first quotation); Exchange of slaves, December 18, 1848, Lucien Hermann, vol. 19, act no. 628, NONA (second quotation).

21. Abrogation of sale, Milly, Mary, and Sam Jones, March 13, 1849, Lucien Hermann, vol. 20, act no. 110, NONA (first quotation); Bill of sale, Horace Ware, January 16, 1850, Theodore Guyol, vol. 15, act no. 35, NONA (second through fourth quotations); Abrogation of sale, John, December 8, 1847, Edward Barnett, vol. 40, act no. 117, NONA; Abrogation of sale, Charlotte and her infant, February 10, 1848, Edward Barnett, vol. 41, act no. 157, NONA; Abrogation of sale, Julia, February 13, 1849, Edward Barnett, vol. 47, act no. 136, NONA.

22. *Kellar v. Williams* (1840), no. 12,928, Orleans Parish Court, NOPL.

23. *McLellan et al. v. Williams* (1856), no. 4299, Supreme Court of Louisiana, UNO.

24. Ibid.

25. Ibid. See also *Thomas McLellan et al. v. Thomas Williams* (1856), Supreme Court of Louisiana, 11 La.Ann. 721.

26. *McLellan et al. v. Williams* (1856), no. 4299 (quotations); *Thomas McLellan et al. v. Thomas Williams* (1856), Supreme Court of Louisiana, 11 La.Ann. 72~~1~~. See also *Times-Picayune* (New Orleans), December 10, 1856.

27. *Daily Picayune*, November 20, 1849 (first through third quotations); Herman Freudenberger and Jonathan B. Pritchett, "The Domestic United States Slave Trade: New Evidence," *Journal of Interdisciplinary History* 21 (Winter 1991), 475, 476; Calvin Schermerhorn, *The Business of Slavery and the Rise of American Capitalism, 1815–1860* (New Haven: Yale University Press, 2015), 201; *New Orleans Weekly Delta*, May 28, 1849; *The Liberator* (Boston), September 6, 1850 (fourth quotation). Frederic Bancroft, *Slave Trading in the Old South*, introduction by Michael Tadman (1931; Columbia: University of South Carolina Press, 1996), 58, and Steven Deyle, *Carry Me Back: The Domestic Slave Trade in American Life* (New York: Oxford University Press, 2005), 120, attributed the boast to William H. Williams. Michael Tadman, *Speculators and Slaves: Masters, Traders, and Slaves in the Old South* (Madison: University of Wisconsin Press, 1989), 207, stated that it was Thomas. By the time Theophilus Freeman's one-time captive Solomon Northup achieved his liberation from bondage, he described the bankrupted Freeman as "a low, miserable rowdy – a broken-down, disreputable man." See Solomon Northup, *Twelve Years a Slave*, ed. Sue Eakin and Joseph Logsdon (Baton Rouge: Louisiana State University Press, 1996), 243. Thomas Williams' wealth made him a target of pickpockets in New Orleans. See *Baltimore Sun*, January 9, 1850; Statement, March 26, 1850, Theodore Guyol, vol. 15, act no. 224, NONA; *Times-Picayune*, April 24, 1853.

28. Cleveland *True Democrat*, quoted in *Anti-Slavery Bugle* (New Lisbon, Ohio), March 3, 1848 (first through third quotations); quoted in Stanley Harrold, *Subversives: Antislavery Community in Washington, D.C., 1828–1865* (Baton Rouge: Louisiana State University Press, 2003), 109 (fourth through eighth quotations). Kenneth J. Winkle, *Lincoln's Citadel: The Civil War in Washington, D.C.* (New York: W. W. Norton, 2013), 32, lists the purchase price at $300.

29. Cleveland *True Democrat*, quoted in *Anti-Slavery Bugle*, March 3, 1848 (first and fifth through eighth quotations); House of Representatives, *Congressional Globe*, 30th Cong., 1st sess., 179 (second through fourth quotations). See also Harrold, *Subversives*, 110; Winkle, *Lincoln's Citadel*, 31–32.

30. Duff Green to W. H. Williams, January 24, 1848, series 1, folder 79, Duff Green Papers #993, SHC (first, second, and seventh through tenth quotations); Wm. H. Williams to Duff Green, January 24, 1848, series 1, folder 79, Duff Green Papers (third through sixth quotations). See also Winkle, *Lincoln's Citadel*, 32.

31. R. Wallach to Gentlemen, January 24, 1848, series 1, folder 79, Duff Green Papers #993 (first quotation); Duff Green to R. Wallach, January 24, 1848, series 1, folder 79, Duff Green Papers #993 (second through seventh quotations); Cleveland *True Democrat*, quoted in *Anti-Slavery Bugle*, March 3, 1848 (eighth quotation); Winkle, *Lincoln's Citadel*, 32–33 (ninth quotation p. 33). "[A]fter the manacles were taken off" Henry Wilson, proclaimed the *True Democrat*, "the chattel … became a *man*." The *True Democrat*'s correspondent, identified only as E.L.S. in the article, was Ezra L. Stevens. See also Harrold, *Subversives*, 111.

CHAPTER 11: THE LOUISIANA STATE PENITENTIARY

1. William Archambeault, ed. Alahna Moore and D. Ryan Gray, "Cabildo Prison," *New Orleans Historical,* http://neworleanshistorical.org/items/show/1255 (accessed March 5, 2018); *Acts Passed at the First Session of the Third Legislature of the State of Louisiana, Begun and Held in the City of New-Orleans on Monday the Eighteenth Day of November, in the Year of Our Lord One Thousand Eight Hundred and Sixteen, and of the Independence of the United States of America the Fortieth* (New-Orleans: J. C. De St. Romes, 1817), 44 (first and second quotations); *Daily Picayune* (New Orleans), February 28, 1841 (third and fourth quotations). See also *Daily Picayune,* March 12, 1841.

2. *New Orleans Commercial Bulletin,* July 27, 1841.

3. Gov. A. B. Roman message to the Senate and House of Representatives, December 13, 1841, State of Louisiana, Messages & Proclamations of the Governor, 1837–1842, p. 382, LSA.

4. Ibid., pp. 382–383 (first quotation), p. 383 (second through fifth quotations), LSA; *The State v. William H. Williams,* Supreme Court of Louisiana (1842, 1844), 7 Rob. (LA) 252, 1844 WL 1414 (La.) (sixth quotation).

5. *Acts Passed at the Second Session of the Fifteenth Legislature of the State of Louisiana, Begun and Held in the City of New-Orleans, December 13, 1841* (New Orleans: J. C. de St. Romes, 1842), 518 (first quotation); *Acts Passed at the First Session of the Sixteenth Legislature of the State of Louisiana, Began and Held in the City of New Orleans, on the 2d Day of January, 1843* (New Orleans: A. C. Bullitt, 1843), 69; Jeff Forret, "Before Angola: Enslaved Prisoners in the Louisiana State Penitentiary," *Louisiana History* 54 (Spring 2013), 143, 144–145; W. F. Griffin, *Minority Report of the Committee on Internal Improvements, in Documents of the First Session of the Fourth Legislature of the State of Louisiana 1852* (New Orleans: Bee Print, 1852), 1; *Louisiana Courier* (New Orleans), April 1, 1844 (second through seventh quotations).

6. Orlando F. Lewis, *The Development of American Prisons and Prison Customs, 1776–1845* (Montclair, N.J.: Patterson Smith, 1967); Blake McKelvey, *American Prisons: A History of Good Intentions* (Montclair, N.J.: Patterson Smith, 1977), chs. 1–2; W. David Lewis, *From Newgate to Dannemora: The Rise of the Penitentiary in New York, 1796–1848* (Ithaca: Cornell University Press, 1965); David Rothman, *The Discovery of the Asylum: Social Order and Disorder in the New Republic* (Boston: Little, Brown, 1971); Michael Ingatieff, *A Just Measure of Pain: The Penitentiary in the Industrial Revolution, 1750–1850* (New York: Pantheon Books, 1978); Adam Hirsch, *The Rise of the Penitentiary: Prisons and Punishment in Early America* (New Haven: Yale University Press, 1992). For an overview of southern penal institutions, see Fletcher Melvin Green, "Some Aspects of the Convict Lease System in the Southern States," in *Essays in Southern History,* ed. Fletcher Melvin Green (Chapel Hill: University of North Carolina Press, 1949), 112–123. Notable studies of antebellum southern state penitentiaries include Marvin E. Gettleman, "The Maryland Penitentiary in the Age of Tocqueville, 1828–1842," *Maryland Historical Magazine* 56 (September 1961): 269–290; Jim Rice, "'This Province, So Meanly and Thinly Inhabited': Punishing Maryland's Criminals, 1681–1850," *Journal of the Early Republic* 19 (Spring 1999): 15–42; James C. Bonner, "The Georgia Penitentiary at Milledgeville, 1817–1874," *Georgia Historical Quarterly* 55 (Fall 1971): 303–328;

Mary Ann Neeley, "Painful Circumstances: Glimpses of the Alabama Penitentiary, 1846–1852," *Alabama Review* 44 (January 1991): 3–16; William C. Nesheim, "The Early Years of the Missouri State Penitentiary: 1833 to 1853," *Missouri Historical Society Bulletin* 28 (July 1972): 246–263; Paul Knepper, "The Kentucky Penitentiary at Frankfort and the Origins of America's First Convict Lease System, 1798–1843," *The Filson Club History Quarterly* 69 (January 1995): 41–66. For the opening dates, see J. Thorsten Sellin, *Slavery and the Penal System* (New York: Elsevier, 1976), 139–141; Edward L. Ayers, *Vengeance and Justice, Crime and Punishment in the 19th-Century American South* (New York: Oxford University Press, 1984), 34–35, 49. On South Carolina's failure to build a penitentiary, see Ayers, *Vengeance and Justice*, 58–59, 294n51; Michael Stephen Hindus, *Prison and Plantation: Crime, Justice, and Authority in Massachusetts and South Carolina, 1767–1878* (Chapel Hill: University of North Carolina Press, 1980), 210–213. Ayers stresses the similarity in the development of penitentiaries North and South. See Ayers, *Vengeance and Justice*, 70–71.

7. *Daily Picayune*, October 8, 1840 (first quotation); *Laws of the State of Louisiana, Relative to the Penitentiary. By-Laws of the Board of Inspectors and Details of the Police and Discipline Adopted by the Warden, with the Approbation of the Board of Inspectors* (Baton Rouge: Hugh Alexander, 1834), 15–16, 12; Brett Josef Derbes, "'Secret Horrors': Enslaved Women and Children in the Louisiana State Penitentiary, 1833–1862," *Journal of African American History* 98 (Spring 2013), 280; *Report of the Board of Control of the Louisiana Penitentiary, January 1858* (Baton Rouge: Office of the Daily Advocate, 1858), 78 (second quotation); *Report of the Board of Directors of the Louisiana Penitentiary* (New Orleans: Emile La Sere, 1854), 5 (third and fourth quotations); *Daily Gazette and Comet* (Baton Rouge), August 26, 1858 (fifth and sixth quotations); *Report on the Penitentiary, 1839* (n.p.: n.p., n.d.), 3.

8. *Laws of the State of Louisiana, Relative to the Penitentiary. By-Laws of the Board of Inspectors*, 3 (first quotation), 11 (second quotation); *Acts Passed at the First Session of the Thirteenth Legislature of the State of Louisiana, Began and Held in the City of New-Orleans, on the Second Day of January, Eighteen Hundred and Thirty-Seven* (New Orleans: Jerome Bayon, 1837), 100; *Report on the Penitentiary, 1839*, (third quotation); *Daily Picayune*, October 8, 1840; Ayers, *Vengeance and Justice*, 59. The Auburn plan permitted prisoners to labor together during the day but required their separation at night. At all times, convicts were to remain silent. By contrast, the Pennsylvania system mandated solitary confinement, with no contact whatsoever among prisoners.

9. *Baton Rouge Gazette*, December 25, 1841 (first quotation); *Acts Passed at the Second Session of the Fifteenth Legislature*, 518 (second quotation), 520 (third quotation). It took a supplementary law passed in 1843 to clarify that free blacks were also candidates for service on the public works. See *Acts Passed at the First Session of the Sixteenth Legislature*, 69.

10. *Daily Picayune*, October 8, 1840; *Report on the Penitentiary, 1839*, 5 (first quotation); *Report on the Penitentiary, by a Joint Committee of the Senate and House of Representatives. J. Bernard, Chairman* (New Orleans: Magne & Weisse, 1845), n.p. (second quotation); *Acts Passed at the Second Session of the Sixteenth Legislature of the State of Louisiana, Begun and Held in the City of New Orleans, on the 1st Day of January, 1844* (New Orleans: Alexander C. Bullitt,

1844), 42 (third and fourth quotations). The law went largely ignored, however, prompting repeated complaints into the 1850s.

11. *Journal of the House of Representatives, First Session – Seventeenth Legislature* (n.p.: A. C. Bullitt, n.d.), 41; *Message of Robert C. Wickliffe, Governor of the State of Louisiana, Together with an Appendix, Containing the Report of the Penitentiary Agents for the Year 1856* (Baton Rouge: Office of the Daily Advocate, 1857), 51; *Acts Passed at the First Session of the Sixteenth Legislature*, 70 (first quotation); *Official Journal of the Proceedings of the House of Representatives of the State of Louisiana. Second Session – Sixteenth Legislature January 1, 1844* (New Orleans: n.p., 1844), 31, 3 (second quotation); *Acts Passed at the Second Session of the Sixteenth Legislature*, 27, 41.

12. *Official Journal of the Proceedings of the House of Representatives of the State of Louisiana. Second Session – Sixteenth Legislature*, 3 (first through third quotations); *Baton Rouge Gazette*, April 30, 1842 (fourth quotation). Susan Wurtzburg and Thurston H. G. Hahn III, *Hard Labor: History and Archaeology at the Old Louisiana State Penitentiary, Baton Rouge, Louisiana* (Fort Worth: General Services Administration, 1991), 5, contend that antebellum black prisoners labored on the levees along the Mississippi River because white men refused to do such dangerous and unhealthy work and because local planters would not risk valuable slaves to do it either. There is no evidence to suggest that Williams' gang worked on levee construction along the Mississippi or its tributaries, as so many postbellum black convicts would.

13. *Acts Passed at the First Session of the Sixteenth Legislature*, 4, 70 (quotation). See also *Acts Passed at the Second Session of the Sixteenth Legislature*, 27, 41.

14. *Acts Passed at the Second Session of the Fifteenth Legislature*, 522 (first through third quotations); *Baton Rouge Gazette*, April 30, 1842 (fourth and fifth quotations); *Baton Rouge Gazette*, May 7, 1842 (sixth and seventh quotations).

15. *Report on the Penitentiary. 1839*, 5 (first quotation), 17; Gov. A. B. Roman message to the Senate and House of Representatives, December 13, 1841, State of Louisiana, Messages & Proclamations of the Governor, 1837–1842, p. 382, LSA; *Report of the Standing Committee on the State Penitentiary Made at the Second Session of the Sixteenth Legislature* (Baton Rouge: n.p., 1844), 13 (second and third quotations); *Journal of the House of Representatives, First Session – Seventeenth Legislature*, 40 (fourth and fifth quotations); Mark Thomas Carleton, "The Political History of the Louisiana State Penitentiary: 1835–1968" (Ph.D. diss., Stanford University, 1970), 10.

16. Gettleman, "Maryland Penitentiary," 286, 288 (quotation); Ayers, *Vengeance and Justice*, 66, 67, 38, 68; Sellin, *Slavery and the Penal System*, 141–143; Knepper, "Kentucky Penitentiary," 64; Carleton, "Political History of the Louisiana State Penitentiary," 6, 10, 12, 14; Wurtzburg and Hahn, *Hard Labor*, 6.

17. *Report on the Penitentiary, by a Joint Committee of the Senate and House of Representatives. J. Bernard, Chairman*, n.p.

18. *Report of the Board of Directors, of the Louisiana Penitentiary to the Governor of Louisiana* (n.p.: n.p., 1852), 6; *Acts Passed at the First Session of the Seventeenth Legislature of the State of Louisiana, Began and Held in the City of New Orleans, on the 6th Day of January 1845* (New Orleans: Magne & Weisse, 1845), 28 (quotation); Forret, "Before Angola," 149.

19. Act No. 268, *Acts Passed By the Fourth Legislature of the State of Louisiana, at Their Session Held and Begun in the Town of Baton Rouge, on the 19th Day of January, 1852* (New Orleans: Bee Office – G. F. Weisse, 1852), 186 (first quotation); Act No. 1, *Acts Passed By the Third Legislature of the State of Louisiana, at Its First Session, Held and Begun in the Town of Baton Rouge, on the 21st January, 1856* (New Orleans: John Claiborne, 1856), 3; *The National Era* (Washington, D.C.), February 10, 1853 (second quotation); G. W. Morse, *Report of the State Engineer*, in *Louisiana Documents 1852* (N.p.: n.p., n.d.), 3 (third quotation); A. D. Wooldridge, *Report of the Internal Improvements of Louisiana, January, 1850*, in *Documents of the First Session of the Third Legislature of the State of Louisiana 1850*, 9 (fourth through ninth quotations).

State engineer Louis Hébert explained that, on April 1, 1857, he had taken out of the penitentiary "one slave, belonging to the State" and "confined in the Penitentiary since 1845 … for safe keeping." Although at first glance, the description sounded like it may have referred to a member of Williams' gang, it did not. Hébert was writing about Dick Glover, another slave committed to the penitentiary in 1845, who was discharged by the governor on March 31, 1857. Hébert dispatched Glover to the public works, where the bondman "labored faithfully" from April 1 to July 15. Glover then "absconded from the [Bayou] Maçon surveying party." In Glover's absence, the state determined that he "should be sold" because he was "incor[r]igible" and made himself, by his "evil propensities, very much disliked by our other slaves." See *Annual Report of the State Engineer, to the Legislature of the State of Louisiana. January, 1858* (New Orleans: John Claiborne, 1858), 8 (first through fourth quotations), 24 (fifth through seventh quotations); *Report of the Board of Control of the Louisiana Penitentiary. January, 1858*, 55.

20. Manuscript Census Returns, Seventh Census of the United States, 1850, Baton Rouge, East Baton Rouge Parish, Louisiana, Schedule 2, Slave Population, NAMS M-432, reel 242, page 321; *Annual Report of the Board of Directors of the Louisiana Penitentiary, to the Governor of the State of Louisiana. January, 1856* (New Orleans: John Claiborne, 1856), 13–18. Unlike all of the Louisiana State Penitentiary's other enslaved prisoners shown in the slave schedule of 1850, twelve who entered the institution in March 1845 did not have a crime listed next to their name, since they had merely been forfeited. Penitentiary officials did not trouble themselves with the details of their crimes. Ten of these twelve were members of Williams' gang. The other two were not but happened to enter the penitentiary the same month.

The notion of "double bonds" derives from the scholarship on enslaved women. See Joan Rezner Gundersen, "The Double Bonds of Race and Sex: Black and White Women in a Colonial Virginia Parish," *Journal of Southern History* 52 (August 1986): 351–372; Deborah Gray White, *Ar'n't I a Woman?: Female Slaves in the Plantation South*, rev. ed. (New York: W. W. Norton, 1999), 23. Philip J. Schwarz, *Twice Condemned: Slaves and the Criminal Laws of Virginia, 1705–1865* (Baton Rouge: Louisiana State University Press, 1988), 30.

Derbes, "Secret Horrors," 281, supplies a chart that vastly overestimates the total number of enslaved prisoners. The overwhelming majority of convict slaves in the Louisiana state prison served life sentences and therefore appeared in multiple penitentiary reports. Adding the total number of slaves from the annual prison census totals, as Derbes does, results in the counting of individual slaves multiple times and an erroneous total.

21. On local jails, see Gilles Vandal, "Regulating Louisiana's Rural Areas: The Function of Parish Jails, 1840–1885," *Louisiana History* 42 (Winter 2001): 59–92; Betty Wood, "Prisons, Workhouses, and the Control of Slave Labour in Low Country Georgia, 1763–1815," *Slavery and Abolition* 8 (December 1987): 247–271.

22. Hindus, *Prison and Plantation*, 145; George P. Rawick, ed., *The American Slave: A Composite Autobiography, Supplement, Series 1*, vol. VI, pt. 1 (Westport, Conn.: Greenwood Press, 1977), 317 (first quotation); George P. Rawick, ed., *The American Slave: A Composite Autobiography*, vol. VIII, pt. 2 (Westport, Conn.: Greenwood Publishing Company, 1972), 193 (second quotation); George P. Rawick, ed., *The American Slave: A Composite Autobiography, Supplement, Series 2*, vol. V, pt. 4 (Westport, Conn.: Greenwood Press, 1979), 1492 (third quotation). See also George P. Rawick, ed., *The American Slave: A Composite Autobiography, Supplement, Series 2*, vol. X, pt. 9 (Westport, Conn.: Greenwood Press, 1979), 4306; George P. Rawick, ed., *The American Slave, Supplement, Series 2*, vol. IX, pt. 8 (Westport, Conn.: Greenwood Press, 1979), 3645.

23. T. Lynn Smith and Homer L. Hitt, "The Composition of the Population of Louisiana State Penitentiary, 1859, 1860, and 1861," *Southwestern Social Science Quarterly* 20 (March 1940), 365; Wood, "Prisons, Workhouses, and the Control of Slave Labour," 248; Rice, "This Province, So Meanly and Thinly Inhabited," 19; Daniel J. Flanigan, *The Criminal Law of Slavery and Freedom 1800–1868* (New York: Garland, 1987), 21; Ayers, *Vengeance and Justice*, 61 (quotation).

24. Flanigan, *Criminal Law of Slavery*, 21; Ayers, *Vengeance and Justice*, 295n56. In the North, gradual or immediate emancipation laws passed in the wake of the American Revolution undermined or eliminated the institution of slavery altogether. The North's slave population was therefore in decline before northern penitentiaries were built. Among northern states, only Pennsylvania, which abolished slavery gradually by law in 1780 and founded its penitentiary a mere decade later, stood a reasonable chance of incarcerating slaves in any numbers. Dozens of runaways from the Upper South and the neighboring states of New York and New Jersey counted among the inmates of Pennsylvania's Walnut Street Prison in the 1790s. See Gary B. Nash, *Forging Freedom: The Formation of Philadelphia's Black Community, 1720–1840* (Cambridge, Mass.: Harvard University Press, 1988), 138. For a demographic study of Walnut Street Prison, see Leslie Patrick-Stamp, "Numbers that are Not New: African Americans in the Country's First Prison, 1790–1835," *Pennsylvania Magazine of History and Biography* 119 (January/April 1995): 95–128. Although Patrick-Stamp's article focuses on the issue of race, it neglects the phenomenon of slave prisoners, making no distinction between slave and free black convicts.

25. Sellin, *Slavery and the Penal System*, 144; Rice, "This Province, So Meanly and Thinly Inhabited," 35. Gettleman notes that, while Maryland's law of 1818 eliminated slaves from the penitentiary, free blacks still entered, numbering one-third of new inmates in 1834 and more than half in 1839. See Gettleman, "Maryland Penitentiary," 276–277.

Flanigan discusses a subsequent effort to imprison slaves in Maryland later in the antebellum period. See Flanigan, *Criminal Law of Slavery*, 22–23.

26. Flanigan, *Criminal Law of Slavery*, 23; Auditor of Public Accounts, Condemned Blacks Executed or Transported, Records – Condemned Slaves, Court Orders, and Valuations, 1846–1857, frames 374, 397, 405, 518, 862, Misc. Reel 2554, LVA; Ayers, *Vengeance and Justice*, 61.

27. *Wm. Gil v. Williams & Davis* (1857), no. 4999, Supreme Court of Louisiana, UNO.

28. *Wm. Gil v. Williams & Davis* (1857), no. 4999; Jeff Forret, *Slave against Slave: Plantation Violence in the Old South* (Baton Rouge: Louisiana State University Press, 2015), 142, 76, 346–347; *Commonwealth v. Thomas* (1839), Executive Papers, David Campbell, Box 6, Folder 2, LVA (first quotation); *Commonwealth v. Malinda* (1840), Executive Papers, David Campbell, Box 7, Folder 8, LVA (all other quotations). See also Joshua D. Rothman, *Notorious in the Neighborhood: Sex and Families across the Color Line in Virginia, 1787–1861* (Chapel Hill: University of North Carolina Press, 2003), 159–160.

29. *Commonwealth v. Landon* (1839), Executive Papers, David Campbell, Box 5, Folder 7, LVA; Bertram Wyatt-Brown, "Community, Class, and Snopesian Crime: Local Justice in the Old South," in *Class, Conflict, and Consensus: Antebellum Southern Community Studies*, ed. Orville Vernon Burton and Robert C. McMath, Jr. (Westport, Conn.: Greenwood Press, 1982), 173–206; *Commonwealth v. Jane* (1838), Executive Papers, David Campbell, Box 4, Folder 6, LVA; *Commonwealth v. Charlotte* (1840), Executive Papers, David Campbell, Box 8, Folder 2, LVA; *Commonwealth v. Nancy* (1839), Executive Papers, David Campbell, Box 5, Folder 3, LVA. The bondwoman Nancy who entered the Louisiana State Penitentiary was definitely the arsonist Nancy Custis, for records describe her as young. The other Nancy, convicted of attempted murder and variously called Nan, Nancy Smith, or Nancy Via, was about twenty years older.

30. *Wm. Gil v. Williams & Davis* (1857), no. 4999; Sellin, *Slavery and the Penal System*, 141; Ayers, *Vengeance and Justice*, 65; Carleton, "Political History of the Louisiana State Penitentiary," 6, 11, 13, 14–15; *Report of the Board of Directors, of the Louisiana Penitentiary to the Governor of Louisiana*, 2 (first and second quotations); Wendell Holmes Stephenson, *Isaac Franklin: Slave Trader and Planter of the Old South* (Baton Rouge: Louisiana State University Press, 1938), 276; *Message of Governor Paul O. Hebert, to the Senate, Vetoing the Penitentiary Bill. March 9th, 1855* (New Orleans: Emile La Sere, 1855), 6 (third quotation); *Daily Gazette and Comet* (Baton Rouge), January 22, 1857 (fourth quotation). See also *Message of Robert C. Wickliffe, Governor of the State of Louisiana, Together with an Appendix, Containing the Report of the Penitentiary Agents for the Year 1856* (Baton Rouge: Office of the Daily Advocate, 1857), 21. Gettleman, "Maryland Penitentiary," 287, describes the Maryland Penitentiary as "mainly an economic enterprise."

31. Most literature on early America's penitentiaries examines institutional development and wholly overlooks the occupants of the cells, and studies of prison populations in most southern states necessarily ignore slaves. One archaeological report on the Louisiana State Penitentiary dismissed enslaved prisoners out of hand, noting only

that, "[s]ince most blacks during the ante-bellum period were slaves and were punished by their owners, few were incarcerated in the penitentiary." Mark T. Carleton's otherwise impressive study of Louisiana's state prison likewise disregards the enslaved inmates. "Before the Civil War," he wrote, "most of Louisiana's convicts were Caucasian." Not until after the war, he continues, did an influx of black prisoners suddenly transform an antebellum institution designed "primarily 'for whites only'" into a repository for African Americans worked under the convict lease system so common in the postwar South. Only the works of Marianne Fisher-Giorlando, Connie H. Nobles, and Brett Joseph Derbes, which analyze Louisiana's inmate population through the lens of gender, have investigated the state's enslaved prisoners, a small fraction of whom were women. Yet like gender, race is a useful category of analysis when exploring Louisiana's antebellum prison population. See Wurtzburg and Hahn, *Hard Labor*, 6; Carleton, "Political History," 12, 16; Marianne Fisher-Giorlando, "Women in the Walls: The Imprisonment of Women at the Baton Rouge Penitentiary, 1835–1862," in *The Wall Is Strong: Corrections in Louisiana*, 3rd ed., ed. Burk Foster, Wilbert Rideau, and Douglas Dennis (Lafayette, La.: Center for Louisiana Studies, University of Southwestern Louisiana, 1995), 16–25; Connie H. Nobles, "Gazing upon the Invisible: Women and Children at the Old Baton Rouge Penitentiary," *American Antiquity* 65 (January 2000): 5–14; Derbes, "Secret History." Carleton's work later appeared as Mark T. Carleton, *Politics and Punishment: The History of the Louisiana State Penal System* (Baton Rouge: Louisiana State University Press, 1971). On women, see also Vernetta D. Young, "All the Women in the Maryland State Penitentiary: 1812–1869," *Prison Journal* 81 (March 2001): 113–132.

32. Forret, "Before Angola," 151–152; *Rapport Annuel du Bureau de Controle du Penitencier de la Louisiane, a l'Assemblee Generale. Janvier, 1861* (Baton Rouge: J. M. Taylor, 1861), 35.

33. *Report of the Board of Directors, of the Louisiana Penitentiary to the Governor of Louisiana*, 1 (quotations). For evidence of the expansion of cells within the penitentiary, see *Report of the Board of Directors of the Penitentiary of the State of Louisiana* (New Orleans: Emile La Sere, 1853), 3; *Report of the Board of Directors of the Louisiana Penitentiary* (New Orleans: Emile La Sere, 1854), 4. The law appears in *Acts Passed by the Fourth Legislature of the State of Louisiana, at Their Session Held and Begun in the Town of Baton Rouge, on the 19th Day of January, 1852* (New Orleans: Bee Office – G. F. Weisse, 1852), 170; Forret, "Before Angola," 149.

34. *Report of the Joint Committee on the Penitentiary* (New Orleans: Emile La Sere, 1854), 4 (first through third and seventh through ninth quotations); *Minority Report of the Committee on the Penitentiary* (Baton Rouge: Winfree & Bryan, 1852), 15 (fourth and sixth quotations); G. W. Morse, *Report of the State Engineer*, in *Louisiana Documents 1852* (n.p.: n.p., n.d.), 4; Geo. W. Morse, *Report of the State Engineer, April 7, 1853*, in *Louisiana Documents 1852* (n.p.: n.p., 1853), 3 (fifth quotation); *Official Journal of the House of Representatives of the State of Louisiana, Session of 1860* (Baton Rouge: J. M. Taylor, 1860), 8 (tenth quotation).

35. *Report of the Board of Control of the Louisiana Penitentiary. January, 1858*, 5 (first, second, and fourth quotations), 6 (third quotation).

36. *Report of the Board of Control of the Louisiana Penitentiary. January, 1858,* 11 (quotations), 6.

37. *Report of the Board of Control of the Louisiana Penitentiary. January, 1858,* 6 (first through fourth and ninth quotations), 11 (fifth quotation), 7 (sixth quotation); *Report of the Board of Control of the Louisiana Penitentiary* (Baton Rouge: J. M. Taylor, 1859), 4 (seventh and eighth quotations).

38. *Daily Picayune,* October 8, 1840 (first quotation); *Acts Passed at the Second Session of the Twelfth Legislature of the State of Louisiana, Began and Held in the City of New-Orleans, the Fourth Day of January, Eighteen Hundred and Thirty Six* (New Orleans: Jerome Bayon, 1836), 155; *Acts Passed at the First Session of the 14th Legislature of the State of Louisiana, Begun and Held in the City of New-Orleans, January 7, 1839* (New Orleans: J. C. De St. Romes, 1839), 76; *Daily Picayune,* October 8, 1840; *Report of the Board of Control of the Louisiana Penitentiary* (Baton Rouge: J. M. Taylor, 1859), 6 (second and fifth quotations), 3 (third quotation); *Daily Picayune,* May 20, 1842 (fourth quotation).

39. *Baton Rouge Gazette,* December 25, 1841 (first through third quotations); *Report on the Penitentiary, by a Joint Committee of the Senate and House of Representatives. J. Bernard, Chairman,* n.p. (fourth and fifth quotations); *Report of the Board of Directors of the Louisiana Penitentiary* (New Orleans: Emile La Sere, 1854), 4 (sixth and seventh quotations); *Annual Report of the Board of Directors, Clerk and Officers of the Louisiana Penitentiary, at Baton Rouge, for the Year Ending December 31, 1854* (New Orleans: Emile La Sere, 1855), 23 (eighth quotation). See also Derbes, "Secret Horrors," 283.

40. *Laws of the State of Louisiana, Relative to the Penitentiary. By-Laws of the Board of Inspectors and Details of the Police and Discipline Adopted by the Warden, with the Approbation of the Board of Inspectors* (Baton Rouge: Hugh Alexander, 1834), 12; *Daily Gazette and Comet,* May 28, 1857 (first quotation), July 14, 1857 (second quotation).

41. *Message of Robert C. Wickliffe, Governor of the State of Louisiana, Together with an Appendix, Containing the Report of the Penitentiary Agents for the Year 1856* (Baton Rouge: Office of the Daily Advocate, 1857), 22 (first quotation); *Daily Gazette and Comet,* July 14, 1857 (second quotation).

42. *Wm. Gil v. Williams & Davis* (1857), no. 4999; Forret, "Before Angola," 158–161; Derbes, "Secret Horrors," 283.

43. *Acts Passed at the Extra Session of the Second Legislature of the State of Louisiana, Held and Begun in the City of New Orleans, on the 4th Day of December, 1848* (New Orleans: Office of the "Louisiana Courier," 1848), 3, 4 (first and second quotations); Derbes, "Secret Horrors," 277, 278, 280, 283, 285 (third quotation); Forret, "Beyond Angola," 159–160.

44. *Special Report of the Committee on the Louisiana Penitentiary, to the Senate of Louisiana* (Baton Rouge: Tom Bynum, 1861), 5 (first quotation); United States War Department, *The War of the Rebellion: A Compilation of the Official Records of the Union and Confederate Armies,* ser. 1, vol. XV (Washington, D.C.: Government Printing Office, 1886), 748; United States War Department, *The War of the Rebellion: A Compilation of the Official Records of the Union and Confederate Armies,* ser. 1, vol. LIII (Washington, D.C.: Government Printing Office, 1898), 532 (second quotation); Derbes, "Secret Horrors," 286, 288. See also United States War Department, *The War of the Rebellion: A Compilation of the Official Records of the Union and Confederate Armies,* ser. 2, vol. VII (Washington, D.C.: Government Printing

Office, 1899), 18; Eliza McHatton-Ripley, *From Flag to Flag: A Woman's Adventures and Experiences in the South during the War, in Mexico, and in Cuba* (New York: D. Appleton and Company, 1889), 25.

CHAPTER 12: CLOSURE

1. *Cincinnati Herald,* reprinted in *Christian Citizen,* November 23, 1844 (first through sixth and ninth and tenth quotations); *The Liberator* (Boston), November 29, 1839 (seventh and eighth quotations).
2. House of Representatives, *Congressional Globe,* 29th Cong., 1st sess., 43; House of Representatives, *Congressional Globe,* 30th Cong., 1st sess. 73.
3. House of Representatives, *Congressional Globe,* 30th Cong., 1st sess., 179, 180, 268. One petition from New Jersey requested that, if the slave trade could not be abolished in Washington, D.C., "the seat of the National Government . . . be removed to some more suitable location." Some voices proposed a site in "the free West." See Senate, *Congressional Globe,* 31st Cong., 1st sess., 564; *Cleveland Herald,* April 14, 1849.
4. Appendix, *Congressional Globe,* 30th Cong., 1st sess., 959.
5. Ibid., 519–520 (quotation 520).
6. Ibid., 959 (first through third quotations), 960 (fourth quotation); *The Liberator,* June 28, 1850 (fifth through seventh quotations).
7. US Constitution, Article I, section 8 (first and second quotations); House of Representatives, *Congressional Globe,* 30th Cong., 2d sess., 38, 55, 83 (third quotation).
8. House of Representatives, *Congressional Globe,* 30th Cong., 2d sess., 106 (first quotation), 323 (second quotation), 415 (third quotation), 416; House of Representatives, *Congressional Globe,* 31st Cong., 1st sess., 1071 (fourth quotation). See also Appendix, *Congressional Globe,* 31st Cong., 1st sess., 1179. Signers of the petition included Jno. Wilson, Vice President of the Board of Aldermen; Silas H. Hill, President of the Common Council; Mayor W. W. Seaton; and twenty-eight others, including Richard Wallach.
9. William L. Van Deburg, "Henry Clay, the Right of Petition, and Slavery in the Nation's Capital," *Register of the Kentucky Historical Society* 68 (April 1970), 141; quoted in *Carlisle Weekly Herald* (Pa.), June 5, 1850 (first through fourth quotations); *Daily Republic* (Washington, D.C.), April 11, 1851 (fifth quotation); Senate, *Congressional Globe,* 31st Cong., 1st sess., 1743 (sixth, seventh, ninth through twelfth, and fourteenth quotations); Appendix, *Congressional Globe,* 31st Cong., 1st sess., 1634 (eighth quotation), 1633 (thirteenth quotation).
10. Senate, *Congressional Globe,* 30th Cong., 2d sess., 324; Senate, *Congressional Globe,* 31st Cong., 1st sess., 1817, 1830; Appendix, *Congressional Globe,* 31st Cong., 1st sess., 1664, 1665. Debate on these matters dominates the *Congressional Globe,* 31st Cong., 1st sess., and its appendix.
11. Senate, *Congressional Globe,* 31st Cong., 1st sess., 948 (first through fourth quotations), 1743 (fifth through seventh and eleventh quotations); Appendix, *Congressional Globe,* 31st Cong., 1st sess., 613 (eighth through tenth quotations). Other than Clay, members

of the Committee of Thirteen from slaveholding states were John Bell of Tennessee, John M. Berrien of Georgia, Solomon W. Downs of Louisiana, William R. King of Alabama, Willie P. Mangum of North Carolina, and James M. Mason of Virginia. Representing the North were Jesse D. Bright of Indiana, Lewis Cass of Michigan, James Cooper of Pennsylvania, Daniel S. Dickinson of New York, Samuel S. Phelps of Vermont, and Daniel Webster of Massachusetts. The final text of the law appears in Appendix, *Congressional Globe*, 31st Cong., 1st sess., 1674; M. Thompson, *Abstract of the Laws of the District of Columbia*, 3d ed. (Washington, D.C.: W. M. Morrison & Co., 1855), 19; Mary Beth Corrigan, "Imaginary Cruelties?: A History of the Slave Trade in Washington, D.C.," *Washington History* 13 (Fall/Winter 2001/2002), 22. In the final bill, the word "transferred" replaced the word "transported," the latter of which may have been a typographical error in the *Congressional Globe*.

12. Appendix, *Congressional Globe*, 31st Cong., 1st sess., 1631 (first and second quotations), 1640, 1641, 1642, 1652 (third quotation), 1630, 1643 (fourth and fifth quotations), 1644.

13. Ibid., 209.

14. Ibid., 957, 613 (first quotation), 1179 (second quotation), 771.

15. Ibid., 1642 (first through sixth and tenth quotations), 1637 (seventh quotation), 1639 (eighth and ninth quotations), 1641, 1649.

16. Ibid., 1669, 1639, 1672.

17. Ibid., 1634, 1664, 1666, 1636, 1667 (first quotation), 1665 (second through fourth quotations).

18. Ibid., 1638, 1642, 1665–1666, 1669, 1673–1674; Senate, *Congressional Globe*, 31st Cong., 1st sess., 1794, 1810, 1817.

19. House of Representatives, *Congressional Globe*, 31st Cong., 1st sess., 1837; Senate, *Congressional Globe*, 31st Cong., 1st sess., 1829–1830, 1848; Appendix, *Congressional Globe*, 31st Cong., 1st sess., 1674 (first quotation), 1643 (second and third quotations), 1665 (fourth quotation).

20. Manuscript Census Returns, Seventh Census of the United States, 1850, Washington Ward 7, Washington, District of Columbia, Schedule 1, Free Population, NAMS M-432, reel 57, page 119A.

21. *A Narrative of Thomas Smallwood, (Coloured man:) Giving an Account of His Birth – The Period He was Held in Slavery – His Release – and Removal to Canada, Etc. Together with an Account of the Underground Railroad. Written By Himself* (Toronto: James Stephens, 1851), 31; *Baltimore Sun*, May 4, 1850 (first and second quotations), August 16, 1850 (third through fifth quotations).

22. *Southern Press* (Washington, D.C.), January 1, 1851; Frederic Bancroft, *Slave Trading in the Old South*, introduction by Michael Tadman (1931; Columbia: University of South Carolina Press, 1996), 91; Alison T. Mann, "Slavery Exacts an Impossible Price: John Quincy Adams and the Dorcas Allen Case, Washington, D.C." (Ph.D. diss., University of New Hampshire, 2010), 232, 233.

23. Fredrika Bremer, *The Homes of the New World; Impressions of America*, vol. I, trans. Mary Howitt (New York: Harper & Brothers, 1853), 492 (first through fourth and seventh quotations), 493 (fifth and sixth quotations).

24. Ibid., 492. A cursory footnote in the book states, "This slave-pen has, I believe, been removed since Miss Bremer's visit." See ibid., 493.

25. Dorothy S. Provine, *Compensated Emancipation in the District of Columbia: Petitions under the Act of April 16, 1862* (Westminster, Md.: Willow Bend Books, 2005), 220.

26. Jerry M. Hynson, *District of Columbia Runaway and Fugitive Slave Cases, 1848–1863* (Westminster, Md.: Willow Bend Books, 1999), 5 (first quotation), 6, 7, 8, 9, 10, 11, 12, 13, 15–16; Walter C. Clephane, "The Local Aspect of Slavery in the District of Columbia," *Records of the Columbia Historical Society, Washington, D.C.* 3 (1900), 240 (second and third quotations); Roy P. Basler, ed., *The Collected Works of Abraham Lincoln,* vol. II (New Brunswick, N.J.: Rutgers University Press, 1953), 253 (fourth quotation).

27. *Republican and Patriot* (Goldsboro, N.C.), July 17, 1851 (first quotation); *Woodville Republican* (Miss.), April 22, 1851 (second quotation); *The Liberator,* June 30, 1854 (third through sixth quotations); *Feliciana Democrat* (Clinton, La.), May 26, 1855 (seventh and eighth quotations).

28. Manuscript Census Returns, Seventh Census of the United States, 1850, Clarke County, Virginia, Schedule 1, Free Population, NAMS M-432, reel 940, page 209B.

29. Manuscript Census Returns, Seventh Census of the United States, 1850, Washington Ward 7, Washington, District of Columbia, Schedule 1, Free Population, NAMS M-432, reel 57, page 117A; Manuscript Census Returns, Eighth Census of the United States, 1860, Washington Ward 4, Washington, District of Columbia, Schedule 1, Free Population, NAMS M-653, reel 103, page 330; *Daily Union* (Washington, D.C.), January 18, 1851; *Springfield Republican* (Mass.), January 20, 1851; *Weekly Messenger* (Boston), January 22, 1851 (quotation); *Charleston Courier* (S.C.), January 23, 1851; *Daily National Intelligencer,* November 22, 1861, April 9, 1862. Neither the 1850 nor the 1860 census shows Ebenezer Rodbird as living in his own home, but he is listed as having a place on First Street West near M Street North in Washington, D.C., in William H. Boyd, *Boyd's Washington and Georgetown Directory. Containing a Business Directory, Congressional and Department Directory and an Appendix of Much Useful Information* (Washington, D.C.: Henry Polkinhorn, 1858), 262. Solomon Northup, *Twelve Years a Slave,* ed. Sue Eakin and Joseph Logsdon (Baton Rouge: Louisiana State University Press, 1996), 22, accurately reported that Rodbird "still live[d] in Washington" in 1853.

30. Manuscript Census Returns, Seventh Census of the United States, 1850, District 19, Chambers County, Alabama, Schedule 1, Free Population, NAMS M-432, reel 2, page 274A; Manuscript Census Returns, Eighth Census of the United States, 1860, St. Clair County, Alabama, Schedule 1, Free Population, NAMS M-653, reel 23, page 191; Manuscript Census Returns, Ninth Census of the United States, 1870, St. Clair County, Alabama, Schedule 1, General Population, NAMS M-593, reel 40, page 46A. Joshua and Mariah Staples' twelve children were Josephine, Miles, Sarah A., Frances, Eliza A., Ervin L., Mary L., Thomas, Edmond, Gustus T., Ida R., and David T.

31. Manuscript Census Returns, Seventh Census of the United States, 1850, Alexandria, Virginia, Schedule 1, Free Population, NAMS M-432, reel 932, page 381A; *Alexandria Gazette* (VA.), September 1, 1834; Inward Slave Manifest, New Orleans, February 5, 1835

(*Uncas*), NARA M1895), reel 7, images 664–665; Inward Slave Manifest, New Orleans, September 29, 1835 (*Uncas*), NARA M1895, reel 7, image 781; Outward Slave Manifest, New Orleans, October 5, 1835 (*Warren*), NARA M1895, reel 21, image 535; Inward Slave Manifest, New Orleans, October 15, 1836 (*Uncas*), NARA M1895, reel 7, image 1214; Outward Slave Manifest, Alexandria, November 3, 1838 (*Uncas*), New-York Historical Society, MS569, Slavery Collection, nyhs_sc_b-05_f-16_020–001, http://cdm16694 .contentdm.oclc.org/cdm/compoundobject/collection/p15052coll5/id/24235/re c/5 (accessed February 25, 2015); Inward Slave Manifest, New Orleans, April 9, 1839 (*Uncas*), NARA M1895, reel 8, image 379; Outward Slave Manifest, Alexandria, November 19, 1839 (*Uncas*), New-York Historical Society, MS569, Slavery Collection, nyhs_sc_b-05_f-16_021-001, http://cdm16694.contentdm.oclc.org/cdm/compoun dobject/collection/p15052coll5/id/24240/rec/4 (accessed February 25, 2015); Outward Slave Manifest, Alexandria, October 9, 1840 (*Uncas*), New-York Historical Society, MS569, Slavery Collection, nyhs_sc_b-05_f-16_015-001, http://cdm16694 .contentdm.oclc.org/cdm/compoundobject/collection/p15052coll5/id/24223/re c/6 (accessed February 25, 2015); *Portland Weekly* (Me.), January 12, 1841; Outward Slave Manifest, New Orleans, January 6, 1846 (*Phoenix*), NARA M1895, reel 24, image 24; Inward Slave Manifest, New Orleans, January 2, 1847 (*Phoenix*), NARA M1895, reel 11, image 756; Inward Slave Manifest, New Orleans, March 27, 1847 (*Phoenix*), NARA M1895, reel 11, image 881; Ralph Clayton, *Cash for Blood: The Baltimore to New Orleans Domestic Slave Trade* (Westminster, Md.: Heritage Books, 2007), 635; Inward Slave Manifest, New Orleans, November 17, 1847 (*Phoenix*), NARA M1895, reel 11, image 1151; Outward Slave Manifest, New Orleans, May 9, 1850 (*Virginian*), NARA M1895, reel 25, image 756; Inward Slave Manifest, New Orleans, June 17, 1850 (*Virginian*), NARA M1895, reel 12, image 950; Outward Slave Manifest, New Orleans, July 25, 1850 (*Virginian*), NARA M1895, reel 26, image 55; Outward Slave Manifest, New Orleans, December 9, 1851 (*Virginian*), NARA M1895, reel 26, image 775; *Alexandria Gazette*, February 11, 1858, May 3, 1860; *Evening Star* (Washington, D.C.), March 11, 1859; *Alexandria Gazette*, June 13, July 10 and 13, 1865; Manuscript Census Returns, Ninth Census of the United States, 1870, Alexandria, Virginia, Schedule 1, General Population, NAMS M-593, reel 1632, page 10B; *Alexandria Gazette*, June 24, August 14, October 14, 1865, August 19, 1865, January 7, 1858, May 14, 1868, February 28, 1859, March 1, April 2, 1867, May 11, December 17, 1871, February 15 and 17, 1873. In addition to his civic roles, Nathaniel Boush also received press coverage for less flattering reasons. See, for example, *Alexandria Gazette*, October 26, 1867, March 7, 1868.

32. Edward E. Baptist, *The Half Has Never Been Told: Slavery and the Making of American Capitalism* (New York: Basic Books, 2014), 344, 345, 359

33. *Cohen's New Orleans and Lafayette Directory, Including Carrollton, City of Jefferson, Algiers, Gretna and M'Donogh, for 1851* (New Orleans: Daily Delta, 1851), 200; *Cohen's New Orleans and Lafayette Directory: Including Carrollton, Algiers, Gretna and McDonogh, for 1852* (New Orleans: Daily Delta, 1852), 240; *Cohen's New Orleans Directory: Including Jefferson City, Carrollton, Gretna, Algiers and McDonogh, for 1853* (New Orleans: Daily Delta, 1852), 274; Bill of sale, Rachel, January 26, 1852, Henry Paul Caire, vol. 4, act no. 3,

NONA; Baptist, *The Half Has Never Been Told*, 84; Charles Gardner, comp., *Gardner's New Orleans Directory, for the Year 1859* (New Orleans: Bulletin Book, 1858), 339; *Cohen's New Orleans Directory, Including Jefferson City, Carrollton, Gretna, Algiers and McDonough, for 1854* (New Orleans: Picayune, 1854); *Cohen's New Orleans Directory 1855* (New Orleans: Picayune, 1855).

34. Will of Thomas Williams, estate records, vol. 5, Butler County, Alabama, LGM013, reel 20, frame 574, ADAH; *Tuskegee Republican* (Ala.), January 8, 1852; Manuscript Census Returns, Eighth Census of the United States, 1860, Butler County, Alabama, Schedule 1, Free Population, NAMS M-653, reel 3, page 75; Manuscript Census Returns, Ninth Census of the United States, 1870, Butler County, Alabama, Schedule 1, General Population, NAMS M-593, reel 5, page 345B; *Tuskegee Republican*, July 14, 1853, April 6, 1854; Hank Trent, *The Secret Life of Bacon Tait, a White Slave Trader Married to a Free Woman of Color* (Baton Rouge: Louisiana State University Press, 2017), 102; Calvin Schermerhorn, *The Business of Slavery and the Rise of American Capitalism, 1815–1860* (New Haven: Yale University Press, 2015), 165–167; Bancroft, *Slave Trading in the Old South*, 378. Michael Tadman, "The Reputation of the Slave Trader in Southern History and the Social Memory of the South," *American Nineteenth Century History* 8 (September 2007), 262, suggests that "[t]he clear pattern seems to have been for established planters to invest some of the profits of planting in the slave trade – rather than to start off as a trader and retire to a plantation." Thomas Williams and the other traders identified in this paragraph did not conform to that model.

35. Eighth Census of the United States, 1860, Butler County, Alabama, Schedule 1, Free Population, NAMS M-653, reel 3, page 75; Will of Thomas Williams, estate records, vol. 5, Butler County, Alabama, LGM013, reel 20, frame 574, ADAH; Guardian books, Macon County, Alabama, LGM137, reel 31, frames 617, 619, ADAH; Manuscript Census Returns, Seventh Census of the United States, 1850, District 21, Macon County, Alabama, Schedule 1, Free Population, NAMS M-432, reel 9, page 249A.

36. Will of Thomas Williams, estate records, vol. 5, Butler County, Alabama, LGM013, reel 19, frame 142 (first quotation), 143, 144 (second quotation), ADAH; Eighth Census of the United States, 1860, Butler County, Alabama, Schedule 1, Free Population, NAMS M-653, reel 3, page 75; Eighth Census of the United States, 1860, Butler County, Alabama, Schedule 2, Slave Population, NAMS M-653, reel 27, pages 222–223.

37. Bill of sale, Westley, March 1, 1858, Hilary Breton Cenas, vol. 70, page 234, NONA (quotation); Jessica M. Lepler, *The Many Panics of 1837: People, Politics, and the Creation of a Transatlantic Financial Crisis* (New York: Cambridge University Press, 2013), 27 (second through fifth quotations). On the panic, see James L. Huston, *The Panic of 1857 and the Coming of the Civil War* (Baton Rouge: Louisiana State University Press, 1987). In June 1855, a "John O'Brien was arrested for assaulting and battering Thomas Williams" on the streets of New Orleans. It is not certain that this was William H. Williams' slave-trading brother. See *Times-Picayune*, June 26, 1855. *Cohen's New Orleans and Southern Directory, for 1856* (New Orleans: Daily Delta, 1855), 265, 281, 282, listed a Thomas H. Williams & Co. as a commission merchant firm and cotton factorage house at 58 Gravier Street. It is unlikely that this was William H. Williams' brother, however, since

the younger Williams sibling never, in any other context, used a middle initial. *Mygatt & Co.'s New Orleans Directory for 1857* (n.p.: n.p., n.d.), 315, listed no Thomas H. Williams & Co. as still operating in the city.

38. *Times-Picayune*, November 4, 1857; Charles Gardner, comp., *Gardner & Wharton's New Orleans Directory, for the Year 1858* (New Orleans: E. C. Wharton's, 1857), 281, 341, 343, 363; *R. G. Dun & Co. Credit Report*, vol. 11 Louisiana, p. 226, BLHBS (quotations). In antebellum New Orleans, several individuals with the surname Scott worked as commission merchants, including A. Scott Co. at 28 Gravier Street in 1842, William P. Scott at 24 Gravier Street in 1843 and later, in 1846, at 62 Camp Street, and T. W. Scott on St. Paul between Poydras and Perdido in 1849. See *New-Orleans Directory for 1842* (New Orleans: Pitts & Clarke, 1842), 267; *New-Orleans Annual and Commercial Directory, for 1843* (New Orleans: Justin L. Sollée, 1842), 295; *New Orleans Annual and Commercial Register for 1846* (New Orleans: E. A. Michel & Co., 1845), 515; *Cohen's New Orleans and Lafayette Directory, Including Algiers, Gretna, and McDonoghville, for 1849* (New Orleans: D. Davies & Son, 1849), 160.

39. Tadman, "Reputation of the Slave Trader," 259, 268n27; *R. G. Dun & Co. Credit Report*, vol. 11 Louisiana, p. 226 (quotations).

40. *Crescent City Business Directory for 1858–59* (New Orleans: Office of the Price-Current, n.d.), 228; Charles Gardner, comp., *Gardner's New Orleans Directory, for the Year 1859* (New Orleans: Bulletin Book, 1858), 268, 307, 327, 357; *R. G. Dun & Co. Credit Report*, vol. 11 Louisiana, p. 226 (quotations).

41. *Acts Passed By the Fourth Legislature of the State of Louisiana, at Its Second Session, Held and Begun in the City of Baton Rouge, on the 17th of January, 1859* (Baton Rouge: J. M. Taylor, 1859), 167 (first quotation), 168 (second quotation); *Times-Picayune*, May 1, 1859 (third quotation).

42. *Times-Picayune*, May 4, 1859 (first and second quotations); *R. G. Dun & Co. Credit Report*, vol. 11 Louisiana, p. 226 (third through seventh quotations).

43. Tadman, "Reputation of the Slave Trader," 259 (first quotation); *R. G. Dun & Co. Credit Report*, vol. 11 Louisiana, p. 226 (second through seventh quotations).

44. *R. G. Dun & Co. Credit Report*, vol. 11 Louisiana, p. 226.

45. Ibid., p. 226 (first through third quotations), p. 248 (fourth through seventh quotations).

46. *Montgomery Daily Mail* (Ala.), April 26, 1861 (first quotation); Will of Thomas Williams, estate records, vol. 5, Butler County, Alabama, LGM013, reel 19, frame 142; National Park Service, Soldiers and Sailors Database, www.nps.gov/civilwar/soldiers-and-sailors-database.htm (accessed April 9, 2018).

47. Will of Thomas Williams, estate records, vol. 5, Butler County, Alabama, LGM013, reel 19, frames 143, 142 (quotation), 146–147, 148–149, ADAH. The dollar figure cited would have been in Confederate currency, but at the time of Thomas Williams' death, that paper still retained its value.

48. Manuscript Census Returns, Ninth Census of the United States, 1870, Butler County, Alabama, Schedule 1, General Population, NAMS M-593, reel 5, page 345B; Will of Thomas Williams, estate records, vol. 5, Butler County, Alabama, LGM013, reel 20, frame 574, ADAH; Will of Thomas Williams, estate records, vol. 5, Butler County, Alabama, LGM013, reel 19, frames 142, 143 (same quotation on each page), ADAH.

CHAPTER 13: PERSEVERANCE

1. *Journal of the House of Representatives of the State of Louisiana, First Session – First Legislature,* 1853 (n.p.: n.p., n.d.), 182 (first quotation); *Staples v. Bouligny* (1845), no. 5342, Supreme Court of Louisiana, UNO (second quotation).

2. Manuscript Census Returns, Seventh Census of the United States, 1850, District 19, Chambers County, Alabama, Schedule 1, Free Population, NAMS M-432, reel 2, page 274A; *Staples v. Bouligny,* Manuscript Census Returns, Eighth Census of the United States, 1860, St. Clair County, Alabama, Schedule 1, Free Population, NAMS M-653, reel 23, page 191; Manuscript Census Returns, Ninth Census of the United States, 1870, St. Clair County, Alabama, Schedule 1, General Population, NAMS M-593, reel 40, page 46A.

3. State of Louisiana, Messages & Proclamations of the Governor, 1837–1842, P86-94, 6483A-1-P, pp. 230, 297, LSA; *Mississippi Free Trader* (Natchez), March 28, 1840; *Williams v. Louisiana,* no. 14157, Orleans Parish Court, NOPL; *Journal of the House of Representatives of the State of Louisiana, First Session – First Legislature,* 1853, 182; *Staples v. Bouligny* (quotation).

4. *Staples v. Bouligny* (first and third through sixth quotations); *Joshua Staples v. Ursin Bouligny* (1845), Supreme Court of Louisiana, 10 Rob. (LA) 424, 1845 WL 1492 (La.) (second quotation).

5. *Staples v. Bouligny* (first through fourth quotations); Legislature, House, Committee on Judiciary, *Report of the Judiciary Committee on the Memorial of W. H. Williams* (New Orleans: n.p., 1855), 6 (fifth quotation).

6. *Times-Picayune* (New Orleans), April 24, 1847; *Journal of the House of Representatives, First Session of the First Legislature of the State of Louisiana* (n.p.: P. K. Wagner, 1847), 94 (quotations).

7. *Journal of the House of Representatives, First Session of the First Legislature of the State of Louisiana,* 102 (first through fourth quotations), 131 (fifth quotation).

8. *Times-Picayune,* February 27, 1850; *Official Journal of the Proceedings of the House of Representatives of the State of Louisiana. First Session – Third Legislature January 21, 1850* (n.p.: n.p., 1850), 84, 104 (first quotation), 109, 112 (second and third quotations), 157.

9. *Journal of the House of Representatives of the State of Louisiana, First Session – Fourth Legislature, January 19, 1852* (n.p.: n.p., n.d.), 117 (first through fourth quotations), 118 (fifth through eleventh quotations); *Times-Picayune,* March 1, 1852.

10. *Journal of the House of Representatives of the State of Louisiana, First Session – Fourth Legislature, January 19, 1852,* 118.

11. Ibid.

12. Ibid.

13. *Times-Picayune,* March 6, 1852 (first quotation); *Journal of the House of Representatives of the State of Louisiana, First Session – Fourth Legislature, January 19, 1852,* 123 (second quotation), 135 (third quotation). The *Times-Picayune,* March 10, 1852, stated that the House Committee of the Whole rejected the bill on March 8, four days later than reported in the House *Journal.*

14. Act No. 268, *Acts Passed By the Fourth Legislature of the State of Louisiana, at Their Session Held and Begun in the Town of Baton Rouge, on the 19th Day of January, 1852* (New Orleans: Bee Office – G. F. Weisse, 1852), 186.

15. *Nailor v. Williams* (1862), Records of the US District Court for the District of Columbia, Case Papers, 1802–1863, Civil Trials #38, Box 1000, Folder 4, NA; *Wm. Gil v. Williams & Davis* (1857), no. 4999, Supreme Court of Louisiana, UNO (quotation).

16. *Journal of the House of Representatives of the State of Louisiana, First Session – First Legislature,* 1853, 182.

17. Ibid., 185.

18. Ibid., 182 (quotation), 190.

19. *Washington Globe,* November 14, 1854 (first quotation), December 18, 1854 (second quotation); *Evening Star* (Washington, D.C.), November 13, 1854; *Washington Union,* November 25, 1854; Manuscript Census Returns, Seventh Census of the United States, 1850, Alexandria, Virginia, Schedule 1, Free Population, NAMS M-432, reel 932, page 387B (third quotation).

20. Jefferson Morley, *Snow-Storm in August: Washington City, Francis Scott Key, and the Forgotten Race Riot of 1835* (New York: Nan A. Talese/Doubleday, 2012), 31, 207; *Nashville Union and American* (Tenn.), August 18, 1854; *Evening Star,* November 13, 1854 (first quotation), February 2, 1855 (second quotation); *Biblical Recorder* (Raleigh, N.C.), July 27, 1854 (third and fourth quotations). For a contemporary description of Columbian College, see Alfred Hunter, comp., *The Washington and Georgetown Directory, Strangers' Guide-Book for Washington. And Congressional and Clerks' Register* (Washington, D.C.: Kirkwood & McGill, 1853), 91.

21. *Evening Star,* November 13, 1854 (first through third quotations); *Washington Globe,* November 14, 1854 (fourth quotation); *Washington Union,* November 25, 1854 (fifth through eighth quotations).

22. *Richmond Enquirer* (Va.), December 5, 1854 (first quotation); *Washington Globe,* December 18, 1854 (second and third quotations); *The South-Western* (Shreveport, La.), January 3, 1855 (fourth quotation); *Evening Star,* December 19, 1854; *Richmond Dispatch* (Va.), January 19, 1855; *Evening Star,* February 2, 1855; *Baltimore Sun,* February 2, 1855; *Richmond Dispatch,* February 2, 1855.

23. *Alexandria Gazette* (Va.), January 20, April 12, 1855 (quotation); *William H. Williams and others v. John Withers and others* (1855), Arlington County, Chancery Record 1855–019, LVA.

24. RSPP, PAR#20885558, Series 2, East Baton Rouge Parish, Louisiana.

25. Legislature, House, Committee on Judiciary, *Report of the Judiciary Committee on the Memorial of W. H. Williams,* 1 (first quotation), 2–3 (second quotation), 3 (third through ninth quotations).

26. Ibid., 4.

27. Ibid., 5 (quotations), 3.

28. Louisiana Legislature, *Journal of the House of Representatives, Second Legislature – Second Session* (n.p.: n.p., n.d.), 121, 129–130; *Times-Picayune,* March 15, 1855 (quotation); *Democratic Advocate* (New Orleans), March 22, 1855. It remains unclear what

dispensation the state legislature made with respect to Albert and Stephen, the two confiscated slaves who died while laboring on the public works. See Legislature, House, Committee on Judiciary, *Report of the Judiciary Committee on the Memorial of W. H. Williams*, 5–6.

29. Act No. 1, *Acts Passed By the Third Legislature of the State of Louisiana, at Its First Session, Held and Begun in the Town of Baton Rouge, on the 21st January, 1856* (New Orleans: John Claiborne, 1856), 3. See also Louisiana Courier (New Orleans), February 8, 1856.

30. *William H. Williams and others v. John Withers and others* (1855), Arlington County, Chancery Record 1855–019, LVA.

31. RSPP, PAR#20885558.

32. Ibid.

33. Ibid.

34. Ibid.; Manuscript Census Returns, Seventh Census of the United States, 1850, Baton Rouge, East Baton Rouge Parish, Louisiana, Schedule 1, Free Population, NAMS M-432, reel 229, page 181A.

35. *Wm. Gil v. Williams & Davis* (1857), Supreme Court of Louisiana, 12 La. Ann. 219, 1857 La. LEXIS 124. Spofford cited at length the recent US Supreme Court verdict in *Marshall v. The Baltimore and Ohio Railroad Co.* (1853). "Bribes, in the shape of high contingent compensation," the court had ruled, "must necessarily lead to the use of improper means and the exercise of undue influence." The promise of financial reward "warm[s] the zeal" of legislators in favor of a desired measure, and if it passes, the individuals whose money exerted sway are corrupted as they come "to believe that any means which will produce so beneficial a result … are 'proper means.'" Moreover, governments are then made "subject … to the combined capital of wealthy corporations," resulting in the nightmare scenario of "universal corruption": "Speculators in legislation, public and private, a compact corps of venal solicitors, vending their secret influences, will infest the capital, of the Union, and of every state, till corruption shall become the normal condition of the body politic." See *Marshall v. The Baltimore and Ohio Railroad Co.* (1853), Supreme Court of the United States, 57 US 314, 16 How. 314, 1853 WL 7690, 14 L.Ed. 953.

36. Jeff Forret, "Before Angola: Enslaved Prisoners in the Louisiana State Penitentiary," *Louisiana History* 54 (Spring 2013), 162; *Times-Picayune*, January 30, 1856; *Report of the Board of Control of the Louisiana Penitentiary, January, 1858* (Baton Rouge: Daily Advocate, 1858), 55 (quotation); *Wm. Gil v. Williams & Davis*; deposition of Thomas Williams, January 24, 1860, *Nailor v. Williams* (1862), Records of the US District Court for the District of Columbia, Case Papers, 1802–1863, Civil Trial #38, Box 1000, Folder 4, NA. The *Times-Picayune*, February 20, 1858, erroneously placed the number of Williams' gang slaves released from the penitentiary at eleven. The confusion derived from the simultaneous release of the bondman Dick Glover to the state engineer, but Glover was not a member of Williams' gang. See *Report of the Board of Control*, 55. The list of Williams' gang slaves in the Board of Control report matches that found in the court record for *Wm. Gil v. Williams & Davis*.

37. *Nailor v. Williams* (1862), Records of the US District Court for the District of Columbia, Case Papers, 1802–1863, Civil Trial #38, Box 999, Folder 1, NA (quotations); *Nailor v. Williams* (1869), Records of the United States Supreme Court, Box 624, Case File #5032, Box 624, NA.

38. Legislature, House, Committee on Judiciary, *Report of the Judiciary Committee on the Memorial of W. H. Williams*, 6 (quotation); *National Republican* (Washington, D.C.), May 9, 1867.

39. *Daily National Intelligencer* (Washington, D.C.), April 19, 1858; Legislature, House, Committee on Judiciary, *Report of the Judiciary Committee on the Memorial of W. H. Williams*, 2 (first quotation), 5 (second and fifth quotations), 6 (third, fourth, and sixth quotations). Williams' death notice was also reported in the *Alexandria Gazette*, April 20, 1858.

CHAPTER 14: VIOLET

1. Steven Deyle, *Carry Me Back: The Domestic Slave Trade in American Life* (New York: Oxford University Press, 2005), 126; L. A. Chamerovzow, ed., *Slave Life in Georgia: A Narrative of the Life, Sufferings, and Escape of John Brown, a Fugitive Slave, Now in England* (London: n. p., 1855), 112 (first quotation), 111–112 (second quotation); *The Liberator* (Boston), November 15, 1834 (third and fourth quotations); Moses Roper, *Narrative of My Escape from Slavery* (1838; Mineola, N.Y.: Dover, 2003), 25 (fifth quotation); Michael Tadman, *Speculators and Slaves: Masters, Traders, and Slaves in the Old South* (Madison: University of Wisconsin Press, 1989), 126–127; Edward E. Baptist, "'Cuffy,' 'Fancy Maids,' and 'One-Eyed Men': Rape, Commodification, and the Domestic Slave Trade in the United States," *American Historical Review* 106 (December 2001): 1619–1650.

2. Hank Trent, *The Secret Life of Bacon Tait, a White Slave Trader Married to a Free Woman of Color* (Baton Rouge: Louisiana State University Press, 2017), 1, 2, 3, 95, 97, 125, 134, 149; Alexandra Finley, "'Cash to Corinna': Domestic Labor and Sexual Economy in the 'Fancy Trade,'" *Journal of American History* 104 (September 2017), 410, 416, 418, 423; Fredrika Bremer, *The Homes of the New World: Impressions of America*, vol. I, trans. Mary Howitt (New York: Harper & Brothers, 1853), 492 (first through third quotations), 493 (fourth quotation). Bacon Tait cohabited with Courtney Fountain, John Hagan with Lucy Ann Cheatam, Hector Davis with Ann Banks, Robert Lumpkin with the bond-woman Mary, and Silas Omohundro with Corinna Hinton. William H. Williams was not the Williams of New Orleans who purchased a young, light-skinned bondwoman as his concubine in H. Mattison, *Louisa Picquet, the Octoroon: or Inside Views of Southern Domestic Life* (New York: the author, 1861).

3. Manuscript Census Returns, Sixth Census of the United States, 1840, Washington, D.C., NAMS M-19, reel 35, page 44; *Daily Union* (Washington, D.C.), February 10, 1848; *Daily National Intelligencer* (Washington, D.C.), February 11, 1848; Manuscript Census Returns, Seventh Census of the United States, 1850, Washington Ward 7, Washington, District of Columbia, Schedule 1, Free Population, NAMS M-432, reel 57, page 119A. Wesley E. Pippenger, comp., *District of Columbia Marriage Licenses Register 1, 1811–1858*

(Westminster, Md.: Family Line Publications, 1994), 645, shows William H. Williams' marriage to Violet A. Milburn, as well as an earlier marriage, on December 3, 1845, between William H. Williams and Sarah Cusins. These were either different William H. Williamses, or William H. Williams' first marriage did not last any more than about two years. A William H. Williams also paid for children's coffins on June 24 and 29, 1845. If this was the slave trader, he may have purchased them for deceased slave children at the Yellow House. See Jane Donovan and Carlton Fletcher, transcribers, *William King's Mortality Books*, vol. II (Westminster, Md.: Heritage Books, 2004), 126.

4. *Cassedy v. Williams* (1843), Records of the US District Court for the District of Columbia, Case Papers, 1802–1863, Civil Trial #98, Box 663, NA (quotations); Manuscript Census Returns, Seventh Census of the United States, 1850, Washington Ward 7, Washington, District of Columbia, Schedule 2, Slave Population, NAMS M-432, reel 57, page 703; *Richmond* (Va.) *Dispatch*, May 3, 1852.

5. Records of the District Courts of the United States, Old Series Case Files, 1801–1878, Entry 115, Box 114, Folder 3969, NA.

6. *Nailor v. Williams* (1869), Records of the United States Supreme Court, Box 624, Case File #5032, NA; Records of the District Courts of the United States, Old Series Case Files, 1801–1878, Entry 115, Box 114, Folder 3969, NA. William H. Williams owned in 1858 a bondwoman named Charlotte and her two children, altogether valued at $950. In 1857, he had reacquired an enslaved convict also named Charlotte, and her three children, out of the Louisiana State Penitentiary. It is theoretically possible that Williams had kept Charlotte and her children for himself, only to have one of the children die within the year. But the similarity of the names is more than likely coincidental. Williams had originally purchased the convict Charlotte to sell, and, knowing her criminal past, would probably not have wanted to have her around his family.

7. *Daily National Intelligencer*, April 26, 1858 (first quotation); *The States* (Washington, D.C.), March 7, 1859 (second through fourth quotations); *Daily National Intelligencer*, December 17, 1858 (fifth quotation); Records of the District Courts of the United States, Old Series Case Files, 1801–1878, Entry 115, Box 114, Folder 3969, NA (sixth and seventh quotations).

8. Manuscript Census Returns, Seventh Census of the United States, 1850, St. Mary's County, Maryland, Schedule 1, Free Population, NAMS M-432, reel 296, page 286B; Manuscript Census Returns, Eighth Census of the United States, 1860, Washington Ward 7, Washington, District of Columbia, Schedule 1, Free Population, NAMS M-653, reel 104, page 806. John and Violet Abell had daughters Flora, Violet L., and Lucy.

9. Manuscript Census Returns, Eighth Census of the United States, 1860, Washington Ward 7, Washington, District of Columbia, Schedule 1, Free Population, NAMS M-653, reel 104, page 806 (first quotation); Manuscript Census Returns, Eighth Census of the United States, 1860, Washington Ward 7, Washington, District of Columbia, Schedule 2, Slave Population, NAMS M-653, reel 105, pages 40–41 (second quotation).

10. *Daily Advocate* (Baton Rouge), February 20 and 28, March 7, 1861; Act No. 1, *Acts Passed By the Third Legislature of the State of Louisiana, at Its First Session, Held and Begun in the Town of Baton Rouge, on the 21st January, 1856* (New Orleans: John Claiborne, 1856), 3 (first quotation); *Official Journal of the House of Representatives, Fifth Legislature – Second Session*, 20, 33–34, 39 (second quotation).

11. Senate, *Congressional Globe*, 30th Cong., 1st sess., 872; House of Representatives, *Congressional Globe*, 31st Cong., 1st sess., 1954 (quotation); House of Representatives, *Congressional Globe*, 33d Cong., 1st sess., 245.

12. House of Representatives, *Congressional Globe*, 37th Cong., 2d sess., 16, 36 (first quotation); Senate, *Congressional Globe*, 37th Cong., 2d sess., 89 (second quotation). On Civil War Washington, emancipation in the District of Columbia, and its aftermath, see Ernest B. Furgurson, *Freedom Rising: Washington in the Civil War* (New York: A. A. Knopf, 2004); Kate Masur, *An Example for All the Land: Emancipation and the Struggle over Equality in Washington, D.C.* (Chapel Hill: University of North Carolina Press, 2010); Kenneth J. Winkle, *Lincoln's Citadel: The Civil War in Washington, D.C.* (New York: Norton, 2013).

13. Senate, *Congressional Globe*, 37th Cong., 2d sess., 1285–1286, 1299–1300.

14. Michael J. Kurtz, "Emancipation in the Federal City," *Civil War History* 24 (March 1978), 254, 255–256; Walter C. Clephane, "The Local Aspect of Slavery in the District of Columbia," *Records of the Columbia Historical Society, Washington, D.C.* 3 (1900), 254. The full text of the Emancipation Act of 1862 is most readily available at www .archives.gov/exhibits/featured-documents/dc-emancipation-act/transcription.html (accessed February 9, 2018) (first and second quotations); Senate, *Congressional Digest*, 37th Cong., 2d sess., 1191 (third quotation).

15. *Congressional Globe*, 37th Cong., 2d sess., 1680 (first quotation); Clephane, "Local Aspect of Slavery," 254, 255; Kurtz, "Emancipation in the Federal City," 251; Page Milburn, "The Emancipation of the Slaves in the District of Columbia," *Records of the Columbia Historical Society, Washington, D.C.* 16 (1913), 113 (third quotation); House of Representatives, *Congressional Globe*, 30th Cong., 2d sess., 212 (second quotation).

16. Eric Foner, *The Fiery Trial: Abraham Lincoln and American Slavery* (New York: Norton, 2010), 60–61, 127, 185, 221, 223, 233–234, 236, 401n52; Eric Foner, "Lincoln and Colonization," in *Our Lincoln: New Perspectives on Lincoln and his World*, ed. Eric Foner (New York: Norton, 2008), 145–146, 151; John G. Nicolay and John Hay, eds., *Abraham Lincoln: Complete Works Comprising his Speeches, Letters, State Papers, and Miscellaneous Writings*, vol. II (New York: Century, 1894, 1922), 222–223 (first quotation), 223 (second and third quotations); *Congressional Globe*, 37th Cong., 2d sess., 1680 (fourth quotation).

17. Ira Berlin, *The Long Emancipation: The Demise of Slavery in the United States* (Cambridge, Mass.: Harvard University Press, 2015), 160; Colbert I. King, "D.C.'s grim, unfinished business, 154 years after emancipation," *Washington Post*, April 15, 2016, www .washingtonpost.com/opinions/ (accessed April 17, 2016).

18. Kurtz, "Emancipation in the Federal City," 256, 259, 260; Milburn, "Emancipation of the Slaves," 117, 118; Joshua D. Rothman, "The End of the Slave Trade," *New York Times*,

March 27, 2015, http://mobile.nytimes.com/blogs/opinionator/2015/03/27/the-end-of-the-slave-trade/?referrer (accessed March 27, 2015).

19. Internal Revenue Service, Tax Assessment List, 1862; Records of the Board of Commissioners for the Emancipation of Slaves in the District of Columbia, 1862–1863, M520 Petitions Filed Under the Act of Apr. 16, 1862: Nos. 401–600, Roll #4, Petition No. 562, May 29, 1862, NA (quotations); Kurtz, "Emancipation in the Federal City," 264; Milburn, "Emancipation of the Slaves," 117, 118; Damani Davis, "Slavery and Emancipation in the Nation's Capital," *Prologue: The Journal of the National Archives* 42 (Spring 2010), 54; Records of the US District Court for the District of Columbia Relating to Slaves, 1851 to 1863, Emancipation Papers Resulting from the Act of Apr. 16, 1862 A-L, NARA microfilm publication M433, Roll #1; Dorothy S. Provine, *Compensated Emancipation in the District of Columbia: Petitions under the Act of April 16, 1862* (Westminster, Md.: Willow Bend Books, 2005), 140. See Petition No. 562, Violet A. Abell, May 29, 1862, in *Civil War Washington*, ed. Susan C. Lawrence, Elizabeth Lorang, Kenneth M. Price, and Kenneth J. Winkle, University of Nebraska-Lincoln, http://civilwardc.org/texts/petitions/cww.00562.html (accessed August 12, 2014).

20. Records of the Board of Commissioners (quotations); Kurtz, "Emancipation in the Federal City," 260, 256–257; Provine, *Compensated Emancipation*, 141; Clephane, "Local Aspect of Slavery," 256; Milburn, "Emancipation of the Slaves," 117. Using the District of Columbia as a guide, at even a measly $300 per slave, the cost to compensate all southern slaveholders at the conclusion of the Civil War would have reached the staggering sum of $1.2 trillion, or almost $18 trillion in 2016 dollars.

21. Senate, *Congressional Globe*, 37th Cong., 2d sess., 1914 (first through third quotations); George P. Sanger, *The Statutes at Large, Treaties, and Proclamations, of the United States of America*, vol. XIII (Boston: Little, Brown and Company, 1866), 353 (fourth quotation); Ralph Clayton, *Cash for Blood: The Baltimore to New Orleans Domestic Slave Trade* (Westminster, Md.: Heritage Books, 2007), 114, 115, 116–117.

22. National Park Service, Soldiers and Sailors Database, www.nps.gov/civilwar/search-soldiers.htm (accessed February 12, 2018). Williams' gang left the Louisiana State Penitentiary more than five years before Union troops liberated the institution in August 1862, but according to one ex-convict, "All the negroes that were in the penitentiary have been uniformed and armed" and recruited into the United States Colored Troops. See United States War Department, *The War of the Rebellion: A Compilation of the Official Records of the Union and Confederate Armies*, ser. 1, vol. XV (Washington: Government Printing Office, 1886), 130.

23. Manuscript Census Returns, Ninth Census of the United States, 1870, St. John the Baptist Parish, Louisiana, Schedule 1, General Population, NAMS M-593, reel 529, page 296A; Manuscript Census Returns, Ninth Census of the United States, 1870, St. Mary Parish, Louisiana, Schedule 1, General Population, NAMS M-593, reel 531, page 492B.

24. On Thomas N. Davis and his legal problems, see Manuscript Census Returns, Seventh Census of the United States, 1850, Washington Ward 4, Washington, District of Columbia, Schedule 1, Free Population, NAMS M-432, reel 56, page 224A; *Times-Picayune* (New Orleans), July 31, 1855; *Augusta Chronicle* (Ga.), February 14, 1852;

State v. Davis (1858), Case #13473, First District Court of New Orleans, NOPL; *Times-Picayune*, March 10, 1858; *State v. Thomas N. Davis* (1868), no. 1430, Supreme Court of Louisiana, 20 La. Ann. 354; Solomon Wolff, comp., *Revised Laws of Louisiana* (New Orleans: F. F. Hansell & Bro., 1897), 236. In the First District Court, Thomas N. Davis' case was no. 17,757. Mary Beth Corrigan, "Imaginary Cruelties?: A History of the Slave Trade in Washington, D.C.," *Washington History* 13 (Fall/Winter 2001/2002), 13; George P. Rawick, ed., *The American Slave: A Composite Autobiography, Supplement, Series 1*, vol. VIII, pt. 3*Mississippi* (Westport, Conn.: Greenwood Press, 1977), 1280 (first and second quotations); Petition for freedom, July 31, 1839, *Hannah Stewart v. Allison Nailor*, in *O Say Can You See: Early Washington, D.C., Law & Family*, ed. William G. Thomas, University of Nebraska-Lincoln, http://earlywashingtondc.org/doc/oscys .case.0136.001 (accessed July 5, 2016) (third through fifth quotations). The Nailor name is often spelled "Naylor," but I have elected to use "Nailor" because that is how it appears more commonly in the sources used here.

25. Gaither & Addison, comp., *The Washington Directory, and National Register, for 1846. In Two Parts* (Washington, D.C.: John T. Towers, 1846), ix; Manuscript Census Returns, Seventh Census of the United States, 1850, Washington Ward 2, Washington, District of Columbia, Schedule 1, Free Population, NAMS M-432, reel 56, page 88B; *Baltimore Sun*, June 14, 1841 (first and second quotations); *Georgetown Advocate*, June 24, 1841; *Washington Globe*, July 28, 1842 (third quotation); *Daily National Intelligencer*, April 12, 1838 (fourth quotation); *Georgetown Advocate*, September 23, 1845; *Daily National Intelligencer*, September 17, 1847 (fifth quotation); Stephen K. Williams, ed., *Cases Argued and Decided in the Supreme Court of the United States* (Rochester, N.Y.: Lawyers Cooperative, 1919), 113 (sixth quotation); *Daily National Intelligencer*, January 18, 1858; *Evening Star* (Washington, D.C.), May 4, 1858.

26. *Alexandria Gazette* (Va.), November 28, 1843 (first and second quotations); *Daily National Intelligencer*, May 5, 1849 (third quotation); Manuscript Census Returns, Seventh Census of the United States, 1850, Washington Ward 2, Washington, District of Columbia, Schedule 2, Slave Population, NAMS M-432, reel 57, pages 655, 657; Manuscript Census Returns, Seventh Census of the United States, 1850, Montgomery County, Maryland, Schedule 2, Slave Population, NAMS M-432, reel 301, page 352; Manuscript Census Returns, Eighth Census of the United States, 1860, Washington, District of Columbia, Schedule 2, Slave Population, NAMS M-653, reel 105, pages 44, 52B; Manuscript Census Returns, Eighth Census of the United States, 1860, Montgomery County, Maryland, Schedule 2, Slave Population, NAMS M-653, reel 485, page 359; Provine, *Compensated Emancipation*, 231 (fourth and fifth quotations). On Nailor's efforts to gain compensation, see also *National Republican* (Washington, D. C.), July 16 and 31, 1862; James D. Walker, "District of Columbia Slave Records," *Journal of the Afro-American Historical and Genealogical Society* 2, no. 1 (1981), 76–77, 78; Petition No. 959, Allison Nailor, July 15, 1862, in *Civil War Washington*, ed. Susan C. Lawrence, Elizabeth Lorang, Kenneth M. Price, and Kenneth J. Winkle, University of Nebraska-Lincoln, http://civilwardc.org/texts/petitions/cww.00959.html (accessed August 12, 2014).

27. *Daily National Intelligencer*, September 18, 1846; *Daily National Tribune*, September 22, 1846; *Daily National Intelligencer*, April 30, September 14, 1863; *Nailor v. Williams* (1862), Records of the US District Court for the District of Columbia, Case Papers, 1802–1863, Civil Trial #38, Box 999, Folder 1, NA.

28. *Nailor v. Williams* (1868), Records of the United States Supreme Court, Case File #5032, Box 624, NA (first through third quotations); *Nailor v. Williams* (1862), Records of the US District Court for the District of Columbia, Case Papers, 1802–1863, Civil Trial #38, Box 999, Folder 2, NA; *National Republican*, May 9, 1867 (fourth through sixth quotations); *Nailor v. Williams* (1869), Supreme Court of the United States, 75 US 107, 19 L. Ed. 348, 1868 US LEXIS 1086, 8 Wall. 107.

29. *Nailor v. Williams* (1862), Records of the US District Court for the District of Columbia, Case Papers, 1802–1863, Civil Trials #38, Box 1000, Folder 4, NA (first and second quotations); *Nailor v. Williams* (1862), Records of the US District Court for the District of Columbia, Case Papers, 1802–1863, Civil Trial #38, Box 999, Folder 1, NA (third through fifth and seventh through sixteenth quotations); *Nailor v. Williams* (1862), Records of the US District Court for the District of Columbia, Case Papers, 1802–1863, Civil Trial #38, Box 999, Folder 2, NA (sixth quotation); Manuscript Census Returns, Seventh Census of the United States, 1850, East Baton Rouge Parish, Louisiana, Schedule 1, Free Population, NAMS M-432, reel 229, page 181A.

30. *Nailor v. Williams* (1862), Records of the US District Court for the District of Columbia, Case Papers, 1802–1863, Civil Trial #38, Box 999, Folder 1, NA; *Times-Picayune*, July 31, 1855 (first quotation); *Nailor v. Williams* (1862), Records of the US District Court for the District of Columbia, Case Papers, 1802–1863, Civil Trials #38, Box 1000, Folder 4, NA (second quotation). Davis claimed receipt of his first payment in April 1856, but he elsewhere placed the timing of events one year too late. Given the date of his agreement with Williams, in February 1855, an April 1855 first payment date seems more likely.

31. *Nailor v. Williams* (1869), Records of the United States Supreme Court, Box 624, Case File #5032, Box 624, NA.

32. *National Republican*, May 9, 1867 (first and fifth quotations); *Nailor v. Williams* (1862), Records of the US District Court for the District of Columbia, Case Papers, 1802–1863, Civil Trials #38, Box 1000, Folder 4, NA (second, third, sixth, and seventh quotations); *Nailor v. Williams* (1869), Supreme Court of the United States, 75 US 107, 19 L.Ed. 348, 1868 US LEXIS 1086, 8 Wall. 107 (fourth quotation).

33. *Nailor v. Williams* (1862), Records of the US District Court for the District of Columbia, Case Papers, 1802–1863, Civil Trials #38, Box 1000, Folder 4, NA.

34. Ibid.

35. *Nailor v. Williams* (1862), Records of the US District Court for the District of Columbia, Case Papers, 1802-1863, Civil Trial #38, Box 999, Folder 1, NA.

36. *Nailor v. Williams* (1862), Records of the US District Court for the District of Columbia, Case Papers, 1802–1863, Civil Trial #38, Box 999, Folder 2, NA (quotations); *Nailor v. Williams* (1862), Records of the US District Court for the District of Columbia, Case Papers, 1802–1863, Civil Trials #38, Box 1000, Folder 4, NA. Information in this

paragraph mostly comes from an unsigned, undated document with no indication of authorship. It reads like jury instructions, however, so I have employed it as such in the text.

37. *Daily National Intelligencer,* January 14, 1865.

38. *Nailor v. Williams* (1862), Records of the US District Court for the District of Columbia, Case Papers, 1802–1863, Civil Trial #38, Box 999, Folder 1, NA (first through seventh quotations); *National Republican,* May 9, 1867 (eighth through eleventh, thirteenth, and fourteenth quotations); *Nailor v. Williams* (1869), Supreme Court of the United States, 75 US 107, 19 L.Ed. 348, 1868 US LEXIS 1086, 8 Wall. 107 (twelfth quotation).

39. *Nailor v. Williams* (1862), Records of the US District Court for the District of Columbia, Case Papers, 1802–1863, Civil Trial #38, Box 999, Folder 2, NA (quotations); Federal Judicial Center, "Supreme Court of the District of Columbia, 1863–1936," www.fjc.gov /history/courts/supreme-court-district-columbia-1863-1936 (accessed February 17, 2018).

40. *Allison Nailor v. Violet A. Williams, administratrix of W. H. Williams,* No. 439, *Daily National Intelligencer,* March 29, 1867; *Daily National Intelligencer,* March 30, April 1 and April 30, 1867; *National Republican,* April 30, 1867; Federal Judicial Center, "Supreme Court of the District of Columbia, 1863–1936," www.fjc.gov/history/courts/supreme-court-district-columbia-1863-1936 (accessed February 17, 2018); *National Republican,* May 9, 1867.

41. *Nailor v. Williams* (1869), Records of the United States Supreme Court, Box 624, Case File #5032, Box 624, NA; *Evening Star,* April 11, 1867.

42. *National Republican,* December 16, 1868 (first quotation); *Nailor v. Williams* (1869), Supreme Court of the United States, 75 US 107, 19 L.Ed. 348, 1868 US LEXIS 1086, 8 Wall. 107 (second through twelfth quotations); *National Republican,* November 2, 1869.

43. Williams, ed., *Cases Argued and Decided in the Supreme Court of the United States,* 113.

44. Ibid., 113 (quotations), 112.

45. Ibid., 113 (first through ninth, twelfth, and thirteenth quotations), 114 (tenth quotation), 115 (eleventh quotation).

46. Records of the District Courts of the United States, Old Series Case Files, 1801–1878, Entry 115, Box 114, Folder 3969, NA; Constitution (Washington, D.C.), July 20, 1859; *Evening Star,* January 14, 1864, December 22, 1864 (first quotation), January 7, 1871 (second quotation), September 13, 1871 (third quotation).

Margaret A. Milburn married Hollis Amidon, a man twenty years her senior, in 1862. Born in New York, Amidon lived in Norfolk, Virginia, prior to moving to Washington, D.C., about 1846. His first wife died, leaving him to care for a young daughter, Mary A. Amidon. In 1850, the father and daughter lived in a household headed by George Milburn's widow, Margaret Milburn. Margaret Milburn's stepdaughter Margaret A. Milburn lived in that same household, as did William H. and Violet Williams, their eldest daughter Olivia, two other members of the Milburn family, and another couple from New York, possible relations of Amidon's. Amidon worked as an upholsterer in 1850 but was described as "a man of rare intellect," no doubt an attractive quality for a professional educator such as Margaret A. Milburn. Amidon went on to work for the US government in both the Treasury Department and the Department of Agriculture.

He died in January 1889, twenty years after his second wife. They did not have any children. Manuscript Census Returns, Seventh Census of the United States, 1850, Washington Ward 7, Washington, District of Columbia, Schedule 1, Free Population, NAMS M-432, reel 57, page 119A-119B; *Evening Star,* January 24, 1889.

After Margaret Milburn died in 1874, some members of the Milburn clan sued to recover Milburn family properties that had fallen into Hollis Amidon's possession after Margaret A. Milburn's death in 1869. They were unsuccessful in wresting the property away from him. See *National Republican,* May 26, 1875; Arthur MacArthur, *Reports of Cases Argued and Determined in the Supreme Court of the District of Columbia, (General Term,) from the January Term, 1875, to the September Term, 1876, Inclusive* (Washington, D.C.: W. H. & O. H. Morrison, 1877), 224–228.

47. Manuscript Census Returns, Ninth Census of the United States, 1870, Seventh Ward, Washington, District of Columbia, Schedule 1, General Population, NAMS M-593, reel 126, page 502; *National Republican,* May 26, 1875; *St. Mary's Beacon* (Leonard Town, Md.), August 8, 1878; Manuscript Census Returns, Tenth Census of the United States, 1880, Leonardtown, St. Mary's County, Maryland, NAMS T-9, reel 514, page 75B.

48. *Evening Times* (Washington, D.C.), November 26, 1895 (first quotation); Manuscript Census Returns, Tenth Census of the United States, 1880, Washington, District of Columbia, NAMS T-9, reel 124, page 36; *National Republican,* August 7, 1868; Twelfth Census of the United States, 1900, Vansville, Prince George's County, Maryland, NAMS T-623, reel 626, page 10; *Evening Star,* October 16, 1901; Thirteenth Census of the United States, 1910, Washington, District of Columbia, NAMS T-624, reel 155, page 6A; Fourteenth Census of the United States, 1920, Washington, District of Columbia, NAMS T-625, reel 213, page 9B; Fifteenth Census of the United States, 1930, Washington, District of Columbia, NAMS T-626, reel 300, page 1B; *Evening Star,* January 4, 1931; Manuscript Census Returns, Tenth Census of the United States, 1880, Washington, District of Columbia, NAMS T-9, reel 124, page 160D; Manuscript Census Returns, Twelfth Census of the United States, 1900, Washington, District of Columbia, NAMS T-623, reel 161, page 5B; Manuscript Census Returns, Tenth Census of the United States, 1880, Washington, District of Columbia, NAMS T-9, reel 124, page 176D; *Evening Star,* September 4, 1895; *Evening Times,* September 4, 1895; *Irish World and American Industrial Liberator* (New York), September 14, 1895; Glenwood Cemetery Records, Washington, D.C., 1854 to 2013, plat book, vol. C, p. 64; Manuscript Census Returns, Sixteenth Census of the United States, 1940, Montgomery County, Maryland, reel m-t0627-01555, enumeration district, 16-50G, page 5B.

49. *National Republican,* August 30, 1879 (quotations); *Evening Star,* December 22, 1884; *Evening Critic* (Washington, D.C.), December 22, 1884. The disgruntled property owners eventually gave up the fight and sold their property. See *Evening Star,* January 30, 1886.

EPILOGUE: THE LEGAL LEGACY OF THE DOMESTIC SLAVE TRADE

1. *Commonwealth v. John* (1839), Executive Papers, David Campbell, Box 6, Folder 3, LVA (quotations). On procedural fairness, see, for example, A. E. Kier Nash, "The Texas Supreme Court and Trial Rights of Blacks, 1845–1860," *Journal of American History* 58 (December 1971), 629.

2. *Commonwealth v. John*; Sixth Census of the United States, 1840, Charles City County, Va., Free Pop., NAMS M-704, reel 553, pp. 127 (Josiah C. Wilson, 37), 130 (John Minge, 44), 130 (James Minge, 19), 134 (Benjamin Harrison, 68), and 136 (George C. Waddill, 12).

3. *Commonwealth v. John*; will of Benskin Hopkins, 1834, Folder 85, Item 14, Southall Papers, Special Collections Research Center, Swem Library, College of William & Mary. In his will, the elder Benskin Hopkins had given his namesake "his choice of my guns." This may well have been the murder weapon. The date of the murder is listed as approximately November 15, 1838, in Executive Papers, David Campbell, Box 7, Folder 7, LVA.

4. *Commonwealth v. John.*

5. *Public Ledger* (Philadelphia), July 30, 1839 (first and third quotations); *Commonwealth v. John* (second and fourth quotations). See also *Tarboro' Press* (Tarboro, N.C.), August 10, 1839.

6. Will of Benskin Hopkins; *William W. Graves, et al. vs. Benskin Hopkins*, 1838, Folder 85, Item 9, Southall Papers; *Public Ledger*, July 30, 1839; *Commonwealth v. Benskin Hopkins*, 1838, Folder 85, Item 13, Southall Papers; *Commonwealth v. James M. Hopkins*, 1839, Folder 85, Item 14, Southall Papers. After Carradus' death, Mildred married Alfred Finch, the administrator of Carradus' estate. See *James M. Hopkins vs. Alfred Finch*, 1843, Folder 85, Item 16, Southall Papers.

7. *Commonwealth v. John.*

8. Jeff Forret, *Slave against Slave: Plantation Violence in the Old South* (Baton Rouge: Louisiana State University Press, 2015), 138, 141; Office of the Governor, Contracts, 1806–1865, Misc. Reel 1648, p. 179, LVA; Executive Papers, Thomas Walker Gilmer, Box 2, Folders 4, 5, LVA; *Daily Picayune* (New Orleans), February 28, 1841; Jeff Forret, "Before Angola: Enslaved Prisoners in the Louisiana State Penitentiary," *Louisiana History* 54 (Spring 2013): 140–147, 156, 167–168; *Report of the Board of Control of the Louisiana Penitentiary. January, 1858* (Baton Rouge: Daily Advocate, 1858), 55.

9. Petition to Thomas W. Gilmer, May 1840, Executive Papers, Thomas Walker Gilmer, Box 1, Folder 5, LVA (first and second quotations); Edwin Grimsley, "What Wrongful Convictions Teach Us About Racial Inequality," Innocence Project, September 26, 2012, www.innocenceproject.org/what-wrongful-convictions-teach-us-about-racial-inequality/ (accessed April 1, 2017); National Registry of Exonerations, *Race and Wrongful Convictions in the United States*, March 7, 2017, a report of the National Registry of Exonerations, Newkirk Center for Science and Society, University of California Irvine (third quotation). For coverage of the report, see Nathanlie Baptiste, "Black People Are More Likely to Go to Prison for Crimes They Didn't Commit: A New Study Details the Role of Racism in Convictions," *Mother Jones*, March 7, 2017, www.motherjones.com/politics/2017/03/black-people-more-likely-wrongfully-convicted (accessed April 1, 2017); Niraj Chokshi, "Black People More Likely to Be Wrongfully

Convicted of Murder, Study Shows," *New York Times*, March 7, 2017, www.nytimes.com /2017/03/07/us/wrongful-convictions-race-exoneration.html?_r=1 (accessed April 1, 2017); Sheryl Estrada, "Black People More Likely to Be Wrongfully Convicted in US, Says Report," DiversityInc, March 17, 2017, www.diversityinc.com/n ews/black-people-likely-wrongfully-convicted-u-s-says-report/ (accessed April 1, 2017); Rebecca Hersher, "Black People Are Wrongly Convicted of Murder More Often, Data Show," National Public Radio, March 7, 2017, www.npr.org/sections/thetwo-way/20 17/03/07/519012758/black-people-are-wrongly-convicted-of-murder-more-often-data-shows (accessed April 1, 2017); Scott Martelle, "When Wrongful Convictions Affect Blacks More Than Whites, Can We Call it a Justice System?" *Los Angeles Times*, March 7, 2017, www.latimes.com/opinion/opinion-la/la-ol-wrongful-convictions-race-2 0170307-story.html (accessed April 1, 2017); Tanzina Vega, "Study: Black People More Likely to Be Wrongfully Convicted," CNN, March 7, 2017, www.cnn.com/2017/03/07/ politics/blacks-wrongful-convictions-study/ (accessed April 1, 2017).

10. Forret, *Before Angola*, 154.

11. Taja-Nia Y. Henderson, "Crucibles of Discontent: Penal Practice in the Shadow of Slavery, Virginia, 1796–1865" (Ph.D. diss., New York University, 2013), 205, 282, 232; Bill Quigley, "Louisiana Number One in Incarceration," *The Huffington Post*, May 10, 2016, /www.huffingtonpost.com/bill-quigley/louisiana-number-one-in-i_b_9888636 .html (accessed April 1, 2017).

12. On the convict lease system, see Douglas A. Blackmon, *Slavery by Another Name: The Re-Enslavement of Black Americans from the Civil War to World War II* (New York: Anchor, 2009); David M. Oshinsky, *Worse Than Slavery: Parchman Farm and the Ordeal of Jim Crow Justice* (New York: Free Press, 1997); Alex Lichtenstein, *Twice the Work of Free Labor: The Political Economy of Convict Labor in the New South* (New York: Verso, 1996).

13. John Kuroski, "Private Prisons: American Slavery, Under New Managment," February 10, 2017, http://all-that-is-interesting.com/private-prisons-us-stats (accessed April 2, 2017); Quigley, "Louisiana Number One in Incarceration"; Cindy Chang, "Louisiana is the World's Prison Capital," *Times-Picayune* (New Orleans), May 13, 2012, updated April 6, 2016, www.nola.com/crime/index.ssf/201 2/05/louisiana_is_the_worlds_prison.html (accessed April 1, 2017); Associated Press, "Louisiana has the Highest Incarceration Rate in the Nation," March 17, 2017, New Orleans CityBusiness, http://neworleanscitybusiness.com/blog/2017/0 3/17/louisiana-has-the-highest-incarceration-rate-in-the-nation/ (accessed April 1, 2017); David Reutter, "Louisiana's High Incarceration Rate Economically Motivated," *Prison Legal News*, March 9, 2017, www.prisonlegalnews.org/news/2017/ mar/9/louisianas-high-incarceration-rate-economically-motivated/ (accessed April 1, 2017); National Institute of Corrections, "Corrections Statistics by State – Louisiana," https://nicic.gov/statestats/?st=la (accessed April 1, 2017).

14. Quigley, "Louisiana Number One in Incarceration"; Chang, "Louisiana is the World's Prison Capital"; Associated Press, "Louisiana has the Highest Incarceration Rate in the Nation," March 17, 2017, New Orleans CityBusiness, http://neworleanscitybusiness

.com/blog/2017/03/17/louisiana-has-the-highest-incarceration-rate-in-the-nation/ (accessed April 1, 2017) (quotation).

15. John Kuroski, "Private Prisons: American Slavery, Under New Management," February 10, 2017, http://all-that-is-interesting.com/private-prisons-us-stats (accessed April 2, 2017) (second quotation); Associated Press, "Louisiana has the highest incarceration rate in the nation" (first quotation); Jeff Asher, "The US Murder Rate Is Up But Still Far Below Its 1980 Peak," https://fivethirtyeight.com/features/the-u-s-mur der-rate-is-up-but-still-far-below-its-1980-peak/ (accessed September 27, 2017). The murder rate did change course and tick upward in both 2015 and 2016. The murder rate in 2016 stood at 5.3 per 100,000 people.

16. Kuroski, "Private Prisons" (quotations); David Reutter, "Louisiana's High Incarceration Rate Economically Motivated." On the phenomenon of private prisons, see Lauren-Brooke Eisen, *Inside Private Prisons: An American Dilemma in the Age of Mass Incarceration* (New York: Columbia University Press, 2018).

17. Chang, "Louisiana is the World's Prison Capital" (first, third through sixth, and eighth quotations); Kuroski, "Private Prisons" (second and ninth quotations); Reutter, "Louisiana's High Incarceration Rate Economically Motivated"; Quigley, "Louisiana Number One in Incarceration"; Associated Press, "Louisiana has the Highest Incarceration Rate in the Nation" (seventh quotation).

18. US Constitution, Thirteenth Amendment, Section 1 (first quotation); Kuroski, "Private Prisons" (second and third quotations); Joshua D. Rothman, "The New History of Slavery and Capitalism," *Aeon*, https://aeon.co/opinions/how-capitalist-was-american-slavery (accessed December 31, 2015); Chang, "Louisiana is the World's Prison Capital"; Michelle Alexander, *The New Jim Crow: Mass Incarceration in the Age of Colorblindness* (New York: New Press, 2012).

19. Dan Berger, "Mass Incarceration and its Mystification: A Review of the 13th," *Black Perspectives*, October 22, 2016, https://www.aaihs.org/mass-incarceration-and-its-mystification-a-review-of-the-13th/ (accessed November 8, 2017); Rashauna Johnson, *Slavery's Metropolis: Unfree Labor in New Orleans during the Age of Revolutions* (New York: Cambridge University Press, 2016), 23, 127, 134, 135, and ch. 4 more generally.

20. *Sunday Herald* (Washington, D.C.), February 25, 1883 (first and second quotations); *The Critic and Record* (Washington, D.C.), April 23, 1891 (third and fourth quotations).

21. *Evening Star* (Washington, D.C.), July 24, 1897.

22. Charles Noble, "Memories of Washington before the Civil War," *Washington Post*, January 31, 1926 (first through third quotations); James Croggon, "In Old Washington," *Evening Star*, October 17, 1908; *Evening Star*, September 11, 1902 (fourth and fifth quotations); *National Tribune* (Washington, D.C.), November 2, 1899; George Rothwell Brown, "Capital Silhouettes: Being Some Sketches in Outline of the Present, With a Glance or Two at the Past," *Washington Post*, March 6, 1924 (sixth through eighth quotations); *Evening Star*, April 16, 1888.

Index

INDEX